ALASKA~YUKON HANDBOOK

ALASKA~YUKON HANDBOOK

SIXTH EDITION

DEKE CASTLEMAN AND DON PITCHER

MOON
PUBLICATIONS INC.

ALASKA-YUKON HANDBOOK
SIXTH EDITION

Published by
Moon Publications, Inc.
P.O. Box 3040
Chico, California 95927-3040, USA

Printed by
Colorcraft Ltd., Hong Kong

ISBN: 1-56691-089-7
ISSN: 1091-336X

Please send all comments,
corrections, additions,
amendments, and critiques to:

**ALASKA-YUKON HANDBOOK
MOON PUBLICATIONS, INC.
P.O. BOX 3040
CHICO, CA 95927-3040, USA
e-mail: travel@moon.com**

Printing History
  1st edition — 1983
  2nd edition — April 1988
  3rd edition — Feburay 1990
    Reprinted — April 1991
  4th edition — March 1992
    Reprinted — April 1993
  5th edition — July 1994
    Reprinted — May 1996
  6th edition — April 1997

Updaters
Andrew Hempstead: British Columbia
Ron Holstrom: Fairbanks, Eagle, Denali Highway
Tom Reale: Northern Southcentral, Matanuska Valley, Prince William
        Sound, and Kenai Peninsula

Editor: Emily Kendrick
Editorial Assistant: Matt Orendorff
Copy Editor: Elizabeth Kim
Production & Design: Rob Warner
Cartographers: Bob Race, Brian Bardwell, Chris Folks, Dave Hurst,
        and Mike Morgenfeld
Index: Gregor Krause

Front cover photo: Blackstone Glacier, by Don Pitcher
All color page photos by Don Pitcher.

Distributed in the USA by Publishers Group West
Printed in Hong Kong

To Melissa J. Rubin
1966-1987
Spirit Soar

CONTENTS

SPECIAL TOPICS

CHARTS

ABBREVIATIONS

AAA—American Automobile Association
AMH—Alaska Mountaineering and Hiking
ANILCA—Alaska National Interest Lands
    Conservation Act
ANSCA—Alaska Native Claims Settlement Act
ANWR—Arctic National Wildlife Refuge
APEX fare—Advance-purchase excursion fare
ATMS—Alaska Travel and Marketing Services
ATV—all-terrain vehicle
AYH—American Youth Hostel
B&B—bed and breakfasts
B.C.—British Columbia
BLM—Bureau of Land Management
CAA—Canadian Automobile Association
CB—Citizens Band
CCC—Civilian Conservation Corps
d—double occupancy
FAI—Fairbanks International Airport
4WD—four-wheel drive
HQ—headquarters
Hwy.—Highway
kg—kilograms
km/h—kilometers per hour

MACS—Metropolitan Area Commuter Service
mph—miles per hour
MV—Motor Vessel
NANA—Northwest Alaska Native Association
NPS—National Park Service
PCL—Pacific Coach Lines
pop.—population
pp—per person
q—quadruple occupancy
REI—Recreational Equipment Inc.
RCMP—Royal Canadian Mounted Police
RV—recreational vehicle
s—single occupancy
SRA—State Recreation Area
t—triple occupancy
UAA—University of Alaska, Anchorage
USGA—United States Geological Survey
X.P.—expeditor
YCC—Youth Conservation Corps
YHA—Youth Hostel Association
YMCA/YWCA—Young Mens/Womens Christian
    Association
YVR—Vancouver International Airport

MAPS

INTRODUCTION

ON THE ROAD

GATEWAYS

SOUTHEAST ALASKA

YUKON TERRITORY

INTERIOR

SOUTHCENTRAL ALASKA

SOUTHWEST ALASKA

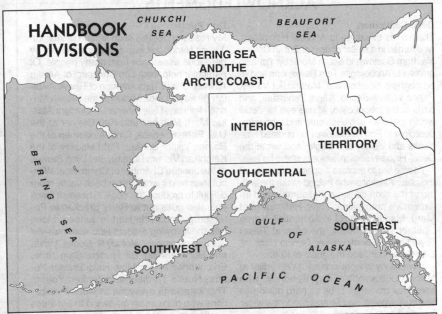

MAP SYMBOLS

▬▬ MAIN ROAD	○ TOWN / VILLAGE	▬ ▬ INTERNATIONAL BOUNDARY
── SECONDARY ROAD	○ CITY	▬ · ▬ STATE BOUNDARY
─ ─ UNPAVED ROAD	■ POINT OF INTEREST	─ ─ FERRY
·─··─ TRAIL	● HOTEL / ACCOMMODATION	⬡ STATE HIGHWAY
╪ BRIDGE		▭ RAILROAD
▲ MOUNTAIN	▱ STAIRS	▨ WATER
⤬⤬ AIRPORT	⛷ SKI AREA/RESORT	◯ CANADIAN PRIMARY HWY.
⛺ CAMPGROUND		⬢ TRANSCANADA HIGHWAY

ACKNOWLEDGMENTS

Deke Castleman

Thanks, as usual, go to Andrew Hemptead, who turned in a stellar update of British Columbia, from Gastown to South Moresby. I'm also grateful to Anchoragite Tom Reale, who updated northern Southcentral, Matanuska Valley, Prince William Sound, Kenai Peninsula, and parts of the Introduction; whose eye for detail would make an eagle jealous; and who introduced me to Ron Holmstrom. Ron updated Fairbanks and vicinity and Eagle, and wrote the Denali Highway section, which is where he lives.

I'd also like to express a special thanks to all the other Alaskans who helped make the writing of the sixth edition a pleasurable and inexpensive proposition: Steve Halloran (and Marg, Maddy, and RJ in abstentia), Karen Shemet, Keith Pollock, the crew at Tiekel River Lodge, Sherry Walker, Denise Hansen, Lisa Kavanagh, and the ghost of Knik.

It was a joy to work with my AYH6 editor at Moon Publications, Emily Kendrick, who somehow manages to be as hard driving as she is easygoing, and as attentive to the writer as she is to the writing.

Finally, there's Patrick Kavanagh to thank, my brother in luggage, recovery, and Alaska. Ding!

Don Pitcher

My research for this sixth edition of *Alaska-Yukon Handbook* was aided enormously by generous assistance from many people. Of particular help were Lou Cancelmi of Alaska Airlines, Shiela Throckmorton of Reeve Aleutian Airways, Linda Mickle of the Alaska Marine Highway, Dale Pihlman of Outdoor Alaska, Marti Marshall and Ken Crevier of the U.S. Forest Service, Cindi Aukerman of the Haines Visitor Bureau, Patti Mackey of the Ketchikan Visitors Bureau, and Lynn Barnes of the Juneau Chamber of Commerce. Without their help it would have been vastly more difficult to produce this book. A heartfelt thank you also goes out to Barry Bracken in Petersburg, and Karla Hart in Juneau, along with the following readers who sent in useful tips and comments: Melody N. Cooke, Lynda and Bob Fanning, Bill Horten, Sam Joffe, Eric Johnson, Tina Moy, Heidi Brewer-Peters, Noelle Tardieu, and Jensen Young. Thanks also to everyone at Moon Publications who once again managed to put these words into a usable form. And a very special thanks to Karen Shemet for her continuing support.

IS THIS BOOK OUT OF DATE?

Writing a guidebook is a lot like taking a snapshot: freezing the image of a place on a giant frame. At the same time, however, it's also like stopping progress: locking the ever-changing details into print. You can't stop progress and you can't slow down time. Although we make herculean efforts to check our facts, the task is an enormous one and sometimes gets away from us. You can help us keep up.

If something we mention no longer exists, if certain suggestions are misleading, if you've uncovered anything new, please write in. Letters from Alaskans and western Canadians are especially appreciated. Although we try to make our maps as accurate as possible, we are always grateful when readers point out any omissions or inaccuracies. If you feel we've overlooked an entire map, please let us know and we'll try to include it in the next edition. When writing, always be as specific and accurate as possible. Notes made on the spot are better than later recollections. Write your comments into your copy of *Alaska-Yukon Handbook* as you go along, then send us a summary when you get home. This book speaks for you, the independent traveler, so please help keep us up to date. Address your letters to:

Alaska-Yukon Handbook
c/o Moon Publications
P.O. Box 3040
Chico, CA 95927
USA

GORDY OHLIGER

INTRODUCTION

THE LAND

The major physical features of western North America continue unbroken into that giant head of land that is Alaska. The Great Plains of the midwestern U.S. extend to become the Mackenzie Lowlands and the North Slope, while the Rockies form an inland spine from deep in Mexico to the Brooks Range. West of the Rocky Mountains a high plateau runs from British Columbia north through the interiors of Yukon and Alaska, then west to the delta of the Yukon River, where it dips into the Bering Sea.

To the west of this plateau, two parallel chains and an intervening depression can be traced all the way from Mexico to Alaska. The Sierra Nevada of California become in turn the Cascades of Oregon and Washington, the Coast Mountains of British Columbia, the St. Elias and Wrangell Mountains, the Alaska Range, and finally the Aleutian Range, which then sinks into the Pacific just short of Asia. Closer to the ocean, California's Coast Range becomes the Olympic Mountains of Washington. Farther north a string of islands from Vancouver to the Queen Char-

lottes and the Alexander Archipelago runs into the St. Elias Mountains, where the two chains unite into a jagged icecapped knot. In Alaska they divide again where the Chugach and Kenai Mountains swing southwest toward Kodiak Island. Between these parallel chains is a 3,000-mile-long depression starting with California's Central Valley, then continuing with Puget Sound, the Inside Passage, the Susitna Basin in Southcentral Alaska, Cook Inlet, and Southwest Alaska's Shelikof Strait. Only four low-level breaks occur in the coastal mountains: the valleys of the Columbia, Fraser, Skeena, and Stikine Rivers. Most of the places described in this book are within or near this mighty barrier, which contains the highest peaks, the largest glaciers, and most of the active volcanos in North America.

Superlatives

Alaska boasts more superlative statistics than any other state in the country (itself a superlative). But all are dwarfed by a single reality: the

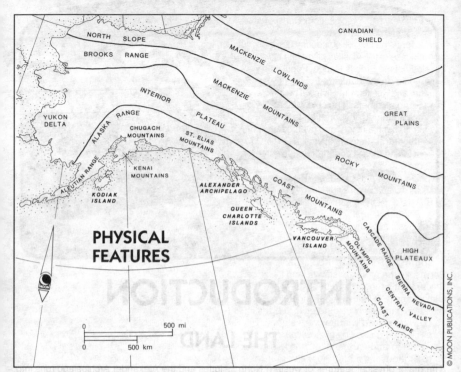

PHYSICAL FEATURES

NORTH SLOPE
BROOKS RANGE
CANADIAN SHIELD
MACKENZIE LOWLANDS
MACKENZIE MOUNTAINS
INTERIOR
PLATEAU
YUKON DELTA
ALASKA RANGE
CHUGACH MOUNTAINS
ST. ELIAS MOUNTAINS
GREAT PLAINS
KENAI MOUNTAINS
ALEUTIAN RANGE
KODIAK ISLAND
ALEXANDER ARCHIPELAGO
COAST MOUNTAINS
ROCKY MOUNTAINS
QUEEN CHARLOTTE ISLANDS
VANCOUVER ISLAND
OLYMPIC MOUNTAINS
CASCADE RANGE
HIGH PLATEAUX
SIERRA NEVADA
CENTRAL VALLEY
COAST RANGE

0   500 mi
0   500 km

© MOON PUBLICATIONS, INC.

sheer immensity of the land. Alaska is so huge, so wild, so underpopulated, that it's almost incomprehensible: it falls right off the edge of your imagination. Consider: Alaska's total land area, 591,000 square miles (375 million acres), is double the size of the next largest state, Texas. A little more than four Alaskas could be jammed into the continental U.S., while almost 300 Delawares could be jigsaw-puzzled into the 49th state. Mount McKinley (also known as Denali), at 20,306 feet, is the highest point in North America; the Aleutian Trench, plunging to 25,000 feet below sea level, is one of the Pacific's deepest ocean troughs. Juneau, with more than 3,000 square miles within its boundaries, has the largest area of any North American city, and the North Slope Borough, at 88,000 square miles (slightly larger than Idaho), is the largest municipally governed entity in the world. Alaska's 45,000-mile coastline is longer than the rest of the country's combined. Though only three percent of the state is covered in glaciers and ice-

fields (debunking the "frozen wasteland" myth—the most common misconception about Alaska), it still has more than 100 times more glacial area than the rest of North America. With all of 605,000 people, Alaska ranks second to last among the states in population, behind only Wyoming. If Manhattan had a relative population density, 17 people would live there. And if all the Manhattanites were transplanted to Alaska, they'd each have 125 acres. Immense.

Five States in One
This book divides Alaska into five regions: Southeast, Interior, Southcentral, Southwest, and the Arctic Coast. (It also covers Seattle, parts of British Columbia, and the Yukon Territory.)

Southeast is Alaska's "Panhandle," a coastal region dissected by the Inside Passage. This intricate network of narrow waterways, with rugged, forested mountains rising from the water's edge, extends along the western edge of Canada from south of Ketchikan up to Skagway. The climate is cool, with very high precipitation. Transportation is limited to ferries and planes.

Interior is the low rolling country between the northern face of the Alaska Range and the southern slope of the Brooks Range. Population centers huddle on the banks of the mighty Yukon, Tanana, and Kuskokwim Rivers. The region has short warm summers, long cold winters, and little precipitation. Transportation is limited to a few roads, bush airlines, and riverboats.

Southcentral stretches along the Gulf of Alaska from the northwest corner of Southeast to the southern edge of the Kenai Peninsula, and up to the peaks of the Alaska Range. The coastal portion is a continuation of Southeast, while the Alaska Range forms the gigantic backbone of the region, with agricultural valleys like the Matanuska and Susitna in between. The climate is mostly coastal maritime, like Southeast's. Transportation is by road, railroad, plane, and ferry.

Southwest includes Kodiak, the Alaska Peninsula, the Aleutian Islands, and the Bristol Bay area. It's rugged and treeless, with a population mostly of Native Aleut and Eskimo. The climate is particularly disagreeable: foggy summers, wind-chilled winters, very stormy, little sun. This area is also one of the world's most active volcano-and-earthquake zones. Four out of 10 of the world's earthquakes occur here, and 40 active volcanos mark the line where the Pacific tectonic plate bumps up against the North American plate. Transportation is mostly by plane, some by boat.

The **Arctic Coast** regions occupy a huge expanse of sparsely populated bush, up the Bering coast all the way around to Barrow and Prudhoe Bay. The very modest population centers are Nome, Kotzebue, and Barrow, with numerous Native villages scattered throughout. The climate is an extreme version of the Interior's: long cold winters, brief cool summers, and a tiny amount of precipitation. Access is almost entirely by plane.

GEOLOGY

Plate Tectonics
Briefly, the huge Pacific plate (the ocean floor) is drifting slowly northeast. It collides with the North American plate, on which the continent rests, along an arc that stretches from the western

Aleutians in the Gulf of Alaska to the Inside Passage—defining one section of the famous Pacific "Ring of Fire." This meeting of plates jams the ocean floor under the continental landmass and gives rise to violent geologic forces: upthrust of mountains, extensive and large earthquakes, volcanic rumblings and eruptions, and movement along fault lines.

Somewhere in the mists of early geologic time, a particularly persistent and powerful collision between the two plates caused the Brooks Range to rise; erosion has whittled its highest peaks to half their original height, at 8,000 feet. Later, a similar episode thrust the Alaska Range into shape. The Pacific plate even today continues to nose under the continental plate, in the vicinity of Yakutat (near where Southeast meets Southcentral). The force of it pushes Mt. Logan, the highest peak in Canada, slowly upward.

Earthquakes
One of the world's most seismically active regions, Alaska has withstood some of the most violent earthquakes and largest tidal waves ever recorded. In the last 90 years, 80 Alaskan earthquakes have registered over 7 on the Richter scale (the famous 1906 San Francisco earthquake is estimated at 7.8-8.3). The most destructive occurred at 5:35 p.m. on Good Friday, March 27, 1964. Now listed in history books at an incredible 9.2 on the Richter scale (newer and more sensitive equipment has upgraded it from a "mere" 8.6 recorded at the time), it remains the strongest earthquake ever recorded in North America. The ensuing tsunamis wiped out nearly every coastal village in Southcentral Alaska, wrought havoc all along the northern Pacific coast, and even created a crest in the canals of Venice in Southern California.

In November 1987, two earthquakes, one 7.5 and the other 7.0, were recorded in the Yakataga Seismic Gap, an active fault zone on the edge of Prince William Sound, in an area where seismologists expect a major quake—over 8.0— to occur sometime in the future.

Volcanos
Like its earthquakes, Alaska's major volcanos occur along the Aleutian chain. In fact, 57 active volcanos stretch along this arc: most have been active in the last 300 years. The largest recorded eruption occurred when Novarupta blew its

top in 1912 (see "Katmai National Park" under "Alaska Peninsula" in the Southwest Alaska chapter), the most cataclysmic natural disaster since Krakatoa cracked 30 years earlier.

In the summer of 1992, Mt. Spurr, an active volcano 78 miles west of Anchorage, erupted with dramatic effects. It threw a cloud of ash nearly 50,000 feet into the air, coating Anchorage with an eighth-of-an-inch-thick layer of ash and closing Anchorage International Airport for 20 hours. If a mere eighth of an inch of ash doesn't sound like much, imagine living inside a fireplace that hasn't been cleaned lately and you'll get an idea of how it felt.

Tsunamis

An earthquake deep below the ocean floor in the Gulf of Alaska or the open Pacific is especially dangerous to the coasts of Alaska and Hawaii, along with the west coasts of Canada and the United States. The activity creates enormous tidal waves (tsunamis), which, though only three to five feet high in open ocean, can travel at speeds exceeding 500 miles an hour. Contrary to popular fears, such a tsunami does not slam into the coast with 20 or 30 feet of water, washing away everything in its path like a flash flood. Instead, the water slowly inundates the land to a depth of four or five feet. Then, after a brief and chilling calm, the wave is sucked back out to sea in one vast undertow. The only means of survival, and not a guaranteed one at that, is to ride it out on a boat. Most of the destruction caused by the great Good Friday earthquake was of this nature, attested to by hair-raising pictures that you'll see in places like Valdez, Seward, and Kodiak.

GLACIATION

A glacier forms in areas of high precipitation and elevation where the snow is allowed to pile up to great depths, compacting the bottom layers into solid ice. The great weight above the bottom ice (along with the forces of gravity), pushes it slowly downward like a giant frozen river, scooping out huge valleys and shearing off entire mountainsides. When the rate of advance is balanced by melt-off, the face of the glacier remains more or less stationary. If the glacier flows more quickly than its face melts, it advances; if it melts faster than it flows, the glacier recedes. All air bubbles are squeezed out of the glacier by this tremendous pressure, which makes glacial ice extremely dense. It's so compacted that the higher frequencies of light cannot escape or penetrate it, which explains the dark blue tinge. And because of its density, it also melts at fantastically slow rates; a small chunk or two will keep a beer in a cooler chilled for a day or two.

Cirques, aretes, and medial moraines are easily identified in this photograph of spectacular Nabesna Glacier in the Wrangell Mountains.

NATIONAL PARK SERVICE, M. WOODBRIDGE WILLIAMS

Signs of the Glaciers

As you travel up the coast or hike in the national parks of the Interior, it's satisfying to be able to recognize and identify glacial landforms. While rivers typically erode V-shaped valleys, glaciers gouge out distinctly U-shaped **glacial troughs.** Valleys and ridges branching from the main valley are sliced off to create **hanging valleys** and **truncated spurs.** A side valley that once carried a tributary glacier may be left as a **hanging trough;** from these hanging valleys and troughs waterfalls often tumble. Alpine glaciers scoop out the headwalls of their accumulation basins to form **cirques.** Bare, jagged ridges between cirques are known as **aretes.**

As a glacier moves down a valley it bulldozes a load of rock, sand, and gravel—known as **glacial till**—ahead of it, or carries it on top. The glacial till dumped by a glacier is called a **moraine. Lateral moraines** are pushed to the sides of glaciers, while a **terminal moraine** is deposited at the point of the face's farthest advance. A **medial moraine** is formed when a pair of glaciers unite. These ribbonlike strips of rubble can be followed back to the point where the lateral moraines converge between the glaciers.

When looking at a glaciated landscape, watch for gouges and scrape marks on the bedrock, which indicate the direction of glacial flow. Watch, too, for **erratics,** huge boulders carried long distances and deposited by the glacier, which often differ from the surrounding rock. Glacial runoff is often suffused with finely powdered till or **glacial flour,** which gives it a distinctive milky-white color; the abundance of this silt in glacial streams creates a twisting, braided course. With a little practice, you'll soon learn to recognize glacial features at a glance.

Permafrost

To picture permafrost, imagine a veneer of mud atop a slab of ice. In the colder places of the Lower 48, soil ecologists measure how much surface soil freezes in winter. In Alaska, they measure how much surface soil thaws in summer. True permafrost is ground that has stayed frozen for more than two years. To create and maintain permafrost, the annual average temperature must remain below freezing. The topsoil above the permafrost that thaws in the summer is known as the **active layer.** With the proper conditions, permafrost will penetrate downward until it meets heat from the earth's mantle. In the Arctic, permafrost begins a few feet below the surface and can extend 2,000 to 5,000 feet deep. This is known as **continuous permafrost,** which almost completely underlies the ground above the Arctic Circle. **Discontinuous permafrost** defines the more southerly stretches of the North, where the permafrost is scattered in patches according to ground conditions.

Frozen ground is no problem—until you need to dig in it. Russian engineers were the first to encounter industrial-scale problems with permafrost during the construction of the Trans-Siberian Railroad. In Alaska, gold mining, especially in deep placer operations, often required up to two years of thawing hundreds of feet of permafrost before dredging could proceed. Today, houses frequently undermine their own permafrost foundations: heat from the house thaws the ground, causing it—and the house above it—to sink. Similarly, road-building clears the insulating vegetation layer and focuses heat on the frozen layer, causing severe "frost heaving," the rollercoaster effect common to roads in Interior Alaska. Most recently, pipeline engineers had to contend with the possibility that the 145° oil flowing through the pipe would have similarly detrimental effects on the permafrost—resulting in potentially disastrous financial and ecological consequences. That's why over half of the Trans-Alaska Pipeline is aboveground, supported by a specially designed and elaborate system of heat-reducing pipes and radiators.

LAND ISSUES

Who Owns All This Real Estate?

In the beginning were the Natives, who shared their vast world with the other creatures of earth and sea and sky and had no concept of owning land. Then came the Russians, who, just by virtue of having arrived, granted themselves ownership of all this earth and sea and sky, and all the creatures in it—including the Natives themselves. Later, the Europeans arrived, and with no less arrogance staked out chunks of Alaska for themselves in the absence of the Russian landlords. Then in 1867 the entire property was sold to the Americans who, over the next 100 years, split up the land into Navy petroleum reserves, Bureau of Land Management parcels, national wildlife refuges, power projects, and the like, to be administered by separate federal agencies, including national park, forest, and military services. By the time Alaska became a state in 1959, only 0.003% of the land was privately owned—mostly homesteads and mining operations—and 0.01% had been set aside for Native reservations, administered by the Bureau of Indian Affairs.

The Statehood Act allowed Alaska to choose 104 million acres to own. But the selection process finally catalyzed the long-simmering feud between the governments and the Native peoples; that, and the issue of ownership of the rights-of-way for the Alaska Pipeline, gave birth to the largest settlement ever secured by an indigenous people. The Alaska Native Claims Settlement Act (ANCSA) of 1971 created 12 Native corporations, among which were divided 44 million acres of land, along with just under one billion dollars in federal funds and state oil royalties. People claiming at least one quarter Native blood were entitled to sign up as stockholders in village and regional corporations. "ANCSA sought to bring Natives into the mainstream of the state economy and culture," writes Chelsea Congdon in the *Cultural Survival Quarterly*, "as corporate shareholders of much of Alaska's resource capital." One Native corporation, Doyon Limited, headquartered in Fairbanks, came away with more than 12 million acres, making it the largest corporate landholder in the U.S.

Boomers and Doomers

ANCSA designated 80 million acres to be withdrawn from the public domain and set aside as national-interest lands (conservation property) by 1978. In the mid- to late '70s, in the wake of the completion of the pipeline, this was the raging land issue, generally divided between fiercely independent Alaskans who protested the further "locking-up" of their lands by Washington bureaucrats, and conservationists who lobbied to preserve Alaska's wildlife and wilderness. Finally, 106 million acres were preserved by these so-called "d2" lands (from section 17:d-2 of ANCSA), which included the expansion of Mt. McKinley National Park (renamed Denali); the expansion of Glacier Bay and Katmai national monuments, which became national parks; and the creation of Gates of the Arctic, Kobuk Valley, Wrangell-St. Elias, Kenai Fjords, and Lake Clark

National Parks, plus the designation of numerous national monuments and preserves, scenic and wild rivers, and new wildlife refuges.

Arctic National Wildlife Refuge

The latest battle between developers and conservationists is whether to allow exploration and drilling for black gold on a 2,300-acre corner of the 1.5-million-acre Arctic National Wildlife Refuge (ANWR), known as Study Area 1002. In a political compromise in 1980, the Alaska National Interest Lands Conservation Act (ANILCA), which set aside millions of acres for parks and wilderness, also called for a federal study to determine if oil and gas could be safely recovered within ANWR. Oil companies are looking ahead to the day when the North Slope reserves finally run dry (by 1995, 18 years after oil began flowing through the pipeline, the North Slope had produced 10.3 billion barrels of crude, with an estimated two billion barrels remaining) and claim that the pipeline's nearly 20 years of operation have proven oil development and environmental protection to be compatible on the North Slope. Also, improved technology has greatly refined development techniques, which further safeguard the wilderness.

Conservationists, on the other hand, know that the caribou herds and 200 other species of wildlife the refuge was installed to protect will be endangered; they argue that this refuge is one of the few places on earth that protect the complete spectrum of Arctic ecosystems.

Often overlooked in the arguments about caribou and petroleum are the Inupiat, known as the Twilight People, of Kaktovik village on Barter Island, which for thousands of years was a crucial link on the trading route between Greenland and Siberia. In the only settlement in the Arctic National Wildlife Refuge, 70% of the villagers depend on subsistence hunting for survival. The battle to open ANWR to drilling flared anew after the *Exxon Valdez* incident and the Gulf War, but Congress has yet to come to any conclusion—and probably won't for some time.

CLIMATE

Granted, over the course of a year, in any given location, Alaska's weather can be extreme and unpredictable. Because of the harshness of the

THE PINEAL GLAND

Most Alaskan life-forms pack a year's worth of living into five months of light, then hibernate through seven months of dark and cold. This is not only a cliché; it's also a fact, based on physiology—the physiology of the pineal gland, to be specific. This gland (shaped like a *pine* cone) sits on a short stem in the oldest and most mysterious section of the human brain. It's a lonely gland, a unique, asymmetrical neuronub, surrounded by large masses of advanced symmetrical tissue. Until recently, it was among the most obscure structures on the human neurological frontier; in fact, only 20 years ago it wasn't even considered a gland but was known only as the pineal "body."

This is somewhat surprising, since its function in other vertebrates has been understood for a hundred years. In fish, reptiles, and birds, the pineal "eye" sits on a long stalk close to the brain's outer frontal section, right between the two regular eyes, where a third eye would be. However, it's not connected to the eyes or any other sensory pathways. Rather, the pineal gland is a simple, efficient photoreceptor, which senses and interprets the relative duration, intensity, and polarizing angles of light in the environment—the primary organ responsible for regulating internal circadian and seasonal rhythms. It tells fish how to navigate, birds when to migrate, and mammals when to sleep and reproduce.

How it works in mammals is the key to understanding the gland's function in humans. Our gland produces a single (that we know of) hormone: melatonin. Melatonin circulates through the body and triggers two known reactions: drowsiness and reduced sex drive. What inhibits melatonin production? Light! The more sunlight—the higher its intensity and the steeper its angle—the less drowsiness and the stronger sex drive we feel. This helps explain many interesting general phenomena, such as why we sleep less deeply when it's not dark, the physiology of "spring fever," and why sex is better during the day. It also explains specific northern occurrences, such as why an amazing 72% of Alaskan babies are conceived between May and September (as opposed to November and February as is commonly believed), and why you can do with a lot less sleep in Alaska in the summer.

winters, comfortable travel to many popular destinations is difficult from early October to late April. Contrary to popular perception, however, the weather can also be quite pleasant. Alaska's spring, summer, and fall are not unlike these seasons elsewhere. It's cool, it's warm; it's wet and dry; sometimes it's windy, sometimes it's muggy, sometimes it's foggy. Maybe it's the worst weather in the world outside, but you're snuggling with your girlfriend in your large new tent after the most exciting raft ride of your life. Maybe it's the crispest, clearest day of your trip, but your camera got soaked in the river and your boyfriend ran off with the raft company bus driver. The weather, here as everywhere, has as much to do with the internal climate as the external. Be happy in the sun. Try to stay happy in the rain. Just keep happy. You're in Alaska.

Superlatives and Trends
It hit 100° F in the state once, in Fort Yukon in 1915. Fairbanks regularly breaks 90° F in July. It gets cold in Fort Yukon too, dropping as low as -78° F (Alaska's record low is -82, recorded in aptly named Coldfoot in 1989). *Any* wind at all at that temperature would make you feel even colder, if that's possible. Thompson Pass near Valdez gets quite a bit of snow, holding the records for the most in 24 hours (five feet), a month (25 feet), and a year (81 feet). But Barrow, at the tip of the proverbial "frozen wasteland," got just three inches of snow in 1936-37. An average of 13 feet of rain falls in Ketchikan every year—what they call "liquid sunshine." But again, one year Barrow squeaked by with only an inch.

Though Alaska retains the reputation of the Great Frozen North, a distinct warming trend has had a noticeable effect on the state. Temperatures warmed abruptly in the summer of 1977 and have remained unusually warm ever since, throughout all the seasons. For example, meteorologists report that in the Interior, only on rare occasions over the past 20 years has the mercury dropped below minus 40. Also, the temperature of the permafrost has risen several degrees. These indications, among others, of the greenhouse effect, have been partially attributed to the thinning ozone layer above the Arctic, similar to the "hole" that appears over the Antarctic every spring. Chlorofluorocarbons (CFCs) are considered the main culprit; Halon, a CFC found in fire extinguishers, is particularly prevalent in the fire-fighting systems of oil and gas developers. The ozone depletion in the Northern Hemisphere is thought to have much more dire consequences than in the Southern, since the north is much more populated.

Climatic Zones

It's possible to generalize about Alaskan weather and distinguish three climatic zones: coastal maritime, Interior, and Arctic. The main factor affecting the coasts—Southeast, Southcentral, and Southwest—is the warm Japanese Current, which causes temperatures to be much milder than the norm at those latitudes. This current also brings continuous rain as the humid Pacific air is forced up over the coastal mountains. For example, it rains in Juneau two out of every three days. However, these mountains shield the Interior plateaus from the maritime air streams, so yearly precipitation there is low, up to a mere 15 inches. The Interior experiences great temperature extremes, from biting cold in winter to summer heat waves. The mountains also protect the coastal areas from cold—and hot!—Interior air masses. The Arctic Zone is characterized by cool, cloudy, and windy summers (averaging 50° F) and cold, windy winters, though not as cold as in the Interior.

THE LIGHT AND THE DARK

If you plan to be in Alaska from late May to late July, you can leave the flashlight at home. If you camped at the North Pole for a week on either side of summer solstice, the sun would appear to barely move in the sky, frying you to a crisp from the same spot overhead as if stuck in space. The Arctic Circle, at 67° latitude, is usually defined as the line above which the sun doesn't set on June 21, nor rise on December 21 (though it's also sometimes defined as the line above which no trees grow, or the line above which the mean monthly temperature never exceeds 50° F).

Barrow lies at 71° latitude, four degrees and roughly 270 miles north of the Arctic Circle. Here the sun doesn't dip below the horizon for 84 days, from May 10 to August 2. (You'll definitely see, and probably buy, the famous postcard with the time-lapse photograph showing the sun tracing a very mild curve: "going down" in the north-northwest, hovering above the horizon, and "coming up" in the north-northeast.)

Fairbanks, 140 miles south of the Circle, has 22 hours of direct sunlight on summer solstice, with the sky (if it's clear) going from a bright orange-blue to a sunset purple to a sunrise pink and back to bright orange-blue in continuous two-hour cycles. Even Ketchikan, at around 55°

In Native mythology the sun is embodied by the female aspect, while the moon is male. The face in the sun is based on a print credited to Johneibo, a Canadian Native (1923-72). Note the tilt of the earth on its axis: this illustrates why Fairbanks stays light for three solid months in summer, dark for three in winter.

N latitude and probably the southernmost point on most Alaskan itineraries, enjoys more than 18 hours of daylight, with the starless dusk a paler shade of twilight. Similarly, in December Ketchikan receives six hours of pale daylight and Fairbanks only three, but at Barrow you wouldn't see the sun at all for nine weeks.

Why?

The explanation for the "midnight sun" lies in the tilted angle at which the earth rotates on its axis. Because of the off-center tilt, the Arctic Circle leans toward the sun in summer; a complete 24-hour rotation of the planet makes little difference in the angle at which the sun's rays strike the North Country. However, the rays do have to travel farther, and they strike Alaska at a lower angle, which you'll notice: the sun never gets nearly as high in the sky here as you're probably used to. Because of the low angle, the rays are diffused over a larger area, thus losing some intensity, which accounts for the cooler air temperatures. And since the sun seems to move across the sky at a low angle, it takes longer to "set" and "rise." In addition, the atmosphere refracts (bends) the sunbeams more dramatically closer to the poles, which causes the low light to linger even after the sun is down. This soft, slanting light is often magical, with sharp shadows, muted colors, silky silhouettes—a photographer's dream (see "On Land," under "Outdoor Recreation" in the On the Road chapter).

Northern Lights

The continual light is a trippy novelty if you're traveling around Alaska for just a few weeks, but when you're there all summer, to paraphrase the commercial, D-A-R-K spells relief. Stars? What a concept! Headlights? Oy vey! From early August on, though, you start losing daylight quickly, to the tune of an hour a week in Fairbanks. Temperatures drop, berries and rose hips ripen, mushrooms sprout, and there's the possibility of experiencing one of life's all-time great thrills: God's light show, the aurora borealis.

The far-flung Eskimo had a variety of mythical explanations for the lights. Many believed that they represented the spirits of ancestors or an-

---

SPARKS IN THE DARK

The stars help guide the northern traveler, and the rhythms of the moon count off the months. But of all the celestial lights, the unpredictable aurora borealis may serve the highest function, stirring our spirits and sparking our imagination in the deadening dark of winter. Some say the northern lights can shine right into the soul and lift a piece of it into the heavens, reflecting there the hope and fear and love and wonder that each of us carries within.

—David and Karen Foster,
Alaska magazine, Oct. 1989

---

imals, while others relegated the lights to malevolent forces. Prospectors preferred to think of them as vapors from rich ore deposits. The Japanese, however, have attributed the most romance to them: a marriage consummated under the lights will be especially fulfilling. Scientists have lately raised some controversy over particular aspects of the aurora, such as that the lights never dip below 40 miles above the earth (though many northerners swear they've seen the lights dancing along the ground); whether or not the lights manifest an electric sound is still a matter of some dissension, and even the experts who believe it don't know why. But these days nearly everyone agrees that the sun, again, is responsible for the show.

When the solar surface sparks, the energy propels a wave of ionized particles (known as the solar wind) through space. When these anxious ions encounter the gases in the earth's atmosphere, a madcap night of oxygen-nitrogen couples dancing begins. The sun's particles and the earth's gases pair off, with the fastest ions grabbing the highest gases. The ensuing friction causes a red or yellow afterglow. The slower ions infiltrate the lower regions, and those encounters glow green and violet. The waving, shimmering, writhing ribbons of color cannot fail to excite your own ions and gases.

FAUNA

If any aspect of Alaska embodies the image of the "last frontier," it's the state's animal kingdom. For millennia, Native hunters, with their small-scale weapons and limited needs, had little impact on wildlife populations. Eskimo and Aleut villages subsisted comfortably on fish, small mammals, and one or two whales a year; the interior Athabascan bands did well on a handful of moose and caribou. This all changed in the mid-1700s with the coming of the rapacious white people. Sea otters, fur seals, and gray whales were quickly hunted to the verge of extinction. By the 1850s, the Alaskan musk ox, largest member of the sheep family, had been annihilated. Wolves, in part because they preyed on the same game as humans, were ruthlessly exterminated.

Conservation measures have nurtured the numbers and today Alaska boasts one of the largest concentrations of animal populations remaining on earth. For example, there are nearly twice as many caribou in Alaska as there are people. There's a moose, and a Sitka black-tailed deer, for every three people. If 80,000 sheep strikes you as an impressive number, consider 40,000 grizzly bears. Bald and golden eagles are commonplace, and while the magnificent trumpeter swan was believed near extinction in the Lower 48, it was thriving in Alaska. Marine mammals, from orcas to the recovering otters, are abundant, and Alaskan waters also contain fish and other sea creatures in unimaginable quantities.

Salmon, halibut, crab, pollock, herring, and smelt, among others, are well known for their positive impacts on Alaska's economy; nearly six *billion* salmon, for example, have been harvested in Alaska, representing a dollar value higher than all the gold recovered there. But the economic value of Alaska's wildlife has only recently begun to be appreciated by state managers. Tourism, Alaska's third-largest industry, is based almost entirely on scenery and wildlife. From the "Tundra Wildlife Safari" at Denali National Park to the $7,000 for each big-game animal killed in the state, Alaska's fauna is one of the country's greatest renewable resources and will remain so, if handled with care.

Note: Visitors to the North should be aware that wildlife may be encountered, up close, almost anywhere outdoors, and even indoors occasionally. Many animals are well prepared to defend their territories against intruders (you), and even the smallest can bite. Never attempt to feed or touch wildlife. It is seldom good for it, you, or those who follow. Any animal that appears unafraid or "tame" can be quite unpredictable, so keep your distance. If you have a pet along, watch it carefully; dogs unfamiliar to locals are often shot first and questioned afterward. Any mosquitoes or other insects reading this are urged not to bother visitors. Hiking in bear country requires special precautions; see the special topic "Coexisting with the Bears" in the Denali section of the Interior chapter. One thing you don't have to worry about is snakes; there are none in Alaska.

LAND MAMMALS

Grizzlies

The grizzly is the symbol of the wild country, the measure of its wildness. Grizzlies once roamed all over North America. In 1800, there were over 100,000 of them; today, less than 300 survive in the Lower 48. Ironically, the grizzly is the state animal of California, where it is now extinct. However, an estimated 32,000-43,000 of these magnificent creatures inhabit Alaska.

You're most likely to see a grizzly at Denali National Park. Denali doesn't have a fatally serious bear problem like Glacier or Yellowstone parks. The estimated 200 Denali grizzlies are still wild, mostly in their natural state. This is especially important for the continued education of the cubs, who are taught how to dig roots, find berries, catch ground squirrels, and take moose calves. However, Denali grizzlies are not afraid of people, and are extremely curious; some have tasted canned beans, veggie burgers, and Oreo cookies. While no one has been killed by a grizzly at Denali, maulings have occurred, usually due to the foolishness of novice hikers and photographers or as a result of improper food storage. Take care, but don't be afraid to go hiking.

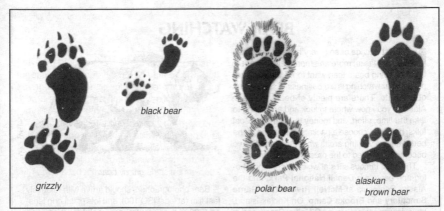

black bear

grizzly

polar bear

alaskan brown bear

The natural grizzly diet is 80% vegetarian. They eat berries, willows, and roots, as well as preying on anything they can take: from ground squirrels to caribou, from foxes to small black bears. And they're challenged by nothing, except humans with high-powered weapons. Grizzlies are racehorse fast and have surprising endurance; they need about 50 square miles for home territory and travel several miles a night. During the day they like to eat, sleep in the sun—often on snow patches—and entertain tourists on the shuttle buses.

Grizzlies are solitary creatures. Full-grown boars and sows are seen together only during mating season, in July. The gestation period is a little over five months, and the sows give birth in December to one to three cubs. The cubs are hairless, weigh one pound each, and remain blind for a week. They stay with the mother for over two and a half years—two full summers. They're then chased away sometime before July of the third summer, when the sow is ready to mate again.

Contrary to popular belief, bears do not hibernate. They do sleep deeply in dens during the winter, sometimes for weeks. But they often get hungry, lonely, or restless, and step outside to forage for frozen roots, berries, and meat. Sometimes a bear will stay out all winter; that's the one that the Natives fear the most: the winter bear. Its fur tends to build up a thick layer of ice, rendering it nearly impenetrable, almost bullet proof. And of course, sows give birth in the deep winter, which they're certainly awake for.

Grizzlies and brown bears were once thought to be different species but now are considered the same. Their basic difference is size, due to habitat. Grizzlies themselves are the world's largest land omnivores, growing to heights of six to seven feet tall and weighing in at 500-600 pounds. However, they're the smaller of the two, because they live in the interior and feed mostly on vegetation. Brown bears are coastal, and with a rich source of fish protein, they have achieved near mythical sizes. Kodiak brown bears retain a reputation for being the largest and most concentrated, reaching heights of over 10 feet and weights of 1,000 pounds. But Admiralty Island brown bears give nothing away in either department.

Moose

The moose is the largest member of the deer family, and Alaska has the largest moose. A bull moose in his prime gets to be about seven feet tall and weighs around 1,200 pounds—all from eating willow stems—about 30 pounds a day of them. They also eat aspen and birch, but willow is the staple of choice. The antlers, which are bone, are shed and renewed every year. Full-size antlers can weigh up to 70 pounds—that's mostly in September during the rut, or impregnation time. Bulls of near-equal rank and size butt their heads together to vie for dominance. You want to be real careful of bulls then. Touchy. The cows have one or two calves, rarely three, in May, and that's when you want to be real careful of the cows, too.

BEAR WATCHING

In the last decade or so a very hopeful trend has begun in Alaska: more and more people want to watch living bears than want to kill them for trophies. Bear watching is big business in some parts of the state. There are plenty of bears to see in Alaska if you know where to look and are willing to take the time, effort, and money to get there. Most folks, however, choose a package trip to one of the better-known viewing areas where the bears have become habituated to the presence of humans.

The most famous sites at which to see and photograph bears are **Denali National Park,** and the Alaska Peninsula at **McNeil River State Game Sanctuary** and **Brooks Camp.** On Kodiak Island, bear viewing centers around **O'Malley Creek,** and in Southeast Alaska at Admiralty Island's **Pack Creek.** All of these are brown-bear sites; the best places to see black bears are **Anan Creek** near Wrangell and **Fish Creek** near Hyder. Polar bears are most likely to be spotted near **Kaktovik,** on the edge of Arctic National Wildlife Refuge. See the appropriate chapters of this book for descriptions of these areas.

grizzly bear

Bear photographers should arrive with relatively fast film (at least ISO 100), and lots of it. Long lenses (300 mm or greater) are useful for those full-face shots at McNeil or Brooks Camp, but bring a range of lenses or a zoom to get more variety in your photos. A tripod is highly recommended if you're shooting with a telephoto, and autofocus cameras are easier to use in fast-moving situations. Be sure to use a fast enough shutter speed to stop the action, generally 1/250 second or faster.

The calves stay with the cow exactly a year, then she chases away the yearlings. Sometimes at the start of the summer season you will spot a huge pregnant cow with a frisky yearling on her heels, and you've never seen a more hassled-looking expression on an animal's face. But that's family life.

Moose don't cover too much territory—about 30 miles a year, mostly in the forest, which provides their natural defense against predators. The word *moose* comes from the Massachusetts Algonquian dialect and means "muncher of little twigs." By the way, the little flap of hair under the moose's chin is known as the moostache.

Harsh winters are deadly to moose. Deep snow and bitter cold can cause one in three moose in central Alaska to perish. Annually, hundreds of moose make their last stand along the snowless railroad tracks between Seward and Fairbanks and are killed by trains that don't stop for them. Other hundreds starve to death. Those hit by cars along roadways are butchered and distributed to the local people. Hunting quotas are drastically reduced until moose numbers recover.

If Alaska moose are the world's largest, Kenai Peninsula moose are Alaska's largest. A Kenai moose holds the Alaskan record: at 10-11 years old, his antlers were just under 75 inches wide, he weighed 1,500-1,600 pounds, and he gave his life for Guinness. Appropriately, the Moose Research Center is on Swanson River Rd., about 50 miles from Soldotna on the Kenai Peninsula, in an area that sustained large forest fires in the late 1940s and in 1969, providing excellent young forage for the prevalent moose. The Research Center was opened in 1969 and has four one-square-mile and two 15-acre pens, which can comfortably contain a dozen or so moose.

Caribou

Caribou are travelin' fools. They're extremely flighty animals—restless, tireless, fast, and graceful. Run and eat, run and eat, is pretty much all they do—and oh yeah, reproduce. Reindeer, in the same species, are smaller and often domesticated. Caribou are peaceful critters and they'll outrun and outdistance their predators, mostly wolves, rather than fight. They like to travel in groups, unlike moose, which are loners.

And they cover 10 times as much territory. Their herding and migrating imperatives are similar to those of the plains bison; they gather in large numbers and think nothing of running 50 miles, almost on a lark. An estimated one million caribou are found in Alaska in 12 major herds.

Caribou are extremely well adapted to their winter environment. They have huge nasal passages and respiratory systems in order to breathe the bitter cold winter air. Thick fur covers almost every inch of their bodies; the fur itself is protected by large, hollow, oily guard hairs. This tends to make caribou look much larger than they really are; a good-size bull weighs 400-500 pounds, a cow about half that. Caribou have the richest milk in the animal kingdom: 20% fat. They've also got huge prancing hooves, immortalized in the Santa Claus myth, which are excellent for running, swimming, disco dancing, and pawing at the snow to uncover the moss and lichens on which they subsist all through the harsh Arctic winter. The word *caribou* comes from the Maine Algonquian dialect and means "scraping hooves."

The caribou is the only member of the deer family whose females grow antlers. Babies are on their feet and nursing within an hour of birth, and at one week they can run 20 miles. If they can't, they'll most likely die, since the herd won't wait. But this helps to keep the herd healthy, controls population growth, and provides food for the carnivores.

The Natives are among the caribou's natural predators. The Natives, at one time, made use of 99% of a caribou carcass. They ate the meat raw, roasted, and stewed. They ate all the organs, even the half-digested greens from the stomach. The little gobs of fat from behind the eyes were considered a delicacy. They used caribou hide almost exclusively for clothes, rugs, blankets, and tents. The leg skins were used to make mukluks; the long strands of stringy sinew provided sewing thread.

Dall Sheep

Named for William H. Dall, one of the first men to survey the lower Yukon (1866), Dall sheep are sometimes called Alaska bighorn sheep, because the Rocky Mountain bighorn is a closely related species. Distinguished by their brilliant white color, the rams grow large curved horns, formed from a specialized skin structure made up of a compacted mass of hair and oil. The horns aren't shed; instead the sheep add another ring to them yearly, so the longer the horns, the older the ram, and the more dominant within the herd. The rams can weigh as much as 175 pounds; the ewes have small spiked horns and average 120 pounds. Their habitat is the high alpine tundra, and they subsist on grasses, mosses, lichens, and flowers. Their bird's-eye view provides an excellent defense. They're also magnificent mountain climbers. Roughly 60,000-80,000 Dall sheep reside in the Chugach, Kenai, Alaska, and Wrangell mountain ranges in Alaska. During summer, the rams migrate high into the ranges, leaving the prime lower grazing grounds for the ewes and lambs.

It's natural that they migrate, the same way it's natural that they have predators. Their alpine tundra habitat is very fragile, and it can take decades to regenerate after overgrazing. Migration and predation thus keep the flock healthy, control population growth, and guarantee the survival of the habitat.

Wolves

Wolves have traditionally been one of the most misunderstood, misrepresented, and maligned mammals, in both fact and fable. We've come a long way from the days when it was believed that wolves were innately evil, with the visage of the devil himself, eating their hapless prey, or little girls in red hoods, alive. But it wasn't until the mid-1940s, when wildlife biologist Adolph Murie began a long-term and systematic study of the wolves in Mt. McKinley National Park, that all the misconceptions composing the accepted lore about wolves began to change.

wolf

BOB RACE

For three years Murie tramped mainly on the plains below Polychrome Pass and became extremely intimate with several wolf families. (His book, *The Wolves of Mount McKinley,* published in 1944, is still considered a classic natural-history text.) Though Murie concluded that a delicate balance is established between predator and prey to their mutual advantage, declining Dall sheep populations, political pressure, and, indeed, tradition forced the park service to kill wolves, which were considered, against Murie's conclusions, to be the cause of the sheep decline. Typically, though, the wolf population was in just as dire straits as the sheep, and for several years no wolves were killed in the feds' traps *due to their scarcity.*

Since then, many researchers and writers have come to incisive conclusions about the wolf. It's been determined that their social systems—within the pack and with the prey—are amazingly complex and sophisticated. The alpha male and female are the central players in the pack, surrounded by four to seven pups, yearlings, and other adults. The dominant female undergoes a long involved courtship by the dominant male (though he might not necessarily always be the biological father of the pups). Territories can be as small as 200 square miles and as large as 800 square miles, depending on a host of influences.

Perhaps the most complex and fascinating aspect of wolf activity is the hunt. Barry Lopez, author of the brilliant *Of Wolves and Men,* argues persuasively that the individual prey is as responsible for its own killing, in effect "giving itself to the wolf in ritual suicide," as the wolf is in killing it. Lopez maintains that the eye contact between the wolf and its prey "is probably a complex exchange of information regarding the appropriateness of a chase and a kill." Lopez calls this the "conversation of death." Further, he points out that domestic stock have had this interspecies language bred out of them. "The domestic horse, a large animal as capable as a moose of cracking a wolf's ribs or splitting its head open with a kick, will almost always panic and run. It will always be killed. The wolf who has initiated a prescribed ritual has received nothing in return; he has met with ignorance in an animal with no countervailing ritual of its own. So he wounds and kills in anger."

With the advent of radio collaring and tracking from airplanes, the movements of individual wolves and packs have continually surprised wildlife biologists. Wolves often travel five to 10 miles an hour for hours at a time. In a matter of days, an individual cut loose from a pack can wind up 500 miles away. Thus wolves are able to select and populate suitable habitats quickly.

Alaska's 6,000-7,000 wolves are reportedly thriving, even though roughly 15% of them are harvested yearly. They've expanded their habitat and their numbers are increasing slowly but surely. They have one extremely fortuitous circumstance in the North Country: the lack of a livestock industry. Ranchers have always been the wolf's worst enemy.

Ground Squirrels and Marmots

These two members of the rodent family, unlike brown, grizzly, and polar bears, are true hibernators: they sleep straight for six months, in a deep coma. This separation between life and death is one of the thinnest lines in the animal world. A ground squirrel's heart slows to about six beats a minute, and his body temperature lowers to just above freezing, around 38° F. (In fact, a zoophysicist at University of Alaska-Fairbanks has found that the core temperature of the arctic ground squirrel, the northernmost hibernator, can drop as low as 26° F—six degrees below freezing! Of course, the squirrels don't "freeze" but "supercool.")

The squirrel takes a breath every couple of minutes. It uses up half its body weight. If you stuck a needle in a hibernating ground squirrel's paw, it would take the animal about 10 minutes to begin to feel it.

Ground squirrels provide a large part of the grizzly and wolf diet, and of scavenger birds' as well, since they're a common kind of roadkill.

Marmots, similar to woodchucks, are often mistaken for wolverines. They live in large rock outcrops for protection and have a piercing whistle, which warns of approaching predators or other possible danger. Look for marmots around Polychrome Pass at Denali Park; ask the driver where exactly.

Elk

Elk, a common sight in the western Lower 48, were also prevalent in Alaska 10,000 years ago but disappeared during the last ice age. In the mid-1920s, Alaskans decided that elk would be an attractive addition to the Territory's big-game species, and a handful of elk were imported from Washington state. After a few years of is-land-hopping, the cervids (deer family) were fi-nally transplanted to their permanent home, Afognak Island off the north coast of Kodiak, and from there they apparently swam to Rasp-berry Island and Kodiak. Though the country was rugged—wet, windy, and choked with alder—the elk thrived in their new homes, and some grew to 1,000 pounds. Within only 20 years (1950), 27 bulls were culled from the herd by resident hunters. Hunting continued up until the late 1960s, after a series of severe winters had decimated the herds. Ten years of protec-tion and mild winters allowed the herds to re-generate; 1,300 elk today reside on Afognak and Raspberry Islands, and around 25 on Ko-diak. Roughly 200 elk are harvested a year.

Musk Ox

The musk ox, a sort of shaggy prehistoric bison, was abundant in the North Country until it was hunted into extinction by the mid-1800s. In the 1930s, several dozen musk ox were trans-planted from Greenland to Nunivak Island in the Bering Sea. Like the elk on Afognak, the musk ox on Nunivak thrived, and the resident Natives used the soft underwool to establish a small cottage industry knitting sweaters, scarves, and caps. And that's what it would have re-mained, a small cottage industry, if it hadn't been for Dr. John J. Teal Jr., a student of Arctic explorer Vilhjalmur Stefansson. Stefansson rec-ognized the potential of musk-ox wool and in-spired Teal to experiment with domesticating them. After spending 10 years with musk-ox on his farm in Vermont, Teal concluded that they were amiable, hardy, and easy to domesticate. So in 1964, he started the Musk Ox Project at the U of A in Fairbanks.

In 1984, the project moved to a farm in the Matanuska Valley, where musk ox are bred to produce qiviut (KEE-vee-ute), the soft under-wool, which is renowned in Alaska for its insula-tion (eight times warmer by weight than sheep wool) and tactile (softer than the finest cash-mere) properties. The qiviut is combed from the animals in the spring; four to seven pounds per musk ox is taken in about three hours. The raw wool is sent to a mill in Rhode Island and then sold to Oomingmak (the Native word for musk ox, meaning "bearded one"), a co-op consisting of 200 members in villages spread throughout western Alaska. Here the qiviut is knitted into garments, which are sold at retail outlets in An-chorage and at the farm. For more information on visiting both, see "Shopping" under "Anchor-age," and "Palmer" in the "Palmer to Valdez" section, both in the Southcentral Alaska chapter.

Lynx

The lynx is the northern version of the bobcat, Alaska's only native cat. Lynx are extremely shy and secretive animals that prey primarily on snowshoe hare. These days, the Kenai Penin-sula provides a good example of the continuing danger to fur-bearing animals. The lynx were hunted heavily in the late 1970s when their pelts were worth up to $500 apiece. The diminished lynx population allowed the snowshoe hare to proliferate. But just as the lynx were regenerating, the hare population crashed according to its seven-year cycle, leaving the lynx without its primary food source. And now the lynx have been reported to be active in urban areas such as Soldotna and Sterling, where they raid chick-en coops and rabbit pens. The Kenai Peninsula, of course, is a "biological island" only marginally connected to the rest of the Alaska habitat, so Kenai lynx are particularly endangered.

But with the hare cycle down throughout Alas-ka, lynx everywhere are hungry in the early 1990s. One of the wild cats actually chased a dog through a pet door into a house near Chugach State Park, and a lynx attacked a do-mestic goat near Fairbanks.

Mountain Goats

These members of the antelope family number between 13,000 and 15,000 in Alaska. They have snow-white coats, shaggy heads, and black-spiked horns up to a foot long, and weigh in between 150 and 300 pounds. They mostly in-habit the coastal ranges and eastern Alaska Range and are frequently seen high on cliffs so precipitous that they would probably scare even Dall sheep.

Sitka Black-Tailed Deer

This deer is neck and neck with moose for the position of second-most prevalent game ani-mal in Alaska behind caribou, with roughly

150,000-175,000 individuals. The Sitka deer prefer a forest environment along the coast—in Southeast, around Prince William Sound, and on Kodiak and surrounding islands—and roam high into the coastal ranges for young shrubs and ripe berries in the late summer months. Males weigh 150 pounds, females 100 pounds.

Black Bear
Sharing the coastal forest habitat with the Sitka black-tailed deer is the black bear, which also comes in cinnamon and glacier blue. Black bears are distinguished from grizzlies and brown bears by their size (much smaller), the shape of their face (much narrower), and the lack of a shoulder hump. Black bears are actually more dangerous to people than grizzlies: there have been more attacks and maulings in Alaska by black bears than by browns.

Others
Alaska has a number of members of the rodent family: shrews, mice, voles, lemmings (along with squirrels, marmots, and porcupines). Long-tailed and least weasels occupy a wide habitat in the taiga and tundra. Martens are another member of the weasel family, similar to though much more aggressive than mink; the pine marten is one of Alaska's most valuable fur-bearers. Wolverines are in attendance, though you'd be very lucky to see one. Red fox are common in Interior and Southcentral, and you're likely to see one at Denali Park; the white Arctic fox is a gorgeous animal, though you'll only see one in pictures.

MARINE MAMMALS

Sea Otters
The mass and brutal slaughter of almost all of these beautiful creatures by Russian, European, and American traders is especially heart-wrenching, simply because the sea otter, of all the sea mammals in northern waters, is so playfully humanlike. James Michener, in his epic *Alaska*, described it thus: "It resembled precisely the face of a bewhiskered old man, one who had enjoyed life and aged gracefully. There was the wrinkled brow, the bloodshot eye, the nose, the smiling lips and, strangest of all, the whispy untended mustache. In fact, this face was so like a

man's that later hunters would sometimes be startled by the watery vision and refrain momentarily from killing the otter lest an involuntary murder take place."

Marine member of the weasel family, the sea otter had one characteristic that would seal its doom: a long, wide, beautiful pelt, one of the warmest, most luxurious and durable furs in existence. Otter furs were so valuable that they fetched up to $5,000 in London or Canton. Once found from the Aleutians to Mexico, otter fur catalyzed the Russian *promyshleniki* to begin overrunning the Aleutians in the mid- to late-18th century, sealing the doom of the Aleuts as well as the otters. In 1803, Aleksandr Baranov (Alexander Baranof) shipped 15,000 pelts back to eastern Russia. Up until the 1840s, otter hunting was the primary industry in the Pacific, and when the Americans purchased Alaska in 1867, nearly a million otters had been killed in the northern Pacific.

(Michener claims that dead sea otters sink and that the number of otters taken represents roughly 20% of those killed. But Jim Rearden, an outdoors writer for *Alaska* magazine, refutes this, stating that sea otters always float when they die.)

During the extreme lawless period in the last quarter of the 19th century, the otters were annihilated. In 1906, schooners cruised the north Pacific for months without taking a single pelt. In 1910, a crack crew of 40 Aleut hunters managed to harvest 16 otters. In 1911, otters were added to the International Fur Seal Treaty, giving them complete protection from everybody. Small, isolated populations of otters had managed to survive in the western Aleutians, and their numbers have increased over the past 80 years to roughly 150,000 today—to the point where they could start to threaten Alaska's shellfish industry. Still, only Native Alaskans have legal rights to hunt the otter.

The *Exxon Valdez* oil spill claimed 5,500 otters; one of the saddest and most enduring images from the disaster was of the uncomprehending face of an otter peering above jet black, greasy water.

Sea Lions
"George Wilhelm Steller, the first white man to set foot in Alaska, described the northern (Steller) sea lion for science in the spring of

1742," writes Marybeth Holleman in the July/August 1991 issue of *Greenpeace* magazine. Two marine mammals ended up with his name: the North Pacific (Steller's) sea cow, a cold-water relative of the manatee; and the Steller's sea lion. "Because of its tameness, its total lack of fear of humans, and the reputed tastiness of its flesh, the sea cow was extinct only 26 years later. Now, 250 years after its discovery, the same fate may await his sea lion."

Steller's sea lions, named after the naturalist aboard Vitus Bering's abortive second exploration of Alaska, are pinnipeds—marine mammals with flippers, not feet. Males can weigh up to a ton; females peak at 600 pounds. Sea lions eat several kinds of fish, but mostly pollock. These playful animals were abundant in Alaskan waters up until quite recently. In 1960, for example, an estimated 140,000 sea lions frolicked in the northern Pacific, in the Gulf of Alaska, and along the Aleutians. But within 25 years, they had fallen to disturbing levels. Commercial hunting was halted in the mid-1970s, but a mere 68,000 remained in 1985. Only four years later, 25,000 sea lions were counted. That same year, they were listed as a threatened species—with only an estimated 66,000 sea lions remaining worldwide.

Speculation on the reasons for this precipitous decline is mostly centered around starvation: the remaining sea lions are small, anemic, and malnourished, and have fewer babies. According to Greenpeace, "The culprit is most likely the burgeoning trawl fishery in the Bering Sea and Gulf of Alaska—a fishery that supplies fast-food fillets, imitation crab legs, and highly prized roe to Japan."

The number of trawlers—huge factory ships that drag thousand-foot nets for miles over the ocean floor—has increased tenfold in the past 10 years. They now "clearcut" the ocean of nearly five *billion* pounds of bottomfish every year, over 10% of which is waste. Small wonder that the sea lions, along with harbor and fur seals and many indigenous seabird populations, are showing signs of decline.

Whales
The largest summer marine visitors to Alaska are the whales. Each spring **gray whales** are seen migrating north from Baja California; in the fall they return south. Also in the spring **humpback whales** move north from Hawaii. The humpback is easily distinguishable for its hump-like dorsal fin, large flippers, and huge tail, which shows as it dives. These 50-foot-long creatures often breach (jump) or beat the surface of the water with their tails, as if trying to send messages. Smaller (30-foot) **minke whales** are also common.

The **killer whale (orca),** which is not actually a whale but the largest of the dolphins (up to 24 feet long), travels in groups hunting fish and other mammals. Its six-foot-high, triangular dorsal fin and its black-and-white piebald pattern easily identify it.

BOB RACE

jumping orca

Fur Seals
The Alaska species of fur seal (*Callorhinus ursinus*) is a kind of "seal bear," as its Latin name suggests. The bulls grow up to seven feet long and can weigh 400 pounds. Tens of thousands of these caterwauling creatures return to the Pribilof Islands yearly to breed. The dominant bulls arrive after eight months at sea in early June, and the noisy fight for the prime beach real estate often results in bloody bulls. The cows show up a couple of weeks later—small (80 pounds), submissive, and steeling themselves for a bloody bounce on the beach. A big stud bull might accumulate 60-70 cows in his harem, and it's exactly as debilitatingly profligate a scene as it sounds. The bulls don't eat, living only off their own fat all summer, and look like skid row derelicts by mid-August when they take off to the North Pacific to eat, sleep, and regain their strength.

The gestation period is one year, and the cows return to the same rookery to give birth. The pups swim away in late October and return after a couple of years as "bachelors." Between two and seven years old, they play in the sand and surf, till the young males have grown big and bad enough to have their way with the cows. (For more information on fur seals, see "Pribilofs Islands" under "The Aleutian Islands" in the Southwest Alaska chapter.)

Walruses

What the Pribilofs are to the fur seal, Round Island in northern Bristol Bay is to the Pacific walrus. Except here, it's a boys-only beach club; the females and babies remain in the northern Bering and Chukchi Seas, where they feed at the relatively shallow bottoms. Sometimes up to 10,000 of these giant 3,000-pound bulls cram themselves onto narrow beaches at the bottom of steep cliffs around the one- by two-mile island. Tony Dawson, wildlife photographer for *Alaska* magazine, writes, "Socially, bull walruses are among the most argumentative in the world, always ready to fight at the drop of a flipper. Most bulls carry dozens of battle scars and scabs on their hides, which are as thick as tire casings. Lips are split and eyes injured or destroyed. Many bulls have chipped, broken, or missing tusks. Earlier breeding battles account for many injuries, but some result from petty disturbances of dozing neighbors."

On the beach, walruses are ungainly, akin to Subaru-sized slugs. But in the water, these big fat fatties are slo-mo smooth.

(To get to Round Island, fly Alaska Air to Dillingham, catch an air taxi to Togiak, and then grab a boat out to the island.)

BIRDS

Alaska is a birdwatcher's paradise. Everywhere you tern, there aren't just a few birds to look at, but dozens, or scores, or hundreds of, say, puffins in Kachemak Bay, and even thousands of, for example, bald eagles in Haines (in October), and even millions of murres in the Pribilofs. Over 400 species of birds have been identified in Alaska, of which 200 species return to just the Pribilofs every summer. Nearly 100 species visit Potter Marsh just a few miles south of Anchorage.

Thus, it's no surprise that birding is big in the North Country. Both birds and birdwatchers travel thousands of miles from all over the world to feed and breed or watch same. Some of the former are extremely rare. The bristle-thighed curlew, for one, has a population of a mere 5,000 worldwide, and their only breeding grounds are in Alaska. Eight of the curlews were banded in the Yukon Delta Wildlife Refuge in 1988, one of which was seen subsequently on Caysan Island in the South Pacific, over 2,000 miles away.

Trumpeter swans, for another, were thought to be nearly extinct in the U.S. until several thousand were "discovered" in the Copper River delta. Many Asian species, such as the greenshank and the Siberian ruby-throat, only foray into the Western Hemisphere as far as western Alaska.

Eagles

As many eagles are found in Alaska as in the rest of the U.S. combined. **Bald eagles** are so common along the coasts that they become almost commonplace—transformed, by familiarity, into the magnificent, high-soaring scavengers and garbage eaters that they are. Still, with their unmistakable white heads, seven-foot wingspans, and dive-bombing salmon-snatching performances, the thrill of watching one is not too quickly gone. Every fall, thousands of bald eagles congregate around Haines for the late salmon-spawning runs nearby, and a lone scraggly black spruce hosting two dozen of the hoary-crowned creatures is not unusual.

Golden eagles, found throughout the Interior, come without the distinctive "baldness" but are no less magnificent for their size, scavenging, and soaring habits. Plentiful around Denali Park, golden eagles perched on the tundra, standing more than three feet tall, have been mistaken for everything from grizzly cubs to adolescent hikers.

eagle

BOB RACE

The **white-tailed eagle** is an Asian raptor; Attu Island in the western Aleutians is its only North American habitat.

Trumpeter Swans

The world's largest waterfowl, these swans boast wingspans as wide as eagles (seven feet) and can weigh up to 40 pounds! They're pure white, and so have figured prominently over the centuries in legends, drama, music, and metaphor. They fly as fast as 60 mph and as high as 10,000 feet on their migrations from Alaska to the Pacific Northwest for the winter (though a group of 500 overwinter in Alaska). They live to be 30 years old and have a hornlike call, which accounts for their given name.

In 1933, trumpeter populations hit an all-time low in the Lower 48—33 individuals—having been hunted for their meat, down, and quills. But several thousand swans were seen by Alaskan bushplane biologists in the early 1950s, and by the early '70s, trumpeters were removed from the Endangered Species list.

Today, of the nearly 12,000 swans in North America, nearly 10,000 spend their summers in Alaska, of which nearly 2,000 are found in the Copper River delta. (A great place to see them is on the road from Cordova to the Million Dollar Bridge.)

Geese

The **Aleutian Canada goose** has made a remarkable comeback from the edge of extinction over the past 20 years. Smaller than Canada geese, Aleutian geese were common throughout the islands up until the 20th century, when decades of fox farming nearly wiped out the geese. Only a few hundred were left alive by the late 1960s, on one fox-free island. Feral foxes were removed from a number of other Aleutians and the geese were reintroduced; by 1987, their numbers (5,800) had regenerated to the point where they were removed from the ranks of the endangered and upgraded to threatened.

Emperor geese, however, have gone in the opposite direction. In the past 20 years their numbers have fallen by half, from 150,000 in the late 1960s to only 70,000 in the late 1980s. Roughly 90% of the world's population of emperor geese nest in western Alaska, the Aleutians, and Siberia.

Snow geese, on the other hand, are plentiful. Huge flocks totaling up to 100,000 birds migrate roughly 5,000 miles each year from central California through Alaska to their nesting grounds on Wrangel Island (in Russia).

Ptarmigan

The ptarmigan is the state bird, and one of the most popular targets of small-game hunters. Ptarmigan—willow, rock, and white-tailed—are similar to pheasant, quail, and partridge in the Lower 48. They reproduce in large quantities, molt from winter white to summer brown, and have a very poor sense of self preservation. The various Alaskan place-names with "Chicken" usually refer to ptarmigan, which the namers had too hard a time spelling.

Others

By the end of your travels you'll be able to identify at least a dozen species of **ducks.** A score of different **seabirds** migrate halfway around the world to nest in their favorite nooks somewhere in Alaska. Crazy **ravens,** frantic **puffins,** dive-bombing **gulls,** scavenging **magpies,** and lame-brained ptarmigan will keep you happily entertained for hours. And you can easily get strung out, lose all sense of time, and miss your tour bus just by trying to identify all the **finches, sparrows, warblers, thrushes,** and **jays** you see flitting everywhere. *Be sure* to bring a bird book, and also strike up conversations anywhere with anybody about the local avifauna—you're sure to hear some interesting words on birds.

MOSQUITOES

The mosquito, contrary to popular belief, is not Alaska's state bird. But skeeters are nearly as much a symbol of the Great North as glaciers, totem poles, and the aurora borealis. Mosquito eggs hatch in water, so the boggy, muskeggy, marshy forests and tundra, plus all the ponds, lakes, creeks, sloughs, and braided rivers of Alaska, provide the ideal habitat for these bothersome creatures. Alaska hosts around three dozen varieties of mosquitoes.

Mosquitoes hibernate in the winter and emerge starting in March and April. Peak season is in late June and early July. The males don't alight or bite, but they do buzz around people's eyes, noses, and ears, which can be as, if not more, annoying than the bites. The males live six to eight weeks, feeding on plant juices; their sole purpose in life is to fertilize the eggs the females produce. They also feed birds and larger insects.

The females live long lives, producing batches of eggs, up to 500 at a time. To nourish the eggs they feed on the blood of humans and mammals, using a piercing and sucking mouth tube. The tube also injects an anti-coagulant, which causes the itch and swelling from a bite. No Alaskan mosquitoes carry the diseases, such as malaria, yellow fever, encephalitis, and elephantiasis, that tropical mosquitoes are known to.

Mosquitoes are most active at dawn and dusk. Windy conditions and low temperatures depress mosquito feeding and breeding. Mosquitoes are attracted to dark colors, carbon dioxide, warmth, and moisture. Mosquito repellent containing DEET (diethylmetatoluamide) is the most effective. If you wear dark heavy clothing (the stinger can pierce light materials), camp in high and dry places that are apt to be breezy, and rub repellent on all exposed skin, you should be able to weather mosquito season without too much difficulty.

FISH

And if you think birds and bird-talk are plentiful, get someone going on fish—you won't be able to shut him or her up or get a word in edgewise for the whole afternoon, guaranteed. The fisheries program in Alaska is extensive, because commercial, sport, and recreational fishing are important to almost every state resident. Commercial fishing is Alaska's second-largest industry, and Alaska accounts for more than half of the nation's total seafood production.

In 1994, nearly 200 million salmon were caught by commercial fishermen and women in Alaskan waters, for a total of nearly a billion pounds, worth more than half a billion dollars (95% of the U.S. market for Pacific salmon). These figures are for salmon *alone*—the figures don't include herring, halibut, pollock, smelt, cod, shellfish, and myriad other commercial fish. Ten million salmon were landed by sport an-

glers, along with Arctic char, northern pike, sheefish, steelhead, rainbow, grayling, etc. The annual sportfishing industry is worth $100 million to Alaska. Below is a brief survey of the most popular fish in Alaska's three million lakes, 3,000 rivers, and 45,000 miles of coastline.

Salmon

Five kinds of salmon—king (or chinook), red (or sockeye), pink (or humpie), silver (or coho), and chum (or dog)—each return to the same bend in the same little creek where they hatched, to spawn and die, ending one of the most remarkable life cycles and feats of migration and single-minded endurance of any living creature. You'll be steeped in salmon lore if only by osmosis by the end of your trip, and you'll get more than your fill of this most delicious and pretty fish.

The **kings** (also known as chinooks, tyees, and springs) are the world's largest salmon, and the world's largest kings spawn in Alaska waters. The average size for a king is 40-50 pounds; 80-pounders are not uncommon. The world sportfish record is 97 pounds, and a few 100-pounders have been caught in commercial nets. Kings generally spend five or six years in salt water before returning to fresh to spawn: the more years spent in the ocean, the larger the fish. They run mostly between mid-May and mid-July.

Reds (sockeye) are the best-tasting salmon and the mainstay of the commercial fishing industry. They average six to 10 pounds and run in June and July; 50 million reds were caught in 1990.

Pinks (humpback) are the most plentiful, with massive runs of up to 150 million fish between late June and early September. They're smallish, three to four pounds, with soft flesh and a mild taste; they're mostly canned.

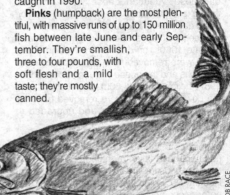

coho salmon

BOB RACE

Silvers (coho) seem to be the most legendary of the salmon, for their speed, agility, and sixth senses. Their spawning growth rate is no less than fantastic, more than doubling their weight in the last 90 days of their lives. Silvers grow seven to 10 pounds and run late, from late July all the way to November.

Chum (dog) are the least valued of the five Pacific salmon *(oncorhynchus)*, even though they average 10-20 pounds, are extremely feisty, and are the most far-ranging, running way above the Arctic Circle. They're known as dog salmon, as they've traditionally sustained working huskies, but chums remain popular with a hard-core group of sport anglers, who consider them terribly underrated.

Halibut

Halibut are the favorite monster fish and can grow so huge and strong that many anglers have an unsurpassed religious experience while catching one. "Chicken halibut" are the common 25-40 pounders, and 100, 200, even 300 pounders are not unusual. (The state-record halibut was a 464-pounder, more than eight feet long, caught near Dutch Harbor in 1996. And some charter-boat operators swear that out there lurking somewhere is a mythical half-ton halibut.) Even though halibut are huge and require 80-pound test line with 20-ounce lead sinkers, they're not the fiercest fighting fish, and one can be caught by just about anyone on a good day's charter from Kodiak, Homer, Seward, or Dutch Harbor. It has a very white flesh, with a fine texture (but it's only tasty if it's very fresh—otherwise, halibut needs dressing up with a lemony tartar sauce).

Pollock

The mainstay of the bottom-fishing industry, Bering Sea pollock has become big business ever since it began being processed into surimi, or imitation crab and lobster. The "strip mining" of pollock in Alaska waters has recently become an international controversy. Asian trawlers are football-field-long factory fishing boats that deploy drift nets up to two acres wide and 100 feet deep and use high-tech fish finders. They trap 20-30 times the sealife that is legal for them to keep, including seabirds and mammals. The male pollock are processed, but the females are stripped of their roe and

then the carcasses are dumped overboard (this is now illegal). Roughly 110 million pounds of pollock carcasses are dumped every year; more than four billion pounds, worth a little less than half a billion dollars, are harvested. International agreements against drift netting have not been ratified by Japan, Taiwan, and South Korea, whose trawlers are common around Alaska.

Smelt

The fattiest fish in northern waters is the Pacific Coast Eulachon, also known as smelt, hooligans, and candlefish (legend claims that the dried fish are so fatty they can be wicked and lit like candles). These silver and white fish are roughly as long and slender as pencils, and run in monumental numbers for three weeks in early summer from Northern California to the Pribilofs. A traditional source of oil, the females are dumped into pits or vats by the ton and left to rot for two weeks. Then fresh water is added and the whole mess is boiled, during which the oil rises to the surface. After skimming, straining, filtering, and sterilizing, roughly 20 gallons of oil (reminiscent of cod liver oil) can be processed from a ton of female smelt. The early males, in addition, are good tasting whether cooked, smoked, dried, or salted.

Aquaculture

The commercial growing and harvesting of shell-fish—oysters, mussels, clams, scallops, and abalone—and seaweed are slowly gathering momentum in coastal Alaska. Today, nearly 50 "farms" are actively engaged in aquacultural activities, mostly supplying Pacific Northwest markets and restaurants with consistently high-quality shellfish. A veritable swamp of regulatory hurdles, however, has inhibited the ocean farming; the one-billion-dollar-plus commercial fishing industry sees it as unwelcome competition. Still, the potential appears gargantuan.

By-products

Fact: One billion pounds of viable fish protein are wasted every year, which equals an astounding 80% of that which isn't wasted! Some fish by-products are processed into something usable, such as pet and livestock food and fertilizer. But fish heads, entrails, flesh left over after filleting, and bones—currently discarded as waste—

could be turned into marketable protein, in the form of fish bonemeal, fish oil and solubles, hydrolized protein, and other products. A large-scale fish by-products industry would also cut way down on pollution from commercial fisheries. Planning is in its early stages.

FLORA

Vegetation Zones

The vegetation of the North Pacific coast and the Yukon/Alaska Interior can be categorized into four main divisions: rainforest, boreal forest, taiga, and tundra. The lush coastal **rainforests** of British Columbia feature giant conifers: Douglas fir, hemlock, cedar, and spruce. Cedar continues into Southeast Alaska, but spruce and hemlock predominate, and Sitka spruce (Alaska's state tree) rivals California redwoods in height, age, beauty—and commercial value, of course. Sparser forests of hemlock and spruce stretch across Southcentral Alaska, with spruce continuing through northern Kodiak Island but not farther west than the adjacent mainland. Dense thickets of alder and willow grow in the higher, subalpine areas near the coast.

The **boreal forest** of the Interior lowlands consists primarily of scattered open stands of white spruce, paper birch, alpine fir, lodgepole pine, and balsam poplar (cottonwood). **Taiga,** the transition zone between boreal forest and tundra, is characterized by sparse and stunted black spruce, dwarf shrubbery (mostly the ubiquitous willow), and swampy areas known as muskegs.

The lower-elevation **tundra,** also known as the moist tundra, starts at treeline, around 2,500 feet. There you find undergrowth similar to that of the taiga, without the trees. The higher-elevation alpine tundra consists of grasses, clinging mosses and lichens, and an abundance of tiny, psychedelically bright wildflowers, including the unforgettable forget-me-not (state flower), with gaze-catching petals the color of Frank Sinatra's eyes.

Trees

There are actually two treelines in Alaska: one is determined by elevation, the other by latitude. Generally, treeline descends in elevation as the latitude ascends. Although alder and poplar do survive in isolated stands near the Brooks Range, the Arctic region on the North Slope is mostly treeless tundra. Dwarf willow, alder, grasses, and moss give the tundra here the appearance of a shag carpet. This tundra belt continues along the shores of the Bering Sea to the Alaska Peninsula and Aleutian Islands. Southward, the Arctic vegetation is gradually replaced by Pacific coastal varieties.

Sitka spruce continues to be logged and clearcut in Tongass National Forest in Southeast Alaska, a controversial boondoggle involving the National Forest Service, U.S. and Japanese logging companies, and local economies. (For details, see the special topic "A Clearcut Issue" in the Southeast Alaska chapter.) A small cottage industry has developed around white spruce cones. Alaska white spruce cones are harvested locally, then sold to makers of Christmas wreaths.

Mainland birch trees have also attracted the attention of the international lumber market. Birch has traditionally been favored locally for building (and heating) log cabins and for bark baskets, dogsleds, and syrup. The whiteness of birch wood makes it attractive to use in cabinets, paneling, countertops, and veneers, as well as toothpicks, chopsticks, and tongue depressors; the pulp is especially favored for white paper. Thus far, however, Alaska's birch hasn't met the standards of quality required by the world market.

Cabbage, Et Al

In 1941, the managers of the Alaska Railroad offered a $25 prize to the grower of the largest cabbage in the state, and since then cabbage growers have been competing. Usually, the largest cabbages at the Tanana Valley State Fair (in Fairbanks in mid-August) weigh in at 65-70 pounds, but the state (and world) record-holding cabbage is still 83 and a half pounds, grown near Wasilla in 1983. Ten-pound celeries, three-pound beets, two-pound turnips, and one-pound carrots are also blue-ribbon earners.

Flowers

Fireweed is a wildflower you'll come to know intimately during your travels in the North. It enjoys sunlight and grows profusely in open areas along roads and rivers. Given proper conditions, tall fireweed can grow to seven feet high; dwarf fireweed is more of a bush. Its long stalk of pink flowers blossoms from bottom to top; sourdoughs claim they can predict the arrival and severity of winter by the speed with which fireweed finishes blooming.

In Southcentral and Interior, **prickly rose** is a common sight. The plant grows stems up to four feet high, with sharp stickers. The flowers have five pink petals; the bright red rose hips ripen in mid-August and contain highly concentrated vitamin C. Pop 'em in your mouth, suck off the slightly tart flesh, spit out the pips, and climb a mountain.

rose hip

Three kinds of **primrose,** also a pinkish red, are another common sight on the tundra. Other red wildflowers of the tundra include **purple mountain saxifrage, moss campion,** and large, bright-pink **poppies.**

White flowers include the **narcissus-flowered anemone,** similar to a **buttercup,** which also grows on the tundra. **Mountain avens** are easily recognizable—they look like white roses. A half-dozen different kinds of white **saxifrage** are widespread throughout the state. Be careful of the local **hemlock:** some are harmless, one is deadly poisonous. Similar is the **yarrow,** with its disk of small white flowers and lacelike leaves, which is a medicinal herb. As soon as you identify **Labrador tea,** you'll notice it everywhere in the forest and taiga. **Cotton grass** looks exactly like its name. **Daisies** and **fleabane** complete this group of plants with white flowers.

Larkspur looks similar to fireweed, only it's a dark purple. It grows on a long stalk and a dwarf bush. **Monkshood** is a beautiful dark blue flower of the buttercup family; **harebells** and **bluebells** are easily identified around Denali. Three kinds of **violets** grow in the boreal forest. Light-purple **lupine** flowers grow in 20-inch clusters. **Asters,** resembling purple daisies, bloom all over the Interior.

While you're hiking, an excellent book to have along is *Wild Flowers of Alaska* by Christine Heller. The photographs are good, the descriptions are usable (if a

blackberry

little technical), and the flowers are conveniently arranged by color.

Berries

Berries are the only fruits that grow naturally in Alaska, and luckily the many varieties are abundant, several are edible, a few even taste good, and only one is poisonous. If you're into berry collecting, get to know poisonous **baneberry** immediately. A member of the crowfoot family, it grows mostly in Southeast and central Interior. The white berries look like black-eyed peas; they ripen to a scarlet red. **Juniper berries** grow throughout Alaska, but the **bog** and **Alaska blueberries** and **huckleberries** are much tastier. Blueberries also grow on poorly drained shady alpine slopes and are generally the first to ripen. **Bunchberries** and **elderberries** are good-tasting but have been known to upset a stomach or two. **Bog cranberries** are best after the first frost, especially when they're a deep purple—deliciously tart. **High-bush cranberries** are common but are best just before they're completely ripe. **Red raspberries** are a lucky find; a couple of great patches grow around the Denali Park Hotel, but nobody'll tell you where. **Wild strawberries** are even better, if you can get to them before the birds and rodents. The several kinds of **bearberries** (blue and red) are tasteless except to bears, and the **soapberry** will remind you of getting caught saying a dirty word as a kid. Pick up *Alaska Wild Berry Guide and Cookbook* by the editors of *Alaska* magazine.

mountain blueberry

Mushrooms

Approximately 500 species of mushrooms are found in Alaska, thrusting up from the fecund forests from Ketchikan to Katmai and the rich tundra from Kantishna to Kotzebue. Most of the mushrooms are harmless to humans, and often edible; a handful are poisonous, such as varieties of amanita (especially the muscaria, or fly agaric, breed) and poison pax. But if you learn to identify such common species as hedgehogs and shaggy manes, you'll enjoy happy hunting, mostly in July and August.

HISTORY

PREHISTORY

The Athabascan Indians of Canada have a legend that tells how, in the misty past, one of their ancestors helped a giant in Siberia slay a rival. The defeated giant fell into the sea, forming a bridge to North America. The forefathers of the Athabascans then crossed this bridge, bringing the caribou with them. Eventually the giant's body decomposed, but parts of his skeleton were left sticking above the ocean to form the Aleutian Islands.

In less fanciful terms, what probably happened was that low ocean levels during the Pleistocene epoch (some 30,000-40,000 years ago) offered the nomadic peoples of northeastern Asia a 50-mile-long and 600-mile-wide land "bridge" over the Bering Sea. One of the earliest records of humans in the Americas is a caribou bone with a serrated edge found at Old Crow in northern Yukon. Almost certainly used as a tool, the bone has been placed at 27,000 years old by carbon dating. The interior lowlands of Alaska and the Yukon Valley, which were never glaciated, provided an ice-free migration route. As the climate warmed and the great ice sheets receded toward the Rocky Mountains and Canadian Shield, a corridor opened down the middle of the Great Plains, allowing movement farther south.

The Athabascans

The Athabascans (or Dene) were the first Indian group to cross the Bering land bridge. Their language is spoken today from Interior Alaska to the American Southwest (among Navajos and Apaches). Way back when (anywhere from 40,000-12,000 years ago), these Indians of the Interior followed the mastodon, mammoth, and caribou herds which supplied them with most of their necessities. Agriculture was unknown to them, but they did fashion crude implements from the raw copper found in the region. Eventually, certain tribes found their way to the coast. The Athabascan-related Tlingits, for example, migrated down the Nass River near Prince Rupert and then spread north through Southeast Alaska. The rich environment provided them with abundant fish and shellfish, as well as with the great cedar logs from which they fashioned community houses, totem poles, and long dugout canoes.

The Eskimo

The Mongoloid Eskimo (commonly known as Eskimos) arrived from Asia probably some 10,000 years ago near the end of the last ice age. Today they are found in Siberia and across Alaska and Arctic Canada to Greenland. Their language, which in Alaska is divided into the Inupiak dialect in the north and the Yup'ik dialect in the south, is unrelated to any other in North America except that of the Aleuts. Like the Tlingits, they too lived near the coast, along the migratory routes of the marine mammals they hunted in kayaks and umiaks. They also relied upon caribou, birds, and fish. Their homes were partly underground and constructed of driftwood, antlers, whale bones, and sod. (The well-known snow-and-ice igloo was exclusive to Canadian Natives.) In the summer skin tents were used at fish camps. The Eskimo did not utilize dogsleds until the coming of the white people.

The Aleut

Marine mammals and fish provided the Eskimo-related Aleuts with food, clothing, and household materials. They were famous for their tightly woven baskets. Prior to the arrival of the Russians in the 1740s, 25,000 Aleut inhabited almost all of the Aleutian Islands; by the year 1800 there were only about 2,000 survivors. The ruthless Russian fur traders murdered and kidnapped the men, enslaved or abandoned the women, and passed on their genes and diseases so successfully that today only 1,000 full-blooded Aleuts remain. The rest intermarried with the conquerors, and scattered groups of their descendants are now found in the eastern Aleutians and the Pribilofs to the north.

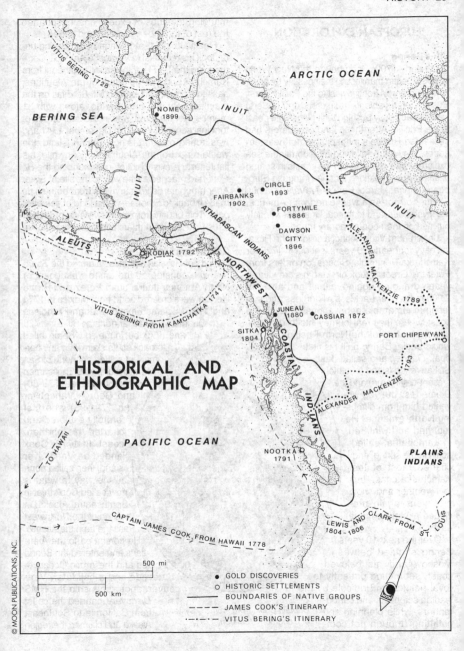

HISTORICAL AND ETHNOGRAPHIC MAP

ARCTIC OCEAN

BERING SEA

INUIT

NOME 1899

INUIT

VITUS BERING 1728

CIRCLE 1893

FAIRBANKS 1902

FORTYMILE 1886

DAWSON CITY 1896

ATHABASCAN INDIANS

INUIT

ALEXANDER MACKENZIE 1789

ALEUTS

KODIAK 1792

NORTHWEST

VITUS BERING FROM KAMCHATKA 1741

JUNEAU 1880

CASSIAR 1872

FORT CHIPEWYAN

SITKA 1804

COASTAL

ALEXANDER MACKENZIE 1793

ALEXANDER MACKENZIE

TO HAWAII

PACIFIC OCEAN

INDIANS

NOOTKA 1791

PLAINS INDIANS

CAPTAIN JAMES COOK FROM HAWAII 1778

LEWIS AND CLARK FROM ST. LOUIS 1804-1806

© MOON PUBLICATIONS, INC.

0   500 mi

0   500 km

● GOLD DISCOVERIES
○ HISTORIC SETTLEMENTS
— BOUNDARIES OF NATIVE GROUPS
- - - JAMES COOK'S ITINERARY
-·-·- VITUS BERING'S ITINERARY

EUROPEAN EXPLORATION

Vitus Bering

In the early 1700s, long before the New World colonists began manifesting their destiny by pushing the American frontier west to the Pacific coast, Russian *promyshleniki* (explorers and traders) were already busy pushing their own frontier east to the Pacific. After these land conquerors had delineated Russia's inhospitable northeastern edges, they were followed by indomitable sea explorers who cast off from the coasts in search of answers to questions that had intrigued Europeans since Marco Polo's *Travels:* mainly, whether or not Asia was joined with America, the mysterious land to the east that was vaguely outlined on then-contemporary maps.

Danish-born Vitus Bering, a sailor in the Russian navy for nearly 20 years, set out in 1725 for Kamchatka Peninsula, Siberia, on orders from Peter the Great. It took him and his crew three years, dragging rigging, cable, and anchors 2,000 miles over trackless wilderness and suffering innumerable deprivations to reach the coast, where their real journey into the uncharted waters of the North Pacific would begin. Bering built his first boat, *Gabriel,* and sailed past St. Lawrence Island (south of present-day Nome) and the Diomedes, but fog prevented him from glimpsing North America. He returned and wintered in Kamchatka, sailed again in the spring, and charted most of the Kamchatka coast, but foul weather and short provisions again precluded exploring farther east.

Over the next 10 years, Bering shuttled between Moscow and his beloved coast, submitting patiently to royal politics and ridicule by the leading scientists and cartographers, while planning and outfitting (though not com-

Captain Cook, from Payne's System of Geography *(London, 1791)*

manding) a series of expeditions that charted the rest of the Siberian coast and Japan.

Finally, in 1741, at the age of 60, Bering undertook his remarkable voyage to America. Commanding the *St. Peter,* he sailed southeast from Kamchatka, came up south of the Aleutians, passed Kodiak, and sighted Mt. St. Elias on the mainland. By that time Bering, along with 31 members of his crew, was in the final throes of terminal scurvy. He died in December 1741 and was buried on what is now Bering Island, the westernmost of the Aleutians. Meanwhile, his lieutenant, Alexis Chirikof, commanding the *St. Paul,* had reached all the way to the site of Sitka. After much hardship, survivors from both ships made it back to Siberia—with a load of sea otter pelts. This bounty from the New World prompted a rush of Russian hunters and traders to Alaska.

Conflicting Claims

Reports of Russian advances alarmed the Spanish, who considered the entire west coast of North America theirs. Juan Perez and Bruno Hecata were ordered north from Mexico in 1774 and 1775. Spanish explorer Juan Francisco Quadra sailed as far north as Sitka in 1775 and 1779, but in the end, Spain failed to back up its claim with any permanent settlement north of San Francisco. It was Englishmen James Cook (in 1776-80) and George Vancouver (in 1791-95) who first carefully explored and charted this northern coast. In 1778, Cook landed on Vancouver Island, then sailed north all the way to what is now called Cook Inlet in Southcentral Alaska, in search of the Northwest Passage from the Atlantic. He continued to the Aleutians and entered the Bering Sea and the Arctic Ocean. A decade and a half later, Vancouver, aboard his ship the HMS *Discovery,* charted the coast from California to Southeast Alaska and claimed the region for England. His was the first extensive exploration of Puget Sound and circumnavigation of Vancouver Island; his maps and charts of this confounding coast were so accurate that they were used for another 100 years.

Exploration by Land
Meanwhile, explorers were reaching the Pacific overland from bases in eastern Canada and the United States. In 1789 a Northwest Company trader, Alexander Mackenzie, paddled down the Mackenzie River to the Arctic Ocean. Four years later, in 1793, he became the first person to cross the entire continent by land, reaching the Pacific at Bella Coola, British Columbia. Other employees of the same aggressive Montreal-based company explored farther south. In 1808, Simon Fraser followed the Fraser River, stopping near the present site of the city of Vancouver; in 1810-11 David Thompson traveled from the headwaters of the Saskatchewan River to the mouth of the Columbia, near present-day Portland. In 1803, after the United States purchased 827,000 square miles of territory west of the Mississippi River from France, Pres. Thomas Jefferson ordered a military fact-finding mission into the area. Led by Lewis and Clark, a group of explorers paddled up the Missouri River to its headwaters and crossed to the Columbia, which they followed to the Pacific (1804-06), helping to open vast expanses of western North America. American fur traders followed close behind. (The Alaskan interior, however, was not properly explored until the gold rush at the end of the 19th century.)

The Fur Trade
The excesses of the *promyshleniki,* who had massacred and enslaved the Aleut, prompted the czar in 1789 to create the Russian America Company, headed by Gregor Shelikof, a fur trader and merchant who in 1784 had established the first permanent settlement in Alaska (at Three Saints Bay on Kodiak Island). Alexander Baranof, a salesman in Siberia, was the first director of the company; he moved the settlement up to present-day Kodiak town, and for the next 20 years, Baranof *was* the law. One of the most powerful men in Alaskan history, he enslaved the remaining Aleuts, warred with the Panhandle Indians, initiated trade with the English, Spanish, and Americans, and sent his trading vessels as far away as Hawaii, Japan, and Mexico. Exhausting the resources of Kodiak and its neighborhood, he moved the company to Sitka, where, according to Merle Colby in his classic 1939 WPA *Guide To Alaska,* ". . . from his wooden 'castle' on the hill surmounting the harbor he made Sitka the most brilliant capital in the new world. Yankee sailors, thrashing around the Horn, beating their way up the California coast, anchored at last in Sitka harbor and found the city an American Paris, its streets crowded with adventurers from half the world away, its nights gay with balls illuminated by brilliant uniforms and the evening dresses of Russian ladies." Except for the Tlingit Indians, who fought bitterly against Russian imperialism, Baranof's rule, extending from Bristol Bay in western Alaska to Fort Ross, California, was complete. His one last dream—of returning to Russia—was never fulfilled. On the voyage back to the homeland, Baranof died at the age of 72.

THE 19TH CENTURY

Political Units Form
In 1824 and 1825, Russia signed agreements with the U.S. and Britain, fixing the southern limit of Russian America at 54° 40' north latitude, near present-day Ketchikan. But the vast territory south of this line was left up for grabs. The American claim to the Oregon Territory around the Columbia River was based on its discovery by Robert Gray in 1792, and on the first overland exploration by Lewis and Clark. Britain based its claim to the region on its effective occupation of the land by the Northwest Company, which in 1821 merged with the Hudson's Bay Company. As American settlers began to inhabit the area, feelings ran high—President Polk was elected in 1846 on the slogan, "Fifty-four Forty or Fight," referring to the proposed northern boundary between America and British territory in the Pacific Northwest. War between Britain and the U.S. was averted when both agreed to draw the boundary line to the Pacific along the 49th parallel, which remains to this day the Canadian/American border. Vancouver Island went

During the Klondike gold rush, tiny cottages and tents crept up the hillsides as Dawson overflowed its narrow plain beside the Yukon River.

PROVINCIAL ARCHIVES OF BRITISH COLUMBIA

to Britain, and the new Canadian nation purchased all the territorial holdings of the Hudson's Bay Company (Rupert's Land) in 1870. In 1871, British Columbia joined the Canadian Confederation on a promise from the leaders of the infant country of a railroad to extend there from the east.

The Russians Bail Out

1863 was a bad year for the Russian America Company. Back in the motherland, Russia's feudal society was breaking down, threatening the aristocracy's privileged status. In Alaska, competition from English and American whalers and traders was intensifying. Food was scarce and supply ships from California were unreliable and infrequent. Worst, perhaps, were the dwindled numbers of fur seals and sea otters, hunted nearly to extinction over the past century. In addition, bad relations with Britain in the aftermath of the Crimean War (1853-56) prompted Czar Alexander the First to fear for the loss of his far-flung Alaskan possessions to the British by force. Finally, the czar did not renew the Company's charter, and the Russian America Company officially closed up shop.

Meanwhile, American technology was performing miracles. Western Union had laid two cables under the Atlantic Ocean from the U.S. to Europe, but neither had yet worked. So they figured, let's go the other way around the world: it was proposed to lay a cable overland through British Columbia, along the Yukon River, across the Bering Strait into Siberia, then east and south into Europe. In 1865, the Western Union Telegraph Expedition to Alaska, led by William Dall, surveyed the interior of Alaska for the first time, revealing its vast land and resources. This stimulated considerable interest in frontier-minded Washington, D.C. In addition, Czar Alexander's Alaska salesman, Baron Edward de Stoeckl, was spending $200,000 of his own money to make a positive impression on influential politicians and journalists.

Secretary of State William H. Seward purchased Alaska on March 30, 1867, for the all-time bargain-basement price of $7,200,000— *two cents* an acre. The American flag was hoisted over Sitka on October 18, 1867. According to Ernest Gruening, first U.S. senator to Alaska, "a year later when the House of Representatives was called upon to pay the bill, skeptical congressmen scornfully labeled Alaska 'Icebergia,' 'Walrussia,' 'Seward's Icebox,' and '[President] Johnson's Polar Bear Garden.' If American forces had not already raised the Stars and Stripes in Sitka, the House might have refused to pick up the tab." (Stoeckl, meanwhile, reimbursed himself the $200,000 he'd invested and sent the other seven million home to Alexander.) Subsequently, Alaska faded into official oblivion for the next 15 years—universally regarded as a frozen wasteland and a colossal waste of money.

Organic Act of 1884

This act organized Alaska for the first time, providing a territorial governor and law enforcement (though not a local legislature or representation in Washington). President Chester Arthur appointed federal district court judges, U.S. attorneys, and marshals. From 1884 to 1900, only one U.S. judge, attorney, and marshal managed the whole territory, all residing in the capital, Sitka. The first three appointees to the court in Sitka were removed in disgrace amidst charges of "incompetence, wickedness, unfairness, and drunkenness." A succession of scandals dogged other federal appointees— and that was only in Sitka; the vast Interior had no law at all until 1900, when Congress divided the territory into three legal districts, with courts at Sitka, Nome, and Eagle.

William H. Dall wrote of Alaska at that time as a place where "no man could make a legal will, own a homestead or transfer it, or so much as cut wood for his fire without defying a Congressional prohibition; where polygamy and slavery and the lynching of witches prevailed, with no legal authority to stay or punish criminals." Kipling's line, "There's never law of God or man runs north of 53," also refers to the young territory of Alaska. In contrast, Colby in his WPA guide commented that the gold rush stampeders, "although technically without civil authority, created their own form of self-government. The miners organized 'miners meetings' to enforce order, settle boundary disputes, and administer rough and ready justice. Too often this form of government failed to cope with [serious problems] . . . yet the profound instinct of the American people for self-government and their tradition of democracy made local self-government effective until the creation of the Alaska Legislature in 1912."

The Search for Gold

Alaska's gold rush changed everything. After the California stampede of 1849, the search moved north. In 1858 there was a rush up the Fraser River to the Cariboo goldfields. In 1872, gold was found in B.C.'s Cassiar region. Strikes in Alaska and the Yukon followed one another in quick succession: at Juneau (1880), Fortymile (1886), Circle (1893), Dawson City (1896), Nome (1899), Fairbanks (1902), and Iditarod (1908).

A very mobile group of men and women followed these discoveries on riverboats, dogsleds, and foot, creating instant outposts of civilization near the gold strikes. Gold also caused the Canadian and American governments to take a serious look at their northernmost possessions for the first time; the beginnings of the administrative infrastructures of both Yukon and Alaska date from those times. Still, in 1896, when Siwash George Carmack and his two Athabascan brothers-in-law discovered gold where Bonanza Creek flowed into the Klondike River in Yukon Territory, this vast northern wilderness could barely be called "settled." Only a handful of tiny non-Native villages existed along the Yukon River from Ogilvie and Fortymile in western Yukon to Circle and Fort Yukon in eastern Alaska, and a single unoccupied cabin sat on a beach at the mouth of the Skagway River at the terminus of the Inside Passage.

But by the end of 1897, 10,000-20,000 stampeders had skirted the lone cabin on their way to the headwaters of the Yukon and the sure fortunes in gold that awaited them on the Klondike. The two trails from Skagway over the coastal mountains and onto the interior rivers proved to be the most "civilized" and successful routes to Dawson. But the fortune-frenzied hordes proceeded north, uninformed, aiming at Dawson from every direction on the compass. They suffered every conceivable hardship and misery from which death (often by suicide) was sometimes the only relief. And those who finally burst through the barrier and landed at the Klondike and Dawson were already two years too late to partake of the "ready" gold.

But the North had been conquered. And by the time the gold rush had spread to Nome, Fairbanks, Kantishna, Hatcher Pass, and Hope, Alaska could finally be called settled (if not civilized).

THE 20TH CENTURY

In the first decade of the new century, the sprawling wilderness was starting to be tamed. The military set up shop at Valdez and Eagle to maintain law and order, telegraph cables were laid across the Interior, the Northwest Passage had been found, railroads were begun at several locations, vast copper deposits were being mined, and thousands of independent pioneer-types were surviving on their own wits and the country's resources. Footpaths widened into wagon trails. Mail deliveries were regularized. Limited self-government was initiated: the capital moved to Juneau from Sitka in 1905; Alaska's first congressional delegate arrived in Washington in 1906; and a territorial legislature convened in 1912. A year later, the first men stood atop the south peak of Mt. McKinley, and the surrounding area was set aside as a national park in 1917. At that time, Alaska's white and Native populations had reached equivalency, at around 35,000 each. Judge James Wickersham introduced the first statehood bill to the U.S. Congress in 1916, but Alaska drifted along in federal obscurity until the Japanese bombed Pearl Harbor.

War

It's been said that war is good for one thing: the rapid expansion of communications and mobility technology. Alaska proves the rule. In the early 1940s, military bases were established at Anchorage, Whittier, Fairbanks, Nome, Sitka, Delta, Kodiak, Dutch Harbor, and the tip of the Aleutians, which brought an immediate influx of military and support personnel and services. In addition, in 1942 alone, the 1,440-mile Alaska Highway from Dawson Creek, B.C., to Delta, Alaska; the 50 miles of the Klondike Highway from Whitehorse to Carcross; the 151-mile Haines Highway; and the 328-mile Glenn Highway from Tok to Anchorage, among others, were punched through the trackless wilderness, finally connecting Alaska by road to the rest of the world. At the war's peak, 150,000 troops were stationed in the territory; all told, the U.S. government spent almost a billion dollars there during the war. (For a full description of the actual fighting, see "War in the Aleutians" under "The Aleutian Islands" in the Southwest Alaska chapter.) After the war, as after the gold rush, Alaska's population increased dramatically, with servicemen remaining or returning. The number of residents nearly doubled between 1940 and 1950.

Statehood

The 1950s brought a boom in construction, logging, fishing, and bureaucracy to Alaska. The decade also saw the discovery of a large oil reserve off the western Kenai Peninsula in the Cook Inlet. The population continued to grow, yet Alaskans still felt like residents of a second-class colony of the U.S. and repeatedly asked for statehood status throughout the decade. Finally, on July 7, 1958, Congress voted to admit Alaska into the Union as the 49th state. President Dwight D. Eisenhower signed the official proclamation on January 3, 1959—43 years after Judge James Wickersham had first introduced the idea.

A little over five years later, the Good Friday earthquake struck Southcentral; at 9.2 on the Richter scale, it remains the largest earthquake ever recorded in the Western Hemisphere. After the tremors and tsunamis had ceased, Anchorage, Whittier, Valdez, Cordova, Seward, and Kodiak lay in shambles, 131 people had died, and damage was estimated at half a billion dollars. But Alaskans quickly recovered and rebuilt with the plucky determination and optimism that still characterize the young state.

The Modern Era

Alaska entered the big time, experiencing its most recent boom, in 1968, when Atlantic Richfield discovered a 10-billion-barrel oil reserve at Prudhoe Bay. In 1969, Alaska auctioned off leases to almost half a million acres of oil-rich country on the North Slope for $900 million, 10 times more money than all its previous leases combined. A consortium of oil-company leaseholders immediately began planning the Trans-Alaska Pipeline to carry the crude from Prudhoe Bay to Valdez. But conservationists, worried about its environmental impact, and Native groups, concerned about land-use compensation, filed suit, delaying construction for four years.

The upshot of those legal actions was passage in 1971 of the Alaska Native Claims Settlement Act (ANCSA) and the Alaska National Interest Lands Conservation Act (ANILCA) in

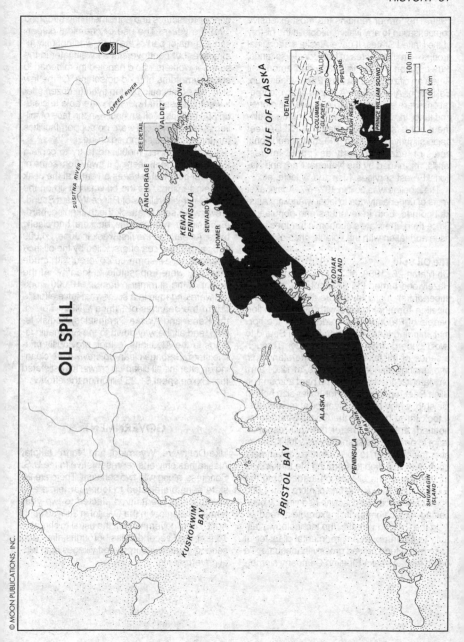

OIL SPILL

GULF OF ALASKA

COPPER RIVER

VALDEZ
CORDOVA
SEE DETAIL

SUSITNA RIVER

ANCHORAGE

KENAI PENINSULA

SEWARD

HOMER

COOK INLET

KODIAK ISLAND

ALASKA

CHIGNIK BAY

PENINSULA

BRISTOL BAY

KUSKOKWIM BAY

SHUMAGIN ISLAND

DETAIL

COLUMBIA GLACIER

VALDEZ

PIPELINE

BLIGH REEF

PRINCE WILLIAM SOUND

100 mi

100 km

© MOON PUBLICATIONS, INC.

1980. The former remains the most extensive compensation to any Native people in the history of the United States. It gave Alaska's aboriginal groups 44 million acres of traditional-use lands, plus a billion dollars to be divided among all American citizens with at least 25% Athabascan, Eskimo, or Aleut blood. A dozen Native corporations were established to manage the money and land, in which each recipient of the settlement holds shares. The latter, ANILCA, set aside slightly more than 100 million additional acres of federal property as "public-interest lands," managed by the National Park and National Forest services, Fish and Wildlife, etc.

The pipeline was built in 1974-77. Again, after years of uncertainty due to legal wrangling, Alaska boomed, both in revenues and population. Since then, the state's economic fortunes have risen and fallen with the volatile price of oil.

The Oil Spill

On March 23, 1989, at 11 p.m., Capt. Joseph Hazelwood turned the 987-foot *Exxon Valdez* supertanker, just a few hours after leaving the pipeline terminal loaded with over 20 million barrels of Prudhoe Bay crude, out of the normal shipping lanes of Prince William Sound to avoid icebergs from Columbia Glacier. Through a series of mistakes and misunderstandings, and ignoring standard procedure, at 12:01 a.m. on March 24 the *Valdez* ran up hard aground on Bligh Reef, opening a tractor trailer-size hole in the ship, which began to leak oil at a rapid rate. It took three hours for the Coast Guard to be notified, and 12 hours for the spill-response team to arrive at the scene. It was a full 72 hours after the oil began to spill before a containment boom was installed to surround the tanker. But as the rest of the oil was off-loaded onto the *Exxon Baton Rouge,* the fate of more than 1,000 miles of Southcentral coastline had already been sealed. The oil began its inexorable spread.

In the following weeks, the technology available to clean up an environmental disaster of such magnitude proved grossly inadequate. To begin with, Alyeska Pipeline Company's emergency procedures and equipment had atrophied over the years. The use of chemical dispersants, a major part of the plan, was not only ineffective, but controversial as well: later in the summer workers who'd handled them began to show symptoms of toxic poisoning. Of the few skimmers that could be deployed (a dozen after a week), those that worked were able to clean up 500 gallons of oil an hour—in the face of millions. And then there were no support facilities for unloading the skimmed crude.

Local fishermen mobilized to try to contain the oil with booms, keeping it away from some of the most bountiful fisheries on earth at the peak of their seasons. As the oil washed up on the wildlife-rich shorelines of Prince William Sound, crews were sent to attack the thickening, hardening sludge with shovels, buckets, and plastic bags. As early as the first week in June, 24,000 birds and 1,000 sea otters, killed by the oil, had been counted—some so covered with crude that they were impossible to identify. At the height of the summer clean-up, 10,000 workers were engaged in a somewhat futile effort to return the beaches of Prince William Sound, the Kenai and Alaska Peninsulas, Kodiak Island, and all the way down to the Shumagin Islands in the Aleutians to their previously pristine state. Garbage clean-up crews were cleaning up after the oil clean-up crews. It's estimated that Exxon spent $1.25 billion on the effort.

GOVERNMENT

Like Delaware, Wyoming, and North Dakota, Alaska has only one representative to the U.S. Congress, along with two senators. There are 20 state senators elected to four-year terms and 40 state representatives elected to two-year terms. They meet in the Capitol in Juneau Jan.-April. Local government is the usual mishmash: 16 first- and second-class boroughs, first- and second-class unincorporated villages, and tribal governments.

ECONOMY

Cost of Living

No doubt about it—this place is expensive. Alaska ranks near the top in the cost of living of all the states. Numerous factors conspire to keep prices high. Most consumer goods must be imported from the Lower 48, and the transportation costs are tacked on along the line. In addition, the transportation and shipping rates within Alaska are similarly high, further inflating the cost of goods and services. In more remote regions especially, lack of competition coupled with steady demand ensures top-dollar prices. And let's not forget how long and cold and dark Alaskan winters are; the cost of heat and utilities is an especial hardship. Alaska ranks first in per-capita energy consumption in the U.S. Because the cost of living is so high, wages tend to keep pace, which in turn adds to the high cost of goods and services. It's a self-perpetuating cycle.

In comparative terms, Alaskans on the average earn more per hour, per week, and per year ($23,788 in 1994, compared to $18,237 national average; eighth highest in the national standings) than the rest of the country. Except for Anchorage and Fairbanks, whose large populations and direct transportation allow for slightly more competitive prices, generally the farther you are in the state from Seattle, the higher the prices—consumer goods in Kotzebue, for example, can be up to 100% more expensive than in Ketchikan. These financial realities apply to residents much more than to short-term visitors: if you're well prepared and you provision yourself adequately in the major commercial centers, any time spent in the bush shouldn't be too painful to the pocketbook. For more tips on budget travel in Alaska, see "Other Practicalities" in the On the Road chapter.

Employment

Some myths die hard. Thanks to the two huge booms of the past 100 years, many outsiders still harbor the impression that all you have to do is get to Alaska and you'll automatically make your fortune in the gold mines and oilfields. It was as false in 1898 and 1975 as it is now. Furthermore, the many (but rarely publicized) busts in the Alaskan economy do not seem to disturb the national perception. Unemployment figures are usually several percentage points above the national average, even during the peak summer season; in winter they can be double the average. In addition, the highly localized industrial base makes Alaskans especially susceptible to hard times: when logging is in trouble, all Southeast suffers; when the fishing season is disappointing, the whole coastline tightens its belt; when oil prices drop, the entire state gets depressed.

However, the employment picture is not as bleak as many residents and state officials would like the rest of the country to believe. You can still come to Alaska and make a fortune, or just make a living and a life—after all, most Alaskans come from somewhere else (only 33.3% of Alaskans were born in the state—the second-lowest such ratio in the country). But the opportunities, it should be stressed, are limited. For example, one out of every three and a half people collecting a paycheck in Alaska works for federal, state, or local government. And the industry that accounts for almost 90% of state revenues (oil and gas) accounts for less than four percent of employment. For a closer look at breaking into the Alaskan job market, see "Employment" in the On the Road chapter.

Permanent Fund

In 1976, with oil wealth about to come gushing out of the south end of the pipeline, voters approved a constitutional amendment calling for a percentage of all oil and mineral revenues to be placed in a Permanent Fund. Money from this account can only be used for investment, not for state operating expenses, which explains why during recent Alaskan recessions, when hundreds of state workers were laid off and state funds were severely cut back, more than seven billion surplus dollars sat untouched in the Fund. It's the only one of its kind in the country: the only state fund that pays dividends to residents, and the largest pool of public money in the country.

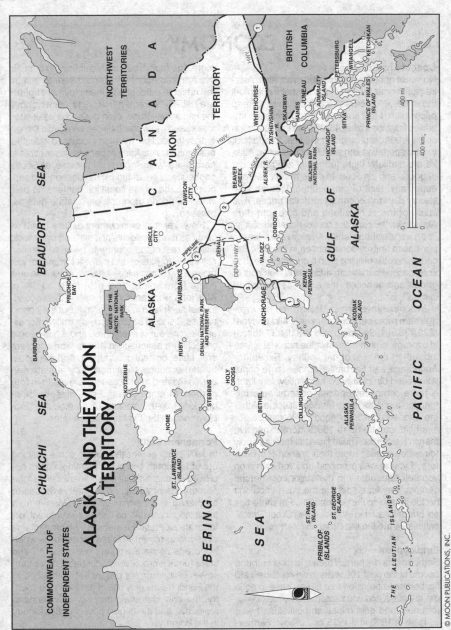

ALASKA AND THE YUKON TERRITORY

COMMONWEALTH OF INDEPENDENT STATES

CHUKCHI SEA

BEAUFORT SEA

NORTHWEST TERRITORIES

CANADA

YUKON TERRITORY

BRITISH COLUMBIA

BERING SEA

ALASKA

PACIFIC OCEAN

GULF OF ALASKA

BARROW

PRUDHOE BAY

TRANS ALASKA PIPELINE

GATES OF THE ARCTIC NATIONAL PARK

KOTZEBUE

NOME

RUBY

FAIRBANKS

CIRCLE CITY

DAWSON CITY

DENALI NATIONAL PARK AND PRESERVE

DENALI

DENALI HWY

ANCHORAGE

VALDEZ

CORDOVA

KENAI PENINSULA

KODIAK ISLAND

HOLY CROSS

STEBBINS

BETHEL

DILLINGHAM

ALASKA PENINSULA

ST. LAWRENCE ISLAND

ST. PAUL ISLAND

ST. GEORGE ISLAND

PRIBILOF ISLANDS

THE ALEUTIAN ISLANDS

BEAVER CREEK

KLONDIKE HWY

ALASKA HWY

WHITEHORSE

TATSHENSHINI R.

ALSEK R.

HAINES

SKAGWAY

JUNEAU

GLACIER BAY NATIONAL PARK

ADMIRALTY ISLAND

CHICHAGOF ISLAND

SITKA

PETERSBURG

WRANGELL

KETCHIKAN

PRINCE OF WALES ISLAND

400 mi

400 km.

The resident dividend program you might hear about distributes a portion of the interest and capital gains income from Permanent Fund assets to all Alaska residents (including children over two) in a yearly check. The size of the checks ranges around $500-1,000. In 1982, the first year of the dividend, each Alaskan received $1,000; in 1985, the dividend only amounted to $425; in 1987, the individual's share of the whopping $1.05 billion in earnings for the 1986 fiscal year was $723. Residents received checks for just under $1,000 in 1996.

Fishing
Alaska accounts for nearly 25% of the entire country's commercial fish production—over a billion pounds, worth more than $1.5 billion. A little more than two-thirds of the value is in salmon and groundfish (pollock and cod), the rest in shellfish, halibut, herring, and others. Six Alaskan ports are among the country's 50 top producers, with Kodiak almost always in the top three. Alaska produces 99% of the U.S. canned salmon stock (200 million pounds). Fishing is Alaska's largest industry in terms of jobs (80,000) and contributes about 22% of the state's revenues—more than tourism, mining, agriculture, and forestry combined.

Agriculture
The percentage of Alaska's land used for farming is as minuscule as the percentage of Alaska's total economy that is accounted for by agriculture. Of the state's 375 million acres (with 17 million suitable for farming), less than 900,000 acres are considered cultivatable; of those, only 30,000 acres are occupied by crops. Of the nearly $15 billion of gross state product, only $27 million comes from agricultural sales. The Matanuska Valley (Palmer/Wasilla) and the Tanana Valley (Fairbanks/Delta) occupy almost 90% of Alaska's usable farmland. Hay, potatoes, milk, vegetables, and barley are the state's top five ag products.

Gold and Minerals
From 1880 to 1980, 30 million ounces of gold were taken from Alaska. Keep in mind, however, that up until 1967, gold was never worth more than $35 per troy ounce, while in 1996 it was worth around $385. From 1900 to 1980, 1.38 billion pounds of copper, and from 1920

to 1980, 29.2 million tons of coal, were mined from Alaskan ground. From 1880 to 1980, excluding gas and oil, $20 billion in minerals were recovered in the state.

Since 1980, upwards of $1.5 billion worth of gold has been mined. The biggest news in Alaska gold production is the Fort Knox Mine, outside the Fairbanks suburb of Fox. Fort Knox opens in November 1997 and will produce millions of ounces over its expected 20 years in production.

Zinc is the state's most valuable mineral, mined primarily at the Red Dog, 90 miles north of Kotzebue. It's worth around $250 million a year. One and a half million tons of coal are mined at Usibelli, near Denali National Park; half is used to fuel interior Alaska power plants, the other half is exported to Korea.

Alaska is the only state that produces platinum, more valuable than gold; half a million ounces have been placer mined from southwestern Alaska. Deposits of zinc, jade, molybdenum, chromite, nickel, and uranium have also been located, though the cost of mining in remote Alaska has generally limited these ventures.

Oil
Everything that moves in Alaska is lubricated with oil, primarily North Slope crude. Without oil, the Alaskan economy would stiffen, shatter, and disappear into thin air. Oil and gas revenues account for 87% of Alaska's entire gross state product. Alaska is so addicted to oil revenue that when the price of a barrel of oil drops $1, the Alaskan budget must be adjusted by $450 million. Yet, this industry only accounts for four percent of the total workforce.

Even pumping nearly 600 million barrels of oil a year, Alaska was still second in production to Texas; Alaska accounts for 23% of the country's oil. Since commercial drilling in Alaska began in 1902, more than four billion barrels of oil have been produced. In 1976, only 67 million barrels flowed from Alaska; in 1977, during which the pipeline was in operation for nearly half the year, 171 million barrels were pumped out of Alaskan ground. In 1978, however, with the pipeline in full swing, almost 450 million barrels were produced. Peak production was in 1988, with 738 million barrels of Prudhoe crude flowing through the pipeline.

The Prudhoe Bay oilfield, largest in North America and 18th in the world, had an estimated 12 billion barrels of oil recoverable with today's technology. A little over nine billion barrels of that had been pumped through the pipeline by early 1995. With oil revenues adding up to $25 billion, exactly $50,000 for every person in the state, you can see why Alaska is the richest state in the Union.

Tourism

Tourism is Alaska's third-largest industry, behind petroleum production and commercial fishing. It's the second largest employer, accounting for 27,000 direct and more than 50,000 indirect jobs. Slightly more than a million annual visitors to Alaska spend more than $1.5 billion in state, nine out of 10 of them arriving May-September.

Approximately 56% of visitors (including business travelers) travel independently; the rest come up on package tours. Ninety percent come from the continental U.S. and Canada. According to the Alaska Visitors Statistics Program, a two-year study conducted for Alaska Division of Tourism, visitors rated Alaska a number-six destination out of a possible seven points. According to the report, the "friendliness and helpfulness" of the people merited a 6.2, "sightseeing and attractions" got a 6.0, and "restaurants and accommodations" averaged 5.1. Favorite activities included flightseeing, day cruising, rafting, fishing, canoeing, and hiking, whereas shopping, dining, and nightlife were low on the list. In order of most visits by all visitors, the top 10 attractions are: Portage Glacier, Inside Passage, Mendenhall Glacier, Glacier Bay, Ketchikan totems, Denali National Park, the pipeline, Sitka's Russian church, University of Alaska museum in Fairbanks, and Skagway's Gold Rush Historic District.

LANGUAGE

A type of pidgin called "Chinook" evolved in the Pacific Northwest in the 18th century. The language was named after the large, powerful Chinook tribe of the Columbia River, which did business with white traders and the Nootka tribe, which held a monopoly on the shells from which the shell money of the Pacific was manufactured. This pidgin first developed between the Chinooks and the Nootkas, and after Europeans arrived, it adopted words from English and French; it was indispensable to traders in Alaska during the entire 19th century. Of the 500 words in the Chinook vocabulary, a few are still used today. Some of the words below have been borrowed from the Eskimo (Native) tongue; the rest derive from the colorful frontier slang of explorers, traders, trappers, prospectors, fishermen, roughnecks, and travel writers.

akutak—Yup'ik Native word for Native ice cream: a combination of whipped berries, seal oil, and snow

Alaskan malamute—a particular breed of working dog used to pull sleds

Alcan—nickname for the Alaska Highway

Arctic Circle—an imaginary line, roughly corresponding to 67° N latitude, which the sun remains entirely above on summer solstice and entirely below on winter solstice

Aurora—goddess of dawn

aurora borealis—the scientific term for the northern lights

baleen—Also known as whalebone, these stiff, flexible whale's "teeth" are woven into baskets by Eskimo men, who display great strength and skill to work with this difficult material.

banya—A small sauna in which rocks surround a wood stove; from a bucket you sprinkle water on the rocks for a steambath and bathe yourself. Russian in origin, banyas are common on Kodiak Island and along the Bering Sea.

barabara—traditional Aleut or Eskimo shelter, made of driftwood and a sod roof

baidarka—an Aleut kayak covered with animal skins

black diamond—hematite jewelry

blanket toss—Originally a means of spotting game on the tundra, this Native event, where six to eight people holding a large blanket toss high in the air and catch the "spotter," is part of most festivals and is demonstrated for tourists in Barrow and Kotzebue.

break-up—The period in late April or early May when the river ice suddenly fractures and begins to flow downstream; it's a particularly muddy, slushy time of year in early spring. Also an apt synonym for divorce, of which Alaska has the country's highest rate (after Nevada, of course).

bunny boot—see "vapor barrier boots"

bush—Borrowed from Africa and Australia, this term generally designates remote areas but specifically refers to the Arctic tundra where all the vegetation is dwarf shrubbery.

cabin fever—Alaskan-size claustrophobia due to the extreme cold and dark of winter

cache—Pronounced "cash." A log hut built on tin-wrapped stilts used to store food and supplies beyond the reach of animals. Nowadays it's a common business name: Book Cache, Photo Cache, Cache 'n' Carry. . . .

Cat—Caterpillar tractor

Chain, The—nickname for the Aleutian Islands

cheechako—A Chinook term meaning "just arrived," used to describe newcomers and visitors, especially those who haven't spent a winter in Alaska or received a dividend check. Some sourdoughs view anyone not born in the state as a cheechako.

chinook—a strong warm wind originating in Prince William Sound which can be particularly destructive in Anchorage

chum—a kind of salmon; also known as dog salmon, after the animals to which it's mostly fed

clean-up—reckoning the amount of gold taken at the end of the season; also a phrase that reached mythical proportions during the summer of 1989

d2—from the section of that name in the Alaska Native Claims Settlement Act; refers to the national-interest lands set aside for national parks and forests, wildlife refuges, preserves, and wild and scenic rivers

Eskimo—from French Canadian *Esquimau,* from northern Algonquin *askimowew,* which means "eater of raw fish." These Natives themselves don't like the name; they refer to themselves as *Inuit,* "People," plural of *inuk,* person.

fish wheel—an ingenious mechanism that uses the current of the river or stream for power to scoop fish into a tank

freeze-up—the time of year, mostly in Northwest and Arctic regions, during which all bodies of water are frozen and the seaports are icebound

gussuk—derogatory Eskimo term for white person

honey bucket—in much of bush Alaska, the local sewage system: a five-gallon plastic bucket used as a toilet. The untreated waste is often dumped into rivers in the summer or onto river ice in winter (for natural "flushing" when the ice breaks up in the spring). Because of the obvious health hazards—not to mention the smell—the state has been trying to bring sewage-treatment facilities to small villages.

hootch—shortened version of the Chinook word "hootchenoo," meaning home-distilled spirits

husky—the generic term for sled dog. A toy poodle hooked up to a sled is technically a husky—for the brief moment before it's eaten by a large **Siberian husky.** Like the malamute, the Siberian husky is a singular breed famous for strength and intelligence.

icefog—caused by an inversion in which warm air traps cold air near the surface, which keeps getting colder and colder . . . until the water vapor in the air freezes, creating floating ice crystals

iceworm—Originally a joke by sourdoughs on cheechakos, the joke was ultimately on the sourdoughs—iceworms actually exist, and you can see specimens of them in the museum in Juneau and at the Portage Glacier visitor center.

Iditarod—famous 1,000-mile dogsled race from Anchorage to Nome in February. The race commemorates an epic dogsled relay that delivered 300,000 units of diptheria serum to Nome, which was threatened by an epidemic. One explanation of the name comes from the term, "rod," a measurement of work accomplished in the gold fields; thus the word is actually a sentence: "I did a rod." Another holds that the name evolved from the name of an Ingalik Indian village on a stream reported as "Khadilotden." It was then reported by the USGS as "Haidilatna," and finally anglicized as Iditarod.

igloo—one of the great myths about Alaskan Natives, whose shelters are never made of ice (see *barabara* above) except in extreme emergencies

Inupiak—a northern Eskimo dialect

iron dog—snowmobile

iron ranger—collection boxes at state parks

kupiak—Eskimo word for coffee

kuspuk—parka worn by Eskimo women, often with a small backpacklike pouch for carrying babies

liquid sunshine—Ketchikan's euphemism for rain

Lower 48—a slightly hostile/humorous Alaskan term used to refer to the rest of the country (except Hawaii)

moose nuggets—small, round, brown turds, bravely made into jewelry by enterprising (usually bankrupt) local artisans

mukluk—boot made by Eskimo women with tough sealskin soles, reindeer-hide uppers, fur and yarn trim, all sewn together with caribou sinew

muktuk—an Eskimo delicacy of the rubbery outer layer of whale skin and fat. Very chewy, it's served raw or pickled.

mush—Popularized by Sgt. Preston of the Yukon (and immortalized in the Crusader Rabbit cartoon episode about the small Canadian village, "If Anyone Can, Yukon"), this command means "Let's go!" to anxious dog teams everywhere. It's a Chinook term adapted from the French word *marchons.*

muskeg—swampy areas covered by moss and scrub

no-see-ums—the tiny biting flies that plague Alaska after mosquito season

nunatak—lonely rock peak jutting out above icefields

Outside—anywhere other than Alaska

Panhandle—nickname for Southeast Alaska

permafrost—permanently frozen ground, with a layer of topsoil that thaws during the summer

petroglyphs—stone-age carvings on rock faces

poke—a miner's moosehide bag full of gold dust and nuggets

potlatch—a Native party to celebrate any old thing. Often the hosts would give away all their possessions to their guests. This exercise in the detachment from all worldly goods was simultaneously an exercise in greed, as the event also conferred upon the guests the obligation to host a bigger potlatch with better gifts.

promyshleniki—early Russian explorers and traders in Alaska

qiviut—wool made from musk-ox fur, supposedly seven times lighter, warmer, and more expensive than down

ruff—fur edge on a parka hood, often of wolf guard hairs

salt chuck—a narrow constriction at the end of a lagoon, where the direction of the water flow depends on the tides (out at low, in at high). The term is mainly used in Southeast Alaska.

skookum—a Chinook word meaning strong or worthy

skookum house—jail

Slope—the gently sloping tundra around Prudhoe Bay; also known as the North Slope. Slope workers are almost always employed by the oil companies.

solstice—first day of summer (June 21) and winter (December 21)

sourdough—a mixture of flour, water, sugar, and yeast that is allowed to ferment before being used to make bread or hotcakes. A portion of the "sponge," removed to use as a yeast substitute for the next loaf, is called "starter." Also means an old-timer.

squaw candy—dried or smoked salmon

surimi—the processed seafood product manufactured from bottom fish (usually pollock) in Kodiak, Unalaska, and other Alaskan ports. It is used in "crab" salads and cocktails, as well as in less expensive sushi.

taiga—Russian word meaning "land of little sticks," which describes the transition zone between the boreal forest and treeless tundra

taku wind—sudden gusts of up to 100 mph that sweep down on Juneau from the nearby icefields

termination dust—the first snowfall that always coats mountaintops at the end of summer, a sign that Alaska's many seasonals are about to be terminated

tillicum—good friend or partner

treeline—the elevation (in Alaska, 2,500 feet) and latitude (generally following the Arctic Circle) above which no trees grow

tundra—another Russian word, meaning "vast treeless plain," used to describe nearly 30% of Alaska's land area

ugruk—sealskin used for making mukluks

ulu—a shell-shaped Eskimo knife that tourists purchase in record numbers and airlines disallow in hand luggage

umiak—an Eskimo kayak similar to a *baidarka*

utilidor—insulated wooden tunnel through which water and sewer pipes pass

vapor-barrier boots—large insulated rubber boots

visqueen—thin clear plastic sheeting

Yup'ik—the dialect of the Bering Coast Eskimo

PEOPLE

In 1996, Alaska's population was 605,000. Of this, roughly 94,000 people (six percent) were of Native descent. There are four groups of Native Alaskans, corresponding to four geographical locations. Southeast Indians consist of **Tlingits, Tsimshians,** and **Haidas.** Interior Indians (who also occupy parts of Southcentral and the Arctic) are **Athabascans. Aleuts** are found along the Alaska Peninsula and the Aleutian Chain. And native Yup'ik and Inupiat (also known as Eskimos) live mostly along the Bering Sea and Arctic Ocean coasts but are also found inland in small villages around the vast northern and western tundra.

The non-Native population is relatively homogeneous, with a small percentage of black and Hispanic residents, Asian and Pacific Islanders, and residents of Scandinavian and Russian descent.

The typical Alaskan is a 29-year-old white male who has lived in Alaska for four years. Alaska has the highest male-to-female ratio in the U.S.: 105 males to 100 females (compared with 95 males to 100 females Outside). But eligible women better hurry: by the year 2000, when Alaska's population is projected to be 625,000, this lopsided ratio will mostly even itself out.

Superlatives

Alaska is the largest and second-least populous (behind Wyoming) of the 50 states, and has the lowest density of people per square mile (0.7)—compare this to Wyoming, which has the second smallest (4.7) or New Jersey (986). Alaska's birth rate of 24.4 per thousand loses out only to Utah's 28.6 per thousand. It's also second to last in number of people born in-state (33.3%); Nevada is last at 23%. Nevada also beats out only Alaska for the highest divorce rate: 17.3 per thousand couples in Nevada, 8.8 in Alaska. Alaska takes last place in its percentage of farm workers (0.1%).

NATIVES

Southeast Natives

One of Alaska's few Indian reservations is at Metlakatla, near Ketchikan. A group of nearly

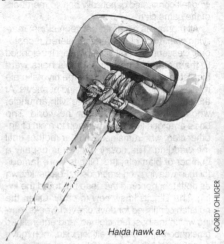

Haida hawk ax

GORDY OHLIGER

1,000 Tsimshian Indians relocated here in 1887 from their traditional homeland, slightly south near Prince Rupert, as a result of disagreements between William Duncan, the tribe's main missionary, and his church superiors (see "Metlakatla" under "Vicinity of Ketchikan" in the Southeast Alaska chapter for the complete story). These "Natives" are thus the only ones not included in the Alaska Native Claims Settlement Act. Similarly, about 800 Haida Indians live on southern Prince of Wales Island at the southeastern tip of Alaska, and the northern extent of the Haida homeland.

The Tlingit (pronounced "KLINK-it") Indians are the traditional dwellers of Southeast Alaska, related to the Interior Athabascans. Blessed with an incredible abundance of food, fuel, furs, and tools, the Tlingits evolved a sophisticated and complex society, religion, and artistry. The primary social unit was the community house, which typically sheltered 50-100 people. The huge trunks of cedar and spruce provided the house posts, often carved and painted with the clan's totemic symbols; slaves were put in the post holes to cushion the connection between totem and earth. One had to stoop to pass through the single door; no windows punctuated the long structure. Ten or so of these clan houses made up a village, and a number of neighboring villages made up a tribe. But these distinctions held little importance to the Tlingits, who felt connected genetically only to members of the same clan.

All marriages occurred between clans; marrying within the clan was considered incestuous. Descent was matrilineal: children belonged to the mother's clan, and a man's heirs were his sisters' children. Therefore the pivotal male relationship was between uncle and nephews. At the age of 10, boys went to live with an uncle, who taught them the ways of the world. The uncle arranged the boy's marriage to a girl of another clan, who remained with her mother until the wedding. The dowry price was usually a number of blankets; the Tlingits were famous for their weaving and embroidery. Feasts, known as potlatch, honored the dead but feted the living. The Tlingits knew how to party. Often the potlatch continued for days or even weeks, during which the host fed, clothed, and entertained a neighboring, usually wealthier, clan, then "gave away" the clan's most valuable possessions to them. It was understood that the hosted clan would reciprocate eventually, with an even greater degree of festivity and generosity.

The Tlingits had an intensely animistic belief system, in which everything, from glaciers to fish hooks, had a spirit. Tlingit shamans were virtually omnipotent, alternately controlling and beseeching *yek,* or karma, on behalf of the tribe. They also professed a complete understanding of the afterlife, "on authority of men who died and came back." Tlingit arts were expressed by men who carved totems for house posts, through the potlatch and other important events, and by women who wove exquisite blankets. Unlike the gentle Aleut, the Tlingits were fierce warriors who were never completely conquered by invading Russians, going head to head and hand to hand every inch of the way, until they settled into an uneasy coexistence.

Athabascans

A restless people—nomadic hunters and migrants—who developed less of a local cultural cohesion, Athabascans are related to the Tlingit of Southeast Alaska and the Navajo and Apache of the American Southwest. These wanderers subsisted on the Interior mammals, mostly caribou and moose, and freshwater fish. They passed the cruel winters in tiny villages of no larger than six houses, with a *kashim,* or community center, as the focal point. They ice-fished and trapped in the dark, using dogsleds as transportation. Their artistic expression was limited mostly to embellishing their clothing with embroidery. The men remained constantly occupied with survival tasks—finding food, building houses, maintaining gear. When the first white explorers and traders arrived in the early 19th century, the Athabascans immediately began to trade with them, learning the new cultures and in turn educating the newcomers in local customs and skills, not the least of which was dogsledding.

Aleuts

As the Athabascans were almost entirely land-based people, the Aleuts were almost entirely dependent on the sea. Clinging to the edge of tiny, treeless, windswept Aleutian islands, they lived in small dwellings made of sealskin-covered frames, with fireplaces in the middle and steam baths attached on the sides (where marriages were consummated without ceremony). They made sea otter skins into clothing and processed walrus and seal intestines into parkas. Their kayaks (called *bidarka*) as well were made of marine mammal skins stretched over a wooden or whale-bone frame. Basketry was their highest artistic achievement, and their dances were distinctly martial, with masks, rattles, and knives.

When the Russian *promyshleniki* invaded the Aleutians in the mid-1700s like furies from hell, around 25,000 Aleuts inhabited almost all the Aleutian Islands and the southern portion of the Alaska Peninsula. Within 50 years, over half had died through violence, starvation, or disease. Most of the rest became slaves and were dispersed around the New World to hunt the sea otter and fight for the Russians. In fact, Aleuts and Koniags (Kodiak Natives) traveled as far south as Catalina Island off the Southern California coast, wiping out the peaceful Gabrielino Indians there, along with the entire otter population, in 1810. Many of the women served as concubines to the Russian overlords, further diluting the Aleut lineage. Today, most Aleuts carry only half or quarter Aleut blood; only 1,000 are considered full-blooded.

Eskimo

Alaskan Natives are commonly known as Eskimo. The term "Eskimo" comes from the French Canadian *Esquimau,* which in turn is derived from the Algonquin *askimowew,* which means "eaters of raw fish." The term includes Eskimo, Yup'ik, and Inupiat peoples of the circumpolar region. Although not derogatory, the Natives prefer to use more specific terms. The most common one—Inuit—simply means "People," the plural of *inuk,* or person. An appropriate appellation in light of their strong traditional sense of community; their society was mostly leaderless, with every able member responsible for contributing to the struggle for survival. The borderline between personal and communal property was fuzzy at best, and theft did not exist. Everything was shared, including wives. All justice was determined by what was deemed best for the community. Marriages, too, were so determined.

A boy entered adulthood after his first kill, and the event was celebrated by a large feast. A girl was considered grown as soon as she began menstruating, which was accompanied by a two-week ritual. The man-child selected a bride, paid a minimal price, and unceremoniously set up house in a hut similar to the Aleuts'—a bone-and-brush framework covered with moss and grass. "Igloos" made of snow and ice were only used as temporary shelters on the trail (and mostly by central Canadian Natives). Fuel was derived from whale oil and driftwood. They ate meat almost exclusively: fish, whale, walrus, caribou, birds. Also, like their relatives the Aleut, they used skin and hides for clothing and boating. Masks are the most visible form of Eskimo art, but they apply an aesthetic touch to almost everything they make.

The Russians had little impact on the remote Eskimo, but their introduction to Western ways by the Boston whalers around the 1850s was swift and brutal. They quickly succumbed to whiskey, and many Native men were shanghaied while unconscious to labor on the white whalers' ships. They learned about prostitution (renting the women) and slavery (selling them). They learned how to use firearms and casually kill each other, usually in a drunken fit. They acquired syphilis, white sugar, canned food, and money.

An encounter between the Eskimo of St. Lawrence Island and a single whaling vessel in 1880, described by Colby in his classic *Guide to Alaska* (1939), sums up the scene: "The master sent members of his crew ashore with bottles of grain alcohol, [for which] the Natives traded ivory, whalebone, and furs. The officers and crew selected a harem from the young women of the village, and paid them in alcohol. When the whaling vessel left, the entire village of 450 Natives was dead-drunk and beggared, for they had even cut up their skin boats to trade for liquor. Around them were plenty of hair seal and walrus, but by the time the village had sobered and collected weapons the game was gone. Only about twenty-five villagers survived."

The whaling years ended just before the gold rush began. But the ruin of the Eskimo culture was total. Gradually, with the help of missionaries and legislators, the Eskimo in the late 19th century turned to reindeer herding, which began to provide income, food, and skins. Today, an estimated 34,000 Eskimo live in Alaska, having doubled their number over the past 50 years. The Eskimo people live in an arc stretching from Siberia to Greenland. Alaskan Eskimo speak two dialects of the common language, Yup'ik along the Bering coast, and Inupiat along the Arctic coast.

NATIVE ARTS AND CRAFTS

Not unlike most other native cultures, Native Alaskan arts and crafts were intricately intertwined with animism, religious ceremony, and utility. Each group worked with its abundant natural resources to produce all the necessities of a lifestyle in which subsistence, religion, and artistic expression were inseparable.

Ivory

The Inupiat Eskimo of northern coastal Alaska are renowned for their use of ivory, harvested (only) by Natives from the tusks and teeth of walruses, as well as from woolly mammoths and giant mastodons uncovered by miners or erosion, so-called "fossil ivory." The ivory is carved, also known as "scrimshawed," and made into various implements. Today you'll see ivory jewelry, *ulu* handles, cribbage boards, and the like. The use of ivory for handicrafts is severely restricted by federal regulations established to protect the walrus; though ivory art is common in gift shops around the North, many carvers are switching to whalebone (skulls and ribs).

Baskets

All Alaska Native groups used available resources to fashion baskets for storage, carrying, and cooking. Birch-bark baskets, often lashed with spruce roots, were made by the forest Athabascans. The coastal Haida, Tlingit, and Tsimshian Indians used the bark of big cedar trees. They also made entire baskets of spruce roots, occasionally weaving in maidenhead ferns for decoration. The Yup'ik and Aleut Natives of western Alaska are known for small delicate baskets fashioned from coastal rye grass. They also process baleen, the long strips of cartilagelike teeth that hang from the upper jaw of whales, and weave the strips into baskets.

The finest examples of the different baskets are displayed in the largest Alaskan museums; commercial baskets sell for anywhere from $30 for simple birch-bark trays to several thousand dollars for large baleen baskets.

Masks

Each Native culture had its traditional mask-making technology and its complex ceremonial uses for masks. Eskimo mask art and ritual were among the most highly developed in the world. Masks, like totems, represented the individual animals and birds that were worshipped, and each mask was believed to embody the spirit, or *inua*, of the animal. The masks of the Athabascans were worn by dancers, accompanied by a tribal choir, to dramatize the tribe's relationship to animal spirits, as well as to entertain guests at feasts. Some believe Aleut masks symbolized the faces of ancient inhabitants of the western Alaska archipelago, though these people were distantly related to the Aleut, if at all.

The use of masks has declined in Alaskan Native cultures, and the art of mask-making isn't as prevalent today as it's said to have been before contact with the Western world. But you will see commercial masks in Native galleries and gift shops around the North; these bear a close resemblance to those of long ago.

Totems

Totem poles were the largest and most dramatic of the Native arts and social images, though today, totemic images are reproduced in every medium and size. Typical totemic characterizations incude highly stylized wolves, whales, bears, ravens, eagles, and beavers, as well as mythological monsters, human ancestors, and religious spirits. These images are a common sight in gift shops all over Alaska and the Yukon. A further description of totem poles is found under "Ketchikan" in the Southeast chapter.

BOB RACE

ON THE ROAD

OUTDOOR RECREATION

Since Alaska is the largest state with the second smallest population, it stands to reason that it has the most outdoors in the country. Also, because Alaska is so vast, so rugged and diverse, and so anything-goes, the range, breadth, and depth of outdoor sports are mind-boggling. And Alaska has sufficient public transportation—by ground, water, and air—to get you to whatever outdoor location you've chosen for your recreation. If you're experienced and well prepared, you can catch the minivan from, say, Glennallen to Kennicott in Wrangell-St. Elias National Park and backpack for a month without seeing another soul. Or start in Bettles and walk west across four national parks in the Brooks Range clear to the Chukchi Sea on the west Arctic Coast. Or put your kayak into Resurrection Bay at Seward and paddle around Kenai Fjords National Park for 10 days. Or put a canoe into the Kobuk River at Ambler and float down to Kotzebue.

Hiking, backpacking, climbing, skiing, dogsledding, snowmobiling, snowshoeing, fishing, hunting, kayaking, canoeing, flightseeing, photographing, and filming are among the more common activities. Recently, mountain biking, windsurfing, and river rafting have dramatically increased in popularity. And for the extremists among you, some of the wilder opportunities for recreation include paragliding and paraskiing, winter camping and ice-fishing, and scuba diving. The possibilities, as they say, are truly limitless.

If you're not all that experienced and would rather leave the planning, preparing, outfitting, and guiding to someone else, you've got a choice of over 500 adventure-travel package operators, offering everything from helicopter skiing on icefields and scuba diving in the Arctic Ocean to ice-climbing on McKinley and skydiving over Turnagain Arm. The best (though still incomplete) compilation of guides and outfitters appears in *Alaska Vacation Planner*, put out every year by the Alaska Division of Tourism. Write: P.O. Box 110801, Juneau, AK 99811, tel. (907) 465-2010. Also check the "Guidepost" section of *Alaska* magazine.

THE PROPRIETORS

National Parks and Preserves

In the federal scheme of things, the National Park Service gets all the glory. The national parks are the country's scenic showcases, and visitors come by the millions, usually to look, occasionally to experience. An unmistakable carnival atmosphere pervades the most popular national parks—in Alaska's case, Denali and Glacier Bay. Here the Park Service is primarily concerned with crowd control, and they take a hefty cut from the proceeds of the concessionaires, which provide the rides, hot dog stands, souvenir booths, and beds. Such hordes come through these gates that lines are long, rides are packed, facilities are maxed out, and much of the backcountry is closed or seriously limited by the permit system. Other national parks, including Kenai Fjords and Wrangell-St. Elias, are accessible by road; these parks are somewhat new and undeveloped, and they only have visitor centers and a couple of rides. The other eight parks and preserves (Aniakchak, Katmai, Lake Clark, Gates of the Arctic, Noatak, Kobuk Valley, and Yukon-Charley Rivers) are so inaccessible that those with any facilities at all are prohibitively expensive for the average traveler, and the others are really no more than a name and a set of boundaries on the map.

People accustomed to Lower 48 national parks are suprised to find that very few trails run through Alaska's baker's dozen. Most of the 54 million acres of national parkland are unforested and in the moist alpine tundra, where trails are not only unnecessary but largely detrimental to the ecology: as soon as the insulating ground cover is removed, the melting permafrost turns the trail into a muddy, impassable quagmire. Even in Denali, the only trails are around the park entrance and hotel area. Some parks (such as Denali and Katmai) require backpacking permits; in the rest you're on your own. Several of the more accessible parks have designated camping areas, but in the others you can pitch your tent on any level patch. For an excellent overview of Alaska's top eight national parks, check out Sierra Club's beautiful and well-written *Guide to the National Parks of the Pacific Northwest and Alaska.*

Forest Service

If the Park Service is in the carnival business, the Forest Service is a huge lumber corporation. Some of its budget is earmarked for visitor facilities and services, but those frivolities take a definite backseat to timber management. Its 23 million acres in Alaska are divided between the two largest national forests in the country: Tongass in Southeast and Chugach in Southcentral. This land is primarily forested. Trails are numerous. Campgrounds are set in beautiful wooded sites, often on lakes, and cost $8-12 pp per night. The Forest Service also manages a large number of wilderness cabins, a few of which are accessible by road, though most are in the Tongass, accessible only by floatplane or boat. Some in the Chugach are on trails, especially around the Cordova area. You must reserve them well in advance, and they cost $25 per night. Write: Alaska Public Lands Information Center, 605 W. Fourth Ave., Anchorage, AK 99501, and make checks payable to U.S. Forest Service. Call (907) 271-2599 for additional information. The Forest Service has a beautiful visitor center at Portage Glacier, 40 miles south of Anchorage, and numerous offices around the state.

State Parks and Recreation Sites

The state manages over 100 park sites, from the 1.5-million-acre Wood-Tikchik State Park outside of Dillingham to the eight-acre Izaak Walton Campground near Sterling on the Kenai Peninsula, and additional lands are continually being added to the system. The state facilities are uniformly less crowded and more accessible than most of the federally managed park and forest lands. About 90% of the sites and parks have trails; about 80% of them have campgrounds.

A usage-fee bill had been rejected by the state legislature several times over the years, but with declining revenues from an oil-price drop the state's park budget was cut almost in half in 1988 and the fees were instituted. State park camping fees are $6-15 per night. A $100 annual pass covers camping at all the parks and recreation areas throughout the state, available at the camping areas (it's $75 for residents).

When you have a choice, always head for a state park or recreation site—they're the best outdoor facilities in Alaska.

Others

The largest amount of wilderness in Alaska, 76 million acres, falls under the auspices of Alaska Fish and Game and the U.S. Fish and Wildlife Service, which manage the state and national wildlife refuges. These departments are in the game management business and permit hunting and fishing on their lands. The feds are also somewhat in the oil business, especially within the Kenai National Wildlife Refuge, and maybe one day in the Arctic Refuge. Some visitor facilities are found at the larger refuges (Kenai and Kodiak): mainly campgrounds ($6-10), hiking trails, canoe routes, and visitor centers.

Finally, the Bureau of Land Management (BLM) is responsible for whatever land is left over. As a result of the 1980 National Interest Lands Act, BLM's acreage shrunk almost in half. Very few restrictions are imposed by BLM (earning them the derisive nickname of the "Bureau of Logging and Mining"), and much mining takes place on these lands, though the miners are pretty peeved these days at having to comply with new, somewhat strict, court-ordered regulations (mostly concerning the quality of runoff water). These tensions are especially evident out the Steese Highway around Central and Circle. A few trails (such as in the White and Pinnell Mountains outside of Fairbanks) and campgrounds are managed by BLM—minimalist, free.

ON LAND

Respecting the Land

Make it your objective to leave no trace of your passing. Litter is pollution. Whenever you are tempted to leave garbage behind, think of how you feel when you find other people's plastic bags, tin cans, or aluminum foil in *your* yard. If you packed it in, you can pack it out. Burying garbage is useless as animals soon dig it up. Be a caretaker by picking up trash left by less-conscientious visitors. In this way, in part, you thank the land for the experiences it has given you.

Along shorelines, the intertidal zone is the best for campfires and human excrement. Human wastes in other areas should be disposed of at least 100 feet from any trail or water source. Bury wastes and carefully burn the toilet paper, if possible. Try to build your fire on sand or gravel and keep it small and under control. Extreme care should be taken during dry periods and in the forest. Refrain from doing anything that might cause even the smallest of accidental fires.

Local People

As you explore, remember that Northerners are fiercely independent people who value their privacy. They can also be overwhelmingly hospitable if you treat them with respect. All Indian reservations are private property; you should always ask the advice of a local resident before camping on one. Never put up your tent in or near a Native village without first asking permission. When visiting a Native village or any small, isolated community, look people straight in the eye and be the first to say hello. Remember, you are the intruder, so you should be the one to make the effort to put them at ease.

Hiking and Camping

Hiking and camping are by far the preferred outdoor recreations for the majority of Alaskans and visitors. These pastimes are available to practically anybody, from three-month old infants to 83-year-old grannies. Here, you don't have to be in particularly good shape, you don't need a big bank balance, and you don't have to have the latest high-tech equipment. Elevation changes are undramatic in the backcountry, affording as slow, steady, and nonstrenuous a pace as required by the weakest hiker. Also, purchasing everything in the "What to Take" section (see "Other Practicalities," below) new is roughly equivalent to splurging on a fancy weekend in the big city—and properly cared for, the equipment should remain useful for at least a decade.

For the size of the Alaskan outdoors, there are very few *trails*—those totalitarian swaths through the wilderness that supervise, magnetize, and hypnotize. It's easy just to pick a direction, especially in the vast taiga and tundra, and go. Also, the perpetual daylight during hiking season allows for additional deviation from normal hiking-camping cycles, providing further freedom. And the definite possibility of encountering a variety and abundance of wildlife is an incalculable bonus.

The few trails that do exist are covered in their respective travel chapters. For more information about hiking, contact the Alaska Public Lands Information Centers in Anchorage, Fairbanks, and Tok.

Photography

Hand in hand with hiking and camping goes photography—of the gorgeous scenery, the fauna and flora, and the special light. Professional photographers can have a literal field day in Alaska, not least because the ideal light conditions—at dawn and sunset everywhere else—continue throughout the long days of low light and long angles in the boreal region. Casual photographers are satisfied with automatic point-and-shoot single-lens reflexes, though the regular 50-55mm lenses don't do justice to either the panoramas or the wildlife. A good set-up would be a couple of camera bodies, a 24mm wide-angle, 80-200mm zoom, and 400mm zoom (a two-ex converter is also handy). A tripod is a must for all the waiting and watching for wildlife; Kodachrome 64 or Fujichrome 100 or 200 will give professional-quality frames. But also take some faster film for those inevitable gray days. And don't be afraid to blow off as much film as your budget can stand, to get those few special shots. A photography class or two are invaluable for learning technique—exposure, bracketing, composition, and the like.

A couple of caveats are in order. A common cause of wildlife incidents is foolish photographers either getting too close or having a false sense of security behind the camera. Your backcountry common sense should remain intact with or without a camera in front of you. Besides, there are times and places to not use a camera—mostly in order not to separate you from a given experience.

Mountain Biking

This relatively new sport seems to be less controversial in Alaska than in the Lower 48, even on Forest Service trails, which are all open to two-wheelers. This is due in part to the fact that hikers aren't entirely limited to trails and can avoid mountain bikers if they're offended by them, as well as the fact that something about Alaska seems to inspire a certain respect for the environment and sensitivity to other people in those sharing the great outdoors. In any event, all trails in the state parks system are still closed to mountain bikers (except a few of the wider ones in Chugach State Park near Anchorage); the state parks people consider mountain bikes *vehicles,* which can easily damage trails, tundra, and people. Still, many local trails, especially around Fairbanks and throughout the Kenai Peninsula, are popular mountain-bike venues. Best is to call the local outdoors stores for recommendations.

Hunting

For all the rules, regulations, and seasons, write for "Alaska Game Regulations," Alaska Dept. of Fish and Game, P.O. Box 3-2000, Juneau, AK 99802.

IN AND AROUND WATER

Beachcombing

A treasure trove of flotsam and jetsam awaits the savvy and the lucky along the thousands of miles of coastline in Alaska. Prizes include glass-ball floats (used by Asian fishermen), life preservers, lantern buoys, whale teeth, ambergris, WW II relics, Russian equipment, and notes in bottles. Beachcombing can be developed into a fine art, consisting of weather and tide patterns, wind and storm conditions, beach accessibility and topography. The experts advise that the best beachcombing is in early May, after the snow cover and before the competition from hikers, anglers, and other beachcombers.

Gold Panning

Panning for gold is not only great fun, it's also a good way to get involved in the history of the North. Besides, there's the chance you'll find a nugget that will become a lifelong souvenir. You might even strike it rich! The amount of equipment required is minimal: an 18-inch plastic gravity-trap gold pan (buy one at any local surplus or sporting-goods store for a couple of dollars), tweezers and an eyedropper to pick out the gold flakes, and a small vial to hold them. Ordinary rubber gloves will protect your hands from icy creek water. An automobile oil dipstick bent at one end is handy for poking into crevices, and a small garden trowel helps dig out the dirt under rocks. Look for a gravel bar where the creek takes a turn, for larger rocks forming ed-

GORDY OHLIGER

dies during high water, for crevices in the bedrock, or for exposed tree roots growing near the waterline. These are places where gold will lodge. Try your luck on any of the old gold-rush creeks; tourist offices can often suggest likely areas. Stay away from commercial mining operations and ask permission if you're obviously on someone's claim.

The principle behind panning is that gold, twice as heavy as lead, will settle to the bottom of your pan. Fill the pan half full of paydirt you've scooped up from a likely spot and cover with water. Hit the rim of the pan seven or eight times, or shake it back and forth. Break up lumps of dirt or clay with your hands and discard any rocks after rinsing them in the pan. Shake the pan again, moving it in a circular motion. Dip the front edge of the pan into the stream and carefully wash off excess sand and gravel until only a small amount of black sand remains. If you see gold specks too small to remove with tweezers, take the black sand out and let it dry. Later dump it on a clean sheet of paper and gently blow away the sand. The gold will remain. That's the basic procedure, though there are many ways to do it. It does take practice; ask a friendly sourdough for advice. Also, many spiked gold panning facilities are found along the roads in the North—commercial, but good places to refine your technique.

Fishing

Fishing is not only great fun but the way to bag some super meals. All you need are a breakdown or retractable rod, a variety of hooks, five flies (salmon fly, black fly, mosquito, gnat, nymph), spinners (rooster tail and shannon), spoons, sinkers, line (four- to eight-pound for fresh water, 12- to 30-pound for salt water—depending on what you're after), and a reel. All but the rod will fit in a small plastic case. For bait, get a small bottle of salmon eggs for fresh water, shrimp for salt water. Have a knife to clean the fish and a small plastic trowel to bury the fish wastes (but pack out all other garbage). While fishing, watch for protected areas with deadfalls or rocks where fish like to hide. You'll have the best luck in the early morning or late evening, or on cloudy days when the sun leaks out to shimmer on the water. So as not to attract bears, keep your catch on a stringer well downstream.

Locals, as always, are the best advice-givers about fishing technique, spots, and regulations, and might even share some secrets. Generally, look for trout, grayling, and whitefish in inland freshwater lakes, the five varieties of northern salmon in bays and rivers, and deep-sea halibut charters mostly in Homer.

Fishing Regulations

Fishing licenses are required almost everywhere. In British Columbia separate licenses are sold for freshwater and saltwater fishing. Nonresidents pay C$23 for saltwater, C$27 for freshwater annual licenses, or C$15 for a three-day license. In Alaska, one-day nonresident sportfishing licenses cost $10, three-day $15, 14-day $30, and annual $50—they're almost always available from charter fishing operators. All-inclusive annual nonresident rates are C$30 in Yukon, US$36 in Alaska. The Alaskan license is valid in national parks; in Canada you need only a special C$4 national-park fishing license (a bargain). Licenses are for sale in most outdoor stores. Ask for brochures outlining local fishing regulations when you buy your license. They often include valuable tips for newcomers. Check open and closed seasons, bag limits, etc., to avoid trouble with the law. Shellfish may be poisonous, so get local advice before taking clams, mussels, etc. For the whole thing, spelled out in minute bureaucratic detail, write for a copy of the regulations booklet to Alaska Dept. of Revenue, Fish and Game Licensing, 1111 W. Eighth St., Room 108, Juneau, AK 99801, tel. (907) 465-2376. For information on fishing charters, available from every seaport in the state, check with local chambers of commerce, or look in the "Guidepost" section of *Alaska* magazine.

Rafting

Whitewater rafting trips are offered by numerous adventure-travel outfitters around the state. A few of the more reasonable, short, and accessible trips include the floats down the Nenana River at Denali, down the Kenai River at Sterling, and down the Lowe River outside of Valdez. A large number of float-trip companies and wilderness outfitters offer overnight, several-day, and up to three-week-long trips down the Charley, Kobuk, Tonsina, Chickaloon, and Nova Rivers, among others. Check the list in the Alaska Division of Tourism's "Alaska Vacation Planner" for many of their names and addresses.

Canoeing and Kayaking

These activities take less, more portable, equipment, and less planning than river rafting, and you can easily canoe Alaska's rivers and kayak its fjords and bays on your own. At least one company in each major town rents canoes and kayaks, and they either give lessons themselves or can put you in touch with someone who does. Many companies also offer guided trips. Well-respected outfits include **Alaska Treks 'n' Voyages,** P.O. Box 625, Seward, AK 99664, tel. (907) 224-3960; **Ageya Kayak Tours,** 2517 Foraker Dr., Anchorage, AK 99517, tel. (907) 243-3274; and **Alaska Discovery,** 418 Franklin St., Juneau, AK 99801, tel. (907) 586-1911.

Windsurfing

The scenery, the space, and the winds combine to make windsurfing a thrill that Alaskans quickly want more of. Turnagain Arm near Girdwood and Portage is the most attractive locale, though some hardy sorts swear by the waters off the coast of Kodiak. Turnagain Arm boasts six- to eight-foot waves, 10- to 15-mph tides, and

steady predictable winds, and it's only a short drive from the Anchorage bowl. Windsurfers can catch some big air in Turnagain Arm; 20 feet isn't unusual. They can also pick up some serious speed; boarders traveling 50 mph have been clocked by passing cars. Turnagain Arm, to be sure, has its dangers as well, primarily the tides, the mudflats, and the biting cold water. But even devoted warm-water boarders swear by the thrills available in Alaskan waters.

Hot Springs

Alaska is a thermally active region, a fact attested to by its more than 100 hot spring sites, of which roughly a dozen are accessible and developed. Accessible, in Alaska, is quite a relative term: possibly the most accessible hot spring in the state is at Chena, 60 miles east of Fairbanks on a well-paved road. But other "accessible" hot springs near Fairbanks include Manley, over 150 hard dirt-road miles, and Circle, a similarly rough distance. Other popular hot springs are in Southeast: White Sulphur and Tenakee on Chichagof Island near Juneau, and Chief Shakes and Baranof on Baranof Island. Contact the Alaska Department of Natural Resources for its map of thermally active areas in Alaska.

IN THE AIR

Flightseeing

Even if you don't go backpacking, rafting, kayaking, gold panning, etc., while you're in Alaska, treat yourself at least once to a small plane or helicopter ride over some spectacular country. Recommended flights include the one from Denali Park around the northern face of the Alaska Range and Mt. McKinley, and the one from Talkeetna around the southern face. The flight over Glacier Bay from Juneau, Haines, or Skagway will leave you hyperventilating for two days. And you won't believe how grand Columbia Glacier really is on the flight over it from Anchorage or Valdez. Scheduled trips such as these usually run $100-150 per person. Chartering a bush plane and pilot for flightseeing routes of your own design can run upwards of $300 an hour for a three- or four-seater; just get a few fellow travelers together and off you go into the wild blue yonder. For more tips on flightseeing, see "By Bush Plane" under "Getting Around" later in this chapter, and "Summer Recreation" under "Anchorage" in the Southcentral chapter.

Fly-in Travel

As mentioned, flying in a real live Alaska bush plane is a spectacular way to see Alaska. It's also the only practical way to access the vast majority of the state's roadless areas. However, before you head out into the wild blue, there are a few things you should know.

First and foremost, you should choose your pilot and/or flight service with care. Just because someone has a pilot's license and is flying in Alaska doesn't mean that he or she is a seasoned bush pilot. You're well within your rights to ask about the pilot's qualifications, and about time spent flying *in Alaska*. The oft-repeated saying is, "There are old pilots and there are bold pilots, but there are no old bold pilots." Given a choice, you want an "old" one—not so much in chronological years, but one that's been flying in and out of the bush for a good long time.

Even if you're just going on a 30-minute flightseeing tour, wear clothing appropriate for the ground conditions. Unplanned stops due to weather or mechanical problems aren't unusual. Warm comfortable hiking clothes, raingear, and lightweight boots or sturdy shoes make for reasonable bush-plane apparel.

Weather is a major limiting factor in aviation. Small planes don't operate on airline-type schedules, with arrivals and departures timed down to the minute. Leave yourself plenty of leeway when scheduling trips, and don't pressure your pilot to get you back to the airstrip so you won't miss your bus, boat, train, dogsled ride, or salmon bake. More than one crash has been the result of subtle or not-so-subtle pressure by clients to fly when it was against the pilot's better judgment.

Before taking off, your pilot should brief all passengers on location of safety and survival equipment and airsickness bags, how to exit during an emergency, and the location and function of the Emergency Locator Transmitter. Ear protection should also be supplied, as most small planes are quite noisy. Just in case, buy a set of foam earplugs at a sporting goods store before you go to the airport. They cost about a buck, weigh nothing, and are perfectly adequate for aircraft noise levels.

You'll probably be asked how much you weigh (don't be coy here—lives are at stake!) and told where you should sit. Weight and balance are critical in little planes, so don't whine about not getting to sit up front if you're told otherwise.

Gear stowage can be a challenge in small planes, especially when transporting people who are heading out on long expeditions. Don't even think of showing up at the airfield with hard-sided luggage. You probably won't be openly mocked, but there will be giggling or exasperated eye-rolling. Internal frame backpacks, duffel bags, and other soft easily compressed and stowed items are much easier to handle. Don't strap sleeping bags and other gear onto the outside of a pack. Lots of small items are much easier to arrange and find homes for than a few bulky things. Also, if you're carrying a canister of red pepper spray to deter bears, tell the pilot beforehand and follow directions for stowage. Most pilots don't want the stuff inside the cabin, so they'll store it in a float if the plane is so equipped, or you can strap it to a strut with duct tape.

As far as what you can expect to pay, most flightseeing operations have preset itineraries and prices. Some companies flying out of the larger towns also have set rates to certain of the more popular destinations. However, for most drop-off trips, you pay for the ride according to engine hours, both coming and going. So if your destination is a spot that's an hour from the airstrip, you pay for four hours of engine time (an hour out and an hour back, twice). Rates run $60-75 per hour for very small planes such as a Super Cub (one passenger) to over $300 per hour for a DeHavilland Beaver, the workhorse of the north. Various Cessna models generally fall between these extremes.

Whenever you fly, leave a flight route, destination, expected departure and arrival times, and a contact number for the flight service with a reliable friend. Then relax and enjoy the scenery—flying in Alaska is a tremendous experience, one that relatively few people get to enjoy, and, in spite of all the cautionary notes listed above, is still a safe and reliable way to get to and see the wilderness.

Paragliding and Paraskiing

Two extreme air sports include paraskiing, which involves wearing skis and a parachute and jumping off very steep cornices, and paragliding, which is a cross between hang gliding and parachuting.

EVENTS

The biggest events in Alaska revolve around the sun and snow. A number of Alaskans, especially those who live in the Interior and the north, believe that the purpose of summer solstice is to compress all the partying encouraged by the light and heat of summer into a single 24-hour period. Fairbanks has at least three "Midnight Sun" activities on solstice. The summer is also the time for town- and city-wide celebrations, such as Golden Days in Fairbanks, River Daze in Nenana, and Colony Days in Palmer. There are fishing derbies in the waters off the coastal towns and athletic competitions, such as triathlons and mountain races, everywhere.

Winter solstice marks the beginning of the winter festivals and dogsled races. The most famous of the former is Anchorage's Fur Rendezvous, of the latter the Iditarod. Every town has some sort of winter carnival that includes dog-mushing, a snow sports competition, and festival of lights with accompanying arts and crafts fairs.

Typically, the major public holidays are also a cause for celebration: July Fourth (Independence Day), Memorial Day (last Monday in May), Labor Day (last Monday in September), Thanksgiving Day (last Thursday in November), New Year's Eve (December 31), etc. The happiest days of the year, though, are around late October and early November when the bulk of the Permanent Fund dividend checks show up in the mailboxes of state residents.

January
Glennallen—Copper Basin 300 Sled Dog Race; Kodiak—Russian Orthodox Masquerade Ball and Starring Ceremony; Sitka—Alaska Airlines Basketball Tournament; Willow—Winter Carnival.

February
Anchorage—Fur Rendezvous, Masters Cross-Country Ski Championships; Cordova—Iceworm Festival; Fairbanks—Yukon Quest Sled Dog Race; Homer—Winter Carnival; Nenana—Ice Classic; Valdez—Ice Climbing Festival; Wasilla—Iditarod Days; Whitehorse—Sourdough Festival.

March
Anchorage—Iditarod Sled Dog Race, Native Youth Olympics; Chatanika—Chatanika Days; Fairbanks—Winter Carnival; Kodiak—Pillar Mountain Golf Classic; Nome—Iditarod Month; Skagway—Windfest Winter Festival; Valdez—Winter Carnival.

April
Craig—Salmon Derby; Cordova—Copper River Shorebird Festival; Girdwood—Alyeska Spring Carnival; Juneau—Folk Festival; Whittier—Crab Festival.

May
Homer—Halibut Derby; Juneau—Ski to Sea Relay Race; Kodiak—Crab Fishing Derby; Nome—Polar Bear Swim; Palmer—Colony Days; Petersburg—Little Norway Festival; Seward—Exit Glacier Run; Talkeetna—Miner's Day Festival; Valdez—Regatta of Ships, Salmon Derby.

June
Anchorage—Midnight Sun Marathon; Barrow—Nalukataq Whaling Festival; Fairbanks—Yukon 800 Boat Race; Kodiak—Freedom Days; Nenana—River Daze; Nome—ARCO-Jesse Owens Games; Sitka—Summer Music Festival; Whittier—Three-Headed Fish Derby.

July
Anchorage—Bluegrass and Folk Festival; Big Lake—Regatta Water Festival; Dawson City—Yukon Gold Panning Championship; Fairbanks—Golden Days, World Eskimo-Indian Olympics; Kotzebue—Northwest Native Trade Fair; Seward—Mount Marathon Race; Talkeetna—Moose Dropping Festival; Valdez—Gold Rush Days.

August
Anchorage—Military Open House and Air Show; Dawson City—Discovery Days; Fairbanks—Tanana Valley Fair; Haines—Bald Eagle Music Festival; Ninilchik—Kenai Peninsula State Fair; Palmer—Alaska State Fair; Seward—Silver Salmon Derby; Talkeetna—Bluegrass Festival.

September
Kodiak—State Fair and Rodeo; Nome—Great Bathtub Race; Kenai, Valdez, Whittier, Wrangell—Silver Salmon Derbies.

November
Anchorage—Great Alaska Shootout; Delta Junction—Winter Carnival; Fairbanks—Athabascan Fiddling Festival; Haines—Bald Eagle Festival; Ketchikan—Festival of Lights.

December
Ketchikan—Festival of Lights; Kodiak—Harbor Stars Boat Parade; Nome—Firemen's Carnival; Talkeetna—Bachelor's Society Ball and Wilderness Women's Contest.

ACCOMMODATIONS

Camping
The only consistent way to sleep cheap in the North is to camp. Unless you're on a prepaid package tour, have friends all over, or own a booming gold mine, don't even briefly entertain the remote possibility of going to Alaska without a tent and sleeping bag. One night in the average Alaskan budget hotel can cost the equivalent of up to a week's food or transportation. Two nights pays for a good tent. Tent camping is free or cheap in most areas, and public showers are available in nearly every town you'll find yourself dirty in. The old A-frame tents are sufficient, but the modern self-supporting dome tents are best: they're lightweight, and a cinch to erect, they don't need to be staked into the often rocky or frozen ground, and you can sit up in them during those long inclement stretches. For peace of mind and dryness of body in those wild and woolly nights in Southeast and South-central, make sure the tent is as waterproof as it can be. (Even so, bring a sponge.) A bivouac bag (self-contained sleeping-bag cover, usually Gore-Tex on the outside) is also handy. A three-quarter-length Therm-a-rest inflatable pad will put a wonderful cushion of air between you and the ground; on top of it you can sleep on gravel, rocks, dead porcupines. . . .

In those few thoughtless towns that don't provide campgrounds within walking distance of the action, you can always wander into the nearby bush and pass the night with relative impunity. Most of the land is owned by some branch of government; so long as you stay out of sight, don't chop down any trees, and are careful with fire, no one is likely to bother you. But avoid places with No Trespassing signs, if possible.

In Canada you may camp anywhere on Crown land without a permit; in Alaska camping is allowed on state land and within the national forests. The national parks of both countries ask that you first obtain a free backcountry-use permit. Camping on public property within city limits, however, is usually prohibited. The lengths to which officials will go to enforce this varies, but probably the worst that might happen is that you'll be asked to leave. Avoid problems and ensure your privacy by keeping your tent well hidden. A dark green tent attracts the least attention.

Campgrounds
Generally, two distinct types of campgrounds are available. State, provincial, and federal government-operated campgrounds all offer a basic outdoor experience with a minimum of facilities, usually just pit toilets and water from pumps. Municipal and private campgrounds usually offer hot showers, laundromats, stores, dump stations, plug-ins, etc. The latter cater primarily to RV drivers, but most welcome tenters. The government campgrounds in both the U.S. and Canada are usually cheaper (rarely more than $15 nightly) than the commercial variety (rarely less than $10). The showers ($3) at the commercial sites are almost always open to noncampers, and are sometimes the only place in town to rinse off. Whenever you are quoted a fee at a campground always assume, unless told otherwise, that it is for your whole group rather than per person.

Hostels
At last count Alaska had 12 official, though highly varied, youth hostels: at Anchorage, Girdwood, Seward (two), Soldotna, Fairbanks, Delta, Tok, Haines, Juneau, Sitka, and Ketchikan. There are also hostels in Vancouver, Victoria, and Banff; all along the Icefields Parkway; and in Jasper. All are accessible by road or ferry, though a few in Alaska are beyond the reach of public transportation

(Delta's, Tok's, and Seward's are at least seven miles outside of town). Males and females have separate dormitories. A sleeping sheet is sometimes required, and always for rent or sale, though you can also use your sleeping bag. All have communal kitchens and reading rooms and require small clean-up chores. Some have washing machines and dryers. Most charge around $12 for members, $15 for nonmembers. Hostels are great places to meet other travelers, but most close during daytime business hours. All addresses and phone numbers are listed in the appropriate travel chapters.

Joining the Youth Hotel Association (YHA) before you leave home is recommended. Write: American Youth Hostels, Inc., 133 I St. NW, Suite 800, Washington, D.C. 20005, USA; or Canadian Hosteling Assn., 333 River Rd., Vanier City, Ontario K1L 8B9, Canada. Wherever and whenever you can, reserve a place at a youth hostel in advance by sending the first night's price, or by calling with a credit-card number.

Hotels

Within these pages you'll find reasonably priced hotels wherever they exist, good-value hotels no matter how expensive they are, and expensive hotels where there's a lack of cheaper ones. In the major package-tour stops and off-the-beaten-track places with limited lodging, what's available is often booked way in advance. Unless you've made reservations, don't count on getting any rooms, especially the good cheap ones, at most Alaskan destinations. Be particularly prepared for this at Denali Park, Valdez, Kodiak, and Skagway, where your choice could be between a $95 room (in the unlikely event that one is available) or camping.

Other Lodging

Bed and breakfasts are booming throughout Alaska and Canada. They're a great way to spend time with local residents in showcase homes, save a little money on accommodations (most start at around $40), and get breakfast thrown in for the price of a night. Some are listed in the specific travel sections of this book; see "Anchorage" in the Southcentral chapter and "Whitehorse" in the Yukon Territory chapter for area-wide associations.

If you're planning to stay a little longer in a particular place, check the classified ads in the newspapers under "Furnished Rooms" or "Rooms for Rent," and the Yellow Pages under "Rooming Houses." You can often get a substantial (50-75%) discount on private rooms (with shared bath and kitchen) for weekly stays.

For indoor sleeping in the great outdoors, check into Forest Service cabins. At $25 per night per cabin, you get up to six bunks, a woodstove, firewood, a table, and an outhouse. Of the nearly 200 cabins in the Tongass and Chugach National Forests, however, only a few are accessible by road; the rest require flying or boating in. These cabins are popular, and the Forest Service accepts applications for reservations six months in advance. Reservations for some of the most-used cabins, especially during hunting and fishing season, are determined by lottery. For addresses to write to for applications, see "Tongass National Forest" under "Introduction" in the Southeast chapter.

FOOD

Home Cooking

The cheapest and healthiest way to eat is to buy groceries and prepare your own meals. A lot can just be eaten cold. Peanut butter, anyone? Raw cookie dough? Freeze-dried food is convenient (but expensive and of varying tastiness) for hikers and campers—add water, heat, and then eat the plastic package instead. Canned food can also be handy, though heavy. Carry your own tea bags, instant oatmeal, pancake mix, fresh and dried fruit, and nuts. Most of the large supermarkets (Carrs and Safeway in the larger towns like Anchorage and Soldotna, Eagle Grocery in smaller towns like Homer and Valdez, and Foodland in Fairbanks) have extensive health-food and bulk sections, plus soup and salad bars where you pay by the pound (usually about $2.85 per). Also, if you can, stop at the roadside produce stands (in Matanuska Valley, mainly) and fish stalls along the coast. The local food won't be cheap, but it will definitely be fresh and tasty, and still less expensive than eating at a restaurant. All hostels have kitchens, or cook on your camp stove.

Restaurants

Don't worry, snappy sustenance is found all over Alaska. You'll feel just as foolish and fat after satisfying a craving for Chicken McNuggets, a Taco Bell Grande, or a bacon quarter-pounder in Anchorage as in your hometown. You won't feel quite so dumb after an Arby's roast beef or Burger King salad bar, though. The good-value restaurants are listed in the "Food" sections of the travel chapters, exhaustively researched with gusto and no little guilt. However, Alaska is not known for its large variety of fine cuisine. Even in Anchorage, Juneau, Fairbanks, and other larger towns, the ethnic options are minimal at best, expensive, and often disappointing. Furthermore, after a week of traveling around Alaska and Yukon, you'll think that all the coffee shops, roadhouses, cafes, and beaneries use the same menu, the same ingredients, the same grill and fryolator, and the same short-order cooks. Basic boring bacon-and-eggs breakfasts are usually $6-7; $5 is a bargain. Your burger and fries are similarly pricey, though a grilled cheese sandwich (American on white bread with liquid margarine) will be slightly cheaper. Fried chicken will start at $8, but spaghetti could be as little as $7. It's always a good idea to have some emergency munchies on hand. This might save you from going into hypoglycemic shock between eateries, which can be very long distances, or from facing yet another unfaceable meal of road food when you finally get to one.

Salmon Bakes

Splurge on these once or twice. The salmon is usually fresh, thick, and delicious (though the halibut is chunked, breaded, and deep-fried—not great, but it will satisfy your grease quotient). Ribs are messy but will address those deep carnivorous instincts, especially in this dog-eat-dog wilderness. Some salmon bakes also have reindeer sausage and crab legs. They all have the requisite macaroni, potato, and infernal three-bean salads, carrot and celery sticks, black olives for every finger, and sourdough rolls. Blueberry cake usually tops off the meal. Different bakes have different takes on second helpings; always ask several different cooks and servers for seconds anyway. Soft drinks are usually included, but beer and wine are extra. Expect to pay $10-15 for lunch, $15-20 for dinner. Discount coupons and nights are often advertised; keep your eyes open and jump on them. The one at Alaskaland in Fairbanks is best; Juneau's is a close second; and the one at Tok is right up there.

OTHER PRACTICALITIES

MONEY AND COMMUNICATIONS

The Whale and the Minnow

Prices are high in Alaska, but that doesn't mean you have to pay them. You can get away without spending a lot of money if you try. Planning is half the battle; budgeting is the other half. If you're driving up, take a friend or rider (or two), and your transportation expenses are immediately slashed. A credit card will give you security and extra time to pay when you get back home. If you buy your Greyhound ticket seven to 30 days in advance, you can go anywhere in the U.S. or Canada at a huge discount. Buy your airline or ferry tickets in the winter or early spring to stretch out the financing of the trip.

Do not even *think* of going to Alaska without a tent. Two nights in a hotel will pay for the tent. Definitely make reservations for the youth hostels in the big towns (Anchorage, Ketchikan, Juneau), and consider becoming a lifetime member of the YHA, much more economical in the long run. Bring a backpacking stove and cook as much food as you can, and utilize the salad bars at supermarkets. With the money you save you can splash out on an occasional restaurant meal and salmon bake.

Study this book carefully beforehand to help you choose the good-value destinations, attractions, and splurges. Then add up the big transportation chunks, the smaller accommodation bits, and a generous $25-40 a day for food and miscellaneous. With a little creativity, flexibility, and minimalism, you can have a whale of a time on a minnow's worth of money.

The Hard Facts

Unless otherwise stated, all prices in this handbook are in the local currency: Canadian dollars in Canada, U.S. dollars in the United States. Assume that all hotel and restaurant prices listed are per person (pp), per day, or per meal. Campground charges are usually per site. The prices and hours of all attractions and services throughout the book refer to the peak season, June-Aug.; discounts are often offered in May and September, when shorter hours are also in effect. Some prices are lower in the off-season, but many businesses close.

Always ask the price of a room, meal, or service before accepting it. Tipping (usually 15% of the bill), as in the Lower 48, is expected at most sit-down eating places fancier than snack bars or takeaway counters. Tourism employees often receive minimum wage and depend on tips for their real income. All transportation fares and traveling times are one-way, unless otherwise noted. Be aware that tickets or exact change are required on all forms of public transport in North America; drivers rarely carry change. Read the instructions before using public telephones in the North. Often you do not pay until your party answers; if you put the coin in before that, it will be lost.

Cash, Traveler's Checks, Exchange
Traveler's checks are the best way to carry money, but buy them from a well-known U.S. company such as Bank of America, Visa, or American Express. European or Japanese traveler's checks are very difficult to cash in North America; even Thomas Cook and Barclay Bank checks are sometimes refused.

If you know you will be visiting Canada, be sure to get a few Canadian-dollar traveler's checks, easily arranged at any large American or European bank. It could save you a lot of trouble if you arrive in Canada outside banking hours (Mon.-Thurs.10 a.m.-3 p.m., Friday 10 a.m.-5 p.m.). Some Canadian and U.S. cash will make your first few hours in the neighboring country less of a hassle. Note that there are no exchange facilities at the borders; Canadians take U.S. dollars at a very poor rate, while Americans often refuse Canadian dollars. Any other currency will most likely be refused. The U.S. dollar hovers around $1.35 Canadian so Americans get a 30-35% discount (though Canadian prices are generally 25% higher than in the U.S.).

Mail and Phone
If you would like to receive mail en route, have it addressed to yourself c/o General Delivery via a post office along the way. American post offices hold General Delivery mail 10 days, Canadian post offices 15 days. If you have mail sent to a Canadian post office and think you might not arrive in time, get a "Holding of Mail" card at any Canadian post office and send it to the appropriate address. Postage stamps in the amount of C$1.50 must be affixed to the card for each month you request mail to be held, up to a maximum of three months. This is an excellent service, but don't bother phoning; verbal requests are not honored.

Note that all mail posted in Canada must carry Canadian postage stamps, just as all U.S. mail must have American stamps. Convenient General Delivery addresses are: Vancouver, B.C. V6B 3P7; Prince Rupert, B.C. V8J 3P3; Whitehorse, Yukon Y1A 2BO; Seattle, WA 98101; Juneau, AK 99801; Fairbanks, AK 99701; Anchorage, AK 99501. Mail takes several weeks to travel from Alaska to Yukon.

The area code in all of Alaska is 907. British Columbia's is 604. Yukon and Alberta share 403.

TIME AND MEASUREMENTS

In 1983, Alaska went from four time zones to two. From Southeast to the western tip of the mainland is on Alaska time, one hour earlier than Pacific time, four hours earlier than Eastern. The western Aleutians are on Hawaii time, two hours behind Pacific time. British Columbia and Yukon are on Pacific time. So when you go from Prince Rupert to Ketchikan, Dawson to Eagle, or Beaver Creek to Tok you gain an hour; from Skagway to Whitehorse you lose an hour.

Just as with currency, all measurements herein are in the local units: metric in Canada, English method in the United States. To compute Celsius temperatures, subtract 32 from Fahrenheit and divide by 1.8. To compute miles from kilometers, multiply by 0.6; to get kilometers from miles multiply by 1.6. Fifty-five mph is 90 km/h. Remember that an imperial gallon is one-fifth larger than a U.S. gallon, so you'll get better mileage!

BORDER CROSSINGS

Immigration officials are trained to be suspicious, so try to look as much like a legitimate short-term visitor as you can. Never admit (or even imply) that you are going to work, study, do business, or live in a country other than your own. Officials may ask to see your money. If you have less than $250, you stand a chance of being refused entry. The best approach is just to be as polite and submissive as you can. Never argue or get angry with an official—it never helps. Dissembling is more effective.

Entry into the U.S.

Everyone other than Canadians must possess a passport and visa to enter the United States. Most Western Europeans and Commonwealth country residents can usually obtain a six-month travel visa easily from American consulates. You must have an onward or return ticket. No vaccinations are required, and you can bring an unlimited amount of money (over US$5,000 must be registered). Be aware that you can wind up crossing a Canadian/U.S. border four times in each direction (Lower 48 into B.C. or Alberta, back into Southeast Alaska, then into Yukon, then back into mainland Alaska). If you're an overseas visitor, make sure you understand the requirements for *re-entering* the United States. Americans returning from Canada may bring back US$400 worth of duty-free merchandise once every 30 days.

Entry into Canada

No visa is required of visitors from Western Europe, most Commonwealth countries, or the United States. Americans can enter Canada by showing a birth certificate or voter-registration card; a driver's license may not be sufficient. Everyone else must have a passport. Travelers under 18 must be accompanied by or have written permission from a parent or guardian to enter Canada. Handguns and automatic weapons are not allowed into Canada. Your home country's driver's license is acceptable in Canada.

WHAT TO TAKE

Camping Equipment

Even in summer, weather conditions in the North can change suddenly and you must be well prepared for rain and cold at any time. Water resistance and warmth (in addition to weight) should be your main criteria when purchasing camping equipment and clothing. Categorize and separate all your things in plastic bags or stuff sacks; pack it that way for convenient access and protection from moisture. If you're planning on hiking and traveling by public transportation, your loaded pack should not weigh more than one-quarter your body weight. Walk around the block with it a few times. Next imagine hiking 10 miles uphill into the rain with that load on your back. Now pack again—lighter this time. You'll still probably end up sending a few things home.

Practice putting up your tent, cooking on your camp stove, etc., before you set out. A foam sleeping pad, or better yet, a Therm-a-rest inflatable pad, provides comfort, insulation, and protection from moisture—essential qualities in the North. (They also double as inflatable rafts on lakes.) Down sleeping bags are useless when wet, especially problematic in Southeast and Southcentral. But they're much lighter and warmer than synthetic-filled bags, and you can always throw them in a dryer for an hour. Synthetic fiber is warmer when wet, less expensive, but heavier and bulkier.

Clothing

Wearing your clothing in layers allows you to add or remove items, depending on the temperature or your level of exertion. Start out with a T-shirt, thermal, or polypropylene top (and bottom). A wool shirt on top of that is comfortable and warm. A wool sweater and waterproof jack-

"ANYTHING TO DECLARE?"

WELCOME TO ALASKA

GORDY OHLIGER

WHAT TO TAKE

Camping Equipment
day pack or shoulder bag
internal-frame pack
nylon tent and rain fly
sleeping bag
sleeping pad
tent-patching tape
waterproofing compound
YH sleeping sheet

Toiletries and Medical Kit
an antibiotic
aspirin or aspirin substitute
Band-Aids
Calmitol ointment
ChapStick
contraceptives
insect repellent
iodine
Lomotil/diarrhea remedy
motion-sickness remedy
nail clippers
one large elastoplast or dressing
shampoo
soap in plastic container
Tiger Balm
toothpaste and toothbrush
unscented stick deodorant
Vaseline
vitamins
water-purification pills
white toilet paper

Essentials
address book
Canadian and American cash
envelopes
extra ballpoint pen
moneybelt with plastic liner
passport or birth certificate
photocopies of important documents
postage stamps
traveler's checks
waterproof notebook, pen or pencil
YH card
Alaska-Yukon Handbook

Food Kit
camp stove
can and bottle opener
canteen or water bottle
corkscrew
fishing tackle
freeze-dried food
litter bag
pen knife or Swiss Army knife
plastic bags
plastic plate
salt
Sierra cup
spoon, fork
tea bags
tin cooking pot
waterproof matches

Accessories
bear bells
candle
compass
fishing line for sewing heavy gear
five yards of rope
padlock and chain or cable
pocket alarm/calculator
pocket flashlight
powdered laundry soap
sewing kit with mini-scissors
sink plug (one that fits all)
sunglasses
towel

Clothing
down vest
mittens, gloves
permanent-press slacks
poncho with grommets
rain pants, parka
rubber thongs
socks
tennis shoes
waterproof hiking boots
wool cap, sweater

et are lighter and more versatile than a bulky overcoat, and a down vest is worth its weight in gold. Down coats are useless in the rain. Hiking boots are a given. The new lightweight high-tops are efficient, though the old tried-and-true work boots are also adequate. Make sure they're waterproof! A pair of old tennis shoes or scuba divers' rubber booties are handy for crossing streams and muskeg. Wear rubber thongs into public showers, around pools, etc. Bring a wool cap and gloves or mittens. A hooded parka comes in handy, though a poncho is adequate and light, and can double as a ground cloth or awning. Make sure it has a grommeted hole in each corner. Plastic rain pants are light and cheap, and will greatly improve the quality of life. Only the most expensive restaurants in the cities expect dressy attire, so bring a sportcoat, suit, dress, or skirt if you plan to hobnob with the nabobs or are on a group tour. But a new pair of permanent-press uniform pants goes a long way toward looking casually presentable, rather than the usual scruffy jeans.

Accessories and Documents
A small pocket calculator with a clock/alarm function is always handy. Carrying a bike cable or length of lightweight chain allows you to attach your pack to something solid if you must leave it in public places, and a padlock locks it (and your tent zippers) in place. Rip-offs are infrequent, but they do occur. Take a five-yard length of rope to hang your food up out of reach of brother bruin or to string out for a clothesline.

Make a couple of photocopies of the information page of your passport, identification, YHA card, transportation tickets, purchase receipt from traveler's checks, eyeglass and medical prescriptions, etc.—you should be able to get them all on one page. Carry these in different places and leave one at home. A soft pouch-type moneybelt worn under your clothes is very safe and handy, but put the documents inside a plastic bag to protect them from perspiration moisture.

Food Kit
A small camp stove is the only way to ensure hot food and drink on the trail. Firewood is often wet or unavailable; other times campfires are prohibited. Look for a stove that is not only light-weight, but burns a variety of fuels. White gas stoves are best. Remember, camping fuel is not allowed on commercial aircraft. Carry your food in lightweight containers. Avoid cans and bottles whenever possible. Dried or freeze-dried foods are light, easy to prepare, and less attractive to animals. Take some high protein/energy foods for hiking. A canteen or plastic water bottle is handy to have along; replenish it whenever you can.

Toiletries and Medical Kit
You'll find a plastic case in which to pack your toiletries or medical kit in the dishware section of any large department or hardware store. Unscented deodorant is best for both bear and bare encounters. Calmitol ointment or aloe gel is good for burns, bites, and rashes. An antibiotic such as sulfatrim apo is useful for serious infections (not VD), but beware of all antibiotics—know when and how to use them. For stomach cramps associated with diarrhea take a painkiller such as Imodium. Moleskin is an effective blister preventative. Take an adequate supply of any personal prescription medicines.

HEALTH AND HELP

Hypothermia
The number-one killer of outdoorspeople in the North, accounting for 85% of all wilderness deaths, is hypothermia. Prolonged exposure to wind and cold plus general physical exhaustion can lead to persistent shivering, drowsiness, disorientation, unconsciousness, and eventual death. The most insidious thing about it is that you probably won't even realize that it's happening to you. To prevent hypothermia always carry good raingear, dress in layers (particularly using wool or polypropylene, not cotton), avoid getting wet, and eat nutritious foods. Wet clothes cause you to lose body heat much faster than do dry clothes. A full 60% of body heat loss occurs through an uncovered head, so wear a waterproof or wool cap.

If you or someone you're with experiences the early-warning signs, get out of the rain and wind, get to a dry, warm place and remove the wet clothes. Cover the victim with a blanket or sleeping bag and a hat, and don't let him fall

GIANDIA

Although Alaska's lakes and streams may appear clean, you may risk a debilitating sickness if you drink untreated water. The protozoan *Giardia duodenalis* is found throughout the state, spread by both humans and animals (including beavers). Although the disease is curable with drugs, it's always best to carry safe drinking water on any trip or to boil water taken from creeks or lakes. Bringing water to a roiling boil for one minute is sufficient to kill Giardia and other harmful organisms. Another option is to use water filters; the latest varieties will get rid of Giardia parasites. Note, however, that these may not filter out other organisms such as Campylobactor bacteria that are just 0.2 microns in size. Chlorine and iodine are not always reliable, taste foul, and can be unhealthy.

asleep. Slowly warm him by placing warm wrapped objects (heated rocks, baked potatoes, etc.) alongside the head, neck, sides, and groin. One of the best ways to rewarm a person is to lie naked next to the victim, using your body heat to warm him (this works best with close friends). Do not try to heat him quickly, since this can lead to a heart attack. If at all possible, get the person to a hospital. Be prepared for hypothermia on all overnight hikes; and if making a day-hike on a wet day, do not go beyond the point where you can beat a hasty retreat to shelter.

Water

Even clear, cold, free-running streams can be contaminated. The best way to avoid contracting parasites from beavers and muskrats upstream is to boil water for 20 minutes before drinking it. If this is not convenient, treat it with chlorine or (better) iodine (about five drops of either per quart) and let it stand for 30 minutes. Purification pills also do the trick. If you're a real purist, you might take one of the water-cleaning devices sold in camping-goods stores; First Need works well and sells for around $35.

Lost in Place

It's easy to become lost in forested areas once you leave the main trail. Do not blunder blindly

on, but stop and look around you. Backtrack to a familiar spot, then either continue on the trail carefully or go completely back to where you began. Don't put your pack down—an excellent way to lose it. Use a compass to find your way to some known point. Panic in the wilderness is a form of culture shock which could spell your end.

Doctors and Mothers

If you're sick or injured and can't afford the prices charged by private doctors and general hospitals, call the local welfare office and ask them to refer you to a low-cost clinic. You may have to wait in line and go during certain limited hours, but there's usually no problem about using their services.

Runaways can send a free message to their parents by calling one of the following toll-free numbers: (800) 231-6946 in the Lower 48; (800) 231-6762 in Alaska/Hawaii. An operator will answer your call and phone your folks anywhere in the U.S. with a message from you. There will be no lectures and nobody will try to find out where you are. Only two questions will be asked, "How are you?" and "Do you need anything?" Let your parents know you're alive and okay.

Information

If you have time to write requests, an excellent selection of free maps and brochures is available from the regional tourism authorities: **Tourism B.C.,** Parliament Buildings, Victoria, B.C. V8W 1X4, Canada, tel. (604) 663-6000 or toll-free from anywhere in North America (800) 663-6000; **Alaska Division of Tourism,** P.O. Box 110801, Juneau, AK 99881, USA, tel. (907) 465-2010; **Tourism Yukon,** P.O. Box 2703, Whitehorse, YT Y1A 2C6, Canada, tel. (403) 993-5575; **NWT Tourism,** Box 1320 (EX), Yellowknife, NT X1A 2L9 Canada, tel. (403) 873-7200 or (800) 661-0788.

A free **highway map** of Washington state is available from the Washington State Dept. of Transportation, Transportation Bldg., Olympia, WA 98504, USA. Write for an index to **maps of Alaska** from the USGS Distribution Branch, P.O. Box 25286, Federal Center, Denver, CO 80225, USA.

For information on Alaska's national parks, write: **National Park Service,** 540 W. Fifth Ave., Anchorage, AK 99501, USA. Free maps of the

Tongass and Chugach National Forests may be obtained from the **U.S. Forest Service,** P.O. Box 1628, Juneau, AK 99802, USA.

For a **ferry timetable** write: Alaska Marine Highway, Pouch R, Juneau, AK 99811, USA. A list of **Alaskan youth hostels** is available from Anchorage International Hostel, 700 H St., Anchorage, AK 99501, USA.

If you are a member of the American Auto-mobile Association (AAA) or Canadian Auto-mobile Association (CAA), or have a friend or relative who is, get their *TourBook* and *CampBook* covering western Canada and Alaska, plus detailed maps. Overseas visitors who belong to an affiliated club in their home country can obtain this material free by showing their membership card at an AAA or CAA office in any large city (look in the phone book).

GETTING THERE

BY AIR

Six airlines offer nonstop service to Anchorage from as far south as Phoenix and as far east as Chicago: **Alaska Airlines,** tel. (800) 426-0333; **United,** tel. (800) 241-6522; **Delta,** tel. (800) 221-1212; **Northwest,** tel. (800) 225-2525; **Continental,** tel. (800) 525-0280; and **Reno,** tel. (800) 736-6247.

Alaska Airlines' Mileage Plan is worth knowing about: travel 10,000 miles in Alaska and get a free upgrade to first class; 15,000 miles gets you 50% off any roundtrip ticket; 20,000 gets you a free Alaska-mainland ticket.

From Canada
Canadian Airways, tel. (800) 426-7000 in the U.S., flies from most Canadian cities to White-horse, Yukon. **Delta Express,** tel. (800) 661-0789 in Canada, (800) 764-1800 in Alaska, flies direct from Whitehorse to Anchorage (and also connects to Yellowknife, Northwest Territories). **Air North Canada,** tel. (403) 474-3999, flies between Fairbanks, Juneau, Whitehorse, and Dawson, with connections to Anchorage. And **Ptarmigan Airways,** tel. (403) 873-4461 or (800) 661-0808, has scheduled service between Whitehorse and Yellowknife, NT.

BY BUS

Greyhound Lines
This giant company, largest of its kind in the world, has thousands of buses and stations all over the U.S. and Canada. Bus travel is very flexible—you buy a ticket and you're on your way (you might have to wait a little while). Also, they're extremely competitively priced and always have several special deals going on, such as substantial discounts for advance purchase.

Greyhound also has an unlimited-travel Ameripass which is valid throughout the United States. The Ameripass is sold for periods of seven days (US$179), 15 days (US$289), and 30 days (US$399), and the ticket is good for one year. The Ameripass will get you as far as Vancouver.

From Vancouver to Whitehorse, the farthest north (and west) that Greyhound goes, the fare is C$309. Or ride to Prince Rupert and grab an Alaska ferry. From Prince Rupert to Whitehorse by bus is C$210. Also check out the Greyhound Canada Pass, which provides substantial discounts for seven to 60 days' worth of bus travel: seven days (C$212), 15 days (C$277), 30 days (C$373), and 60 days (C$480).

All Greyhound regular-fare tickets are valid for one year, and unlimited stopovers are allowed. Greyhound buses run around the clock so you can save a lot on hotels. Instead of going straight through, however, stop off once in a while for a night or two in some of the exciting cities along the way. Remember, you're on holiday! There's almost always a YMCA, a YH, a campground, a roadside ditch, a cheap motel, or even a luxury hotel where you can arrange accommodations. For information, call (800) 231-2222 in the U.S. and (800) 661-8747 in Canada.

Magic Buses
Green Tortoise travel is more than just a bus ride—it's a vacation and a cultural experience in itself. This alternative bus line uses recycled Greyhounds with the seats ripped out and foam-

MAIN HIGHWAYS

A ELLIOT HIGHWAY
B RICHARDSON HIGHWAY
C TAYLOR HIGHWAY
D EDGERTON HIGHWAY / McCARTHY ROAD
E STERLING HIGHWAY
F SEWARD HIGHWAY
G COPPER HIGHWAY
H HAINES HIGHWAY
I ATLIN ROAD

© MOON PUBLICATIONS, INC.

rubber mattresses laid in their place on elevated platforms. Up front there's a lounge area with seats and tables, which converts to another sleeping area at night—just roll out your sleeping bag and forget everything. Food is usually included in the fare for the long-distance trips such as Alaska. Unlike Greyhound, you're allowed to drink beer and wine on board (in moderation), but tobacco smoking is prohibited. One of the best things about these trips is the people—alternative travel attracts good company. The removal of the seats eliminates barriers and leads to new friendships. This is a friendly, unprivate way to travel, though not inexpensive.

Green Tortoise has two trips each summer to Alaska, one in late June and the other in late July. Each bus holds 32 passengers and two drivers. Book no later than January to ensure a space; these buses fill up fast. The trip to Alaska is described by Green Tortoise sales agents as "rugged"—you camp along the way in tents. The trips take a month, leaving from Eugene, Portland, or Seattle and winding up in Fairbanks or Anchorage. You can also catch the bus down from Alaska. The fare is $1,500, plus $250 for food. The fare includes the ferry ride from Bellingham to Skagway.

Despite the casual approach, Green Tortoise buses are reliable and have a good safety record. For more information write: Green Tortoise Alternative Travel, P.O. Box 24459, San Francisco, CA 94124, USA; or call (800) 227-4766 nationwide (outside California), (415) 821-0803 in California.

Others
Inland Coach Lines, tel. (250) 385-4411, offers excellent service the length of Vancouver Island, from Victoria to Port Hardy, with connections in Port Alberni for Tofino. At Port Hardy, catch a B.C. Ferry to Prince Rupert, where you can connect to an Alaska state ferry.

Once you reach Whitehorse, however, the bus situation goes a little downhill. **Alaskon Express,** Gray Line's public transportation arm, tel. (907) 277-5581, runs into Alaska three times a week. **Alaska Direct,** tel. (800) 780-6652, has three trips a week from Whitehorse to Anchorage and Fairbanks. **Norline Coaches,** tel. (403) 633-3864, runs from Whitehorse up to Dawson.

Within Alaska many small companies provide local and short hops around the state; all services are listed in the travel chapters. Note, however, that these companies change with the wind, so always research and reconfirm the information herein.

BY FERRY

Ferries plying the Inside Passage from Bellingham to Skagway cruise up an inland waterway and through fjords far wilder than Norway's, surpassing even a trip down the coast of Chile to Punta Arenas. One difference is that the North American journey is cheaper and more easily arranged than its South American or Scandinavian counterparts. Another difference is the variety of services, routes, and destinations for this 1,000-mile historic cruise. The **Washington State Ferries,** Colman Dock, Seattle, WA 98104, tel. (206) 464-6400 (in Washington call toll-free 800-542-7052) offers regular service throughout Puget Sound and to Vancouver Island. **Black Ball Transport,** 430 Belleville St., Victoria, B.C. V8V 1W9, tel. (250) 381-1551, sails between Victoria and Port Angeles. **B.C. Ferries,** 112 Fort St., Victoria, B.C. V8V 4V2, tel. (250) 669-1211, has commuter service between Vancouver Island and the B.C. mainland, plus long-distance ships through the Canadian Inside Passage from Port Hardy at the northern tip of Vancouver Island to Prince Rupert on the B.C. mainland's north coast, and from Prince Rupert to the Queen Charlotte Islands.

The **Alaska Marine Highway,** P.O. Box 25535, Juneau, AK 99802, tel. (800) 642-0066, operates two ferry networks: one from Bellingham throughout Southeast Alaska (see the Southeast Alaska "Introduction" for details), the other through Southcentral Alaska from Cordova to Dutch Harbor. The two systems do not connect, but Alaska Airlines' flight from Juneau to Cordova makes it possible to travel almost the whole distance from Bellingham to Dutch Harbor by regular passenger ferry (ferry Bellingham-Juneau, plane Juneau-Cordova, ferry Cordova-Kodiak-Dutch Harbor). The ferries operate year-round and fares are 25% lower Oct.-April. Also, a little-known service provided at all the Alaska ferry terminals is a computer printout

ALASKA MARINE HIGHWAY

Alaska Marine Highway's flagship Columbia *sails from Seattle to Skagway once a week in the summer.*

describing the sights and travel practicalities of all the towns en route. And they're amazingly up to date. Ask when you're there.

BY CAR

Getting to Alaska by car is by far the cheapest, easiest, most dependable, and most flexible means of mobility. Its advantages over public transportation are manifold, so to speak. You can start anywhere, and once there, you can go anywhere there's a road, anytime you feel like it, stopping along the way for however long you decide, carrying anything (so long as it's legal, of course) or anyone you like. The roads in the North Country are especially fun, and you have some of them pretty nearly to yourself. On a few roads you rarely see another car. It's very open, unconfined, uninhibiting—a large part of the spell of the North. All you have to do is keep gas and oil in the car. And a good spare tire.

Highways North

You can drive all the way up and back. Alternatively, put the car on the ferry one way. The **Alaska Highway** (nicknamed the Alcan) is now

55 years old. Gone are the days when you had to carry extra fuel and four spare tires, when you had to protect your headlights and windshield with chicken wire, and when facilities were spaced 250 miles apart. Today, almost the entire road is paved and wide enough for two trucks to pass each other without one having to pull over. Gas stations are located almost every 50 miles, and roadhouses and inns are numerous. Still, this road passes through 1,440 miles of somewhat inhospitable wilderness. Frost heaves and potholes are not uncommon. Mechanics are few and far between and parts are even scarcer. Gas prices are no laughing matter. If you're coming from anywhere east of Idaho or Alberta, you can hit Mile 0 of the Alaska Highway through Edmonton without having to backtrack east at all. But if you're heading north from the West Coast, or through the Canadian Rockies, you'll probably wind up in Prince George and have to head east a bit to Dawson Creek.

You can also head west out of Prince George on the Yellowhead and take the **Cassiar Highway** north from Meziadin Junction to just west of Watson Lake in Yukon Territory. This 458-mile road is scenically stunning and most of it is now paved; services are a little less frequent than on the Alaska Highway.

Go Prepared

A few common-sense preparations can eliminate all but the most unexpected problems. A gas credit card is invaluable—Chevron, Texaco, and Shell are most useful. You can expect to get hit hard by gas prices, especially along the Alcan and the remoter stretches in Alaska. But along the main Interior and Southcentral thoroughfares, prices are only a few cents higher than Outside. And in the cities, gas may be cheaper than the cheapest in your home town.

A reliable car is a must. If you have the slightest doubt about it, good luck! Get the car closely serviced before setting out; when you ask your mechanic "Will it make it to Alaska?" you won't be kidding. If you get stuck somewhere, there might not be another mechanic for 100 miles. And tow trucks have been known to charge $5 *a mile*. Since you'll be tempted to drive hundreds of miles off the beaten track, the best investment you can make in your car is five steel-belted radial tires. Even with big gashes and holes, they'll still roll under you. Bring a pressure gauge and check the tires frequently. A few spare hoses (and hose tape) and belts take up little room and can come in very handy. Spare gas and oil filters are also useful, due to the amount of dust on the gravel roads in the dry months. Water is an absolute necessity; carry at least a five-gallon jug. Take tools even if you don't know how to use them. Someone usually comes along who doesn't have tools but knows what to do. It's a good idea to carry a roll of baling wire and a tube of superglue, to rehang or rejoin the inevitable part that jars loose, falls off, or gets dragged along the highway.

Be very careful around road construction crews, especially graders. Graders leave a mound of fill in the middle of the road, which they spread along the surface. Occasionally you wind up on the wrong side of the mound and have to cross over to the right side of the road. Hidden rocks can really tear up the underside of your car. Where there's construction, often a pilot car will lead you through the muddy maze; follow it closely so as not to get stuck. A lot of salt is laid down on the roads, especially in the mountains, so wash the car thoroughly at the first opportunity to minimize the rust, which never sleeps.

Finally, by driving the whole way in one direction and putting the car on the ferry in the other, you can take different routes up and back.

OTHER WAYS TO ALASKA

By Train

A **Canrailpass** is available in Canada for 13 days' travel out of 30 on VIA Rail trains. The Pass costs C$535. Even with the pass, reservations are required; call toll-free in the U.S. (800) 561-9181, in Canada (800) 561-3952. With trains running from both Prince Rupert and Vancouver, a train trip is a creative way to begin or end your journey north.

Driveaways

Driveaway cars are another way of getting around North America. You pick up a car from an agency in one city, pay a deposit, then drive the car to the destination, where your deposit is refunded. If you have a rider or two to share the gas and driving, it's especially cheap and efficient transportation. Non-Canadians and non-Americans are welcome but should have an International Driver's License. Aaacon is one of the largest driveaway agencies in the U.S.; look for others in the Yellow Pages under "Auto Transporters." The classifieds in the daily newspapers of the big cities, especially on the West Coast (under "Travel and Transportation"), often have advertisements for private driveaways and riders to share expenses, sometimes even to Alaska. In Alaska, people looking for drivers or riders to the Lower 48 frequently advertise in the classifieds.

Package Tours

Seven- to 21-day whirlwinds around Alaska-Yukon are available from a growing number of retail and wholesale tour packagers. All will book you onto one of a variety of cruise ships up the Inside Passage, reserve your first-class (for Alaska) hotel rooms, roll you between them on luxury motorcoaches and superdome railcars, and offer options for local and overnight side trips. Many are escorted by tour directors, and some even include all meals in the price. Many people choose this route for convenience, comfort, and security, though they certainly pay for what they get.

Holland America-Westours, 300 Elliot Ave. W, Seattle, WA 98119, tel. (206) 281-3535 or (800) 426-0327, is the granddaddy of the Alaska package program. Chuck West, one of the most colorful characters in the history of Alaska tourism, actually started the entire industry in 1948 doing city tours of Fairbanks in his private car and built Westours into a huge, debt-ridden operation, which he had to sell to the shrewd Dutch of Holland America Lines in the early 1970s. In January 1989, Carnival Cruise Lines bought Holland America, including its worldwide cruise-ship operation, Alaska Gray Line ground division, and the 18-hotel Westmark chain. Changes for the '90s remain to be seen, but if a moderately priced tour is what you want, in many ways their old motto—"Westours *is* Alaska"—is accurate. Six cruise ships, all in the 1,075- to 1,500-passenger range, leave Vancouver and call at ports in Southeast, Kenai Peninsula, and Prince William Sound.

Chuck West went on to start up another tour company, TravAlaska, now known as **Alaska Sightseeing/Cruise West,** Fourth and Battery Bldg. Suite 700, Seattle, WA 98121, tel. (206) 441-8687 or (800) 426-7702. Their cruise ships are small (all carry less than 100 passengers) and intimate; you get a more personalized and low-to-the-ground look at Alaska. You can read all about the fascinating background to the whole Alaska tourism industry in Chuck West's autobiography, *Mr. Alaska: The Chuck West Story,* from Weslee Publishing, Seattle.

An excellent package tour, if you can pay the price and get on one of them (book early), is offered by **Tauck Tours,** P.O. Box 5027, Westport, CT 06881, tel. (203) 226-6911 or (800) 468-2825, which uses Westours' facilities. One of the largest domestic package-tourism com-

panies, Tauck's tours are all escorted and have a system all their own.

The five-star tour is on **Cunard's** 600-passenger *Sagafjord,* 800-passenger *Dynasty,* and 116-passenger *Sea Goddess II.* Write: 555 Fifth Ave., New York, NY 10017, tel. (800) 1-CUNARD.

Princess Tours, 2815 Second Ave., Seattle, WA 98121, tel. (800) 421-0522, competes head-on with Westours. Princess is higher class, both the cruise ships and ground facilities, than Westours. Its ships are all larger and more Love Boatish.

Canadians and Germans should contact **Atlas Tours,** P.O. Box 4340, Whitehorse, Yukon Y1A 3T5, tel. (403) 668-3161.

Other tour operators include **Celebrity, Clipper, Hanseatic** (out of Germany), **Norwegian Cruises, Royal Caribbean, Royal Cruise, Seabourn, Society Expeditions,** and **World Explorer.** For all the info, contact your travel agent, or write for the *Alaska Vacation Planner,* P.O. Box E-301, Juneau, AK 99811, tel. (907) 465-2010.

Two tips: It's preferable to take a "southbound" tour, which means you fly into Anchorage, see the mainland first, then finish off with your luxury four-day cruise down to Vancouver. That's because the ground portion can be grueling, but then you can just relax onboard the ship for the final leg. Also, be aware that the tour companies mostly target the retired market, which can be fun for nonelders who can get into the spirit, but which isn't exactly a "Love Boat"-type experience for swinging singles.

GETTING AROUND

By Plane and Package Tour
In Alaska, often the only way to get from here to there is through the air. To find the best-value fares, always compare the airlines to the big tour companies. You can usually get a better deal from the tour companies, which charge wholesale airfares and then add on the conveniences to compete with the regular coach fare. For example, the best APEX fare between Anchorage and Nome is generally only a few dollars more expensive than the entire Gray Line tour price, which also includes one night's lodging, two city tours, and transfers. Also, always

check the ads in the daily newspapers, where the tour companies often advertise up to 50% reductions in their local package-tour prices.

Still, when you come right down to it, unless you're really into gold-rush history or Native culture, you might rather skip Nome or Barrow altogether and go flightseeing over Denali and Glacier Bay and cruise Prince William Sound for the same price. (Though you might seriously consider Alaska Airlines' new tours to Russia.) Even when the airfare alone seems substantially cheaper, by the time you add the airporter van both ways and rent a bike or car to see the sights, you might as well take the tour. Besides, the tours themselves can be very good value. All this is contingent, of course, on short time; if you have unlimited days to explore, say, Kodiak, and lots of planning leeway, get the cheapest deal and really stretch your travel dollars.

By Bush Plane

All these factors are, of course, predicated on large domestic carriers flying to your destination. If they don't, you're in for a guaranteed adventure with the small, local, colorful bush airlines, which almost always deliver exciting, personalized experiences. These airlines have regularly scheduled, mostly competitively priced (though usually expensive) flights to towns and attractions (Eagle or McNeil State Game Preserve, for instance) that either have no public ground transportation or simply can't be reached overland—which accounts for over three-quarters of the state.

The planes usually seat nine, 10, or 16 passengers, and they fly no matter how many passengers are along, for the regular fare (if the weather's cooperating). But if you're heading to a really remote cabin, fjord, river, glacier, or park, that's when you'll encounter the famous Alaskan bush pilots and the famous Cessna two-, three-, and four-seaters. And their infamous "charter rates," upwards of $300 an hour flying time, which can make Alaska Airlines' fares look like the bargain of the century. But you'll have quite a ride—landing on tiny lakes with pontoons, on snow or ice with skis, on gravel bars with big fat tires; and flying through soupy fog by radar or instinct, loaded to the gills with people, equipment, extra fuel, tools, mail, supplies, and anything else under the sun. Make sure you agree on all the details beforehand—charges, drop-off and pickup times and locations, emergency and alternative procedures, tidal considerations, etc. Never be in much of a hurry; time is told differently up here, and many variables come into play, especially weather and maintenance. If you're well prepared for complications, and have a flexible schedule and a loose attitude, one of these bush hops will no doubt be among your most memorable experiences in the North Country, worth every penny and minute that you spend. Also see "In the Air" under "Outdoor Recreation" earlier in this chapter.

By Train

Except for the White Pass and Yukon Route excursion between Skagway and Fraser, and the kids' choo-choo around Alaskaland in Fairbanks, Alaska-Yukon's only train is the Alaska Railroad, running 470 miles between Seward and Fairbanks (with a seven-mile spur between Portage and Whittier). The train—historic and a bit exotic—is also much roomier and slower than the tour buses but is about the same price (and occasionally even on time). Two daily expresses (May 19-September 18), one northbound and one southbound, run between Anchorage and Fairbanks (10 hours, $135). Fairbanks to Denali costs $50, Anchorage to Denali $96.

Princess Tours and Westours hook their two-deck superdome Vistacruiser coaches to the end of the train, for which you pay an additional 35% (meals extra—$9 for brunch, $18 for dinner). There are also plenty of Denali packages, train-plane combinations, and family discounts. A shuttle train transports passengers through the Chugach Mountains between Portage and Whittier several times a day ($8). The train also runs all the way to Seward daily ($45 one-way, $70 roundtrip). Write: Alaska Railroad, Passenger Services, P.O. Box 107500, Anchorage, AK 99510; or call (907) 265-2494 in Anchorage, or (800) 544-0552.

By Ferry

Alaska Marine Highway serves almost every town in Southeast Alaska, plus most of the coastal towns in Southcentral, Kodiak Island, the Kenai and Alaska Peninsulas, all the way out to Dutch Harbor in the eastern Aleutians. The two systems do not interconnect, but the Alaska Airlines flight from Juneau to Cordova is an easy, though very expensive, transition. Five of the nine ferries have staterooms, and eight have solariums where you can spread out your sleeping bag (or sleep inside in the lounges). Note that the *Bartlett,* which cruises Prince William Sound, doesn't have showers, but the other long-distance ferries do. All except the tiny shuttle between Ketchikan and Metlakatla have food service. It's a very relaxing and friendly way to travel around the state, and prices are extremely reasonable, especially compared to airfare.

Write: Alaska Marine Highway, P.O. Box 25535, Juneau, AK 99802, tel. (907) 465-3941 or (800) 642-0066, for a copy of the schedules and fares or to make reservations (especially recommended to book staterooms or passage for your car).

Note that the southern terminal of the Alaska ferry system is no longer in Seattle; it's now in Bellingham, WA, 85 miles north; see "Bellingham" under "Seattle and Vicinity" in the Gateways chapter.

By Bus

Bus services, highly developed in B.C. and Yukon, become a little less so when you enter Alaska. Nonetheless, you can get to most major destinations by bus or minibus, and most minor destinations (on the road) by van. Except for the big tour companies' buses, plus Alaskon Express (Gray Line), most bus companies are small local affairs, which are covered in the relevant travel sections of this book. Note, however, that some crucial connections are not serviced every day. Also be aware that buses in Alaska and Yukon do not run at night. Everyone arriving from Skagway or Edmonton/Prince George will have to spend a night in Whitehorse. All passengers transiting Yukon to Anchorage must overnight in either Beaver Creek or Tok. Accommodations are at your own expense, so take this into consideration when calculating your costs.

Finally, be acutely aware that the small bus and van services come and go with regularity (they're not very profitable). Always check and double check that the company 1) exists, 2) is in operation, 3) does the route you're interested in, and 4) will die with dignity if they leave you stranded and you catch back up with them.

By Car

Your own car is without a doubt the most convenient, reliable, and inexpensive way to get around the small part of Alaska that has roads. It's best to bring the car with you; trying to buy one at inflated Alaskan prices is not recommended and selling it at the end of your stay is problematic. Rental cars are prohibitively expensive in the outback towns and can be difficult to come by in the major cities. Gasoline is often cheaper in the larger towns than in the Lower 48, which helps offset the higher prices you pay the closer you get to the end of the roads, and the

very high prices beyond the roads. For more info and an in-depth look at bringing your car to Alaska, see "By Car" under "Getting There," above.

By Bicycle

Inveterate cyclists have a love affair with bike riding that makes the relationship between car and driver look like a one-night stand. If you're indifferent to or can overcome the hardships (hills, trucks, rain and wind, bugs, time, security considerations, sore muscles, etc.), the advantages of bikes are unassailable. They're free to operate, nonpolluting, easy to maintain, and great exercise. They also slow down the world and attract the immediate friendly and curious attention of the locals. Taking along a bicycle is an excellent idea, and most of the ferries will let you bring it at no extra charge. Almost all of the bus companies and railways will carry your bike as accompanied baggage for a nominal amount, although a few want you to have it in a box. Most airlines also accept bicycles as luggage, as long as they're boxed before check-in. Before you buy a ticket, compare prices, then ask each airline about taking a bicycle.

Alaska can be just as hard on bikes as on cars, however, if not harder. Fifteen-speed mountain bikes are recommended to better handle the rough roads. Know how to fix your own bike, and take along a good repair kit as bicycle shops are few and far between. You should have spare tubes and tires, a patch kit, a pump, extra cables, a spare chain, a chain tool, and perhaps even extra wheels. Carry your gear in saddlebag panniers lined with plastic bags. Fenders are nice in wet weather. Warm, waterproof clothing is essential, particularly rain pants, poncho, rain hat, wool shirt, wool socks, and waterproof shoes. Bicycling gloves, shorts, and clear goggles are also necessary. Everything you need may be purchased in Seattle, Vancouver, or Anchorage.

Short-distance bicycles are available for rent, usually at no more than $12 per day, in every major town and are an excellent way to see the local sights, especially in fair weather.

Hitchhiking

One of the best ways to meet the local people and get where you're going at the same time is to stick out your thumb and hitch. Hitchhiking is possible, at least part of the year, throughout the North; mostly what you need are time and patience. If standing by the roadside for hours sounds boring, read a book: *Hitchhiker's Guide to the Galaxy* by Douglas Adams, Michener's epic *Alaska,* or Kesey's *Sailor Song* are good ones. But be sure to put it down and make eye contact with the drivers. Otherwise, it's easy for them to ignore you. Opinions vary on walking down the road and hitching, but in Alaska it's safer to hitch near civilization, though it's often easier to get a ride if you're in the middle of nowhere. Most of the North is uninhabited, so if you get stuck you'll have no trouble finding a place to pitch your tent when night falls.

In the hierarchy of hitchhiking, one or two women get rides easiest (but at the most physical risk), then couples, then solo males, then solo males with guitars, then two guys, and last, two guys and a dog. Having small children with you often helps. If you're from somewhere other than Canada or the U.S., a flag on your backpack might assist you in getting a lift. Often the people who stop are former hitchhikers themselves. When you get a ride, offer to contribute for gas, and at stops, try to be the one who pays for cigarettes or soft drinks. Buying the driver lunch will make you both feel good and is a lot cheaper than a bus ticket. Ask people you meet on ferries and at campgrounds if they can give you a lift. A good number of the motorists leaving the ferry at Haines head for Fairbanks or Anchorage. Tape a notice outside the ship's cafeteria offering to share the gas and driving in exchange for a ride. If you have your own car, save money by looking for riders to share expenses. Noticeboards outside tourist offices are great clearinghouses for people offering or looking for rides. In the big towns, check the classifieds in the daily papers.

SUGGESTED ITINERARIES

One Week

If you only have a week, one option is to take the ferry ride from Bellingham to Juneau or Skagway roundtrip (takes six days); or ride the ferry one-way, tour Juneau, Glacier Bay, Skagway, or Whitehorse, for example, then fly back from Juneau or Whitehorse. The other option is to fly to and from Anchorage, see the city briefly, then head up to Denali National Park (what most people would do), down to the Kenai Peninsula, or over to Prince William Sound. One week will allow you to do one, of the above three, leisurely and in depth, two of the three at a steady clip and somewhat superficially, and all three frantically.

Two Weeks

Two weeks is the length of the average package tour to Alaska. In two weeks you can ride the ferry from Bellingham to Skagway, stopping off at, say, Juneau overnight. Spend a night in Skagway, a night in Whitehorse, then go overland to Fairbanks. A few nights in Fairbanks and Denali will get you ready for Anchorage; from there you can choose between the Kenai Peninsula and Prince William Sound as described above.

Alternately, you could ride the ferry to Juneau, fly to Cordova and connect up with the Southwest ferry system, and do Prince William Sound and the Kenai Peninsula that way, then wind up in Anchorage. If your planning is tight and your timing is right, you might even be able to jam in Denali. That's starting to border on hysteria, though. Also, keep in mind that by the end of their package journeys, most tourists need a vacation!

Three Weeks

Three weeks is about the minimum required to drive at least one-way. It's a long three days from anywhere in the Pacific Northwest up the Alaska or Cassiar Highways. But with your own car, you can cover as much ground as you like, as fast as you like. It's light most of the summer, so you don't have to worry about missing the scenery if you drive at night. You can sleep when you're dead. If you really want to crank up the mileage, drive to Whitehorse, then Dawson, then Eagle, then Tok. From Fairbanks, you can get out there, going to hot springs at Manley or Central. Head down to Denali and Anchorage, then take in the whole Kenai Peninsula, and/or put your car on the *Bartlett* or *Tustumena* to do the whole Prince William Sound excursion. Riding back on the ferry will save a lot of wear and tear on your wheels and your lower back.

Four Weeks or More

If you have all this time, and the big bucks, you can get as far out there as you want. Head up the Dempster Highway from Dawson several hundred miles to Inuvik, Northwest Territories, near the Arctic Ocean. Or head up to Coldfoot above the Arctic Circle on the Dalton outside of Fairbanks. Or get to Cordova or Kodiak on the Southwest ferry system. You could also take the *Tustumena* for a week's ride to Dutch Harbor in the Aleutians. Or pay the price and go to McNeil River, Katmai, Nome, Barrow, or the Pribilofs. To travel around Alaska for a month or more, you need to read this whole book very carefully.

EMPLOYMENT

Alaska occupies a special place in the national imagination; a mystique and magnetism surround even the word itself with a singular vibration. Fur, gold, war, statehood, oil, fish, cruise ships—Alaska's life and times are as exotic and electric as the northern lights. For many people, the state assumes a symbolic dimension, vague of correlation yet strong of sensation: somewhere *beyond*. Adventure. The freedom dream. For other people the lure of Alaska is measured directly in dollars: get rich quick in the land of the Klondike and the pipeline. Those who want to synthesize the dream and the dollars often wind up as seasonal employees.

Boiled down to its essence, at a summer job in Alaska you'll mostly be working with tourists or fish. The government is another alternative for summer jobs in Alaska, through land-management bureaucracies like the national park and forest services.

FISHING AND CANNERIES

For work on fishing boats, there's almost always a waiting list that stretches from the end of the pier through town all the way to cabins in the hills. And everyone on it has at least five years' seniority. Many canneries are unionized, and even if they're not, they may also have waiting lists for entry-level positions. However, it's still eminently possible to find work—a lot of work—at them. Canning is loud, wet, foul, hard, long, hot, cold, and rank . . . which isn't bad if you don't mind that sort of thing. You might, however, lose your appetite for fish. Also, many canneries open and close in a month, depending on the catch; be prepared to relocate occasionally to other canneries to start from scratch. But, in a good season you can make big bucks at canneries, working like 84 hours a week (the infamous "seven twelves") at $6-8 an hour, $9-11 overtime.

FEDERAL ARCHIVES, SEATTLE

This cannery, photographed in Metlakatla, Alaska, in 1916, was less automated than the ones you may work at, but one thing hasn't changed: you might lose your appetite for fish.

You can wind up in some pretty remote places, so find out beforehand whether the company pays for your transportation costs plus housing and food. A lot of fish-processing companies are based in Seattle. Track down the Seattle Yellow Pages in your local library for applicable listings and call the likely looking—in January, February at the latest, when the fishing companies do their early hiring. Ask as many questions as you can; you'll quickly learn the lay of the Seattle scene. You'll also learn a lot about the seasons: crab, halibut, salmon, cod, pollock, etc. If you're in Seattle in May or early June, you can also call to see who needs last-minute fill-ins.

After that, the only way to get a cannery job is to go to the canneries themselves, in Cordova, Valdez, Seward, Homer, Dutch, Ketchikan, Juneau, etc. You show up every morning at 5 a.m. until you're hired, and depending on the catch, you work till you drop, or you get laid off the next day. Nothing too secure about it. But if you do lose the one job, you follow the crowd down to the next cannery. If you're in Alaska in the middle of the summer and are serious about working in the commercial fishing industry, a good idea is to call the tourism information people or directory assistance or the library or somebody in each town, get the names of the canneries, and call them. By the end of the day you'll know all you need to know about the work possibilities.

TOURISM JOBS

Tourists don't smell nearly as bad as dead fish, and they tip much more readily. They aren't so cold and slimy, either—most of them, anyway. Every summer, tourists descend on the place by the packed planeload carrying cash, credit cards, and traveler's checks in their pockets. If you position yourself in their path, you can profit from this modern-day gold rush. In addition, the tourist trail for the most part is where adventure awaits: immense and spectacular wilderness areas such as Denali and Glacier Bay National Parks; isolated, historic bush communities such as Valdez, Skagway, Dawson; and wild and woolly cityscapes such as Fairbanks and Anchorage.

In order to become a toll collector on the tourist trail, you must first understand that the big money is in the package-tourism end of the industry. Your typical Alaskan tourist is a retired senior citizen from the Midwest on a 15- to 17-day package tour which includes 10 or so days busing, railroading, and flying around the state, plus a three- to five-day sail down the Inside Passage on cruise ships. He/she carries two suitcases, sleeps in seven different hotels, rides on nine different buses, eats roughly 30 meals on the mainland, and spends upwards of $500 cash on food, souvenirs, and miscellaneous. The bargain packages pay transportation, lodging, and baggage handling: the expensive tours include meals and gratuity.

Tour-Company Jobs

The large package-tour companies have numerous entry-level positions: basically warm young bodies to throw at the onslaught of warm old bodies. Jobs are almost entirely centered on transportation and sales and service. These include bus drivers, expeditors, and tour company sales reps.

Tour-bus driving in Alaska is one of those jobs that appears glamorous and exciting but turns out to be one of the more grueling, burn-out positions on the circuit. Moneywise, however, it's the best entry-level position. First-year drivers for the tour companies generally conduct the "city tour" (Anchorage, Fairbanks, Juneau, Ketchikan), the airport shuttle, and transfers to local attractions. First-year drivers used to do the 375-mile marathon trip between Anchorage and Fairbanks, but this is the exception, now that most package tourists ride the luxury train cars along this run (see below for employment details on the train). Plan to look like a fool all through May and June as you "develop" your rap. It's not unusual to have a busload of tourists (or worse, Alaskans!) behind you, a microphone in front of you, driving along and trying to knowledgeably describe country you've never seen before. And see how far a tour's worth of sick jokes and Geritol show tunes gets you.

Second-year routes are much more lucrative, and much more demanding, than first. On the Fairbanks-Whitehorse-Skagway run, for example, you drive three days (two nights) with the same group, with which—if you're good—you can develop a high-tip rapport. Similar runs include Anchorage-Valdez and the new Fairbanks-Prudhoe Bay overnighter. (The very senior drivers can work up to the three-night Fairbanks-Dawson-Whitehorse run.) Not only do you drive the coach, but you also give the guided narration, spot wildlife, answer the same questions day in and day out, serve lunch, sing, recite Robert Service, cheerlead, and occasionally fish a wallet or a bracelet out of the chemical toilet.

Gray Line and Princess Tours run the vast majority of these buses. You must possess a valid bus driver's license before applying, often with stringent clean-record requirements. Plan on $1,200-1,400 a month to start, with the all-important tips, year-end safety and attendance bonuses, and a small (or no) charge for housing. Bus driving will definitely test your endurance.

Shuttle and tour-bus driver jobs in places like Denali are jealously guarded positions, with five-year employees the norm, 10-year drivers not uncommon, and even 15-year lifers to be found. Shuttle/tour drivers at Denali are very well-paid: in the $12-18 an hour range. Tour drivers are also well-tipped. These positions are highly competitive, and a background in natural science and interpretation is almost mandatory for applicants.

Another endurance challenge is the variety of positions on the "domecars"—luxury coaches that are hooked up to the back of Alaska Railroad trains to transport the package tourists between Anchorage and Fairbanks. These include **car managers, bartenders, waitpeople, narrators,** and **kitchen crew.** Schedules are generally as follows: based in Anchorage, you do the 16-hour run to Fairbanks, changing passengers at Denali. You serve three meals, then stay overnight in company apartments in Fairbanks, and do it in reverse the next day. Day off, then another roundtrip, then three days off. The car manager and waitpeople make good money, but keep in mind that carrying those bowls of soup on rocking and rolling train cars is hard on the legs and nerves, and the hours are long.

Another entry-level possibility in working for the large tour companies is the all-purpose **expeditor** (X.P.) position, a combination greeter, chaperone, cheerleader, trouble-shooter, luggage counter, and gofer. Expediting is possibly the most demanding firing-line job on the tourist trail, with long hours and lots of problems. It's commonly stressful due to the hundreds of tourists needing to be handled at each location at various times of day. But it's a good foot in the door: the pay is fair, you get to see a lot of behind-the-scenes operations, free housing is often included, and some expeditors step right up the ladder into bus driving or management.

Most large hotels in the state have travel desks in their lobbies peopled by **tour company sales reps.** They function as sort of in-house travel agents, selling tours and working closely with other tour companies and the airlines. This is good training for travel agenthood.

A job at **Westours** is the best bet for package-tour companies, being Alaska-size and fairly well organized. Holland America/Westours/Gray Line/Westmark Hotels is by far the biggest tour operator in the state. They own numerous cruise ships, countless motorcoaches, and 18 hotels around Alaska. They hire scads of bus drivers, train-car personnel, expeditors, sales and service reps, tour escorts, and some management personnel out of their Seattle office: Personnel, Westours, 300 Elliot Ave. W, Seattle, WA 98119. The hotels do their own hiring on-site.

The other major package tour company based in Seattle is Princess Tours. It's similar to, though smaller and more upscale than, Westours. Contact: Personnel, Princess Tours, 2815 Second Ave., Suite 400, Seattle, WA 98121.

These companies send out applications starting around November, have a filing deadline of February 15, then interview in March and hire in April. That means a two- to three-month wait for word on your first summer; if you survive your dues-paying year, rehire is generally automatic. But for that first year, if you stay loose and get hired in April, you're going to Alaska in May with a potentially lucrative job in your pocket.

Hotels and Restaurants

Let's face it. Entry-level positions in hotels and restaurants are the dregs. You'll probably be hard-pressed to decide which you'd rather do less: housekeeping, laundry, desk clerk, reservations, dishwasher, gift shop, or night kitchen cleaner. For your first year you're pretty much guaranteed a dull, low-paying, drudge of a job. That's the bad news. The good news is, in hotels, there's generally some room to maneuver—in the restaurants and coffee shops, for example. At many places, busing positions are the only shot you'll have at tips your first year. (Not to mention a shot at the restaurant-quality food which, especially as compared to employee food, can be critical to the quality of your experience.) Also, if a waiter or waitress is 86'd, you could be in line for an instant promotion. Similarly, there might be openings for line and prep cooks, sandwich and salad makers, and bakers. It's tough work, but you'll never starve. Bartenders and cocktail waitresses are often replaced every season. Some hotel gift shop positions are open to first-year employees and offer sales incentives. Even if you do wind up cleaning toilets, at least you'll be there, with freedom just outside the door. And if you keep your senses tuned, you're bound to run across some kind of opportunity, like people quitting, or overtime in another department. In addition, if you can just hang in for the 11-14 weeks of your contract, you'll be in a good position to move up the lackey ladder and pick those packaged pockets the following year.

And that's the crux: boastable Alascams take a few seasons to evolve. After you pay your dues the first year, all kinds of doors can open: luggage handler (with an automatic 25-50 cents a head for package tourists), waitperson (with your usual 15% tacked on to grossly overpriced meals), bus driving, even junior management (for career-minded, Horatio Alger types). At that point, you start to experience the essence of scamology Alaska-style—making a year's pay in four to five months, leaving the other seven to eight for school, travel, or just goofing off. In fact, many seasonals really catch the Alaska bug and opt to stay all year.

Most hotels in Alaska, especially the ones open year-round, do their own hiring on-site. It's chancy, but this could be a good way to pick up work if you're mostly interested in traveling and only want to stop to make money if you have to. However, you can get hired in spring in Seattle for, say, Westmark's seasonal hotels (Skagway, Tok, Valdez, etc.).

Where to Do It
The main consideration in determining where you want to work is where you want to live. Would you prefer to be around the coastline, rugged mountains, and glaciers (and rain, rain, rain) of Southeast, Southcentral, and Southwest? Or would you rather bask in the hotter, drier, less spectacular Interior? Another consideration is housing. The large tour companies and outback hotels often provide housing at a nominal (or no) cost to employees. This is the most secure and convenient arrangement, especially if it's your first year. In addition, food plans (three squares a day deducted, with the cost of housing, from your paycheck) are also available. Again, you take your chances finding your own affordable housing after getting a job in a city hotel, most of which don't accommodate their employees.

Best Bets
Denali National Park combines the most favorable conditions for entry-level opportunities in Alaskan tourism. The park itself is the size of Connecticut; you take one 85-mile road in and out, on free shuttle buses. The hiking, wildlife viewing, photography, joyriding, and party possibilities are limitless. The weather is a cross between the wet maritime and dry Interior patterns. Denali is the second-most-popular tourist attraction in the state. The vast majority of package tourists remain only one night, with roughly 500 rooms turning over every 24 hours. Four large hotels (three run by the same company) employ approximately 2,000 seasonals in positions ranging from dishwashers to waitress/entertainers to oarsmen to tour-bus drivers. There is room to maneuver, even in your first year, and good opportunities for advancement if you decide to make a multiseason commitment (and don't screw up). Numerous smaller lodges, campgrounds, and restaurants offer fall-back and possible moonlighting positions. For applications, write: Personnel, ARA, 825 W. Eighth Ave., Suite 200, Anchorage, AK 99501, tel. (907) 279-2653; and Personnel, Princess Tours, 2815 Second Ave., Suite 400, Seattle, WA 98121.

Glacier Bay National Park is equally awesome but much smaller and more isolated (the only way in is by plane or boat); many flashy tourists nonetheless. Write: Glacier Bay Lodge or Gustavus Inn, Gustavus, AK 99826.

FEDERAL GOVERNMENT JOBS

Government workers have always been a mainstay in Alaska's economy. Local, state, and federal employees today comprise a third of the workforce, making government Alaska's largest employer. These agencies are also important sources of temporary and volunteer employment, accounting for thousands of seasonal jobs each year in Alaska.

Federal Seasonals

Seasonals do much of the grunt work for federal agencies in Alaska: surveying roads, laying out timber sales, fighting fires, building cabins and trails, counting fish, picking up garbage in campgrounds, patrolling backcountry areas, and working in visitor centers. Most of these jobs begin in June and last until mid-September. Much of the work happens outdoors and can be arduous. Clearing a survey line through head-high devil's club is no fun, particularly when you're providing cocktail hour for mosquitoes. Even worse is the prospect of returning soaking wet to camp, where you and three others crowd into a small cabin. But for the hard-core outdoor enthusiast, the advantages of getting paid to work in some of the most spectacular country imaginable far outweigh most discomforts and inconveniences.

Applying

Federal government jobs in Alaska have always been attractive to those who enjoy the outdoors. Unfortunately, Alaska's unspoiled beauty is such a drawing card that seasonal jobs are at a premium, and new openings are usually taken by those who have already worked for the federal government in the Lower 48 or as volunteers in Alaska.

The application period for some seasonal positions ends as early as January 15, so be sure to begin your job search very early. Forms vary between the agencies, but it's always a good idea to have a completed **SF-171** (Application for Federal Employment) and your résumé available for short-term job openings. In most cases your application will be rated by a personnel clerk who scores your qualifications. Often they must go through hundreds of such applications, so yours is only part of a big pile of work. As a result, you're not likely to get VIP treatment. To combat this, make your application as readable as possible (typed is best), and try to address the issues you will be rated on. This means reading the job descriptions carefully and trying to show how you measure up to each qualification.

Once your application has been rated, it is sent to the person who actually does the hiring. The employer looks through those rated most highly and selects the best-qualified person (you, of course). Or so the theory goes. In reality, certain things beyond paper qualifications work in favor of certain applicants. Those with rehire status from the past year are usually given highest priority. Being from Alaska is also a major help (sometimes a requirement), as is being a veteran or of the "correct" race or sex to fulfill hiring quotas. Getting to know the employer can be a great benefit. One way is to directly contact the employer with a letter or phone call. If possible, it's even better to make an appointment and meet with him or her before hiring time. For more information on current federal job openings, contact the individual agencies such as the Park Service or Forest Service (see below for addresses).

VOLUNTEER JOBS

Volunteers are becoming an increasingly important part of the federal seasonal work force all over the nation, and Alaska is no exception. Most of the naturalists on board Alaska's ferry system are volunteers, as are many field workers. The biggest employers of volunteers are the Forest and the Fish and Wildlife Services, but the Park Service, Bureau of Land Management, and U.S. Geological Survey also use volunteers. Federal agencies vary greatly in their treatment of volunteers. Some (most egregiously the Park Service) offer only the barest essentials and require that you pay for your own transportation to and from Alaska. The Forest Service has the best volunteer program, which sometimes includes a free ride from your home and back, free food and lodging, and all the adventure you could ask for.

Why You Should Volunteer

Why volunteer for a federal position when you could be putting away money from a cannery job? It all depends on what's most important to you—money, or an interesting and educational job. After a summer of sliming fish, you have the skills necessary to, well, slime fish. But after a season of building forest trails, you'll know how to operate a chain saw and small boats, will have lived in places other folks pay thousands of dollars to visit, and will have great stories to tell your envious friends. For many, volunteering is a wonderful opportunity to work in Alaska without having to fight tooth and nail for a job. Noncitizens, too, can volunteer for work in the federal government (paying jobs require U.S. citizenship).

Why You Shouldn't Volunteer

The federal volunteer program has proven immensely popular, but it's not for everyone. For many college students, summers are a time to earn survival money, and they can't afford the time off. Many federal workers are upset that paying jobs are being lost to people willing to work for nothing. At one time, experienced volunteers were able to look forward to a chance for a paying job the following year, but today those prospects are slim. Also, not all volunteer work is enjoyable. At its worst you may be viewed as simply a warm body willing to slave for three months with no pay. And some employers seem to enjoy testing the mental stability of their volunteers by cooping them up in remote field camps for weeks or months at a stretch. Be sure you find out the specifics before you make a volunteer commitment.

Getting Volunteer Jobs

Short-term volunteer jobs are sometimes available if you're in the right place at the right time. If you have specific skills in such areas as fisheries or wildlife biology, surveying, or carpentry, you may be able to walk into a week-long trip into the wilderness courtesy of Uncle Sam. It's worth a try. For longer-term positions you need to apply well in advance (Jan.–March generally). If you have persistence, a few skills, and physical endurance, you're almost assured of a volunteer position—if you start searching early enough and apply to a variety of places. Contacting the agencies directly will give you the best idea of what positions are available and what the work will be like. The **Student Conservation Association,** Box 550C, Charlestown, NH 03603, produces an excellent catalog listing voluntary conservation jobs throughout the U.S., including many in Alaska. This is probably the easiest way to find out what's available, but you'll stand out from the crowd more by applying directly to the agencies.

U.S. FOREST SERVICE

Paid Seasonal Positions

The U.S. Forest Service, one of Alaska's largest government employers, has a variety of paid positions in the Tongass and Chugach National Forests. Competition for these jobs is intense.

In recent years, fewer than 100 openings have occurred throughout the state, with two-thirds of these going to rehires. Apply for Forest Service seasonal positions using either the standard federal government application (SF-171) or the easier form OF-612. Closing dates are generally in early December for the following summer season. For **Tongass National Forest** job information, contact the U.S. Forest Service Information Center, 101 Egan Dr., Juneau, AK 99801, tel. (907) 586-8880. For **Chugach National Forest** job information, contact them at 2221 E. Northern Lights Blvd., Anchorage, AK 99508, tel. (907) 271-2500.

Volunteer Positions

Alaska's national forests use hundreds of volunteers each year. There is no central clearinghouse for these applications; but you can get more information about Tongass or Chugach volunteer jobs at the above addresses. Deadlines vary, but the sooner you apply, the better your chances. Many positions are listed in the Student Conservation Association catalog (described above). Since all "hiring" is done at the district level, you may be better off writing to the individual Forest Service district where you would most like to work. Get addresses for the various district offices by contacting the Tongass or Chugach offices listed above.

NATIONAL PARK SERVICE

Paid Seasonal Positions

The National Park Service manages 55 million acres of park and preserve land in Alaska, but has only 200 or so seasonal jobs. Alaska's national parks lure many job seekers, so competition for the seasonal openings is intense. Glamor jobs such as studying Dall sheep in the Brooks Range are nearly impossible to get unless you have all the right skills, education, and experience, and know the person doing the hiring. Unfortunately, bribery doesn't help.

Park Service seasonal hiring policy is currently changing due to severe budget cuts, and many Alaska parks now hire their own workers directly, although some still hire seasonals from the national registers. You'll need to contact the various parks directly for details, and be sure to fill out form OF-612. Get a list of Alaska park addresses and phone numbers from: National Park Service, Alaska Regional Office, 2525 Gambell St., Anchorage, AK 99503, tel. (907) 257-2574. They also have copies of the standard seasonal application (form 10-139) used by some parks. Attempts at filling out this application have been known to drive normal people to the brink of insanity. Where else would you be asked to describe everything from your technical rock-climbing ability to your knowledge of colonial pioneer homemaking? A good night's sleep, several cups of coffee, and a willingness to exaggerate should pull you through.

Volunteers in the Parks (VIPs)
If you don't want to go the insanely competitive paid seasonal route, Alaska's national parks and preserves also offer approximately 130 volunteer positions each year. Here your chances are better, although still only half of the applicants are accepted. Volunteers are generally "hired" for the entire summer, but the cheapskate agency even makes volunteers pay for their own transportation and food. The NPS does supply lodging (and occasionally a stipend). There is no central application center for VIP work, so contact the Alaska Regional Office for a list of the park addresses. Or, get in through the Student Conservation Association (see above).

FISH AND WILDLIFE SERVICE

Paid Seasonal Positions
The U.S. Fish and Wildlife Service manages Alaska's 16 national wildlife refuges, covering a staggering 77 million acres. The Fish and Wildlife Service hires approximately 90 seasonal workers each year as biological technicians and park technicians, as well as laborers. Competition is cutthroat, and you'll be battling it out with over 3,000 qualified applicants! If you're not extremely well qualified (strong wildlife or fisheries biology education plus lots of related experience), it is probably not worth your time to apply. Write or call them to get a complete listing of job requirements and application procedures: U.S. Fish and Wildlife Service, 1011 East Tudor Rd., Anchorage, AK 99503, tel. (907) 786-3301. Their Internet address is http://www.usgs.gov/doi/avads.

Volunteer Jobs
Even the volunteer program for Alaska wildlife refuge work is competitive. Each year the Fish and Wildlife Service selects approximately 175 volunteers from a pool of over 300 applicants. The jobs may include taking census of waterfowl in the Yukon delta, operating a fish weir, or working with peregrine falcons. Living conditions vary greatly, but all food and lodging are supplied. You must supply your own transportation to and from Alaska, however. Applications should be submitted before April, and most positions last June-August. For more information, write or call: Volunteer Coordinator, National Biological Survey, U.S. Fish and Wildlife Service, 1011 East Tudor Rd., Anchorage, AK 99503, tel. (907) 786-3512.

BUREAU OF LAND MANAGEMENT

The Bureau of Land Management (BLM) manages extensive portions of Alaska, and is responsible for mining activities on all federal land. In Alaska, the agency employs only a few seasonals in land management (primarily in surveying), but is well known for its strong fire fighting program based in Fairbanks. Each year the BLM hires approximately 250 firefighters, dispatchers, and smoke jumpers to suppress fires in the northern half of the state. (The Alaska Division of Forestry is responsible for forest fire control in the southern half.) For more on BLM seasonal work, contact: Personnel Office, Bureau of Land Management, 222 W. Seventh Ave. #13, Anchorage, AK 99513-7599. For fire fighting jobs, call (907) 271-3162; for surveying positions, call (907) 271-3758. Call (907) 271-3122 for a recorded listing of permanent and seasonal positions with the BLM.

OTHER FEDERAL JOBS

National Marine Fisheries Service
The National Marine Fisheries Service hires a number of seasonals each year as biological technicians, fish and wildlife biologists, clerk/typists, and other positions. Contact them at: U.S. Dept. of Commerce—NOAA, Western Administrative Support Center, 7600 Sand Point Way

NE, Bin C15700, Seattle, WA 98115, tel. (206) 526-6357.

Army Corps of Engineers
The Corps of Engineers is responsible for maintaining navigable waterways, harbors, and rivers. In Alaska, the Corps hires approximately 50 temporary summer employees each year. Most of the jobs are based in Anchorage rather than in the field. Unlike some other agencies, the Corps gives no preference to Alaskan residents, and most of the hires come from Outside. For more information, contact: Army Corps of Engineers, Alaska District, Pouch 898, Anchorage, AK 99506, tel. (907) 753-2838.

JOBS WITH THE STATE OF ALASKA

Although recent years have seen state funding cutbacks, Alaska continues to be an excellent employer. Wages often run considerably higher than for similar federal jobs, and the perks are noticeably better. Although you must be a resident to apply for state jobs, the requirement is easily met. A resident is "anyone living in Alaska at the time of application with no intention of permanently leaving." For complete information on state employment, ask for a copy of "How to apply for a job with the State of Alaska" from: Division of Personnel, Public Services Unit, P.O. Box C, Juneau, AK 99811, tel. (907) 465-8910.

Seasonal Jobs
Although most state employees work year-round, some are only employed for a few months each year, primarily the summer. These "permanent seasonals" can be found in a number of state agencies, including Fish and Game, Environmental Conservation, and Natural Resources. The jobs are primarily technical: fish and wildlife technician, park ranger, fish and wildlife enforcement officer, and others. To be hired, you need to get on the state job registers, especially the fish and wildlife technician register. It may take quite a while to get an official rating, so get your application in the previous fall for a summer job. Most hiring takes place in April and May. Write to the above address to get a state application form. They do not accept applications from out of state.

Volunteer Positions
The State of Alaska employs more than 120 volunteers in a number of positions, primarily in the summer months. Volunteers in the state parks work on trails, as backcountry rangers, at information counters, and as campground hosts. The benefits are quite limited, and you'll need to provide your own transportation to and from Alaska. U.S. citizenship is required. Apply before April for most jobs. For more info, write or call: Volunteer Program, Alaska State Parks, 3601 C St., Anchorage, AK 99503, tel. (907) 269-8708. Contact them via e-mail at volunteer@dnr.state.ak.us.

The Alaska Department of Fish and Game also has a few volunteer jobs doing such work as counting fish or meeting the public. For details, contact them at: Alaska Department of Fish and Game, Personnel Office, P.O. Box 3-2000, Juneau, AK 99802, tel. (907) 465-4140.

GORDY OHLIGER

GATEWAYS

SEATTLE AND VICINITY

Seattle is one of the best places to begin an Alaskan holiday. Since the gold rush days, the city has served as the gateway to Alaska and the Yukon, with air, rail, bus, and automobile routes converging here. It's a direct flight north from nearby Sea-Tac Airport to Anchorage, and just an hour and a half by bus to Bellingham, the southern terminus of Alaska Marine Highway's ferry system. Seattle is, of course, a major attraction in its own right, good for several days (or years) of adventurous sightseeing. Fascinating day-trips beckon from all sides, and the beauty of Seattle's waterways complements the grandeur of the Olympic Mountains to the west, the Cascades to the east, and Mount Rainier to the southeast, giving you a taste of the magnificence waiting farther north. For details on Seattle and other sights in Puget Sound, check out *Washington Handbook* by Don Pitcher (Moon Publications).

SIGHTS

Pike Place Market
Start your day with breakfast at the Pike Place Market at the corner of Pike Place and the waterfront end of Stewart St. downtown. Farmers have been bringing their produce to Pike Place since before WW I; the sensual market—open daily—is one of Seattle's best free shows: browse among the fruits and vegetables, herbs and spices, fish, baked goods, flowers, and crafts. For a market map and newsletter, head to the **information booth** near the market entrance on the corner of Pike St. and First Avenue.

The main focal point is beneath the famous "Public Market Center" neon sign. Enter here to meet Rachel, the fat bronze market pig. Follow the throngs of tourists to **Pike Place Fish,** right behind Rachel. You can't miss the famous flying fish and the raucous repartee. As you head north from here, small tables are crowded with peddlers hawking artwork, handicrafts, T-shirts, fresh produce, and a myriad of other goods. A longtime favorite restaurant within the market is **Athenian Inn,** where several scenes in *Sleepless in Seattle* were filmed. Great views of Elliott Bay here. Another old-time favorite (opened in 1908) is **Lowell's Restaurant,** where market locals still come for coffee every morning.

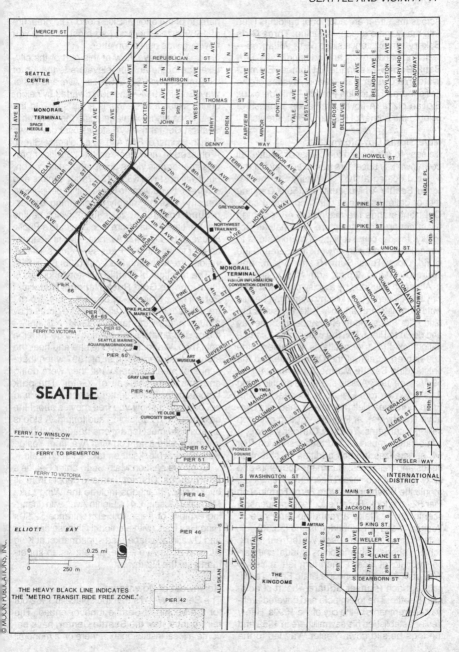

SEATTLE

THE HEAVY BLACK LINE INDICATES
THE "METRO TRANSIT RIDE FREE ZONE."

Across the street are additional buildings filled with many more shops, including: **Three Girls Bakery**—in existence since 1912, **Milagros**—featuring Mexican folk art and handicrafts, **Left Bank Books**—selling leftist tomes, **Emmett Watson's Oyster Bar**—serving oysters on the half shell, and **Cuchina Fresca**—with delicious Sicilian pizza. A flower stall adds a splash of color to the corner of Pike and First Streets.

More Sights Downtown

It's easy to get around the center of Seattle: all downtown city buses are free every day 6 a.m.-7 p.m. Located at 100 University St., the delightful **Seattle Art Museum** has 155,000 square feet of gallery space, a gift shop, and a cafe. Out front stands the distinctive 48-foot-high "Hammering Man" sculpture by Jonathan Borofsky. Inside, climb a flight of marble steps to three floors filled with artwork from around the world. Open Tues.-Sun. 10 a.m.-5 p.m., and Thursday 10 a.m.-9 p.m.; admission costs $6.

Although bounded by a noisy overhead freeway and cluttered with kitschy shops, the Seattle waterfront is worth a stroll. Take the stairs behind Pike Place (north end) under the freeway and down to Pier 59 on the waterfront. A combination ticket ($11 for adults) is available for the 180-degree screen at the **Omnidome** and the outstanding **Seattle Marine Aquarium** at Pier 59. Vintage 1927 Aussie streetcars rumble along Alaskan Way from Pier 70 to Pioneer Square. From there, head left (north) and check out **Creative Northwest,** at Pier 55—a good gift shop selling local items. **Ye Olde Curiosity Shop,** a combination museum and tourist shop on Pier 54, specializes in such oddities as shrunken heads and mummies, plus inane souvenirs and tacky curios. If you haven't been on the ferries yet, go into the **Washington State Ferry Terminal** on Pier 52 for a look. For an excellent, inexpensive scenic cruise, take a roundtrip ferry ride to Vashon Island or Bainbridge Island ($3.50).

Now head south, past Waterfront Park, schlock shops, fish-and-chips stands, and harbor-tour ticket kiosks, then turn left at Yesler Way, just a little beyond the State Ferry Terminal, to reach **Pioneer Square**—heart of gold-rush Seattle. The totem pole and covered archway are remnants of the city of the 1890s. Henry Yesler established his sawmill here in 1852 and the logs he slid down Yesler Way led to the naming of the original Skid Road. The great fire of 1889 razed the area, so most of what you now see was built soon after.

For a bird's-eye view of this part of the city, take one of the antique elevators to the top of the **Smith Tower** ($2) at Second Ave. and Yesler Way. Built in 1914—and now dwarfed by neighboring skyscrapers—this is a fun step into the past. For a higher vantage point, the **Columbia Seafirst Center** rises 76 stories over downtown from the corner of Fifth Ave. and Columbia Street. A glassed-in view deck on the 73rd floor provides panoramic views across the entire region, but it will cost you $3.50 ($1.75 for seniors and children). If you want to delve a little deeper into the city, take the highly entertaining **Underground Tour** ($5.50 for adults), which begins several times a day from Doc Maynard's Public House at 610 E. First Avenue. This is Seattle's answer to the famous Paris sewer tours. Reservations are recommended; call (206) 682-4646.

The highlight of Seattle's historical district is the **Klondike Gold Rush National Historical Park,** 117 S. Main St., open daily 9 a.m.-5 p.m., free. As soon as you walk in, you're greeted by a huge print of the famous "Golden Stairs"—the most dramatic and enduring image from the gold rush. Wander around to see and hear the story of that mad summer of 1897 when thousands of men dropped what they were doing and answered the call of "Gold!" The park rangers at the visitor center are very helpful and will be glad to show you free movies about the gold rush in the adjoining auditorium. A stop is an absolute must for anyone headed north. To get there, take a right on First Ave. from Yesler, walk several blocks, then take a left on Main.

Continue east on Main St. to enter Seattle's **International District,** home to people from all over Asia. Attractions include the Wing Luke Memorial Museum, 414 Eighth Ave., with changing exhibits of Asian folk art (entrance $2.50); Hing Hay Park, with a colorful Chinese pagoda; and Uwajimaya Japanese supermarket at King St. and Sixth Ave.—the largest Asian supermarket in the Northwest.

Northwest of Downtown

The Seattle World's Fair took place in 1962 but for the people of Seattle it never ended. The fairgrounds, now the **Seattle Center,** have become a local institution. Get there on a monorail that leaves from Fifth Ave. and Pine downtown and costs 90 cents one-way. Entry to the grounds is free. In the **Center House** is a large indoor pavilion with dozens of fast-food counters selling specialties from around the world. You can ride up the 605-foot **Space Needle** (an overpriced $7), or take in the outstanding **Pacific Science Center's** museum, IMAX big-screen flick, and Laserium shows ($8 for everything). **Seattle Children's Museum** ($4.50) and **Fun Forest** amusement park will keep the kids happy for a while.

When you've had your fill of the center, walk out to First Ave. N and board bus no. 15 or no. 18, or head up Elliot to 15th Ave. to the south end of Ballard Bridge. The bulk of the Pacific Northwest fishing fleet is based at the Salmon Bay Terminal just west of the bridge. From here grab bus no. 17 or head west on Shilshole Ave. to one of Seattle's most interesting sights, the narrow Hiram M. Chittenden or **Ballard Locks,** which permit navigation between Puget Sound and Lake Washington. Finished in 1916, they're still very busy. The public is welcome to observe their operation and enjoy the beautiful surrounding gardens daily, free. The visitor center here is open daily 10 a.m.-7 p.m. in the summer. At the large fish ladder just on the other side of the locks you can look a salmon in the eye from late June to early September.

BOB RACE

North of Downtown
Located north of Chittenden Locks, the fine **Woodland Park Zoo** is open daily 9:30-6 p.m. Admission is $7. Another fun place to relax is **Green Lake Park,** where a paved trail circles the scenic lake. Dozens of other city parks await your aching bones—relax, sunbathe, and people-watch.

One of Seattle's best museums and one of the finest of its kind anywhere is the **Burke Museum,** N.E. 45th St. and 17th Ave. NE in the University District. This well-arranged and colorful collection features Northwest Coastal Indian

artifacts, and is open daily 10 a.m.-5 p.m.; $3. The museum is at the north edge of the large, parklike University of Washington campus, originally the site of the 1909 Alaska-Yukon-Pacific Exposition. Numerous buses, many running north on Third Ave., shuttle between downtown and the University District. Or take the exit off I-5 and park in one of the many lots.

South of Downtown
The world-class **Museum of Flight** is one of Seattle's premier attractions, featuring dozens of aircraft, from a 1950s Aerocar to an M-12 Blackbird spy plane. It's located at 9404 E. Marginal Way South, tel. (206) 764-5720, and is open daily 10 a.m.- 5 p.m., Thursday till 9 p.m.; admission $6. Other sights south of downtown include the **Rainier Brewery,** open for free tours Mon.-Sat. 1-6 p.m.; and the **Kingdome,** where professional football and baseball games are played.

Other Sights
Half a dozen museums, fascinating neighborhoods, dozens of tours, several breweries and wineries, floating bridges, nearby waterfalls; and of course all the activities on the vast Puget Sound, rugged Olympic Peninsula, and mighty Cascades; and the usual city food, shopping, and entertainment, will keep you busy till your time and/or money run out—unless you remember in the nick of time that this is only the *beginning* of your journey to Alaska.

ACCOMMODATIONS

If you're on a tight budget, stay at one of the motels near the airport on Pacific Hwy. S (Hwy. 99) or north of the Ship Canal on Aurora Ave. (Hwy. 99), rather than in run-down city-center hotels. From either area Metro buses can take you downtown. The Seattle Convention & Visitors Bureau offers a **Seattle Hotel Hotline,** tel. (800) 535-7071, where you can make hotel reservations at no charge. The **Seattle Inter-**

national AYH-Hostel is cheap, clean, and perfectly located—just down from Pike Place Market at 85 Union St., tel. (206) 622-5443. Beds cost $16-19.

Three private hostels offer alternatives to the AYH: **Vincent's Backpackers Guest House,** 527 Malden Ave. E, tel. (206) 323-7849 or (800) 600-2965; **American Backpackers' Hostel,** 126 Broadway Ave. E, tel. (206) 720-2965; and **Green Tortoise Backpacker's Guest House,** 715 Second Ave. N, tel. (206) 282-1222. Another relatively inexpensive lodging choice is the **Downtown YMCA,** 909 Fourth Ave., tel. (206) 382-5000. The **Seattle B&B Association,** tel. (206) 547-1020, keeps tabs on who has space at a dozen of the nicer B&Bs in town.

INFORMATION

For information on Seattle attractions and events, plus maps and other assistance, contact the **Seattle/King County Convention & Visitors Bureau,** located at 800 Convention Place in the Washington State Convention and Trade Center, on the Galleria level. They are open Mon.-Fri. 8:30-5 p.m., Sat.-Sun. 10 a.m.-4 p.m. While here, be sure to pick up the *Seattle Visitors Guide,* a compendium of local entertainment, restaurants, shopping, and sights. Call them for a big packet of Seattle information at (206) 461-5840. A Seattle events calendar, tour maps, flyers for all the attractions, and schedules for all the public bus transportation and Gray Line tours and airporters are available. The Convention & Visitors Bureau also maintains small visitor centers next to the Space Needle (summers only). At Sea-Tac Airport, the Travelers Aid stations have limited local info and brochures.

If you're a member, the **AAA Travel Store** at 330 Sixth Ave. N is a good source of maps and area information plus travel guidebooks, luggage, and other travel-related accessories.

The **National Forest and Parks Outdoor Recreation Information Center,** 915 Second Ave., Room 442, tel. (206) 220-7450, has information on Forest Service and Park Service lands throughout Washington. It's open year-round Mon.-Fri. 8:30 a.m.-4:30 p.m. For good free maps of British Columbia and Canada, visit the **Canadian Government Tourist Of-**

fice, Sixth Ave. and Stewart, Plaza 600, fourth floor. For a map of British Columbia go to **Tourism B.C.,** 720 Olive Way at Eighth Avenue. The **Youth Hostel Association** office, 419 Queen Anne Ave. N, Suite 108, near Seattle Center, tel. (206) 281-7306, sells memberships and has local information. They offer some excellent group trips around Washington in the summertime. Office hours are Mon.-Fri. noon-4 p.m. **CIEE Student Travel,** 219 Broadway, Suite 17, Seattle, tel. (206) 329-4567, sells cheap air tickets to Europe and Asia. Check out the **Greenpeace** office, 4649 Sunnyside Ave. N in the Good Shepherd Center near Goldies on 45th, for information on local environmental issues.

Exchange foreign currency at the airport; at **First Interstate Bank,** 1215 Fourth Ave., tel. (206) 292-3111; or at **Rainier Bank,** 1301 Fifth Ave., tel. (206) 621-4111.

Books

A number of guidebooks on the Seattle area and Washington state can fill in all the holes in coverage that are beyond the scope of this book. The most complete and up-to-date guidebook to the area is **Seattle Access,** published by Harper Perennial, and available in local bookstores. *Seattle Best Places,* published by Sasquatch Books, details many of the finer aspects of the city. Moon Publications' own *Washington Handbook* by Don Pitcher covers the state in depth. *Seattle Best Places* and *Northwest Best Places* from Sasquatch Press in Seattle emphasize more upscale places. Dozens of other guides, one-way on everything from bed and breakfasts and touring Washington's wine country to hiking, kayaking, and birding in the area, are available at bookstores around town. A great local bookstore is **Elliot Bay Book Company,** 101 S. Main St., with a huge section on Northwest titles, and books literally overflowing the store.

TRANSPORTATION

Airport

Sea-Tac International Airport is 12 miles south of downtown Seattle, halfway to Tacoma. A small **tourist information counter** is on the central baggage-claim level, north end. The air-

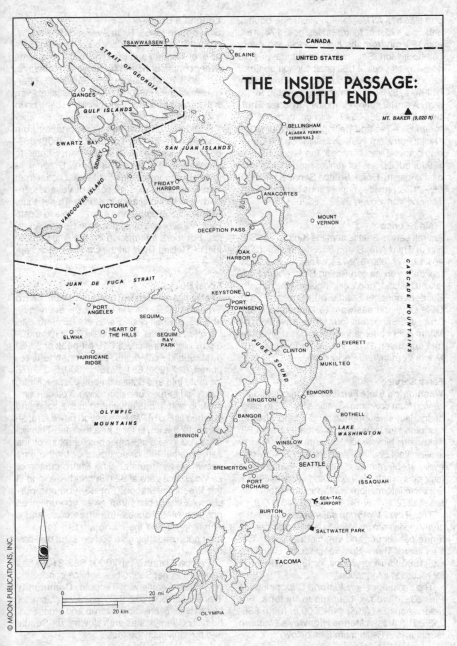

THE INSIDE PASSAGE:
SOUTH END

MT. BAKER (9,020 ft)

CANADA
UNITED STATES

TSAWWASSEN
BLAINE

STRAIT OF GEORGIA

GANGES

GULF ISLANDS

BELLINGHAM
(ALASKA FERRY
TERMINAL)

SWARTZ BAY

SIDNEY

SAN JUAN ISLANDS

FRIDAY
HARBOR

ANACORTES

VANCOUVER ISLAND

VICTORIA

MOUNT
VERNON

DECEPTION PASS

OAK
HARBOR

JUAN DE FUCA STRAIT

KEYSTONE

PORT
TOWNSEND

PORT
ANGELES

SEQUIM

ELWHA

HEART OF
THE HILLS

SEQUIM
BAY
PARK

CLINTON

EVERETT

MUKILTEO

HURRICANE
RIDGE

PUGET SOUND

EDMONDS

CASCADE MOUNTAINS

KINGSTON

BOTHELL

OLYMPIC
MOUNTAINS

BANGOR

LAKE
WASHINGTON

BRINNON

WINSLOW

BREMERTON

SEATTLE

PORT
ORCHARD

ISSAQUAH

SEA-TAC
AIRPORT

BURTON

SALTWATER PARK

TACOMA

0   20 mi
0   20 km

OLYMPIA

© MOON PUBLICATIONS, INC.

port also has ATMs, foreign exchange booths, and coin lockers. Metro buses nos. 174, 184, and 194 run from the airport into town every half-hour Mon.-Sat., hourly on Sunday, $1.10 one-way off-peak, $1.60 peak. Or hop on **Gray Line**'s airporter to six downtown hotels every half-hour, $7.50; the timetable is posted at the stop. A similar service is run by **Airporter Shuttle**, tel. (800) 235-5247, with connections between Sea-Tac and Bellingham (including the Alaska Ferry terminal), and Blaine on the Canadian border. Direct service to the Alaska Ferry is $29 for adults, $26 for seniors, and $15 for children under 16. **Quick Shuttle Service,** tel. (800) 665-2122, provides connections between Sea-Tac and Vancouver, B.C., for $29.

Train Service
Amtrak serves Seattle from the King Street Station at Third Ave. S and S. King St., tel. (206) 464-1930 or (800) 872-7245. The Coast Starlight has daily service connecting Seattle with Portland, Oakland, and Los Angeles. The Empire Builder connects Seattle with Spokane, Salt Lake City, and eastward to Minneapolis and Chicago. Service is four times a week. The Mount Baker International provides daily trains to Vancouver, B.C., via Edmonds, Everett, Mount Vernon, and Bellingham.

Ferry Service
Washington State Ferries have frequent daily service from downtown Seattle's Pier 52 to Bainbridge Island, Bremerton, and Vashon Island. roundtrip fare for walk-on passengers is $3.50. Take your bicycle for 50 cents extra. A ferry leaves West Seattle (Fauntleroy) for Southworth every 40-50 minutes. Also from that dock, a ferry runs over to Vashon Island every half-hour. For more information on Washington State Ferries, call (206) 464-6400 or (800) 843-3779.

The *Royal Victorian* sails between Seattle and Victoria from mid-May to late September, offering passenger and vehicle transport. The ferry leaves Thurs.-Sun. from Pier 48. Call (206) 625-1880 for reservations, or (800) 668-1167 for recorded information.

The passenger-only *Victoria Clipper* leaves Pier 63 for the two-hour trip to Victoria. For reservations call (206) 448-5000 or (800) 888-2535. The **Alaska Marine Highway**'s southern terminus is in Bellingham (see below).

Longhaul Buses
Greyhound Lines, Ninth Ave. and Stewart, tel. (800) 231-2222, offers daily bus service to cities all over Canada and the U.S., with departures every couple of hours. **Northwest Trailways,** tel. (206) 728-5955 or (800) 366-3830, operates from their station at 1936 Westlake Ave., with service throughout the Northwest and on to Vancouver, B.C.

The most unusual bus transportation from Seattle is the **Green Tortoise,** tel. (800) 867-8647, a twice-weekly bus ride from Seattle to Los Angeles that takes 48 hours. Green Tortoise also operates trips to the east coast from San Francisco, plus all sorts of voyages, including month-long treks to Alaska, 16-day tours of the national parks, and even travels to Costa Rica, Mexico, and other places in Central America. For more information on the "magic bus" turn to "Getting There" in the On The Road chapter.

Local Buses
Seattle has an excellent city bus system. **Metro Transit** buses run 6 a.m.-1 a.m. every day, about every half-hour. Fares are 85 cents during off-peak hours, $1.10 peak (6-9 a.m. and 3-6 p.m.) within the city; $1.10 off-peak or $1.60 peak outside city limits. Exact change is required. Call (206) 684-1716 or (800) 542-7876 for route info and details on bus passes. Metro has a Ride Free Zone downtown. You can simply hop onto a bus anywhere in the zone and ride free till 8 p.m. Whenever you pay a fare, always ask the driver for a free transfer. This will allow you to take any other bus, or return on the same, within two or so hours or by the time shown on the transfer. The Metro customer service offices are at 821 Second Ave. and in the Westlake Station. For $3, you can purchase a visitor pass that gives you unlimited rides on Metro buses, the streetcars, and a roundtrip ride on the monorail. Buy the pass after noon and they give you an extra half-day free.

Pierce Transit, tel. (800) 562-8109, has southern Puget Sound bus service connecting downtown Seattle with Tacoma. **Community Transit,** tel. (800) 562-1375, provides commuter bus service connecting Everett and other Snohomish County cities with downtown Seattle and the University District.

BELLINGHAM

The friendly and picturesque small city of Bellingham is 85 miles north of Seattle and 55 miles south of Vancouver. It serves as a jumping-off point for northbound travelers aboard the Alaska Marine Highway's MV *Columbia,* flagship of the ferry fleet.

Sights
Downtown's outstanding **Whatcom Museum** spreads over four structures on Prospect St., including an ornate red-brick building that served as city hall from 1892 to 1939. A single entrance charge ($3) provides access to all four buildings. The ferry departs from Bellingham's historic **Fairhaven** neighborhood, a delightful place to explore, with a multitude of shops, galleries, and fine restaurants. Be sure to drop by **Village Books** at 1210 11th St. for a taste of class.

Accommodations and Camping
The **Bellingham and Whatcom County Convention and Visitors Bureau,** 904 Potter St., tel. (360) 671-3990 or (800) 487-2032 (recorded message), keeps track of local lodging availability during the summer months. Great budget accommodations are available at the **AYH Hos-**

BELLINGHAM

TO VANCOUVER

ELDRIDGE AVE

TO AIRPORT

HOLLY ST

■ WHATCOM MUSEUM

BUS TERMINAL

CONVENTION & VISITORS BUREAU

CHESTNUT ST.

MAPLE ST.

LAUREL ST.

STATE ST.

BELLINGHAM BAY

LAKEWAY

EXIT 253

DR.

■ MALL

EXIT 252

10th ST.

12th ST.

24th ST.

32nd ST.

BELLINGHAM CRUISE TERMINAL

YOUTH HOSTEL HARRIS AVE.

DONOVAN AVE

OLD FAIRHAVEN PKWY.

FAIRHAVEN

TO SEATTLE

EXIT 250

0   0.5 mi
0   0.5 km

© MOON PUBLICATIONS, INC.

tel in a beautiful location in the Fairhaven Rose Garden, tel. (360) 671-1750. It's a long uphill walk from the ferry terminal (or take bus no.1 from the downtown city bus terminal for 25 cents). They serve an all-you-can-eat pancake breakfast each morning. Call for advance reservations (strongly advised May-September). Someone's there to answer the phone all day on weekends, but only after 5:30 p.m. weekdays. Note that the hostel fills up fast on the Thursday night before the Friday sailing of the *Columbia.*

Budget motels in the $30-40 d range include: **Evergreen Motel,** 1015 Samish Way, tel. (360) 734-7671 or (800) 821-0016; **Motel 6,** 3701 Bryon St., tel. (360) 671-4494 or (800) 466-8356; **Shangri-La Downtown Motel,** 611 E. Holly St., tel. (360) 733-7050; **Lions Inn Motel,** 2419 Elm, tel. (360) 733-2330; and **Aloha Motel,** 315 N. Samish Way, tel. (360) 733-4900.

Call the **Whatcom County B&B Guild,** tel. (360) 676-4560, for details on the finest local B&Bs, including the following Victorian-era places: **The Castle,** tel. (360) 676-0974; **North Garden Inn,** tel. (360) 671-7828 or (800) 922-6414; **DeCann House B&B,** tel. (360) 734-9172; and **A Secret Garden B&B,** tel. (360) 671-5327 or (800) 671-5327.

The closest public campsites are seven miles south of town at **Larrabee State Park.** Call (800) 452-5687 for campsite reservations. Additional campsites are approximately 14 miles north in **Birch Bay State Park.**

Information
The **Convention and Visitors Bureau** is off I-5 exit 253 at 904 Potter St., tel. (360) 671-3990 or (800) 487-2032 (recording). It's open daily 9 a.m.-6 p.m. in the summer, and daily 8:30 a.m.-5:30 p.m. the rest of the year. In the summer, the Bellingham Cruise Terminal (where the Alaska ferry docks) also has an information booth, open Thursday and Friday only. The **area code** in the Bellingham vicinity is 360.

Transportation
Bellingham Cruise Terminal sits on the edge of the city's historical district, and serves as the home for the Alaska ferry and ferries to the San Juan Islands and Victoria. To get there, simply take the Old Fairhaven Parkway, exit 250 from I-5, and go right on 12th St. and left on Harris Ave. down to the waterfront. A much more scenic

and satisfying (though longer) route is to cruise to and from I-5 on Chuckunut Drive. Or from downtown Bellingham it's about four miles; just head north on 12th and State Streets. The terminal has reservation and ticketing booths for the Alaska Marine Highway, which provides passenger and vehicle ferry service to Prince Rupert and Southeast Alaska destinations. Alaska ferries usually depart on Friday evenings year-round; call (206) 676-8445 or (800) 642-0066, for details and a schedule. The terminal is open Thursday and Friday each week, in time for Alaska ferry arrivals and departures, and also has a restaurant and gift shop (but you're better off heading to Fairhaven).

Bellingham International Airport is a few miles north of town just off of I-5 (exit 258). Horizon Air and United Express fly in and out. **Airporter Shuttle,** tel. (360) 733-3600 or (800) 235-5247, has daily service to Sea-Tac Airport, while **Quick Shuttle,** tel. (800) 665-2122, runs vans to Vancouver and Seattle destinations, including Sea-Tac.

Both **Greyhound** tel. (360) 733-5251 or (800) 231-2222, and **Northwestern Trailways,** tel. (800) 366-3830, provide nationwide bus connections from the Amtrak depot in Fairhaven. **Whatcom Transit,** tel. (360) 676-7433, offers local bus service Mon.-Sat. for just 25 cents.

Amtrak, tel. (800) 872-7245, provides daily train connections north to Vancouver, B.C., and south to Mount Vernon, Everett, Edmonds, and Seattle aboard the Mt. Baker International. Trains stop at the Fairhaven depot.

VANCOUVER

Canadians consider Vancouver their most beautiful city, and certainly no other in North America is so spectacularly located. A wall of snow-capped mountains faces Vancouver on the north, and wide bays and inlets encircle it on the other three sides. Abundant park lands and beaches offer outdoor experiences not usually associated with thriving metropolises, but with unforgettable vistas of modern buildings clustered against the forested hillsides.

Vancouver is still a young city. Although Capt. George Vancouver sailed into Burrard Inlet in 1792 and made the area known to the world, permanent white settlers did not arrive until 70 years later. A rough-and-tumble loggers' shantytown established itself on the site about that time, but it was the settlements along the Fraser River that received early official attention and benefitted from the 1858 Cariboo gold rush. All this changed in 1887, when Canada's first transcontinental railway reached Vancouver and the city became the country's major Pacific port. Today Vancouver is Canada's third-largest city with 490,000 residents; the region has nearly 1.5 million (B.C. has 3.4 million). It is an exciting city to visit and, for Canadians, the gateway to the Pacific coast. Also, due to U.S. maritime laws, all Inside Passage cruise ships tie up to Vancouver's piers at Canada Place.

SIGHTS

The West End

For many, the highlight of the city is beautiful **Stanley Park** (bus no. 11 from W. Pender St.), occupying a large peninsula jutting out into Burrard Inlet. A walk along the seawall promenade offers totem poles, beaches, honking geese, and a series of splendid views. Stanley Park also has a zoo (free), an aquarium (C$10), snack bars, and lots of lawns and scenic spots where you can sit and watch the world go by. If you like your action a little faster, head to one of a number of bike rental places around the corner of Denman and Robson Streets.

Walk back to town along Robson St. for Vancouver's best window-shopping. Locally known as Robsonstrasse, this street's many delicatessens, tea rooms, and small shops have a European flavor. In summer the restaurants move some of their tables into the open air.

Downtown

Landscaping and a balance between open spaces and offices help make **Robson Square** the architectural showplace of the city. Filling three city blocks along Howe, south from Georgia St., features include the central plaza with its excellent Food Fair and the sloping glass roof of

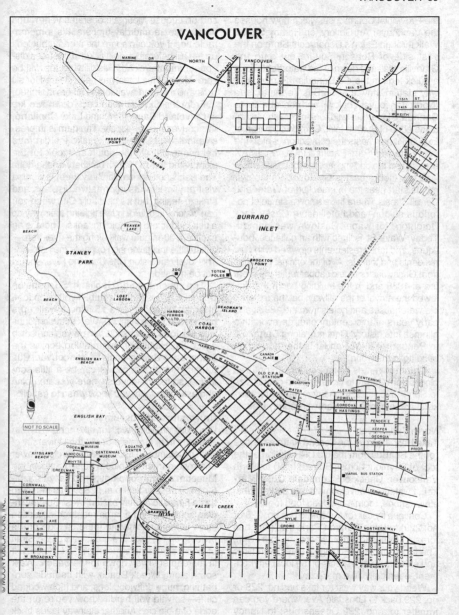

VANCOUVER

NOT TO SCALE

the Provincial Courthouse, which now houses the Vancouver Art Gallery, on Hornby Street. Walk through Eaton's Department Store on the east side of Robson Square out onto the Granville Mall and down to the waterfront. Take a quick look in the old Canadian Pacific Railway station, now the SeaBus Terminal (see "North Vancouver," below), and continue out to **Canada Place,** the wild-looking "sailbuilding" at the edge of Burrard Inlet. Canada's pavilion at Expo86, it now hosts the convention center, the many-starred Pan Pacific Hotel, an IMAX screen, and the docking facilities for cruise ships.

A few blocks east is **Gastown.** Vancouver got its start near the intersection of Water and Carrall Streets, where there's now a statue of notorious saloon- and hotelkeeper Gassy Jack Deighton, for whom Gastown was named. Today, Water St. is lined with art galleries, boutiques, and fancy restaurants crowded with chic residents and tourists. All of the original buildings from Gassy Jack's time disappeared in the great fire of 1886 and in the building boom that followed the arrival of the railway, but the restored old warehouses and hotels from the 1890s and early years of this century offer an evocative glimpse into history. Continue along Carrall St. to Pender. At 8 W. Pender is the "narrowest building in the world."

Chinatown runs along Pender St. for three blocks from Carrall to Gore; second only in size to San Francisco's, its many restaurants, markets, and emporia are worth a leisurely look.

North Vancouver

Take Hwy. 1 across the Second Narrows Bridge (or the SeaBus from the old CPR station at the foot of Seymour across Burrard Inlet) to North Vancouver. Check out **Lonsdale Quay Market,** a waterfront development with parks, pubs, stalls, shops, rooms, and food food food.

Continue by car (or transfer to bus no. 228 or no. 229) to **Lynn Canyon Park.** The park has forests, trails, and a river where you can swim. The highlight is the Ecology Center, with films and exhibits on all aspects of the local environment, open daily 10 a.m.-5 p.m.

Wend your way west (or take bus no. 228 or no. 229 back to Lonsdale Ave. where you can transfer to a no. 232 Queens bus) to Nancy Greene Way and the **Grouse Mountain Skyride.** The cable car (C$16.50) to the ski re-sort on Grouse Mountain operates year-round for sightseers and day-trippers. It's a memorable ride if you can spare the money, but look up the hill before buying a ticket: if the trees disappear into the clouds, visibility on top will be zero. Much of the forest has been cleared for ski runs and the area available to hikers is limited.

From the Skyride head back down two km to **Cleveland Dam** (1954) and **Lake Capilano,** Vancouver's water supply. The dam is impressive in itself, but be sure to take the dirt road below the dam to the south and look for the signposted trail to the fish hatchery on the right. The Capilano Salmon Hatchery (free) is worth a visit anytime for its informative displays and striking setting, but it's best July-Oct. when you can watch the returning fish fighting their way up a fish ladder into the holding tanks. There is an excellent 30-minute walk along the river here—consult the trail guide sign opposite the hatchery. This lovely area along the Capilano River should not be missed.

The much-touted "Capilano Suspension Bridge" (C$7) is farther south. If you're on foot, after the hatchery it's a 15-minute walk up a paved road to the highway. Walk south on Capilano Rd. to Ridgewood Dr., where you can catch a no. 246 Highlands bus running across the Lions Gate Bridge back to Vancouver. Bus routes in North Vancouver can be a little confusing, so tell the drivers where you are going and ask them to let you know when to get off.

University and Museums

Drive out W. 10th Ave. (or take a no. 10 10th Ave. bus from Granville St.) to the University of British Columbia (UBC). Go via the clock tower and rose garden (in bloom June-Sept.) to the **Museum of Anthropology,** open daily 11 a.m.-5 p.m., Tuesday till 9 p.m., C$6. This museum has a fantastic display of Northwest Coastal Indian sculpture and a large research collection open to visitors. Around the east side of the building and in back is a great view of the Strait of Georgia from the adjacent cliff. Just to the left is a steep stairway down to the beach. Walk south along Wreck Beach, with its nude sunbathing, huge driftwood logs, and high wooded cliffs—so wild you hardly know you're on the edge of a big city. Another stairway leads back up to the UBC campus. When you get to the top of the stairs, turn left and walk between the red brick residences to the **Nitobe Japanese Garden** on campus. The UBC campus covers a large, beautifully landscaped area with many buildings worth looking into. Wander at will. If you're weary and hungry, try the Student Union Building with its large cafeteria **(The Subway)** and pub **(The Pit).**

From UBC head back on the coast road along English Bay (or on a no. 14 Hastings bus back along Broadway to MacDonald, where you transfer to a no. 22 Knight bus to go as far as Cypress Street). Go due north on Cypress to the totem pole flanking a group of museums on the south side of English Bay at the entrance to False Creek. The **Vancouver Museum** has exhibits on Vancouver history and a good cafeteria with a fine view. Above is the **Planetarium,** C$6. And nearby is a small **Maritime Museum** (C$6.50). The RCMP ship *St. Roch,* first to traverse the difficult North West Passage between the Pacific and Atlantic Oceans in both directions (during the 1940s), can be seen at no charge every day in the same building as the Maritime Museum. All these facilities are open daily 10 a.m.-5 p.m., closed Monday in winter. The unusual mushroom dome over the Centennial Museum contains a planetarium. If the sun is shining, walk west along the shore to Kitsilano Beach to join the local sun worshippers. There's also an outdoor saltwater swimming pool here which you may use for C$1.50.

Along Howe Sound

A good day-trip from Vancouver and one which no rail buff will want to miss is on the Royal Hudson, a train pulled by an authentic 1930s steam locomotive. This is a six-hour roundtrip excursion from North Vancouver station to the logging town of Squamish. May-Sept., Wed.-Sun. the train pulls out at 10 a.m. for the two-hour journey past Horseshoe Bay and up Howe Sound to Squamish. In Squamish there is ample time for lunch and a visit to the local pioneer museum in the park near the station. The trip may be a little touristy; still, the scenery is hard to beat. Combine the train trip with Harbor Ferries' **MV** *Brittania* for the return trip. The three-hour journey back down the fjord gives you a taste of what to expect on the Inside Passage cruise to Skagway—snowcapped mountains, thick forests, eagles, and seals. You also get to see Vancouver Harbor from end to end with a knowledgeable commentary from the captain. The roundtrip costs C$62. Transfers from the train station to Harbor Ferries' dock are included. Call (604) 984-5246 for ticket information and reservations; the seller will explain where to catch the city bus to the station.

INFORMATION

By far the best source of information about Vancouver, Victoria, Vancouver Island, and the rest of British Columbia is Moon Publications' *British Columbia Handbook.* This guide is absolutely indispensable for anyone going overland to the Yukon and Alaska: across to Victoria, up Vancouver Island, then back across to Prince Rupert, and onto the Alaska ferries to Haines or Skagway; or going by train to Prince Rupert and ferry to Alaska; or driving up the Cassiar or Alaska Highways (see the back of this book for ordering information).

Seven **Travel InfoCentres** are scattered around Vancouver, the best places to get face-to-face information on Vancouver and the province. The main one is at 200 Burrard St., tel. (604) 683-2000, open daily 8 a.m.-6 p.m., closed on Sunday in winter. Be sure to collect a map of the city (free), the *Accommodations* booklet for B.C. (invaluable), and all the brochures, schedules, etc., that you have room for. The other InfoCentres are at Delta, Richmond, Coquitlam, North Vancouver, Vancouver International Airport, and Tsawwassen Ferry Terminal.

Detailed topographical maps for hikers are available from **World Wide Books and Maps,** 736 Granville St., tel. (604) 687-3320.

Western Canada Wilderness Committee, 20 Water St., tel. (604) 683-8220, publishes information sheets on local environmental issues. **Vancouver Public Library,** 35 W. Georgia St., tel. (604) 331-3600, is open Mon.-Wed. 10 a.m.-9 p.m., Thurs.-Sat. 10 a.m.-6 p.m.; this is a brand new nine-story library with a million books on the shelves. **Duthie Books,** Robson and Hornby, is the best bookstore in the city. **Mountain Equipment Co-op,** 428 W. Eighth Ave., sells camping equipment, guidebooks, and youth-hostel membership cards.

The most knowledgeable travel agency in Vancouver is **Westcan Treks,** 1965 W. Fourth, tel. (604) 734-1066.

The **area code** for Vancouver and vicinity is 604. For interior B.C., including Vancouver Island, it's 250.

TRANSPORTATION

By Air
Vancouver International Airport (YVR) is 20 km south of downtown Vancouver. Transit bus no. 100 leaves from outside the terminal's upper level (departures) to the right. Pay C$1.50 (exact change only) and ask for a transfer. Just after the large bridge change to the no. 20 Vancouver bus, which runs straight up Granville into town. The no. 100 bus leaves the airport every 30 minutes Mon.-Sat., hourly on Sunday; service continues until after midnight. Alternatively, grab the **Express Bus airporter** from Level Two, leaving every half-hour for downtown (C$11).

The **Travel Infocentre,** on Level Three, is open daily 8 a.m.-11 p.m.—very helpful with maps and brochures. There is no bank, but a currency-exchange booth open daily 6 a.m.-10:30 p.m. gives about two percent less than the banks downtown. Coin lockers are plentiful and cost C$1 a day. The airport is open 24 hours a day so crash here if you're arriving or leaving in the wee hours. Don't feel guilty about stretching out your sleeping bag because a C$40 international departure tax is built into tickets, on top of which you must now pay an "airport improvement tax" when you check in: C$15 for international flights, C$10 within North America, C$5 within British Columbia.

By Boat
B.C. Ferries has frequent service throughout the day from Tsawwassen, 30 km south of Vancouver, to the Gulf Islands and Swartz Bay (for Victoria). The ferry to Nanaimo on Vancouver Island leaves frequently from Horseshoe Bay, a 10-minute drive west of Vancouver, as does the ferry to Langdale (for the Sunshine Coast). To get to the Tsawwassen ferry terminal by public transportation, take bus no. 601 South Delta from Howe St. to Ladner Exchange, where you transfer to a no. 640 bus to the ferry. West Vancouver Transit has frequent service, usually every 30 minutes daily, to Horseshoe Bay. Look for the blue bus (C$1.50) in front of the Hudson's Bay Co. at Georgia and Seymour streets.

The **SeaBus** crosses Burrard Inlet to North Vancouver from the old railroad station at the foot of Seymour Street. There is service every 15 minutes weekdays, every 30 minutes evenings and weekends. The fare is $1.50 and city bus transfers are both given and accepted.

By Bus
Greyhound, 1150 Station St. (in the VIA Rail station), tel. (800) 661-8747 (Canada only), sells

The arrival of the first train on May 23, 1887, heralded Vancouver's emergence as the major metropolis of western Canada.

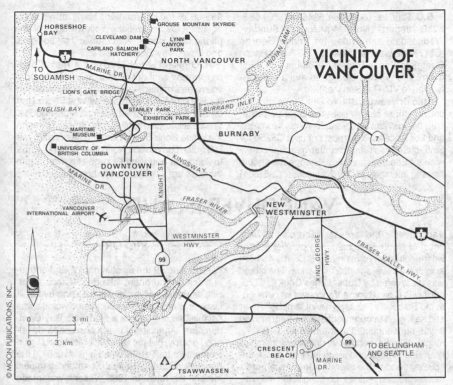

VICINITY OF VANCOUVER

tickets to Prince Rupert (C$181), Whitehorse, Yukon (C$309), and points throughout Canada. The Canada Travel Pass can be bought at any Greyhound depot in Canada. It must be purchased at least seven days in advance and gives unlimited travel on all domestic Greyhound routes (including Vancouver to Seattle). See the "Getting Around" section of the main Introduction for prices.

Pacific Coach Lines, tel. (604) 662-8074, has service every two hours 5:45 a.m.-7:45 p.m. from the Greyhound terminal to Victoria (C$25.50, includes ferry and tax). **Maverick Coach Lines,** tel. (604) 662-8051, has a bus from the same terminal twice a day to Powell River. The 8:30 a.m. bus is the one to take if you want to see anything along the way. (It lays over in Powell River for two hours, then returns to Vancouver by 10 p.m.) The fare (C$25.25 each way) includes both ferries. From Powell River, B.C., ferries operate a regular service to Nanaimo on Vancouver Island.

Local

All Vancouver city buses, the SkyTrain, and SeaBus charge a flat rate of C$1.50 (exact *change* required—no bills) regardless of distance traveled in off-peak hours. Fares go up to C$3 for out-of-the-way travel during rush hour. All give transfers valid for stopovers and roundtrips for up to 90 minutes. Ask about Day-Passes—good value if you're using public transportation to get around.

Other Travel Options

VIA Rail has service to all points east of Vancouver. The terminal is at 1150 Station St. near Main and Pryor behind the SkyTrain station, tel. (800) 561-8630 in Canada, (800) 361-3677 in the States. One-way to Jasper costs C$156, and all the way to the other end of the line at Halifax, Nova Scotia, C$741. The Canrail Pass, C$535, is good for 13 days of travel out of 30.

B.C. Rail, tel. (604) 984-5246 or (800) 663-8238, departs North Vancouver Sunday, Wednesday, and Friday for Prince George (C$177 one-way) via Whistler (C$27) and Prince George to Prince Rupert (C$89 but you must overnight in Prince George to make the connection to VIA Rail Services).

Auto Driveaway, 211 W. First St., North Vancouver (three blocks from the SeaBus terminal), has driveaway cars to Toronto, Montreal, and Los Angeles. You must put up a C$250 refundable deposit and pay the gas, but otherwise it's free transportation. Europeans should have an International Driver's License. Call (604) 985-0936 for information. Many other such agencies are listed in the Yellow Pages of the phone book under "Automobile Transporters and Driveaway Companies."

Hitchhiking is prohibited on the Trans-Canada Highway east out of Vancouver. However, if you're determined, take bus no. 330 Ferguson (no Sunday service) from Hastings St. and get off at the first stop after the Port Mann Bridge. Walk back to the highway and smile. To reach the White Rock/Blaine border crossing into the U.S., take bus no. 351 North Bluff from Howe St. to Johnston and King George Highway. From there it's easy to hitch to the border.

VANCOUVER ISLAND

Vancouver is the largest island off the west coast of North America. Lying parallel (northwest-southeast) to mainland B.C., it's 454 km long and an average of 97 km wide. The island was discovered by Capt. James Cook in 1776, but it was Capt. George Vancouver who, by entering Discovery Passage near Campbell River and sailing on through Johnstone Strait, proved it was not connected to the mainland. Today, roughly 380,000 people live on the island, mostly around Victoria and along the east coast; the southern end of the island is one of Canada's fastest growing regions. Logging is the main industry, with clearcutting prevalent in the north, followed by fishing, tourism, and mining. A spine of snowcapped mountains runs down the center of the island, isolating the wild, rugged west coast. Much of the west coast is inaccessible, making Pacific Rim National Park a haven for backpackers.

Vancouver Island is an entire vacation destination of its own, and if you're tempted to halt your northbound progress here, you'll find enough wilderness, coast and ocean, villages, medium-sized towns, and cosmopolitan capitals to keep you happily occupied for weeks; just have *British Columbia Handbook* along for company. Otherwise, grit your teeth, maybe spend a few days checking out the highlights, and make your way to Port Hardy at the northern tip—where the trip to Alaska officially kicks off.

VICTORIA

Without a doubt the most intriguing and unusual place on the entire island is Victoria itself, with its British civility, island-type homey familiarity, and large and wild backyard. Victoria was established in 1843 as a Hudson's Bay Company fort. Agricultural lands were soon developed nearby, but the little settlement didn't gain momentum until 1858, when a gold rush on the Fraser River brought a flood of American miners through the town. In 1868, Victoria was made capital of the crown colony of British Columbia. Today, nearly three-quarters of the people on Vancouver Island live in this small city of 300,000 and on the adjacent Saanich Peninsula. The many historic sites, parks and gardens, and tourist side shows, along with a distinct European air and compact size, make Victoria an inspiring gateway to the Inside Passage and beyond.

Downtown Sights
Most walking tours begin at the **Parliament Buildings** (1898), which dominate Victoria's Inner Harbor. Together with the **Empress Hotel** (1908), they lend the city a monumental air. Free tours of Parliament leave regularly weekdays from the front door and are well worth taking. Across the street is the ultra-modern **Royal B.C. History Museum,** tel. (250) 387-3701,

VICTORIA

open 9:30 a.m.-7 p.m. in summer, 10 a.m.-5:30 p.m. in winter, C$7.50. Largest in western Canada, and one of the best around, the rich collection of art, artifacts, and photos envelops all of your senses in the entire realm of living history of British Columbia; allow a half-day here.

Thunderbird Park, beside the museum, has totem poles and replicas of large Northwest Indian houses. Helmcken House (1852), just behind the totem poles, is one of the oldest houses in the province still at its original location (open daily, C$4). Just a block south on Douglas St. is the entrance to **Beacon Hill Park.** This century-old reserve extends all the way to the

Juan de Fuca Strait. From the shore is a splendid view of the Olympic Mountains. A 39-meter-high totem pole, numerous ponds, and flower gardens add to the park's allure.

Bastion Square, heart of the 1890s city at Yates and Wharf, gets its name from a bastion of old Fort Victoria (1843), which once stood here. The old courthouse, built in 1889, is now the **Maritime Museum,** and the square, with its trees and benches, is a perfect picnic or people-watching place. **Centennial Square,** a few blocks north at Pandora and Government Sts., is another historic district. Victoria's colorful **China-town** is just north of here at Government and

Fisgard Streets. Downtown Victoria is full of side-show "attractions," such as Undersea Gardens, Miniature World, Crystal Garden, and Royal London Wax Museum—all are expensive.

To the Castle
Walk up Courtney St. to the impressive facade of **Christ Church Cathedral.** Many old tombstones from Victoria's first cemetery stand in the park beside the church. Continue east on Rockland Ave. for 15 minutes through a peaceful residential area to **Government House,** home of the lieutenant-governor. The beautiful gardens surrounding the estate are open to the public daily (free). Leave the gardens through the second gateway and head north on Joan Crescent to **Craigdarroch Castle** at no. 1050. This towering Victorian mansion, built by coal magnate Robert Dunsmuir in 1890, is now open daily for tours (C$6). Ask if you can shoot a little nine-ball in the rumpus room. Also in this area is the **Art Gallery of Greater Victoria,** 1040 Moss St. (C$4.50). Walk back to town along Fort St. past many antique shops.

Butchart Gardens
These famous gardens, 20 km north of Victoria on Saanich Inlet, originated almost 90 years ago, when Canadian cement pioneer Butchart and his wife began collecting flora from around the world and planting it at their quarry. Today, the gardens contain roughly 5,000 varieties of flowers, trees, and shrubs, many rare and exotic. They're open 9 a.m.-10 p.m. in summer, 9 a.m.-5 p.m. in winter. The best time to go is in the early evening, to appreciate the fading light and the nighttime illumination effects. Admission is C$13 adult, C$7 ages 13-17, C$2 ages five to 12 during the peak season (approximately mid-April through October). Take Highway 17 north and follow the signs.

Information
The **Tourism Victoria Travel Information Centre,** 812 Wharf St. on the Inner Harbor, tel. (250) 382-2127, is open daily 9 a.m. to 7 p.m. They have stacks of maps and promo brochures on Victoria and the surrounding area. **Department of Environment, Land, and Parks,** 780 Blanshard St., provides free brochures on B.C.

wildlife. Whether you need a topographical map for hiking or only a big souvenir map of the island, **Crown Publications,** 521 Fort St., tel. (250) 386-4636, will have it.

TRANSPORTATION

By Boat
The Port Angeles ferries dock at adjoining wharfs in Victoria's Inner Harbor. **Black Ball Transport**'s Port Angeles ferry sails twice daily in winter, four times a day in summer, passenger US$6.50 one-way, car and driver US$27; call (206) 457-4491 in the U.S. or (250) 386-2202 in Victoria for information. Clear U.S. Immigration at Port Angeles.

The Anacortes ferry to Friday Harbor, San Juan Island (US$6), leaves Sidney daily at 12:30 p.m. For current schedules and fares, call **Washington State Ferries** at (206) 464-6400 in Seattle; (604) 381-1551 in Victoria. Seventeen ferries run daily between Swartz Bay (Vancouver Island) and Tsawwassen (Lower Mainland), passenger C$8.50 one-way, car and driver C$25. For ferries to and from Vancouver, see above.

Victoria Line ferries, tel. (800) 668-1167 (Canada) or (800) 683-7977 (U.S.), depart from Pier 48 daily at 1 p.m. for Victoria's Ogden Point, C$27 pp each way, C$60 for a regular car and driver, summer only.

Victoria Express, tel. (250) 361-9144, has ferries that depart three times daily from Port Angeles for Victoria's Belleville Passenger Ferry Terminal; C$20 roundtrip.

By Bus
Buses on Vancouver Island are operated by **Island Coachlines,** tel. (604) 385-4411 (same telephone as the former Pacific Coach Lines). From Victoria, six buses daily run to Nanaimo, C$16.10 each way; to Campbell River, C$36.80; and to Port Hardy at the northern end of the island C$77.85. (Only the 6:20 a.m. bus goes to Port Hardy, arriving at 4:30 p.m.).

Bus Connections
Bus no. 70 Pat Bay Highway (C$2.25) runs from Douglas St. in downtown Victoria right to the Swartz Bay ferry terminal hourly every day. This

same bus passes within a block of the Sidney ferry terminal for the Washington State ferry to Anacortes. At Tsawwassen, catch the no. 640 Valley-To-Sea bus (C$1.75), also hourly every day, to Ladner Exchange, where you transfer to the bus to downtown Vancouver. If you're going to the Vancouver International Hostel, hang onto your transfer and ask the driver where you change to the Fourth Ave. bus.

Trains and Longhaul Buses

Buses on Vancouver Island are run by **Island Coach Lines,** 710 Douglas St., Victoria, tel. (604) 385-4411. ICL has a bus every two hours to Vancouver, C$25.50. Six buses a day run from Victoria to Nanaimo (C$16.10) and Campbell River (C$36.80) and one a day goes all the way to Port Hardy (C$77.85). Only the 6:20 a.m. bus continues to Port Hardy (arriving at 4:30 p.m.). Stopovers are allowed. There are coin lockers (C$2) at the ICL depot behind the Empress Hotel if you need a place to leave your luggage for the day. If you

prefer trains, a diesel rail car goes from Esquimalt to Courtenay daily at 8:15 a.m., C$32 one-way (seven-day APEX $19). No bicycles are carried. Take bus no. 23, no. 24, or no. 25 to the station. Call (250) 383-4324 for reservations.

Local Buses and Hitching

The local bus system publishes *Rider's Guide,* which you can have for the asking at the Info-Centre. Or call (250) 382-6161 for specific questions. Usual fares are C$1.50; they also sell day passes and offer tourist discounts.

To hitch north to Nanaimo, take bus no. 50 Goldstream to Brock and Jacklin, very close to the Trans-Canada Highway. To hitch to Port Renfrew for the West Coast Trail, take a no. 61 Sooke bus from Western Exchange to Sooke (C$2.25), which is on Highway 14 on the way to the trailhead. The Sooke bus only runs every couple of hours, so call (250) 382-6161 for the schedule before leaving. Timetables for all bus routes are available free at the tourist information offices.

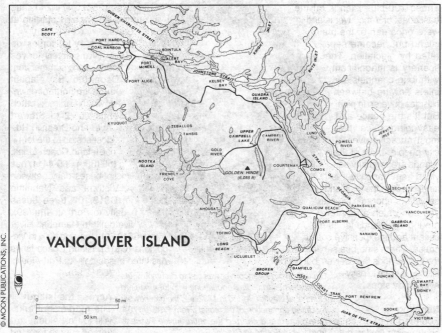

VANCOUVER ISLAND

The Route North

You can drive/bus to Port Angeles and then connect to the ferry to Victoria from there. Or take the B.C. ferry from Tsawwassen southwest of Vancouver to Swartz Bay northeast of Victoria. Whichever you choose, once on Vancouver Island you'll drive, bus, or hitch up the highway to Port Hardy on the far north tip, where the B.C. ferry *Queen of the North* runs to Prince Rupert every other day from May-September. From there, you can catch Greyhound up the Yellowhead to the Alaska Highway as far as Whitehorse, or connect to the Alaska State Ferries through Southeast Alaska as far as Haines or Skagway, both of which have road connections to mainland Alaska. For information on air transport from Canada, see the "Getting There" section in the On The Road chapter.

TOWARD THE MIDNIGHT SUN

Gulf Islands

These 100-plus islands off the east coast of Vancouver Island were once part of the main island but became separated by glaciation. The scenery is magnificent, with long channels and inlets flowing between hillsides covered in pine. But it's the peace and easygoing pace that most attract droves of city people. Most of the islands are regularly serviced from Vancouver Island, but from the mainland service is sporadic. See if you can catch a day ferry around the islands for an excellent and inexpensive scenic cruise. There's no bus service on the Gulf Islands themselves, but hitchhiking on them is easy— everybody stops.

Nanaimo

Founded in 1852 as a coal-mining settlement,

Captain George Vancouver was first to circumnavigate Vancouver Island. His negotiations with the Spaniard Quadra, at Nootka Sound in 1792, laid the groundwork for British domination of this coast. From 1792 to 1794, he explored and charted the entire Inside Passage from Puget Sound to Glacier Bay.

downtown Nanaimo and its Small Boat Harbor are attractive, with excellent views. Don't judge the city by the jumble of parking lots, shopping centers, and strip suburbia you find on the outskirts. Old Nanaimo is worth a stopover. Along the waterfront past the museum is the **Bastion,** a wooden fort built in 1853 by the Hudson's Bay Company to protect the coal-mining families against Indian attack.

Excellent hiking and camping are found on **Newcastle Island,** just offshore from downtown Nanaimo. A self-guide folder for the nine-km nature trail on Newcastle is available free from the Nanaimo tourist office. June-Aug. an hourly passenger ferry goes from Nanaimo to the island (C$4.25 roundtrip). The entire island is a provincial park, with no cars to contend with; camping $11. The Gabriola ferry (C$3.50 roundtrip) leaves approximately every hour from the landing in downtown Nanaimo. Campsites (C$12) are available at Page's Resort, tel. (250) 247-8931; Haven-by-the-Sea on Gabriola, an easy three-km walk from the ferry, tel. (250) 247-9211, has rooms and cabins starting at C$49.

The ferry to Horseshoe Bay (Vancouver) leaves hourly during summer from Departure Bay, about three km north of downtown Nanaimo; catch bus no. 2 to Stewart Ave. and Brechlin Rd., closest stop to the terminal. **Island Coach Lines,** tel. (604) 385-4411, has six buses daily between Victoria and Nanaimo (C$16.10), three buses daily to Port Alberni ($9), five daily to Campbell River (C$18.50), and nine daily to Victoria (C$15). Island Coach Lines has three buses daily to Port Alberni (C$12.90).

PROVINCIAL ARCHIVES OF BRITISH COLUMBIA

Across the Island

The road from Parksville to Port Alberni traverses superb forested

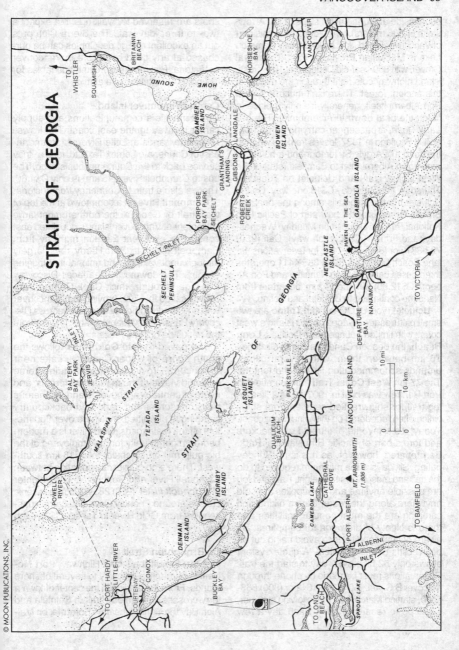

STRAIT OF GEORGIA

TO WHISTLER

SQUAMISH

BRITANNIA BEACH

HOWE SOUND

HORSESHOE BAY

VANCOUVER

GAMBIER ISLAND

BOWEN ISLAND

LANGDALE

GIBSONS

GRANTHAM'S LANDING

ROBERTS CREEK

SECHELT

PORPOISE BAY PARK

SECHELT INLET

SECHELT PENINSULA

GABRIOLA ISLAND

HAVEN BY THE SEA

NEWCASTLE ISLAND

NANAIMO

DEPARTURE BAY

STRAIT OF GEORGIA

TO VICTORIA

SALTERY BAY PARK

JERVIS

MALASPINA STRAIT

TEXADA ISLAND

LASQUETI ISLAND

PARKSVILLE

POWELL RIVER

QUALICUM BEACH

HORNBY ISLAND

DENMAN ISLAND

BUCKLEY BAY

CAMERON LAKE

CATHEDRAL GROVE

VANCOUVER ISLAND

MT. ARROWSMITH (1,806 m)

PORT ALBERNI

ALBERNI INLET

SPROUT LAKE

TO BAMFIELD

TO LONG BEACH

TO PORT HARDY / LITTLE RIVER

COMOX

COURTENAY

10 mi

10 km

© MOON PUBLICATIONS, INC.

countryside along the north slope of Mt. Arrowsmith (1,806 meters), which dominates this part of Vancouver Island. Just beyond lovely Cameron Lake is MacMillan Provincial Park (Cathedral Grove), with 850-year-old Douglas firs. The cross-island highway cuts right through the middle of this ancient forest. There isn't much to see in Port Alberni itself; generally it's only a place to catch the boat down to Alberni Inlet. The MV *Lady Rose,* a passenger-carrying cargo boat built in Scotland in 1937, leaves from the wharf at the bottom of Argyle St. for four-and-a-half-hour runs down Alberni Inlet to Bamfield (start of the West Coast Trail) and Ucluelet on Tuesday, Thursday, and Saturday C$18 one-way. On the Ucluelet trip the ship sails among the beautiful Broken Group Islands, now part of Pacific Rim National Park, to Ucluelet on Monday, Wednesday, and Friday (C$20 each way). Call (250) 723-8313 or (800) 663-7192 for reservations. Island Coach Lines, tel. (604) 385-4411 operates three buses daily between Nanaimo and Port Alberni (C$12.90) with the 11 a.m. departure from Nanaimo continuing to Ucluelet and Tofino.

Ucluelet (yoo-CLOO-let) and **Tofino** are two small picturesque villages on the island's west coast, with limited but adequate facilities. **Long Beach,** the best on Canada's coast, stretches 16 km between them, with several campgrounds accommodating RVers and tenters. The 77-km **West Coast Trail** from Bamfield to Port Renfrew was built in 1907-12 as a lifesaving trail for shipwrecked seamen from ships which often foundered on this windswept coast. Today, it's a favorite of intrepid backpackers and forms part of Pacific Rim National Park. Be prepared, however, as this is no Sunday outing. Six days is the minimum required to do the trail and most hikers take eight. Rain and fog are possible anytime and no supplies are sold anywhere along the route. Beach hiking and camping are the most popular activities and there is plenty of driftwood for campfires. Be aware of tidal conditions to avoid being cut off below cliffs by rising waters. A quota system allows only 52 hikers per day to start the trail. Reservations must be made by phone through Discover B.C., tel. (604) 387-1642 or (800) 663-6000, starting March 1 for the following summer, C$25 pp to receive a spot. Each day a few spots are reserved for walk-ups, but expect a two- to three-day wait. The Sierra Club puts out an excellent trail guide. Copies can be purchased at any good bookstore in Vancouver or Victoria. Pick up a copy of the tide tables for Tofino, B.C., while you're at it.

Central Vancouver Island

Courtenay is a communications and supply center halfway up the east coast. The Powell River ferry lands at Little River, 11 km northeast of Courtenay. Comox Taxi Ltd. runs a jitney service back to the Courtenay bus station. The bus to Campbell River (45 km) is only C$4.60. There's also a train to Courtenay from Victoria.

Campbell River is a boomtown at the top of the Strait of Georgia, the northernmost large settlement of Vancouver Island's populated east coast; the excellent 236-km highway from Campbell River to Port Hardy runs largely through undeveloped and uninhabited logging country. The downtown area faces Discovery Passage, through which Capt. George Vancouver sailed in 1792, proving that Vancouver was an island. An hourly ferry runs across Discovery Passage to Quadra Island, leaving from the east side of Tyee Plaza.

The paved road to **Gold River** follows the south shore of Upper Campbell Lake near Strathcona Provincial Park, affording some splendid views of the mountains, forests, and rivers of central Vancouver Island. Numerous trails crisscross the park, and backcountry camping is permitted anywhere over 800 meters off the main roads. Gold River is a modern bedroom community for the employees of the big pulp mill on Muchalat Inlet, 16 km southwest. There's no public transportation between Campbell River and Gold River. The freighter **MV** *Uchuck III,* tel. (250) 283-2325, runs scenic cruises around Friendly Cove and carries passengers from Gold River to Tahsis, C$23 each way.

On Broughton Strait

Just two km off the Island Highway, **Port McNeill** is primarily a gateway to several offshore islands. From the landing in the center of town a ferry crosses Broughton Strait to Sointula and Alert Bay throughout the day. **Sointula,** on Mal-

The Kwakuitl Indians of coastal B.C. painted these huge, 1.5 meter-long raven masks black, red, and white. Shredded cedar bark fell to the shoulders; a long cape covered the body.
The spectacle of a line of squatting dancers, masks swinging from side to side, hinged beaks opening and clapping to the beat of their batons, must have been overwhelming.

colm Island, is a friendly little community descended from Finnish settlers who came looking for utopia in the early years of this century. Many still speak Finnish and the blond heads and Nordic landscape make it easy to imagine you're in Scandinavia. **Alert Bay,** on five-km-long Cormorant Island near the mouth of the Nimpkish River, was established in 1870 when a salmon saltery was set up. In 1878 the Kwakiutl Indian mission was moved here from Fort Rupert near Port Hardy. Today the population of 1,800 is half-Indian, half-white. The picturesque town with its large frame houses and fishing boats winds along the water's edge; the Indian village is to the left of the ferry landing, the whites' town to the right. Alert Bay is probably the most intriguing coastal town in northern B.C., but you won't read much about it in the offical tourist brochures because the locals want to keep it to themselves.

Port Hardy

Port Hardy, near the north end of Vancouver Island 485 km from Victoria, is a medium-size tourist town where you catch the B.C. Ferry to Prince Rupert on the northern coast of mainland Canada. Since the ferry departs at 7:30 a.m. you'll need to spend the night, and since the arriving ferry from Rupert pulls up around 10:30 p.m., accommodations can get rather tight on turnaround night. The best campground is halfway (four km) between the ferry terminal at Bear Cove and downtown: **Quatse River Campground,** on Byng Rd. (go left at the totem-pole fork, then turn left into the camp-

ground), tel. (250) 949-2395, has 62 large sites under towering spruce trees, C$14. Just across the street is the **Pioneer Inn,** tel. (250) 949-7271, which has rooms for C$62 s, C$72 d, and an excellent cafeteria-style coffee shop where the "trucker's breakfast" will keep you stuffed until dinnertime. **Wildwoods Campsite** is only three km down Bear Cove Rd. from the ferry terminal, but it isn't particularly comfortable for tenting. And **Sunny Sanctuary Campground,** just before Hardy Bay Rd., is an RV parking lot that looks like a wagon train in a defensive circle. **Seagate Hotel,** right on the wharf, tel. (250) 949-6348, has rooms for C$72 s, C$80 d. The coffee shop at **Glen Lyon Inn,** on Hardy Bay Rd. along the waterfront, tel. (250) 949-7115, C$59 s or d, has an excellent view of the Small Boat Harbor.

You can see the new Bear Cove ferry terminal from the waterfront at Port Hardy, but it's eight km around by road. A minibus (C$5.35) conveniently leaves the bus station on Market St. 90 minutes prior to all ferry sailings; if you call (250) 949-6300 they'll pick you up from any of the area campgrounds or hotels at no extra cost. This minibus and the big Island Coach Lines buses, tel. (604) 385-4411, to Campbell River (C$41) and Victoria (C$77.45) also meet arrivals of the ferry from Prince Rupert.

Queen of the North

Flagship of the huge B.C. Ferry fleet, this comfortable vessel can accommodate 750 passengers and 160 cars. It departs Port Hardy once every two days (in June, July, and September on odd-numbered days, in August on even-numbered days) at 7:30 a.m., C$98 one-way, C$202 car one-way, and arrives in Prince Rupert at 10:30 p.m. Lately, they've been allowing drivers to check in 9:30-11 p.m. the night before the sailing. You are assigned a place in line and can camp in the parking lot in your vehicle; they wake you when they start loading.

It's a lovely trip 274 nautical miles up the almost uninhabited middle Inside Passage, especially if the weather's clear. The route enters open Pacific just beyond the north end of Vancouver Island and can be particularly rough during the two-hour sail through Queen Charlotte Sound. Open Pacific is also encountered for an

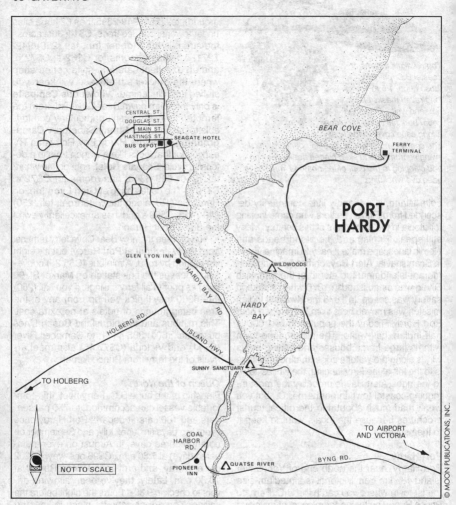

CENTRAL ST
DOUGLAS ST
MAIN ST
HASTINGS ST
BUS DEPOT
SEAGATE HOTEL

BEAR COVE

FERRY
TERMINAL

PORT
HARDY

GLEN LYON INN

WILDWOODS

HARDY BAY RD

HARDY
BAY

HOLBERG RD.

ISLAND HWY

SUNNY SANCTUARY

TO HOLBERG

COAL
HARBOR
RD.

QUATSE RIVER

BYNG RD.

PIONEER
INN

TO AIRPORT
AND VICTORIA

NOT TO SCALE

© MOON PUBLICATIONS, INC.

hour at Milbanke Sound. Have breakfast in the cafeteria, then splurge on the lunch buffet around 2 p.m.—it's a better deal than the dinner buffet. The individual john compartments on the "'tween decks" are large and private enough that activities therein are only limited by your imagination. Pick up from the gift shop the excellent *B.C. Ferries Guide to the Inside Passage*, C$2. And study the "wall of history" about the discovery and exploration of the Inside Passage.

GORDY OHLIGER

PRINCE RUPERT AND THE NORTH COAST

Rainy Rupert! Prince Rupert is a fair-sized city on Kaien Island near the mouth of the large Skeena River, at the north end of the Canadian Inside Passage. Hooked up to the rest of the world by road, rail, ferry, and airline, most travelers pass through Rupert on their way to or from Vancouver Island, the Queen Charlottes, the B.C. interior, and Alaska. Being such a major crossroads and gateway, the city has abundant and reasonable facilities for travelers and plenty of action. You couldn't ask for a better place to cool your heels while waiting for a connection. Prince Rupert is called the "City of Rainbows," though as one local put it, "It doesn't *stop* raining long enough for any rainbows to shine."

History

This area had been an important trade center for thousands of years before the Hudson's Bay Co. built Fort Simpson, 30 km north of present-day Prince Rupert, in 1834. The local Tsimshian Indians had evolved into prosperous middlemen in the trade of precious metals, furs, slaves, etc., between the powerful tribes to the north and south. An uneasy truce prevailed between the Indians and the settlers, as Fort Simpson, the most important post between Vancouver and Sitka, began to attract the inevitable missionaries, prospectors, loggers, fishermen, and homesteaders. William Duncan of Metlakatla fame (see below) served here until 1862. A gold strike up the Skeena River (Skeena means "River of Trouble," as many Indians died after eating poisonous shellfish found near its mouth)

in the 1870s led to the opening of the first sawmill on the north coast in 1875, eight km north of Fort Simpson, which continued to mill cedar, spruce, and hemlock till 1969.

The Grand Trunk Railroad, Canada's second transcontinental line, was originally intended to terminate at Fort Simpson, until at the last moment it was decided that a better harbor was situated at Kaien Island. The western end of the line was begun in 1906, and a national contest was sponsored to name the new city; $250 was awarded for "Prince Rupert," named for the first governor of Hudson's Bay Company. The tent town, strictly overseen by the railroad company, was finally put up for sale in 1909, and the boom was on. The first lots, sold for $500 in 1910, fetched $17,000 a year later. The first train pulled into Rupert in April 1914, but by then WW I had halted the boom, and by 1919 poor management had bankrupted the Grand Trunk, which was reorganized into the Canadian National Railway in 1923. Fishing and logging became the economic bases, and today Rupert's role as a transportation hub still accounts for numerous canneries, a monstrous pulp mill, and transshipment terminals for much of Canada's grain and coal.

SIGHTS

First visit the **Museum of Northern B.C.** (donation), 100 First Ave. E, tel. (250) 624-3207, open Mon.-Sat. 9 a.m.-8 p.m., Sunday 9 a.m.-

5 p.m. in summer; and Mon.-Sat. 10 a.m.-5 p.m. the rest of the year. The area's history is graphically displayed in a number of excellent exhibits, especially those on the Tsimshian Indians and Fort Simpson. Don't miss the great videos of constructing the Grand Trunk and of early halibut and salmon fishing. An art gallery is in the back room, and a good selection of local-interest books is sold in the gift shop. The **Visitor Info-Centre,** tel. (250) 624-5637, in the lobby is very helpful; read the bulletin board and brochures closely, then ask, ask, ask.

Behind the museum is a **carving shed,** where totems are sometimes in progress. Walk around the courthouse beside the museum to enjoy the attractive gardens and scenic views. The "sunken gardens" were an ammunition dump during WW II. Across First Ave. from the museum and overlooking the harbor is the **Northern Mariners Memorial Park,** a tribute to those who have lost their lives at sea.

To dig really deep into Rupert's past, head for the **Regional Archives,** 123 Third St., tel. (250) 624-3326, open 10 a.m.-4 p.m. Then go over two blocks to Fifth St. and head up to **Roosevelt Park.** Prince Rupert was an important Allied transportation base during WW II and at one time 7,000 U.S. soldiers slept in the barracks on this hill. Stop off at the map to orient yourself and read some history, then continue up to **Totem Park,** across from the hospital, a little higher with a less obstructed view of town and the harbor.

Get High

But for the high point of Prince Rupert, head down McBride St. (or grab the no. 53 bus to the Civic Centre) and go two km on the access road to the 732-meter Mt. Hays Gondola (or walk up the 4WD track a little ways for views over the harbor). A visitor survey in 1992 found that the number-one attraction in Prince Rupert was this gondola, which at the time ran year-round. Shortly after the survey was taken the gondola closed, and there are no plans to reopen it. It used to take seven minutes flat to get the bird's-eye view of the city, the harbor, the islands, and the mountains in the distance. But now you have to do it the aerobic way: a hard three-hour hike up the second-steepest gondola ground in North America.

Other Hikes

Get your map of the Linear Trails from the Info-Centre. These trails link the Prince Rupert township to the ferry terminal via Park Avenue Campground, and the Gondola to Roosevelt Park. A linear trail also starts at Seal Cove. To get there, take the no. 51 Seal Cove bus to the seaplane base at the end of the line. The road southeast from the bus stop leads past a series of abandoned WW II ammunition bunkers to the Department of Fisheries wharf. Walk back to the corner where the bus turns and continue along the abandoned railway line. This follows the shoreline below a high wooded bluff back past the Small Boat Harbor to Cow Bay and cannery row.

About two km south of the Alaska/B.C. ferry terminals is an overgrown concrete bunker and gun emplacement built during the war to protect Prince Rupert against a Japanese naval strike. A hike this way also offers excellent views of Chatham Sound and the surrounding waterways. Follow the railway tracks past two No Trespassing signs and keep going until you see the bunker above you to the left. More bunkers are several km farther down the line near Ridley Island, but they can be hard to find. If you're determined, continue south until you reach three small bunkers beside the tracks. Just beyond these is a bridge over the railway. Scramble up onto the bridge and look back to the northwest. Many wartime fortifications are swallowed by the bush here. Hitch a ride back to town on the road from Ridley Island and you'll have gone right around Kaien Island. Or, if you're willing to risk arrest or a fatal accident, walk boldly along the railway tracks past the pulp mill to Prince Edward. But don't stop on the railway bridge to admire the rushing waters at the narrows, as a sudden train could spell your end. Continue down the road seven km to the cannery museum, or catch a bus back to town.

PRACTICALITIES

Accommodations

Prince Rupert has an amazing amount of reasonable accommodations—but being such a crossroads town, it can be eventful trying to find a good cheap room if you don't have reserva-

TO SEAL COVE

TO TERRACE

PRINCE RUPERT BLVD.

YELLOWHEAD HWY.

HAYS COVE CIRCLE

HAYS CREEK

11th AVE.

COW BAY

4th AVE.

EAST 6th AVE.

EAST 6th AVE.

EAST 8th AVE.

PRINCE RUPERT

McBRIDE ST.

INFOCENTRE AND MUSEUM

WATER TAXI DOCK

PUBLIC LIBRARY

CIVIC CENTRE RECREATION COMPLEX

EARL MAH AQUATIC CENTRE

WANTAGE RD.

1st ST.

VIA RAIL

2nd ST.

3rd

PRIDE O' THE NORTH MALL

PRINCE RUPERT HARBOUR

AIRPORT LIMOUSINE TERMINAL AND RUPERT MALL

CITY HALL

RUPERT THEATRE

6th ST.

7th ST.

TAYLOR

GOLF COURSE

LAUNDROMAT

BUS DEPOT

ROOSEVELT PARK

1st AVE.

2nd AVE.

3rd AVE.

SUMMIT AVE.

CRUISE SHIP DOCK

GONDOLA HILL

GRAIN ELEVATOR

PARK AVE.

LINEAR TRAIL

KOOTENAY

SLOAN AVE.

LINEAR TRAIL

LINEAR TRAIL

2nd AVE.

PARK AVE.

AVE.

MT. HAYES (732 m)

NOT TO SCALE

B.C. FERRY
ALASKA STATE FERRY
TO PRINCE RUPERT AIRPORT
& DIGBY ISLAND TERMINAL

© MOON PUBLICATIONS, INC.

tions. You should know when you'll be here, since you'll either be arriving or departing on a scheduled ferry. Do yourself a favor and call ahead to reserve your bed.

Cheapest is **Pioneer Rooms,** 167 Third Ave. E, around the corner from the Museum of Northern B.C., tel. (250) 624-2334, C\$23 s, C\$35 d, shared bath on each of their three floors. Even though it's a C\$7 cab ride from the ferry terminal, this place fills up fast after the ferries arrive.

If that happens, the **Aleeda Motel,** 900 Third Ave. W, tel. (250) 627-1367, is recommended; C\$65 s, C\$70 d, all with baths and some with kitchenettes, which you can sometimes get for no extra charge. The **Slumber Lodge,** tel. (250) 627-1711, across the road from the Aleeda, is C\$55 s, C\$60 d and includes breakfast; the **Inn on the Harbour,** 720 First Ave. W, tel. (250) 624-9107, has views over the harbor for C\$60 s, C\$65 d (pretty rough). If you want to splurge, try a 10th-floor room atop the **Highliner,** tel. (250) 624-9060, from C\$78 d.

The **Park Avenue Municipal Campground** is a one-km, 10-minute walk toward town from the ferry terminals, tel. (250) 624-5861. It's open to register 9 a.m.-midnight; C\$16 for full hookups, C\$11 for tent sites, which includes showers. Good for city camping—treeless, grassy, some tents, mostly RVs. The alternative is **Prudhomme Lake Provincial Park** (C\$11), 20 km out of town on Hwy. 16.

Eagle Bluff B&B, Cow Bay Rd., tel. (250) 627-4955, is a great little place built over the water and overlooking the marina. It's all of 100 meters from cafes, galleries, and restaurants. The rooms are basic but clean and comfortable; the C\$50 s and C\$60 d includes a light breakfast.

Food

Breakfast around town is good and cheap—C\$4 for bacon and eggs. **Smitty's Pancake House** is in Pride O' the North Mall. The **Slumber Inn** restaurant is good and opens at 5 a.m. The coffee shop at **Moby Dick Motor Inn,** on Second Ave., also serves big but boring budget bacon-and-eggs breakfasts, open 24 hours; it's the best value of the downtown bunch, but it's the busiest (read: slowest service). Or try **Raffles Inn** on Third Ave., with specials starting at C\$3.

The **Stardust** has good Chinese—cheap and plentiful. **Zorba's** is recommended for good authentic Greek, but get your Greek pizza at **Rodhos.** At **La Gondola,** flash your headlights from the carpark to place your order for takeaway food. **Smiles Seafood** is recommended highly by Rupertites. Shop at the Rupert Mall, or at Safeway near the museum, open daily.

There's also a concentration of cafes and restaurants down at Cow Bay. Casual **Smiles,** tel. (250) 624-3072, has been serving seafood for more than 60 years; fish and chips go for C\$6. **Cow Bay Cafe,** tel. (250) 627-1212, has indoor and alfresco tables right over the water; fun. **Cowpuccino's Coffee House,** tel. (250) 627-1395, offers plentiful coffees and provides newspapers and magazines to go with your cuppa.

Entertainment

Drink, dance, and try not to get your face punched in. **Popeye's Pub** in the Rupert Hotel is where the 21-year-olds hang out, the kind of place where the hard-rocking band plays its heart out, ends every song with a bang, and nobody claps (not even the dancers), though one drunk guy invariably shouts out, "Rock 'n' roll!" **Surf Club,** corner of Second Ave. W and Fifth St., is for the over-30 crowd, where the band plays Top 40, or '50s and '60s rock, ends a song with a bang, but doesn't wait for the crowd not to clap, launching instead right into a sick joke or another two-minute classic. At the **Empress** across the street, you're on your own. For a quieter experience, head out to **Solly's Pub** at Seal Cove and **Breakers Pub** at Cow Bay, or look for out-of-town entertainers at the **Moby Dick Inn's** nightclub.

Play bingo nightly at **Totem Bingo,** Third Ave. W and First Street. Hang out with the 15-year-olds at **Fourth Avenue Amusements,** Second Ave. W and Fourth St., for pinball, foosball, or eight-ball. Or play some serious nine-ball with the 17-year-olds at **International Billiards,** Second Ave. W and Sixth Street. In fact, Rupert has more pool tables per capita than anywhere else in the North, including a beautiful giant snooker table at the Belmont. **Famous Players Theatre,** Second Ave. W and Fifth St., tel. (250) 624-6770, shows three separate films, C\$7.50.

Services and Information

You're never wanting for time or temp. here: both are displayed from the top of the landmark Highliner Inn. They might not be right, which is more fun. Another InfoCentre is found at Park Avenue Campground.

The **library** is on McBride between Sixth and Seventh. Rupert has a good bookstore, too: **Star of the West,** 518 Third Ave. W, tel. (250) 624-9053, open weekdays 9 a.m.-9 p.m., Saturday 9 a.m.-6 p.m. Also check out the gallery in back.

The **Earl Mah Aquatic Centre,** McBride St. next to the Civic Centre, has a pool, a hot tub, saunas, and fitness machines, only C$4.50 for use of the lot; call (250) 627-7946 for hours.

TRANSPORTATION

By Air

Canadian Regional, tel. (250) 624-6292, has three flights daily from Vancouver via Terrace to Rupert (and back to Vancouver), C$271 one-way; the APEX fare starts at C$260 roundtrip. The airport is on Digby Island across the harbor; Canadian Air has a check-in at the Rupert Square Mall, Second Ave. W between Third and Sixth Sts., two hours before departure. From there, a bus transfers you via ferry to the airport. The bus is technically free, though the ferry charges C$12 pp, which you pay to the bus driver. Go figure. **Air B.C.,** 112 Sixth St., tel. (250) 624-4554, flies the same route. **Water Taxi,** tel. (250) 624-3337, has a workers' ferry several times a day from the second dock south from the foot of McBride St. (C$2.50), if you want to try to save a few bucks—it's a five-km walk from the drop-off to the airport.

Local air transportation is provided by a few seaplane companies at Seal Cove (see "Other Hiking" under "Sights," above). **Harbour Air,** tel. (250) 627-1341, is the largest, with service to Port Simpson (C$35) and Kitkatla (C$65). They also fly to Sandspit and Q.C. City (C$170) and Masset (C$116) in the Queen Charlottes. There's no service to Ketchikan; their Masset service operates three times daily, permitting you to combine sea (ferry to Skidegate), land (hitch to Masset), and air (seaplane back to Rupert) travel on a visit to these islands. You can

also charter their various planes for scenic flights, from C$396 an hour.

By Sea

Both the B.C. and Alaska ferry terminals are two km from downtown. City buses show up once every two to three hours, if that, but a shuttle bus (C$3.50) meets the B.C. (not Alaska) ferries; call (250) 624-5645 for hotel pickup. A cab to downtown costs C$5, to Pioneer Rooms at the far end of town, C$6. If it's late and you're camping, just walk the one km to the campground. Or walk the kilometer to the corner of Pillsbury and Kootenay, where bus no. 52 passes every half-hour 7:30 a.m.-5:30 p.m., except Sunday.

B.C. Ferries' (tel. 250-624-9627) *Queen of the North* makes a roundtrip between Port Hardy

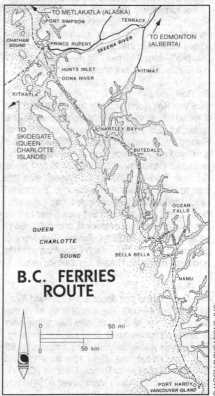

B.C. FERRIES
ROUTE

© MOON PUBLICATIONS, INC.

on Vancouver Island and Prince Rupert every two days. Southbound, the ferry leaves Prince Rupert on odd-numbered days in June, July, and September, even-numbered days in August, at 7:30 a.m. and arrives in Port Hardy at 10:30 p.m.; northbound just reverse the ports and days. The ferry makes a stop in Bella Bella, a surprisingly large town, once a week. The fare is C$98 one-way, car C$202.

Queen of Prince Rupert sails to Skidegate Landing on the Queen Charlottes four to six days a week, depending on the month. The sand-and-a-half-hour ride leaves Rupert Wed.-Sun. at 11 a.m, Monday 9 p.m. (Thursday and Saturday are summer sailings only), C$21.75 one-way, C$83 car only. From Skidegate, the ferry leaves at 11 a.m. on Monday and Tuesday, 11 p.m. on Thursday and Friday (and Saturday in August).

For local ferry trips, see "Vicinity of Prince Rupert," below. For Alaska Marine Highway information, see "By Ferry" under the "Getting There" section in the On The Road chapter, and "Alaska Marine Highway" in the Introduction of the Southeast Alaska chapter.

By Rail
The **VIA Rail** depot is at the foot of Second St.; a wooden ramp descends right down to the water, tel. (250) 627-7304. Trains depart Prince Rupert Wednesday, Friday, and Sunday at 8 a.m. and arrive Prince Rupert Monday, Thursday, and Saturday at 8 p.m.; C$89 to Prince George, C$140 to Jasper. Connect with the train to Vancouver at Prince George. You travel along the historic Skeena River route; get a window seat on the right for best views. For further information and reservations, call (800) 561-8630 anywhere in British Columbia. The depot is only open two hours on each side of the arrivals and departures and has a few coin lockers.

By Bus
The **Greyhound** bus depot is at 822 Third Ave., tel. (250) 624-5090. The depot is open weekdays 8:30 a.m.-8:30 p.m. and has a few coin lockers. All buses these days are nonsmoking. Two buses arrive daily, at 9:45 a.m. and 6:30 p.m. Two depart too, at 11:15 a.m. and 8:30 p.m. It's 12 hours to Prince George (C$87), where you connect to Vancouver (C$181) or Whitehorse (C$201).

Getting Around
Prince Rupert has an adequate local transit system, which can get you practically anywhere in and around town within an hour. Fare is C$1, exact change, or C$2 to ride all day. Buses run commuter hours during the week, later on Friday nights, limited on Saturday, not at all on Sunday. Schedules/route maps are available on any bus, or call (250) 624-3343 for info. **Budget** rents cars, starting at C$40 a day plus 25 cents per km, tel. (250) 627-7400, with an office in Rupert Mall. **Tilden's** rates are the same, tel. (250) 624-5318.

For transportation to and from the ferry docks, see "By Sea" above.

Tours
To reach **Gray Line,** call (250) 624-6124. A number of charter and tour boats operate out of Rupert, all organized into **Seashore Charters,** tel. (250) 624-5645. Fishing charters run C$40-60 pp an hour, C$150 pp per day; check the Yellow Pages. A two-hour harbor tour is C$50 pp (minimum four people), and a crab-fishing picnic is C$60 pp (minimum four).

VICINITY OF PRINCE RUPERT

Around Chatham Sound
Digby Island is the one to the left as the ferry arrives. Site of an old Norwegian settlement, many of the old houses remain, as does Wahl's Boat-yard (now closed) at Dodge Cove, where wooden fishing boats were once built. An old wharf and more dilapidated buildings are at Casey Cove, one bay over. There are some interesting hikes around the cove area. Rupert Water Taxi leaves from its dock (at the foot of McBride St., Wednesday and Friday 11:30 a.m. and 3:30 p.m., C$2.50, extra sailings on school days) for Dodge Cove and makes for a cheap harbor ride.

Port Simpson, 30 km north of Rupert, was a Coast Tsimshian settlement before Hudson's Bay Co. built a fort there in 1834. The white population grew steadily till the turn of the century but quickly subsided as soon as the Grand Trunk Railroad terminus was located at Prince Rupert. The fort was abandoned in 1904 and burned down in 1912, and now it's again a settlement of the Coast Tsimshian. A fish-pro-

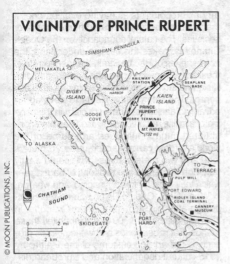

VICINITY OF PRINCE RUPERT

© MOON PUBLICATIONS, INC.

Washington, D.C., where he received permission for the Tsimshian to homestead in Alaska. In 1887, Duncan led 823 Indians to Annette Island, Alaska, where they founded a new Metlakatla (see "Metlakatla" under "Vicinity of Ketchikan" in the Southeast Alaska chapter). The original town burned down in 1901, and today no buildings remain from Duncan's time.

The best way to see the village is on an **Archaeological Harbour Tour,** which departs daily at 1 p.m. from the InfoCentre (C$20). The villagers used this service to get to and from Rupert.

Port Edward
A scenic 20-km ride from Rupert brings you to the **North Pacific Cannery Village Museum,** 1889 Skeena Dr., tel. (250) 628-3538, open in the summer daily 10 a.m.-7 p.m., the rest of the year Wed.-Sat. 10 a.m.-4 p.m., admission C$5. Built in 1889, this is the oldest remaining cannery village on North America's west coast. At its peak, the cannery employed 400 workers of several nationalities. It canned its last fish in 1972; a museum society to sponsor its restoration was formed in 1985, and in July 1987 ownership was transferred to Port Edward village. In the cannery building itself are the displays, including a 10-meter relief map of local salmon-spawning routes, a seven-meter map of the Skeena River hand-drawn on sailcloth, early maritime charts, and salmon-fishing artifacts. Also check out the Iron Chink and can-making machinery in the back room. Walk along the boardwalk past the former living quarters, which now house an art gallery, a coffee shop, and a store—note the ledgers with 1937 prices: six cents for a package of Jello, 20-cent bottles of vinegar, 15-cent bottles of ketchup. The large wharf is a fine place to get a tan from sitting in the English rain.

Far West Bus Lines, tel. (250) 624-6400, does a roundtrip to Port Edward (C$1.50) and the cannery (C$2.50) four times on weekdays, twice on weekends.

cessing plant there is owned by the Indians. The only way to get there these days is to fly with Harbor Air (C$35 one-way), which leaves from the Seal Cove seaplane base; or you could ask around the docks for a lift.

Centurion 4 is the other small B.C. Ferry that departs Prince Rupert from the small downtown dock for Kincolith, a small Indian settlement up the Portland Inlet. It departs Monday and Friday at 8 a.m., arriving back in Rupert around 3:30 p.m., C$15 roundtrip. There is no longer a B.C. ferry up the spectacular Portland Canal to Stewart, though you can catch an Alaska ferry in Ketchikan to Hyder.

Metlakatla
This small Indian village, eight km west of Rupert by boat, was founded in 1862 by Anglican missionary William Duncan on an ancient Tsimshian site. A sawmill and a trading post were set up, and these people became self-supporting. The church Duncan built in 1874 seated 1,200 people, at the time the largest church west of Chicago and north of San Francisco. In later years Duncan clashed with church authorities who wanted to impose the elaborate Episcopalian ritual on the Indians. When Duncan demurred, the Episcopal bishop had local officials seize the land on which the mission sat in an attempt to force Duncan to obey. Instead, he traveled to

THE QUEEN CHARLOTTE ISLANDS

The Queen Charlotte Islands (pop. 6,000) form a chain 300 km long, separated from the Canadian mainland continental shelf by the stormy 50-

Missionary William Duncan converted the Tsimshians into model Christians, but he obliterated all traces of Tsimshian culture in the process.

to 130-km-wide Hecate Channel. Although there are 150 islands in all, the two largest, Graham and Moresby, account for most of the group's land area. Narrow Skidegate (SKID-uh-git) Channel slices these two apart near the middle of the group. Snowcapped mountains run down the west coast of the archipelago, with a wide area of lowland and rolling hillside on the east toward the middle and northern end of the chain. For the most part, the Queen Charlotte Islands are a remote, wild, and natural land where deer and eagles still outnumber people, where the world's largest black bears are found, and where the temperate rainforest grows like a thick green jungle. If you are looking for a unique experience, this is the place.

History
Juan Perez was the first European to sight the islands, in 1774; however, the Charlottes had been the homeland of the Haida Indians for centuries. The Haida are considered by contempo-

rary anthropologists as having evolved one of the world's most sophisticated hunter-gatherer societies. The natural abundance on the Queen Charlottes makes this easy to understand: the rich fisheries of Hecate Strait, the teeming life in the tidepools, mushrooms and berries, and prolific game animals provided the Haida with a rich pantry. This allowed the Haida to develop an advanced artistic tradition, especially in the carving of argillite, a soft black slate. They also constructed huge longhouses and some of the world's largest canoes—craft up to 25 meters long and two meters across that could easily transport 40 people and two tons of baggage— which they used for trading, raiding, and whaling.

When Capt. George Dixon named the archipelago after his ship, the *Queen Charlotte,* in 1787, an estimated 8,000 Haida inhabited these islands. But missionaries and white officials proscribed the art and customs of the Haida; by 1915 cultural degeneration and European diseases had reduced their numbers to 588. Today their descendants live in Haida village, near Masset, and in Skidegate; 5,000 whites also inhabit the group, mostly along Skidegate and Masset Inlets.

Preparations
Bring as much as you can of what you'll need to the Queen Charlottes—these islands are remote. Especially be prepared for *rain*—which is always happening somewhere on the islands, usually where *you* are. A good raincoat and waterproof rubber boots are a must. August and September are the best months to take your chances with the weather; bring a sponge, anyway. Also bring food, camping equipment, and basic supplies. For the most part, prices are only slightly higher than on the mainland, but selections are limited.

Skidegate
B.C. Ferries' *Queen of Prince Rupert* docks at Skidegate. The **Haida Gwaii Museum** (C$3), just 500 meters east of the ferry landing, is open Tues.-Fri. 10 a.m.-5 p.m., weekends 1-5 p.m. The museum has a good collection of argillite carvings, century-old totem poles, and fascinating displays of fauna, insects, and birds; there's also a platform for viewing gray whales as they rest on their northward migration (April-May). Skidegate village, a small Haida commu-

nity (pop. 470), is 2.5 km up the road. The **Band Council Office** on the waterfront is built in the form of a traditional longhouse.

The ferry MV *Kuvuna,* which leaves Skidegate 12 times daily 7:30 a.m.-10:30 p.m. on its 20-minute trip over to Alliford Bay on Moresby Island and the road to Sandspit (C$3 roundtrip, C$8.50 car), is the only public transportation on the islands. Also check out the numerous tours that leave from Skidegate.

Queen Charlotte City

Second-largest town on the islands (pop. 1,000), Q.C. City is five km west of the ferry landing and an easy hitch. Most of the islands' govern-

QUEEN CHARLOTTE ISLANDS

ment offices are here, plus half a dozen small lodging houses. But make your first stop at the **Visitor Reception Centre,** tel. (250) 559-4742, open daily 8 a.m.-5 p.m., and be sure to buy the *Guide to the Queen Charlotte Islands* for only C$3.95. Make your arrangements here in Q.C. City for over 40 kayaking, fishing, sailing, flightseeing, and sightseeing tours. Call **Kallahin Expeditions,** tel. (250) 559-8455, for any info and to book ahead.

The best-value and oldest (dating back to 1910) place to stay is **Premier Creek Lodging,** tel. (250) 559-8415; C$30 s, C$55 d. Or stay at **Spruce Point Lodging** on Seventh St., tel. (250) 559-8234, for C$55 s, C$65 d (bed and breakfast); or the **Premier Hotel,** Third Ave., tel. (250) 559-8415, C$25 or C$56 d, with sweeping views of the harbor. **Gracie's Place,** Third Ave., tel. (250) 559-4262, captures the essence of the Queen Charlottes at C$50 s, C$60 d. **Haydn Turner Park** at the west end of the road through Q.C. City has 10 sites (C$5, if anyone shows up to collect), pit toilets, and huge trees. Eat at **Margaret's Cafe** or **Claudette's Place.**

Sandspit

It's 13 km by paved road from the ferry landing on Moresby Island to the island's only settlement, Sandspit, a logging and communications town (pop. 730) with good beaches. Gwaii Haanas/South Moresby National Park Reserve is the island's main drawing card. Sandspit also boasts the only airstrip in the group. Best of several B&Bs is **Moresby Island Guesthouse** on Beach Rd., tel. (250) 637-5300, C$30 s, C$55 d. The stunning **Sandspit Inn,** tel. (250) 637-5334, will put you up for the night while putting you back C$76 d. Or head down to **Gray Bay Campground** on a secluded beach 15 km south of Sandspit. Gray Beach is as far south as you can drive on Moresby Island; the rest of the way south to Cape St. James, accessible only on tours or by sea kayak, could be the wildest land in the North Pacific. The logging road heads west from Gray Bay by Skidegate Lake and down to Moresby Camp on Mosquito Lake, then back up to the ferry landing. This is a long day's drive, and an even longer hitchhike.

An information facility is at the airport. Canadian Airlines flies jets in and out of the airport to Prince Rupert and Vancouver. Budget Rent-A-Car has an office here, tel. (250) 637-5688.

Again, a dozen tour operators offer tours of the island and park; contact Kallahin Expeditions in Q.C. to lead you in the right direction.

Gwaii Haanas/South Moresby National Park Reserve

This park, established in 1988, was a victory for environmentalists and Haida and a defeat for the logging companies. It's co-managed by Parks Canada and the Gwaii Haanas. Part of the deal cut with the loggers and fishermen was the establishment of a man-made harbor in Sandspit. Slated for completion in 1997, it will be the home base for sightseeing and fishing charter boats. The park itself is accessible by boat, floatplane, and helicopter. Approximately 50 commercial operators offer services within the park.

The park comprises 138 islands with a total land area of only 1,470 hectares, but more than 1,500 km of shoreline. More than 500 Haida archaeological sites are located in the park, including five deserted villages. Best known is Ninstints on Sgan Gwaii island. Abandoned in the 1890s, rotting longhouses and dozens of mortuary (totem) poles remain. It's a UNESCO World Heritage Site.

For further information on the park, call Parks Canada in Sandspit at tel. (250) 637-5362.

Naikoon Park

Naikoon (Long Nose) Provincial Park covers a large flat area in the northeast corner of Graham Island. Park HQ, tel. (250) 557-4390, is in Tlell, 40 km north of Skidegate, where there's a 31-site campground (C$11) and a picnic area. Tlell is home to a number of back-to-the-land weavers, potters, and artisan types, which provides a welcome contrast to the island's rough-and-ready loggers. **Tlell River House,** tel. (250) 557-4211, has a bar, a restaurant, and lodging, C$52 s, C$60 d. **Hltunwa Kaitza B&B,** tel. (250) 557-4664, charges C$30 pp; it's a nice walk to the beach.

A five-km trail leads up the north side of Tlell River onto the beach and past the wreck of the *Pesuta,* a log barge grounded during a fierce storm in 1928. The East Beach Hike starts here and goes all the way to Tow Hill at the northern tip of the island, a four- to eight-day hike (89 km). The beach is open to 4WDs, which use it very regularly.

To Tow Hill

Continue northwest from Tlell to **Port Clements** (pop. 470)—check out the museum (open daily 1-5 p.m., donation), the market, a couple of bars, and a restaurant. Stay at the **Golden Spruce Motel,** tel. (250) 557-4325, C$40 s, C$45 d. Then head up to **Masset** (pop. 1,400 but dropping fast as the Canadian Forces Base closes), largest settlement on Graham Island. Stop in at the InfoCentre just before town. Accommodations are limited; try **Naikoon Park Motel,** tel. (250) 626-5187, C$45 s or d; or **Copper Beech House** by the dock, tel. (250) 626-3225. There's also a small campground on Tow Hill Rd., C$8. The town itself has little of interest, but the surrounding countryside more than makes up for it. Do head to **Haida** or Old Masset, two km west of Masset, to visit the museum, crafts shops, and a few totem poles. **Harbour Air,** tel. (250) 627-1341, flies to Prince Rupert twice daily, C$116 one-way.

Tow Hill is 26 km east of Masset, the last 13 along a gravel road. Three trails begin by the Heillen River bridge at the base of the hill. The **Blow-hole Trail** (one km) leads down to fantastic rock formations by the shore and a view of the spectacular basalt cliff on the north side of Tow Hill (109 meters). From here a second trail climbs to the top of Tow Hill for a view of the sandy beaches that arch in both directions along the north coast of Graham Island for as far as you can see. The longest trail is the **Cape Fife Trail** (10 km), which cuts across to the east side of the island. From there you can hike up to Rose Point at the very northeastern tip of the archipelago, where the Haida believe the world began. Then come back down North Beach to Tow Hill, a total of 31 km, a one- to three-day hike.

An established campground (windy) is beside the road just west of Tow Hill, but backcountry camping is allowed anywhere in Naikoon Park. For more info, contact **Naikoon Park HQ,** P.O. Box 19, Tlell, B.C. V0T 1Y0, tel. (250) 557-4390.

Transportation

Except for the local ferry between Skidegate and Alliford Bay, there is no public transportation. The locals are good about picking up hitchhikers, but cars can be few. Hitching the main roads is a piece of cake, though, compared to getting really out there on the logging roads, especially when you remember how many black bears are around. Most logging roads are open to the public on weekends and after 6 p.m. weekdays. During working hours on Moresby Island you must get permission from TimberWest, tel. (250) 637-5436 (in Sandspit) to travel on them. MacMillan-Bloedel controls most of the logging roads on Graham Island and has offices in Q.C. City, tel. (250) 559-4224, and in Juskatla, tel. (250) 557-4212.

Queen Charlotte City and Masset have **bicycle rentals.**

You might consider renting a car from **Budget,** which has offices in Q.C. City, Sandspit, and Masset, tel. (250) 637-5688, starting at C$72 plus 25 cents a km; pickup trucks and 4WDs start at C$65 plus 30 cents. **Rustic Car Rentals** is in Q.C. City, tel. (250) 559-4641, C$45 per day plus 20 cents a km. Make your reservations far in advance.

Most people arrive on the excellent B.C. Ferries service from Prince Rupert at Skidegate (C$21.75, C$83 car only), which runs five to six times a week in summer, four in the off-season. The ferries remain overnight at Skidegate, enough time to see the town. While a quick roundtrip is certainly better than nothing, campers and naturalists will want to spend longer in the islands.

Canadian and **Air B.C.** have daily flights from Vancouver to Sandspit, from C$250 roundtrip. All flights are met at the airport by Twin Services, which transports passengers to Q.C. City for C$6. **Harbour Air,** tel. (250) 627-1341, flies to Prince Rupert twice daily from Q.C. City and Sandspit (C$170 one-way) or Masset (C$116 one-way) and has other scheduled flights around the islands. **South Moresby Air Charters,** tel. (250) 559-4222, in Q.C. City, flies everywhere; popular charters include Hot Spring Island, from C$310 roundtrip for three people; and Ninstints, from C$510 roundtrip.

For information on the Queen Charlottes, write to the **Queen Charlotte Islands Chamber of Commerce,** P.O. Box 38, Masset, B.C. V0T 1M0, tel. (250) 626-5211. And be sure to pick up their excellent *Guide to the Queen Charlotte Islands,* C$3.95, which has everything you need to know, including exact distances between towns.

Rennell Sound

A logging road leads northwest from Q.C. City 55 km to Port Clements through the heart of Graham Island. Halfway along is a road, which leads as far west as it is possible to drive in Canada, to Rennell Sound. The final descent to this rugged piece of coastline is a mere 24% gradient. Here you'll find great beachcombing (Japanese glass floats are the prize) and a free campground with pit toilets along the shoreline. Back on the main logging road, continue past Juskatla to the unfinished Haida canoe and one of the world's only golden spruce trees.

GORDY OHLIGER

SOUTHEAST ALASKA

INTRODUCTION

For many people, the name Alaska conjures up images of bitterly cold winters and sunshine-packed summers, of great rivers, enormous snowcapped mountains, and open tundra reaching to the horizon. If that is your vision of the state, you've missed its Garden of Eden, the Southeast. Almost entirely boxed in by British Columbia, Southeast Alaska's "Panhandle" stretches 500 miles along the North American coast. Everything about this beautifully lush country is water-based: the rain that falls on the land, the glaciers that drop from giant icefields, and the ocean that surrounds it all. Gray-blue clouds play a constant game of hide-and-seek with the verdant islands; deep fjords drive up between snow-covered summits; waterfalls plummet hundreds of feet through the ever-green forests to feed rivers rich in salmon; brown bears prowl the creeks in search of fish; bald eagles perch on treetops beside the rugged, rocky coastline; and great blue glaciers press down toward the sea.

The Land

Southeast Alaska is composed of a mountainous mainland and hundreds of islands, varying from rocky reefs that barely jut out of the sea at low tide to some of the largest islands in North America. Collectively, these islands are called the Alexander Archipelago. This ragged shoreline stretches for more than 11,000 miles and includes over 1,000 named islands, the largest being Prince of Wales, Chichagof, Baranof, Admiralty, Revillagigedo, and Kupreanof—names that reflect the English, Russians, and Spaniards who explored the area.

The Rainforest

Much of Southeast is covered with dense rainforests of Sitka spruce (the state tree), western hemlock, Alaska yellow-cedar, and western red cedar. Interspersed through the rainforests are open boggy areas known as muskegs, with a scattering of stunted lodgepole pines and cedars. Above the treeline (approx. 2,500 feet)

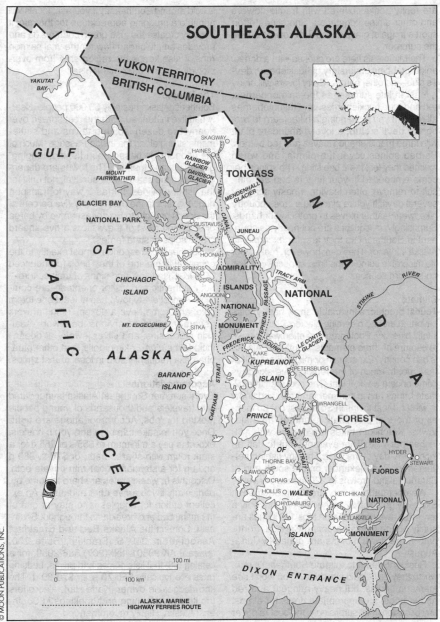

SOUTHEAST ALASKA

YUKON TERRITORY
BRITISH COLUMBIA

YAKUTAT BAY

GULF

MOUNT FAIRWEATHER

SKAGWAY

HAINES

RAINBOW GLACIER

DAVIDSON GLACIER

TONGASS

MENDENHALL GLACIER

GLACIER BAY

NATIONAL PARK

OF

GUSTAVUS

ICY BAY

JUNEAU

PELICAN

HOONAH

TENAKEE SPRINGS

CHICHAGOF ISLAND

ADMIRALITY

ANGOON

ISLANDS

TRACY ARM

NATIONAL

STIKINE RIVER

MT. EDGECUMBE

SITKA

MONUMENT

FREDERICK SOUND

LE CONTE GLACIER

PACIFIC

ALASKA

KUPREANOF ISLAND

BARANOF ISLAND

KAKE

PETERSBURG

CHATHAM STRAIT

WRANGELL

PRINCE

FOREST

OCEAN

OF

CLARENCE STRAIT

MISTY

HYDER

STEWART

THORNE BAY

KLAWOCK

CRAIG

HOLLIS

HYDABURG

WALES

FJORDS

NATIONAL

KETCHIKAN

METLAKATLA

ISLAND

MONUMENT

CANADA

DIXON ENTRANCE

0   100 mi
0   100 km

ALASKA MARINE
HIGHWAY FERRIES ROUTE

© MOON PUBLICATIONS, INC.

are rocky peaks covered with fragile flowers and other alpine vegetation. Shorelines often sport a fringe of grass dotted with flowers during the summer.

The rainforests here are choked with a dense, ankle-grabbing understory of huckleberry, devil's club, and other shrubs. Berry lovers will enjoy a feast in late summer as the salmonberries, red and blue huckleberries, and thimbleberries all ripen. If you're planning a hike, learn to recognize **devil's club,** a lovely, abundant plant with large maple-shaped leaves and red berries. Barbed spines cover the plants, and when touched they feel like a bee sting. The spines become embedded in your fingers and are difficult to remove, often leaving a nasty sting for several days. If you're planning a cross-country hike, wear leather gloves to protect your hands. Surprisingly, mosquitoes are not nearly as abundant in Southeast as they are, for example, in Alaska's Interior. They can, however, make your life miserable some of the time, especially during no-see-um season.

Climate

Tourist brochures invariably show happy folks cavorting around gleaming glaciers under a brilliantly blue sky. Photographers often wait weeks to capture all three elements; Southeast Alaska is rain country! Expect rain or mist at least half of the time. In much of the region, blue-sky days come once a week, if that. The cool maritime climate brings rain in summer, and rain and snow in winter. Most towns in Southeast get 80 inches or more of precipitation, and of the major towns, Ketchikan takes top honors with 162 inches per year. That averages out to half an inch every day of the year. The tiny fishing settlement of Port Alexander on the south end of Baranof Island drowns in 220 inches per year!

Weather patterns vary greatly in Southeast; Skagway gets just 22 inches a year, but only a few miles away, precipitation tops 160 inches annually on the peaks bordering Canada. Fortunately, the driest months are generally June-August.

Residents learn to tolerate Southeast's rain, which they call "liquid sunshine." You won't see many umbrellas, but heavy raingear and red rubber boots are appropriate dress for almost any occasion. (Not surprisingly, the best raingear is sold around Southeast.) If you ask, locals will admit to a grudging appreciation for the rain; it not only creates the lush green countryside and provides ample streamflow for the vital salmon runs, it also keeps the region safe from overcrowding by the drier-minded set.

The People

Southeast Alaska has only 65,000 people. Nearly half live in Juneau, with the rest spread over nearly two dozen isolated towns and settlements strung along the Inside Passage. Much of the economy is based upon fishing, logging, governing, and tourism. The towns are dependent upon the sea for their survival, not only for the fish it provides, but as a way to transport huge log rafts to the mills. Ninety-five percent of the goods brought to Southeast arrive by barge or ship, and most of the visitors arrive aboard cruise ships or state ferries.

Southeast corresponds almost exactly to the ancestral homeland of the Tlingit (pronounced "KLINK-it") Indians, and signs of their culture—both authentic and visitor-oriented—are common. Almost every town has at least one totem pole, and some have a dozen. Tlingit artwork generally includes carvings, beadwork, sealskin moccasins, and silver jewelry. It doesn't include the *ulus,* Eskimo dolls, and other paraphernalia frequently sold in local tourist shops.

Accommodations

Every summer Southeast Alaska is inundated with travelers and thousands of young people looking for jobs. Accommodations are tight. Once you forsake camping and youth hostels, expect to pay a minimum of $55 s or $65 d for a stark room with shared bath, or $70 s, $80 d and up for a standard room with private bath. Discounts or weekly rates are hard to come by, particularly if you arrive after mid-June. An excellent option for couples is to stay at one of the many bed and breakfasts throughout Southeast. Contact the **Alaska Bed and Breakfast Association,** 369 S. Franklin, Suite 200, Juneau, AK 99801, tel. (907) 586-2959, for a catalog ($3) that lists places and prices. Lodging rates are typically $60-70 s, or $70-80 d. The knowledgeable owner, Karla Hart, also offers trip itinerary planning and bookings in Southeast Alaska. Highly recommended.

For those on a tighter budget, campgrounds are plentiful throughout Southeast, and most main towns have youth hostels. (Note, however, that most campgrounds and hostels are open only from mid-May to mid-September.) Camping is allowed anywhere in the Tongass National Forest except day-use areas, but is generally prohibited within city limits. If you have more money and are willing to spend it, some incredible places to bed down are available. These include remote lodges and resorts where the scenery is grand and the service impeccable.

GETTING THERE

Visitors come to Southeast by three primary means: cruise ship, jet, and ferry. Cruise ships are easily the most popular method—nearly 500,000 people travel this way each year—but also the most expensive and the least personal. In general, cruise ships are for folks who want everything presented to them via a canned bus tour of town or a quick helicopter flight over the glacier, rather than discovering on their own. This book is not likely to be of much interest to the average cruise ship traveler. The smaller tour boats, such as those operated by **Alaska Sightseeing/Cruise West,** tel. (800) 426-7702, offer more personal voyages that emphasize the natural world. But they're very expensive. With a little planning, you can cover the same ground (or water or air) for far less cash.

The second option, by air, is more popular with independent travelers. **Alaska Airlines,** tel. (800) 426-0333, has daily flights from Seattle, with connections to Juneau, Ketchikan, Wrangell, Petersburg, Sitka, and Gustavus. Floatplanes connect these towns to smaller places and provide access to even the most remote corners of the Panhandle, such as Elfin Cove, Tokeen, and Port Alexander. These flights are detailed in subsequent chapters.

ALASKA MARINE HIGHWAY

Only three Southeast towns (Haines, Skagway, and Hyder) are connected by road to the rest of the continent. All the others, including Juneau, the state capital, are accessible only by boat or plane. This lack of roads—hopefully they will never be built—has led to an efficient public ferry system, the best in the Western Hemisphere and the longest in the world. Most ferries sail between Prince Rupert, B.C., and Skagway ($124), stopping along the way in the major towns. There is also weekly service from Bellingham, Washington, all the way to Skagway ($246), with stops along the way. It takes three days to travel all the way from Bellingham to Skagway. Less popular, but equally scenic, is the summertime service from Hyder/Stewart ($126 to Skagway). In the larger towns, summer service is almost daily, but in the smallest settlements ferries may be up to two weeks apart.

History
One of the first actions of the newly created Alaska State government in 1959 was to establish a state ferry system. Originally it consisted of just a single boat, the 100-foot-long snub-nosed *Chilkat* (no longer in service), but after passage of a 1960 state bond, three new ships were built: the *Matanuska, Malaspina,* and *Taku.* Over the next decade the *Tustumena, Bartlett, Le Conte,* and flagship *Columbia* (418 feet long with a thousand-passenger capacity) were added to the fleet. The *Aurora* was christened in 1977, and a brand-new 380-foot ship comes online in 1998. It will be capable of sailing across the Gulf of Alaska, providing much-needed connections between Southeast and Southcentral Alaska. Service has gradually expanded over the years so that today the only substantial Southeast town without ferry service is Gustavus—where residents don't want the influx of RVers it would bring.

The Ferry System Today
Southeast Alaska is served by the *Columbia, Malaspina, Matanuska, Taku, Le Conte,* and *Aurora.* The *Tustumena* and *Bartlett* operate between Southcentral Alaskan ports. The smaller vessels, *Le Conte* and *Aurora,* primarily serve the more remote villages such as Hoonah, Pelican, or Angoon. All the vessels carry vehicles and have a cafeteria, free shower facilities (except the *Bartlett*), and lockers (for now); and the larger ships also have private cabins and more spacious facilities. The *Le Conte* and *Aurora* take you to quieter villages relatively un-

SOUTHEAST ALASKA FERRY PASSENGER FARES (SUMMER 1997 RATES)

	Seattle (Bellingham)	Prince Rupert	Hyder	Ketchikan	Metlakatla	Hollis	Wrangell	Petersburg	Kake	Sitka	Angoon	Hoonah	Juneau	Haines	Skagway	Pelican
Ketchikan	164	38	40													
Metlakatla	168	42	44	14												
Hollis	178	52	54	20	22											
Wrangell	180	56	58	24	28	24										
Petersburg	192	68	70	38	42	38	18									
Kake	202	80	82	48	52	48	34	22								
Sitka	208	86	88	54	58	54	38	26	24							
Angoon	222	100	102	68	72	68	52	40	28	22						
Hoonah	226	104	106	74	78	74	56	44	38	24	20					
Juneau	226	104	106	74	78	74	56	44	44	26	24	20				
Haines	240	118	120	88	92	88	70	58	58	40	38	34	20			
Skagway	246	124	126	92	96	92	76	64	64	44	42	40	26	14		
Pelican	248	126	128	96	100	96	78	66	52	40	38	22	32	46	54	
Tenakee	226	104	106	74	78	74	56	44	32	22	16	16	22	34	40	32

touched by the glamorizing effects of tourism. You'll be able to talk with more locals and can walk right up to the ship's prow to watch the islands slip by.

Ferries generally stop for one or two hours in the larger towns, but less than an hour in the smaller villages. You can go ashore while the vessel is in port. Unfortunately, in 1996 the state suddenly yanked the lockers out of all of Alaska's ferry terminals, claiming unnamed "security" reasons. Blame it on creeping paranoia, but you will no longer have a place to safely store things in the terminals. Despite the recent lack of lockers, the ferry terminals are generally well stocked with local information brochures. Most of the terminals open only an hour or two before ship arrivals, closing upon their departure. A baggage cart transports luggage from the terminal to the ship if you want to save your back a bit. There is a limit of 100 pounds of luggage per person, but this is only enforced if you are way over and the ship is full.

Life Onboard

Many travelers think of the ferry as a floating motel—a place to dry off, wash up, relax, sleep, and meet other travelers while at the same time moving on to new sights and new adventures. Ferry food is reasonably priced (by Alaskan standards) and is fairly good, but many budget travelers stock up on groceries before they board to save money.

For a bit of entertainment, try flying a kite from the back deck. Be sure it's a cheap one, however, since you can't chase it if it gets away. Another popular toy is a hackey sack. And if you bring a musical instrument along, *you'll* provide the entertainment. Also be sure to bring earplugs if you are a light sleeper since things can get pretty noisy sometimes, especially in the solarium.

Staterooms or Solarium?

Staterooms offer privacy (for a price), as well as a chance to get away from the hectic crowding of midsummer. There are several types of rooms, but all Southeast ferries have bunk beds and private baths with showers—so you can avoid the morning shower lineup. (Some cabins on Southwest Alaska's *Tustumena* ferry don't have private baths.) Rooms start at $227 for a two-berth cabin from Bellingham to Haines, or $98 for a two-berth cabin from Prince Rupert to Haines. Lower rates, of course, for shorter distances. Note that these costs are in addition to the ferry rates.

If you don't mind hearing others snoring nearby, you can save a bundle and make new friends with fellow voyagers. There's often plenty of space to stretch out a sleeping bag in the recliner lounge (an inside area with airline-type seats), as well as in the solarium. Pillows and blankets are available for rent on most sailings. The **solarium**—a covered and heated area high atop the ship's rear deck—has several dozen deck chairs to sit and sleep on, making it a favorite hangout for backpackers, budget travelers, cannery workers, and high school basketball teams. It's also a great place to enjoy the passing panorama and to make new friends. The solarium is so popular that at some embarkation points (particularly Bellingham), there's often a mad dash up the stairs to grab a place before all the chairs are taken. To be assured of a deck chair, get in line five hours ahead of time if you're coming aboard in Bellingham in midsummer. When the weather is good you're also likely to see the rapid development of a tent-city on the rear deck, often held down with duct tape (usually sold in onboard gift shops).

Show Time

Between early June and Labor Day, the *Columbia, Malaspina, Matanuska,* and *Taku* have Forest Service interpreters on board. They provide videos and slideFish and Game shows, give talks, answer questions, hand out Smokey Bear pins to the kids, and generally spoon-feed the Forest Service line. Be sure to pick up a **Tongass National Forest map** ($4) from them, and take a look at their "Opportunity Guide" for up-to-date info on each town. This is a good place to ask about various Forest Service cabins in Southeast (see below). Alaska Department of Fish and Game interpreters are also on some ships.

In addition to these naturalist-types, ferry passengers are often given the chance to watch or work with various artists and performers in the **Arts on Board** programs. These include concerts, Native craftwork, and more. Feature movies are shown on the video monitors every day.

Getting Tickets

See the "Southeast Alaska Ferry Passenger Fares" chart for a listing of summer 1996 fares. Get ferry schedules and make reservations by calling (800) 642-0066 or by writing Alaska Marine Highway, P.O. Box 25535, Juneau, AK 99802-5535. You can also access rate and schedule information, as well as make reservations, on the State of Alaska web page at http://www.state.ak.us. Since most travel in Southeast centers around the ferry schedules, it's a good idea to request a copy of the schedule before making any solid travel plans. Reservations for the summer can be made as early as

Erecting your own nylon stateroom on deck outside the solarium is a common practice on the long journey north from Bellingham up the Inside Passage.

DAVID STANLEY

December, and travelers taking a vehicle should book as early as possible to be sure of a space. Before you get ready to board, it's always a good idea to call the local ferry terminal to make sure the ferry is on schedule.

Although there is usually space for walk-on passengers, it's a smart idea to make advance reservations for ferries out of Bellingham. This is especially true for cabins. Reservations are required for anyone with a vehicle, and are generally available six months in advance. If you can't get on in Bellingham, take a ferry to Victoria on Vancouver Island, a bus (or hitch) to Port Hardy, and a ferry to Prince Rupert. This will cost slightly more, but will be far more exciting. The ferry system says that ferry reservations are required for all sailings, but space is usually available for last-minute foot passengers out of Prince Rupert and within Southeast Alaska. Exceptions to this are during the Southeast Alaska State Fair in mid-August (all Haines-bound ferries are jammed), and ferry sailings in Prince William Sound. The ferry system charges an extra fee of up to $41 (the amount varies depending upon your destination) to carry bicycles, canoes, kayaks, and inflatable boats aboard. These are listed in the schedule as "alternate means of conveyance."

Discounts
Those driving a car to Alaska may be able to save money by riding the ferry during the off-season (Oct.-April). These typically include discounts for drivers (summertime drivers must pay for both their car and themselves), and for children in the winter holiday season. Contact the Alaska Marine Highway for these special promotional rates.

Seniors over 65 can take advantage of special bargain fares. In the summer, they can travel between Alaskan ports (not, however, between Ketchikan and Prince Rupert or Bellingham) on the *Le Conte* and *Aurora* for 50% of the regular full fare. During the rest of the year, the discounted fares are expanded to all vessels within Alaska. Some restrictions apply during each season. The discounts do not apply to vehicles or staterooms, and you do not need to be an Alaskan to obtain the discounts. Contact the ferry system for further details. Substantial discounts are also available for people with disabilities; see the latest Alaska Marine Highway brochure for specifics.

TONGASS NATIONAL FOREST

Three times larger than any other national forest in the country, Southeast Alaska's Tongass National Forest is America's rainforest masterpiece. Within these 16.8 million acres are magnificent coastal forests, dozens of glaciers, snow-capped peaks, an abundance of wildlife, hundreds of verdant islands, and a wild beauty that has long since been lost elsewhere. Originally named Alexander Archipelago Forest Reserve in 1902, the area became Tongass National Forest in 1907 by proclamation of Pres. Theodore Roosevelt. It was later enlarged to include most of the Panhandle. Between the Forest and Park Services, nearly 95% of Southeast is federal property.

Recreation
The Tongass is a paradise for those who love the outdoors. It has dozens of scenic hiking trails and over 1,000 miles of logging roads accessible by mountain bike (if you don't mind the clearcuts and can avoid the logging trucks and flying gravel). The islands contain hundreds of crystal-clear lakes, many with Forest Service cabins on them. Fishing enthusiasts will enjoy catching salmon, cutthroat trout, and other fish from these lakes, the ocean, and the thousands of streams that empty into bays. The Inside Passage is composed of a wonderful maze of semi-protected waterways, a sea kayaker's dream come true. Particularly popular with kayakers are Misty Fjords National Monument, Glacier Bay National Park, and the waters around Sitka and Juneau, but outstanding sea kayaking opportunities can be found throughout Southeast. If you have a sea kayak, access is easy, since they can be carried on the ferries. Ask the Forest Service recreation staff in the local district offices for info on nearby routes and conditions.

Wilderness Areas
Less than five percent of the Tongass has been logged or otherwise developed, so it isn't necessary to visit an official wilderness area to see truly wild country. However, 21 wilderness areas total well over five million acres in the national forest, offering outstanding recreational opportunities. The largest are **Misty Fjords National Monument** (2.1 million acres) near Ketchikan, and

Admiralty Island National Monument (956,000 acres) near Juneau. Other major wildernesses include **Tracy Arm-Ford's Terror** (653,000 acres) south of Juneau, **Stikine-Le Conte** (449,000 acres) near Wrangell, **Russell Fjord** (349,000 acres) near Yakutat, **South Baranof** (320,000 acres) south of Sitka, and **West Chichagof-Yakobi** (265,000 acres) near Pelican. Six new wilderness areas (totaling over 300,000 additional acres) were created when Congress passed the Tongass Timber Reform Act of 1990.

Several wilderness areas, such as the remote islands off the west coast of Prince of Wales (Coronation, Maurelle, and Warren Islands) are exposed to the open ocean and are inaccessible for much of the year, even by floatplane. Others, such as the Stikine-Le Conte, Admiralty Island, Russell Fjord, and Petersburg Creek-Duncan Salt Chuck wilderness areas are relatively accessible. There are developed trails or canoe/kayak routes within the Misty Fjords, Admiralty Island, Stikine-Le Conte, Tebenkof Bay, and Petersburg Creek-Duncan Salt Chuck wilderness areas. See subsequent chapters for specific information.

Forest Service Cabins
Tongass National Forest has over 145 public recreation cabins throughout Southeast. These are a wonderful way to see the *real* Alaska. Most cabins are rustic, one-room Pan-Adobe log structures 12 by 14 feet in size with bunk space for four to six people. They generally have a woodstove with cut firewood (some have oil stoves), an outhouse, and rowboats at cabins along lakes. You'll need to bring your own bedding, cookstove, cooking and eating utensils, Leatherman or Swiss Army knife, food, playing cards, candles, flashlight, matches, and mousetraps. (Some of this will probably be there, but it's better to be sure by bringing your own.)

Getting Out
Many Forest Service cabins can only be reached by floatplane. These flights can be very expensive, averaging approximately $280/hour in a Cessna 185 (two people with gear) or $400/hour in a Beaver (up to five people with gear), but even those on a tight budget should plan to spend some time at one of these cabins. A few can be reached by hiking from towns (Ketchikan, Petersburg, and Juneau), cutting out the expensive flight. If you're considering a flightseeing trip anyway, make it to one of these remote cabins where you get to see what the country is really like. This is one splurge you won't regret.

Cabin Reservations
Cabin reservations can be made in person at any ranger district office (Ketchikan/Misty Fjords, Thorne Bay, Craig, Wrangell, Petersburg, Sitka, Hoonah, Juneau/Admiralty Island, or Yakutat), or by writing or calling one of the offices listed below. The Forest Service charges $25 per night for the cabins, with all fees going toward the maintenance of these facilities. They are reserved on a first-come, first-served basis up to six months in advance, some of the most popular cabins are even chosen by lottery. As of this writing, no credit card reservations were possible, though that may change in the future. The Forest Service publishes brochures describing recreation facilities, and can also supply **Tongass National Forest maps** ($4) that show the locations of all Forest Service cabins. Both the **Forest Service Information Center,** Centennial Hall at 101 Egan Dr., Juneau, AK 99801, tel. (907) 586-8751, and the **Southeast Alaska Visitor Center** in Ketchikan, tel. (907) 228-6220, can provide information and cabin reservations for all of the Tongass.

GORDY OHLIGER

KETCHIKAN

After the 36-hour ferry ride up from Bellingham, Ketchikan is most first-timers' introduction to Alaska. Along the way they've heard tales from sourdoughs (and those who claim to be), talked to Forest Service naturalists, and watched the logging towns and lush green islands of British Columbia float past. As the ferry pulls into Tongass Narrows an air of expectancy grows among the newcomers who are about to take their first steps in Alaska.

The state's fourth largest city (pop. 8,000, plus another 6,000 in nearby areas), Ketchikan bills itself as "Alaska's First City," and even its zip code—99901—seems to bear this out. Many ferry passengers don't bother to stop here, instead hurrying on toward Juneau and points north. Because downtown is two miles away, they only have time for a superficial bus tour or a walk to the grocery stores for provisions. But with its great scenery, fine local trails, unusual museums, the world's largest collection of totem poles, a bustling downtown, and famous Misty Fjords nearby, Ketchikan deserves a longer stay.

The Setting
Located 90 miles north of Prince Rupert, Ketchikan clings to a steep slope along Ton-

gass Narrows, on Revillagigedo (ruh-VEE-ya-he-HAY-do) Island; locals shorten the name to "Revilla." Fortunately, it doesn't bear the one-time viceroy of Mexico's full name: Don Juan Vicente de Guemes Pacheco de Pedilla y Horcasitas, Count of Revilla Gigedo! The town is "three miles long and three blocks wide," forming a continuous strip of development along the waterfront from the ferry terminal to beyond Thomas Basin. Because of this, Tongass Avenue—the only through street—is one of the busiest in the entire state. Be ready for traffic jams in this hectic, bustling small city with a redneck, working-class atmosphere.

Much of Ketchikan is built on fill, on pilings over the water, or on hillsides with steep winding ramps for streets. Fishing boats jam the three boat harbors (there are almost as many boats as cars in Ketchikan), and the two canneries and two cold-storage plants run at full throttle during the summer. Floatplanes are constantly taking off from the narrows. For several decades Ketchikan's pulp mill was the biggest employer in Southeast Alaska, processing spruce and hemlock for the production of rayon and cellophane. The pulp mill closed in 1997, throwing 500 local people out of work. Two other Louisiana-Pacific

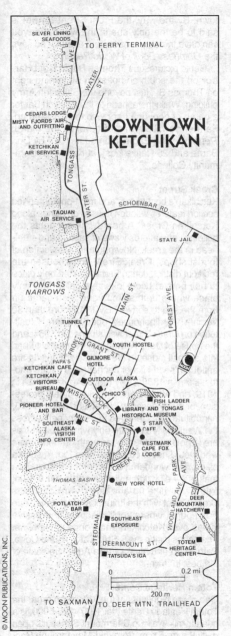

DOWNTOWN KETCHIKAN

SILVER LINING SEAFOODS

TO FERRY TERMINAL

WATER ST.

AVE.

CEDARS LODGE
MISTY FJORDS AIR AND OUTFITTING

KETCHIKAN AIR SERVICE

TONGASS

WATER ST.

SCHOENBAR RD.

TAQUAN AIR SERVICE

STATE JAIL

TONGASS NARROWS

MAIN ST.

FOREST AVE.

TUNNEL

FRONT ST.

GRANT ST.

YOUTH HOSTEL

GILMORE HOTEL

PAPA'S KETCHIKAN CAFE

KETCHIKAN VISITORS BUREAU

OUTDOOR ALASKA

CHICO'S

PIONEER HOTEL AND BAR

MISSION ST.

DOCK ST.

FISH LADDER

LIBRARY AND TONGASS HISTORICAL MUSEUM

SOUTHEAST ALASKA VISITOR INFO CENTER

MILL ST.

CREEK ST.

5 STAR CAFE

WESTMARK CAPE FOX LODGE

PARK AVE.

THOMAS BASIN

NEW YORK HOTEL

POTLATCH BAR

STEDMAN ST.

SOUTHEAST EXPOSURE

WOODLAND AVE.

DEER MOUNTAIN HATCHERY

DEERMOUNT ST.

TATSUDA'S IGA

TOTEM HERITAGE CENTER

0   0.2 mi

0   200 m

TO SAXMAN   TO DEER MTN. TRAILHEAD

sawmills still employ 500 workers in the area, but these may also close. The company blames economic losses stemming from the 1990 Tongass Timber Reform Act. Environmentalists counter that the shutdown was inevitable due to the mill's outmoded equipment and poor pollution record (Ward Cove is heavily contaminated with toxic waste). Ketchikan's economy will survive the closure.

Ketchikan is one of the rainiest places in Alaska, with more than 13 feet a year, or an average of half an inch per day. Luckily, May-Aug. are the driest months, but expect to get wet nevertheless. Locals adapt with "Ketchikan sneakers" (red rubber boots) and Helley Hanson raingear; umbrellas are the mark of a tourist. Residents pride themselves on almost never canceling baseball games, and enjoy weekend picnics at Ward Lake in a downpour. Weather predicting is easy in Ketchikan: if you can't see the top of Deer Mountain, it's raining; if you can, it's *going* to rain.

History

The name Ketchikan comes from *Kitcxan,* a Tlingit word meaning "Where the Eagles' Wings Are," a reference to the shape of a sandspit at the creek mouth. The sandspit was dredged in the 1930s to create Thomas Basin Boat Harbor. Rumor has it that several bodies were found then, and suspicious fingers were pointed toward the denizens of nearby Creek Street, the local red-light district. One of Southeast Alaska's youngest major towns, Ketchikan began when the first of many salmon canneries at the mouth of Ketchikan Creek opened in 1885. By the 1930s it had become the "Salmon Capital of the World" (13 canneries), and Alaska's largest town. Overfishing caused salmon populations to crash in the 1940s, and the fishing industry was supplanted in the 1950s by a new pulp mill that turned the town into a major logging center. The mill closed in 1997, but commercial fishing has rebounded due to strict fishing controls and increased hatchery production. The number of cruise ship visitors to Ketchikan keeps increasing each year and is now approaching 500,000 annually. This means that some days see half a dozen ships of various sizes tied up in Tongass Narrows, and downtown is often overrun.

SIGHTS

Southeast Alaska Visitor Center

A great place to start your exploration of Ketchikan is the striking Southeast Alaska Visitor Center (SEAVIC), 50 Main St., tel. (907) 228-6214. Opened in 1995, it's one of four interagency public land information centers in Alaska; this one is operated by the U.S. Forest Service. It's filled with impressive exhibits—including a full-scale rainforest—that offer an educational portrait of the land and people of Southeast. The 13-minute multimedia show is a must-see. Also here is a very helpful trip planning room filled with maps, trail guides, and books. You can buy the above in the gift shop; you can also make reservations for Forest Service cabins at the information desk. The center is open daily 8:30 a.m.-4:30 p.m. April-Oct., and Tues.-Sat. 8:30 a.m-4:30 p.m. the rest of the year. Entrance to the exhibits and audiovisual show costs $3 (free for children under five).

More Downtown Sights

The small but interesting **Tongass Historical Museum** at 629 Dock St. (the library building), tel. (907) 225-5600, is open daily 8 a.m.-5 p.m. mid-May through September; and Wed.-Fri. 1-5 p.m., Saturday and Sunday 1-4 p.m. October through mid-May. Admission is $2. The museum contains local historical items plus permanent exhibits on Native culture and commercial fishing. Outside is **Raven Stealing the Sun Totem,** and not far away stands the **Chief Johnson Pole** (an older version is inside the Totem Heritage Center). Tiny Whale Park occupies the intersection across from the Forest Service office and is home to the **Chief Kyan Totem,** raised in 1993 to replace an older version. The older one was reputed to reward those who touched it by bringing money within a day. It's worth a try on the new one, but don't head immediately to Las Vegas on the basis of this claim.

Check out some of Ketchikan's many long aerobic **stairways** up to hillside homes and outstanding vistas. The best ones start from the tunnel at Front and Grant Sts., and from the intersection of Main and Pine Streets. If you have a bike (or better yet a skateboard), you may want to test your mettle on Schoenbar Rd., the route blasted out of a very steep hillside behind

town. By the way, the Front Street **tunnel** is said to be the only one in the world that you can drive through, around, and over! Or so says the *Guinness Book of World Records.*

Get to picturesque **Thomas Basin Boat Harbor** on the south end of town by turning right on Thomas St., just beyond the Salvation Army building. While there, head to the Potlatch Bar for a game of pool or a beer with local fishermen. Farther down Stedman St. notice the mural, *Return of the Eagle* (painted in 1978 by Don Barrie and 25 Native kids), at Ketchikan Community College.

Creek Street

Ketchikan's best-known and most-photographed section features wooden houses on pilings along Ketchikan Creek. A boardwalk connects the buildings and affords views of salmon and steelhead in the creek. Now primarily a collection of tourist shops, Creek Street once housed the red-light district, during Prohibition the only place to buy booze. Local jokesters call it "the only place where both salmon and men came up from the sea to spawn." By 1946 more than 30 "female boardinghouses" operated here. Prostitution on Creek Street was stopped in 1954, and the house of **Dolly Arthur** was eventually turned into a small museum ($3 admission). Inside are antiques, secret liquor caches, and risqué photos. Born in 1888, Dolly moved to Ketchikan in 1919, and worked at the world's oldest profession for many decades. When she died in 1975, her obituary was featured in newspapers across the West. Dolly's is open only when cruise ships are in port and is fun to tour with grandmothers who would never otherwise step foot in such a place. The wonderful collection of memorabilia makes it well worth a visit. A **cable car** ($1 up; free if you hike up and ride down) connects Creek Street with the luxurious Westmark Cape Fox Lodge, where you'll discover impressive vistas over Ketchikan and Tongass Narrows. The shops inside the **5-Star Cafe**—Soho Coho, Parnassus, and Alaska Eagle Arts—are some of the best in town.

Totem Heritage Center

One of the highlights of the Ketchikan area, the Totem Heritage Center, tel. (907) 225-5900, is a quarter-mile walk up Deermount Street. It's open daily 8 a.m.-5 p.m. from mid-May through Sep-

TOTEM POLES

These largest of all wooden sculptures were carved in cedar by the Tlingit, Haida, Tsimshian, Kwakiutl, and Bella Bella peoples of the Pacific Northwest. Their history is not completely known, but early explorers found poles in villages throughout Southeast Alaska. Apparently, totem-pole carving reached its heyday in the late 19th century with the arrival of metal woodworking tools. The animals, birds, fish, and marine mammals on the poles were totems that represented a clan, and in combination, conveyed a message.

Totem poles were very expensive and time-consuming to produce; a clan's status could be determined in part by the size and elaborateness of their poles. In a society without written words to commemorate people or events, the poles served a variety of purposes. Some totem poles told of a family's history, others of local legends, and still others served to ridicule an enemy or debtor. In addition, totems were used to commemorate the dead, with a special niche at the back to hold the ashes of a revered ancestor.

GORDY OHLIGER

Totem poles were never associated with religion, yet early missionaries destroyed many and, as recently as 1922, the Canadian government outlawed the art in an attempt to make the Natives more submissive. Realizing that a rich heritage was being lost due to neglect, skilled Native carvers worked with the CCC during the 1930s to restore older totems and create new ones. Today, active carving and restoration programs are taking place in Saxman, Ketchikan, Sitka, and Haines.

---

tember, and Tues.-Fri. 1-5 p.m. the rest of the year, admission $3.50 (free for children under five). The center was established in 1976 to preserve a collection of 33 original totem poles and house posts retrieved from abandoned village sites. Unlike other totems in the area, these works are not brightly painted copies or restorations but were carved more than a century ago to record Tlingit and Haida events and legends. Guides answer your questions and put on a short video about the totem recovery program. During the winter, the center has special classes in carving, basketry, beading, and other Native crafts. Surrounding the building is a short trail with signs identifying local plants. Out front is the Fog-Woman pole, crafted by noted carver Nathan Jackson.

Deer Mountain Tribal Hatchery

Just across a footbridge from the Totem Heritage Center is Deer Mountain Tribal Hatchery on Ketchikan Creek. Signboards explain and illustrate the process of breeding and rearing king and coho salmon, and visitors can feed the fish. Kings arrive from the Pacific Ocean to spawn at the hatchery late in the summer; look

for them in the creek. A **fish ladder** to help them get past the falls is visible from the Park Ave. bridge. If too many fish return to spawn, the state opens Ketchikan Creek to dipnet fishing by locals, creating a rather astounding scene. Thousands of pink (humpback or humpies) salmon also spawn in the creek each summer. Another good place to see spawning humpies is **Hoadly Creek,** a half-mile south of the ferry terminal.

The hatchery is run by the Ketchikan Indian Council, with tours for $3, including the chance to dress up in Tlingit regalia for photos. It is open daily 8:30 a.m.-4:30 p.m. from early May to late September. Watch performances of "Salmon Boy," a dramatization of an ancient legend, at 10 a.m. and 2 p.m. daily in the summer.

Totem Bight State Historical Park

Totem Bight, eight miles northwest of the ferry terminal, has 15 Haida and Tlingit totems and a realistic replica of a clan house complete with a brightly painted facade and cedar-scented interior. No charge. Be sure to pick up the fine brochure describing the poles and their meanings. The totems, carved from 1938 to 1941, are replicas of older poles. They are surrounded by a stand of young hemlock trees and a view across Tongass Narrows. Although hundreds of tour buses come here each summer, no city buses reach Totem Bight, so you'll have to walk or hitch here unless you have wheels.

Saxman

This Native village (ironically named for a white schoolteacher) is a 2.5-mile walk or hitch south of Ketchikan. Saxman is crowded with the largest collection of standing totem poles in the world—more than two dozen. Most were brought from their original sites in the 1930s and restored by Native CCC workers; others came from a second restoration project in 1982. The oddest pole is topped with a figure of Abraham Lincoln in commemoration of the settlement of a war begun by the U.S. revenue cutter *Lincoln*. Probably the most photographed is the Rock Oyster Pole, which tells the story of a man who drowned after his hand became caught in an oyster.

DAVID STANLEY

Saxman totem pole

Saxman (pop. 400) has recently thrown itself into the tourism maelstrom with the completion of a cedar **Beaver Clan House** and a **carving shed** for totems, masks, and other woodworking. The carving shed (free; open Mon.-Fri. 9 a.m.-4 p.m.) is a must-see, especially when master carvers Nathan Jackson or Israel Shotridge are at work. A gift shop sells tourist junk, or head downhill a block for authentic local crafts from the **Saxman Arts Co-op,** tel. (907) 225-4166. They even carry the famous Tlingit button blankets, but be ready to drop $1,250 to own one. Tours of Saxman ($30; mainly for the cruise-ship crowd) include performances in the clan house by the Cape Fox Dancers, and a theatrical production of an old legend. Tickets are available at the gift shop, tel. (907) 225-5163.

RECREATION ON LAND

The Ketchikan area is blessed with an abundance of hiking trails and remote wilderness cabins maintained by the U.S. Forest Service. Several are described below; go to the Southeast Alaska Visitor Center for reservation information. If you arrive in Ketchikan unprepared for a cabin stay, **Alaska Wilderness Outfitting,** tel. (907) 225-7335, rents such supplies as outboard motors, coolers, stoves, and dishes (but not sleeping bags).

Deer Mountain

The best hike from Ketchikan is up to the 3,000-foot summit of Deer Mountain (six miles, or four hours roundtrip). Begin by following Ketchikan Lakes Rd. a half-mile up toward the old city dump from Deermount and Fair Streets. Take the first left—the road to Ketchikan Lakes, source of the city's drinking water—and then an immediate right. The trail starts from a small parking lot and climbs along an excellent but strenuous path through dense Sitka spruce and western hemlock forests. There's an incredible view in all directions from the top of Deer Mountain, but right into July you'll have to cross snowbanks to reach the summit. (Raingear works fine for sledding down again.)

Just before the final climb to the peak, a trail to the left leads around the north slope and on to tiny **Blue Lake** and **John Mountain** (3,238 feet). Entirely above the timberline, this portion can be hazardous for inexperienced hikers. Carry a map and compass since it's easy to become disoriented if the clouds drop down. A Forest Service A-frame **shelter cabin** ($25) is at Deer Mountain below the north slope a half-mile beyond the fork; space for eight hikers. No stove, but the cabin is well insulated. It's also often vandalized by local jerks. Make reservations (and ask about the current conditions) at the Forest Service district office in Ketchikan, 3031 Tongass, a half-mile south of the ferry terminal (or at SEAVIC). You can also find places to camp near the summit of Deer Mountain and at Blue Lake.

Another 1.5 miles beyond Blue Lake is a steep drop-off that requires careful climbing. After this, the primitive trail (designated by orange markers) continues to John Mountain and then down to Lower Silvis Lake where it meets a gravel road. Follow this road the final two miles to the Beaver Falls power plant and a salmon hatchery that may or may not be in operation. Nearby is an old cannery where tours are given to cruise ship folks. With luck you can hitch the 13 miles back to town from here, but there isn't a lot of traffic. The total distance from the Deer Mountain trailhead to the hatchery is 12 miles. If you do this trek in the opposite direction, you'll need to sign the log book just past the entrance gate and next to the hatchery. Stop by the Southeast Alaska Visitor Center for maps and other details on this long hike.

Ward Lake Area

Two good trails are near the Forest Service campground at Ward Lake. The one-and-a-third-mile **Ward Lake Nature Trail** is an easy loop with interpretive signs and good steelhead and salmon fishing. **Perseverance Trail** begins on the right side just before Three-C's Campground. Park on the left side of the road. The two-mile climb begins in a gravel path along the creek, and then follows a "stairway-to-heaven" boardwalk, passing through several muskegs along the way. Originally built by the CCC in the 1930s, it has been rebuilt several times since. When wet it gets quite slippery, but at least it isn't muddy. Unfortunately, the interesting trail ends in a quagmire at Perseverance Lake, so don't plan on camping there.

To get an idea of how the Saxman-based Cape Fox Native Corporation is mismanaging its lands, head another four miles up the road beyond Ward Lake. This unbelievably huge clearcut is so bad that even the Forest Service makes it a point to put up boundary signs stating "Entering Private Land." Unfortunately, this sort of operation is typical of Native corporations in Alaska. An even worse clearcut is visible from the ferry as you head north from Ketchikan. Is this what's meant by the "We are stewards of our heritage" line one hears from Native leaders?

Naha River

The Naha River watershed, 20 miles north of Ketchikan, contains one of the finest trail and cabin systems in Southeast. The river once supported astounding runs of sockeye salmon and is still a popular salmon, steelhead, and trout fishing area for locals. At one time the town of **Loring** (established 1888) at its mouth had the world's largest fish cannery and was the main point of entry into Alaska. Today, it's a tiny settlement of retirees and vacation homes. **Heckman Lake,** six miles upriver, supported the world's largest and most costly salmon hatchery at the turn of the century. The hatchery failed, however, and all that remains are the overgrown ruins. The pleasant and recently rebuilt six-mile **Naha River Trail** begins at Naha Bay, follows the shore of Roosevelt Lagoon, then climbs gently up to Jordon and Heckman Lakes. Both lakes have Forest Service cabins ($25/night) with rowboats. A third cabin will be added to Heckman Lake by 1998. Approximately half the trail is boardwalk. At the mouth of Roosevelt Lagoon is an interesting salt chuck where the direction of water flow changes with the tides. Covered picnic tables are nearby. More picnic tables are two miles up the trail at a small waterfall, a good place to watch black bears catching salmon late in the summer. Access to the Naha area is either by sea kayak, by floatplane, or by having someone drop you off in a skiff; contact Knudsen Cove Marina, tel. (907) 225-8500 or (800) 528-2486. **Taquan Air,** tel. (907) 225-8800 or (800) 770-8800, offers day-trips into Naha, with a drop-off at Naha Bay and a pickup six hours later at the lake for $129 pp.

Other Cabins

Lake Shelokum, 40 miles north of Ketchikan, has a free three-sided shelter near a hot springs. A two-mile trail stretches from the shelter to Bailey Bay, passing the scenic lake and a very impressive waterfall. Be prepared for lots of mosquitoes and a stream crossing. Access is very expensive, approximately $600 roundtrip for a Cessna 185 with space for two people and gear. Ketchikan Ranger District has many other cabins worth visiting. Favorites include **Lake McDonald, Reflection Lake, Helm Creek,** and **Blind Pass.** Contact the district office for details.

Cycling

Rent mountain bikes by the hour or day from **The Pedalers,** tel. (907) 723-1088, located in the Spruce Mill shops downtown. Southeast Exposure (described above) also rents bikes and offers cycling tours.

RECREATION ON THE WATER

Whatever you do, *do not* take the "Mountain Lake Canoe Adventure" offered by one local company. This is one of those made-for-cruise-ship-suckers tours that includes a chance to paddle around Connell reservoir (built to supply water for the now-defunct pulp mill) while trying to ignore the concrete dam and the trees killed when the water level rose. There are a number of excellent alternatives to this falderal. Geoff Gross of **Southeast Exposure,** 507 Stedman St., tel. (907) 225-8829, offers sea kayaking instruction ($40 for two hours), plus day-trips to nearby areas, starting at $50 (children $30) for a three-hour tour of Tongass Narrows. Rent single fiberglass kayaks for $35/day and doubles for $50/day (less for more than six days or for plastic kayaks). Folding kayaks are available for folks flying to remote Forest Service cabins on lakes. Southeast Exposure also does extended trips into Misty Fjord (described below) and to the remote Barrier Islands along the south end of Prince of Wales. The latter costs $1,200 pp for an eight-day expedition (including transportation and supplies).

Southeast Sea Kayaks, tel. (907) 225-1258, is a smaller newer company that also offers guided kayak trips, including a two-and-a-half-hour paddle along Tongass Narrows for $65, plus longer trips to George Inlet and the Naha River area. They rent double fiberglass kayaks and offer transport for their or your own kayaks. Very friendly folks, too.

The best local on-the-water deal is through the **Ketchikan Parks and Recreation Department,** 2721 Seventh Ave. (next to the high school), tel. (907) 225-9579. Their office is open Mon.-Fri. 8 a.m.-5 p.m. They rent fully equipped canoes, basketballs, and other sports equipment, as well as skis and snowshoes in the winter months, and sometimes offer sea kayaking classes.

Rent skiffs from **Knudsen Cove Marina,** 13 miles north of town, tel. (907) 247-8500 or (800) 528-2486; **Clover Pass Resort,** 15 miles north of town, tel. (907) 247-2234; **Mountain Point Boat Rentals,** 5660 S. Tongass Ave., tel. (907) 225-1793; and **Salmon Falls Resort,** 17 miles north of town, tel. (907) 225-2752 or (800) 247-9059. Several of these also rent rods and reels.

Charter fishing is available from many different outfitters in Ketchikan; see the visitors bureau for a complete listing, or stop at one of their booths along the cruise ship dock. The **Ketchikan Yacht Club,** tel. (907) 225-3262, sponsors low-key races a couple of times a week in the summer, and the skippers are always looking for volunteer crew members. It's a fun way to sail with the locals for free.

ACCOMMODATIONS

See the "Ketchikan Accommodations" chart for a complete listing of local lodging choices. The **Ketchikan Youth Hostel,** downtown in the basement of the Methodist church at Grant and Main, tel. (907) 225-3319, costs $8 for members and $11 for nonmembers. Open 6 p.m.-9 a.m., doors are locked at 11 p.m.; if your ferry gets in after that, call the hostel promptly upon arrival and they'll open for you, but only if they have space. It's a very good idea to reserve ahead to be sure, since there are precious few reasonably priced options in town. The hostel, open only from Memorial to Labor Days, is nothing fancy—we're talking foam mattresses on the floor—but is very friendly and clean, with free coffee, kitchen facilities, and showers. It's a great place to meet other travelers. There's a four-night maximum stay.

Ketchikan's other "budget" option is **Rain Forest Inn,** 2311 Hemlock St. (just up the hill from Carrs), tel. (907) 225-7246. The crowded dorms are $25 pp with space for 14 men but no women,

KETCHIKAN ACCOMMODATIONS

Note: Ketchikan charges an 11.5% tax on these lodging rates.

Ketchikan Youth Hostel; Grant and Main; tel. (907) 225-3319; $8-11 pp; hostel facility, dorms with mats on floor, community kitchen, open Memorial Day to Labor Day

Rain Forest Inn; 2311 Hemlock St.; tel. (907) 225-7246; $25 pp in crowded men's dorm; $35 s in semiprivate rooms; $47 s in private rooms; community kitchen, recreation room, see rooms first

New York Hotel; 207 Stedman St.; tel. (907) 225-0246; $69 s, $79 d; restored historic hotel, classic place, continental breakfast

Gilmore Hotel; 326 Front St.; tel. (907) 225-9423; $70 s, $75 d; courtesy van, rooms can be very noisy (downstairs bar)

Ingersoll Hotel; 303 Mission St.; tel. (907) 225-2124; $84 s, $94 d; continental breakfast, small rooms, courtesy van, AAA approved

Super 8 Motel; 2151 Sea Level Dr.; tel. (907) 225-9088 or (800) 800-8000; $85 s, $93 d; free van to ferries

The Cedars Lodge; 1471 Tongass Ave.; tel. (907) 225-1900; $85-160 s or d; courtesy van

Best Western Landing; 3434 Tongass Ave.; tel. (907) 225-5166 or (800) 428-8304; $105-155 s, $110-160 d; fitness center, courtesy van to ferry and town, AAA approved

Westmark Cape Fox Lodge; 800 Venetia Way; tel. (907) 225-8001 or (800) 544-0970; $155 s or d; courtesy van, AAA approved

BED AND BREAKFASTS

House of Stewart B&B; 3725 S. Tongass Hwy. (four miles south of Ketchikan); tel. (907) 247-3725; $50 s, $60 d; rural location near beach, two guest rooms, full breakfast; $75 s or d in apartment with kitchen (no breakfast), private entrance

Alaskan Home Fishing B&B; 12 miles north; tel. (907) 225-6919 or (800) 876-0925; $55-105 s, $75-125 d; courtesy van, hot tub, full breakfast, fishing package trips available

Innside Passage B&B; 114 Elliot St.; tel. (907) 247-3700; $60 s, $70-100 d; hillside house on stairway, harbor views, near ferry, two guest rooms with shared bath or apartment with private bath and entrance, full breakfast

Granny & Papa B&B; 1940 Second Ave.; tel. (907) 225-9514; $70 s, $85 d; new place, harbor views, seven guest rooms, private baths, full breakfast

Captain's Quarters B&B; 325 Lund St.; tel. (907) 225-4912; $70-75 s or d; custom home with view, three guest rooms, private baths, continental breakfast

Millar St. House B&B; 1430 Millar St.; tel. (907) 225-1258 or (800) 287-1607; $75 s or d; 1920s historic home, ocean views, two guest rooms, private baths and entrances, continental breakfast, very friendly

Alder St. B&B; 410 Alder St.; tel. (907) 247-9871; $75 s or d; near ferry terminal, one guest room, cedar deck, private entrance, full breakfast

D&W B&B; eight miles north; tel. (907) 225-3273; $75 s or d; two-bedroom apartments, fix-your-own breakfast

Oyster Ave. B&B; 2259 S. Tongass Hwy. (two miles south of Ketchikan); tel. (907) 225-3449; $75 s or d; new cottage, quiet location, deck, kitchen, continental breakfast

Velda's Victorian B&B; 609 Pine St.; tel. (907) 225-4940; $75 s or d; one guest room, private bath, continental breakfast

Robbins & Company B&B; 320 Bawden St.; tel. (907) 225-4232; $75 s or d; one-bedroom condo, continental breakfast

Blueberry Hill B&B; 601 E. First St.; tel. (907) 247-2583; $75 s, $80 d; two guest rooms, private baths, full breakfast

Whale Tail B&B; 11 miles north; tel. (907) 225-3380; $78 s or d; three guest rooms, shared or private baths, full breakfast

Oakes House B&B; 10 miles north of Ketchikan; tel. (907) 225-1705; $99 s or d; two guest rooms and apartment, private baths, sauna, continental breakfast

a reflection of Alaska's skewed demographics! Women or couples can get a shared room for $35 pp or a private room for $47 pp. During midsummer, spaces may not be available at all—especially in the private rooms—so be sure to reserve well in advance. The inn has a TV/recreation room, communal kitchen, washing machine, no curfew, and lots of chain-smokers. No alcohol allowed. Warning: Some readers have complained of filthy conditions and poor management at Rain Forest Inn; women may not feel safe here. Check out the rooms before putting down any money on this place.

Some of the nicer local lodging options are the various B&Bs, such as **Innside Passage B&B, Captain's Quarters B&B, House of Stewart B&B,** and **Oyster Ave. B&B.** See the lodging chart for specifics on these and others. Your best bet may be calling **Ketchikan Reservation Service,** tel. (907) 247-5337 or (800) 987-5337. They book rooms in most of Ketchikan's 20 or so B&Bs, priced $60-80 d.

The historic **New York Hotel** is a pleasant eight-room hotel that has been painstakingly restored to its Roaring '20s heyday condition. Good downtown location, but things can get a bit noisy with street traffic at night. If you're on a *very* tight budget and are desperate for a place for a week or more, you might try **Union Rooms Hotel,** 319 Mill St., tel. (907) 225-3580. Take a look at the rooms before putting down any money here. At the other end of the spectrum is the elaborate **Westmark Cape Fox Lodge,** tel. (907) 225-8001 or (800) 544-0970.

Camping

There are no campsites in town, but in a pinch folks have been known to camp in the small city park a few blocks uphill and directly across from the ferry terminal. Don't leave a tent up during the day if you try this.

The Forest Service operates three excellent campgrounds in the scenic Ward Lake area north of town. All have running water, outhouses, picnic tables, and a seven-day camping limit, and can be reserved ($8.25 extra) by calling (800) 287-2267. Hitching from town is relatively easy. Head five miles north from the ferry terminal and turn right just before the pulp mill at Ward Creek Road. Ward Cove is a good place to see eagles and salmon, so stop for a look before heading up to the lake. The first and

most popular camping area is **Signal Creek Campground,** three-quarters of a mile up the road, and along the shore of Ward Lake ($8). A quarter-mile farther is the tiny **Three-C's Campground;** $8. During the winter this is the only one open. Another 1.5 miles north is **Last Chance Campground;** $10.

Settler's Cove State Park, 16 miles north of the ferry, charges $6 for campsites but is primarily used by RVers. The beach here is a popular picnic spot. While at Settler's Cove, be sure to hike the 100-yard trail that ends at a platform overlooking an impressive falls. The creek is a good place to watch spawning pink salmon. **Clover Pass Resort,** 12 miles north of the ferry, tel. (907) 247-2234, charges $20 for full RV hookups.

FOOD

Although not renowned for its food, Ketchikan has a number of places worth a visit. On Sundays, 9 a.m.-2 p.m., the **VFW Hall** at 311 Tongass (one-half mile south of the ferry) serves up filling all-American breakfasts. Located right across from the ferry terminal, **The Landing Restaurant,** tel. (907) 225-5166, is a very popular breakfast place. If you just want to relax and enjoy looking over busy Tongass Narrows, stop by **Coffee Connections,** 521 Water St., for a cup of espresso or a pastry. **5-Star Cafe,** on the north end of Creek St., serves earthy sandwiches, soups, salads, and espresso coffees (locally roasted Ravens Brew brand). 5-Star also has breakfasts. Note the inlaid five-pointed star on the floor; the cafe was originally a dance hall and bordello. It's a good place to meet the artist/greenie crowd. Head upstairs to **Jeremiah's** for lunch and dinner, including a Friday noontime buffet that's worth a try.

Another favorite of locals is **Roller Bay Cafe** inside the bowling alley at 2050 Sea Level Dr., tel. (907) 225-0690. You'll also find Godfather's Pizza at Roller Bay, completing this rather bizarre mix of businesses. Get fresh juices, smoothies, herbal teas, and organic vegan fare at **The Sun Dance,** 432 Dock St., tel. (907) 247-6551.

Papa's Ketchikan Cafe, 314 Front St. (upstairs), tel. (907) 247-7272, serves well-prepared meals including gourmet pizzas, Italian sandwiches, salads, soups, and burgers. It's

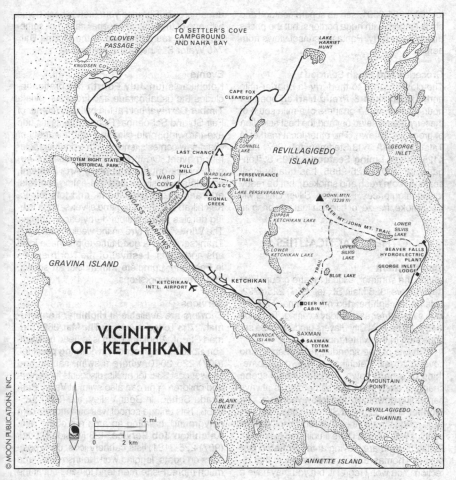

VICINITY OF KETCHIKAN

open for lunch and dinner only. Also popular for pizzas is **Harbor Lights Pizza,** 2131 Tongass Ave., tel. (907) 225-7111. Harbor Lights has a great selection of beers at decent prices and a fine view of Bar Harbor. More pizza at **Chico's,** 435 Dock St., tel. (907) 225-2833, but the house specialty is authentic Mexican food.

New York Hotel Cafe, 207 Stedman St., specializes in gourmet seafood and has an espresso bar. Very good. **Annabelle's,** 326 Front St., tel. (907) 225-6609, wins the "best atmosphere" prize among Ketchikan restaurants, and has an irresistible menu of seafood (including delicious

chowders), pasta, and steaks. There are daily specials as well as cocktails and espresso. A fine place to impress that special person you met on the ferry.

The best local chicken sandwiches, salmon burgers, and hamburgers can be found at the tiny **Burger Queen** just north of the Front Street tunnel. Definitely recommended. **McDonald's** is in the shopping mall, three-quarters of a mile south of the ferry, and the local **Subway** is downtown at 415 Dock Street.

Héen Kahídi Restaurant and Lounge inside the Cape Fox Westmark, 800 Venetia Way, tel. (907) 225-8001, serves superb seafood and steak dinners with huge portions, but the prices match the quality. Fantastic sunset views from here.

Groceries and Fresh Seafood

The closest store to the ferry (a quarter-mile north) is **Alaskan & Proud Market,** open 24 hours. **Carrs,** three-quarters of a mile south of the ferry, has a salad bar and the best selection of groceries in town. The other local market is **Tatsuda's IGA,** 633 Stedman, tel. (907) 225-4125. **Silver Lining Seafoods,** 1705 S. Tongass, tel. (907) 225-9865, has quality local seafood (both fresh and smoked), but be ready for sky-high prices. For a fee, Silver Lining will also smoke, freeze, or can fish that you bring in.

OTHER PRACTICALITIES

Entertainment

During the summer, a local theatre group, First City Players, 338 Main St., tel. (907) 225-4792, puts on the lighthearted melodrama, *Fish Pirate's Daughter* each Friday evening. The price is $8 pp. The First City Players produce more serious stuff in the winter months.

With lots of free-spending fishermen and no cover charges, Ketchikan is known as something of a party town. The live music scene changes each year, but something is always happening downtown; just follow your ears. The **Pioneer Bar,** 122 Front St., often has a country band rolling through the tunes, but things can get pretty rowdy here. If Dave Rubin and his rockin' Potlatch Band are playing at the **Potlatch Bar** next to Thomas Basin, make tracks in that direction. You won't regret it, but you may have a hard time finding space to breathe. Other places for live music are **Raven's Roost** and **First City Saloon.** First City tends to bring in the better-known bands. The **Alaska Bar,** 116 Front St., has a motto worth putting into practice: "Celebrating the repeal of Prohibition every day!"

Jeremiah's, across from the ferry, has mellow rock tunes five nights a week. It's a nice place to get romantic. The finest bar views are from the **Cape Fox Westmark,** overlooking town above Creek Street. The **Arctic Bar,** near the Front St. tunnel, has a pleasant patio hanging over Tongass Narrows, and attracts the biker/fisherman crowd. Surprise your friends back home with one of their risqué baseball caps. For something more raunchy, head to the **Marine Bar,** 740 Water St., the local strip joint.

Events

Ketchikan's fun **July Fourth** celebration includes the usual parade and fireworks, plus a **Timber Carnival** held at the ball field (corner of Fair St. and Schoenbar Road). Events include axe-throwing, pole-climbing, and a variety of chain-saw contests, ending with a dramatic pole-felling event. On the second Saturday of August, check out the **Blueberry Arts Festival,** complete with slug races, pie-eating contests, arts and crafts exhibitions, and folk music. Ketchikan also has king and silver salmon fishing derbies and a halibut derby each summer. The **Winter Arts Faire** on the weekend following Thanksgiving is a good time to purchase local arts and crafts. **Festival of the North** arrives in February, complete with music, art shows, and various workshops.

Services

Showers are available at **Highliner Laundromat,** 2703 Tongass Ave.; or **The Mat,** 989 Stedman Street. A better option is to head up Madison St. to the high school **swimming pool,** tel. (907) 225-2010, where a swim, sauna, and shower cost $3-5 for adults, discounts for seniors and children. You can also swim at Valley Park Grade School in Bear Valley, tel. (907) 225-8755. This unique school was built atop its own playground, creating an area out of the rain. **Ketchikan Job Service,** 423 Mission St., tel. (907) 225-3181, lists cannery jobs, crew positions on boats, logging work, tourism jobs, and much more. Fishermen tend to hang out at the Potlatch and Arctic Bars, or you might try checking local bulletin boards on the public docks. The **Seamen's Center,** 423 Mission St., tel. (907) 225-6003, is a great place to go if you live on the sea. There's a TV room, showers, washers and dryer, plus a library. Those looking for work on a boat might try talking to folks here. **Mountain Point,** 5.5 miles south of Ketchikan, is a good spot to try your luck at salmon fishing from the shore. Locals do much of their shopping at **Plaza Portwest Mall,** centering around Carrs and McDonald's, with a couple dozen other shops, including Bon Marché, Jay Jacobs,

Zales, and Plaza Sports. Get fast cash from **ATMs** at First Bank and National Bank of Alaska downtown, and at the Carrs and A&P grocery stores.

Information

The **Ketchikan Visitors Bureau** is right on the downtown dock at 141 Front St., tel. (907) 225-6166. It's open Mon.-Fri. 8 a.m.-5 p.m. and Sat.-Sun. 7 a.m.-4 p.m. (longer when the cruise ships are docked) May-Sept.; and Mon.-Fri. 8 a.m.-5 p.m. the rest of the year. Pick up their free map with a walking tour of local sites.

The outstanding **Southeast Alaska Visitors Information Center** (a.k.a. SEAVIC, not to be confused with the Civic Center) is on the downtown dock at 50 Main St., tel. (907) 228-6214. Pick up a Tongass map ($4) and make Forest Service cabin reservations here for the Ketchikan area and other parts of Tongass National Forest. Open daily 8:30 a.m.-4:30 p.m. April-Oct., and Tues.-Sat. 8:30 a.m.-4:30 p.m. the rest of the year. See "Sights" above for details on SEAVIC.

The Forest Service offices for **Ketchikan and Misty Fjords** ranger districts (open Mon.-Fri. 8 a.m.-5 p.m.) at 3031 Tongass, tel. (907) 225-2148, are a half-mile south of the ferry terminal. Be sure to talk to the staff here if you're planning a hiking or kayaking trip into the surrounding country. They can also make cabin reservations. The main **post office** is next to the ferry terminal on the north end of town, and a branch post office is downtown in the Great Alaskan Clothing Company at 422 Mission Street.

Arts and Crafts

A surprisingly creative town, Ketchikan is home to a number of fine artists; it even made it into a national ranking of the "100 best small art towns in America." Because of all the tourists, downtown is crowded with all sorts of gift shops selling trinkets and trashy art to folks who should know better. Head to the better places. These include **Alaska Eagle Arts,** tel. (907) 225-8365, downstairs in the 5-Star Cafe building on Creek St.; and **Soho Coho,** tel. (907) 225-5954, just upstairs. The latter is owned by Ketchikan's best known and loopiest artist, that master of all things weird and fishy, **Ray Troll.** You can find T-shirts with his designs all over the West. Check out his latest design concepts on the bul-

letin board; when I last visited, it was a Gen-X fly fisher with a fishing lure through his tongue. Twisted, but funny. For more artwork, head to the gallery of the **Ketchikan Area Arts Council,** 338 Main St., tel. (907) 225- 2211. "Wearable art" is on sale here, too.

Books

Ketchikan's **public library,** 629 Dock St., tel. (907) 225-3331, is open Sunday 1-5 p.m., Mon.-Wed. 10 a.m.-8 p.m., and Thurs.-Sat. 10 a.m.-6 p.m. Inside, find an excellent collection of Alaskana. An afternoon of reading at the tables along the big windows overlooking Ketchikan Creek is a pleasant alternative to soaking in the rain. You can also watch nature videos on a TV (with headphones). A book-lover's bookstore, **Parnassus Bookstore,** tel. (907) 225-7690, is upstairs in the 5-Star Cafe building on Creek Street. Sit down and talk with the friendly owner, Lillian Ference, about the latest Ketchikan news. Parnassus stocks an especially impressive collection of women's books. The other bookstore in town is **Waldenbooks** in Plaza Portwest Mall.

TRANSPORTATION

Ferry

Ketchikan's ferry terminal is two miles northwest of downtown, right next to the post office. The terminal is open Mon-Fri. 9 a.m.-4:30 p.m., and when ships are in port. Call (907) 225-6182 during business hours, or (907) 225-6181 for recorded arrival and departure times. During the summer, ferries provide service to Hyder/Stewart ($40) two or three times a month, and almost-daily runs to Prince Rupert ($38), Hollis ($20), Metlakatla ($14), Wrangell ($24), and points north. Ferry service to Bellingham ($164) is once a week.

Buses and Tours

The **city bus** ($1 each direction) runs throughout Ketchikan (including from the ferry terminal to town) every half-hour Mon.-Fri. 5:30 a.m.-9:30 p.m. and Saturday 6:45 a.m.-7 p.m. Schedules are available at the visitors bureau. In town, catch it at the library or near the tunnel at Front and Grant Streets. It's generally quite easy to hitch around Ketchikan, though you're considerably less likely to be picked up if you're soak-

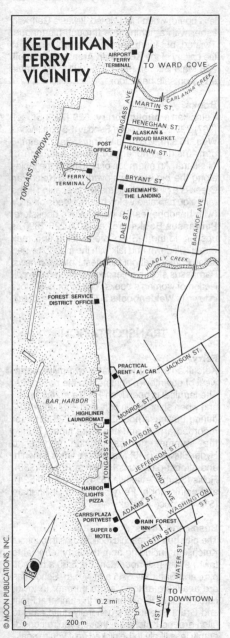

KETCHIKAN
FERRY
VICINITY

AIRPORT
FERRY
TERMINAL

TO WARD COVE

CARLANNA CREEK

TONGASS AVE

MARTIN ST.

HENEGHAN ST.

ALASKAN &
PROUD MARKET

POST
OFFICE

HECKMAN ST.

TONGASS NARROWS

FERRY
TERMINAL

BRYANT ST.

JEREMIAH'S/
THE LANDING

DALE ST.

BARANOF AVE

HOADLY CREEK

FOREST SERVICE
DISTRICT OFFICE

PRACTICAL
RENT - A - CAR

JACKSON ST.

BAR HARBOR

HIGHLINER
LAUNDROMAT

MONROE ST.

MADISON ST.

JEFFERSON ST.

TONGASS AVE

2ND AVE

HARBOR
LIGHTS
PIZZA

CARRS/PLAZA
PORTWEST

SUPER 8
MOTEL

ADAMS ST.

RAIN FOREST
INN

WASHINGTON ST

AUSTIN ST.

WATER ST.

TO
DOWNTOWN

1ST AVE

© MOON PUBLICATIONS, INC.

0   0.2 mi

0   200 m

ing wet. Local **tour buses** meet most ferries and provide two-hour city tours for $20. If you are staying in town and want a tour, head to the visitors bureau, where a number of tour operators have booths. Rates start at $15 for a quick, hour-long tour. These are mostly for cruise ship visitors. Also popular with the same crowd are the two-hour waterfront cruises ($45) offered by **Outdoor Alaska,** tel. (907) 225-6044. A better deal is their two-hour Saturday evening cruise for $15, including hors d'oeuvres.

Cabs and Cars

The local taxi companies are **Alaska Cab Co.,** tel. (907) 225-2133; **Sourdough Cab,** tel. (907) 225-5544; and **Yellow Taxi,** tel. (907) 225-5555. They charge about $8 from the ferry to downtown, $9 from downtown to Saxman, or $44 per hour (up to five people).

Because Ketchikan's sights are so spread out, renting a car is a good idea, particularly if you're able to get several folks together on the deal. Rental rates start around $45 from **Practical Rent-A-Car,** tel. (907) 225-8778 or (800) 233-1663; and **Alaska Car Rental,** 2828 Tongass, tel. (907) 225-5000 or (800) 478-0007 (in Alaska). **Avis,** at the airport, tel. (907) 225-4515 or (800) 331-1212, charges more, and you'll need to add on the ferry fee ($5 each way) from the airport. All three companies include unlimited mileage on their cars, but the limited roads around Ketchikan keep you from driving an unlimited amount, unless you just want to drive up and down Tongass Avenue.

By Air

Ketchikan Airport is on Gravina Island, directly across Tongass Narrows from the ferry terminal. The **airport ferry,** tel. (907) 225-6800, $2.50 pp roundtrip, operates every half-hour daily 6:15 a.m.-9:30 p.m.; more frequently in the summer. The **Airporter Bus,** tel. (907) 225-5429, has shuttle service into town from the airport for an exorbitant $8-12 each way. The price varies, depending upon your destination, and includes the ferry fare. They meet all jets.

Alaska Airlines, tel. (800) 426-0333, has flights from Ketchikan to Juneau, Petersburg, Sitka, Wrangell, and other cities in Alaska and the Lower 48. **Taquan Air,** 1007 Water St., tel. (907) 225-8800 or (800) 770-8800, has daily floatplane service to Coffman Cove ($69), Craig ($76), Hollis ($49), Hydaburg ($80), Kasaan, ($43), Klawock ($76), Metlakatla ($26), Prince Rupert ($91), and Thorne Bay ($51), as well as a variety of logging camps on Prince of Wales Island and elsewhere. They also fly every Monday and Thursday to Hyder ($80). **Ketchikan Air Service,** 1427 Tongass Ave., tel. (907) 225-6600 or (800) 656-6608, has daily scheduled service to Coffman Cove ($75), Craig/Klawock ($75 from the airport), Hollis ($53), Juneau ($132), Kake ($175), Kasaan, ($50), Petersburg ($117), Point Baker ($110), Point Protection ($110), Thorne Bay ($55), Whale Pass ($85), and Wrangell ($107). They also fly to the many logging camps, fishing villages, and resorts on Prince of Wales.

Taquan and Ketchikan Air, along with **Island Wings Air Service,** tel. (907) 225-2444; Seaborne Aviation, tel. (907) 225-3424; **Promech Air,** tel. (907) 225-3845 or (800) 860-3845; and **Misty Fjords Air and Outfitting,** 1285 Tongass, tel. (907) 225-5155, all have flightseeing trips to Misty Fjords (around $130 pp for 90 minutes) and offer air-taxi service to nearby Forest Service cabins. Island Wings is a unique one-woman business run by Michelle Masden, one of the few female commercial floatplane pilots in Alaska. Expect to pay around $280/hour for a Cessna 185 (two people with gear), or $400/hour for a Beaver (up to five people with gear). Taquan Air and Ketchikan Air Service also have shorter sightseeing trips, including a 15-minute flight over Ketchikan ($35 pp), and a three-hour trip to Anan Creek, where you can watch black bears catching salmon ($198 pp).

VICINITY OF KETCHIKAN

MISTY FJORDS NATIONAL MONUMENT

The 3,600-square-mile Misty Fjords National Monument is the largest national forest wilderness in the U.S., covering the east side of Revillagigedo Island, the adjacent mainland all the way to the Canadian border, and the long narrow Behm Canal that separates island and mainland. Misty contains a diversity of spectacular scenery—glaciers, rainforests, narrow fjords, and rugged mountains—but is best known for the spectacular cliffs that rise as much as 3,000 feet from the ocean. Almost unknown until its establishment in 1978, Misty Fjords is today one of the highlights of an Alaskan trip for many visitors. Be forewarned, however, it's an expensive highlight.

Flightseeing and Boat Tours
On any given summer day, flightseeing planes constantly take off from Tongass Narrows for trips over the monument. Ninety-minute flightseeing trips cost approximately $129 pp (including a water landing) from **Misty Fjords Air and Outfitting,** tel. (907) 225-5155; **Taquan Air Service,** tel. (907) 225-9668 or (800) 770-8800; or **Ketchikan Air Service,** tel. (907) 225-6608 or (800) 656-6608.

Another excellent way to see Misty is by boat. **Outdoor Alaska,** 220 Front St., tel. (907) 225-6044, runs top-notch cruises into Misty Fjords from June to Labor Day. Prices begin at $145 pp ($110 for children) with lunch included for an 11-hour cruise, or $185 pp ($150 for children) for a faster trip that includes a flightseeing return back to Ketchikan (or vice versa). Trips depart only on Sunday, Tuesday, Thursday, and Saturday. Ask about discounts if you take your chances and book standby the day before.

Kayak Trips
The best way to see Misty Fjords is from a kayak. You can paddle there from Ketchikan, but only if you're experienced and adequately prepared. For $180 roundtrip, Outdoor Alaska does drop-offs and pickups at the head of Rudyerd Bay. Those with folding kayaks may opt for flying one way and taking the boat the other direction. Pickup points are anywhere along their daily tour route. **Southeast Exposure,** 507 Stedman St., tel. (907) 225-8829, provides four-to eight-day kayak trips into Misty that start at $655 pp. These are coordinated with Outdoor Alaska's drop-off runs. If you are going on your own, rent kayaks from Southeast Exposure for $35/day for singles or $50/day for doubles (discounts for longer periods). Kayakers should be

warned that flightseeing planes and cruise ships may impact your wilderness experience in Rudyerd Bay, but other areas get far less use.

Trails, Cabins, and Information

Misty Fjords National Monument has 14 recreation cabins ($25/night). Those near magnificent **Rudyerd Bay** are very popular, and reservations must be made months in advance. There are also 10 trails that take you from saltwater to scenic lakes, most with cabins or free three-sided shelters. Two of the best trails lead up to shelters at Punchbowl and Nooya Lakes. The three-quarter-mile **Punchbowl Lake Trail** switchbacks up from Rudyerd Bay, passing spectacular Punchbowl Creek Waterfall on the way. Punchbowl is one of the finest short hikes in Southeast Alaska. Both brown and black bears may be encountered on any of these trails, so be certain to make plenty of noise and to hang all food. The Forest Service maintains a floating bunkhouse/barge for its field crews near Winstanley Island, and there is usually someone onboard who can answer your questions.

Before heading out on any overnight trips into Misty, talk with staff at the District Office, 1817 Tongass, tel. (907) 225-2148; or write to Misty Fjords National Monument, Box 6137, Ketchikan, AK 99901. They can provide information on trail conditions, campsites, and what to expect. Be sure to request a copy of their excellent map of Misty Fjords ($3).

METLAKATLA

Twelve miles southwest of Ketchikan on the western shore of Annette Island is the planned community of Metlakatla (pop. 1,500). Metlakatla (meaning "Saltwater Channel" in Tsimshian) is Alaska's only Indian reservation, a status that was reaffirmed in 1971 when its residents refused to join other Native groups under the Alaska Native Claims Settlement Act. It is the only predominantly Tsimshian settlement in Alaska and the only place in the United States where fish traps are still legal.

The quiet, conservative town has a strong religious heritage and the air of a pioneer village. Large frame houses occupy big corner lots, while vacant lots yield abundant berry crops. There seems to be a church on every corner—eight in all, none of them Catholic. Children are also abundant—nearly a third of the population in grade-school! Like much of Southeast, Metlakatla boasts a flourishing cannery, cold-storage facility, fish hatchery, and sawmill. Most of Annette Island is wooded mountainous terrain reaching up to 3,500 feet, but the town of Metlakatla spreads out across a large, relatively flat portion of the island that contains many muskegs and lakes.

History

In 1887, a Tsimshian Indian group left Canada in search of religious freedom in Alaska. They discovered an abandoned Tlingit settlement on Annette Island offering a sheltered bay, gently sloping beaches, and a beautiful nearby waterfall. Under the direction of Anglican missionary William Duncan, who established a similar community in Metlakatla, Canada (see "Vicinity of Prince Rupert" under "Prince Rupert and the North Coast" in the Gateways chapter), 823 Tsimshian followers began clearing a townsite. The converts took new Christian names, dressed in suits, and abandoned much of their cultural heritage. At Metlakatla, Alaska, the settlers established a sawmill to produce lumber for the construction of houses and the first cannery.

The most ambitious building erected was a 1,000-seat church, "The Westminster Abbey of Alaska." It burned in 1948 but was replaced by a replica six years later. In 1891, the U.S. Congress granted the Tsimshians the entire 86,000-acre island as a reserve, a right they jealously guard to this day. Duncan maintained his hold over most aspects of life here until 1913 when a government school opened. (Duncan's paternalism extended in other directions, too: rumors persist that the bachelor fathered many Metlakatla children.) He opposed the school, preferring that education remain in the hands

BOB RACE

METLAKATLA

of his church. The ensuing conflict led to intervention by the U.S. Department of the Interior in 1915, which seized the sawmill, cannery, and other facilities that had been under his personal control. Duncan died three years later, but his memory is still revered by many, and his influence can still be seen in the healthy little Indian settlement of today. For a fascinating account of Father Duncan and the two Metlakatlas, read Peter Murray's *The Devil and Mr. Duncan* (Sono Nis Press, Victoria, B.C.).

During WW II, the U.S. Army constructed a major military base seven miles from Metlakatla on Annette Island. The base included observation towers (to search for Japanese subs), a large airfield, hangars, communications towers, shore batteries, and housing for 10,000 men. At the time the airport was built, it was the most expensive one ever constructed by the government—everything kept sinking out of sight into the marshy muskeg. Until construction of an airport on Gravina Island in 1973, this airfield was used for jet service to Ketchikan, forcing passengers to land on Annette and fly by floatplane to Ketchikan. With the area's notorious weather, delays were common; many times it

took longer to get the last dozen miles to Ketchikan than the 600 miles from Seattle to Annette Island.

Sights
Father Duncan's Cottage, tel. (907) 886-6926—where the missionary lived from 1894 until his death in 1918—is open as a museum Mon.-Fri. 10 a.m.-noon ($1) or by request on weekends, tel. (907) 886-7363. The old photographs of Metlakatla and the fascinating assortment of personal items owned by Duncan make a stop here a must. The rather run-down **William Duncan Memorial Church** (built in 1954) stands at the corner of Fourth Ave. and Church Street. Duncan's grave is on the left side. Also visit the New Small Boat Harbor where a traditional **longhouse** (open Mon.-Fri. afternoons) has been erected to stimulate local arts and crafts and to help recover the cultural traditions lost because of Duncan's missionary zeal. Inside are a small library and a model of one of the four floating fish traps used on the island. One of these traps is often visible near the ferry terminal. See "Transportation and Tours" below for details on dance performances at the longhouse. Annette Island Can-

FISH TRAPS

The floating fish trap was developed in 1907 and quickly proved an amazingly efficient way to catch salmon. The traps were constructed with heavy wire netting that directed migrating salmon into progressively smaller enclosures. All one had to do was wait. The traps were hated by most Alaskans because they were owned by "Outsiders" who could afford the high construction and maintenance costs, and because their efficiency took jobs from local fishermen. Their efficiency also robbed many streams of needed brood stock. For many years these traps brought in over half of Southeast Alaska's salmon catch. Locals got even by stealing fish from the traps, and those who did often became folk heroes. As a territory, Alaska had no say in its own affairs, but when statehood came in 1959, the first act of the state legislature was to outlaw all fish traps. Only the Annette Island Reservation (which manages all waters within 3,000 feet of the island, and sets its own fish and game regulations) still operates the floating fish traps.

nery and Cold Storage dominates the waterfront, and the lumber mill is not far away.

Hiking

Unlike almost everywhere else in Alaska, there are no bears on Annette Island, a relief to those who fear encounters with bruins. A short hiking trail runs from the corner of Milton St. and Airport Rd. on the southeast edge of town along **Skaters Lake,** a large pond where native plants and ducks can be observed. **Yellow Hill,** a 540-foot tall fragment of 150-million-year-old sandstone, is unique in Southeast Alaska. The rock is rich in iron and magnesium, giving it a lovely desertlike yellow color set off by gnarled old lodgepole pines. An easy boardwalk trail (20 minutes one-way) leads up to its summit where you get panoramic vistas of the western side of Annette, along with the snowcapped peaks of nearby Prince of Wales Island. A noisy wind generator disturbs your peace at the top. Get there by walking or hitching 1.5 miles south from town on Airport Rd. to the signed trailhead on the right side. Some people claim to see George Washington's profile in Yellow Hill.

Two trails access alpine lakes in the mountains east of Metlakatla. The **Chester Lake Trail** starts at the end of the road, a quarter-mile beyond the ferry terminal. From the trail you get views over the impressive **Chester Lake Falls,** which first attracted Duncan's flock to Annette Island. The trail climbs very steeply up steps and a slippery path along a waterline used for power generation. Plan on 45 minutes to reach beautiful Chester Lake, where there is a small dam. From this point, the country is above timberline and it's possible to climb along several nearby ridges for even better views. Good camping sites are available, but be careful coming up the steep, slippery path with a pack.

Farther afield and not quite as scenic is the **Purple Lake Trail.** Take Airport Rd. four miles south of town and turn left near the Quonset huts at the unmarked Purple Mt. Road. Follow it two miles to the power plant. The unmarked trail heads directly up a steep jeep road. After a 30-minute climb, you reach a saddle and from there you can head up adjacent ridges into the alpine or drop down to Purple Lake (10 minutes). Another place worth a look is the aptly named **Sand Dollar Beach** on the southwest end of the island. Ask locally for directions.

By Bike

The flat country around Metlakatla contains a labyrinth of dirt roads built during WW II, and if you have a mountain bike or car, they're well worth exploring. You'll find abandoned structures of all types: huge communication towers, strangely quiet empty hangars, old gun emplacements, and a major airport with no planes. From the south end of the road network are excellent views of Prince of Wales and Duke Islands, as well as the open sea beyond Dixon Entrance. This is the southernmost road in Alaska.

Practicalities

Metlakatla Hotel and Suites, tel. (907) 886-3456, has rooms; or try Bernita Brendible, tel. (907) 886-7563, who also makes traditional spruce-root baskets. Several other locals produce craftwork: Ray Holt, Jack Hudson, and Jimmy Casperson; ask locally for directions.

Meals (mainly burgers and Mexican fare) are available at **JV Burger Bar** and several other little places, but in general you're better off heading to **Leask's Market** for food. Check the bulletin board here for such items as hand-carved fossil ivory or fresh Ooligan grease (if you don't know what it is, you probably won't like it). Note that Metlakatla is (officially) a dry town, and alcoholic beverages are not allowed on the island.

The staff at the mayor's office in the **municipal building,** tel. (907) 886-4868, may be able to provide some local information or try the **Metlakatla Indian Community Council Chamber,** tel. (907) 886-4868. Camping is discouraged, and visitors who want to stay on Annette Island more than five days must obtain a special permit from the city. A local sponsor is required, and fishing is not allowed. The **Lepquinum Activity Center,** next to the high school, houses an Olympic-size swimming pool, plus a weight room, sauna, and showers. Out front is **Raven and the Tide Woman Totem,** with a descriptive plaque. Although Metlakatla is only a dozen miles away from Ketchikan, it gets 118 inches of precipitation per year, 44 inches less than Ketchikan. Locals celebrate the establishment of Metlakatla each year on **Founder's Day,** August 7. As with most other American towns, Metlakatla also has festivities on July Fourth.

Transportation and Tours

Metlakatla's **Ferry terminal** is a mile east of town. Ferries generally stop for only a half-hour or so. During the summer, the *Aurora* connects Metlakatla and Ketchikan four days a week for $14 one-way. Local cops often check passengers for smuggled booze on arrival. On Saturdays, the ferry schedule allows for an early Ketchikan departure and a return trip that evening, a good opportunity to visit this interesting little town. For a taxi ride to town, call Dee White at (907) 886-1212. **Taquan Air Service,** tel. (907) 225-8800, (800) 770-8800, flies daily between Ketchikan and Metlakatla for $36 roundtrip.

A **Metlakatla Tour & Salmon Bake** is offered during the summer months for $89 pp. This includes roundtrip floatplane transport from Ketchikan, a tribal dance in regalia at the longhouse, a tour of the fish cannery and fish traps, and an all-you-can-eat dinner of baked salmon or halibut. Call (907) 247-8737 or (800) 643-4898 for details.

HYDER AND STEWART

The twin towns of Hyder, Alaska, and Stewart, British Columbia, lie at the head of the long, narrow Portland Canal that separates Canada and the United States. The area's remoteness has kept it one of the relatively undiscovered gems of the entire Pacific Northwest coast. Most people arrive via the stunning drive down Highway 37A from Meziadin Junction into Stewart, passing beautiful lakes, majestic glaciers, high waterfalls, spectacular mountain peaks, the narrow Bear River Canyon, and finally the mountain-rimmed, water-trimmed towns. The ferry trip through Portland Canal gives close-up vistas of one of the wildest stretches along the British Columbia and Alaska coastlines. Early in the season numerous black bears frolic along the shore, and porpoises are common in the fjord.

The town of Stewart (pop. 2,200), lies at the mouth of the Bear River, while tiny Hyder (pop. 100), is three km down the road next to the Salmon River. They are as different as two towns could possibly be. Stewart is the "real" town, with a hospital, churches, schools, a museum, a pharmacy, a bank, and the other necessities of life; it bills itself as Canada's northernmost ice-free port. In contrast, Hyder, "the friendliest ghost town in Alaska," makes the most of its flaky reputation. Between the two settlements lies an international boundary that is virtually ignored. There are no border check stations. Residents buy their liquor in Alaska and send their kids to school in British Columbia. Everyone uses Canadian currency and the Canadian phone system (area code 604). The Royal Canadian Mounted Police patrol both Stewart and Hyder. You can, however, mail letters from a post office in either country, saving postage and the hassles of shipping parcels internationally.

History

In 1793, Capt. George Vancouver, searching for the fabled Northwest Passage, turned into Portland Canal. For days his men worked their boats up the narrow fjord, but when they reached its end after so many miles he was "mortified with having devoted so much time to so little purpose." Over a century later the area finally began to develop. In 1896, Capt. David

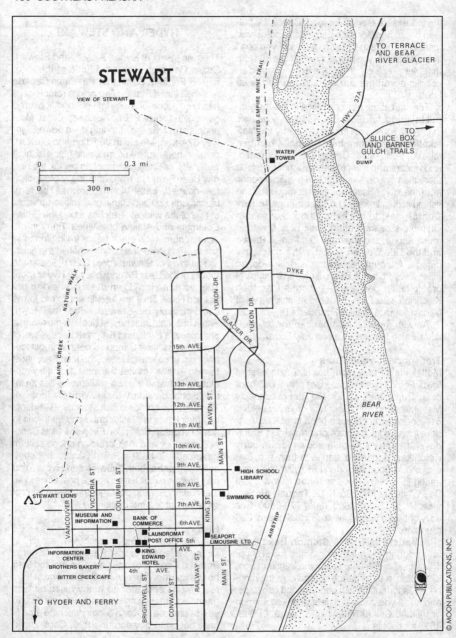

STEWART

VIEW OF STEWART

UNITED EMPIRE MINE TRAIL

TO TERRACE AND BEAR RIVER GLACIER

HWY. 37A

WATER TOWER

TO SLUICE BOX AND BARNEY GULCH TRAILS

DUMP

0   0.3 mi

0   300 m

NATURE WALK

RAINE CREEK

DYKE

YUKON DR.

YUKON DR.

GLACIER DR.

15th AVE.

13th AVE.

12th AVE.

11th AVE.

10th AVE.

9th AVE.

8th AVE.

7th AVE.

6th AVE.

5th AVE.

4th AVE.

RAVEN ST.

MAIN ST.

KING ST.

BEAR RIVER

HIGH SCHOOL/ LIBRARY

SWIMMING POOL

AIRSTRIP

VICTORIA ST.

COLUMBIA ST.

VANCOUVER

STEWART LIONS

MUSEUM AND INFORMATION

BANK OF COMMERCE

LAUNDROMAT

POST OFFICE

SEAPORT LIMOUSINE LTD.

INFORMATION CENTER

BROTHERS BAKERY

BITTER CREEK CAFE

KING EDWARD HOTEL

BRIGHTWELL ST.

CONWAY ST.

RAILWAY ST.

MAIN ST.

TO HYDER AND FERRY

© MOON PUBLICATIONS, INC.

MOON

Gilliard of the Army Corps of Engineers (for whom Gilliard Cut in the Panama Canal was later named) explored the region and left behind four stone storehouses, Alaska's first masonry buildings. Prospectors soon arrived and found an incredible wealth of gold, silver, and other minerals in the nearby mountains. Stewart received its name from two of its earliest settlers, Robert and John Stewart. The adjacent Alaskan town was initially named Portland City, but postal authorities, wary of yet another Portland, vetoed it. Instead, the town was named after Frederick B. Hyder, a Canadian mining engineer.

Gold fever and the prospect of a transcontinental Canadian railway terminus attracted more than 10,000 newcomers to the area. The steep, mountainous terrain was difficult to build on; much of Hyder was constructed on pilings driven into the mudflats. The planned railroad made it only a few miles out of town, but in 1919 prospectors struck it rich. The Premier Gold and Silver Mine was, until its 1948 closure, the largest gold mine in North America. After it shut down, the local population dwindled to less than a thousand until development of the Granduc copper mine in the 1960s. To reach the rich Leduc ore vein, workers dug the longest tunnel ever built from one end, 18 km. A devastating avalanche in 1965 buried 40 men in a tunnel entrance, killing 27 of them. The mine operated until 1984 when it was closed down and completely dismantled; the site was restored to a relatively natural condition.

The spectacular Stewart/Hyder area served as the location of several B-movies: *Bear Island, The Thing,* and *Iceman.* Recent years have also seen sporadic promises of new gold, silver, coal, or asbestos mines, but times have been hard of late. As one local told me, "The Moose Park Graveyard is full of people still waiting for Hyder to boom."

Sights
The fine **Stewart Historical Society Museum** (C$2) at Columbia and Sixth, tel. (604) 636-2568, is housed in the old Fire Hall (1910). It has wildlife specimens on the first floor as well as numerous historical items both upstairs and out front. Many of the items are from the region's rich mining history. It is open Mon.-Fri. 1-4 p.m.,

Saturday and Sunday noon-5 p.m. or by appointment.

On the U.S. side of the international border stands a tiny stone **storehouse** built in 1896 by Captain Gilliard. The building looks like an old jail and once served that purpose, but for much of its life it was a shoe repair shop. On the mudflats in front of Hyder are hundreds of old pilings, remnants of what was once a town of 1,000 people. The straight row of pilings in front of Stewart is all that remains of the aborted transcontinental railroad.

Nearby Sights
About five km out of Hyder is **Fish Creek.** In summer (especially August) its waters are filled with pink salmon, along with some of the world's largest chum salmon—some weighing up to 14 kg. A viewing platform here provides an excellent vantage point over an artificial spawning channel where black bears catch salmon. Nearby are remains of an old brothel operated by Dolly, Ketchikan's best-known madam. No U.S. Forest Service cabins are near Hyder, but the beautiful **Chickamin Cabin** on Texas Lake may be available.

The old Premier and Big Missouri gold mines are 48 km beyond Hyder. Before heading out, be sure to ask about the snow level along the road. **Tide Lake** is the site of the world's greatest yearly snowfall: 28 meters in 1971.

Gorgeous **Bear River Glacier,** 37 km east of Stewart on Highway 37A, should not be missed. Like its more famous cousin, Juneau's Mendenhall, it is a "drive-up glacier" with the highway passing close to its base. The small lake in front is often filled with icebergs.

Hiking
The easiest local trail, **Raine Creek Nature Walk,** takes off from the Raine Creek Campground and follows the creek 2.5 km to the north end of town. The mountains around Stewart and Hyder are crisscrossed with old mining roads, great both for day-hikes and camping. The short and scenic **Barney Gulch/Sluice Box Trail** begins near the dump, just across the Bear River on the north edge of town. The **United Empire Mine Trail** starts from Quarry Rd. north of Stewart, and climbs to a viewpoint overlooking the Bear River Valley.

Ore Mountain Trail originates 13 km northeast of Stewart at Clements Lake, a good place for canoeing. An attractive campsite (free) is available near the trailhead. This four-km trail gains 1,100 meters as it climbs an old mining road to a small alpine lake. Plan on two and a half hours one-way for the hike. The Titan Trail starts near the bridge over Fish Creek (10 km out of Hyder) and climbs eight km up to the alpine. You'll also discover the remains of a 1920s mine up here. For maps and more info on these and other local hikes, contact the Stewart office of the British Columbia Forest Service at Eighth and Brightwell, tel. (604) 636-2663.

Accommodations and Camping

The best local hotel is Hyder's Grandview Inn, tel. (604) 636-9174, with rooms for C$60 s, or C$67 d. Sealaska Inn, tel. (604) 636-9003, also in Hyder, charges C$48 s or d with private baths and C$28 s or C$32 d in simple rooms with shared baths. RV hookups also available. Rooms can also be found at Stewart's King Edward Hotel/Motel, tel. (604) 636-2244, for C$55-65 s or C$65-73 d, but watch out for the tax, which tacks on another 15% (no tax on the Alaskan side).

Stewart Lions Campground in Stewart has tent spaces for C$10, and RV hookups for C$15. It's quietly situated on the edge of town and has a cookhouse, free firewood, and pay showers. The tenting area is across the creek.

Food

Several places serve meals in Stewart. Fong's Garden at Fifth and Conway has Chinese food and stays open late. The King Eddy is the locals' place with All-Canadian grub. Tourists prefer Bitter Creek Cafe, an upscale place in this otherwise homey and rough-at-the-edges town. The food includes pasta, Mexican, pizza, burgers, seafood, and nightly specials, along with espresso and an outside deck for a beer on a sunny summer day. Slow service because everything is made fresh. Get baked goods from Brothers Bakery, right next door.

Over in Hyder, Border Cafe, tel. (604) 636-2379, is a family restaurant serving breakfasts, burgers, and fish & chips. Sealaska Inn, tel. (604) 636-2486, offers burgers, steaks, and pizzas. They also serve booze. Get espresso from Salmon River Outpost, tel. (604) 636-9019,

and groceries from Dean's Groceries in Hyder (Canadian tax-free shopping), tel. (604) 636-2422. Other Hyder places sell guns, ammo, fireworks, and booze—all essentials of Alaskan life, but harder to find in Maple Leaf country.

Watering Holes

Hyder has two bars for fewer than a hundred inhabitants, and getting "Hyderized" is an experience that attracts folks from all over the world. Bartenders claim that the tradition began when prospectors would tack up a dollar bill on the wall, in case they were broke next trip into town. Today the walls of the Glacier Inn are papered with over thousands of dollars in signed bills left by previous initiates, creating the "world's most expensive wallpaper." Becoming Hyderized is cheap and lasts a lifetime (you even get an official card), but it could also prove expensive if you fail the test. Warning: it involves that frat house favorite, Everclear.

Events

The Stewart/Hyder International Rodeo in early June features team roping, bull riding, barrel racing, and other contests. Canada's Independence Day (July 1) and the American Independence Day (July 4) provide the opportunity for a four-day party in Stewart and Hyder. International Days, as it's called, features various events, including parades, pig races, and fireworks.

Information and Services

The Stewart Information Center is on Fifth near Victoria, and is open Mon.-Fri. 10 a.m.-4 p.m. The small Hyder Information Center sits on the right side as you enter town, and is open daily (except Wednesday) 9 a.m.-1 p.m., June to mid-September. The U.S. Forest Service has a summertime office/info center in Hyder; stop here for details on bear viewing up the road. For swimming, showers, and a weight room, head to Stewart High School pool on Main Street. The public library is also at the high school. Wash clothes at Shoreline Laundromat in Stewart. There are no U.S. banks in the area, but Stewart has a Bank of Commerce.

Transportation

Alaska ferry service to Hyder/Stewart offers an excellent alternative to the usual routes north. From mid-May to mid-September the *Aurora* sails every two or three weeks from Ketchikan to the Stewart dock, leaving Ketchikan Tuesday morning and arriving in Hyder by mid-afternoon. It stays approximately three hours before heading back to Ketchikan. The fare is US$40 one-way. Stewart does not have a ferry terminal building and you must purchase tickets onboard the ship. Considering a bit of international drug-running on the unguarded Hyder/Stewart border? Be forewarned that U.S. Customs in Ketchikan "greets" all Hyder and Stewart ferry passengers.

Taquan Air Service, tel. (907) 225-8800 or (800) 770-8800, flies every Monday and Thursday between Ketchikan and Hyder for US$80 one-way/US$194 roundtrip. This is also the only time mail goes in or out of the Hyder post office.

Fjording Ventures Cruises, tel. (800) 916-0250, offers cruises on Portland Canal aboard a 60-foot Swedish motorsailer. The cost is US$75 for the buffet breakfast cruise, and US$100 for a gourmet dinner cruise.

PRINCE OF WALES ISLAND

With more miles of roads than the rest of Southeast Alaska combined, a beautifully wild coastline, deep U-shaped valleys, rugged snow-topped mountains, and a wealth of wildlife, you might expect America's third-largest island (after Kodiak and Hawaii) to be a major tourist attraction. Instead, Prince of Wales (POW) has a reputation as a place to avoid. The island provides over half the timber cut on Forest Service land in Alaska, and is a major source of timber for Native corporations such as Sealaska. As a result, much of the island has been heavily logged, with huge clearcuts gouged out of the hillsides, particularly along the extensive road network.

Actually, POW's notoriety is its saving grace as well: the towns are authentically Alaskan, with no pretext of civility for the tourists. The 6,000 or so people who live here are friendly, and the many roads offer good opportunities for a variety of recreation not available elsewhere in Southeast. Mountain bikers will enjoy riding on the logging roads when they aren't in use. The island is very popular with hunters from other parts of Southeast, and the roads provide easy access to many bays for fishing. Black bears and deer are common sights, and wolves are occasionally seen.

Prince of Wales has several small towns along with many logging camps, some on floathouses and others with more permanent structures. State land sales and a strong timber market have helped turn POW into an economically booming area in recent years. The island's largest settlement is Craig, on the west coast, but Klawock, Thorne Bay, and Hydaburg are also growing. Rainfall amounts on POW range 60-200 inches per year, depending upon local topographic conditions. As an aside, this is one of four Prince of Wales Islands on the planet. The others are in Canada's Northwest Territories, in Queensland, Australia, and in Malaysia.

CRAIG

Just across a short bridge from the western shore of POW Island lies the town of Craig (pop. 1,500), overflowing Craig Island. Named after Craig Miller, founder of an early fish cannery here, it was originally called the even more prosaic "Fish Egg," after the herring eggs found here which are considered a Tlingit delicacy. Fishing and logging are the mainstays of Craig's economy, giving it a likable rough edge. The town has two fish-processing plants where summer jobs are sometimes available. No real "sights" in town, but as you enter Craig you pass the recently erected **Healing Heart Totem Pole.** Black bears and bald eagles are often seen at the dump, located a mile north of town (look for the Entering Klawock Heenya Land sign). You can thank a Native corporation, Shaan-Seet Inc., for the giant clearcut glaring down on Craig.

Accommodations
Travelers often camp under the trees near Craig's ball field. Simple rooms are available at **TLC Laundromat** on Cold Storage Rd., tel. (907) 826-2966. Showers are also available if you're camping. Find nicer rooms at **Ruth Ann's Motel,** tel. (907) 826-3377; and **Haida Way Lodge,** tel. (907) 826-3268 or (800) 347-4625. The homiest place to spend a night is **Inn of the Little Blue Heron,** tel. (907) 826-3606, which faces the south boat harbor. Other places

to stay include **Bucarelli Bay B&B,** tel. (907) 826-2951; **Shelter Cove Lodge,** tel. (907) 826-2939; **Windy Way Lodge,** tel. (907) 826-3084; and **Fish, Fur, & Feathers,** tel. (907) 826-2309.

Food

Meal prices are high on POW; your best bet is to stock up in Ketchikan or at the grocery store in Craig: **Thompson House,** tel. (907) 826-3394. Here you'll find a deli and bakery. Located downtown, **Ruth Ann's Restaurant,** tel. (907) 826-3377, serves good food with a front-row view of the harbor. Nice place. You won't go wrong ordering fish and chips. **Panhandle Bar & Grill** has Italian food and a big beer and wine selection. Other places for food are the **Shelter Cove Restaurant,** tel. (907) 826-2939; and even a new **Burger King** next to the grocery store. The **Hill Bar** sometimes has live music.

Information and Services

The Forest Service's **Craig District Office,** tel. (907) 826-3271, faces the south boat harbor. Folks here can supply maps and recreation info, including a listing of more than a dozen charter fishing operators. There's an **ATM** at the National Bank of Alaska office in Craig. Contact the **Prince of Wales Chamber of Commerce,** tel. (907) 826-3870, for additional information on the area. The town has a fine new indoor **swimming pool** complete with water slide, jacuzzi, sauna, and weight room. **Craig's Dive Center,** tel. (907) 826-3481 or (800) 380-3483, offers custom dive trips to the undiscovered clear (and cold) waters off Prince of Wales Island. Skiff rentals are available in Craig from **Fish, Fur, & Feathers,** tel. (907) 826-2309.

KLAWOCK

Six miles from Craig is the Tlingit village of Klawock (pop. 770), home to the oldest cannery in Alaska (1878), along with a bustling sawmill, state fish hatchery, and POW's only airport (all other settlements have floatplane service). Klawock is best known for its **Totem Park** (21 poles) which dominates the center of town. These brightly painted poles, all originals, were moved from the old abandoned village of Tuxekan (20 miles north) in the 1930s and restored. Showers are available at **Black Bear Laundromat** next to Thorne Bay Road. Also here is a Quik Stop market.

Accommodations

Log Cabin Resort, tel. (907) 755-2205 or (800) 544-2205 (outside Alaska), has tent spaces and rustic cabins along the beach. Rent one of their canoes or skiffs to explore Big Salt Lake and nearby islands. Other gear, including fishing poles and even crab pots, can also be rented. **Fireweed Lodge,** tel. (907) 755-2930, has rooms, as does **Klawock Bay Inn,** tel. (907) 755-2929. The latter also has skiff rentals. Lodging is also available at **Forget Me Not Inn,** tel. (907) 755-2340; **Klawock Bay Inn,** tel. (907) 755-2959; and **Prince of Wales Lodge,** tel. (907) 755-2227.

Food

Best pizzas on Prince of Wales—including a pesto and artichoke version—are found at **Papa's Pizza,** tel. (907) 755-2244. The restaurant at **Fireweed Lodge,** tel. (907) 755-2930, serves breakfast and dinner, as does **Dave's Diner,** tel. (907) 755-2986. Another good place is **Captains Table,** tel. (907) 826-3880. Get groceries at the **Alaskan & Proud (A&P) Market,** tel. (907) 755-2722.

OTHER TOWNS

Thorne Bay

The growing settlement of Thorne Bay (pop. 580) calls itself "the biggest logging camp in the U.S." It's also billed as a "planned city," but the plan seems based upon chaos, mud, abandoned vehicles, and a heavy dose of mobile homes and shacks. Thorne Bay has to be one of the ugliest settlements in Southeast; that alone should be reason enough for a visit!

Lodging options at Thorne Bay include: **McFarland's Floatel B&B,** tel. (907) 828-3335; **Boardwalk Wilderness Lodge,** tel. (907) 828-3918; **Boulton's Landing,** tel. (907) 247-3458; **Deer Creek Cottage,** tel. (907) 828-3393 or (800) 830-3393; **Southeast Retreat,** tel. (907) 828-8835 or (907) 755-2994; and **Treetops Lodge,** tel. (907) 828-3989. McFarland's also rents skiffs. Ten miles north of town on Forest Hwy. 30 is **Sandy Beach Picnic Area,** an attractive beach (rare in Southeast) where you can pitch a tent. Thorne Bay's **POW Island Logging Show and Fair** takes place in late July or early August each summer, with ax throwing, tree climbing, hooktender races, bucking, and other events, plus small town fair displays.

Get groceries from **Thorne Bay Market,** tel. (907) 828-3306, and booze from **Riptide Bar,** tel. (907) 828-3353.

Hydaburg

Forty-two miles south of Craig, Hydaburg (pop. 420) is the largest Haida settlement in Alaska. The Haida Indians are relative newcomers to the state, arriving in this Tlingit land around 1700. Originally from Canada's Queen Charlotte Islands, they were given parts of POW in compensation for the accidental killing of a Haida chief by

Klawock totems

GORDY OHLIGER

the Tlingits. Hydaburg was established in 1911 when three nearby Haida villages combined into one. Hydaburg has the prettiest setting on POW, situated along scenic Sukkwan Strait. Most of the houses, however, are very plain BIA-style boxes. The gravel road to Hydaburg was only completed in 1983, opening the town to the outside world. In town is a nice collection of totems restored by the CCC in the 1930s, along with a new one erected in 1991. For food you're best off heading to **Do Drop Inn Groceries,** but fast food is available at **JJ's** or the **Sweet Shop.** Ask locally for folks with rooms for rent available.

Logging and Fishing Towns

The tiny logging communities of **Whale Pass** (pop. 80) and **Coffman Cove** (pop. 190) each have a general store and gas pumps. Stay at **Coffman Cove Cabin,** tel. (907) 329-2251. On the far northern end of POW are the minuscule fishing/retirement villages of **Port Protection** (pop. 60) and **Point Baker** (pop. 40). Both have small general stores and a number of floathouses but are accessible only by boat or floatplane. A long boardwalk connects homes in Port Protection, and lodging on a weekly basis only is available at **Wooden Wheel Cove Lodge,** tel. (907) 489-2288. In Point Baker, stay at **Land's End Fish Camp,** tel. (907) 559-2216. The latter also serves meals and has whalewatching trips and skiff rentals. If you have the bucks (over $2,000 for three nights), **Waterfall Resort,** tel. (800) 544-5125, is pretty hard to beat. Located on the south end of POW in a refurbished fish cannery, Waterfall has become extremely popular with the elite crowd. Great fishing, three big meals daily, and positively pampered guests.

A CLEARCUT ISSUE

One frequently hears Prince of Wales Island described as "nuked," a consequence of logging on both U.S. Forest Service and Native corporation land. Logging is a major economic pillar in Southeast Alaska, and provides well-paying work in such towns as Ketchikan, Craig, Thorne Bay, Wrangell, and Kake—places where other employment opportunities are scarce. Unfortunately, logging leads to unsightly clearcuts that affect other important Southeast Alaska industries, especially fishing and tourism.

The first large-scale logging in Tongass National Forest began during WW II when Sitka spruce was needed for airplane construction. But until the 1950s, logging's impact was minor. In 1954 the first pulp mill opened in Ketchikan. A Japanese corporation built a second in Sitka five years later, and today thousands of people work in the timber industry in Southeast Alaska. To supply these mills, the forest service signed unprecedented 50-year contracts giving the two companies nearly 300 million board-feet of timber each year at prices well below timber management costs. This controversial boondoggle was institutionalized in 1980 with passage of the Alaska National Interest Lands Conservation Act (ANILCA), which mandated a cut of 450 million board-ee each year from the Tongass, to be funded by a $40 million annual appropriation to the forest service for road building and timber management. The Tongass Timber Reform Act of 1990 attempted to end the worst of this. The Clinton administration is encouraging a shift away from logging toward other economies. The closures of the Sitka pulp mill in 1993 and the Ketchikan pulp mill in 1997 have lessened the pressure to log Forest Service lands.

Clearcutting is not only an eyesore visible from the ferries and roads, it also damages old-growth ecosystems. Within 20 years after logging, cut-over land is densely covered with trees and bushes. Although these provide wildlife habitat for a while, as the trees grow taller an impenetrable thicket develops. Thinning crews attempt to open up these stands by cutting out the smaller and weaker trees. Once these forests reach 50 years of age they appear similar to old-growth forest from a distance, but actually they differ greatly. Old-growth forests have an almost continuous understory of huckleberry, devil's club, salmonberry, skunk cabbage, rusty menziesia, and other plants that provide food and cover for many animals. In contrast, second-growth forests lack many of these understory plants, making for great hiking but very poor wildlife habitat.

One of the most infamous clearcuts on forest service land anywhere in the country is the six-square-mile scalping at Staney Creek near the center of Prince of Wales. In 1993, this area was the site of a major pink salmon die-off that biologists attributed to higher stream temperatures caused by logging. Later that same year, heavy rains led to landslides on roads built through some of POW's clearcuts. Due to persistent criticism, the Forest Service has now reduced clearcut sizes to less than 40 acres.

Unfortunately, private corporations created by the Alaska Native Claims Settlement Act of 1971 have taken the lead in the cut-and-run game. Unlike the Forest Service—which ostensibly manages its lands for multiple use and is accountable to the public—private corporations are managing much of their land for only one purpose: to cut the timber as fast as possible to make as much money as possible. The timber is almost gone from most of the village corporation lands, and even timber giant Sealaska's supply—300,000 acres of trees—will only last another decade or so.

The big profiteers out of this are the Japanese and Korean corporations who get Alaskan timber for fire-sale prices. The big losers are the Native people who will have decimated their land for a short-term boom. The resulting eyesores have prompted even the Forest Service to distance itself by placing Entering Private Land signs on Sealaska Corporation borders. It's too late for many areas, but people are finally becoming aware that cutting all the trees on all the land at once does not provide a long-term economic base. Two things are certain for the future: clearcut logging will continue to be one of the major uses of forest land in Southeast Alaska, and it will continue to generate controversy.

RECREATION

Camping
You can camp almost anywhere on POW's National Forest land, but avoid trespassing on Native lands (these are generally quite easy to identify since the trees have been scalped off them for miles in all directions). **Eagles Nest Campground** ($25/night) is just east of the intersection of the Klawock-Thorne Bay Rd. and Coffman Cove Road. Also here is a pleasant

pair of lakes (Balls Lakes—named for, well, you figure it out) with a short path down to tent platforms overlooking the water. This is a good place for canoeing.

Hiking and Cabins

There are only a few trails on POW. One of the best and most accessible is the 1.5-mile **One Duck Trail** southwest of Hollis. The trailhead is on the east side of the Hydaburg Rd., two miles south of the junction with the Craig-Hollis Road. It heads up sharply to an Adirondack shelter (free) on the edge of the alpine where the scenery is grand and the hiking is easy. Be sure to wear rubber boots since the trail can be mucky.

The **Soda Lake Trail** (marked) begins approximately 14 miles south of the junction along the Hydaburg Road. This 2.5-mile trail leads to a pungent collection of bubbling soda springs covering several acres. There are colorful tufa deposits (calcium carbonate, primarily) similar to those in Yellowstone but on a vastly smaller scale. **Control Lake,** at the junction of the Thorne Bay and Big Salt Lake Roads, has a nice cabin ($25/night) with a rowboat. Twenty other Forest Service cabins are scattered around POW, most accessible only by floatplane or boat. For world-class steelhead and salmon fishing, reserve one of the four cabins in the Karta River area north of Hollis. The five-mile-long **Karta River Trail** connects Karta Bay to the **Salmon Lake Cabin** and provides panoramic views of surrounding mountains. This is now part of the 40,000-acre Karta Wilderness. **Harris River Trail** is an almost level half-mile path that takes off from the Hydaburg Rd. between Hollis and Hydaburg. Watch for the sign.

Spelunking

Prince of Wales Island has the best-known and probably the most extensive system of caves in Alaska, and spelunkers keep finding more. In 1994, the 35,000-year-old bones from a brown bear were discovered in one of these caves. Two of them—**El Capitan Cave** and **Cavern Lake Cave**—are open to the general public. Both are located on the north end of the island near Whale Pass. The Forest Service offers free tours of El Capitan Cave between late May and mid-September; call (907) 828-3304 for

details. Bring your own hard hat, flashlights (three is best), warm clothing, and hiking boots. Reservations are recommended.

No tours at Cavern Lake Cave, but you can explore it on your own. A stream flows out of this cave. Contact the Forest Service for directions.

Canoeing

The **Sarkar Canoe Trail** is an easy 15-mile loop canoe route with boardwalk portages connecting seven lakes. The trailhead is at the south end of Sarkar Lake, on the northwest side of Prince of Wales, off Forest Rd. 20. A more strenuous route is the 34-mile-long **Honker Divide Canoe Route.** This paddle-and-portage route begins near Coffman Cove at the bridge over Hatchery Creek on Forest Rd. 30, and works up Hatchery Creek to Lake Galea, which has a Forest Service cabin ($25/night). You may need to line the canoe up shallow sections of the creek. The route then continues over Honker Divide on a mile-long portage to the upper Thorne River before heading downstream all the way to Thorne Bay. There is a two-mile portage to avoid dangerous rapids and falls. The route is strenuous and should only be attempted by experienced canoeists. For more information on either of these excellent canoe routes, contact the Thorne Bay Ranger District Office at Box 1, Thorne Bay, AK 99950, tel. (907) 828-3304.

Sea Kayaking

With its hundreds of miles of rugged coastline, and numerous small islands, inlets, and bays, POW offers tremendous opportunities for sea kayakers. One of the wildest areas is the 98,000-acre **South Prince of Wales Wilderness,** but access is difficult and much of the area is exposed to fierce ocean storms. Nearby **Dall Island** has exploring possibilities, but parts of it are being logged. On beaches exposed to the open sea, you occasionally find beautiful Japanese glass fishing floats that have washed ashore. **Southeast Exposure,** 507 Stedman St., Ketchikan, tel. (907) 225-8829, offers sea kayaking trips to the myriad **Barrier Islands** on the south end of Prince of Wales. These trips cost $1,200 pp for an eight-day expedition (including transportation and supplies). Highly recommended.

In Craig, you can rent sea kayaks from Cheryl Fecko, tel. (907) 826-3425. Sylvia Geraghty in New Tokeen also rents sea kayaks. Tiny **New Tokeen** (pop. three!) has a small store, and is accessible by boat from Naukati or floatplane from Ketchikan. It's a good place to start explorations of fascinating Sea Otter Sound. Three other wilderness areas along POW's outer coast—**Maurelle Islands, Warren Island,** and **Coronation Island**—offer remote and almost unvisited places to see whales, sea otters, and nesting colonies of seabirds. You're likely to see a few fishermen, but nobody else.

TRANSPORTATION

By Ferry
The Alaska state ferry *Aurora* connects POW with Ketchikan ($20) almost daily during the summer months. Reservations for vehicles are highly recommended. Ferries to Petersburg generally depart on Mondays and are less crowded. The ferry terminal is in **Hollis,** tel. (907) 530-7115, and is open a half-hour before arrivals and one hour prior to departures. There are no services in Hollis other than phones and a toilet, and it's 25 miles to Klawock, the nearest town. Make reservations in Craig, downstairs in Thibodeau's Mall, tel. (907) 826-3432; open Mon.-Fri. 9 a.m.-5 p.m. only.

The *Aurora* tends to arrive in the late evening and depart early to mid-morning, making hitching somewhat difficult; in general, however, hitching is fairly easy on the island, though you may have to wait awhile for a ride. **Prince of Wales Transporter** in Klawock, tel. (907) 755-2348, has vans that meet most ferry dockings. Call in advance from Ketchikan to be sure they'll be meeting your ferry.

By Air
Two air taxi operators, **Ketchikan Air Service,** tel. (907) 225-6608 or (800) 656-6608; and **Taquan Air Service,** tel. (907) 225-8800 or (800) 770-8800, fly every day between Ketchikan and the major towns on POW, offering rates within a few dollars of each other: Coffman Cove ($69), Craig ($76), Hollis ($49), Hydaburg ($80), Kasaan, ($43), Klawock ($76), Point Baker ($110), Point Protection ($110), Thorne Bay ($55), and Whale Pass ($85). In addition, both also have daily flights to the many logging camps and fishing communities that dot the island. Folks with a folding sea kayak may want to take advantage of these flights as an inexpensive way to reach remote parts of POW. Example: Roundtrip airfare from Ketchikan to the Karta Bay cabin will set you back at least $440 for a charter flight, but just $43 pp if you buy seat fare to nearby Kasaan on these daily flights!

The Road System
For a good road map, pick up the **Prince of Wales Road Guide** ($3) at Forest Service offices in Ketchikan, Craig, or Thorne Bay. Be sure to check out the photo on the back cover that shows a logging truck heading up a POW road. It's labeled "A Forest At Work," as though this were the sole purpose of publicly owned forests! Pretty obvious that "nonworking" forests—such as wilderness areas—are lazy and good for nothing.

Because of its extensive road network (over 2,000 miles and increasing at 80 miles per year), some visitors take mountain bikes to POW. There are some excellent stretches of paved road (including the entire distance from Hollis to Craig), and enjoyable vistas, but be prepared for wet weather, huge logging trucks, and many miles of rutted and rough gravel roads. Ask at the Forest Service offices in Ketchikan or Craig where logging is underway. Avoid these roads, unless you don't mind watching a loaded truck bearing down on you! Some travelers to POW rent a car from **Practical Rent a Car** in Klawock, tel. (907) 826-2424. Taxi service is available from three Klawock companies: **Screaming Eagle Taxi,** tel. (907) 755-2699; **Irish Setter Cab,** tel. (907) 755-2217; and **Jackson Cab,** tel. (907) 755-2557.

WRANGELL

Wrangell (pop. 2,600) is a small, quiet, friendly, and conservative settlement near the mouth of the Stikine River. The streets are filled with folks in pickup trucks, their dogs hanging out the back, and country tunes on the radio. Wrangell is quite unlike its neighbor, prim and proper Petersburg. Wrangell's inner harbor resonates with salmon and shrimp processing plants, fishing boats, and seaplanes, while totem poles guard historic Chief Shakes Island. Surrounding the harbor are old buildings on piles, wooded hillsides, and snowcapped mountains. Wrangell is compact enough that visitors can hoof it around to the most interesting sites in an hour or two and still have time to buy beer for the ferry. To see the area right, however, you should spend a couple of days, or longer if you're interested in visiting the mighty Stikine River.

HISTORY

Redoubt Saint Dionysius
Third-oldest community in Alaska, Wrangell is the only one to have been governed by four nations: Tlingit, Russian, British, and American. Tlingit legends tell of an ancient time when advancing glaciers forced them to abandon their coastal life and move to what is now British Columbia. As the ice retreated following the last ice age, the Stikine River was their entryway back to the newly reborn land. When the Tlingits discovered that the river suddenly disappeared under a glacier, they sent old women to explore, expecting never to see them again. One can only imagine their astonishment when the women returned to lead canoes full of people out to the coast.

For many centuries the Tlingits lived in the Stikine River area, paddling canoes upstream to catch salmon and trade with interior tribes. Similarly, the river figured strongly in Wrangell's founding. Russians began trading with Stikine Indians in 1811; by 1834 the British were trying to move in on their lucrative fur trading monopoly. To prevent this, Lt. Dionysius Zarembo and a band of men left New Archangel (present-day

Sitka) to establish a Russian fort near the Stikine River mouth. The settlement, later to become Wrangell, was originally named Redoubt St. Dionysius. When the British ship *Dryad* anchored near the river, the Russians boarded the vessel and refused to allow access to the Stikine. The *Dryad* was forced to return south, but a wedge had been driven in Russia's Alaskan empire. Five years later the Hudson's Bay Co. acquired a long-term lease to the coastline from the Russian government. Redoubt St. Dionysius became Fort Stikine, and the Union Jack flew from town flagpoles.

Gold Fever
The discovery of gold on Stikine River gravel bars in 1861 brought a boom to Fort Stikine. Hundreds of gold-seekers arrived, but the deposit proved relatively small and most soon drifted on to other areas. With the transfer of Alaska to American hands in 1867, Fort Stikine was renamed Wrangell, after Baron Ferdinand Petrovich von Wrangel, governor of the Russian-American Company. Its population dwindled until 1872 when gold was again discovered in the Cassiar region of British Columbia. Thousands of miners quickly flooded the area, traveling on steamboats up the Stikine. Wrangell achieved notoriety as a town filled with hard-drinking rabble-rousers, gamblers, and shady ladies. When the naturalist John Muir visited in 1879 he called it "the most inhospitable place at first sight I had ever seen . . . a lawless draggle of wooden huts and houses, built in crooked lines, wrangling around the boggy shore of the island for a mile or so in the general form of the letter S, without the slightest subordination to the points of the compass or to building laws of any kind."

By the late 1880s, the second gold rush had subsided and lumbering and fishing were getting started as local industries. The Klondike gold rush of the late 1890s brought another short-lived boom to Wrangell as the Stikine was again tapped for access to interior Canada, but Skagway's Chilkoot Trail became the preferred route. With its rowdy days behind, Wrangell set-

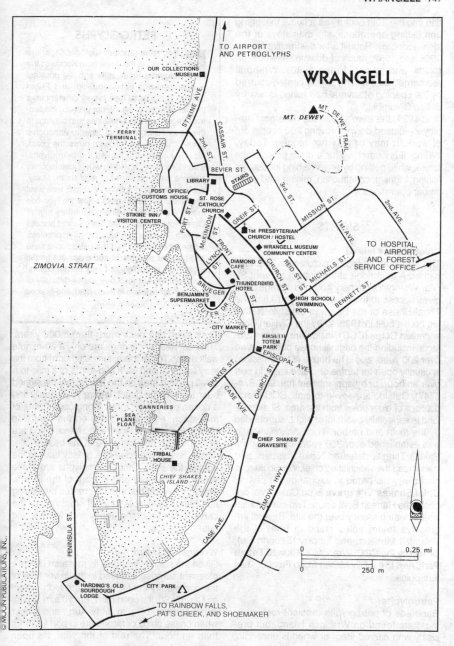

WRANGELL

TO AIRPORT
AND PETROGLYPHS

OUR COLLECTIONS
MUSEUM

MT. DEWEY

MT. DEWEY
TRAIL

FERRY
TERMINAL

STIKINE AVE.

2nd ST.

CASSAIR ST.

BEVIER ST.

3rd ST.

MISSION ST.

2nd AVE.

LIBRARY

STAIRS

POST OFFICE/
CUSTOMS HOUSE

ST. ROSE
CATHOLIC
CHURCH

GREIF ST.

FORT ST.

McKINNON ST.

1st PRESBYTERIAN
CHURCH / HOSTEL

WRANGELL MUSEUM/
COMMUNITY CENTER

TO HOSPITAL,
AIRPORT,
AND FOREST
SERVICE OFFICE

STIKINE INN /
VISITOR CENTER

LYNCH ST.

FRONT ST.

DIAMOND C
CAFE

REID ST.

CHURCH ST.

MICHAELS ST.

1st AVE.

ZIMOVIA STRAIT

BRUEGER ST.

THUNDERBIRD
HOTEL

BENJAMIN'S
SUPERMARKET

OUTER DR.

HIGH SCHOOL/
SWIMMING
POOL

BENNETT ST.

CITY MARKET

KIKSETTI
TOTEM PARK

EPISCOPAL AVE.

SHAKES ST.

CANNERIES

CASE AVE.

CHURCH ST.

CHIEF SHAKES'
GRAVESITE

SEA
PLANE
FLOAT

TRIBAL
HOUSE

CHIEF SHAKES
ISLAND

ZIMOVIA HWY.

PENINSULA ST.

CASE AVE.

0   0.25 mi

0   250 m

MOON

HARDING'S OLD
SOURDOUGH LODGE

CITY PARK

TO RAINBOW FALLS,
PAT'S CREEK, AND SHOEMAKER

tled into the 20th century as a home to logging and fishing operations, still mainstays of the local economy. Rebuilt after destructive fires in 1906 and 1952, much of downtown is now on rockfill and pilings. In the 1980s, Wrangell reemerged as a mining supply center, spurred by the opening of several new mines in nearby British Columbia.

In 1994, the town's sawmill—its largest employer—closed down, throwing 200 people out of work. It may or may not reopen. Today, Wrangell is searching for a more prosperous future, while getting by on remaining industries: fishing, tourism, construction, mining, and small timber operations.

SIGHTS

Chief Shakes Island

This is the centerpiece of picturesque Wrangell harbor. A footbridge at the bottom of Front St. near Wrangell's cannery and cold storage plant gives access to the island. Here you'll find the Tribal House of the Bear, an old-style Native log house built in 1939-40 by the Civilian Conservation Corps (CCC). Inside are various artifacts, including the original house posts carved over 200 years ago. The house ($1 admission) is usually open for ferries or cruise ships in port over an hour, or by appointment (tel. 907-874-3747). Outside are seven totems, CCC reproductions of older poles from the area. Shakes Island is especially beautiful at night, surrounded by the town and harbor. The Shakes lineage was established over 300 years ago, after the Stikine Tlingits defeated Niska invaders and then forced the vanquished chief, We-Shakes, to give away his name in exchange for peace. **Chief Shakes VI's grave** is on Case Ave. opposite the Hansen Boat Shop. Two carved killer whales watch silently over the site. Several impressive totem poles stand in front of the Wrangell Museum and Library (Second St.), carved by the CCC. Wrangell's **Kiksetti Totem Park,** next to the City Market along Front St., has four poles.

Petroglyphs

Hundreds of petroglyphs (ancient rock carvings) are found on Wrangell Island, but precisely who carved them or when is uncertain.

PETROGLYPHS

Petroglyphs (ancient rock carvings) are found along the coast from Kodiak to the Columbia River, although the greatest concentration is between Sitka and Puget Sound. The coastal type is very different from the petroglyphs of the interior plateau and central Oregon, but has similarities with carvings in the Amur River region of Siberia. Although a single style can be followed down the coast, no one knows who carved the petroglyphs, when they were carved, or why. Contemporary Natives have no knowledge of them. Many, such as the designs from Wrangell, face west and were carved on rocks below the high-tide mark. Were they territorial boundary signs? Greetings to returning salmon? Sacred places? As with Stonehenge, we can only speculate. Some have posited that the petroglyphs were just the idle doodles of some ancient graffiti artist. This is unlikely not only from a cultural perspective, but also due to the difficulty of pecking out a design in these hard, fine-grained rocks using only stone tools.

They may date back more than 8,000 years. The best nearby carvings are only a 20-minute walk away. To get there, turn left (north) from the ferry terminal and walk two-thirds of a mile to a small parking area on the left. Follow the signed boardwalk to the beach where you'll easily find a dozen petroglyph rocks along upper parts of the beach, especially those on the right side (facing the water). Most face seaward and are near the high-tide line. One of the best, a killer whale, lies on the edge of a grassy lawn to the right of the path. Other petroglyphs are in the Wrangell Museum and in front of the library. Petroglyph rubbings can be created by placing rice paper (available in local stores) over the carvings and rubbing lightly with ferns found near the beach.

Wrangell Museum

Given the size of Wrangell, its museum ($2) is a pleasant surprise. Housed in the lower floor of the community center next to the high school on Church St., it's open Mon.-Fri. 10 a.m.-5 p.m. and Saturday 1-5 p.m. May-Aug., and longer when cruise ships or ferries are in port for more than an hour. The rest of the year, it's open

Mon.-Fri. 10 a.m.-noon and 1-4 p.m. Petro-glyphs, old photographs, Tlingit artifacts, and local relics are crowded into this provocative museum. The staff is a good source of information about the town. A slide program of Wrangell is shown on request and the museum shop sells books on local and regional history. Call (907) 874-3770 for more information.

Mount Dewey

A half-mile path winds up Mt. Dewey (actually more of a hill) from Third St. behind the high school. It's a steep 15-minute climb up to this viewpoint over Wrangell. You could probably find a place to camp up here in a pinch. On a wild stormy night in 1879, John Muir did just that. He, however, also decided to build a huge bonfire atop the hill, its flames dancing off the clouds. Muir later wrote, "Of all the thousands of campfires I have elsewhere built none was just like this one, rejoicing in triumphant strength and beauty in the heart of the rain-laden gale." To the Native people below, however, the fire ignited fears of evil spirits, and as Muir's partner noted, "the Tlingits ever afterward eyed Muir askance, as a mysterious being whose ways and motives were beyond all conjecture." During the 1920s, a dance pavilion crowned the top of Mt. Dewey; nothing remains of it today.

Other Sights

Wrangell is home to the oldest Protestant church building in Alaska, the **First Presbyterian Church**, as well as the oldest Roman Catholic parish, **St. Rose of Lima Catholic Church**. Appropriately located on Church St., both were founded in 1879. The large red neon cross atop the Presbyterian church is one of only two in the world used as a navigational aid (the other is in Rio). For something completely different, you might want to stop in at **Our Collections** (free) on your way to the petroglyphs. The place looks like a cross between granny's attic and a yard sale, and represents more than 50 years of collecting by the Bigelow family. Open when cruise ships and ferries are in town, tel. (907) 874-3646.

GORDY OHLIGER

As you step off the ferry you will be greeted by local kids selling **garnets** for 25 cents to $10 depending upon the size. These imperfect but attractive stones come from a nearby garnet ledge along the Stikine River, deeded to the Boy Scouts in 1962 by a former mayor. Local children may collect the stones for free, but adults must pay $10 for a permit (available at the museum). At one time the mine was owned by the Alaska Garnet Mining and Manufacturing Co., the world's first corporation composed entirely of women.

TRAILS AND CABINS

Anan Creek Bear Observatory

Anan Creek, 27 air miles south of Wrangell on the mainland, has an observation platform (complete with three-sided shelter) that provides a good place to watch black bears catching salmon and steelhead. The best viewing is a half-mile upstream from this, below a second falls, but be sure to make lots of noise when walking up this primitive trail to keep from surprising a bear. No food is allowed along these trails, and dogs cannot be brought into the area. The best time to visit is mid-July through mid-August, the peak of the pink salmon run. The **Anan Creek** Forest Service cabin ($25/night) is just a mile away on a good trail, but is often booked months in advance, so make reservations early.

Many visitors to Anan Creek arrive on flights from **Sunrise Aviation**, tel. (907) 874-2319 or (800) 874-2311. The charter cost is $396 roundtrip for a Cessna 206 (room for up to four people with gear), but they try to match you up with others heading to Anan to spread this around. Two companies offer guided day-trips to Anan Creek by boat: **TH Charters**, tel. (907) 874-2985 or (800) 874-2085; and **Breakaway Adventures**, tel. (907) 874-2488. Those with a sea kayak may want to paddle along the east side of Wrangell Island to Anan Bay. En route, be sure to visit scenic **Berg Bay**, an area rich in moose, mountain goats, grizzlies, deer, geese, and other wildlife. A Forest Service cabin ($25/night) is available here, and a trail leads from the cabin along Berg Creek for several miles into a cirque basin with old mine ruins.

Hiking Trails

Scenic **Rainbow Falls Trail,** a moderately steep three-quarter-mile hike, begins across the road from Shoemaker Bay Campground, five miles south of town. More ambitious bodies can continue three miles up the trail to **Shoemaker Overlook** (1,500 feet). The trail accesses large ridgetop muskeg areas and ends at a three-sided Adirondack-style shelter offering a panoramic vista of Zimovia Strait. The trail and shelter provide an excellent opportunity for an overnight camping trip. The trail is steep and often muddy, but is being improved with a boardwalk. Check with the Forest Service for current conditions.

Logging roads crisscross most of Wrangell Island, providing good cycling opportunities for mountain bike enthusiasts if you enjoy seeing cut-over land. Those with wheels may want to visit several areas on the island. **Long Lake Trail,** 28 miles southeast of Wrangell along Forest Rd. 6271, is a half-mile boardwalk that ends at an Adirondack shelter complete with a rowboat, fire grill, and outhouse. In the same vicinity is a 300-foot path to **Highbrush Lake,** where you'll find a small boat to practice your Olympic rowing skills. Individuals with disablities may want to try fishing at **Salamander Creek,** 23 miles south of town on Forest Rd. 6265, where ramps lead right up to a pad along the creek. Good fishing for king salmon here, along with three campsites. For info on cabins and other trails around Wrangell, visit the Forest Service's **Wrangell Ranger District office** at 525 Bennett St. (on the way to the airport).

Cabins

There are 21 different Forest Service cabins ($25/night) near Wrangell. The closest is at **Virginia Lake,** a $225 roundtrip flight for three people and gear. See below for air taxi companies. Another nearby cabin is at **Kunk Lake,** across Zimovia Strait from the south end of the Wrangell Island road system. Access is by kayak, or skiff if you can get someone to run you across. A 1.5-mile trail climbs to a new three-sided shelter at the lake. From here, it's a relatively easy climb into high-elevation muskeg and alpine areas that cross Etolin Island.

PRACTICALITIES

Accommodations

Wrangell's **Youth Hostel,** tel. (907) 874-3534, is in the Presbyterian church at 220 Church Street. The cost is $10 pp, and it's open only in the summer from mid-June to Labor Day. This is nothing fancy, but does include a kitchen and shower facilities. It's open 5 p.m. to 8 a.m., with mats for sleeping. For other lodging options, refer to the chart "Wrangell Accommodations."

Camping

Free tent camping is allowed (no vehicles or RVs) at **City Park** just beyond the ball field, two miles south of the ferry on the water side of Zimovia Highway. The official limit is 24 hours, but this is not strictly enforced. There is more camping at **Shoemaker Bay RV Park,** five miles south of town, but you'll find yourself right alongside

---

WRANGELL ACCOMMODATIONS

Note: Wrangell adds a seven percent tax plus a $4 room tax to these rates (not applied to the hostel).

Wrangell Hostel; 220 Church St.; tel. (907) 874-3534; $10 pp; dorm accommodations

Rooney's Roost B&B; 206 McKinnon; tel. (907) 874-3622; $45-60 s or d; three guest rooms, shared or private bath, full breakfast

Stikine Inn; Front St.; tel. (907) 874-3388; $55 s, $65 d

Thunderbird Hotel; 223 Front St.; tel. (907) 874-3322; $55 s, $65 d

Harbor House Lodge; 645 Shakes Ave.; tel. (907) 874-3084 or (800) 488-5107; $55 s, $65 d with shared baths; $110 d for two-bedroom apartment with kitchen and sun room; bikes available

Roadhouse Lodge; four miles south; tel. (907) 874-2335; $60 s, $67 d; courtesy van

Grand View B&B; two miles south Zimovia Hwy.; tel. (907) 874-3225; $60 s or d; basement apartment, private bath, continental breakfast

Harding's Old Sourdough Lodge; 1104 Peninsula Ave.; tel. (907) 874-3613; $65 s, $75 d; sauna and steambath, courtesy van

the highway. The cost is $8 for RVs or tents. Call (907) 874-2381 for details. One advantage of this campsite is its proximity to the Rainbow Falls and Shoemaker Overlook Trails (see above). You'll find other campsites 14 miles south of town and up Forest Rds. 16 and 6267. These offer impressive views across Zimovia Strait, and are free. Still more campsites are farther out.

Food and Entertainment

Wrangell eating places leave much to be desired. The **Diamond C Cafe,** just up the street, tel. (907) 874-3677, has standard American fare, decent breakfasts, and good homemade soups for lunch. **Maggie's and Son Pizza,** 214 Front St., tel. (907) 874-2353, sells homemade pizza by the pie or slice; or you might try **J & W's** (open summers only), a couple of doors down, for greasy fast food. Ask around the harbor for local fishermen selling fresh shrimp (Wrangell's specialty) or salmon.

Benjamin's Supermarket, on Outer Dr., tel. (907) 874-2341, has a deli with inexpensive sandwiches. **City Market** on Front St., tel. (907) 874-3336, is Wrangell's other grocery store. Locals hang out in the **Marine Lounge,** 274 Shakes St., tel. (907) 874-3005; **Totem Bar,** 116 Front St., tel. (907) 874-3533; and the **Brig Bar,** 532 Front St., tel. (907) 874-3442.

Events

Wrangell's big winter event is **Tent City Days,** held the first weekend of February. Featured activities include bed races, the Shady Lady Fancy Dress Ball, beer drinking contests (both official and unofficial no doubt), food booths, a pancake feed, a tall-tales contest, and beard judging. In late May, visit Wrangell for a **King Salmon Derby.** The main summer event is the town's **July Fourth** celebration.

Information and Services

The small **Wrangell Visitor Center,** tel. (907) 874-3901 or (800) 367-9745, is housed inside the Stikine Inn on Front St. and is open when cruise ships are in port. If they're closed, get info from the museum, or pick up a copy of the *Wrangell Guide* (free) at the ferry terminal.

The **library** has a good collection of books about Alaska. **B.B. Brock's Bookstore,** next to the city dock on Front St., tel. (907) 874-3185, has Alaskan titles. Housed inside the Stikine Inn,

Eagle's Wing Art Gallery is a small cooperative gallery with pottery, stained glass, and other works by local artisans. Golfers may want to check out Wrangell's **Muskeg Meadows Golf Course,** an eight-hole version near the airport. But bring bright orange balls; there's lots of "rough" here.

The Forest Service's **Wrangell Ranger District Office,** tel. (907) 874-2323, is on Bennett St., three-quarters of a mile from town on the left side of the road. They have info on local hiking trails, the Stikine River, and 23 nearby recreation cabins ($25/night). The **Alaska Department of Fish and Game** office, tel. (907) 874-3822 is on Front St. in the Kadin Building. Wrangell's excellent **swimming pool** ($1.50 for adults; $1 for students and children) at the high school, tel. (907) 874-2381, is the place to go for showers if you're camping out. Fishing and sightseeing **charters** are available through a number of local outfits; get brochures from the visitor center. The **Wrangell General Hospital,** tel. (907) 874-3356, is on Airport Road.

Transportation

Wrangell's **ferry terminal,** tel. (907) 874-2021, is right in town. Ferries head both north and south almost daily during the summer months. The terminal is open only for vessel arrivals and departures. Call (907) 874-3711 for recorded ferry departure information. **Star Cab,** tel. (907) 874-3622, and **Porky's Cab,** tel. (907) 874-3603, both charge $5 to transport a carload of people and gear to the campsites in City Park, and $6 from the airport to town. **Garnet Express,** tel. (907) 874-2714, offers bus tours of Wrangell that include the totem park, Chief Shakes Island, petroglyphs, and more. The cost is $7, free for kids under 12.

The airport is 1.5 miles from town on Bennett Street. **Alaska Airlines,** tel. (800) 426-0333, has daily flights from Wrangell to Juneau, Ketchikan, Petersburg, and Sitka, along with other Alaskan and Lower 48 cities. **Ketchikan Air Service,** tel. (907) 874-2369 or (800) 656-6608, flies to Juneau ($125), Kake ($105), Ketchikan ($107), Klawock ($140), and Petersburg ($68). Both Ketchikan Air Service and **Sunrise Aviation,** tel. (907) 874-2319 or (800) 874-2311, provide charter flights to nearby Forest Service cabins. Forty-five-minute Le Conte Glacier and Stikine River flightseeing trips cost around $95 pp. Rent cars at the airport from **Practical Rent-A-Car,** tel. (907) 874-3975.

THE STIKINE RIVER

Seven miles north of Wrangell is the Stikine River, one of the top 10 wild rivers of Canada and the fastest navigable river in North America. The river begins its 330-mile journey to the sea high inside British Columbia's Spatsizi Wilderness Park. The 55 mile-long Grand Canyon of the Stikine, just above Telegraph Creek, B.C., has thousand-foot walls enclosing fierce whitewater. River travel is easier below Telegraph Creek all the way to Wrangell, between high peaks of the coast range, past glaciers and forested hills. At one spot on the river, 21 different glaciers are visible! These glaciers dump tons of silt into the river, coloring it a milky gray; at the mouth of the Stikine, the sea takes on this color for miles in all directions. So much for the advertisements about glacially pure water. Each spring bald eagles flock to the river to eat hooligan, a fish that spawns here, with numbers often topping 1,000 birds.

Running the River

The Stikine River is a popular destination for kayakers, canoeists, and river rafters. (It is even more popular with local jetboaters, so don't expect peace and quiet in the lower reaches.) You can either float down the river from Telegraph Creek, B.C., or work your way upriver to the Canadian border (30 miles) and then float back. You will need to go through Customs, tel. (907) 874-3415, at the Wrangell airport if you cross the border. It's open Mon.-Fri. 8 a.m.-5 p.m. An agent is frequently stationed along the river just across the Canadian border; call (604) 627-3003 in Prince Rupert for details. Heading upriver is not as difficult as it might sound, and the route is well documented. Be extremely cautious, however, when crossing the mouth of the Stikine by canoe, especially during the bigger tides and when the wind is blowing. The Forest Service publishes an excellent guide and map ($3) of Stikine canoe/kayak routes, available from the Wrangell Ranger District, tel. (907) 874-2323. Canoe or kayak rentals are not available in Wrangell, but you can bring your own along on the ferry.

Camping and Cabins

The lower Stikine is a multichanneled, silt-laden river nearly a mile wide in places. The route is spectacular, wildlife crowds the banks, campsites are numerous, and 13 Forest Service cabins ($25) are available. One of the finest is the **Mount Rynda Cabin** along crystal-clear Andrew Creek, a spawning area for king salmon. You may also want to stay in one of the two cabins near **Chief Shakes Hot Springs.** At the springs you'll discover two wooden hot tubs (one enclosed), great places to soak those aching muscles. Note, however, that macho Wrangellites run loud jetboats up here, and the facility is often crowded and dirty on summer weekends, especially when the river is high enough to get boats up the side channels (generally in mid-July). It's the local party place. You can escape the crowds at the main hot springs by finding your own undeveloped springs in surrounding areas.

The upper portion of the Stikine is a vastly different river, with less noise and development than on the U.S. side of the border, and a drier, colder climate. The vegetation reflects this. The historic settlement of **Telegraph Creek** is accessible by road from the rest of B.C., or you can charter a small plane from Wrangell. The upper river is some of the wildest whitewater anywhere; canoeists and kayakers intent on running the river would do best to begin at Telegraph Creek.

Tours

Both **Roadhouse Lodge** in Wrangell, tel. (907) 874-2335; and **Stikine Riversong Lodge** in Telegraph Creek, tel. (604) 235-3196, will help you set up raft trips down the Stikine. Telegraph Creek is 160 miles upriver from Wrangell. Riversong also has lodging, supplies, and a pleasant cafe. Several charter boat operators in Wrangell provide day-trips or longer voyages by power boats up the Stikine River and in surrounding areas, including Anan Creek, Leconte Glacier, and Shakes Glacier. These include **Breakaway Adventures,** tel. (907) 874-3455; **Stickeen Wilderness Adventures,** tel. (907) 874-2085 or (800) 874-2085; and **Alaska Waters Inc.,** tel. (800) 347-4462. The Wrangell Visitor Center has a list of two dozen local charter boat operators with similar services.

PETERSBURG

Southeast Alaska's picture-postcard town, Petersburg (pop. 3,300) sits at the northern tip of Mitkof Island along Wrangell Narrows. Great white walls of snow and ice serve as a dramatic backdrop for the town. "Peter's Burg" was named after Peter Buschmann, who built a sawmill here in 1897, followed by a cannery three years later. With ample supplies of fish, timber, and glacial ice, the cannery proved an immediate success—32,750 cases of salmon were shipped that first season. Unlike boom-and-bust Wrangell, the planned community of Petersburg has kept pace with its expanding fishing base. Many of the present inhabitants are descended from Norwegian fishermen, who found that the place reminded them of their native land. The language is still heard occasionally on Petersburg's streets, and Norwegian rosemaling (floral painting) can be found on window shutters of the older homes.

Petersburg is a prosperous and squeaky-clean town with green lawns (a rarity in Alaska), tidy homes, and a hardworking heritage that may appear a bit cliquish to outsiders. Its high school and grade school were recently rated Alaska's finest. Although the town has a lumber mill, fishing is still the main activity here, with salmon, halibut, herring, crab, and shrimp all landed. The odor of fish hangs in the air, and bumper stickers say "Quit Beefing, Eat Seafood." Petersburg has the most canneries in Southeast Alaska (four) and is home to Alaska's largest halibut fleet. Overall, the town is the 10th most important fishing port, by volume, in America. It is a self-sufficient, inward-looking community that only tolerates tourism instead of promoting it.

Wrangell Narrows

Between Wrangell and Petersburg the ferry passes through tortuous Wrangell Narrows, a 46-turn nautical obstacle course that resembles a pinball game played by ship. This is one of the highlights of the Inside Passage trip and is even more exciting at night when the zigzag course is lit up like a Christmas tree. Be up front to see it. The larger cruise ships are too big to negotiate these shallow waters between Kupre-

anof and Mitkof Islands, thus sparing Petersburg from the tourist blitz and glitz other Southeast towns endure.

SIGHTS

In Town

Petersburg's main attraction is its gorgeous harbor and spectacular setting. The sharply pointed peak visible behind Petersburg is **Devil's Thumb,** a 9,077-foot mountain 30 miles away on the U.S.-Canadian border. The **Sons of Norway Hall** (1912), built on pilings over scenic Hammer Slough, bears traditional Norwegian rosemaling designs on its exterior. Inside is the **Husfliden** crafts shop that sells locally made Scandinavian handicrafts. Next to Sons of Norway is the *Valhalla,* a replica of the original Viking boats. It was built in 1976 and sailed in the parade of ships bicentennial celebration in New York Harbor. Walk up the wooden street along **Hammer Slough** to see the interesting old homes hanging over this tidal creek. The boat harbors usually have several Steller's sea lions cruising around.

Clausen Memorial Museum ($2), Second and Fram Sts., tel. (907) 772-3598, is open Sunday 12:30-4:30 p.m. and Mon.-Sat. 9:30 a.m.-4:30 p.m. in the summer, and Saturday 1-4 p.m. the rest of the year. Inside, find the world's largest king salmon (a 126-pound monster) and chum salmon (36 pounds), along with the Cape Decision lighthouse lens, an old Tlingit dugout canoe, and other historical exhibits. Outside is a fishy sculpture and fountain by Carson Boysen.

Nearby Sights

A good place to watch eagles is **Eagle's Roost Park,** north of the Petersburg Fisheries cannery. Upwards of 30 eagles can be seen at one time along here when the tide is low. An active eagle nest is two miles north of town along the road. Whales, seals, and sea lions are frequently seen in Frederick Sound near **Sandy Beach Park** north of town. Hike to the west side of Sandy Beach Park to discover ancient petroglyphs on the rocks. Discerning individuals may also see the remnants of an ancient Tlingit fish trap near here. In late summer pink salmon spawn in the tiny creek that flows through the park. Icebergs from Le Conte Glacier are common along the north side of Frederick Sound and sometimes drift across to Petersburg, especially in winter. See "Hiking and Cabins" below for trails in and around Petersburg.

Heading out the Road
South of town, the main road is paved for 18 miles, with a gravel road continuing another 16

miles to the southeast end of Mitkof Island. From this point you have excellent views of the nearby Stikine River mouth and the whitecapped peaks of the Coast Range. Canoeists or kayakers (with transportation) may want to start their trip up the Stikine from here rather than at Wrangell.

Approximately eight miles out is a small turnoff to **Falls Creek,** a pleasant picnic spot. Stop here to look at the fish ladder (built in 1959) used by coho and pink salmon, as well as steelhead. A **trumpeter swan observatory** is set up on Blind Slough 16 miles south of Petersburg. A dozen or so of these majestic birds over-

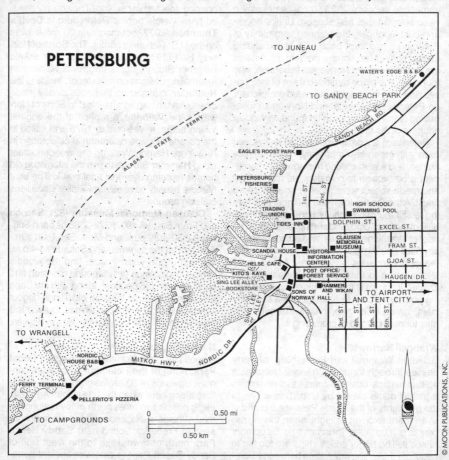

PETERSBURG

COMMERCIAL SALMON FISHING

Three types of salmon-fishing boats are commonly seen along the Pacific coast.

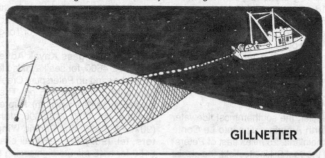

GILLNETTER

The **gillnetter** is easily recognized by the large drum at the stern of the boat. Fish are caught by the gills in the long nylon net played out from the drum and removed by hand as the net is wound back in.

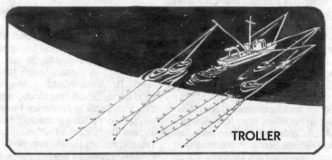

TROLLER

Trollers use tall poles that stick straight up from the boat when not in use. To catch fish they are extended over the sides with up to eight trailing lines and hooks. The hooked fish are pulled in either hydraulically (power trollers) or by hand (hand trollers).

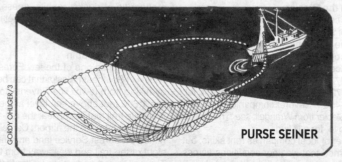

GORDY OHLIGER/3

PURSE SEINER

The **purse seiner** is the largest of the types. It is recognizable by the power block in the rigging to haul the net in, and by a skiff that is usually perched astern. A net with floats along the top edge and weights at the bottom is pulled out around a school of fish by a person in the skiff. When the fish are surrounded, the bottom is closed like a purse and the net is pulled out by the power block.

winter here and other waterfowl abound during spring and fall migrations. **Crystal Lake Fish Hatchery,** 18 miles south of Petersburg, tel. (907) 772-4772, produces king, coho, and chum salmon. Blind Slough flows away from the hatchery and is a great place to explore by canoe or kayak. Or, try ice skates in the winter months.

LE CONTE GLACIER

Le Conte Glacier, the southernmost tidewater glacier in North America, dips into Le Conte Bay on the mainland, 25 miles east of Petersburg. Part of the vast Stikine Icefield, the glacial ice was once used by local fishermen to keep their catches cold on the way to market in Seattle. Today, locals use it to cool their drinks. Le Conte Bay is home to 2,000 harbor seals. The entire area is included within the 448,841-acre **Stikine-Le Conte Wilderness.**

There are no Forest Service cabins in Le Conte Bay, but an excellent one ($25/night) is on **Mallard Slough,** near its entrance. A 1.5-mile trail connects the cabin and Le Conte Bay, where you're likely to find icebergs high and dry at low tide. A fine trip for experienced sea kayakers is to head up the Stikine River from Wrangell and then into Le Conte Bay, 10 miles north, before crossing Frederick Sound and continuing on to Petersburg. Total distance is approximately 50 miles (longer if you explore the Stikine River or Le Conte Bay).

Getting to the Glacier
The visitor center has a complete listing of boat charters for sightseeing and fishing around the area. Some of the best include the following: **Kaleidoscope Charters,** tel. (907) 772-3736; **Alaskan Scenic Waterways,** 114 Harbor Way, tel. (907) 772-3777; **Real Alaska Adventures,** tel. (907) 772-4121; and **Sights Southeast,** tel. (907) 772-4503. Several companies also visit Le Conte Glacier from Wrangell; see "The Stikine River," above, for a listing.

A number of local companies rent skiffs, but be forewarned that weather conditions across Frederick Sound can sometimes change abruptly, so don't go out unless you have considerable experience in small boats. Also be sure to stay well away from the face of Le Conte Glacier. There are other hazards near the glacier—in-

cluding hidden ice below the water that suddenly breaks loose and rises to the surface—so it really isn't a good idea to do this without a guide. If you still want to rent a boat, try Scandia House, tel. (907) 772-4281; or Tongass Marine, tel. (907) 772-3905.

Contact **Tongass Kayak Adventures,** tel. (907) 772-4600, for sea kayaking tours around the harbor and up Petersburg Creek. Four-hour trips with guide are $45 pp. They also rent kayaks (three-day minimum). **Kupreanof Flying Service,** tel. (907) 772-3396; **Nordic Air,** tel. (907) 772-3535; and **Pacific Wing Air Charters,** tel. (907) 772-9258, all charge around $150 for a 45-minute flightseeing trip over the glacier (up to three people).

HIKING AND CABINS

Stop by the **Forest Service district office** (upstairs from the post office) for detailed maps of local hiking trails and 25 nearby cabins ($25/night). A pleasant walk takes off from Nordic Dr., three miles from town and just beyond Sandy Beach, and continues down a mile-long boardwalk to **Frederick Point.** Along the way, you get a taste of muskeg, rainforest, and a creek that's packed with salmon in August. You can return to town along the beach. A short in-town boardwalk leads through the muskeg from the top of Excel St. to the senior center (Mountain View Manor) on 12th Street. The center is crowded with flowers outside, along with a menagerie of ducks, rabbits, geese, turkeys, and chickens. Right across the street is the Forest Service's area office.

Ravens Roost Cabin
Petersburg has one of the few Forest Service cabins in Southeast Alaska that can be reached by hiking from town. The Ravens Roost cabin lies 1,600 feet above sea level at the end of a four-mile trail that starts near the red-and-white water tower next to the airport. Camping is permitted on Forest Service land anywhere out of sight of the trail and well away from the cabin. The trail traverses muskeg for the first mile and becomes very steep (and often mucky) for the next mile through the forest before breaking into open muskeg again along a ridge. Here the trail is in better condition and you are treated to

grand views of Devil's Thumb and the surrounding country. Keep your eyes open for wolf tracks. The path ends at a two-level Forest Service cabin with space for up to eight people. Allow three hours for the hike up and be sure to make advance reservations for the cabin through the Forest Service ($25/night). A minor caution: folks occasionally wander up and beg to stay illegally in the cabin with those who have paid, so it's possible that you may have to contend with a freeloader or two.

Come wintertime, Ravens Roost cabin becomes a popular cross-country ski center, with access either by skis or helicopter. A five-mile ski/snowmobile trail connects the cabin to Twin Creek Road (7.5 miles south of Petersburg). A second ski route provides a three-mile loop trip from Twin Creek Road. Both of these trails can also be hiked in the summer.

Three Lakes Recreation Area

Very popular with locals for picnicking, fishing, and berry picking is the beautiful Three Lakes Recreation Area along Forest Service Rd. 6235, 33 miles southeast of town. You can hitch there, but it's a long hike back to town if your thumb is numb. Each lake has a rowboat and picnic table and you may want to camp nearby at the old three-sided shelter built by the CCC along tiny **Shelter Lake.** An easy three-mile boardwalk loop trail connects the lakes; a brushed-out primitive trail continues from Sand Lake to nearby Ideal Cove, 1.5 miles away. Be sure to wear your rubber boots for this primitive trail, although street shoes are fine on the boardwalk. The three main lakes (Sand, Hill, and Crane) are named after the sandhill cranes that announce each spring.

Kupreanof Island Trails and Cabins

On nearby Kupreanof Island, the Petersburg Mountain and Petersburg Lake trails provide good hiking and great views. Both paths begin at the state boat dock on Bayou Point directly across Wrangell Narrows. Ask around Petersburg harbor for people willing to provide skiff transportation for a fee, or stop by Alaskan Scenic Waterways, 114 Harbor Way, tel. (907) 772-3777.

For **Petersburg Mountain Trail,** walk north (right) up the road 1.5 miles to the trail marker. Be prepared for a very steep, muddy, and brushy path, rising 3,000 feet in a distance of only 2.5 miles. From the top, however, you'll be rewarded with outstanding views of the entire Petersburg area.

Petersburg Lake Trail provides an easy 6.5-mile hike to a Forest Service cabin ($25/night) on Petersburg Lake within the 46,777-acre **Petersburg Creek-Duncan Salt Chuck Wilderness.** Check with the Forest Service for current trail conditions. A diamond-shaped sign marks the trailhead along the shore. Fish the creek for coho salmon, steelhead, and cutthroats. Another option is to fly in to Petersburg Lake (approximately $100 for three people and gear) and hike back out. From Petersburg Lake it's possible to continue another 10.5 miles along a primitive but brushed-out trail to the Forest Service's Salt Chuck East Cabin ($25/night). The trail is nearly level the entire distance and offers spectacular views of Portage Mountain.

On the south end of Kupreanof Island is **Kah Sheets Lake,** where the Forest Service has an A-frame cabin ($25/night) that is now wheelchair accessible (great for older folks and families, too). The very popular (reserve early!) cabin is a 30-minute flight from Petersburg (approximately $200 roundtrip for three people and gear). A three-mile trail leads from the lake to Kah Sheets Bay, where you can fish for coho and sockeye salmon. A second Forest Service cabin sits along the bay.

The newest place to stay is the **West Point Cabin** ($25/night) in Portage Bay on the north end of Kupreanof Island. This is a great spot to watch for whales, and the beach makes for good hiking.

Thomas Bay Area

Several of the most popular local Forest Service cabins ($25/night) are in the country around Thomas Bay, on the mainland approximately 20 miles from Petersburg. Spectacular Baird and Patterson Glaciers feed into this bay. Be sure to reserve months ahead to ensure a spot. **Cascade Creek Cabin** is on the salt water and is accessible by either air or charter boat. Backpackers will love **Cascade Creek Trail,** one of the best (and steepest) paths in Southeast. This three-mile path climbs 3,000 feet from the cabin to Falls Lake, passing cascading water much of the way. A new three-sided shelter (free) sits along the shore of Falls Lake, and there's good fishing for rainbow trout. Hikers can continue two more miles up the trail beyond Falls Lake to Swan Lake. **Swan Lake Cabin** is on the opposite end of the lake from the trailhead and offers great views of the rocky mountain country. Contact the Petersburg Forest Service office for details on current trail conditions and access.

ACCOMMODATIONS

With nearly a thousand transient cannery workers clamoring for housing in Petersburg, travelers often have a hard time finding a place to stay during the summer. Unfortunately, there is no youth hostel in Petersburg, and no cheap lodging.

Water's Edge B&B, 705 Sandy Beach Rd., tel. (907) 772-3736 or (800) 722-5006, is a fine place if you want peace and quiet. The owners are a retired fisheries biologist and a schoolteacher, and their beachfront room overlooks Frederick Sound where sea lions, ducks, and whales are often seen just offshore. Rooms, including a continental-plus breakfast, run $70-

80 s, $80-90 d. Highly recommended. Another good local place is **Nordic House B&B,** 1106 Nordic Dr., tel. (907) 772-3620. It offers four guest rooms with private or shared baths, plus continental breakfast; $65-75 s, $75-85 d.

For additional lodging possibilities, see the chart "Petersburg Accommodations."

Camping

Finding a place to camp in Petersburg can be a problem during the summer. The only designated camping area close to town is **Tent City,** about two miles out, between the airport and Sandy Cove. This campground (alias "Visqueen Acres") consists of 52 wooden tent platforms built over the wet muskeg and connected by boardwalk to a covered cooking/partying area with cold running water, firewood, toilets, coin-operated showers, and phones. The facility becomes home to dozens of cannery workers during the summer and is often full by June, though a few places are kept for short-term campers. Travelers often have a hard time finding space, and those who do should be ready for a noisy

---

PETERSBURG ACCOMMODATIONS

Note: Petersburg adds a nine percent tax to lodging rates. Accommodations are arranged from least to most expensive.

Narrows Inn; across from the ferry; tel. (907) 772-4284; $55 s, $65 d; very plain

Harbor Day B&B; 405 Noseeum; tel. (907) 772-3971; $55 s, $70 d; newer home, two guest rooms, shared bath, breakfast buffet

Nordic House B&B; 1106 Nordic Dr.; tel. (907) 772-3620; $65-75 s, $75-85 d; four guest rooms, private or shared baths, continental breakfast

Broom Hus B&B; 411 S. Nordic; tel. (907) 772-3459; $65 s, $80 d; apartment unit, private entrance, continental breakfast

Rainsong B&B; 1107 Wrangell Ave.; tel. (907) 772-3178; $65-70 s, $70-75 d; two-bedroom apartment, full kitchen, continental breakfast

Sea Breeze B&B; 313 Sandy Beach Rd.; tel. (907) 772-3279; $70 s, $80 d; one guest room, private bath, continental breakfast

Mountain Point B&B; five miles south of town; tel. (907) 772-4669; $70 s, $80 d; one guest room, private bath, continental breakfast

Tides Inn; First and Dolphin Sts.; tel. (907) 772-4288; $70 s, $85 d; AAA approved

Scandia House; Nordic Dr.; tel. (907) 772-4281 or (800) 722-5006; $75 s, $85 d; new hotel, continental breakfast, courtesy van

Water's Edge B&B; 705 Sandy Beach Rd.; tel. (907) 772-3736 or (800) 868-4373; $70-80 s, $80-90 d; great views, quiet location, continental plus breakfast

Mitkof Island Guest House; 606 S. Nordic Dr.; tel. (907) 772-3800; $145 s or d; historic building, furnished three-bedroom apartment, sleeps six, full kitchen

night. Tent City costs $5 pp/day or $30 pp/week. Call (907) 772-9864 for details. City Cab has a CB at Tent City that you can use to call for a ride to town ($4 for two people) or to check on times to report for work at the canneries. Tent City is open May-Sept. only.

It may not be legal, but good camping sites can also be found by walking east a half-mile along the beach from Sandy Beach Recreation Area. The sites are in the woods near the shore.

Those with a vehicle or willing to try hitching should head south 22 miles to the Forest Service's excellent **Ohmer Creek Campground.** This is a quiet place in a flower-filled meadow along Blind Slough, with tap water available. Not far away is the quarter-mile long, wheelchair-accessible **Ohmer Creek Trail,** complete with interpretive signs. This is a beautiful old-growth rainforest walk, with good steelhead fishing in the spring.

RVers often head to **Le Conte RV Park,** Fourth St. and Haugen Dr., tel. (907) 772-4680; or **Twin Creek RV Park,** seven miles south of the ferry terminal, tel. (907) 772-3244, where full hookups cost $15-20/night. These also have a few tent spaces.

FOOD

For an all-American greasy-spoon breakfast or lunch (try their fish and chips basket) visit the **Homestead Cafe** downtown on Main Street. It's open 24 hours, but you may want to bring a gas mask if you don't smoke, since the air gets pretty dense, especially in the morning when the good old boys talk fishing. **Helse Cafe** at Sing Lee Alley and Gjoa St., tel. (907) 772-3444, serves inexpensive earthy lunches. Another good lunchtime option for a cheap, quick meal is one of the downtown **street vendors.**

AlasKafe Coffeehouse, upstairs on the corner of Nordic and Excel, tel. (907) 772-5282, serves panini sandwiches, pastas, salads, desserts, and espresso. A good hangout with several outdoor seats; open Tues.-Saturday.

Seafood

Given the importance of fishing in the local economy, it comes as no surprise that Petersburg has a number of places offering fresh seafood. The **Coastal Cold Storage Fish Market** on Excel

and Main St., tel. (907) 772-4171, makes up delicious fresh seafood specials daily, including shrimp cocktail, soups, fish chowders, salads, beer-batter halibut, and other deli specials. You can also purchase fresh fish, crab, scallops, and other seafood and have them ship it for you. Open lunches year-round, and dinners in the summer. Budget watchers should try the docks to buy fresh-caught crab, halibut, or shrimp. **Tonka Seafoods,** tel. (907) 772-3662, has a small fish-processing plant that specializes in premium quality smoked salmon. You can tour the plant.

International Eats

For some of the best pizzas in Alaska head to **Pellerito's Pizzeria** across from the ferry terminal, tel. (907) 772- 3727. These are *not* those frozen-dough, slap-on-the-Ragu versions that pass for pizza elsewhere. They have both whole pizzas and pizzas by the slice, plus a big choice of microbrewed beers. Next to Pellerito's is **Joan Mei Chinese Restaurant,** tel. (907) 772-4221, serving breakfast, American grub, and all-too-Americanized Chinese food. Pellerito's and Joan Mei are the only Petersburg restaurants open on Sunday evenings. Another pizza place is **Harbor Lights Pizza** on Sing Lee Alley, tel. (907) 772-3424. The pizzas don't come close to those produced by Pellerito's, but they do offer an unusually good Canadian bacon cheeseburger, and a fine location.

Groceries

Prices for food and other items are higher in Petersburg than in other Southeast towns. The friendliest place for groceries is **Hammer and Wikan** with a new store at 1300 Haugen Dr., tel. (907) 772-4246, but **Trading Union,** tel. (907) 772-3881, tends to be a little cheaper. Get natural foods at **Helse Foods** on Sing Lee Alley, tel. (907) 772-3444.

OTHER PRACTICALITIES

Events and Entertainment

Petersburg's **Little Norway Festival,** held each year on the weekend nearest Norwegian Independence Day (May 17), is the town's biggest event. The three-day festivities include boat races, folk dancing, Norwegian costumes, pancake breakfasts, and a big seafood smorgasbord. The **American Independence Day** (July Fourth) is another time for fun and games, and the annual salmon derby in late May is always popular with locals.

The annual **Petersburg Canned Salmon Classic** is a contest to guess the number of cans of salmon packed by local canneries each year; $2,500 goes to the person who guesses closest. It's awarded in mid-August. The last three weeks of October make up the **Octoberfest Artshare**, with concerts, plays, and art events.

Live music, booze, and a clientele of local toughs make for good fights in **Kito's Kave** on Sing Lee Alley. **AlasKafe**, tel. (907) 772-5282, features Saturday night jam sessions and poetry readings. For something even more low-key, **The New You**, 104 Haugen Dr., tel. (907) 772-4466, has a relaxing jacuzzi.

Information

The **Petersburg Visitor Information Center** is on the corner of First and Fram Sts., tel. (907) 772-4636, and is open Sunday noon-4 p.m., Mon.-Fri. 8 a.m.-4 p.m., and Saturday 9 a.m.-5 p.m. For up-to-date local info, pick up a copy of Petersburg's free *Viking Visitor Guide* here or at the ferry terminal. The visitor center staff can also make reservations for Forest Service cabins in the area. The Forest Service publishes a map ($3) of the Petersburg area *(Mitkof Island Road Guide)*, available from their office upstairs in the post office building on Main St., tel. (907) 772-3871. It details the whys and wherefores of logging on the island, and even describes a tour of local clearcuts for the truly dedicated timber beast. (The blurb on the back cover gives you an idea of its biases: "Timber Harvest Prepares the Way.") The map is a must if you're planning to ride a mountain bike around the island.

Shopping and Services

Sing Lee Alley Bookstore, tel. (907) 772-4440, next to the Sons of Norway Hall, has an excellent collection of Alaskan books and other choice reading material. Get cash 24 hours from **ATMs** at First Bank, 103 N. Nordic Dr; and National Bank of Alaska, 201 N. Nordic Drive. The **post office** is on the corner of Nordic and Haugen. The town **library**, open Mon.-Thurs. noon-9 p.m., Friday and Saturday 1-5 p.m., is upstairs in the municipal building on Nordic Drive. Coin-operated **showers** are available downtown next

to the harbormaster's office ($1 gives you eight minutes of hot water). Showers ($1.75; $2.75 with towel) are also available from **Glacier Laundry** on Nordic Drive. For a better deal, head to the public **swimming pool** at Petersburg High School, tel. (907) 772-3304. A fine community gymnasium is nearby, complete with a weight room and racquetball courts.

Transportation and Tours

Petersburg is strung out along Wrangell Narrows, with the **ferry terminal** a mile south of town center. During the summertime, ferries run almost daily both northbound and southbound from Petersburg. They usually stop for an hour or two, long enough to walk into town or at least check out the nearby harbor. The purser will let you know when you need to be back onboard. The ferry terminal, tel. (907) 772-3855, opens two hours prior to ship arrivals and generally stays open a half-hour after it departs.

City Cab, tel. (907) 772-3003, charges $4 pp for transport from the ferry to Tent City. Rent cars from **Allstar Rent-A-Car** at Scandia House, tel. (907) 772-4281; or **Avis**, in Tides Inn, tel. (907) 772-4288 or (800) 331-1212. Bike rentals and tours are available from **Northern Bikes,** 110 N. Nordic Dr., tel. (907) 772-3978.

Petersburg Airport is a mile southeast of town on Haugen Drive. **Alaska Airlines,** tel. (907) 772-4255 or (800) 426-0333, has daily service to Juneau, Ketchikan, Sitka, Wrangell, and other places in Alaska and the Lower 48. **Ketchikan Air Service,** tel. (907) 772-3443 or (800) 656-6608, has daily flights to Juneau ($112), Kake ($55), Ketchikan ($117), Klawock ($150), and Wrangell ($68). **L.A.B. Flying Service,** tel. (907) 772-4300 or (800) 426-0543, also has air taxi service to Kake ($56) and Juneau ($115). **Pacific Wing,** tel. (907) 772-9258; **Kupreanof Flying Service,** tel. (907) 772-3396, and **Nash West Aviation,** tel. (907) 772-3344, all provide air charter service to Forest Service cabins and nearby sites (around $200/hour for two people and gear).

KAKE

The small Tlingit village of Kake (pop. 700) lies along the northwest shore of Kupreanof Island, halfway between Petersburg and Sitka. Kake's single claim to fame is being home to the world's tallest totem pole, exhibited at the 1970 World's Fair in Osaka, Japan. The 132-foot pole is unique in that it contains figures representing all the Tlingit clans on a single pole. Kake is also the starting point for sea kayak trips into two large wilderness areas on nearby Kuiu Island.

History

During the 1800s the Kake tribe had a reputation as one of the fiercest in Southeast. Richard Meade (1871) recorded the following incident: "In 1855 a party of Kakes, on a visit south to Puget Sound, became involved in some trouble there, which caused a United States vessel to open fire on them, and during the affair one of the Kake chiefs was killed. This took place over 800 miles from the Kake settlements on Kupreanof Island. The very next year the tribe sent a canoe-load of fighting men all the way from Clarence Straits in Russian America to Whidby's Island in Washington Territory, and attacked and beheaded an ex-collector—not of internal revenue, for that might have been pardonable—but of customs, and returned safely with his skull and scalp to their villages. Such people are, therefore, not to be despised, and are quite capable of giving much trouble in the future unless wisely and firmly governed." John Muir later described a visit to a Kake village where human bones were scattered all over the ground, reminders of previous battles: "Chief Yana Taowk seemed to take pleasure in kicking the Sitka bones that lay in his way, and neither old nor young showed the slightest trace of superstitious fear of the dead at any time." Needless to say, the people of Kake treat outsiders in a more friendly manner today.

Practicalities

Waterfront Lodge, tel. (907) 785-3472, has rooms for rent, as do **Keex' Kwaan Lodge/Hotel,** tel. (907) 785-6471; and **Rocky Pass Resort,** tel. (907) 785-3175. The **Nugget Inn,** tel. (907) 785-6469, serves meals. In town are three grocery stores; **SOS Value-Mart,** tel. (907) 785-6444, is the largest. Kake has a laundromat and liquor store but no bank. For local info, contact the City of Kake at (907) 785-3804. Camping facilities are not available and much of the land around Kake is privately owned, but camping is permitted on Forest Service land, two

miles south of town. Charters and tours are becoming available as Kake residents begin to enter the tourism business. Kake is one of the drier towns in Southeast, with 50 inches per year of precipitation. The town has a fish hatchery and cold storage plant but no Forest Service office. Ask at the Forest Service office in Petersburg about the Cathedral Falls, Goose Lake, and Hamilton River Trails. **Big John Cabin** ($25/night) on Big John Bay is accessible via the road network from Kake.

Transportation

The ferry *Le Conte* visits Kake twice a week, heading both east to Petersburg ($22) and west to Sitka ($24). The ferry docks 1.5 miles from the center of town. There is only a covered shelter area, but no phone. The ferry usually stops just long enough to load and unload cars (a half-hour or so). There are daily flights between Kake and Petersburg ($56) by **Alaska Island Air,** tel. (907) 772-3130 (in Petersburg); **L.A.B. Flying Service,** tel. (907) 785-6435 or (800) 426-0543; and **Wings of Alaska,** tel. (907) 772-3536 or (800) 478-9464. L.A.B. also flies to Juneau ($95), while **Taquan Air,** tel. (907) 785-6411 or (800) 770-8800, flies daily to Sitka for $80 and Angoon for $80. **Ketchikan Air Service,** tel. (907) 785-3139 or (800) 656-6608, flies daily between Kake and Juneau ($85), Ketchikan ($155), Klawock ($175), Wrangell ($105), and Petersburg ($55).

Kuiu Island

If you have the time, equipment, and skill, nearby Kuiu (pronounced "Q-U") Island provides excellent kayaking and canoeing opportunities. The area is filled with an enjoyable network of islands and waterways. The Forest Service has cleared four portages ranging from one to four miles in length, making it possible to do a variety of loop trips. Plan on at least a week and be sure to check with the Forest Service on current trail conditions, especially the Alecks Creek Portage. Be cautious along portions of Kuiu Island exposed to ocean swells, particularly near Point Ellis. Three Forest Service cabins ($25/night) are along the route. Also of interest are the protected waters of scenic **Rocky Pass** separating Kupreanof and Kuiu Islands. Because of the numerous reefs, the pass is treacherous for boats, but can be run in a kayak if you traverse with the tidal flows. Some supplies are available at the Gedney Harbor Fish-buying Scow, but check with Petersburg Fisheries in Petersburg first to see what is available.

Two wilderness areas encompass the south and west sides of Kuiu Island; other parts have been very heavily logged in recent years. Dozens of interesting islands, islets, and coves crowd the west side of Kuiu in the 67,000-acre **Tebenkof Bay Wilderness,** while the south end includes the newly established 60,000-acre **Kuiu Wilderness.** Wilderness rangers patrol these areas from kayaks. The Forest Service publishes a detailed map of Kuiu Island with descriptions of all portages and routes. Get a copy of **Kuiu Island/Tebenkof Bay Canoe/Kayak Routes** ($3) from Petersburg Ranger District, Box 1328, Petersburg, AK 99833, tel. (907) 772-3871. Experienced kayakers will enjoy the paddle between Kake and Petersburg around the south end of Kupreanof Island. There is open water in places, but a good portion of the route is protected and the state ferry makes it easy to get between Kake and Petersburg.

SITKA

Sitka (pop. 9,100) is everybody's favorite Southeast Alaska town. Look out on the gemlike setting of Sitka Sound on a typical summer day. Fishing boats head out to sea from the four harbors, passing the hundreds of islands dotting the sound. Cruise ships steam by, their decks crowded with tourists as they pass Mt. Edgecumbe, the Fuji-like snowcapped volcano that adorns Sitka's outer waters. Back in town, other visitors glance inside the Russian church that dominates Sitka's center, wander along totem-pole-lined paths in Sitka National Historical Park, and climb up the sharply rising wooded peaks behind town. The people who make this their home are similarly diverse, ranging from back-to-the-land ecofreaks to beer-guzzling, case-hardened fishermen. This surprising diversity and the gorgeous setting make Sitka a detour well worth the effort. Be forewarned, however, to expect rain—the town soaks in 94 inches a year. By the way, Sitka lays claim to being the "biggest city in America"; its boundaries encircle Baranof Island, fully 4,710 square miles! (New York City covers only 301 square miles.)

Peril Strait

Located on the western shore of Baranof Island, "Sitka-by-the-Sea" is Southeast Alaska's most remote ferry stop, and the only major one to front on the Pacific Ocean. Getting to Sitka by ferry requires a long detour through the scenic but treacherous Peril Strait that separates Baranof and Chichagof Islands—a great place to watch for eagles perched on trees along the shore. (Make sure the shipboard naturalist points out the "flamingos" that perch atop one tall spruce tree!) During larger tides, fierce currents prevent ferries from going through, and the ships must time their passage to coincide with a high or low slack tide. The passage narrows to only 300 feet wide in one spot (24 feet deep). When the tide is really cooking, the buoys are often bent far over by the wild currents. This has one side benefit: the ferry is forced to stay for three hours or so in Sitka, long enough for you to get a taste of this fascinating town. But to see this pretty place better, be sure to stay awhile.

HISTORY

Russian America
First established as a base for collecting sea otter pelts, Sitka has a long and compelling history. In 1799, Alexander Baranof—head of the Russian American Company—founded the settlement under a charter from the czar. Baranof built his original fort, Redoubt St. Michael, near the present Alaska ferry terminal, only to see it

Russian emblem

LOUISE FOOTE

destroyed by a Tlingit attack in 1802. (There is evidence that the British, long enemies of the Russians, assisted the Tlingits in the fort's destruction.) Two years later, Baranof returned with 120 soldiers and 800 Aleuts in 300 *baidarkas,* defeating the Tlingits in what was to become the last major resistance by any Northwest Coast Indians. The Russians rebuilt the town, then called New Archangel, on the present site and constructed a stockade enclosing what is now downtown Sitka. New Archangel soon became the capital of Russian America and a vital center for the sea otter and fur seal trade with China. Although the Tlingits were invited back in 1821 (Native leaders say the Russians begged them to return), the groups coexisted uneasily. Tlingits built their houses just outside the stockade, facing a battery of eight Russian cannons.

Once labeled the "Paris of the North Pacific," New Archangel quickly became the Northwest's most cosmopolitan port. By 1840, it was already home to a library of several thousand volumes, a museum, a meteorological observatory, two schools, a hospital, an armory, two orphanages, and dozens of other buildings. The wealthier citizens lived in elaborate homes filled with crystal and fine lace, but as with czarist Russia itself, the opulence of Sitka did not extend beyond a select few. Slavelike working and living conditions were forced upon the Aleut sea otter hunters.

America Takes Over

An emotional ceremony at Sitka in 1867 marked the passage of Alaska from Russian to American hands, and most of the Russians returned to their motherland, including many third-generation Sitkans. Even today, there are locals who speak Russian. Although the town served as Alaska's first capital city for three decades, its importance declined rapidly under the Americans, it was almost a ghost town by the turn of the century. The territorial government was moved to the then-booming mining town of Juneau in 1900.

During WW II, Sitka became a major link in the defense of Alaska against Japan. Hangars remain from the large amphibious air base just across the bridge on Japonski Island (Fort Ray), and the barracks that once housed 3,500 soldiers were turned into Mt. Edgecumbe High School, Alaska's only boarding high school for

Natives. The boarding school is now fully integrated.

Sitka's largest employer—until 1993—was a Japanese-owned pulp mill five miles east of town. The mill closed mainly due to the high cost of production and competition from mills elsewhere. Before it closed, the mill gained national attention for dumping large quantities of cancer-causing dioxin into nearby Silver Bay, and for being one of the primary forces behind the clearcut logging of Tongass National Forest. Many Sitkans still work in the fishing and tourism industries, or for the government. The mill's closure did not have nearly the devastating effect the prophets of doom had predicted; in fact Sitka seems to be doing just fine, fueled by tourism and the arrival of increasing numbers of retirees, many from California. However, this has unfortunately had a negative side effect, as local property taxes have risen dramatically.

SIGHTS

St. Michael's Cathedral

The most striking symbol of Russian influence in Sitka is St. Michael's Cathedral. Originally built in 1848, the building burned in 1966 but was replaced by an identical replica a decade later. The original Russian artifacts and icons, including the Sitka Madonna (purportedly a miraculous healer), were saved from the fire and have been returned to their original setting in this, the mother church for all of Alaska's 20,000 Russian Orthodox members. The church ($1 donation), tel. (907) 747-8120, is open daily 7:30 a.m.-5:30 p.m. except during services in the summer, with longer hours when cruise ships are in port, and reduced hours in winter.

Other Downtown Sights

One of the finest views of Sitka is from the unusual cable-stayed, girder-span bridge that crosses Sitka harbor to Japonski Island. On a clear day, you'll have a hard time deciding which direction to look: the mountains of Baranof Island rise up behind the town, while the perfect volcanic cone of Mt. Edgecumbe (3,000 feet) on Kruzof Island dominates the opposite vista. Beside the old post office on Lincoln St. a stairway leads up to **Castle Hill,** a tiny state park

St. Michael's Cathedral

commemorating the spot where the ceremony transferring Alaska to the U.S. was held on October 18, 1867. The Kiksadi Indian clan inhabited this hill for many generations prior to the Russian arrival. After defeating the Indians, Alexander Baranof built his castlelike house here, but the building burned in 1894. The splendid view makes Castle Hill a must.

The most prominent downtown feature is the large yellow **Alaska Pioneers Home** (built in 1934), housing elderly Alaskans with 15 or more years of state residence. The Pioneer Home crafts shop is open weekdays 8 a.m.-5 p.m. The **Prospector** statue out front was based upon William "Skagway Bill" Fonda, an Alaskan pioneer. Across the road is a **totem pole** bearing the Russian coat of arms, three old English anchors, and a couple of Indian petroglyphs.

On a hill just west of the Pioneer Home stands a reconstructed **Russian blockhouse** from the stockade that kept the Indians restricted to the area along Katlian Street. It's open Sunday afternoons during the summer. **Kogwantan and Katlian Streets,** directly below the blockhouse, are a picturesque mixture of docks, fish canneries, shops, and old houses, one with its exterior entirely covered in Tlingit designs. The main **Russian Orthodox cemetery** (400 graves dating from 1848) caps the wooded hill at the end of Observatory Street. The grave of the Russian Princess Maksoutoff is at the end of Princess St., and a few other old graves are near the blockhouse. Cemetery buffs might also be interested in the small **Sitka National Cemetery,** accessible via Jeff Davis St. beside Sheldon Jackson College. It's the oldest national cemetery west of the Mississippi.

The **Isabel Miller Museum,** tel. (907) 747-6455, in the Centennial Hall, is open daily 8 a.m.-6 p.m. in summer, and Tues.-Sat. 10 a.m.-4 p.m. in winter. A donation is requested. The museum houses a small collection of interesting local artifacts from the past 120 years. The scale model of Sitka in 1867 (the year Alaska became a U.S. territory) is especially evocative of the Russian period. A beautiful old chair made entirely of whalebone is also notable. Out front is a 50-foot carved and painted replica of a **Tlingit war canoe.**

Russian Bishop's House

Now administered by the National Park Service, the Russian Bishop's House (donation requested) is Sitka's oldest building and one of just four Russian buildings still standing in North America. Built in 1842, the carefully restored building was home to Ivan Veniaminov, bishop of Alaska and later head of the entire Russian Orthodox Church hierarchy in Moscow. The Park Service spent $5 million restoring this structure over a period of 15 years. The first floor houses exhibits describing the building and its occupants, as well as the exploits of Russia's American colony. The second floor has been fully restored to its 1853 appearance and is filled with original furnishings and artifacts. Access to the second floor is with guided groups only during an informative half-hour tour. Tours cost $2 pp; entrance to the lower level remains free. The Bishop's House is open daily 9 a.m.-1 p.m. and 2-5 p.m. during the summer or by reservation the rest of the year. Winter tours are given

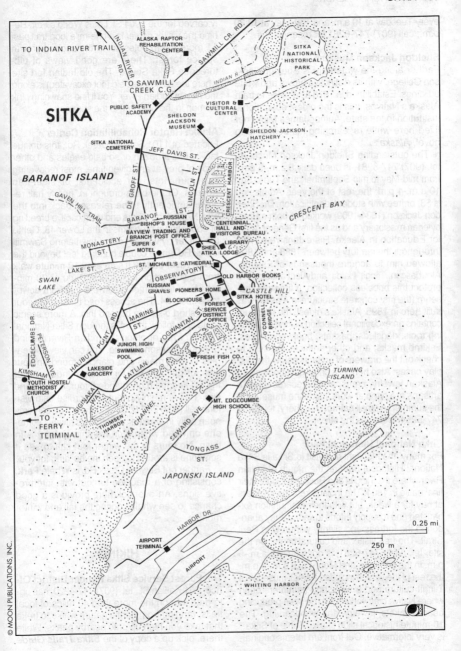

SITKA

BARANOF ISLAND

TO INDIAN RIVER TRAIL

ALASKA RAPTOR REHABILITATION CENTER

TO SAWMILL CREEK C.G.

INDIAN RIVER RD

SAWMILL CR. RD

INDIAN R.

SITKA NATIONAL HISTORICAL PARK

PUBLIC SAFETY ACADEMY

SHELDON JACKSON MUSEUM

VISITOR & CULTURAL CENTER

SHELDON JACKSON HATCHERY

SITKA NATIONAL CEMETERY

JEFF DAVIS ST.

LINCOLN ST.

CRESCENT HARBOR

CRESCENT BAY

GAVEN HILL TRAIL

DE GROFF ST.

BARANOF ST.

RUSSIAN BISHOP'S HOUSE

BAYVIEW TRADING AND BRANCH POST OFFICE

MONASTERY ST.

SUPER 8 MOTEL

CENTENNIAL HALL AND VISITORS BUREAU

SHEE ATIKA LODGE

LIBRARY

LAKE ST.

ST. MICHAEL'S CATHEDRAL

OBSERVATORY

OLD HARBOR BOOKS

SWAN LAKE

RUSSIAN GRAVES

PIONEERS HOME

BLOCKHOUSE

CASTLE HILL

SITKA HOTEL

FOREST SERVICE DISTRICT OFFICE

O'CONNELL BRIDGE

PETERSON AVE

EDGECUMBE DR.

HALIBUT PGINT RD

MARINE ST.

KATLIAN

KOGWANTAN ST.

JUNIOR HIGH/ SWIMMING POOL

FRESH FISH CO.

KIMSHAM

YOUTH HOSTEL/ METHODIST CHURCH

LAKESIDE GROCERY

SIGINAKA WAY

THOMSEN HARBOR

TO FERRY TERMINAL

SITKA CHANNEL

MT. EDGECUMBE HIGH SCHOOL

TURNING ISLAND

SEWARD AVE.

TONGASS ST.

JAPONSKI ISLAND

HARBOR DR.

AIRPORT TERMINAL

AIRPORT

WHITING HARBOR

0.25 mi

250 m

© MOON PUBLICATIONS, INC.

every Tuesday at 10 a.m. and Thursday at 12:30 p.m.; call (907) 747-6281 for reservations.

Sheldon Jackson Museum

Farther along the waterfront is Sheldon Jackson College, with its distinctive brown and white buildings. Established in 1878 as a place to train Alaska's Natives, this is the oldest educational institution in the state. Author James Michener lived here while researching his best-selling novel, *Alaska.*

The outstanding Sheldon Jackson Museum, tel. (907) 747-8981, is open daily 8 a.m.-5 p.m. from mid-May to mid-September, and Tues.-Sat. 10 a.m.-4 p.m. the rest of the year. Admission is $3, or free with student identification. Dr. Sheldon Jackson (1834-1909) worked as both a Presbyterian missionary and as the first General Agent for Education in Alaska. His extensive travels throughout the territory between 1888 and 1898 allowed him to acquire thousands of Eskimo, Athabascan, Tlingit, Haida, and Aleut artifacts. To protect this priceless collection, a fireproof museum (the first concrete structure in Alaska) was built here in 1895. Alaska's oldest, the museum contains an exceptional selection of kayaks, hunting tools, dogsleds, baskets, bentwood boxes, Eskimo masks, and other artifacts. Be sure to check out the drawers of artifacts below the display cases. Also here is a small gift shop selling Alaskan jewelry, crafts, and notecards. Native artisans are often at work inside the museum in the summer. A small **salmon hatchery,** tel. (907) 747-5254, is across the street.

Sitka National Historical Park

For many, the highlight of a visit to Sitka is Sitka National Historical Park, at the mouth of Indian River where the Tlingits and Russians fought their final battle in 1804. The Indians kept the invaders at bay for a week, but with their ammunition exhausted and resupply efforts thwarted, they abandoned the fortress and silently withdrew to Peril Strait. The free visitor and cultural center on the site, tel. (907) 747-6281, is open daily 8 a.m.-5 p.m. in the summer, and Mon.-Fri. 8 a.m.-5 p.m. the rest of the year. It includes a small museum of Tlingit culture and a workshop (summers only) where Native craftworkers can be seen producing bead blankets, jewelry, and woodcarving. The 10-minute historical slide show, "Battle of Sitka," is very informative. Out front are totems originally carved for the 1904 St. Louis World's Fair. Behind the visitor center is a one-mile loop trail past 11 more totem poles set in the second-growth spruce forest. There are good views of picturesque Sitka Sound. The old Indian fort site where the battle was held (not excavated) is along the nearby Indian River. You'll find spawning pink salmon in the river late in the summer.

Alaska Raptor Rehabilitation Center

Located at 1101 Sawmill Creek Rd., this unique facility has a dozen or so bald eagles and other birds of prey at any given time, most recovering from gunshots, car accidents, or steel-trap wounds. Of the birds brought in, nearly half recover sufficiently to be released back into the wild. Most of the others end up in captive breeding or educational programs in the Lower 48. Get to the center by walking out of town along Sawmill Creek Rd. and a couple hundred feet beyond the Indian River bridge. It's an easy 10-minute walk from Sitka National Historical Park, or 20 minutes from the center of town. A taxi from downtown costs $4. The access road takes off to your left a short distance beyond this. A more scenic route is to follow the trails through Sitka National Historic Park or along the Indian River behind Sheldon Jackson College. You can view the eagles in their mews and glance around on your own, or pay $10 ($5 for children under six) for the full-fledged (pun intended) tour, lecture, and film. This is mainly oriented to cruise ship visitors; call (907) 747-8662 for details. The center is open daily in summer, and there's always someone on hand when a cruise ship or ferry is in town. No tours in the winter, but call to see if someone is around to open the building for you.

Farther out Sawmill Creek Rd. is **Whale Park,** consisting of a roadside turnout with interpretive signs. An overlook here provides a good chance to see whales during the fall and winter months.

HIKING

The **Forest Service Sitka Ranger District Office,** 201 Katlian St., tel. (907) 747-4220, has up-to-date info on the more than 40 miles of local trails, ranging from gentle nature walks to treks that take you high up onto nearby peaks. While there, pick up a copy of the *Sitka Trails Guide.*

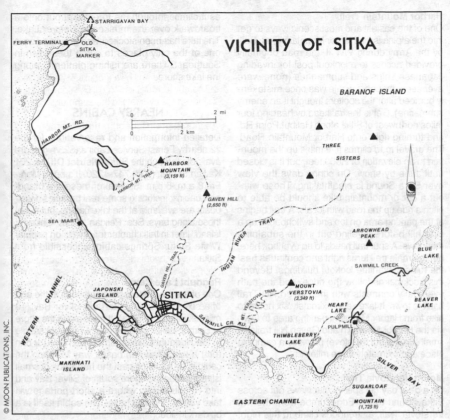

VICINITY OF SITKA

($4) for complete details. Call **Rain Forest Hiking Tours**, tel. (907) 747-8902, for guided hikes around Sitka.

Indian River Trail

One of the finest of Sitka's trails, this is an easy valley hike within walking distance of town. The route follows a clear salmon spawning stream through typical rainforest, with a chance to see brown bear and deer. Begin by taking Indian River Rd. (unmarked) beside the Public Safety Academy along Sawmill Creek Road. Follow it past the gate about a half-mile to the city water pumphouse. The gentle trail leads from here up along the Indian River and a tributary to the right as far as a lovely 80-foot waterfall in a V-shaped valley. The last mile of the trail is brushed out but not well maintained. Watch for berries along the

trail and fish in the stream. Allow six hours roundtrip to cover the 5.5-mile trail.

Gaven Hill Trail

For the more adventurous, Gaven Hill Trail provides access to alpine areas near Sitka with great vistas. Recently reconstructed, the "stairway to heaven" wooden trail starts at the end of Baranof St. and climbs three miles to the top of 2,650-foot Gaven Hill. (Bear right at the junction with Cross Trail just under a mile up.) Gaven Hill Trail then switchbacks to a long ridge that opens onto subalpine meadows before a steep final climb up the last 200 feet of elevation. From here, it's relatively easy to follow rock cairns on through the alpine, connecting to the Harbor Mountain Trail. This makes an outstanding loop hike with impressive vistas of Sitka Sound.

Harbor Mountain Trail

One of the easiest and most scenic ways to get into the alpine is via Harbor Mountain Trail. Built by the Army during WW II, the road originally provided access to a lookout post for invading Japanese ships and submarines (none were ever seen, though a whale was once mistakenly bombed after the spotters thought it an enemy submarine). Get to the trailhead by heading four miles northwest of Sitka along Halibut Point Rd. and turning right onto Harbor Mountain Road. The gravel road climbs five miles up the mountain to an elevation of 2,000 feet, but it is closed until June by snow. On sunny days the view over Sitka Sound is breathtaking. Those without a car or mountain bike should be able to hitch a ride up the road with locals. A trail begins at the parking area on top and switchbacks up a side hill before leveling out in the subalpine meadows. A spur trail heads to an overlook here, but the main trail turns right and continues past the ruins of wartime lookout buildings. Beyond this, rock cairns follow the ridge, and the path eventually connects with the Gaven Hill Trail back to town. It takes approximately six hours to hike from Harbor Mountain parking area to town via the Harbor Mountain and Gaven Hill trails. A small survival hut (no stove) provides a camping place approximately three miles in.

Mount Verstovia Trail

On a clear day get spectacular views out across Sitka Sound to Mt. Edgecumbe from the Mt. Verstovia Trail, a strenuous climb to this high, pointed peak overlooking Sitka. The steep 2.5-mile trail begins on the west side of the Kiksadi Club, two miles east of town on Sawmill Creek Road. The trail is brushy and very poorly maintained, and inexperienced hikers have gotten lost here. You'll pass some old Russian charcoal pits (signposted) only a quarter-mile from the trailhead. The route switchbacks to a ridge, which you follow to the shoulder of Mt. Verstovia. The true summit is farther northeast along the ridge. Allow four hours for the return trip as far as the "shoulder" (2,000 feet), six hours roundtrip to the top (2,550 feet).

Beaver Lake Trail

This excellent mile-long trail begins at the bridge in Sawmill Creek Campground seven miles east of town. The path gains 250 feet in elevation as it climbs through the forest and out onto a boardwalk over the muskeg to Beaver Lake. The lake has been stocked with grayling and is one of the only places to catch these fish in Southeast. There are fishing platforms along the lake shore.

NEARBY CABINS

Detailed information and reservations for the 22 nearby Forest Service cabins ($25/night) are available through the **Sitka District Office,** 201 Katlian St., tel. (907) 747-4220. It's open Mon.-Fri. 8 a.m.-5 p.m. Several of these are brand-new cabins, including some real beauties. Rowboats are available at the lake cabins, but not at those along bays. See "Pelican" under "Chicagof Island" later in this chapter for details on popular White Sulfur Springs cabin, accessible from Sitka.

Redoubt Lake Cabin

One of the most accessible cabins is at the end of a six-mile trail that starts in Silver Bay (10 miles southeast of Sitka). It goes along the shore of Salmon Lake and then over a 600-foot saddle to the Redoubt Lake cabin. If you have (or can rent) a sea kayak, an easier way to reach the cabin is by paddling past the hundreds of small islands along the shore south of Silver Bay and into Redoubt Bay, where a short portage will take you to Redoubt Lake. The cabin itself is a bit dark inside.

Mount Edgecumbe

Mount Edgecumbe, a 3,000-foot volcanic cone that looks like Mt. Fuji, can be climbed along a 6.5-mile trail that starts on the southeast shore of Kruzof Island. The last mile is above timberline through red volcanic ash. The island is 10 miles west of Sitka and can be reached by kayak (beware of ocean swells) or by arranging for a skiff drop-off (approximately $125 roundtrip) through a local charter boat operator. Stay in **Fred's Creek Cabin** at the trailhead, or in a free three-sided shelter halfway up the peak. Wonderful views from atop this dormant volcano.

Lake Eva Cabin

The Lake Eva Cabin, 27 miles northeast of Sitka on Baranof Island, is entirely wheelchair-accessible, including the dock, outhouse, and fishing platform. It's a great place for those with young children or physical disabilities. Good fishing for sockeye salmon, cutthroats, and steelhead. On the east side of Lake Eva (opposite the cabin) a trail leads three miles through beautiful old-growth forests to Hanus Bay. Lake Eva is a half-hour floatplane trip from Sitka (approximately $440 roundtrip for two people and gear).

Plotnikof Lake Cabin

One of the most scenic local cabins is on the edge of Plotnikof Lake, a narrow four-mile-long lake bordered by steep mountainsides and many waterfalls. The cabin is a very expensive 45-minute floatplane trip from Sitka in the spectacularly rugged South Baranof Wilderness Area. Bring fuel oil for the oil-burning stove here. A one-mile trail connects Plotnikof Lake to the similarly impressive **Davidof Lake,** which also has a Forest Service cabin.

Baranof Lake Cabin

This cabin is located on the upper end of three-mile-long Baranof Lake, and its remote setting offers definitive wilderness accommodations. The cabin looks out from a small stand of spruce trees across the blue-green lake to a waterfall. If you have an outboard, or fly in with a folding kayak, you can cruise down the lake to the outlet. From here, a trail leads a half-mile to the little settlement of **Baranof Warm Springs,** where a privately owned (and not especially well maintained) hot springs is available. **Taquan Air,** tel. (907) 747-8636 or (800) 770-8800, flies to Baranof Warm Springs from Sitka for $70.

Kruzof Island Cabins

Brent's Beach Cabin is on the eastern shore of Kruzof Island, approximately 15 miles northwest of Sitka. There is a white-sand beach out front (rare in Southeast), and interesting caves and lava domes just up the shore. Also on Kruzof Island is **Shelikof Cabin,** on the island's west side. Access is by boat to Mud Bay, followed by a seven-mile hike along a logging road and newly rebuilt trail to the cabin. (If you have the money, helicopter access is also possible.) The cabin features an impressive ocean view and sandy beaches, and is relatively close to Sitka.

Other Popular Cabins

Sevenfathom Bay Cabin is a new A-frame cabin 22 miles south of Sitka along a Baranof Island inlet. The cabin is a 20-minute boat ride from the hot tubs at **Goddard Hot Springs** and near the edge of the South Baranof Wilderness Area. The spacious **Samsing Cove Cabin** sleeps 10 folks comfortably and is just six miles south of Sitka. Built in 1991, the cabin is very popular with Sitkans.

Families (or couples wanting to relax in spacious accommodations) may be interested in a truly outstanding place, the **Allan Point Cabin,** 16 miles north of Sitka. The impressive two-story log cabin (sleeps 10) commands a fine view across Nakwasina Sound from its location on the northeast end of Halleck Island. Access to all of these cabins is primarily by boat or kayak from Sitka, though some are also reachable by floatplane. Either rent a skiff (if you have the skills) or get one of the many local charter operators to drop you off. Completed in 1994, the **Piper Island Cabin** is an A-frame structure 30 miles north of Sitka. Access is by skiff or kayak.

OTHER RECREATION

Kayaking

The protected waters near Sitka provide excellent kayak access to many Forest Service cabins and trails. Larry Edwards of **Baidarka Boats** rents double fiberglass kayaks for $45/day, singles for $35/day, and folding double kayaks for $55/day. Weekly rates are lower, and instruction is available for all levels. Call (907) 747-8996 or write him at P.O. Box 6001, Sitka, AK 99835, to reserve a kayak. The shop is above Old Harbor Books at 201 Lincoln Street. Baidarka also offers guided kayak trips for $50 d for a half-day, or $95 d for all day. This is the only place in the U.S. to buy Nautiraid folding kayaks, a superior design to the better-known Kleppers. Request Baidarka's free catalog detailing the various kayaks and kayaking equipment. A local charter boat operator, Sitka's Secrets, tel. (907) 747-5089, provides kayak drop-offs for a fee. A similar service is offered by **Southeast Alaska Canoe Adventures,** tel. (907) 747-5011, who also do sailing cruises.

Sitka Sound Ocean Adventures, tel. (907) 747-6375, offers guided kayak day-trips ($50 pp for two hours) and rents kayaks ($50/day for a double). The other company renting kayaks in town is Sitka Sea Kayaking Adventure, tel. (907) 747-7425 or (800) 791-2673. They deal primarily with the cruise ship crowd.

Boating and Fishing

St. Lazaria Islands National Wildlife Refuge is a great place to see tufted puffin colonies, along with storm petrels, auklets, whales, seals, and sea lions. **Raven's Fire,** tel. (907) 747-5777; **Steller Wildlife & Exploring,** tel. (907) 747-6157; and **Bare Island Charters,** tel. (907) 747-4900, all offer day and overnight trips to the refuge. For other charter boat and fishing opportunities, pick up a listing from the visitors bureau. Recommended is **Sitka's Secrets,** tel. (907) 747-5089, run by two experienced wildlife biologists. **Allen Marine Tours,** tel. (907) 747-8100, offers jetboat trips to Salisbury Sound, 25 miles north of Sitka, where you'll discover sea otters and other marine critters. Experienced boaters may want to rent skiffs from **Baranof Sportsmans Vacations,** tel. (907) 747-4937; or **Sitka Sound Ocean Adventures,** tel. (907) 747-6375.

A favorite locals' relaxation place is **Goddard Hot Springs,** accessible only by boat or floatplane. The M.V. *Raven's Fire,* tel. (907) 747-6157, takes folks there on day-trips for $90 pp, minimum of four people. They'll also transport kayaks for $15. Other local charter boats offer a similar service.

Scuba divers are increasingly discovering the beauty of local waters during the winter months (when the sea is clearer). **Southeast Diving and Sports,** 203 Lincoln St., tel. (907) 747-8279, has scuba gear for rent, and can direct you to local charter boat operators willing to take you out. They also rent mountain bikes, as does **J&B Bike Rentals** downtown, tel. (907) 747-8279.

ACCOMMODATIONS

See the chart for a listing of Sitka accommodations. Also the Sitka Convention & Visitors Bureau maintains a complete listing of private apartments and houses available. When you call for reservations, be sure to ask if the lodging places provide free ferry or airport shuttle ser-

vice. The **Sitka Youth Hostel** (open June 1 to August 31 only) is in the Methodist church at 303 Kimsham Rd., tel. (907) 747-8356. Follow Halibut Point Rd. out of town toward the ferry and turn right on Peterson St. across from McDonald's. Head a couple blocks uphill to the hostel, on the right side of the road just beyond Wachusetts Avenue. If you're arriving by ferry, the shuttle bus ($5 roundtrip) will drop you at the door. Lodging is $7 pp for AYH members, $10 pp for nonmembers, sleeping bag required. The hostel is open 6 p.m.-9:30 a.m., with an 11 p.m. curfew. It has cooking facilities and a very friendly staff that usually accommodates travelers arriving or departing by ferry at any hour of the night; call ahead to make sure they'll be open for you. There's almost always space.

Beyond the hostel, prices rise dramatically. Built in 1939, **Sitka Hotel** is relatively inexpensive and has recently undergone a complete remodeling. Choose from 14 different **bed and breakfasts** for more homey surroundings. One of the most distinctive (and expensive at $150 d) is **Rockwell Lighthouse,** a modern, furnished three-bedroom home built in the shape of a lighthouse. Access is by skiff (provided). **Raven's Nest House** is on Berry Island, 3.5 miles from town, and is accessible only by skiff (provided). It's a beautiful remote place owned by longtime Alaskans.

Camping

No campgrounds are near downtown Sitka, but the Forest Service provides camping at each end of the road. The excellent **Starrigavan Campground** ($8) is seven miles northwest of town and three-quarters of a mile beyond the ferry terminal. Open all year, but no services Oct.-April. Make advance reservations by calling (800) 280-2267 ($8.25 extra fee). Campsites to the left of the road face onto a rocky beach while those to the right border Starrigavan Creek, where you can watch spawning coho salmon in late summer. Starrigavan fills up with RVs in July and August, but there are six walk-in sites on the ocean side of the campground (water isn't available on this side of the road, however). Starrigavan also has an **artesian well** with wonderfully fresh spring water, some of which is bottled commercially under the "Misty Fjords" label and sold in the Lower 48. Sitka locals often drive out to fill big bottles for themselves.

SITKA ACCOMMODATIONS

Note: Sitka adds an eight percent bed tax to these rates. Accommodations are arranged from least to most expensive.

Youth Hostel; 303 Kimsham St.; tel. (907) 747-8356; $7-10 pp in dorm rooms; sleeping cots, open June-Aug.

Sitka Hotel; 118 Lincoln St.; tel. (907) 747-3288; $45 s, $50 d with bath down the hall; $55 s, $59 d with private bath; historic hotel, newly remodeled

Potlatch Motel; 713 Katlian St.; tel. (907) 747-8611; $75 s or d; courtesy van, kitchenettes available

Cascade Inn; 2035 Halibut Point Rd.; tel. (907) 747-6804 or (800) 532-0908; $75-125 s or d; kitchenettes available

Super 8 Motel; 404 Sawmill Creek Rd.; tel. (907) 747-8804 or (800) 800-8000; $97 s, $103 d

Westmark Shee Atika Lodge; 330 Seward St.; tel. (907) 747-6241 or (800) 544-0970; $131 s or d

Camp Coogan Bay Hideaway; six miles from Sitka; tel. (907) 747-6375; $135 for up to eight; floathouse accessible by skiff only

BED AND BREAKFASTS AND GUEST HOUSES

Abner's B&B; 200 Seward St.; tel. (907) 747-8779; $40 s, $50 d; turn-of-the-century home, one guest room, private bath, full breakfast

Jerry's Waterfront B&B; 2037 Halibut Point Rd.; tel. (907) 747-7265; $45-65 s or d; waterfront deck, two guest rooms, full breakfast, open May-Oct.

Bed Inn 518; 518 Monastery St.; tel. (907) 747-3305; $50 s, $60 d; two guest rooms, shared bath, continental breakfast

Karra's B&B; 230 Kogwantan St.; tel. (907) 747-3978; $50-65 s, $65-80 d; four guest rooms, shared baths, full breakfast

Seaview B&B; tel. (907) 747-3908; $55-60 s or d; one guest room, continental breakfast

Creek's Edge Guest House; 109 Cascade Creek; tel. (907) 747-6484; $55-105 s, $65-105 d; modern home overlooking Sitka Sound, antiques, three guest rooms, full breakfast

Alaska Ocean View B&B; 1101 Edgecumbe Dr.; tel. (907) 747-8310; $59-99 s, $79-119 d; three guest rooms, shared or private baths, full breakfast, AAA approved

AAA Inn; tel. (907) 747-1076; $60-80 s or d; two guest rooms, continental breakfast

Mt. View B&B; 201 Cascade Creek Rd.; tel. (907) 747-8966; $60-80 s $70-90 d; five guest rooms, full breakfast, AAA approved

Helga's B&B; 2821 Halibut Point Rd.; tel. (907) 747-5497; $60-65 s, $70-75 d; new home, five guest rooms, private baths, continental breakfast, AAA approved

Wild Strawberry Lodge; 724 Siginaka Way; tel. (907) 747-8883 or (800) 770-2628; $62-75 s or d; primarily a fishing lodge, 12 guest rooms, shared or private baths, full breakfast

Archangel B&B; 200 New Archangel St.; tel. (907) 747-6538; $65 s or d; one guest room, continental breakfast

Biorka B&B; 611 Biorka St.; tel. (907) 747-3111; $65 s, $70 d; two guest rooms, private bath and entrance, full breakfast

By the Sea B&B; 1713 Edgecumbe Dr.; tel. (907) 747-3993; $65 s, $70 d; two guest rooms, shared bath, full breakfast, open mid-May through August

Gaven Hill B&B; one mile south; tel. (907) 747-4986; $65-75 s or d; one guest room, continental breakfast

Pacific Sunset B&B; tel. (907) 747-1020; $65-75 s or d; two guest rooms, full breakfast, open April-Nov.

Eagle's Landing B&B; 3005 Barker St.; tel. (907) 747-5936; $65-80 s or d; log home with view, two guest rooms, continental breakfast, open mid-May to mid-Sept.

Shoreline Apartment; 3301 Halibut Point Rd.; tel. (907) 747-8508 or (800) 327-5131; $65-100 s or d; beachfront apartment, continental breakfast

Hannah's B&B; 504 Monastery St.; tel. (907) 747-8309; $70 s, $75 d; two guest rooms, newly remodeled, private entrance and bath, continental breakfast

(continues on next page)

SITKA ACCOMMODATIONS

(continued)

Vonnie's B&B; 101 Shelikof Way; tel. (907) 747-6401; $70-90 s or d; sauna, hot tub, two guest rooms, full breakfast

Annahootz B&B; tel. (907) 747-6498 or (800) 746-6498; $75 s or d; one bedroom suite, continental breakfast

Seaside B&B; 2924 Halibut Point Rd.; tel. (907) 747-6066; $75-95 s or d; covered porch with view of Sitka Sound, two guest rooms, full breakfast

Sportsman's Inn; 714 Etolin St.; tel. (907) 747-3934; $100 s or d; two guest rooms, hot tub, sauna

A Crescent Harbor Hideaway; 709 Lincoln St.; tel. (907) 747-4900; $105 s or d; private apartment in restored historical home, full kitchen, make-your-own breakfast

Swan Lake Guest Cottage; tel. (907) 747-6388; $125 for up to six; two-bedroom cottage

Rockwell Lighthouse; P.O. Box 277; tel. (907) 747-3056; $150 s or d; three-bedroom house with kitchen (sleeps eight) on small island three-quarters of a mile from Sitka, rate includes a skiff

Raven's Nest House; Berry Island; tel. (907) 747-5165; $245 for up to four; luxurious and remote location on 10-acre island, hexagonal cabin, boat access only (included), skylight loft, hot tub, outdoor deck, full kitchen, sea kayaks available

---

The quarter-mile boardwalk **Estuary Life Trail** (wheelchair accessible) leads along the edge of the marsh from the campground, and connects with a three-quarter-mile **Forest and Muskeg Trail.** Placards describe points along this easy trail. On the road between the ferry and campground are interpretive display signs marking the site of **Old Sitka**—burned by the Tlingits in 1802.

The unmaintained and little-used **Sawmill Creek Campground** (free, but no water) is up Blue Lake Rd. six miles east of town. The campground is a bit remote, making it hard to reach on foot, and the road is too rough for RVs. Park RVs ($16) at **Sealing Cove RV Park** on Japonski Island, tel. (907) 747-3439. **Sitka Sportsman's RV Park,** tel. (907) 747-6033, has RV spaces ($15) just a block south of the ferry terminal.

FOOD

Something Fishy

Sitka is blessed with a range of options for those who love fish and other seafood. **Van Winkle & Daigler Frontier Cuisine,** tel. (907) 747-3396, at the foot of the bridge to Japonski Island, has seafood, pasta, prime rib, and more, but is famous for their halibut fish and chips. This is the real thing, Alaskan style. Similarly great fish and chips can be had just up the street and up the

stairs at **Marina Restaurant.** The Marina bakes the best pizzas in town. The **Channel Club,** three miles out on Halibut Point Rd., tel. (907) 747-9916, broils up outstanding seafood and steaks, or you can do some grazing on the large salad bar (best in Sitka). **Bayview Restaurant,** tel. (907) 747-5440, upstairs in Bayview Trading, 407 Lincoln St., serves every possible type of burger (including one with caviar). For Russian fare, try their borscht or piroshki. While in the building, get a free cup of "Russian Tea," a sweet concoction of questionable authenticity containing instant tea, spices, and Tang.

All-American

Get great burgers, milk shakes, and other fast food at **Lane 7 Snack Bar,** 331 Lincoln St. (next to the bowling alley), tel. (907) 747-6310. They also serve a surprisingly good breakfast. **MoJo Cafe,** 256 Katlian St., tel. (907) 747-0667, is the place to go for inexpensive and delicious lunchtime sandwiches, soups, and salads, or for light breakfasts of pastries, scones, bagels, and espresso. Although primarily a takeout place, Mojo has a few tables. It's open Mon.-Thurs. till 2 p.m., and Friday only till 10 a.m. If you're on your way into or out of town by plane, stop by the airport's **Nugget Restaurant,** tel. (907) 966-2480, where the fresh-baked pies are famous. Of course, there is always the **McDonald's** a mile out on Halibut Point Rd. for industrial-strength junk food. With the harbor-

and-mountains view, this McD's certainly has one of the most impressive vistas in the entire corporate chain. There's also a **Subway** sandwich shop, tel. (907) 747-6502, behind the Westmark on Seward Street. Get delicious sweets from **Chocolate Moose,** 120 Lincoln St., tel. (907) 747-5159.

Ethnic Eats

For Chinese food, head to **Twin Dragon Restaurant,** tel. (907) 747-5711, next to the Pioneer Bar on Katlian Street. A bit heavy on the MSG for some folks. **El Dorado,** at 714 Katlian St., tel. (907) 747-5070, across from the Forest Service area office, has decent Mexican food and pizzas at Alaskan prices.

Coffeehouses

A great place to spend time is the **Backdoor Cafe,** tel. (907) 747-8856, a small espresso shop behind Old Harbor Books on Lincoln Street. The Backdoor is the literary/greenie hangout, and has tasty bagels and pastries made at their sister shop, Mojo Cafe. Coffee is also available at **Highliner Espresso,** 303 Lincoln St., tel. (907) 747-4924.

Grocers

Sea Mart, two miles from town along Halibut Point Rd., tel. (907) 747-6266, has a salad bar, deli, bakery, and the most complete selection of groceries in Sitka. Closer to town are **Lakeside Grocery,** 705 Halibut Point Rd., tel. (907) 747-3317; and **Market Center Supermarket,** 210 Biorka St., tel. (907) 747-6686. The **Fresh Fish Company,** tel. (907) 747-5565, behind Murray Pacific on Katlian St., sells fresh local salmon, halibut, shrimp, snapper, and smoked salmon. They will also smoke fish that you bring in. **Alaska Native Seafoods,** 236 Lincoln St., tel. (907) 747-7483, has fresh and smoked fish, crab, and Alaskan meats.

ENTERTAINMENT AND EVENTS

On the Town

The **Rookies Grill,** tel. (907) 747-3285, two miles out on Sawmill Creek Rd., has live music on weekends, and TV sports the rest of the week. Decent bar grub on the menu, too. Another place to try for live music is the **Pilot House,** 713 Katlian Ave., tel. (907) 747-4707. Fishermen and would-be crewmembers hang out at the sometimes-rowdy **Pioneer Bar** on Katlian St., tel. (907) 747-3456. The P-Bar's walls are crowded with photos of local fishing boats, and the blackboard often has ads for boats; you might try tacking up a "help available" notice.

Dance and Theater Performances

When cruise ships are in town, Centennial Hall auditorium comes alive with half-hour performances of traditional Russian, Ukranian, and Moldovian dance by the **New Archangel Dancers** ($6). The 40 dancers are all women, though some dress in male costumes. The troupe has toured extensively, visiting Japan, Russia, Europe, and the Caribbean in recent years. Call (907) 747-5940 for details.

For a very different dance program, the **Noow Tlein and Gajaa Heen Dancers** give periodic Tlingit performances through the summer months inside Centennial Hall. These half-hour productions cost $5 and are offered when cruise ships are in port. A new **Native Cultural Center** that will house not only these performances, but eventually a collection of cultural artifacts from the Sitka tribe, is being constructed. The center is located next to the Pioneers Home. For more information on Native dancing, call the Sitka Tribe at (907) 747-7290 or (888) 270-8687.

Even more unique are the **Tlingit Dinner Theater** productions by Robert Sam, a Tlingit storyteller. Performed in the round, with illustrative dinnerware created by his wife, Doe Stahr, this is a fascinating way to experience the past while enjoying a halibut dinner. Performances ($40 pp) take place at the Westmark Shee Atika banquet room several times a week. Call (907) 747-8882 for details.

Events

Each June, the renowned **Sitka Summer Music Festival** attracts musicians from all over the world. Chamber music concerts are given Tuesday, Friday, and Saturday evenings in Centennial Hall, but the most fun is the annual Houseparty Concert. Reserve early. Concert tickets may be hard to come by, but you can always visit rehearsals for free. For advance tickets and more info contact Sitka Summer Music Festival, P.O. Box 3333, Sitka, AK 99835, tel. (907)

747-6774. Another cultural event is the **Sitka Writers Symposium** in mid-June, which attracts nationally known writers.

In late May, visitors can join locals in the **Sitka Salmon Derby,** where the top fish is often a 60-pound-plus king salmon. **July Fourth** is another time for fun, with a parade, races, softball tournament, live music, dancing, and fireworks. On Labor Day weekend, the **Mudball Classic Softball Tournament** attracts teams from around the nation for fun in the muck. As the town where Alaska was officially transferred from Russian to American hands, Sitka is also the place to be on **Alaska Day.** A celebration of "Seward's Folly" is held each October 18 with dances, traditional Russian costumes, a parade, and a reenactment of the brief transfer ceremony.

OTHER PRACTICALITIES

Information

The Centennial Building houses a small information desk, or stop by the **Sitka Convention & Visitors Bureau,** upstairs at 303 Lincoln St., tel. (907) 747-5940, open Mon.-Fri. 8 a.m.-5 p.m. Their e-mail address is scvb@ptialaska.net. For up-to-date local info pick up the free summer newspaper supplement, *All About Sitka* at the ferry terminal or visitors bureau. The Forest Service's Sitka area office is the bright red building at Katlian St. and Siginaka Way, tel. (907) 747-6671, but a better place for local info is their **Sitka District Office** at 201 Katlian St., tel. (907) 747-4220. Get the latest weather info (in great detail) by pushing the button on the box above the ramp to Crescent Harbor.

Shopping and Services

The **Sitka Crafters Mall,** 110 American St., tel. (907) 747-6544, sells works from some 30 different artists and craftworkers. Showers ($2) are available at **Homestead Laundry** on Katlian St. adjacent to the Forest Service supervisor's office; and at **Duds and Suds,** across from McDonald's on Halibut Point Road. A better deal is the public **swimming pool** (tel. 907-747-8670) in the Blatchley Middle School at 601 Halibut Point Rd., where you can swim, sauna, and shower for $2.50 ($1.25 for students and seniors). The pool at Sheldon Jackson College is also open to the public daily.

Sitka's main **post office** is on Sawmill Creek Rd., 1.5 miles south of town, but a substation is in McDonald's Bayview Trading Co., corner of Lincoln and Lake Streets. **ATMs** can be found at the National Bank of Alaska downtown, and at the walkup booth of First Bank in front of Subway at Lake and Seward Streets. For fishing or cannery work head to the **Job Service Office** in the Municipal Building at 304 Lake St. (tel. 907-747-3423), or talk with folks on the docks and in local bars.

Booked Up

Old Harbor Books on Lincoln St. has a fine collection of books on Alaska and a pleasant coffee shop in the back. The owner is a local Greenpeace activist (as is his upstairs neighbor, Larry Edwards of Baidarka Boats), so this is a great place to catch up on environmental issues affecting Southeast Alaska. The **public library,** tel. (907) 747-8708, next to Centennial Hall downtown, has a free paperback exchange with plenty of titles along with a phone for free local calls. They also have binoculars to watch whales, seals, and porpoises from the library windows that overlook the bay. The curved benches out back make a pleasant lunch spot when it isn't raining. Library hours are Sunday 1-5 p.m., Tues.-Thurs. 10 a.m.-9 p.m., Friday 10 a.m.-6 p.m., and Saturday 1-5 p.m.

TRANSPORTATION

Ferry Service

State ferries reach Sitka up to five times a week during the summer ($26 from Juneau). The larger ferries often stop for three hours; the Saturday "turnaround" runs put the *Le Conte* in Sitka for six hours. (It's used by residents of Hoonah and Angoon for a shopping visit to the big city of Sitka.) The ferry terminal, tel. (907) 747-8737 (live) or (907) 747-3300 (recording), is open two hours prior to ship arrivals. Note that, unlike all other stops along the route, the Sitka terminal posts arrival, rather than departure, times. Because of the difficult tidal conditions in Peril Straits, a small mechanical problem can lead to a six-hour delay since ferries must hit the straits at just the right time, or wait for the next tide. Because of this, be sure to confirm the departure time so you don't end up sitting in the ferry terminal for six hours.

Wheeling around Sitka

The terminal is seven miles north of town, but despite the distance you'll have time for a quick tour, even if you don't stay. Most folks ride the **tour buses** (tel. 907-747-8443) that meet the ferries for $5 roundtrip, or $10 with a tour that includes the cathedral and Sitka National Historical Park. Many places (including the raptor center) open even for the 4 a.m. ferry arrivals. **Sitka Tribe Tours,** tel. (907) 747-3770 or (888) 270-8687, offers a Native slant to tours of Sitka's sights.

Hitching both into and out of town is easy and almost always faster than the buses. Besides, this gives you a chance to talk with locals rather than getting a canned package tour. Taxis cost approximately $13 one-way from the ferry to town, or $35 for a one-hour tour. The companies are **Arrowhead Taxi,** tel. (907) 747-8888; and **Sitka Cab,** tel. (907) 747-5001.

Rent cars from **Allstar Rent-A-Car,** tel. (907) 966-2552 or (800) 722-6927; or from **Avis,** tel. (907) 966-2404 or (800) 478-2847. The rates are with unlimited miles, not a big deal with only a few miles of roads in town, but book ahead since the rental agencies are busy in the summer. Rent **bikes** from Southeast Diving and Sports, 203 Lincoln St., tel. (907) 747-8279.

By Air

The airport is on Japonski Island, just under a mile from town by road. **Alaska Airlines,** tel. (800) 426-0333, flies to Juneau, Ketchikan, Petersburg, Wrangell, and other cities in Alaska and the Lower 48. **Taquan Air,** 475 Katlian St., tel. (907) 747-8636 or (800) 770-8800, has scheduled daily floatplane service to the villages of Angoon ($80), Baranof Warm Springs ($70), False Island ($70), Hoonah ($100), Kake ($90), Pelican ($100), Port Alexander ($90), Little Port Walter ($90), Rowan Bay ($90), and Tenakee Springs ($80). Both Taquan Air and **Mountain Aviation** at the airport (cheaper rates), tel. (907) 966-2288, provide charter flights to nearby Forest Service cabins, and flightseeing trips. Expect to pay around $250/hour for two people with gear in a Cessna 185 or $380/hour for a Beaver that seats four or more with gear.

CHICHAGOF ISLAND

HOONAH

The predominantly Tlingit village of Hoonah (pop. 950) nestles in Port Frederick, 20 miles south of Glacier Bay. Port Frederick has served as a home for the Tlingits since the last ice age drove them out of Glacier Bay and across Icy Strait to the north coast of Chichagof Island. There they found a protected bay they called Huna, meaning "place where the north wind doesn't blow." The Northwest Trading Company opened a store here in 1880 and missionaries added a church and school the following year. A cannery opened in 1912, operating until 1953. The attractive old cannery still stands a mile north of town on the entrance to Port Frederick, but the old village and many priceless Tlingit cultural items were destroyed by a fire in 1944. The people rebuilt their village on the ashes.

Today Hoonah is far from being the prettiest town in Alaska. The weathered clapboard houses are unpainted, and junk cars pile up in the yards. It's the sort of town where the eagle calls blend with the sounds of motorboats and mufflerless dump trucks. There are dogs in every house and children playing on every porch. The liquor store has a sign out front: NO CORK BOOTS. Life in Hoonah follows a slow pace—residents half-complain that they are unable to go anywhere without meeting someone who wants to talk the hours away. Hoonah's economy is a blend of logging, commercial fishing, and traditional activities such as deer hunting, fishing, and berry picking.

The impressive cliff faces of **Elephant Mountain** (2,775 feet) guard the southern flank of

Hoonah. Unfortunately, two Native corporations, Huna Totem and Sealaska, have logged much of their land near town, selling off a centuries-old heritage to pay off debts resulting from appeals to their land claims. Hoonah is now surrounded by a spiderweb of logging roads on both Native and Forest Service land, making this a good place to explore by mountain bike if you're ready for clearcuts and can dodge the many logging trucks.

Practicalities

The **Hoonah Cultural Center,** tel. (907) 945-3600, has a small free museum with local artifacts, open Mon.-Fri. 10 a.m.-3 p.m. There are no campgrounds, but you should be able to find a camping spot above the upper edge of town. For Hoonah info, head to **City Hall,** tel. (907) 945-3664. The **Forest Service Hoonah District Office,** Box 135, Hoonah, AK 99829, tel. (907) 945-3631, at the south end of town, has limited local trail and kayaking information. Get from them a copy of the detailed *Hoonah Area Road Guide* map ($3) if you plan to spend any time in the Hoonah or Tenakee area.

Mary's Inn Restaurant, tel. (907) 945-3228, a nonprofit vocational school and boardinghouse for local youths, is a good place to get burgers, fresh baked goods, or more substantial meals while helping out a great program. **Huna Totem Lodge,** tel. (907) 945-3393, has rooms for rent and serves meals in its restaurant. Lodging is also available at **Tina's Room Rentals and Apartments,** tel. (907) 945-3442; **Hubbard's B&B,** tel. (907) 945-3414; and **Snug Harbor Lodge,** tel. (907) 945-3636. Hoonah has two small grocery stores (including the L. Kane Store established in 1893) and a laundromat with coin-operated showers. Showers are also available in the harbor building or at the **swimming pool** tel. (907) 945-9911, next to the high school. Hoonah also has a bank, a tavern, a variety store, a liquor store, a cold storage facility (mostly local hires), and a logging camp. A few miles southwest of town near Game Point is the only agricultural commune in Southeast, Mt. Bether Bible Center.

Transportation

Hoonah's tiny **ferry terminal,** tel. (907) 945-3293, is a half-mile from town. The *Le Conte*

typically arrives six days a week and generally stops for approximately 45 minutes, long enough for a quick jog into town and back. Across from the ferry terminal is a tiny but interesting old cemetery. Four air-taxi operators fly into Hoonah daily. **Wings of Alaska,** tel. (907) 945-3275 or (800) 478-9464; **Haines Airways,** tel. (907) 945-3701; **L.A.B. Flying Service,** tel. (907) 945-3661 or (800) 426-0543; and **Skagway Air,** tel. (907) 789-2006, all fly between Juneau and Hoonah for $45. Haines Airways also flies to Haines ($84) and Gustavus ($50). **Taquan Air,** tel. (907) 747-8636 or (800) 770-8800, flies to Sitka for $100.

Nearby

The Hoonah area offers almost nothing in the way of developed trails or other recreation facilities. If you have a car, the quarter-mile **Bear Paw Lake Trail,** 18 miles south of town on Road 8508, leads to a good lake where you can catch trout or coho salmon. Kayakers and canoeists may want to paddle the 40 miles from Hoonah to Tenakee Springs. The route goes to the head of Port Frederick, where there is a 100-yard portage into Tenakee Inlet. Neka Estuary in Port Frederick is a good place to see bears. A Forest Service cabin ($25/night) is available at nearby **Salt Lake Bay,** but a considerable amount of logging has beaten you there. Ask at the Hoonah Forest Service office for details on these and other possible kayak trips in the area.

PELICAN

If you're looking for a place to get away from it all, it's hard to get more remote than the tiny, picturesque fishing village of Pelican (pop. 230) inside narrow Lisianski Inlet on the western shore of Chichagof Island. During the summer Pelican's population doubles with the arrival of fishermen and cold storage workers. (Pelican received its name from *The Pelican,* a fishing boat owned by the town's founder; there are no pelicans in Alaska.) Tiny Pelican has achieved notoriety as a party town, particularly when festivities reach their peak each July Fourth. Featured attractions include a beer-can throwing contest, a tug-of-war (inevitably won by the women), and a wet T-shirt contest.

The centerpiece of Pelican's boardwalk thoroughfare is the rowdy **Rosie's Bar and Grill** where Rosie still holds down the fort. Rosie's, tel. (907) 735-2265, rents rooms. The town also has a general store, laundromat, and restaurant, as well as a large cold-storage plant operated by Pelican Seafoods. Showers are available at the laundromat, or try the steam baths at the local liquor store (no joke). **Kyak Jack's,** tel. (907) 735-2260, rents sea kayaks in Pelican.

Accommodations

Otter Cove B&B, tel. (907) 735-2259 or (800) 962-8441, has accommodations in a pretty shoreside house just a short walk from town for $55 s, $65 d, including a full breakfast. Open Feb.-Oct., they also offer special package deals that include access to White Sulfur Springs. **Lisianski Inlet Wilderness Lodge,** tel. (907) 735-2266 or (800) 962-8441, two miles west of Pelican, offers a pricey but idyllic setting for a splurge trip. Rooms are $110-160 s or d, including a full breakfast. Access is by boat, and they also rent skiffs. The lodge is open May to mid-September. A variety of package trips are also available at the lodge for around $375 pp/day. These include sleeping arrangements, meals, guide service, use of kayaks and skiffs, and roundtrip airfare from Juneau to Pelican.

Transportation

Ferry service to Pelican arrives only once or twice a month. The *Le Conte* usually stays for two hours and then turns around for the return trip to Juneau ($32 one-way). **Glacier Bay Airways,** tel. (907) 789-9009; **Loken Aviation,** tel. (907) 735-2244 or (800) 478-3360; and **Wings of Alaska,** tel. (907) 735-2284 or (800) 478-9464, have daily flights between Juneau and Pelican for $80. **Taquan Air,** tel. (907) 735-2210 or (800) 770-8800, flies from Sitka for $100.

West Chichagof-Yakobi Wilderness

On the northwestern shore of Chichagof Island is the wildly rugged 264,747-acre West Chichagof-Yakobi Wilderness. The coastline is swept by ocean storms and winds. Sea otters have been reintroduced to portions of this scenic shore, and sea lions, brown bears, marten, and deer are common. The coast is deeply indented with many small bays, lagoons, and inlets. It also supports areas of distinctive open spruce forest with grassy glades. Except for White Sulfur Springs, this wilderness gets very little recreational use due to its remoteness and the storms that frequently make it a dangerous place for small boats and kayaks.

One of the most popular Forest Service cabins in Southeast (make reservations well in advance) is at **White Sulfur Springs,** accessible only by boat, sea kayak, helicopter, or floatplane (the growth of pond lilies may make it impossible for planes to land on the pond). The springs are a 20-mile kayak trip from Pelican. Much of the trip is through the protected waters of Lisianski Inlet and Strait, but the last five miles are exposed to the open ocean and require great care. The cabin ($25/night) has a wonderful hot springs bathhouse overlooking Bertha Bay just 50 feet away. Note, however, that the springs are free and open to the public, so fishermen, kayakers, and others from nearby Pelican will probably disturb your solitude. **Lisianski Wilderness Lodge,** tel. (907) 735-2266 or (800) 962-8441, offers kayak rentals and skiff dropoffs at the cabin from Pelican.

Elfin Cove

This tiny fishing settlement (pop. 50) tops the north end of Chichagof Island, and is considered one of Alaska's prettiest towns. The setting is hard to beat, right on the edge of the wild waters of Cross Sound yet protected within a narrow harbor. The town has two grocery stores and lodging facilities, with showers and a sauna during the summer months. **Tanaku Lodge,** tel. (800) 482-6258, has accommodations, but only by the week. Be ready to drop $2,400 pp all inclusive. Other lodges include **Elfin Cove Sport Fishing Lodge,** tel. (907) 239-2212; **Inner Harbor Lodge,** tel. (907) 239-2245; and **Shearwater Lodge & Charters,** tel. (907) 239-2223. During the summer, **Wings of Alaska,** tel. (907) 789-0790 or (800) 478-9464; and **Loken Aviation,** tel. (907) 789-3331 or (800) 478-3360, offer service between Juneau and Elfin Cove for $80 one-way. The waters of Cross Sound and Icy Strait separate Chichagof Island from Glacier Bay National Park. This is one of the best areas to see whales in Southeast Alaska, especially near Point Adolphus. Charter boats offer day-trips from Glacier Bay to Elfin Cove during the summer months. Also nearby is the 23,000-acre **Pleasant-Lemesurier-Inian Islands Wilderness,** established in 1990.

TENAKEE SPRINGS

Residents of the tiny hamlet of Tenakee Springs (pop. 110) include retirees and counterculture devotees, and a few local fishermen. Many Juneau folks have second homes here. Tenakee's houses stand on stilts along the shoreline; some have "long-drop" outhouses over the water. The town has only one street, a dirt path barely wide enough for Tenakee's three vehicles (its oil truck, fire truck, and dump truck). Everyone else walks or uses three-wheelers and bicycles. This simplicity is by choice—when rumors arose that the Forest Service would complete a road to Hoonah, locals became alarmed and successfully blocked the idea.

Tenakee is best known for its hot **mineral springs,** in a building right beside the dock. The springs feed a small concrete pool with an adjacent changing room. There are separate hours for men (2-6 p.m. and 10 p.m.-9 a.m.) and women (6-10 p.m. and 9 a.m.-2 p.m.), but after midnight the rules tend to relax a bit. If the ferry is in town for more than a half-hour, be sure to take a quick dip in the pool.

Practicalities

You can pitch your tent two miles east of town along Indian River, but be sure to hang your food since brown bears are sometimes a problem. Trails extend out of town for several miles in both directions along the shore. The trail south

of town reaches eight miles to an old cannery and a homestead at Coffee Cove. Beside the dock is **Snyder Mercantile Co.,** tel. (907) 736-2205, which has groceries and supplies, and rents cottages. Tenakee Springs has a small library, an impressive new hillside grade school, and two bars. Unfortunately, a devastating fire in 1993 destroyed the town's largest lodging place, Tenakee Inn. This was a big loss to the community because, other than the springs, it was the main focus of life here. Lodging options now include **Patch B&B,** tel. (907) 736-2258; and **Tenakee Hot Springs Lodge,** tel. (907) 736-2400.

Tenakee does not have a Forest Service office, but if you are considering a kayak trip in the area, contact the Hoonah District Office, P.O. Box 135, Hoonah, AK 99829, tel. (907) 945-3631, for the *Hoonah Area Road Map* ($2), a detailed guide that includes Tenakee.

Transportation

Tenakee is a popular weekend vacation spot for both Juneauites and travelers. The ferry *Le Conte* arrives in Tenakee four times a week with a schedule that makes it possible to stopover for a Friday night before returning to Juneau the following evening ($22 one-way). There is no ferry terminal and cars cannot be off-loaded. The ferry usually stays in town only a brief time, sometimes not even long enough to get off the boat for a walk. **Wings of Alaska,** tel. (907) 736-2247 or (800) 478-9464, has daily flights between Tenakee and Juneau ($65), as well as Angoon ($65). **Taquan Air,** tel. (907) 736-2210 or (800) 770-8800, flies every day between Sitka and Tenakee for $80. **Loken Aviation,** tel. (907) 789-3331 or (800) 478-3360, flies between Pelican and Juneau ($80) six days a week.

JUNEAU

America's most beautiful state capital, Juneau (pop. 30,000) is a thriving slice of civilization surrounded by rugged Inside Passage scenery. The city perches precariously on a thin strip of land at the mouth of Gold Creek. Behind it rise the precipitous summits of Mt. Juneau and Mt. Roberts; out front Gastineau Channel separates it from Douglas Island and the town of Douglas.

The city abounds with cultural and artistic attractions, and the adjacent wild country provides a broad sampling of Southeast Alaska—from glacially capped mountains to protected coves where sea kayakers relax. In 1992, *Outside Magazine* ranked Juneau as one of the top five most livable small cities in America, noting that "the beauty of the place is almost blinding."

Juneau is a government town, where nearly half the people work in state, federal, or city agencies. It is the only state capital with no roads leading in or out. Tourism provides another mainstay for the local economy, fed by an annual influx of more than 470,000 visitors, primarily aboard luxury cruise ships. On summer days, up to five different ships tie up simultaneously, disgorging an onslaught of 7,500 passengers. (To avoid the worst of the rush, get here before July or after August.) Juneau has a small fishing fleet and provides workers for a major silver mine on nearby Admiralty Island. Efforts to reopen Juneau's long-abandoned AJ Gold Mine were halted in 1997 when explorations turned up less gold than expected.

Juneau may be small in population, but its boundaries extend to the Canadian border, covering 3,100 square miles—larger than any other American city (except Sitka, with a staggering 4,710 square miles). Less than half of Juneau's population actually lives downtown. The rest are spread into Douglas (across the channel), Mendenhall Valley (10 miles northwest), and other surrounding areas. As might be expected, these areas exhibit diverse personalities. Even the weather varies, with an average of 92 inches of rain each year downtown, but only 55 inches in nearby Mendenhall Valley.

Downtown Juneau is marked by a mix of modern government offices and older wooden structures, many dating from the turn of the century. Across the bridge is Douglas Island and the bedroom community of Douglas. The town now consists of a few shops, but at its peak in 1915 when the Treadwell Gold Mine was operating, Douglas housed 15,000 miners. The road north from downtown Juneau is Southeast's only divided highway. Heading north, you first reach Mendenhall Valley, Juneau's version of suburbia: three shopping malls, a slew of fast fooderies, and hundreds of pseudo-rustic split-level homes and condos. But you can also see something most suburbs don't have: a drive-up glacier spilling out from the massive Juneau Icefield. The road continues north from Mendenhall Valley for another 30 miles, passing Auke Lake, the ferry terminal, and scattered homes along the way, and ending at scenic Echo Cove.

HISTORY

Gold in the Hills

In October 1880, two prospectors—Joe Juneau and Richard Harris—arrived at what would later be called Gold Creek. Along its banks was a small Tlingit fishing camp of the Auke tribe. Chief Kowee showed the prospectors gold flakes in the creek, and the resulting discovery turned out to be one of the largest gold deposits ever found. Harris and Juneau quickly staked a 160-acre townsite. The first boatloads of prospectors arrived the next month, and almost overnight a town sprouted along the shores of Gastineau Channel. Three giant hard-rock gold mines were developed in the area, eventually producing some seven million ounces of gold, worth over $3 *billion* at today's prices! Compare that to the $7.2 million the U.S. paid Russia for Alaska only 13 years before the discovery.

The **Alaska Juneau (AJ) Mine** proved the most successful, operating for more than 50 years. Built in Last Chance Basin behind Juneau, its three tunnels connected the ore source to the crushing and recovery mill site on Gastineau Channel. Inside the mine itself was a maze of tunnels that eventually reached over 100 miles in length. Because the ore was low grade—it could take 28 tons of ore to yield one ounce of gold—enormous quantities of rock had to be removed. At its peak, the mill (still visible just south of town) employed 1,000 men to process 12,000 tons of ore a day. Tailings from the mill were used as the fill upon which much of downtown Juneau was constructed. (Franklin St. was originally built on pilings along the shore.) The AJ closed down in 1944 due to wartime labor shortages and never reopened.

The **Perseverance Mine** operated between 1885 and 1921, with a two-mile tunnel carrying ore from Gold Creek to the mill four miles south of Juneau. It eventually ran into low-grade ore and was forced to close.

The best known Juneau-area mine was the **Treadwell,** on Douglas Island. The Treadwell Complex consisted of four mines and five stamping mills to process the ore. It employed some 2,000 men who were paid $100 a month, some of the highest wages anywhere in the world at

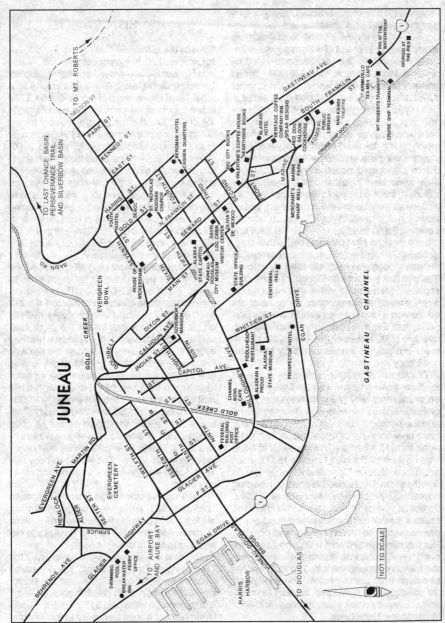

NOT TO SCALE

© MOON PUBLICATIONS, INC.

the time. The men enjoyed such amenities as a swimming pool, Turkish baths, tennis courts, bowling alley, gymnasium, and 15,000-volume library. The giant Treadwell stamping mills where the ore was pulverized made so much noise that people in downtown Douglas had to shout to be heard. Everything changed on April 21, 1917, when the ground atop the mines suddenly began to collapse, swallowing first the gymnasium and swimming pool, then the fire hall. Sea water rushed in, filling the tunnels as the miners ran for their lives. Amazingly, all apparently escaped alive. (The only missing miner was reportedly later seen in a nearby tavern before he skipped town.) Only one of the four mines was not destroyed in the collapse, and that one closed five years later.

Later Years

Juneau became the capital of Alaska in 1906 as a result of its rapid growth and the simultaneous decline of Sitka. Several attempts have been made to move the capital closer to the state's present power center—Anchorage. In 1976, Alaskan voters approved a new site just north of Anchorage, but six years later, when expectations for petro-billions had settled into reality, voters thought better of the move and refused to fund it. Juneauites breathed a sigh of relief and went on a building spree that only ended with the sudden drop in state oil revenue from the 1986 oil price plummet. Recent years have seen ever-increasing tourism (mainly from cruise ships) and a renewed focus on mining developments.

SIGHTS

Juneau is jam-packed with things to see and do, from glaciers to salmon-bakes to tram rides. It's the sort of place that travelers love. Many interesting places are right downtown—including two museums, numerous historic buildings, unusual shops, and even a library-with-a-view. Farther afield are dozens of hiking trails, several easily accessible glaciers, and such attractions as an informative new fish hatchery, a brewery, old mining buildings, a stone church, and much more. Even on a rainy day, you'll find something fun to do in Juneau.

Alaska State Museum

Anyone new to Juneau should not miss the outstanding Alaska State Museum, at 395 Whittier St., tel. (907) 465-2901. It's open summers Mon.-Fri. 9 a.m.-6 p.m., Saturday and Sunday 10 a.m.-6 p.m., and winters Tues.-Sat. 10 a.m.-4 p.m.; admission $3 (free on Saturday; students free anytime). Inside, you'll find an impressive collection of Native artifacts (including wildly creative Yup'ik Eskimo spirit masks) and exhibits relating to the Russian-American period and other aspects of Alaskan history. The museum also includes a gallery of contemporary fine arts, and brings in special exhibits each summer. But the highlight is the circular stairwell which houses a full-size bald eagle nest and other Alaskan wildlife.

Juneau-Douglas City Museum

The fine Juneau-Douglas City Museum ($2), tel. (907) 586-3572, at Fourth and Main Sts. is open summers Mon.-Fri. 9 a.m.-6 p.m., Saturday and Sunday 10 a.m.-6 p.m., and winters Thurs.-Sat. noon-4:30 p.m., or by appointment. Inside is an interesting collection of maps, artifacts, photos, and videos from Juneau's rich gold-mining history. Be sure to check out the three-dimensional model of Perseverance Mine with its intricate maze of tunnels. Other displays include a turn-of-the-century store and a hands-on history room that's popular with kids (no matter what their age). The museum has a small gift shop, as well as several free brochures describing **walking tours** of historic Juneau; 60 remaining downtown buildings were built before 1904!

State Office Building

Enter the modernistic State Office Building (locally known as the SOB) from Willoughby Ave. and take the elevator up to the eighth floor. Here you'll discover a 1928 Kimball organ, a lovingly preserved totem pole from the 1880s, the Alaska State Library, and an incredible panoramic view from the observation deck (great for bag lunches). The huge airy lobby is also a fine place to stay dry on a rainy day; Friday at noon you'll enjoy the added bonus of an organ recital.

Governor's Mansion

Just up Calhoun Ave. from the SOB is the large white Governor's Mansion. Built in 1912 in the New England colonial style, it overlooks much of

Juneau from its hilltop location. The mansion is open for free guided tours, but only if you reserve a couple of weeks in advance by calling (907) 465-3500, and are willing to give up your firstborn son. Out front is a totem pole carved in 1939-40. Near its base are the figures of a mosquito and a man, representing the Tlingit tale of the cannibalistic giant Guteel and his capture by hunters in a pit. The hunters built a fire to kill him, but just before he died he warned, "Even though you kill me, I'll continue to bite you." His ashes swirled into the air, becoming the mosquitoes that fulfill Guteel's promise. More than 20 other **totems** are scattered around downtown. Most are recent carvings, but some date to the 19th century. Pick up the "Totem Pole Walking Tour" brochure from the Juneau-Douglas City Museum to find them all.

State Capitol

Back on Fourth St. is the marble Alaska State Capitol. Completed in 1931, it was originally the federal office building and post office. Not at all like a traditional state capitol, from the outside it could be easily mistaken for an ostentatious Midwestern bank, complete with wide steps and marble columns. A 1993 Juneau ballot measure attempted to have it replaced, but local voters refused to boost their sales tax to fund a new building. Things are at a stalemate since representatives from other parts of the state refuse to fund anything new in Juneau; many still have dreams of moving the Capitol building to the Anchorage area. Hopefully, they will never win; Anchorage doesn't need any more power in Alaska. Free tours of the bank—oops—Capitol are available every half-hour Mon.-Sat. 9 a.m.-4:30 p.m. Check out the impressive historical photos by Winter and Pond on the second floor. You may sit in on the legislature when it is in session Jan.-May.

House of Wickersham

The historic House of Wickersham, 213 Seventh St., tel. (907) 465-4563, offers a good view of Juneau and the surrounding country. The house is open Sunday noon-4 p.m. and Mon.-Sat. 9 a.m.-4 p.m. from mid-May through September, with brief tours. Closed winters. Admission is $2.50. This was home to Judge James Wickersham (1857-1939), a man who had a major impact upon Alaskan history. As Alaska's longtime delegate to Congress he introduced the first statehood bill in 1916—43 years before it passed—and was instrumental in the establishment of a territorial legislature, McKinley National Park, the University of Alaska, and the Alaska Railroad. Be sure to take a gander at the beautiful ivory carvings that Judge Wickersham collected from around the state.

Mount Roberts Tramway

The newly opened Mt. Roberts Tramway provides a fast way into the high country above Juneau. The tram starts at the cruise ship dock on the south end of town and climbs 2,000 feet up the mountain, providing panoramic views of the surrounding land and water. The six-minute ride ends at an observation deck, a restaurant, gift shops, and a theater where you can watch a free film about Tlingit culture. Guided hikes (fee charged) are offered, or you can strike out on your own across the alpine country. The tram costs $17 for adults, and $10 for children ages seven to 12. No charge for children under seven. It's open daily 8 a.m.-10 p.m. May-Sept.; call (907) 463-3412 for details.

More Downtown Sights

One of Juneau's most photographed sights is **St. Nicholas Russian Orthodox Church** (built in 1894) at Fifth and Gold. It's open daily 9 a.m.-6 p.m. from mid-May through September; tel. (907) 586-1023 (no winter tours). A $1 donation is requested. Inside are icons and artwork, some dating from the 1700s.

Marine Park, along Shattuck Way, with its lively mix of people and picturesque views, is a good place to relax after your tour of downtown. Directly across the street a bright mural depicts the Haida creation legend. **Evergreen Cemetery,** between 12th and Seater Sts. on the north side of town, has the graves of Juneau's founders: Joe Juneau, Richard Harris, and Chief Kowee.

Behind town, the road climbs 1.5 miles up Basin Rd. to the old AJ Gold Mine. The former compressor building here has been turned into the **Last Chance Mining Museum.** Inside, you'll find a collection of mining paraphernalia. It's open daily 9:30 a.m.-12:30 p.m. and 3:30-6:30 p.m. from mid-May to late September. Admission costs $3; free for children under 10.

Gastineau Salmon Hatchery

The elaborate and impressive Douglas Island Pink and Chum (DIPAC) salmon hatchery is three miles north of town at 2697 Channel Dr., tel. (907) 463-5114. Here you can learn about salmon spawning and commercial fishing, watch fish moving up one of the state's largest fish ladders, and check out the saltwater aquariums and underwater viewing windows. The facility (open Mon.-Fri. 10 a.m.-6 p.m., and Sat.-Sun. noon-5 p.m.) includes several shops and a visitor center. Entrance costs $2.75 for adults, $1 for kids. Very interesting place, and well worth the entrance fee. It is open May-Sept. only. Try your own hand at fishing by renting poles and lures from the **Catch-A-Bunch** tackle shack nearby. Open July-September.

Mendenhall Glacier

Southeast's best-known drive-up ice cube, Mendenhall Glacier is without a doubt Juneau's most impressive sight. This moving river of ice pushes down from the 1,200-square-mile Juneau Icefield and is 12 miles long and up to 1.5 miles wide. Since 1750, the glacier has been receding, and is now several miles farther up Mendenhall Valley. It is presently retreating at more than 100 feet each year, although some scientists believe that it may begin advancing within the next decade.

The **Mendenhall Visitor Center,** tel. (907) 789-0097, shows free videos and contains a large relief map of the area. The center is open daily 8:30 a.m.-5 p.m. in summer; weekends only 8:30 a.m.-5 p.m. the rest of the year. Use the spotting scopes to check the slopes of nearby Bullard Mountain for mountain goats. Forest Service naturalists lead walks on nearby trails and can answer your questions. Walk up at least one of the excellent trails in the area if you want to come away with a deeper appreciation of Mendenhall Glacier (see "Hiking and Cabins" below).

Although it's 11 miles northwest of town, the glacier is easily accessible by city bus. Have the driver let you off when the bus turns left one mile up Mendenhall Loop Road. It's a one-mile walk up the road from here to the glacier. Buses run both directions around Mendenhall Loop Road. On the way back you can catch a bus heading either direction since both eventually drop you off downtown. The **Glacier Express,** tel. (907) 789-0052 or (800) 478-0052, has direct bus service to the glacier from downtown for $8 roundtrip. All local tour buses go to Mendenhall; see "Sightseeing Tours" under "Transportation" below for details.

University

The campus of the University of Alaska Southeast (2,600 students) is a dozen miles northwest of Juneau on beautiful Auke Lake. The view across the lake to Mendenhall Glacier makes it one of the most attractive campuses anywhere. City buses reach the university hourly Mon.-Saturday. Also here is **Chapel By the Lake,** a popular place for weddings with a dramatic backdrop of mountains and the Mendenhall Glacier. Across the highway, **Auke Bay Fisheries Lab** has a small saltwater aquarium and fisheries displays. It's open Mon.-Fri. 8 a.m.-4:30 p.m.

Alaskan Brewery

For something completely different, take the city bus to Anka St. in Lemon Creek and walk two blocks to Shaune Drive. Follow it a block to the small Alaskan Brewery building on the left. Free tours are given Tues.-Sat. every half-hour 11 a.m.-4:30 p.m. (tel. 907-780-5866). You're given a glass of beer at the end of the tour. Bottling takes place on Thursdays. Available only in Alaska and the Pacific Northwest, the beer is pricey but is very popular with both locals and visitors. Their Alaskan Amber and Alaskan Pale Ale have won top prize in several national beer competitions. The brewery also sells attractive T-shirts, hats, and other items.

Shrine of St. Terese

Twenty-three miles northwest of Juneau is a beautiful Catholic chapel built in 1939, the Shrine of St. Terese, tel. (907) 780-6112. The cobblestone chapel is hidden away on a bucolic little wooded island connected to the mainland by a 400-foot causeway. It's open daily, with Sunday service at 1 p.m. This is a nice, quiet place to soak up the scenery or to try your hand at fishing for salmon from the shore. The trail to Peterson Lake is nearby (see "Hike-in Cabins" below).

HIKING AND CABINS

The Juneau area has an amazing wealth of hiking paths leading into the surrounding mountains. For a complete listing, pick up a copy of *Juneau Trails* ($4) from the Forest Service Information Center in Centennial Hall at 101 Egan Dr., tel. (907) 586-8751. This is also the place to go for hiking and cabin information in Juneau. Rubber boots are recommended for all these trails, though you could get by with leather boots on some of the paths when the weather is dry.

Guided Hikes

The **City Parks and Recreation Department** offers guided day-hikes in summer, and cross-country ski trips in winter into areas around Juneau every Wednesday and Saturday 9:30 a.m.-3 p.m. The Wednesday outings are for adults only (no, they are not X-rated). Pick up a schedule from their office at 155 S. Seward St., tel. (907) 586-5226, or check the Thursday edition of the *Juneau Empire*.

Juneau Hikes & Tours, tel. (907) 586-4323, leads nature hikes in the backcountry around Juneau. Downtown walking tours (mainly for folks off the cruise ships) are offered by **Alaska Sightseeing/Cruise West,** tel. (907) 563-6300; Alaska Travel Adventures, tel. (907) 789-0052 or (800) 478-0052; and **Gray Line,** tel. (907) 586-3773.

Mendenhall Glacier Trails

The short **nature trail** near Mendenhall Visitor Center offers a fine chance to view spawning sockeye salmon in late summer. Even shorter is the handicapped-accessible **Photo Point Trail** right in front of the visitor center. The relatively easy **East Glacier Loop Trail** (3.5 miles roundtrip), also begins near the center and pro-

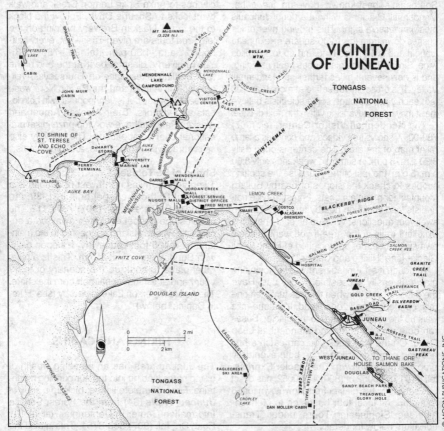

VICINITY OF JUNEAU

vides good views of the glacier. For a longer hike, follow the **East Glacier Loop Trail** 1.5 miles out to the junction with the Nugget Creek Trail. This trail continues along the creek another four miles to a decrepit Adirondack shelter. Vegetation along the East Glacier Trail consists of brush and trees established since the glacier's recent retreat, while trees along the Nugget Creek Trail are much older.

My favorite Mendenhall trail is the **West Glacier Trail** (seven miles roundtrip), which begins from the end of Montana Creek Rd., just beyond the Mendenhall Lake Campground: incredible views of the glacier and icefalls en route. Experienced ice-climbers use the path to access the glacier itself. Finally, for the really ambitious there's a primitive route up 3,228-foot **Mount McGinnis** from the end of the West Glacier Trail, an additional four miles (six hours) roundtrip. This trail is generally covered with snow until late summer, but offers panoramic vistas of the entire Juneau area—on clear days.

Douglas

Remains of the **Treadwell Mine,** destroyed by the collapse and flood of 1917, offer a fascinating peek into the past. Pick up the "Treadwell Mine Historic Trail" brochure from the Juneau-Douglas City Museum for a description of the area. The trail starts from the south end of St. Ann's Ave. in Douglas and passes the crumbling remains of old buildings. Get there by catching the hourly Douglas bus ($1) in Juneau and riding it to the end of the line at Sandy Beach. Keep right on the main trail to reach the **Treadwell Glory Hole,** once the entrance to a network of shafts under Gastineau Channel, but now full of water and wrecked cars. A waterfall drops into the hole. Return to the fork in the trail and continue down to the shore to see remains of more buildings and pieces of old mining machinery. Mine tailings dumped into Gastineau Channel created an attractive sandy beach along the shore here (Sandy Beach Park). Just to the south is a steep-sided pit where the mine collapsed in 1917. Walk back along the beach and past the Small Boat Harbor to Douglas Post Office, where you can catch a bus back to Juneau.

Mount Roberts

The most convenient way to get a panoramic view of Juneau and Gastineau Channel is by climbing Mt. Roberts, directly behind town. On summer weekends, you're bound to meet dozens of others on this enjoyable climb, including ironman-type joggers. A 2.5-mile trail (five hours roundtrip) begins at the east end of Sixth St., rising 2,500 feet in elevation through the rainforest. It ends at a large wooden cross just above the timberline. The hike is strenuous, but you're rewarded with spectacular views on clear days. There may be snow above this point until late July. The trail continues up to **Gastineau Peak** (3,666 feet), six miles (four hours roundtrip) from town, then on along the ridge to the summit of Mt. Roberts (3,819 feet), nine miles (five hours roundtrip) from town. Experienced hikers with a map and compass may want to continue along the ridge, eventually connecting up with other trails in the area. Weather conditions change rapidly on these ridgetops, so be aware of incoming clouds and never hike into fog.

The easiest way to the top of Mt. Roberts is on the new tramway (described above). A fast six-minute lift raises you to the 2,000-foot level, at the edge of the alpine. The tram, tel. (907) 463-3412, costs $16 for adults, and $10 for children ages six to 12. No charge for children under six.

Up Gold Creek

Some of the finest hiking around Juneau is found in the old gold mining areas up beyond the end of Basin Rd., a pleasant half-hour walk from town. You could easily spend several days exploring this scenic area. In Last Chance Basin, 1.5 miles up Basin Rd., are the fascinating remains of the **AJ Mine.** A number of paths lead around the compressor building (which now contains the Last Chance Mining Museum described above), a locomotive repair shop, and a variety of remains from the heyday of gold mining. For more details of the area, pick up the "Last Chance Basin Walking Tour" brochure from the Juneau-Douglas City Museum.

Perseverance Trail leads past Last Chance Basin to Silverbow Basin, site of the Perseverance Mine, three miles away (three hours roundtrip). The **Mount Juneau Trail** branches off from Perseverance Trail a half-mile up. It's very steep and only suitable for experienced hikers, but offers unparalleled vistas across Gastineau Channel. Plan on seven hours roundtrip. Directly across from the Mt. Juneau trailhead is a short path down to Ebner Falls. Continue another mile out Perseverance Trail to the **Granite Creek Trail** (1.5 miles one-way), which follows the creek up past several waterfalls into the alpine. Just before Silverbow Basin yet another side trail leads right to the Glory Hole, which is connected to the AJ Mine by a tunnel. Old mining ruins are at the end of the trail, but signs warn of potential hazards from toxic tailings at the mine site.

Point Bridget State Park

Point Bridget is a delightful park along the edge of Lynn Canal, 38 miles north of Juneau, and near Echo Cove. It's a great place to hike if you have the wheels to get there or want to try hitching. Several paths lace this 2,850-acre park, including the **Point Bridget Trail** (seven miles roundtrip) which takes hikers out to a fine vantage point across Lynn Canal to the Chilkat Mountains. Sea lions, harbor seals, and humpback whales are often seen from here. Before heading out, pick up a park map from the Dept. of Natural Resources, 400 Willoughby Ave., tel. (907) 465-4563.

Hike-in Cabins

The Juneau area has four very popular Forest Service cabins ($20/night) that can be reached by hiking trails or in the winter on skis. Be sure to make advance reservations, especially for weekends. Some of these fill up six months in advance. Located on a scenic alpine ridge, the **John Muir Cabin** overlooks Auke Bay and the surrounding islands. Get there by following the **Spaulding Trail** a half-mile, turning left onto the **Auke Nu Trail,** and continuing another 2.5 miles to the cabin. The trail starts from a parking area on the right side of the road 12 miles northwest of town and just beyond the Auke Bay Post Office.

The **Peterson Lake Cabin** lies at the end of a 4.5-mile trail. Although it's mostly boardwalk, rubber boots are highly recommended. The trailhead is on the right, 24 miles northwest of town, and just beyond the Shrine of St. Terese. Experienced hikers or cross-country skiers with a map and compass may want to cross the alpine ridges from Peterson Lake to the John Muir Cabin (2.5 miles away), where they can head back along the Auke Nu and Spaulding trails.

The **Dan Moller Cabin** on Douglas Island lies at the end of a three-mile trail. Get there by taking the Douglas bus to West Juneau. Get off the bus on Cordova St. (across from the Breeze Inn) and hike three blocks up the street. Turn left onto Pioneer Ave.; the trail begins from a small parking lot next to 3185 Pioneer Avenue. One of the most popular wintertime skiing trails in the area, it leads up to the beautiful alpine country of central Douglas Island.

Eagle Glacier Cabin faces this magnificent glacier, and is accessed via the **Amalga (Eagle Glacier) Trail** that begins 28 miles north of town. The path is relatively easy to hike, passes the cabin at the 5.5-mile point, and ends at the Eagle Glacier, 7.5 miles from the trailhead. The cabin faces across a lake to the glacier, offering some of the most dramatic vistas anywhere. Wear rubber boots for the often-muddy trail.

Yet More Cabins

In addition to these hike-in cabins, there are five other Forest Service cabins on the mainland around Juneau, plus another 15 on nearby Admiralty Island. Access to these cabins is by floatplane or sometimes by sea kayak. For more details on all Forest Service cabins in the area, contact the Forest Service Information Center downtown or the district office near Nugget Mall. The newest is **Berners Bay Cabin,** just eight kayak miles from the north end of Glacier Highway. The location is grand, with fine vistas across the bay, good fishing, a beautiful waterfall, and lots to explore on the two-mile-wide river delta just north of here. But book early on this cabin; it's guaranteed to fill up early! Travelers can fly in to the cabin, but most choose to take their own kayaks in or rent them ($50/day for a double kayak) from the **Juneau Outdoor Center** in downtown Douglas, tel. (907) 586-8220.

Two close and extremely popular cabins (they fill up several months in advance) are on **Turner Lake,** 20 miles east of Juneau. Great fishing for cutthroat trout and incredible waterfall-draped rock faces on all sides. The flight in takes you near the enormous Taku Glacier, an added bonus. Expect to pay $250 roundtrip (two people and gear) for a floatplane into the cabin. See "Transportation" for a list of local air taxi operators.

RECREATION

Sea Kayaking

In business for more than 25 years, **Alaska Discovery,** 5449 Shaune Dr., tel. (907) 780-6226 or (800) 586-1911, is one of Alaska's oldest and most respected wilderness expedition companies. Emphasizing low-impact travel and camping, Alaska Disco guides lead groups of six to 12 people throughout the state. Examples are: a three-day all-around-Douglas-Island sea-kayaking trip, $495 (from Juneau); Hubbard Glacier six-day sea-kayaking trip, $1,550 (from Yakutat); 10-day Tatshenshini River rafting trip, $2,100 (from Haines); Arctic National Wildlife Refuge 10-day trip, $2,900 (from Fairbanks); and seven-day Noatak River, $2,100 (from Kotzebue). In addition to these long voyages, Disco has guided kayaking day-trips from Juneau ($125 pp) or Glacier Bay ($119 pp), as well as bear watching/canoeing day-trips to **Pack Creek** ($349 including roundtrip airfare). You can reach them on the Internet at http://www.gorp.com/akdisc.htm.

Other companies offering guided sea kayaking trips from Juneau include **Greatland Guides of Alaska,** tel. (907) 463-4397; **Adventure Sports,** tel. (907) 789-5696; and **Absolutely Alaska,** tel. (907) 789-0841.

BOB RACE

Rent kayaks from the **Juneau Outdoor Center** in downtown Douglas, tel. (907) 586-8220. They also offer limited training for beginners, and can do kayak deliveries to areas around Juneau such as Berners Bay. Other companies renting kayaks include **Adventure Sports,** 8345 Old Dairy Rd., tel. (907) 789-5696; and **Out of Bounds/Adlersheim Lodge,** 34 miles north of Juneau, tel. (907) 789-7008 or (800) 435-5932.

Kayak Express, tel. (907) 780-4591, operates a very helpful kayak drop-off service (plus charter fishing and whalewatching trips) to Gustavus ($125 one-way), Hoonah ($125 one-way), Oliver's Inlet ($75), and other points in the area. **Auk Nu Tours/Glacier Bay Tours & Cruises,** tel. (907) 586-8687 or (800) 820-2628, provides kayak drop-offs to Gustavus, but make advance reservations to be sure they have space onboard. Other companies with kayak drop-offs include **Bird's Eye Charters/Timeline Cruises,** tel. (907) 586-3311; **Adventure Bound Alaska,** tel. (907) 463-2502 or (800) 228-3876; and **Absolutely Alaska,** tel. (907) 789-0841.

Floating Mendenhall River

Alaska Travel Adventures, tel. (907) 789-0052, provides three-and-a-half-hour raft trips down the Mendenhall River during the summer. This is mainly for the cruise ship folks. The cost is $89 pp for adults or $59 pp for children. Experienced rafters and canoeists also float the river, but be sure to ask the Forest Service for the details. The river is not particularly treacherous, but a number of people have died in independent boating accidents here. Alaska Travel Adventures twice dumped rafters in the river in 1996, though nobody was killed.

Boats

See the Davis Log Cabin Visitor Center for a complete listing of more than 30 **charter boat** operators in Juneau. All sorts of options are available, from half-day fishing and whale-watching ventures to two-week cruises around Southeast. Day rates start around $110 pp. If you want to do it on your own, rent a skiff and fishing gear from **Alaska Ship Chandlers,** 1000 Harbor Way, tel. (907) 789-7301. **Alaska Research Voyages,** tel. (907) 463-5511, operates a 54-foot sailing vessel. Guests go along on one- and two-week voyages, and participate in scientific research and natural history work.

Skiing and Snowboarding

Come wintertime, the **Eaglecrest Ski Area** on Douglas Island, tel. (907) 586-5284, provides excellent skiing opportunities (including night skiing). Thirty ski trails are available; maximum vertical drop is 1,400 feet. Adult lift tickets cost $24 per day. Cross-country skiers can get a special two-ride pass for $7 that takes them into the beautiful alpine meadows. Eaglecrest is generally open Thanksgiving to early April. Call (907) 586-5330 for a recording of current snow conditions. The lifts do not run during the summer.

Out of Bounds, tel. (907) 789-5952 or (800) 435-5932, operates a nationally known heli-skiing/snowboarding operation out of Adlersheim Lodge, 34 miles north of Juneau. Guests pay $2,500 per week to ski or snowboard 75,000 vertical feet of untracked terrain in the Juneau Icefield. Lodging is in bunk rooms, with all meals included. The peak snow season is Feb.-April.

Taku Glacier

Historic **Taku Glacier Lodge,** tel. (907) 586-8258, sits just across the Taku Inlet from the glacier. This beautiful old log structure was built in 1923. Black bears and eagles are frequent visitors (the bears were Juneau garbage bears that would have been shot if they had not been brought here). Three-hour visits to the lodge cost $175 pp, and include the scenic flight here over Taku Glacier, along with a big salmon dinner. This is primarily oriented to the cruise ship crowd, so expect to see lots of other folks if you go on a day when several ships are docked. No overnight visits to the lodge; it's open from mid-May through September.

River Expeditions, tel. (907) 463-6788 or (907) 586-2959, features a different sort of trip up the Taku. Guests are flown into a remote wilderness lodge on the Canadian side of the border, where they stay in a rustic log cabin and get to explore the surrounding country. Then they float downriver on a raft, catch a jetboat up the Tulsequah River, and return to Juneau by plane. The cost is $488 pp for one night, or $588 pp for two-night stays, including food, transportation, and raingear.

Cycling

Cycle Alaska, tel. (907) 364-3377, offers three-hour bicycle tours around Juneau ($50-60) along with bike rentals. You can also rent bikes from **Mountain Gears,** 210 N. Franklin St., tel. (907) 586-4327, a full-service bicycle shop. **Gray Line,** tel. (907) 586-3773, has an easy bike ride for lazy pedalers: they drive you up the Eaglecrest road, and you ride down. This three-hour tour costs $55.

More Playing Around

The **Augustus Brown Swimming Pool,** at the high school, 1619 Glacier Ave., tel. (907) 586-2055, has an excellent pool, coed sauna, and workout equipment for just $2-3.50 per visit. Golfers may want to head to **Mendenhall Golf Course,** tel. (907) 789-7323, a nine-hole course near the airport.

ACCOMMODATIONS

A full range of options is available to travelers staying in Juneau. See the "Juneau Accommodations" chart for a complete listing of Juneau lodging places. Bags and backpacks can be stored at the Alaskan Hotel, 167 S. Franklin St., tel. (907) 586-1000 ($1.50/bag/day). During the off-season, the Davis Log Cabin Visitor Center will temporarily store bags for free.

Hostel

One of the finest youth hostels in Alaska, Juneau International Hostel is in a lovely old home at 614 Harris St., tel. (907) 586-9559, just a few blocks up the hill from downtown. In addition to dorm space for 48 people, the hostel has a comfortable community room, kitchen facilities, and washer and dryer. It does not have a TV (hooray!). The hostel is open year-round, but is closed daily 9 a.m.-5 p.m. The doors are locked at 11 p.m. (10:30 p.m. in winter), putting a damper on your nightlife. Lodging here costs $10 pp ($7 for AYH members), with a maximum stay of three nights. Rooms are clean and the managers are friendly, but things are often crowded. Be sure to reserve ahead in summer, or get here early to be sure of a place.

Bed and Breakfasts

Couples may want to spend the extra money to stay in one of more than 35 Juneau B&Bs. Prices are generally around $75-85 d; some places are less expensive while others top $150 d. Accommodations run the gamut from old min-

JUNEAU ACCOMMODATIONS

Note: Add an 11% sales and bed tax to these motel rates (except for the hostel). See the text for details on B&B accommodations in Juneau. The accommodations are arranged from least to most expensive.

Juneau Youth Hostel; 614 Harris St.; tel. (907) 586-9559; $7 pp for AYH members, $10 pp for non-members; bunk accommodations, 11 p.m. curfew

Alaskan Hotel; 167 S. Franklin St.; tel. (907) 586-1000 or (800) 327-9347; $55 s, $65 d with bath down the hall; $70 s, $80 d with private bath; kitchenettes available, often noisy (bar downstairs)

Bergman Hotel; 434 Third St.; tel. (907) 586-1690; $55 s, $65 d; older hotel, bath down the hall, smoky place

Adlersheim Lodge; 34 miles north along Lynn Canal; tel. (907) 789-5952 or (800) 435-5932; $65 s or d; remote lodge with impressive setting, three rustic log cabins and main lodge, meals available

Driftwood Lodge; 435 W. Willoughby; tel. (907) 586-2280 or (800) 544-2239; $68 s, $78 d; courtesy van

Inn at the Waterfront; 455 S. Franklin St.; tel. (907) 586-2050; $60-72 s, $69-81 d with shared bath; $77-101 s, $86-110 d with private bath; historic building, continental breakfast

Super 8 Motel; 2295 Trout St.; tel. (907) 789-4858 or (800) 800-8000; $88 s, $97 d; courtesy van

The Prospector Hotel; 375 Whittier St.; tel. (907) 586-3737 or (800) 478-5166 in Alaska, or (800) 331-2711 elsewhere in U.S.; $90-135 s or d; AAA approved

Silverbow Inn and Restaurant; 120 Second St.; tel. (907) 586-4146; $99 s, $109 d; continental breakfast; historic building, AAA approved

Breakwater Inn; 1711 Glacier Ave.; tel. (907) 586-6303 or (800) 544-2250; $99-109 s or d

Best Western Country Lane Inn; 9300 Glacier Hwy.; tel. (907) 789-5005 or (800) 528-1234; $106-126 s, $115-140 d; continental breakfast, courtesy van, AAA approved

Best Western Country Lane Inn; 9300 Glacier Hwy.; tel. (907) 789-5005 or (800) 528-1234; $108 s, $110 d; continental breakfast, courtesy van

Airport Travelodge; 9200 Glacier Hwy.; tel. (907) 789-9700 or (800) 578-7878; $115 s, $125 d; indoor pool, jacuzzi, courtesy van, AAA approved

Best Western Grandma's Feather Bed; 2358 Mendenhall Loop Rd.; tel. (907) 789-5566 or (800) 528-1234; $126-150 s or d; jacuzzis, courtesy van

Baranof Hotel; 127 N. Franklin St.; (907) 586-2660 or (800) 544-0970; $142 s or d

Westmark Juneau; 51 W. Egan Dr.; tel. (907) 586-6900 or (800) 544-0970; $156 d

Whale's Eye Lodge; Shelter Island; tel. (907) 789-9188 or (800) 478-9188; $280 d; remote homestead with sea kayaking, fishing, and whalewatching

ers' cabins to gorgeous log hillside homes with views out over Juneau. Pick up the "Juneau Visitors Guide" brochure at the visitor center for a listing of local places, or check out their rack for flyers from many of the B&Bs. Note that not all places calling themselves B&Bs operate the same way, or have the same amenities.

A few recommended B&Bs include the following: **Crondahl's B&B,** tel. (907) 586-1464; **Jan's View B&B,** tel. (907) 463-5897; **Cashen Quarters B&B,** tel. (907) 586-9863; **Glacier Trail B&B,** tel. (907) 789-5646; **Mt. Juneau Inn,** tel. (907) 463-5855; **Raven's Roost,** tel. (907) 586-6811; **The Mullins House B&B,** tel. (907) 586-3384; and **Blueberry Lodge B&B,** tel. (907) 463-5886.

Karla Hart, at the **Alaska Bed & Breakfast Association,** 369 S. Franklin, Suite 200, Juneau, AK 99801, tel. (907) 586-2959, can make B&B reservations for you. She knows the various places well, and can direct you to one fitting your needs. It's a good idea to reserve ahead during the summer. The B&B Association can also reserve space in many other Alaskan towns.

Hotels and Motels

Lodging prices in Juneau match those elsewhere in Alaska—they are high. The least expensive place is **Alaskan Hotel.** Built in 1913, the Alaskan is Juneau's oldest lodging place. It was recently renovated, returning it to its traditional Victorian glory. The Alaskan also has a hot tub, jacuzzi, and sauna available ($21 an hour for two or three people; half price weekdays noon-4).

Camping

Both of the Forest Service's campgrounds in the Juneau area are far from downtown and open only mid-May to mid-September; call (907) 586-8800 for details. The campgrounds charge $8 per site and have firewood, water, and toilets. (You can pitch a tent here for free in the off-season, but will have to haul your own water in and garbage out.) **Auke Village Campground** is 16 miles out Glacier Hwy. on Point Louisa. Get there by turning left from the ferry and walking or hitching two miles on the road. The area is secluded, with a nice beach and views of nearby islands. Its only problem is access to Juneau—the nearest city bus stop is four miles away. **Mendenhall Lake Campground,** a larger area with great views across Mendenhall Lake to the glacier and access to many hiking trails, has seven backpacker units and 54 sites for vehicles. From the ferry terminal, turn right and go two miles to De Hart's Store, then left onto Loop Road. Follow it three miles to Montana Creek Rd., then another three-quarters of a mile to the campground. From Juneau, take the city bus to where Montana Creek Rd. intersects Mendenhall Loop Road. Walk up Montana Creek Rd., bear right at the "Y" after a half-mile, then continue another half-mile to the campground (well marked). Note that the rifle range is near the Mendenhall Lake Campground, so you may be awakened by gunfire some mornings. Don't worry, the drug wars haven't come to Juneau yet. Make reservations for Mendenhall Lake Campground by calling (800) 280-2267 ($8.25 extra for reservations).

Although there are no official campgrounds closer to Juneau, backpackers sometimes head up Basin Rd., with several tolerable spots in the trees nearby. Farther afield, you'll find places to pitch a tent up the Mt. Roberts or Perseverance trails. Some people also camp at beautiful Echo Cove, 40 miles northwest of Juneau on the Glacier Highway. Getting there without wheels is the primary drawback.

Recreational vehicles can generally overnight in Juneau shopping mall parking lots for free, and the city of Juneau (tel. 907-586-5255) maintains limited RV facilities at **Savikko Park** ($5; no showers) and **Norway Point** (free). Full service facilities ($16; open year-round) are available at **Auke Bay RV Park,** tel. (907) 789-9467, located 1 1/2 miles southeast from the ferry terminal. Reservations are recommended for Auke Bay, and a two-night minimum stay is required. Get details from the **Good Sam RV Information Center** at Nugget Mall.

FOOD

One of Juneau's strong points is a wide variety of restaurants with quality food and not-as-expensive-as-Barrow prices. Hang out with the bureaucrats at the cheapest—and blandest—place in town, the **cafeteria,** Room 241 in the Federal Building at Ninth St. and Glacier Ave. (open Mon.-Fri. 7 a.m.-3:30 p.m.). The absolutely best place to get a breakfast or lunch in Juneau is **Channel Bowl Cafe,** 608 Willoughby Ave., tel. (907) 586-6139. In spite of its location (in the bowling alley) and its funky decor ('50s-style Naugahyde diner stools and Formica tabletops), the Channel has great all-American cooking. You're likely to meet everyone from fishermen to state legislators inside. There's always some irreverent witticism posted on the sign out front. A fun place with good food.

Just up the street—but light years away in terms of style—is the **Fiddlehead Restaurant and Bakery,** 429 W. Willoughby Ave., tel. (907) 586-3150, with a nouvelle cuisine menu of fresh sourdough breads, locally caught seafood, homemade soups, and vegetarian specialties. Be prepared to drop $25 pp or more for dinner in the upstairs Fireweed Room, where you'll find a full bar. Definitely recommended if you have the bucks. Prices are considerably cheaper downstairs, but the international menu is more limited. The best locally baked breads come from **Silverbow Inn,** 120 Second St., tel. (907) 586-4146. The restaurant here is pricey, but meals aren't as notable as their impressive wine list.

The Cook House, tel. (907) 463-3658, next to Red Dog Saloon downtown, serves up gigantic burgers (at a humongous $13 price), along with steaks and fish specials. Over in Douglas is **Mike's Place,** 1102 Second St., tel. (907) 364-3271, owned by the same family since 1914. Fine steaks and seafood (try the blackened halibut for $17), along with a big salad bar ($7). The best prime ribs in Juneau can be found at **Prospector Hotel,** 375 Whittier St., tel. (907) 586-3737. The best local place for Asian food is **Canton House,** 8585 Old Dairy Rd., tel. (907) 789-5075.

Mexican Food
Armadillo Tex-Mex Cafe, 431 S. Franklin St., tel. (907) 586-1880, is well known for its delicious south-of-the-border fare, especially tasty nachos with a spicy salsa. Most meals start around $10, but a bowl of homemade chili and cornbread is a deal for $6.50. Extraordinarily popular with both locals and travelers, for good reason. **Olivia's de Mexico,** downstairs at 222 Seward St., tel. (907) 586-6870, has more traditional Mexican food, fair prices, and big portions.

Pizza and Italian
Juneau's best-known pizza joint is **Bullwinkle's,** tel. (907) 586-2400, directly across from the State Office Building on Willoughby Ave. and also in Mendenhall Valley next to Super Bear Market. Daily lunch pizza specials start around $6 and the popcorn is always free. You'll get better and more authentic pizza at **Pizzeria Roma,** in the Merchant's Wharf building at 2 Marine Way, tel. (907) 463-5020; and at **Pizza Verona,** 256 S. Franklin St., tel. (907) 586-2816. **Vito 'N Nick's,** 9342 Glacier Hwy., tel. (907) 789-7070, makes tasty deep-dish pizzas, along with sandwiches, Italian dinners, and monstrous homemade cinnamon rolls (famous locally).

Salmon Bakes
Juneau has two excellent salmon bakes with all-you-can-eat salmon dinners and free bus transport from town. **Thane Ore House Salmon Bake,** tel. (907) 586-3442, four miles south of town, charges $19 for a dinner of salmon, halibut, BBQ ribs, salad, baked beans, and corn bread, or $27 for a dinner and the "Gold Nugget Revue" musical comedy. Kids under 12 pay half price. **Gold Creek Salmon Bake,** tel. (907) 586-1424, in Last Chance Basin behind town, charges $22 pp (kids $12) for similar food. Gold Creek is particularly popular with locals.

Fishy Business
Giorgio at the Pier, on the south end of town at 544 S. Franklin St., tel. (907) 586-4700, is Juneau's most elaborate seafood place, with waterfront dining and a bar that looks like a Spanish galleon. The menu emphasizes fresh seafood, from clam chowder to broiled Alaskan prawns. This is Juneau's dress-up place. Another dependably fine place for creatively prepared seafood is the Fiddlehead Restaurant (described above). Two local places sell freshly smoked salmon: **Taku Smokeries,** 230 S. Franklin, tel. (907) 463-3474; and **Alaska Seafood Co.,** 5434 Shaune Dr. (across from the Alaskan Brewery), tel. (907) 780-5111. You might also try walking the docks to buy fresh fish or crab. **The Hanger,** on Merchants Wharf at 2 Marine Way, tel. (907) 586-5018, is a very popular pub with seafood, steaks, burgers, and sandwiches. Historic photos line the walls. A great place to watch the sun go down.

Coffee Shops
Several pleasant coffee shops serve espresso and pastries in Juneau. **Heritage Coffee Co.** at 174 S. Franklin St., tel. (800) 478-5282, is easily the most popular and crowded, and is open till 11 most nights during the summer. A great place to meet tree-huggers, state government yuppies, hip high schoolers, and Gore-Tex-clad vacationers. Walk down the halls of this building to view the wonderful historic photos of Juneau. **Valentine's Coffee House & Bakery,** 111 Seward, tel. (907) 463-5144, is smaller, but also extremely popular. Out in Nugget Mall near the airport is **Vintage Fare Cafe,** tel. (907) 789-1865, with good breakfasts and lunches, plus espresso.

Fast Food
If all Juneau's fine food is not to your liking, and you just want a cheap burger, be assured that Juneau also has two **McDonald's** restaurants (downtown and in Mendenhall Valley), along with a combination **Subway/Taco Bell** on the corner of Front and Seward downtown, and a **Taco Bell** in Mendenhall Mall. **Pizza Hut** and **Kentucky Fried Chicken** have outlets in Mendenhall Valley. Downtown Juneau has several **street vendors** who sell quick, cheap, and tasty lunchtime food such as bagels, burgers, chicken, and tacos. Wander around to see what looks interesting. Sure beats the local McD's!

Grocers
You'll find no-frills grocery shopping and harried clerks at **Fred Meyer,** tel. (907) 789-6503, nine

miles northwest of town along Glacier Highway. Nearby, notice the old hip-roofed barn that was once home to the Juneau Dairy. Other grocers out in Mendenhall Valley are **Family Grocer,** near the airport, tel. (907) 789-3399; **Carrs Quality Center,** 3033 Vintage Blvd., tel. (907) 790-5500; and **Super Bear Supermarket** in Mendenhall Mall, tel. (907) 789-0173. In town, head to friendly **Alaskan & Proud Market** (better known as A&P, but not to be confused with the East Coast chain), 615 Willoughby Ave., tel. (907) 586-3101 or (800) 478-2118, for a complete selection of fresh produce and meats. Carrs, A&P, and Fred Meyer are all open 24 hours a day. **Rainbow Foods,** Seward and Second Sts., is the local natural foods market. You might also try the **Costco** store in Lemon Creek, 5225 Commercial Way, tel. (907) 780-6740, for megaquantity food purchases, though most visitors won't find much need for case-lots of tuna fish.

ENTERTAINMENT

The Bar Scene
Juneau has an active nightlife, with plenty of live music almost every night of the week. The famous **Red Dog Saloon,** tel. (907) 463-3777, on S. Franklin St. has sawdust on the floor and honky-tonk or rock music in the air every day and night during the summer. A block up the street is the **Alaskan Bar,** at the Alaskan Hotel, 167 S. Franklin, tel. (907) 586-1000, a much quieter place with blues or folk music most nights. It is very popular with locals, who head here in the summer to escape the hordes at the Red Dog. The Alaskan has a turn-of-the-century decor and you can hear lawyer shoptalk from any seat in the place during the legislative session. Traipse a couple of doors down to the old Senate Building and take the elevator four flights up. **The Penthouse,** tel. (907) 463-4141, has windows overlooking the city lights, Top-40 rock videos, a glitzy dance floor, and a decor that takes you back to the disco era. The cover charge is $2. Across the street is the **Rendezvous,** 184 S. Franklin, tel. (907) 586-1270, where you'll find very loud rock 'n' roll on weekends and a lowlife crowd. The **Fiddlehead Restaurant and Bakery,** 429 W. Willoughby Ave., tel. (907) 586-3150, often has piano music or jazz in its upstairs Fireweed Room (cover charge). This is a fine place

for a romantic getaway. Located behind the Nugget Mall near the airport, **Hoochi's Sports Pub,** 2525 Industrial Blvd., tel. (907) 789-0799, has a big dance floor, 10 TVs, and country or rock music five nights a week. **The Hanger,** on the wharf at 2 Marine Way, tel. (907) 586-5018, has live music periodically, and is especially popular with state government workers after 5 p.m. Get here early for the window seats facing the waterfront. They have more than 100 brews on tap or in bottles. The elaborately furbished Galleon bar inside **Giorgio at the Pier,** 544 S. Franklin St., tel. (907) 586-4700, has pop-rock tunes frequently in the summer.

Performing Arts and Music
Housed in a clan house style structure along the shoreline where the cruise ships dock, **Naa Kahidi Theatre** mixes Native tales, songs, and dances. The production includes stories from Tlingit, Gwich'in, and other groups, with puppetry, masks, and colorful regalia. The group has toured extensively throughout the U.S. and Europe, and their hour-long performances are $16 for adults, $10 for kids under 12. The schedule changes through the summer, but performances take place at least once a day May-September. Watch for discount coupons in the *Juneau Guide* or *Capital Weekly.*

    Perseverance Theater, tel. (907) 364-2421, is a respected Douglas-based group that puts on plays Sept.-May. On Friday evenings 7-8:30 (mid-June to mid-August), **Marine Park** in downtown Juneau comes alive with free musical performances, ranging from classical to Middle Eastern folk. Call (907) 586-2787 to see who's playing.

EVENTS

Call (907) 586-5866 for a recorded listing of upcoming events and activities in Juneau. **July Fourth** is Juneau's day to play. The usual parades and fireworks (see them from Douglas Island for the most impressive backdrop) are joined by dog Frisbee-catching and watermelon-eating contests, along with a sand castle contest at Sandy Beach Park. If you're around in April, don't miss the week-long **Alaska State Folk Festival,** which attracts musicians from Alaska and the Pacific Northwest. Performances are free, and you can also attend workshops and dance to some of the hottest folk and blue-grass bands anywhere. Lots of fun. Each May, culture comes to town with the **Juneau Jazz and Classics,** a 10-day series of performances and workshops by local musicians and guest artists. Those who like to fish should throw in their line at the annual **Salmon Derby** in early August. A top prize of $35,000 in cash and prizes makes it the big summer event for locals. Even Robert Redford once took part.

INFORMATION AND SERVICES

Juneau's Visitor Information Center is in the **Davis Log Cabin** at 134 Third St., tel. (907) 586-2201. Modeled after Juneau's first church, this picture-perfect cabin (rebuilt in 1980) is itself a tourist attraction. Hours are Mon.-Fri. 8:30 a.m.-5 p.m., Sat.-Sun. 9 a.m.-5 p.m. during the summer (May-Sept.), and Mon.-Fri. 8:30-5 p.m. the rest of the year. (If you want to avoid the cruise ship mobs, ask to see the ship schedule posted at Davis Log Cabin. Get your rear out of downtown anytime they have five ships anchored up at the same time.) For Internet info, head to http://www.juneau.com.

Four other locations in Juneau are staffed by visitors bureau personnel in kiosks in the summer: **Marine Park** (open when cruise ships are in town), **Cruise Ship Terminal** on S. Franklin St. (open when cruise ships are in town), the **airport** (open for flight arrivals), the ferry terminal (open for ferry arrivals). RVers may want to stop at the **Good Sam RV Info Center** in Nugget Mall; open Mon.-Fri. 10 a.m.-6 p.m., Sat.-Sun. noon-4 p.m.

For up-to-date local information, pick up a copy of the annual *Juneau Guide* (free) at the ferry terminal or the visitor center. A **"Juneau Walking Tour"** map is also available at the visitor center, with German, French, Spanish, Chinese, and Japanese translations. Change foreign bills at **Thomas Cook Foreign Exchange** on 127 N. Franklin St., tel. (907) 586-5688; open daily in the summer. **Crew Quarters,** across from the library on S. Franklin, has telephones, and is particularly popular with Indonesian and Filipino crew members from the cruise ships.

Tongass National Forest Information
The U.S. Forest Service Information Center in Centennial Hall at 101 Egan Dr., tel. (907) 586-8751, is open daily 8 a.m.-5 p.m. during the summer (Mon.-Fri. 8 a.m.-5 p.m. the rest of the year). Inside, find a tremendous amount of information on recreation activities throughout Southeast. The staff has Forest Service personnel able to answer almost any question about the outdoors. This is the place to make reservations for Forest Service cabins throughout Southeast, to find out about trips to Glacier Bay or Tracy Arm, to pick up free brochures and maps, or to buy books on local hiking trails. On rainy days, stop by for films on whales, eagles, glaciers, bears, and other topics. Special events are held here throughout the winter months.

The Forest Service District offices for **Juneau Ranger District** and **Admiralty Island National Monument** are at 8465 Old Dairy Rd., tel. (907) 586-8800, 10 miles northwest of town near Nugget Mall. The folks here have a first-hand knowledge of the local terrain and can also make cabin reservations. Call (907) 465-4116 for recorded fishing information courtesy of the Alaska Dept. of Fish and Game.

Services
The main **post office** is in the downtown Federal Building, and a branch post office is on Seward St. near Second Street. Coin-operated **showers** ($1.50) are available at **Harbor Wash Board,** 1114 Glacier Ave., and at the **Auke Bay Harbormaster's Office.** You can also shower at **Zach Gordon Youth Center,** 396 Whittier St.; **Auke Bay Boat Harbor;** and the **Alaskan Hotel.** A better deal is the high school **swimming pool,** 1619 Glacier Ave., tel. (907) 586-2055, where $3 buys access to a shower, pool, sauna, and weight-lifting equipment. Plus, you get to check out the pallid-skin Juneauites. Laundromats include the above-mentioned Harbor Wash Board and **Mendenhall Laundromat** in the Mendenhall Mall Shopping Center, tel. (907) 789-2880.

OTHER PRACTICALITIES

Arts and Crafts
Wm. Spear Designs, next to the Alaskan Hotel on S. Franklin St., tel. (907) 586-2209, has the complete collection of colorful enameled pins by this local artisan with an international reputation. A former lawyer, Spear does work covering the spectrum from UFOs to dinosaurs. **Rie**

Muñoz Gallery, in Jordan Creek Mall (near the airport), tel. (907) 789-7411, features works by several of Alaska's finest artists, including prints by Rie Muñoz and JoAnn George. **Mt. Juneau Artists,** 211 Front St. (above Subway), tel. (907) 586-2108, is the town's arts and crafts cooperative, with a wide range of artwork. Other places of note are **Gallery of the North,** 406 S. Franklin St., tel. (907) 586-9500; **Portfolio Arts,** 210 Ferry Way, tel. (907) 586-8111; and **R.T. Wallen Gallery,** 217 Seward St., tel. (907) 586-3009. Scads of other galleries and gift shops sell artwork and trinkets to the cruise ship crowd. The quality varies widely, but nearly everything is overpriced, particularly anything by a Native artisan. Unfortunately, the romanticized paintings, carvings, and sculpture depicting these original Alaskans hunting seals in kayaks or carving totem poles meets head-on a much sadder picture of inebriated Natives leaning against the windows of downtown Juneau bars.

Shopping
Most locals do their shopping out the road at Nugget Mall, Mendenhall Mall, or the trio of monster-marts: Fred Meyer (near the airport), Kmart (in Lemon Creek), and Costco (near the Alaskan Brewery). Hard to believe a city the size of Juneau can support all three. Undoubtedly the smaller stores are in for tough times now that the big boys have muscled their way into town.

The **Salvation Army Thrift Store** beside Channel Bowl on Willoughby Ave. sells warm clothes, paperbacks, and lots more. More bargains near the airport are at **St. Vincent De Paul's,** 8617 Teel, tel. (907) 789-5535. The **Foggy Mountain Shop,** 134 N. Franklin St., sells camping gear, topographic maps, and sports equipment. They also rent skis and rollerblades. The best place for rugged raingear, boots, and outdoor clothes is the **Nugget Store** in Nugget Mall. While there, check out the mall's nine-foot-tall stuffed brown bear. **Taku Tailor,** in Emporium Mall (behind the Heritage Coffee Co. downtown) does a nice job on repairs of packs and tents.

Equipment Rental
Gearing Up, 369 S. Franklin Ave., tel. (907) 586-2549, rents sleeping bags with sleeping pads ($25 for two days), tents ($25 for two days), one-and two-burner stoves ($12-18), and

raingear and boots ($10-14). Owner Renee Gayhart requests some advance notice and requires a minimum deposit. You can also arrange with her for pickup and drop-off of the equipment. But don't ask Renee about her secret hiking and camping spots.

The Literary Scene
Juneauites enjoy three different public libraries. The award-winning **main library,** tel. (907) 586-5249, is on the top floor of the parking garage on S. Franklin Street. There's a wonderful view of all the activity in Gastineau Channel from the outside walkway. Visitors may want to stop by the freebie shelves near the entrance for a trashy novel to read. Hours are Mon.-Thurs. 11 a.m.-9 p.m., Fri.-Sun. noon-5 p.m. The **Valley branch** in Mendenhall Mall, tel. (907) 789-0125, is open Sunday noon-5 p.m., Mon.-Fri. noon-9 p.m., and Saturday 10 a.m.-6 p.m. The **Douglas library** at Third and E Sts., tel. (907) 586-5249, is open Mon.-Wed. 3-9 p.m., Thursday 11 a.m.-5 p.m., Saturday and Sunday 1-5 p.m. The **Alaska State Library** is on the eighth floor of the State Office Building, and is open Mon.-Fri. 9 a.m.-5.

Big City Books, 100 N. Franklin St., has an impressive selection of Alaskan books and topographic maps. A few doors down is another good shop, **Hearthside Books,** tel. (907) 586-1760 or (800) 478-1000, which also has a store in the Nugget Mall near the airport, tel. (907) 789-2750. For bargain-basement prices on used books, stop by the library's secondhand bookshop in Mendenhall Mall. **The Observatory,** 235 Second St., tel. (907) 586-9676, has used books—including the largest collection of out-of-print Alaskana—plus first editions and antiquarian maps.

SEACC
The Southeast Alaska Conservation Council (SEACC), 419 Sixth St., tel. (907) 586-6942, has material on environmental issues, plus activist T-shirts. This is the primary environmental group in Southeast and has a reputation as a highly effective organization both locally and in Washington, D.C. Members receive a quarterly newsletter and periodic notices of important environmental issues. You can join for $25/year. Their mailing address is P.O. Box 21692, Juneau, AK 99802. Reach them via e-mail at seacc@igc.apc.org.

TRANSPORTATION

By Ferry

Juneau's **ferry terminal,** tel. (907) 789-7453 or (800) 642-0066, is 14 miles northwest of town at Auke Bay. Ferries arrive and depart daily during the summer, headed north to both Haines ($20) and Skagway ($26), southwest to Sitka ($26), and south to other towns. Arrivals are often very late at night, so be ready to stumble off in a daze. Ferries generally stay one to two hours in Auke Bay. The terminal is open three hours before departures of the larger ferries, two hours before *Le Conte* or *Aurora* departures, or one hour before any vessel arrivals. Several covered picnic tables are behind the terminal where you can crash out if you have an early-morning departure. Call (907) 465-3940 for recorded ferry schedule info.

A local bus company, **MGT,** tel. (907) 789-5460, meets all ferries year-round and charges $5 for the ride into town, or $5 from the ferry to the airport. They can also deliver you to the ferry from Juneau if you make reservations the night before 6-8 p.m. Upon request, they will stop at most downtown lodging places, including the youth hostel. A cab ride to town will set you back $20 or so, but hitching to town is relatively easy during the day. You can also walk the two miles from the ferry terminal to De Hart's Store, where hourly city buses ($1.25) will pick you up Mon.-Sat. 7 a.m.-11:30 p.m.

By Air

Juneau airport is nine miles northwest of downtown Juneau. Express **city buses** ($1.25) arrive hourly in front of the airport between 8 a.m.-5 p.m. On weekends or later hours (till 11:15 p.m.) you can catch the regular city bus behind Nugget Mall, a half-mile away. If you're in a hurry, **Island Waterways,** tel. (907) 780-4977, charges $7 one-way for direct service to the downtown Westmark and Baranof hotels. They meet most (but not all) flights. **Gray Line,** tel.

(907) 586-3773, offers a similar shuttle service to town or back to the airport for $8.75 one-way. Juneau airport closes 10 p.m.-5 a.m. Inside the terminal, take a look at the glass cases with various stuffed critters, including a huge polar bear (upstairs). The upstairs cafeteria offers impressive vistas out across Mendenhall Glacier. A good place to see waterfowl and eagles is the **Mendenhall Wetlands** that surround the airport. An overlook provides a view from Egan Highway on the way into Juneau.

Air North, tel. (907) 789-2007 or (800) 327-7651, flies classic DC-4s and DC-3s between Juneau and Whitehorse, Yukon, and onward to Dawson and Fairbanks. **Alaska Airlines,** tel. (800) 426-0333, has daily flights into Juneau from Seattle, and on to Anchorage and Fairbank. Alaska's jets also connect Juneau with Cordova, Yakutat, Gustavus, Sitka, Petersburg, Wrangell, Ketchikan, and points south all the way to Mexico. Some of Alaska's flights to Anchorage stop at Yakutat and Cordova. A one-way ticket to Cordova, though painfully expensive at $186, is an excellent way to connect to Southcentral Alaska. You get to see out-of-the-way Cordova, and the spectacular Copper River delta country, and you can catch the southwest ferry to Valdez ($30) and on to Whittier via Columbia Glacier ($58), then through to Anchorage ($33) via Alaska Railroad. You can save a bit if you miss Valdez and the Columbia Glacier by going directly by ferry from Cordova to Whittier ($58).

Options abound for small plane service to communities around Juneau. **Wings of Alaska,** tel. (907) 789-0790 or (800) 478-9464, has daily service to Angoon ($70), Cube Cove ($45), Elfin Cove ($85), Gustavus ($65), Haines ($59), Hoonah ($45), Pelican ($80), Skagway ($70), and Tenakee Springs ($65). **Loken Aviation,** tel. (907) 789-3331 or (800) 478-3360, offers daily flights to Angoon ($70), Elfin Cove ($80), Hobart Bay ($90), Pack Creek ($70), Pelican ($80), and Tenakee ($70). **Skagway Air,** tel. (907) 789-2006, flies to Hoonah ($45), Gustavus

($60), Haines ($80), and Skagway ($70) daily. **L.A.B. Flying Service,** tel. (907) 789-9160 or (800) 426-0543, has daily service to Excursion Inlet ($56), Gustavus ($56), Haines ($65), Hoonah ($48), Kake ($95), Petersburg ($115), and Skagway ($81). **Haines Airways,** tel. (907) 789-2336, flies daily to Haines ($55), Hoonah ($45), and Gustavus ($80). **Ketchikan Air Service,** tel. (907) 790-3377 or (800) 656-6608, has daily service between Juneau and Kake ($85), Ketchikan ($132), Klawock ($184), Petersburg ($112), and Wrangell ($125). **Air Excursions,** tel. (907) 697-2375 or (800) 354-2479, offers the cheapest flights to Gustavus: $50.

Charter Trips

Charter service to nearby Forest Service cabins and flightseeing trips are available from the above-listed companies and from two others: **Alaska Coastal Airlines,** tel. (907) 789-7818; and **Ward Air,** tel. (907) 789-9150. Both of these also have excellent safety records and have been around for many years. Expect to pay around $340/hour for a Beaver (seats six people or four with gear) or $240/hour for a Cessna 206 (seats four people or two with gear). One way to save money on a flight into a Forest Service cabin is by hopping on a mail flight that passes near the cabin. Example: a charter to Admiralty Island's Lake Florence costs $380 roundtrip, but you can do the same trip by getting dropped off from the Angoon mail plane for only $140 roundtrip. Note, however, that this is for one person; for groups it is often less expensive to charter since the plane costs the same amount for one or four people.

Flightseeing

Wings of Alaska, tel. (907) 789-0790 or (800) 478-9464, has flightseeing trips (45 minutes) over the Juneau Icefield for $100 pp. Glacier Bay tours are available for $140 pp, but you'll find lower rates and shorter flying distances out of Haines or Skagway. **Air Excursions,** tel. (907) 697-2375 or (800) 354-2479, also offers flightseeing trips from Juneau.

 Temsco Helicopters, tel. (907) 789-9501, has 50-minute Mendenhall Glacier tours costing $142 pp (including a 25-minute stop on the glacier), while **ERA Helicopters,** tel. (907) 586-2030 or (800) 843-1947, offers hour-long tours of the spectacular Juneau Icefield for $162 pp. ERA's

flights land on Norris Glacier, and spend more time flying over the icefield. Locals prefer this one because of the greater sightseeing opportunities. A third company, **Coastal Helicopters,** tel. (907) 789-5600, has shorter flights that land on Herbert Glacier for $120 pp. All three companies provide transportation from downtown to their landing pads and also provide chartered flights to the glaciers for heli-hiking or skiing.

Sightseeing Tours

MGT, tel. (907) 789-5460, runs two- to two-and-a-half-hour tours of the city and Mendenhall Glacier for $12.50 pp. They meet all ferries. Several other companies also offer van or bus tours of Juneau, including: **Alaska Native Tours,** tel. (907) 463-3231; **Island Waterways,** tel. (907) 780-4977; **Gray Line,** tel. (907) 586-3773; and **Juneau Custom Tours,** tel. (907) 789-8400.

City Buses

Capital Transit buses ($1.25 exact change only) operate daily, connecting Juneau, Douglas, and Mendenhall Valley. Buses to and from Mendenhall Valley run every half-hour 7 a.m.-11 p.m. (9 a.m.-5 p.m. on Sunday), with both regular and express service (weekdays only). Bus service to Douglas is hourly. For details, call (907) 789-6901 or pick up route maps and schedules from the various visitor centers or at the ferry terminal or airport. Schedules are also posted at the bus stop outside the downtown Federal Building.

Trolleys

Two trolleys provide access to downtown Juneau. One of these, the **Trolley Car Company,** tel. (907) 586-1233, covers most of downtown on a daily basis May-Sept. 9 a.m.-6 p.m. Fares are $10 for all day; free for kids under five. This red trolley features a narrated tour. Gray Line operates a green **downtown trolley** to shuttle folks around the town center; $3 roundtrip or $5 for all day.

Taxis

The local taxi companies are **Taku Glacier Taxi,** tel. (907) 586-2121; **Alaska Taxi & Tours,** (907) 780-6400; and **Capital Cab,** tel. (907) 586-2772. A cab ride from downtown to the ferry terminal will set you back $20, but might be worth it if you get several people together.

Car Rentals

With nearly 100 miles of roads in the Juneau area, renting a car is a smart idea, especially if you can get several people in on the deal. **Rent-A-Wreck,** tel. (907) 789-4111, has the cheapest rates (and the oldest cars). Also try **Mendenhall Auto Center,** 8725 Mallard St., tel. (907) 789-1386 or (800) 478-1386; or **Evergreen Ford,** 8895 Mallard St., tel. (907) 789-9386. The national chains have offices at the airport: **Allstar/Practical,** tel. (907) 790-2414 or (800) 722-0741; **Avis,** tel. (907) 789-9450 or (800) 331-1212; **Hertz,** tel. (907) 789-9494 or (800) 654-3131; **National,** tel. (907) 789-9814 or (800) 227-7368; and **Payless,** tel. (907) 780-4144 or (800) 729-7219. Most of these companies can pick up or drop off visitors downtown or at the airport (by prior arrangement). Rates start around $35-40/day. Tip: cars rented in Skagway or Haines have mileage restrictions, so people on a

budget sometimes rent a car in Juneau for a week or two, put it on the ferry to Haines, and drive all over Alaska and the Yukon before returning to Juneau. You may have to pay an extra insurance fee if you do this, however.

TRACY ARM-FORDS TERROR WILDERNESS

Located 50 miles southeast of Juneau, the 653,000-acre Tracy Arm-Fords Terror Wilderness contains country that rivals Glacier Bay National Park, but costs half as much to reach. The wilderness consists of a broad bay that splits into two long glacially carved arms—Tracy Arm and Endicott Arm. (Fords Terror splits off as a separate channel halfway up Endicott Arm.) Within Tracy Arm, steep-walled granite canyons plummet 2,000 feet into incredibly deep and nar-

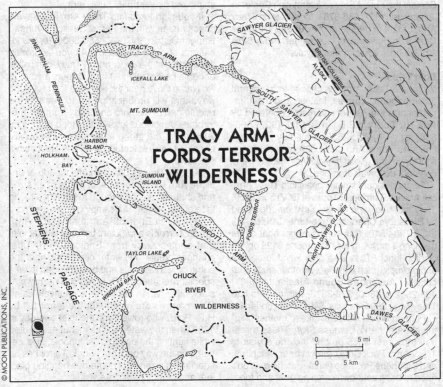

© MOON PUBLICATIONS, INC.

row fjords. We're talking rocks-to-the-waterline here. The fjords wind past waterfalls to massive glaciers, their icebergs dotted with hundreds of hair seals. Humpback whales are a common sight, as are killer whales (orcas). Look closely on the mountain slopes and you're bound to see mountain goats, especially near North Sawyer Glacier. John Muir noted that the fjord was "shut in by sublime Yosemite cliffs, nobly sculptured, and adorned with waterfalls and fringes of trees, bushes, and patches of flowers, but amid so crowded a display of novel beauty it was not easy to concentrate the attention long enough on any portion of it without giving more days and years than our lives can afford." Modern-day visitors come away equally impressed.

Two glaciers—Sawyer and South Sawyer—cap the end of Tracy Arm. Sawyer Glacier is retreating up bay at 85 feet per year, while South Sawyer is heading up at over 300 feet per year. Contact the Forest Service Information Center in Juneau, tel. (907) 586-8751, for details on Tracy Arm, or talk to people at the **Juneau Outdoor Center** in downtown Douglas, tel. (907) 586-8220, where you can rent kayaks.

Boat Trips

Visitors to Tracy Arm can choose from several different boats. Largest, fastest, and most impersonal is the 78-foot catamaran operated by **Auk Nu Tours,** 76 Egan Dr., tel. (907) 586-8687 or (800) 820-2628. A full-day roundtrip cruise to Tracy Arm costs $99 pp including a light lunch and use of binoculars. The company does not do kayak drop-offs.

For trips aboard smaller boats into Tracy Arm, call **Alaska Rainforest Tours** at (907) 586-2959. They can book you on the *Seymour*, operated by **Birds Eye Charters/Time-Line Cruises,** tel. (907) 790-2510. This 16-passenger boat offers day-long Tracy Arm trips for around $125 pp, including lunch. They also offer kayak drop-offs and pickups for an extra fee. Another small boat option is **Adventure Bound Alaska,** tel. (907) 463-2502 or (800) 228-3876, with cruises into Tracy Arm, $99 for adults, $49 for kids under 18.

For something different, take a "mother ship" trip aboard the *Wilderness Swift.* These three-day trips cost $365 pp and include a visit to Tracy Arm, Pack Creek (brown bear watching), and Stephens Passage (whalewatching). You'll need to bring your own camping gear and food,

since nights are spent camping out on the shore. The groups are limited to a maximum of six people. Call Alaska Rainforest Tours at (907) 586-2959 for details.

On Your Own

There are no trails in the Tracy Arm-Fords Terror Wilderness, but experienced sea kayakers discover spectacular country to explore. Unfortunately, kayakers in Tracy Arm should be prepared for a constant parade of giant cruise ships, leaving large wakes and plenty of engine noise to contend with. (Sound travels a long way over the water. Wilderness rangers report being startled to suddenly hear loudspeakers announcing, "Margaritas will be served at 1630 in the aft lounge.") You can, however, escape the boats by hiking up the ravines into the high country, or by heading into the less-congested waters of Endicott Arm where the big cruise ships and power boats rarely stray.

If you plan to go into Tracy Arm in a kayak, check ahead with the Forest Service's Juneau Ranger District, tel. (907) 586-8800, for the locations of good campsites. As you approach the glaciers at the upper end of Tracy, campsites become harder to find. Many boaters anchor in No Name Cove near the entrance to Tracy Arm. Kayakers will probably prefer to head to the middle part of the fjord and away from the motorboats. Ambitious folks (with a topo map) may want to try the steep half-mile cross-country climb up to scenic **Icefall Lake** (1,469 feet above sea level).

Massive **Dawes Glacier** jams the top of Endicott Arm with thousands of bergs of all sizes and shapes, making it tough to get close to the face of the glacier. But camping spots are more numerous in Endicott Arm than Tracy Arm. **Fords Terror** is a turbulent but spectacular inlet that angles away from Endicott Arm. Tidal changes create wild water conditions near the entrance, so kayakers and boaters need to take special precautions. Only run the narrows at slack tides, when the water is relatively calm. (The narrows are named for the terror felt by H.R. Ford, who rowed into the inlet one day in 1889 when the water was calm, but nearly died while fighting the currents, whirlpools, and icebergs on the way back out.) Fords Terror has no tidewater glaciers, but numerous hanging glaciers and craggy peaks are visible.

Chuck River Wilderness

Twelve miles south of Tracy Arm is **Windham Bay,** entrance to Chuck River Wilderness. This small wild area currently receives very little use, but offers good fishing for all five species of salmon and a chance to explore the ruins of Southeast's oldest mining community, Windham Bay. Good hiking also up the mile-long **Taylor Creek Trail** from Windham Bay to Taylor Lake.

Endicott River Wilderness

Although it encompasses 94,000 acres, this is believed to be the least-visited wilderness area anywhere in America. A few hunters are the primary visitors each year. Located some 60 miles northwest of Juneau, the wilderness borders on Glacier Bay National Park and includes the Endicott River watershed along the eastern slope of the Chilkat Range. The country is spruce and hemlock forests, mixed with alders. Trails are nonexistent, and access from Lynn Canal is virtually impossible. See the Forest Service's Juneau Ranger District office for more information on this decidedly off-the-beaten-track area.

ADMIRALTY ISLAND

Just 20 miles west of Juneau lies the northern end of Admiralty Island National Monument, and the massive Kootznahoo Wilderness. At nearly a million acres, the wilderness covers 90% of Admiralty, making it the only large island in Southeast that has not been extensively logged or developed. The Tlingit name for Admiralty—Kootznahoo—means "Bear Fortress." The island is aptly named: it has perhaps 1,500 brown bears, giving it some of the highest bear densities anywhere on earth. Eagles are extraordinarily abundant along the shoreline, and the cries of loons haunt Admiralty's lakes. This is truly one of the gemstones of Southeast Alaska.

ANGOON

Located along Admiralty's southwestern shore, the Tlingit village of Angoon (pop. 650) is the island's lone town. It sits astride a peninsula guarding the entrance to Kootznahoo Inlet, an incredible wonderland of small islands and saltwater passages. Tourism is not encouraged in Angoon but people are friendly. Locals have cable TVs and microwave ovens, but smokehouses sit in front of many houses and you'll hear older people speaking Tlingit. Angoon weather generally lives up to its reputation as Southeast Alaska's "Banana Belt"; yearly rainfall averages only 38 inches, compared to three times that in Sitka, only 40 miles away. By the way, the word "hootch" originated from the potent whiskey distilled by the "Hoosenoo" Indians of Admiralty in the 19th century. Today, Angoon is a dry town with a reputation as a place where traditional ways are encouraged. As with most other Bush towns, it is far from attractive, with lots of trash strewn about.

History

The village of Angoon still commemorates an infamous incident that took place more than a century ago. While working for the Northwest Trading Company, a local shaman was killed in a seal hunting accident. The villagers demanded 200 blankets as compensation and two days off to honor and bury the dead man. To ensure payment, they seized two hostages. Unaware of Tlingit traditions, the company manager fled to Sitka and persuaded a U.S. Navy boat to "punish them severely." On October 26, 1882, the town was shelled, destroying most of the houses. All the villagers' canoes were smashed and sunk, and all their winter supplies burned. Six children died from the smoke and the people nearly starved that winter. In a U.S. Congressional investigation two years later, the shelling was called "the greatest outrage ever committed in the United States upon any Indian tribe." Finally, in 1973, the government paid $90,000 in compensation for the shelling, but the Navy has never formally apologized.

Unlike most other villages in Southeast, the people of Angoon have fought hard to preserve their island from logging and development. Unfortunately, they were unable to stop the timber-mining presently destroying some of Admiralty's most scenic country. Atikon Forest Products, a Native-owned corporation, has already logged right down to the water around Peanut and Kathleen Lakes (30 miles north of Angoon), and beautiful Lake Florence is fast becoming the final victim. This is what happens when money talks. On the north end of Admiralty Island is the Greens Creek Mine. It was one of the largest silver mines in the country until 1993, when it closed due to low silver prices. Aside from these developments and a few other old logging scars and homesites, Admiralty Island is pristine wilderness.

Sights

Even if you don't stay overnight in Angoon, get off the ferry and walk across the road and down to the beach. From there you can look up to a small **cemetery** with old gravestones and fenced-in graves. Another interesting cemetery is near the end of the peninsula a half-mile behind the **Russian Orthodox church** in town. A number of rustic old houses line the shore, one with killer whales painted on the front. A hundred feet uphill from the post office are five memorial **totems** topped by representations of different local clans. Near Angoon Trading you get a great view of the narrow passage leading into **Kootznahoo Inlet,** where tides create dangerous rapids.

Accommodations and Food

Angoon has several places to stay. **Favorite Bay Inn,** tel. (907) 788-3123 or (800) 423-3123, on the edge of town near the boat harbor, charges $69 s or $109 d with breakfast included. **Kootznahoo Lodge,** tel. (907) 788-3501, a few hundred feet closer to town, costs $75 s or $85 d. It also rents skiffs ($100/day), and serves meals for guests. Another place to stay is **Sophie's Place B&B,** tel. (907) 788-3194. **Whaler's Cove Sportfishing Lodge,** tel. (907) 788-3123 or (800) 423-3123, has package weekly rates for anglers in search of salmon and halibut; open May-October.

Angoon has no official camping facilities, but people sometimes pitch tents at the trashed-out picnic area just to the right of the ferry terminal along the beach. It is 2.5 miles to town along the road or a pleasant 1.5-mile walk north along the rocky beach.

Both **Angoon Trading,** tel. (907) 788-3111; and the smaller **City Market,** tel. (907) 788-

3178, have a limited and rather expensive selection of groceries and other supplies. City Market is the local hangout for kids, with snacks, hot dogs, nachos, and ice cream.

Transportation

The ferry *Le Conte* visits Angoon six times a week (three times in each direction), staying just long enough to unload and load vehicles. The Juneau-Angoon fare is $24. The dock (no ferry terminal) is 2.5 miles out of town, so you won't get to see Angoon up close unless you disembark. "Taxis" meet most ferries, or you can hitch or walk the dirt road to town. **Wings of Alaska,** tel. (907) 788-3530 or (800) 478-9464; and **Loken Aviation,** tel. (907) 789-3331 or (800) 478-3360, have daily floatplane service between Angoon and Juneau for $70. Wings also flies to Tenakee for $65. **Taquan Air,** tel. (907) 788-3641 or (800) 770-8800, flies to Sitka every day for $80, and to Kake for $80.

CROSS-ADMIRALTY CANOE ROUTE

Admiralty Island is ideally suited for people who enjoy canoeing or sea kayaking. Kootznahoo Inlet reaches back behind Angoon through a labyrinth of islands and narrow passages, before opening into expansive Mitchell Bay. From there you can continue to Salt Lake or Kanalku Bay, or begin the Cross-Admiralty Canoe Route—a chain of scenic lakes connected by portages (one over three miles long). Using this 42-mile route you should reach Seymour Canal in four to six days (the record is 12 hours). Along the way are six Forest Service cabins ($25/night) and six Adirondack shelters (free), so you won't have to sleep out in the rain all the time.

Kootznahoo Inlet

Twice each day, tidal fluctuations push water through the narrow passages of Kootznahoo Inlet into Mitchell Bay and Salt Lake. At full flood or ebb tide, the water becomes a torrent that creates some of the fastest-flowing stretches of salt water in the world (13 knots). These strong tidal currents create eddies, whirlpools, standing waves, and even falls, depending upon the tides and the stage. To avoid these Class III whitewater conditions, be sure you reach the narrow passages at slack tide. Use a tide chart, adding approximately two hours to the Juneau times for the passage through the inappropriately named Stillwater Narrows. Inside Mitchell Bay and at Salt Lake the tides are delayed even longer, up to three hours beyond Juneau tides. If you aren't sure how to read the tide charts or need more info on running Kootznahoo Inlet, talk to folks at the monument office in Juneau.

Practicalities

Be sure to make cabin reservations well in advance by contacting the **U.S. Forest Service Information Center** in Centennial Hall at 101 Egan Dr., Juneau, tel. (907) 586-8751. Also be certain to request a copy of the **"Admiralty Island National Monument Canoe/Kayak Route"** map ($3). It includes detailed info on navigating Kootznahoo Narrows and crossing the island. Trail conditions may vary along the canoe route. The Distin Lake-to-Thayer Lake trail is in poor condition, but other trails on the route are in better shape, with long stretches of puncheon or boardwalk.

Guided canoe treks are no longer offered across Admiralty, perhaps a reflection of the aging of the baby boomer generation. This means that those who do go will have the great place even more to themselves. Most canoeists and kayakers bring their own boats along on the ferry, but you can rent canoes in Angoon; call Favorite Bay Inn at (907) 788-3123 or (800) 423-3123. For more specific information on the canoe route, contact the office of **Admiralty Island National Monument** at 8461 Old Dairy Rd., Juneau, AK 99801, tel. (907) 586-8790.

Thayer Lake Lodge makes an excellent break in the middle of the canoe route (if you take a bit of a detour). The facilities are comfortably rustic and you get three big meals a day as well as use of the lodge's boats and fishing gear. Besides, you get to meet some real old-time Alaskans. Highly recommended if you have the cash. For reservations, contact Thayer Lake Lodge, P.O. Box 211614, Auke Bay, AK 99821, tel. (907) 225-3343 (winter) or (907) 789-5646 (summer).

If you're really ambitious (and experienced) it's possible to cross Admiralty Island and then continue up Seymour Canal, eventually reaching Juneau. Only a few hardy souls try this, however, because the canoes that work so well on the lakes can be dangerous in the open water of

Seymour Canal, and sea kayaks are impractical for the long portages of the canoe route.

SEYMOUR CANAL

The Seymour Canal area is popular with sea kayakers, offering beautiful country, relatively protected waters, and the chance to see eagles, brown bears, and other wildlife. Most kayakers head south from Juneau, crossing the often-rough Stephens Passage and entering Oliver Inlet. A boat tramway makes it easy to bring kayaks across to upper Seymour Canal, a mile away. Alaska State Parks maintains the **Oliver Inlet Cabin** ($35) at the northern tip of Seymour Canal. For reservations contact Alaska State Parks, 400 Willoughby Center, Juneau, AK 99801, tel. (907) 465-4563.

In Seymour, you'll find many coves and islands to explore, and have a chance to view bears that are protected from hunting. If you're adventurous, climb up the nearby peaks to get fantastic views of the entire area. A three-sided shelter (free) is available in **Windfall Harbor.** Bears can be a real problem in Seymour Canal so be sure to select camping spots carefully (preferably on a small island) and hang all food.

Pack Creek

Located along the west side of Seymour Canal, this is one of the best known places to see brown bears in Alaska. Pack Creek fills with spawning humpback and chum salmon during July and August, and they in turn attract the bears, which in turn attract people. Most visitors arrive on day-trips from Juneau via the local air taxis. Others come aboard kayaks and boats, or with commercially guided groups.

Because of its popularity with both bears and people—and the potential for conflicts between the two—Pack Creek has very stringent rules. Only 24 people per day are allowed during the peak of the bear-viewing season (July 10 to August 25). If you plan to visit during this time, make reservations early in the year by contacting the Forest Service Information Center, Centennial Hall, 101 Egan Dr., Juneau, AK 99801, tel. (907) 586-8751. Four of the 24 permits are held for late arrivals, and are available three days in advance of your visit. These are in high demand, however, and are chosen by lottery from the applicants who show up. Contact the Forest Service for specifics. Fees are now charged to every visitor to help pay management costs. As of this writing, the exact amount was still being debated, but it may be $50 pp in the peak season, and $30 pp in the shoulder season. If you're coming outside the peak viewing season, you will still need to pick up a permit, but don't need advance reservations. Be sure to bring raingear and rubber boots even if you're only coming for the day. During the summer, Forest Service and Fish and Game personnel at Pack Creek will be happy to answer your questions, so it is not necessary to come with a guide (unless you can't get in otherwise).

Loken Aviation, tel. (907) 789-3331 or (800) 478-3360, has daily summertime flights to Pack Creek for $140 roundtrip. All the other air taxi services in Juneau can also provide charter service to Pack Creek. If you get a group of four or more folks together on a charter, the cost drops considerably.

Guided Trips

Several guide companies offer trips to Pack Creek; contact the Forest Service for a complete list. The following companies are likely to have space available on a last-minute basis,

and are a good option if you can't get a permit (and have the cash). **Alaska Discovery,** 5449 Shaune Dr., tel. (907) 780-6226 or (800) 586-1911, has day-trips to Pack Creek that include charter air service, experienced guide, lunch, rubber boots, and raingear. You pay a lot for this coddling: $349 pp. They also have five-day canoe trips around Seymour Canal (including Pack Creek) for $1,400 pp, including airfare from Juneau. Everything is supplied except personal gear and sleeping bags.

Wilderness Swift Charters has excellent three-day, two-night trips that include a day among the glaciers in Tracy Arm, a day at Pack Creek, and a third day whalewatching in Stephens Passage. These "mother ship" trips are a way to see a wide range of country for a low cost: $365 pp (prices may be lower in early summer). Travelers are dropped on shore each night, so you will need to provide your own camping gear and food. You can bring along a kayak for no extra charge, but many folks simply like to relax in the evening. The group size is limited to six people for this outstanding travel option. Call Alaska Rainforest Tours at (907) 586-2959 for details. **Fish & Fly Charters,** tel. (907) 790-2120, also offers guided day-trips to Pack Creek.

GLACIER BAY NATIONAL PARK

America's national parks are this country's version of Mecca, places where hordes of pilgrims are drawn, in search of a fulfillment that seems to come from experiencing these shrines of the natural world. Since Glacier Bay's discovery by John Muir in 1879, the spectacles of stark rocky walls, deep fjords, and giant rivers of ice calving massive icebergs into the sea have never ceased to inspire and humble visitors.

Established as a national park in 1925, Glacier Bay received major additions in the Alaska National Interest Lands Conservation Act (ANILCA) of 1980. The park and preserve now cover more than 3.3 million acres and contain 18 glaciers that reach the ocean, making this the largest concentration of tidewater glaciers on earth. These glaciers originate in the massive snow-capped Fairweather Range, sliding down the slopes and carving out giant troughs that become fjords when the glaciers retreat. **Mount Fairweather,** rising 15,320 feet, is Southeast Alaska's tallest peak. On a clear day, it is prominently visible from park headquarters, 72 miles away. The vegetation of Glacier Bay varies from a 200-year-old spruce and hemlock forest at Bartlett Cove to freshly exposed moraine where

tenacious plantlife is just starting to take hold. (Around Bartlett Cove you'll see extensive areas of Sitka spruce killed by a recent bark beetle infestation.) Wildlife is abundant in the park: humpback whales, harbor porpoises, harbor seals, and bird rookeries can be seen from the excursion boats and kayaks. Black bears are fairly common.

History

Glacier Bay has not always looked as it does today. When Capt. George Vancouver sailed through Icy Strait in 1794, he found a wall of ice more than 4,000 feet thick and 20 miles wide. Less than 100 years later (1879) when Hoonah Indian guides led John Muir into the area, he discovered that the glaciers had retreated nearly 50 miles, creating a new land and a giant bay splitting into two deep fjords on its upper end. The bay was shrouded by low clouds, but Muir, anxious to see farther into the country, climbed a peak on its western shore: "All the landscape was smothered in clouds and I began to fear that as far as wide views were concerned I had climbed in vain. But at length the clouds lifted a little, and beneath their gray

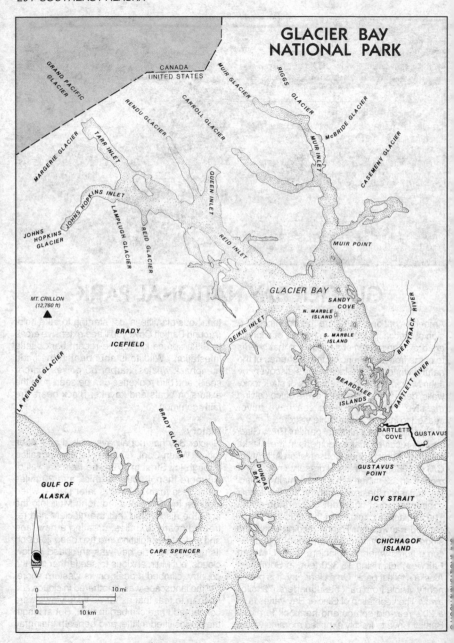

GLACIER BAY
NATIONAL PARK

fringes I saw the berg-filled expanse of the bay, and the feet of the mountains that stand about it, and the imposing fronts of five huge glaciers, the nearest being immediately beneath me. This was my first general view of Glacier Bay, a solitude of ice and snow and newborn rocks, dim, dreary, mysterious. I held the ground I had so dearly won for an hour or two, sheltering myself from the blast as best I could, while with benumbed fingers I sketched what I could see of the landscape, and wrote a few lines in my notebook. Then, breasting the snow again, crossing the shifting avalanche slopes and torrents, I reached camp about dark, wet and weary and glad." Today's traveler is less likely to take such pains to see this grand place.

The rapid retreat of the glaciers over the last 200 years has caused the land to rebound, much like a sponge that has been squeezed and then re-forms. The process is astoundingly rapid by geological standards; around Bartlett Cove it is rising nearly two inches a year and even faster farther up the bay. Ask the park rangers to point out some of the changes in vegetation because of this rebound effect.

Visiting Glacier Bay

The vast majority of the over 300,000 visitors who come to Glacier Bay each year arrive aboard luxury cruise ships; they're given a talk by a Park Service naturalist as the ship heads up the west arm of the bay and never set foot on the land itself. Most other visitors stay in Glacier Bay Lodge, venturing out only to walk the two short trails in Bartlett Cove or cruise up to the glaciers on a speeding tour boat. The tiny percentage who come to actually see and touch their national park rather than view it in a park naturalist's slide show are often prevented from doing so by prohibitive costs. It is somewhat ironic that the park is most accessible not to those who really want to experience the place on the ground and on the water, but to those who would rather look out on its glaciers from their stateroom windows.

The nearest tidewater glacier is 40 miles from Bartlett Cove park headquarters. To see these glaciers, expect to spend at least $379 pp from Juneau for a fast two-day trip that includes a night at Glacier Bay Lodge. You could save some by camping, but it still isn't cheap. A visit to

Glacier Bay is a wonderful experience, but there are few options for the budget traveler, and you should probably make other plans if you're pinched for cash. Note also that things wind down after Labor Day, as facilities close for the winter months and boats stop running up the bay after mid-September.

Bartlett Cove Hiking Trails

There are several enjoyable walks in the Bartlett Cove area. The mile-long **Forest Trail** loops between the lodge and the campground. **Bartlett River Trail** (three miles roundtrip) leads from near the backcountry office to the rivermouth, with opportunities to observe wildlife. For a satisfying beach walk, head south from the campground along the shore. If you're ambitious, it is possible to walk to **Point Gustavus** (six miles) or on to **Goode River** (13 miles). Follow the river upstream a mile to Gustavus, where you can walk or hitch back on the road. Beach walking is easiest at low tide; the backcountry office has tide charts. Note that none of these trails goes anywhere near the tidewater glaciers for which the park is famous.

Campground

An excellent free campground at Bartlett Cove comes complete with bear-proof food storage caches, outhouses, and a three-sided shelter with a woodstove (great for drying your gear after a kayak trip up the bay). The campground is only a half-mile from Glacier Bay Lodge and almost always has space. Running water is available next to the nearby backcountry office. All cooking must be done below the high tide line (where the odors are washed away every six hours) to reduce the chance of bear problems. See "On Your Own" below for info on camping elsewhere within the park.

GUSTAVUS AREA

There are two basic centers for visitors to Glacier Bay: Gustavus (outside the park) and Bartlett Cove (10 miles away and inside the park boundaries). The airport, main boat dock, small store, and several lodging houses are in the community of **Gustavus** (pop. 250). The town consists of equal parts park employees, fishermen, and folks dependent upon the tourism trade. It's one of the only places in Southeast Alaska that has enough flat country to raise cows. **Bartlett Cove** has Park Service Headquarters, a campground, Glacier Bay Lodge (with bar and restaurant), boat dock, and a **backcountry office** (open daily 8 a.m.-7 p.m. during the summer). The Park Service offers interpretive walks every day plus evening talks and slide shows upstairs in the lodge. Bartlett Cove and Gustavus are connected by a shuttle bus ($10 one-way).

Accommodations

During the summer Glacier Bay is packed with flashy tourists, so don't expect any bargains. The least expensive place (after camping) is **Glacier Bay Lodge,** tel. (800) 622-2042, where $28 gets you dorm space (jammed six to a room). The lodge is right in Bartlett Cove (park

headquarters), and has an overpriced restaurant, a nice bar, plus a big stone fireplace that makes a cozy place to sit on a rainy evening, even if you're not a guest. Laundry facilities and coin-operated showers are available at Glacier Bay Lodge. Luggage or gear storage is available for $2/day, or you can store things free in the shed next to the backcountry office (not locked, however).

Several other lodging options are available in nearby Gustavus; see the accompanying chart "Glacier Bay Accommodations" for specifics. Contact the **Gustavus Visitors Association,** Box 167, Gustavus, AK 99826, tel. (907) 697-2451, for a complete listing of local establishments. Honeymooners or others with an urge to splurge should look into staying at one of the excellent upscale lodges that serve three big gourmet meals each day: **Gustavus**

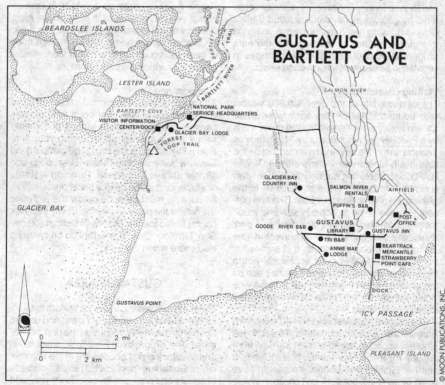

GLACIER BAY ACCOMMODATIONS

Note: All addresses are for Gustavus, AK 99826. Most places provide free transport to and from the Gustavus airport or boat dock, along with bikes to ride on the dirt roads. Lodging places are arranged from least to most expensive.

Glacier Bay Lodge; Bartlett Cove; tel. (907) 697-2226 or (800) 622-2042; $28 pp in dorms; $130 s, $153 d in private rooms; AAA approved

Noah's Ark B&B; P.O. Box 131; tel. (907) 697-2307; $35 s, $70 d; four guest rooms, continental breakfast

Goode River Bed & Breakfast; P.O. Box 37; tel. (907) 697-2241; $60-70 s, $60-80 d; three-story log home with four guest rooms, small log cabin, shared baths, full breakfast, open mid-May to mid-Sept.

Salmon River Rentals; P.O. Box 13; tel. (907) 697-2245; $70 s or d; cozy cabins with microwave and hot plates

Tri Bed & Breakfast; P.O. Box 214; tel. (907) 697-2425; $70 s, $90 d; comfortable cabins, full breakfast

The Growley Bear B&B; P.O. Box 246; tel. (907) 697-2730; $70 s, $140 d; log cabin, four guest rooms, private baths, full breakfast, open May-Sept.

A Puffin's Bed and Breakfast; P.O. Box 3; tel. (907) 697-2260 or (800) 478-2258; $85 s or d; modern cabins, private baths, full breakfast, open May to mid-Sept.

Spruce Tip Lodge; P.O. Box 2909; tel. (907) 697-2215; $110 s, $185 d; three meals, log cabin lodge, three bedrooms, shared or private baths, open year-round, B&B rates available

Bear's Nest Cabins; P.O. Box 216; tel. (907) 697-2440; $125 s or d; unique round cedar cabin, private bath

W.T. Fugarwe Lodge; P.O. Box 280; tel. (907) 697-2244; $120 s, $240 d; three meals, open June to Labor Day

Annie Mae Lodge; Box 80; tel. (907) 697-2346 or (800) 478-2346; $120-135 s, $195-225 d; quiet newer lodge on Goode River, 11 guest rooms, shared or private baths, three meals included, open year-round

Gustavus Inn; Box 60; tel. (907) 697-2254 or (800) 649-5220; $135 s, $270 d; luxury accommodations, shared or private baths, three gourmet meals included, open mid-May to mid-Sept.

Glacier Bay Country Inn; P.O. Box 5; tel. (907) 697-2288 (summers) or (801) 673-8480 (winters); $158 s, $256-275 d; luxury accommodations, three gourmet meals included, open year-round

---

Inn, tel. (907) 697-2254; or **Glacier Bay Country Inn,** tel. (907) 697-2288. These places get a lot of favorable press, and advance reservations are essential, especially for Gustavus Inn, the oldest and most famous. Its picturesque garden provides fresh vegetables all summer long.

Food and Supplies

In Gustavus, **Strawberry Point Cafe,** tel. (907) 697-2227, is a fine place for a cup of coffee and fresh pastries in the morning. Meals are also available at **Glacier Bay Lodge,** tel. (907) 697-2225, in Bartlett Cove. For outstanding gourmet seafood dinners, make reservations at **Gustavus Inn,** where a few spots are held for nonguests; tel. (907) 697-2255. Head to **Salmon River Smokehouse,** tel. (907) 697-2330, where you can check out the salmon and halibut as

they cure. Salmon River serves smoked fish, along with chowders and homemade bread. The other place to eat is **Bear's Nest Restaurant,** tel. (907) 697-2440; reservations only. Very small.

The small grocery store at Gustavus, **Beartrack Mercantile,** tel. (907) 697-2358, sells essentials for a price, but it's better to bring all your own food from Juneau. They don't sell booze, so bring your own, or head to the bar at Glacier Bay Lodge for drinks.

Fishing

Fishing, primarily for halibut and salmon, is a big attraction for many visitors, and most of the lodges offer special package deals for anglers. Get a list of local charter boat operators from the Park Service in Bartlett Cove, or see their brochures at the airport or in Juneau.

TRANSPORTATION

Getting There

There is no state ferry service to either Glacier Bay or Gustavus. Locals have kept the ferry out, fearing it would inundate the area with RVs and lead to major developments. Residents receive most of their supplies by barge every two weeks. **Auk Nu Tours,** tel. (907) 586-8687 or (800) 820-2628, operates a daily ferry service between Juneau and Gustavus from mid-May to mid-September. The fare is $85 roundtrip or $45 one-way. They also transport bikes for $10, and kayaks for $25. You can add on a wildlife and whalewatching cruise around Pleasant Island for $78, or get a combination roundtrip transport plus the wildlife/whalewatching cruise for $119.

Many visitors fly by jet from Juneau to Gustavus on **Alaska Airlines,** tel. (800) 426-0333; $130 roundtrip (sometimes less). Book ahead to be sure of getting on these very popular flights. The trip takes only 15 minutes in the air, so the flight attendants don't even have time to throw bags of peanuts at you. More rewarding are flights by **Glacier Bay Airways,** tel. (907) 789-9009; **Wings of Alaska,** tel. (800) 697-2236; **L.A.B. Flying Service,** tel. (907) 789-9160 or (800) 426-0543; and **Haines Airways,** tel. (907) 789-2336 (all Juneau phone numbers). They offer more personal service and the small planes fly lower, providing excellent on-the-way sightseeing for around $140 roundtrip. **Air Excursions,** tel. (907) 697-2375 or (800) 354-2479, has the cheapest connections between Juneau and Gustavus: $100 roundtrip. Haines Airways also flies from Gustavus to Haines ($89) and Hoonah ($50); and L.A.B. flies to Skagway ($120) and Haines ($110); while **Skagway Air,** tel. (907) 789-2006, flies between Gustavus and Skagway ($81), Juneau ($60), and Haines ($70).

Note that it's illegal to transport white gas and other potentially explosive fuels in any commercial aircraft, so be sure your gas stove and fuel bottles are empty before you reach the airport. White gas can be purchased in Bartlett Cove next to the visitor center or in Gustavus at Beartrack Mercantile. Also, you can't carry "bear mace" on the jets, though the floatplanes will sometimes carry it in the floats.

The airport in Gustavus is 10 miles from Bartlett Cove/Park Headquarters. A **shuttle bus** meets all Alaska Airlines flights, transporting you to Bartlett Cove for an absurd $10 each direction. Hitching eliminates this extortion, but traffic can be downright scarce in tiny Gustavus. Actually, it is easier to hitch to Gustavus from Bartlett Cove, so you may want to pay the $10 to get to Bartlett Cove and then hitch back when you leave. **TLC Taxi,** (907) 697-2239, provides passenger and kayak transport ($15 for one person or $22 for two) from anywhere in the Gustavus area. Add $10 each way if you're carrying a hardshell kayak. **B.W. Rent-A-Car,** tel. (907) 697-2403, rents cars for $50/day, and you don't even need to fill up the tank at the end.

Flightseeing

Air Excursions, tel. (907) 697-2375 or (800) 354-2479; **Alaska Seair Adventures,** tel. (907) 697-2215; and **L.A.B. Flying Service,** tel. (907) 789-9160 or (800) 426-0543, all provide flightseeing trips. Air Excursions has a special plane that's a favorite of photographers; it flies low and slow for good aerial photos. If you have a folding kayak, these companies can provide drop-offs up the bay if you want to charter a flight. Most people travel to the head of Glacier Bay on boats instead. Flightseeing trips over Glacier Bay are also available from Juneau, Haines, and Skagway, but prices are generally higher since you'll need to fly farther.

Getting to the Glaciers

A number of boats (and many cruise ships) offer tours of Glacier Bay during the summer. Most of these two-to-four-day trips depart from Juneau, but one boat—the *Spirit of Adventure*—offers daily tours and kayaker drop-offs from Bartlett Cove. Day-trips on this 220-passenger high-speed catamaran cost $151 for adults, or $75 for kids under 13. A Park Service naturalist is onboard to provide information on the animals and sights along the route. A light lunch is served. Make reservations at Glacier Bay Lodge, or by calling Glacier Bay Tours & Cruises at (907) 463-5510 or (800) 451-5952.

Another *Spirit of Adventure* option is to pay $299 pp for a day-long trip that includes a flight from Juneau to Gustavus followed by a trip up the bay and another flight back to Juneau that evening. A more popular option is to fly to Gustavus, take a trip up the bay, return for a night at Glacier Bay Lodge, then take the Auk Nu ferry back to Juneau for a very full two days. The cost is $379 per person. See below for information on sea kayak drop-offs from the *Spirit of Adventure*.

Glacier Bay Tours & Cruises operates several other boats in Glacier Bay, with a wide variety of "soft adventure" tour options. Travelers on their **Wilderness Explorer** have access to sea kayaks to explore on their own when the boat is anchored up. Some of their other cruises are even softer, more of the couch-potato variety. For details on any of these, call Glacier Bay Tours & Cruises at (907) 463-5510 or (800) 451-5952.

Some people prefer the **Spirit of Glacier Bay,** a slower boat that leaves Juneau on Sunday and Wednesday in the summer. The boat has a Park Service naturalist onboard within the park. They do not offer day trips out of Bartlett Cove, nor do they provide kayaker or camper drop-offs. They *do* provide three- or four-night voyages that include excellent meals (prime rib, seafood, freshly baked bread . . .), stateroom accommodations, and a leisurely cruise up the West Arm of Glacier Bay. Both sailings include visits to Glacier Bay and Sitka, and the longer one adds a circumnavigation of Admiralty Island (but it doesn't stop at Pack Creek). These cost a not-so-leisurely $1,225-1,635 pp for the three-night sailing, and $1,635-2,179 pp for the four-night version. Be sure to reserve months ahead for these very popular trips. The *Spirit of Glacier Bay* has a foredeck perfect for watching wildlife or photographing glaciers, and the ship's slow speed (11 knots versus 30 knots for the *Spirit of Adventure*) means the wind doesn't force you inside. For details, contact Alaska Sightseeing/Cruise West, tel. (907) 586-6300 or (800) 426-7702.

Guided Kayak Trips
Alaska Discovery, tel. (907) 463-5500 (in Juneau), (907) 697-2411 (in Gustavus), or (800) 586-1911, has six-hour kayak trips from the Bartlett Cove dock in the summer. These include kayak and gear, guide, food, and boots for $119 pp. This is a good way to learn the basics of sea kayaking. Alaska Discovery also offers several excellent but pricey longer trips into Glacier Bay National Park. Kayak trips of the bay cost $1,890 pp for eight days, plus airfare

from Juneau. They also offer 10-day trips to Icy Bay for $1,975 per person. These trips are based out of Yakutat.

Spirit Walker Expeditions, tel. (907) 697-2266 or (800) 478-9255, runs excellent sea kayak tours, including overnight trips to nearby Pleasant Island. All sorts of longer voyages are available, all the way up to seven-day trips to remote islands off Chichagof Island. They do not guide within Glacier Bay National Park. In addition, you can rent kayaks in Gustavus from **Sea Otter Kayak,** tel. (907) 697-3007. Doubles go for $50/day, singles for $40/day.

ON YOUR OWN

Backcountry Camping
No trails exist anywhere in Glacier Bay's backcountry, but Park Service rangers can provide good info on hiking and camping up the bay. Camping is allowed in most areas within the park. Exceptions are the Marble Islands—closed because of their importance for nesting seabirds—and a few other areas closed because of the potential for bear incidents. A gas stove is a necessity for camping since wood is often unavailable.

Free permits (available at the backcountry office) are recommended before you head out. Park naturalists have special camper orientations each evening, including info on how and where to go, bear safety, and minimum-impact camping procedures. Bears have killed two people within the park in the past decade or so, and to lessen the chance of this happening, free bear-proof containers are supplied to all kayakers and hikers before they head out. A small storage shed beside the backcountry office is a good place to store unneeded gear while you are up the bay. Note that firearms are not allowed in Glacier Bay National Park.

Sea Kayaking
An increasingly popular way to visit Glacier Bay is by sea kayak. Some folks bring their own folding kayaks on the plane, or pay $25 to bring them from Juneau aboard the ferry run by Auk Nu tours, but most people rent them from the friendly proprietors of **Glacier Bay Sea Kayaks** in Bartlett Cove for $50/day ($40/day for five to nine days' use). Contact them at P.O. Box 26,

Gustavus, AK 99826, tel. (907) 697-2257, for details. Reservations are a must during mid-summer, since only a few boats can be transported into Glacier Bay at a time. Kayak rentals include a two-person boat, paddles, life vests, spray skirts, flotation bags, and a brief lesson. Glacier Bay Sea Kayaks also rents raingear and rubber boots, and will help set up your trip, including making the all-important boat reservations.

Another option is rent a kayak in Juneau from the **Juneau Outdoor Center,** tel. (907) 586-8220, and take it with you to Glacier Bay. **Kayak Express,** tel. (907) 780-4591, will transport you and the kayak from Juneau to Gustavus or Point Adolphus on their boat for $125 one-way. Recommended.

Kayakers (and hikers) heading into Glacier Bay are often dropped off by the high-speed *Spirit of Adventure*. The cost for a drop-off and pickup is $174 pp; if you paddle back on your own, a drop-off costs $88 pp. Call (907) 463-5510 or (800) 451-5952 for details. Before heading out on any hiking or kayak trip, be sure to talk with Park Service personnel in Bartlett Cove. You'll also need to be in Gustavus airport by 3 p.m. the day before to go through all the hoops (getting to Bartlett Cove, renting the kayak, going through the Park Service camping and bear safety session, and getting your kayak onboard the *Spirit of Adventure*). This means you cannot take the evening Alaska flight; it arrives too late in the day.

Heading Up Bay

Several focal points attract kayakers within Glacier Bay. The **Beardslee Islands,** in relatively protected waters near Bartlett Cove, make an excellent two- or three-day kayak trip and do not require any additional expenses. Beyond the Beardslees, Glacier Bay becomes much less protected and you should plan on spending at least a week up bay if you paddle there. (It is 50 miles or more to the glaciers.) Rather than attempting to cross this open water, most kayakers opt for a drop-off. The locations change periodically, so ask at the backcountry office for specifics. The *Spirit of Adventure* (see above) provides daily trips into both arms of Glacier Bay. Roundtrip drop-off and pickup service costs $174 pp. **Muir Inlet** (the east arm

of Glacier Bay) is preferred by many kayakers because it is a bit more protected and is not used by the cruise ships or most tour boats. The **West Arm** is more spectacular—especially iceberg-filled Johns Hopkins Inlet—but you'll have to put up with a constant stream of large and small cruise ships. If the boat operators have their way, even more ships can be expected in future years.

Kayaking opportunities at Glacier Bay are described in *Discover Southeast Alaska with Pack and Paddle* by Margaret Piggott. For information on hiking, pick up a copy of *Hiking in Muir Inlet* at the backcountry office. They also sell topographic maps of the park and a variety of local guidebooks.

TATSHENSHINI AND ALSEK RIVERS

Along the western edge of Glacier Bay National Park flows the Tatshenshini River, considered one of the world's premier wilderness rafting routes. Bears, moose, mountain goats, and Dall sheep are all visible along the route. The river passes through Class III whitewater and spectacular canyons along its way to the juncture with the Alsek River. **Alaska Discovery,** tel. (907) 780-6226 or (800) 586-1911, has several trips each summer down this spectacular route, as well as down the more remote and less-explored Alsek. A 12-day river-rafting trip isn't cheap—$2,550 pp, but the price includes a van ride from Haines to the put-in point at Dalton Post in the Yukon, and a spectacular helicopter portage around the Class VI rapids of Turnback Canyon. One of the real treats of this trip is paddling past the seven-mile-wide Alsek Glacier. The trip begins and ends in Juneau.

Another good company offering trips is **Chilkat Guides,** tel. (907) 766-2491. Many other American and Canadian companies feature float trips down the "Tat" and Alsek Rivers. For their addresses or info on running the rivers on your own (permit required), contact Glacier Bay National Park and Preserve, Gustavus, AK 99826, tel. (907) 697-3341. Only one launch is allowed per day, with half of these set aside for commercial guides. Alaskon Express can provide bus transportation from Haines to the put-in point at Dalton Post.

GORDY OHLIGER

HAINES

The pleasant and friendly town of Haines (pop. 1,400) provides a transition point between the lush greenery of Southeast and the more rugged beauty of the Yukon and Alaska's Interior. As the ferry sails north to Haines on the Lynn Canal—at 1,600 feet deep it's the longest and deepest fjord in North America—the Inside Passage gets narrower, and you sense that this unique waterway, and your passage on it, are coming to an end. To the east, waterfalls tumble off the mountainsides, while to the west, glaciers lumber down from the icefields of the Chilkat Range. The long river of ice you see 40 minutes before Haines is **Davidson Glacier. Rainbow Glacier,** also on the left, hangs from a cliff just beyond. Both originate from the same icefield that forms part of Glacier Bay National Park.

Haines lies 90 miles north of Juneau, straddling a narrow peninsula between Chilkoot and Chilkat Inlets. Its mountain-ringed setting seems to define the word spectacular: from the ferry you catch a glimpse of the white Victorian buildings of Fort Seward backdropped by the 6,500-foot tall Cathedral Peaks. Haines has a wealth of outdoor experiences, almost as many for those without cash as for those with. Plenty of hiking trails run up surrounding peaks, camping is right next to town, and travelers will discover a pleas-

ant mixture of working stiffs and artisans. Haines has been gradually changing from a conservative, traditional town to one where residents have a more environmentally friendly attitude. In fact, for now, the greenies are in the majority.

Unlike nearby Skagway where a tidal wave of tourists inundates the town daily, Haines only sees a single large cruise ship each week during the summer. Most Haines visitors arrive by ferry and head on up the highway (or vice versa), but Haines is also becoming a popular weekend getaway for Canadians from Whitehorse. With "only" 60 inches of precipitation a year, the weather here is decidedly drier than points farther south. And, on top of that, the people of Haines are some of the friendliest in Alaska.

History
Long before the arrival of whites to the Haines area, the Tlingit people of the Chilkoot and Chilkat tribes established villages nearby. Fish were plentiful, as were game animals and berries. The area's "mother village" was Klukwan, 20 miles up the Chilkat River, but another large Chilkoot village nestled near Chilkoot Lake, and a summer camp squatted just northwest of present-day Haines. The Chilkat people were renowned for their beautiful blankets woven

DIANA LASICH HARPER

Chilkat blanket

from mountain goat wool and dyed with an inventive mixture of copper nuggets, urine, lichen, and spruce roots. The blankets were (and are) worn during dance ceremonies. Today they are also exceedingly valuable.

In 1879, the naturalist John Muir and the Presbyterian minister Samuel Hall Young reached the end of Lynn Canal. The Reverend Dr. Young was looking for potential mission sites to convert the Natives to Christianity. Muir was along for the canoe ride, wanting a chance to explore this remote territory. While there, they met with members of the Chilkat tribe at a settlement called Yendestakyeh. Both men gave speeches before the people, but the Chilkats were considerably more interested in Muir's "brotherhood of man" message than Dr. Young's proselytizing. Muir wrote: "Later, when the sending of a missionary and teacher was being considered, the chief said they wanted me, and, as an inducement, promised that if I would come to them they would always do as I directed, follow my councils, give me as many wives as I liked, build a church and school, and pick all the stones out of the paths and make them smooth for my feet." Two years later the mission was established by two Presbyterian missionaries (Muir had other plans) and the village was renamed Haines, in honor of Mrs. F.E.H. Haines of the Presbyterian Home Missions Board. She never visited her namesake.

During the Klondike gold rush, an adventurer and shrewd businessman named Jack Dalton developed a 305-mile toll road between Haines and the Yukon along an old Indian trade route, charging miners $150 each to use his Dalton Trail. Armed men never failed to collect. To maintain order among the thousands of miners, the U.S. Army established Fort William H. Seward at Haines. Named for Alaska's "patron saint," it was built between 1900 and 1904 on 100 acres of land deeded to the government by the Haines mission. Renamed Chilkoot Barracks in 1922 (to avoid confusion with the town of Seward), it was the only military base in all of Alaska for the next 20 years.

In 1942-43 the Army built the 150-mile Haines Highway from Haines to Haines Junction as an emergency evacuation route from Alaska in case of invasion by the Japanese. After WW II, the post was declared excess government property and sold to a veterans' group that hoped to form a business cooperative. The venture failed, but many stayed on, making homes in the stately old officers' quarters. The site became a National Historic Landmark in 1978 and its name was changed back to Fort Seward.

Today the town of Haines has a diversified economy that includes fishing (no canneries, however), tourism, and government jobs. Haines has also recently become something of a center for the arts, attracting artists and craftsworkers of all types, from creators of stained glass to weavers of Chilkat blankets. Halfway between Haines and Juneau is the site of a large gold mine currently in the planning stages. If opened, the Kensington Mine would lead to effluent being dumped into the pristine waters nearby where salmon and halibut are caught.

SIGHTS

The **Sheldon Museum**, tel. (907) 766-2366, on Main St. has a fine collection of Tlingit artifacts (including Chilkat blankets) and items from the gold rush. Upstairs, you can watch the excellent Audubon Society video, "Last Stronghold of the

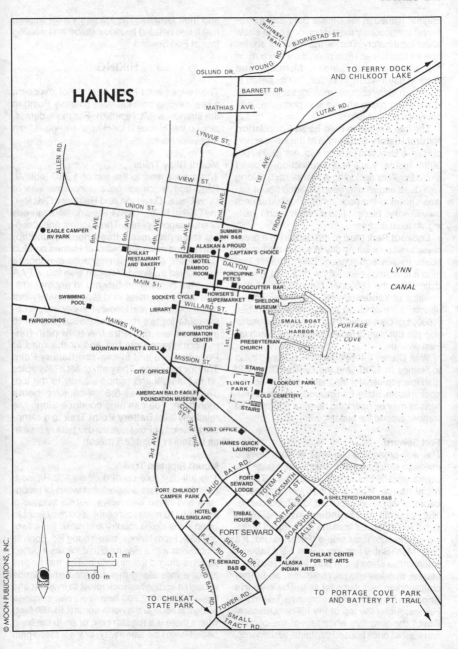

HAINES

MT.
RIPINSKI
TRAIL

BJORNSTAD ST.

YOUNG RD

OSLUND DR.

TO FERRY DOCK
AND CHILKOOT LAKE

BARNETT DR.

MATHIAS AVE.

LUTAK RD.

LYNVUE ST.

ALLEN RD.

VIEW ST.

UNION ST.

6th. AVE.

5th. AVE.

4th. AVE.

3rd. AVE.

2nd. AVE.

1st. AVE.

FRONT ST.

● EAGLE CAMPER
RV PARK

CHILKAT
RESTAURANT
AND BAKERY

SUMMER
INN B&B

ALASKAN & PROUD

CAPTAIN'S CHOICE

THUNDERBIRD
MOTEL
BAMBOO ROOM

DALTON
ST.

PORCUPINE
PETE'S

MAIN ST.

FOGCUTTER BAR

SWIMMING
POOL

SOCKEYE CYCLE

WILLARD ST.

SHELDON
MUSEUM

LYNN
CANAL

■ FAIRGROUNDS

LIBRARY

HAINES HWY.

VISITOR
INFORMATION
CENTER

1st. AVE.

SMALL BOAT
HARBOR

PORTAGE
COVE

MOUNTAIN MARKET & DELI

MISSION ST.

PRESBYTERIAN
CHURCH

CITY OFFICES

STAIRS

AMERICAN BALD EAGLE
FOUNDATION MUSEUM

TLINGIT
PARK

LOOKOUT PARK

COY
ST.

OLD CEMETERY

STAIRS

POST OFFICE

3rd. AVE.

2nd. AVE.

HAINES QUICK
LAUNDRY

BAY RD.

MUD

FORT
SEWARD
LODGE

TOTEM ST.

BLACKSMITH
ST.

PORT CHILKOOT
CAMPER PARK

HOTEL
HALSINGLAND

TRIBAL
HOUSE

PORTAGE
ST.

A SHELTERED HARBOR B&B

SOAPSUDS
ALLEY

FORT SEWARD

F.A.A. RD.

SEWARD DR.

FT. SEWARD
B&B

ALASKA
INDIAN ARTS

CHILKAT CENTER
FOR THE ARTS

MUD BAY RD.

TOWER RD.

TO PORTAGE COVE PARK
AND BATTERY PT. TRAIL

TO CHILKAT
STATE PARK

SMALL
TRACT RD.

0   0.1 mi

0   100 m

© MOON PUBLICATIONS, INC.

Eagles" (filmed at the Chilkat Bald Eagle Preserve) continuously most days, or a slide show about local history. The museum ($3 for adults; free for kids under 18) is open daily 1-5 p.m. in the summer, and Sunday, Monday, and Wednesday 1-4 p.m. in winter. The museum is also open many summer mornings and at other times when cruise ships are in port (generally several nights a week).

The free **American Bald Eagle Foundation Natural History Museum** is at the intersection of Haines Hwy. and Second Ave., tel. (907) 766-3094. Inside, you'll find a collection of dead stuffed critters (including a manta ray!), along with dead eagles overhead. A video about eagles shows in the back room. Trophy hunters may like this place; I find it barely worth visiting. At least it's free.

Lookout Park (next to the harbor) is a great place to sit on a sunny day to watch the fishing boats, eagles, and scenery. Bring a lunch. Behind it is a small cemetery with Tlingit graves dating from the 1880s. An old building, all that remains of **Yendestakyeh,** is just beyond the airport, 3.5 miles from town. The mission bell (1880) that once called Tlingit peoples to worship now sits out front of the Presbyterian church on First Avenue.

Walt Disney's *White Fang* was filmed next to Haines in 1990, and the **Dalton City** gold rush town created for the movie is at the Southeast Alaska State Fairgrounds. A few businesses may be operating here, or you can just wander around the buildings.

Fort Seward

The well-preserved buildings of Fort Seward make an excellent place to explore. Inside the central parade ground are replicas of a **Tlingit tribal house,** along with a Yukon **trapper's cabin** complete with pelts and a food cache. The nonprofit **Alaska Indian Arts,** tel. (907) 766-2160, operates from the old hospital building on the southeast side of Fort Seward. It's open Mon.-Sat. 9 a.m.-noon and 1-5 p.m., and when cruise ships are in port. Inside you'll find master woodcarvers, silversmiths, and other craftsworkers with items for sale. The **Wild Iris Shop** here has the most attractive T-shirts in Haines. Along the top of the hill is **"Officers' Row,"** the attractive white turn-of-the-century homes that once housed captains, lieutenants,

and their families. The Haines visitor bureau has a free detailed historical guide and walking tour of Fort Seward.

HIKING

The Haines area has a number of excellent hikes, ranging from the easy (Battery Point) to the strenuous (Mt. Ripinski). For more details, pick up the "Haines is for Hikers" pamphlet from the visitor center.

Mount Riley Trails

Three trails lead to the top of 1,760-foot Mt. Riley, from which you get a panoramic view of Lynn Canal, Davidson and Rainbow Glaciers, the Chilkat River, Taiya Inlet, and 360 degrees of snowcapped peaks. The shortest and steepest route (two miles, three hours roundtrip) starts three miles southeast of Haines on Mud Bay Road. A small parking area is opposite the marked trailhead. You can also follow FAA Rd. from behind Fort Seward to another trail. This one is four miles long (approximately four hours roundtrip) and follows the city water supply route for two miles before splitting off to join the more direct trail. A third path (unmarked) starts from the end of the road at Portage Cove and follows the Battery Point Trail for two miles. The path to Mt. Riley splits off to the right and climbs steeply to the top. The total length is 5.5 miles (five hours roundtrip). You can also continue along the relatively level **Battery Point Trail** to a campsite at Kelgaya Point and across pebbly beaches to Battery Point (2.5 miles).

Mount Ripinski Trail

The full-day hike up and down Mt. Ripinski (3,900 feet) offers unparalleled views of mountains and inland waterways, but it's strenuous and long (10 miles roundtrip). You may want to camp in the alpine country and make this a two-day hike. From Haines, take Young Rd. north till it intersects with a jeep road that follows a buried pipeline around the mountain. The trail begins about a mile along this dirt road and climbs through a spruce/hemlock forest to muskeg and finally alpine at 2,500 feet. You can continue along the ridge to the north summit (3,160 feet) where there is a register box, or on to the main peak. Return the same way, or via a steep path that takes you down to a saddle and then to the Haines Highway, seven miles northwest of Haines. Mount Ripinski is covered with snow until mid-summer, so be prepared. Don't go in bad weather and do stay on the trail in the alpine areas.

Seduction Point Trail
For a gentle, long, and very scenic beach walk, head to Chilkat State Park campground, seven miles southeast of Haines on Mud Bay Road. Seduction Point is on the end of the peninsula separating Chilkoot and Chilkat Inlets, a six-mile hike from the campground. The trail alternates between the forest and the beach, and

it's a good idea to check the tides to make sure that you're able to hike the last beach stretch at low tide. This hike also makes a fine overnight camping trip. Call the State Park Office in Haines, tel. (907) 766-2292, for locations of campsites along this trail.

PRACTICALITIES

Accommodations
The youth hostel in Haines, **Bear Creek Camp,** is 2.5 miles south of town on Small Tract Rd., tel. (907) 766-2259. Dorm spaces are $15 pp and private cabins $37 (sleeps four). Tent spaces

---

HAINES ACCOMMODATIONS

Note: The city of Haines adds a five percent sales tax to lodging rates.

Bear Creek Camp; three miles south; tel. (907) 766-2259; $15 pp in hostel, $37 for up to four in cabins; bike and hot tub rentals

Hotel Halsingland; Fort Seward; tel. (907) 766-2000, (800) 542-6363 in the U.S., or (800) 478-2525 in Canada; $39 s, $49 d in small rooms with shared bath; $83 s, $87 d with private bath; historic hotel

Fort Seward Lodge; Fort Seward; tel. (907) 766-2009 or (800) 478-7772; $45 s, $55 d with shared bath; $60 s, $70 d with private baths; kitchenettes for $75 s, $85 d

Officer's Inn B&B; Fort Seward; tel. (907) 766-2000, (800) 542-6363 in the U.S., or (800) 478-2525 in Canada; $50-84 s, $55-89 d; historic home, 14 old-fashioned guest rooms, continental breakfast

Mountain View Motel; Mud Bay Rd.; tel. (907) 766-2900 or (800) 478-2902; $59s, $64 d; kitchenettes available

Summer Inn B&B; Second and Main; tel. (907) 766-2970; $60 s, $70 d; historic place, five guest rooms, full breakfast

Thunderbird Motel; Dalton St.; tel. (907) 766-2131 or (800) 327-2556; $62 s, $72 d

Chilkat Eagle B&B; Fort Seward; tel. (907) 766-2763; $65 s, $75 d; historic building, three guest rooms, shared or private baths, full breakfast

Eagle's Nest Motel; Haines Hwy.; tel. (907) 766-2891 or (800) 354-6009; $68 s, $79 d; courtesy van, AAA approved

Chilkat Valley Inn B&B; nine miles north of Haines; tel. (907) 766-3331 or (800) 747-5528; $70 s, $80 d; beautiful location, A-frame home, full breakfast

A Sheltered Harbor B&B; 795 Beach Rd.; tel. (907) 766-2741; $70 s, $80 d; five guest rooms private baths, full breakfast

Porcupine Pete's Restaurant and Hotel; tel. (907) 766-2909; $70-90 s or d; older downtown hotel

Fort Seward B&B; Fort Seward; tel. (907) 766-2856 or (800) 615-6676; $72 s, $85 d; historic place, full breakfast

Fort Seward Condos; Fort Seward; tel. (907) 766-2425; $85 s or d; historic building, one-and two-bedroom apartments sleep five, full kitchen, two-day minimum stay

Captain's Choice Motel; Dalton and Second; tel. (907) 766-3111 or (800) 247-7153; $88 s, $98 d; courtesy van, nicest in town, AAA approved

Bear's Den; tel. (907) 766-2117; $90 for up to four; furnished apartment, two-day minimum stay

Riverhouse B&B; tel. (907) 766-2060 or (800) 478-1399 in Alaska; $115 s or d; beautiful Chilkat River cottage, hot tub, garden deck, bikes, wind and solar power, self-serve continental breakfast

cost $10 d. Kitchen facilities and bike and hot tub rentals are available. The hostel is a clean and friendly place to stay, but reservations are strongly advised in the summer. If it's full, pitch a tent out front. Free shuttle to and from the ferry, and they'll also pick up from the visitor center.

Hotel Halsingland is a beautiful old Victorian hotel that originally served as the commanding officer's quarters at Fort Seward. In addition to the standard rooms, they have inexpensive shared-bath rooms. **Riverhouse B&B** offers the most luxurious accommodations in Haines. This attractive modern cottage features a hot tub, wind and solar power, a garden deck, and a third-floor balcony with impressive mountain views. **Fort Seward B&B** occupies a beautiful home that once housed Haines's chief surgeon. **Chilkat Valley B&B** is notable for its location atop a cliff overlooking the Chilkat River.

More lodging options are listed in the chart "Haines Accommodations."

Camping

The best campsite near Haines is at **Portage Cove State Wayside** ($6), only three-quarters of a mile from town. Water and outhouses are available, but there is no overnight parking—the site is for hikers and cyclists only. The location is quiet and attractive, and eagles hang around nearby. Located behind Hotel Halsingland, **Port Chilkoot Camper Park,** tel. (907) 766-2000 or (800) 542-6363 in the U.S., or (800) 478-2525 in Canada, has wooded campsites, showers, and a laundromat on the premises. There's always tent space. If you have a vehicle or don't mind hitching, stay at one of the two excellent state-run campgrounds, both with drinking water, toilets, and picnic shelters. **Chilkat State Park** ($6), seven miles southeast of Haines, has a fine hiking trail to Seduction Point; and **Chilkoot Lake State Recreation Site** ($10), five miles northwest of the ferry, has good fishing and a lovely view over the turquoise-blue lake. More camping at **Mosquito Lake State Park,** 27 miles north of Haines.

RVers park at the gravel lot named **Oceanside RV Park,** tel. (907) 766-2444, on Main St.; or at the fancier but sterile **Haines Hitch-Up RV Park** on Haines Highway, tel. (907) 766-2882. No tents allowed. The other local RV parking lots are **Eagle Camper RV Park,** 955 Union St.,

tel. (907) 766-2335; **Salmon Run RV Campground,** two miles northeast of the ferry terminal, tel. (907) 766-3240; and **Swan's Rest RV Park,** near Mosquito Lake, 27 miles north of Haines, tel. (907) 767-5662.

Food

Haines has a variety of restaurants with fair prices (by Alaskan standards). For filling breakfasts and lunches, along with friendly service, head to the **Bamboo Room** on Second Ave., tel. (907) 766-9101. Check the board for daily specials. **Lighthouse Restaurant,** at the foot of Third and Main St., tel. (907) 766-2442, is an old favorite that serves famous buttermilk pies. For sourdough pizzas, try **Porcupine Pete's** on Main St., tel. (907) 766-9199. **Chilkat Restaurant and Bakery** on Fifth Ave., tel. (907) 766-2920, has all-you-can-eat Mexican meals on Friday nights and fresh salmon and halibut other evenings. It's a bit on the pricey side. Their baker rolls out great pastries. A personal favorite is **Mountain Market & Deli,** Third and Haines Hwy., tel. (907) 766-3340, where you'll find fresh baked goods, soups, sandwiches, and espresso. It's the center for the longhair and peasant-dress crowd. Also here is a natural foods market.

Get groceries from **Howser's Supermarket** on Main St., tel. (907) 766-2040; or **A&P Market,** Third and Dalton, tel. (907) 766-2181. Ask around the boat harbor to see who's selling fresh fish or prawns. **Dejon Delights Smokery,** at Fort Seward, tel. (907) 766-2505, has freshly smoked salmon for sale or will smoke fish that you catch. An all-you-can-eat **salmon bake** ($21) is held nightly in the tribal house at Fort Seward. Go light on the trimmings to save room for more of the tasty fish. Some of the best local seafood dinners—along with burgers, fish & chips, and other favorites—can be found at **Hotel Halsingland,** tel. (907) 766-2000, (800) 542-6363 in the U.S., or (800) 478-2525 in Canada. Not far away at **Fort Seward Lodge,** tel. (907) 766-2009, all-you-can-eat crab dinners are served nightly.

Entertainment

If you hit the bar at **Fort Seward Lodge,** be sure to ask for a "Roadkill," the flaming house drink that's guaranteed to set your innards on fire. They also have live music on weekends, as does the **Fogcutter Bar** downtown. The **Chilkat Dancers,** an acclaimed Tlingit dance group, give performances ($10 for adults, $5 for students) on evenings when cruise ships are in port; call (907) 766-2160 for details. The costumes (including priceless Chilkat blankets) and dances are all entirely authentic, offering a glimpse of revitalized Tlingit culture. They perform in the Chilkat Center for the Arts, located in Fort Seward's old recreation hall.

Events
In late April, the **Actfest-Alaska Community Theater Festival** features theatrical groups from all over the state. Performances and theater workshops take place at the Chilkat Center for the Arts. On the longest day of the year (June 21) a **Kluane to Chilkat Bike Relay** attracts teams of cyclists for an exciting 160-mile race that ends in Haines. The **Haines Rodeo** comes to town on July Fourth weekend.

Every year during the third week in August some 15,000 visitors from all over Alaska and the Yukon flock to Haines for the five-day-long **Southeast Alaska State Fair.** Events include a horse show, logging contest, farmers' market, parade, pig races, dog show, and hundreds of exhibits of all types. Concerts every evening feature nationally known artists at no extra charge. Don't miss this one! The **Alaska Bald Eagle Festival** in mid-November offers talks, slide shows, live birds, Tlingit dancing, art exhibits, and other attractions.

Services
Get cash from **ATMs** inside Howser's Supermarket and the First National Bank of Anchorage. Showers are available at **Port Chilkoot Camper Park,** behind Hotel Halsingland, and **Haines Quick Laundry,** across from Fort Seward Lodge. Another option is the fine **swimming pool,** tel. (907) 766-2666, next to the high school, where $3 ($1.50 for seniors or students) gets you a shower and swim. The public **library** is on Third Ave., tel. (907) 766-2545, and has used books for 25 cents. The **post office** is on Haines Highway near Fort Seward. Get topographic maps from **Chilkoot Gardens** at Second Ave. and Main Street. For something completely different, check out the nine-hole **Weeping Trout Golf Course** on Chilkat Lake. (Weeping trout?) Access is only by boat or floatplane!

Shopping
Haines is the home of several fine galleries. **Chilkat Valley Arts,** 207 Willard St., tel. (907) 766-2990, has quality silver jewelry. Next door, **Form & Function Art Gallery** features carved wood objects, beadwork, prints, and baskets; carvers and beaders at work daily. Get Alaskan and other books from **The Babbling Book,** on Main next to Howser's, tel. (907) 766-3356. Haines is home to one of several birch syrup producers in Alaska—**Birch Boy Products,** tel. (907) 767-5660. The syrup is sold locally in gift shops. Don't expect the smoothness of maple syrup; birch syrup has a bit of a bite to it, but is quite good on ice cream and when blended with sugar syrup.

Information
The **Haines Visitor Information Center,** tel. (907) 766-2234, (800) 458-3579 (U.S. outside Alaska), or (800) 478-2268 (Canada), is on Second Avenue. It's open Mon.-Fri. 8 a.m.-8 p.m., and Sat.-Sun. 10 a.m.-1 p.m. and 2-7 p.m. from mid-May to mid-Sept., and Mon.-Fri. 8 a.m.-5 p.m. the rest of the year. Their Internet address is http://www.haines.ak.us. Stop here first to talk to the very friendly and knowledgeable staff, to leave notes on the message board for fellow travelers, or to get a cup of coffee or tea. Packs can generally be left here while you walk around town. Ask about the free guided **walking tours** available from the visitor center, and pick up a copy of the free *Visitors Guide to Haines* here or at the ferry terminal. If you arrive in town without fishing gear, you can rent rods and reels from the Halsingland Hotel at Fort Seward.

Tours
The visitor center has a complete listing of local guide companies and charter boat operators. **Chilkat Guides,** tel. (907) 766-2491, offers an excellent four-hour float trip down the Chilkat River for $75 ($35 for ages seven to 14). This is a leisurely raft trip (no whitewater) with good views of the Chilkat Mountains, glaciers, and eagles. They also have a two-day, fly-in/raft-out trip that begins with a flight to Le Blondeau Glacier, followed by a float trip down the gentle Tsirku River to Klukwan where a van returns you to Haines. This trip is $350 per person.

Alaska Cross Country Guiding & Rafting, tel. (907) 767-5522, offers a similar trip into the backcountry. Guests are flown to the base of Le Blondeau Glacier for a night in a remote cabin. The next day you can explore the surrounding country before rafting back down the Tsirku River and past the Chilkat Bald Eagle Preserve to Haines. The cost is $450 pp, plus the air taxi service ($200 for up to three people).

Dan Egolf of **Alaska Nature Tours**, tel. (907) 766-2876, leads educational three-hour trips ($45 for adults, $25 for kids) to the eagle-viewing area along the Chilkat River and other places. Ask about his longer day-trips, hiking tours, and telemark ski tours in the high country. **Chilkoot Lake Tours,** tel. (907) 766-2891 or (800) 354-6009, offers two-hour boat tours of this pretty lake. **River Adventures,** tel. (907) 766-2050 or (800) 478-9827 (inside Alaska), runs half-day jetboat tours up the Chilkat River.

Deishu Expeditions, tel. (907) 766-2427, has guided sea kayak trips around Haines, and an overnight guided trip to Davidson Glacier ($255 pp, all inclusive). They also rent kayaks if you want to go on your own.

Tanani Bay Kayak & Canoe Rentals, tel. (907) 766-2804, rents sea kayaks and canoes for $16 s or $26 d. Pickup and delivery are provided for a fee.

Haines Carriage & Trolley Co., tel. (907) 766-3308 or (907) 766-2715, offers horse-drawn carriage rides around Haines. **Yeshua Guided Tours,** tel. (907) 766-2334 or (800) 765-2556, leads van tours of the eagle preserve. A 90-minute tour tour is $20 pp; all day costs $65 pp.

TRANSPORTATION

Ferry Service
The Haines ferry terminal, tel. (907) 766-2111, is 3.5 miles north of town on Lutak Highway. Ferries arrive in Haines almost every day during the summer, heading both north to Skagway ($14) and south to Juneau ($20). They generally stop for 90 minutes.

The **Haines-Skagway Water Taxi,** tel. (907) 766-3395, is an excellent option if you need a break from the ferries and don't have a car. The boat connects Haines and Skagway twice each day in summer (mid-May to mid-Sept.), and costs $18 one-way or $29 roundtrip ($5 extra for bikes). Rates are half-price for kids. This is a

fine way to see wildlife, fjords, glaciers, and waterfalls at a leisurely nine-knot pace. **Silver Eagle Transport,** tel. (907) 766-2418, has a 65-foot landing craft that transports both vehicles and passengers between Juneau and Haines on a daily basis.

Haines Taxi, tel. (907) 766-3138; and **The New Other Guys Taxi,** tel. (907) 766-3257, both charge $6 to town from the ferry terminal. Rent mountain bikes ($6/hour or $30/day) from **Sockeye Cycle,** tel. (907) 766-2869, in the alley behind Howser's Market. They also offer bike tours of Haines for $10. Both Sockeye Cycle and Deishu Expeditions, tel. (907) 766-2427, rent kayaks.

By Air
The airport is 3.5 miles west of town on the Haines Highway. **Wings of Alaska,** tel. (907) 766-2030 or (800) 478-9464, flies daily to Juneau ($59) and Skagway ($40). **Skagway Air,** tel. (907) 789-2006, flies to Gustavus ($70) each day. **Haines Airways,** tel. (907) 766-2646, has daily service to Juneau ($55), Gustavus ($89), Hoonah ($84), and Skagway ($30). **L.A.B. Flying Service,** tel. (907) 766-2222 or (800) 426-0543, also flies to Gustavus ($110), Hoonah ($89), Juneau ($65), and Skagway ($30). The flight between Juneau and Haines is pretty spectacular; on clear days you'll be treated to views of glaciers along both sides of Lynn Canal. Both Haines Airways and L.A.B. offer hour-long Glacier Bay **flightseeing** trips for $80-100 pp.

Mountain Flying Service, a few doors down from the visitor center, tel. (907) 766-3007 or (800) 766-4007, offers flightseeing trips for $85 pp for one hour, $149 pp for a two-hour flight.

Heading North
The paved highway north from Haines is the most direct route to Fairbanks (665 miles) and Anchorage (775 miles). For cyclists it's much easier than the Klondike Highway out of Skagway. If you are thinking of driving to Skagway from Haines, think again. It's only 15 water or air miles away, but 359 road miles. Take the ferry!

Alaskon Express (Gray Line's public transportation), tel. (800) 544-2206, provides bus service between Haines and Haines Junction ($73), Whitehorse ($85), Tok ($145), Glennallen ($175), Fairbanks ($180), and Anchorage ($185). You

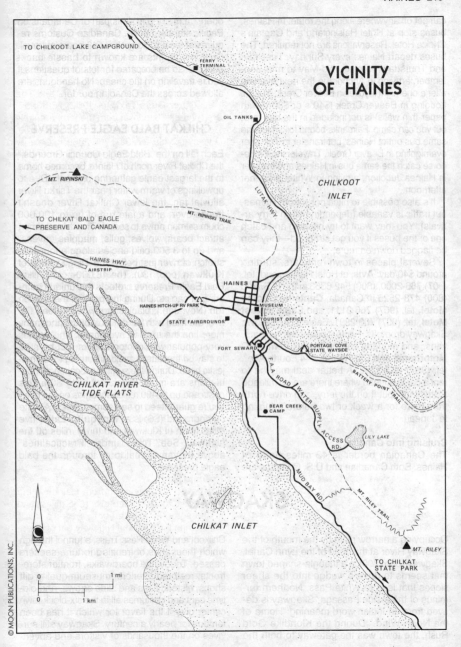

VICINITY OF HAINES

TO CHILKOOT LAKE CAMPGROUND

FERRY TERMINAL

OIL TANKS

CHILKOOT INLET

MT. RIPINSKI

LUTAK HWY

MT. RIPINSKI TRAIL

TO CHILKAT BALD EAGLE PRESERVE AND CANADA

HAINES HWY AIRSTRIP

HAINES

HAINES HITCH-UP RV PARK

STATE FAIRGROUNDS

CHILKAT RIVER TIDE FLATS

MUSEUM

TOURIST OFFICE

FORT SEWARD

PORTAGE COVE STATE WAYSIDE

BATTERY POINT TRAIL

F.A.A. ROAD

WATER SUPPLY ACCESS RD.

BEAR CREEK CAMP

LILY LAKE

CHILKAT INLET

MUD BAY RD.

MT. RILEY TRAIL

MT. RILEY

TO CHILKAT STATE PARK

© MOON PUBLICATIONS, INC.

0   1 mi

0   1 km

can get off anywhere along the route. In Haines, buses stop at Hotel Halsingland and Captain's Choice Hotel. Reservations are not required. The buses depart Haines every Sunday, Tuesday, and Thursday morning, mid-May to mid-September, arriving in Anchorage the next evening after a one-night layover in Beaver Creek, Yukon. Lodging in Beaver Creek ($40 s or $80 d with paper-thin walls) is *not* included in the bus fare, but you can camp. Fairbanks-bound folks take the same bus out of Haines, but transfer in Tok after overnighting in Beaver Creek. Travelers to Whitehorse catch the same bus in Haines and transfer in Haines Junction, arriving in Whitehorse that afternoon.

It's also possible to hitch north from Haines, but traffic is variable (depending upon ferry arrivals). You may want to try hitching and catch one of the buses if you get stranded—they can be flagged down en route.

Several places in town rent cars, starting around $40/day: **Avis,** at Hotel Halsingland, tel. (907) 766-2000, (800) 542-6363 in the U.S. and (800) 478-2525 in Canada; **Captains Choice Motel,** tel. (907) 766-3111; and **Eagle's Nest Motel,** tel. (907) 766-2891. Eagle's Nest allows Skagway drop-offs. Recreational vehicles, cars, vans, and mopeds can be rented from **ABC Motorhome and Car Rental,** 444 Fourth Ave., tel. (907) 983-3222. A better deal may be to rent a car in Juneau where there are no mileage restrictions, put it on the ferry, and drive north from there for a week or two before returning to Juneau.

Cruising into Canada

The Canadian border is 42 miles north of Haines. Both Canadian and U.S. Customs are open 7 a.m.-11 p.m. (this part of Canada is on Pacific standard time). Canadian Customs requires at least $150 cash for 48 hours of travel. Customs agents are known to hassle backpackers, so be prepared for lots of questions if you're traveling on the cheap. No handguns are allowed across the Canadian border.

CHILKAT BALD EAGLE PRESERVE

Each fall on the "Bald Eagle Council Grounds," the Chilkat River north of Haines becomes home to the largest eagle gathering on earth. Due to upwellings of warm water near the Tsirku River alluvial fan, the lower Chilkat River doesn't freeze over, and a late run of up to 100,000 chum salmon arrive to spawn. The dying salmon attract bears, wolves, gulls, magpies, ravens, and up to 3,500 bald eagles along a four-mile stretch of river just below the Tlingit village of **Klukwan** (pop. 130). The 48,000-acre Chilkat Bald Eagle Preserve protects this unique gathering of eagles. During the peak of the salmon run (Nov.-Jan.), black cottonwoods along the river are filled with hundreds of birds, and many more line the braided riverbanks. The area is very popular with photographers, but be sure to stay off the flats to avoid disturbing these majestic birds. During the summer, local eagle populations are much lower, but, with 80 active nests and up to 400 resident eagles on the river, you're guaranteed to see some eagles. A state campground ($6) is at **Mosquito Lake,** five miles north of Klukwan and three miles off the highway. See "Tours" under "Practicalities" above for van or boat tours through the bald eagle preserve.

SKAGWAY

Occupying a narrow plain by the mouth of the Skagway River at the head of the Lynn Canal, Skagway (pop. 700) is a triangle-shaped town that seems to drive a wedge into the sheer slopes that lead to White Pass. Northern terminus of the Inside Passage, Skagway is derived from an Indian word meaning "Home of the North Wind." During the Klondike Gold Rush, the town was the gateway to both the Chilkoot and White Pass Trails, a funnel through which thousands of frenzied fortune-seekers passed. Today, the boardwalks, frontier storefronts, restored interiors, museum-quality gift shops, historic films and slide shows, and old-time cars and costumes all in the six-block town center give it the flavor for which it has been famous for nearly a century. Skagway still survives on the thousands of visitors and adventurers who come each summer to continue on the trail that led to gold. This is the most popular cruise port in Alaska, and the 1,500 summer residents (it dwindles to 400 or so in winter) are snowed under by up to 5,000 cruise ship visitors in a single day. (Up to five ships can dock at once!)

Independent travelers often leave Skagway with mixed feelings. The town is fun to visit and has lots to see and do, but seems well on the way to becoming a schmaltzy shadow of its former self, sort of a Disneyland version of the gold rush era. If you're looking for authentic Alaska, look elsewhere. Of course, once you escape to the surrounding mountains on the Chilkoot Trail, it's easy to forget the crowds below. One way to avoid most of the crowds is to get here before mid-May or after mid-September. Typically, there are only a handful of days all summer without cruise ships.

Skagway's weather is decidedly different from the weather in the rest of the Southeast. It only gets 22 inches of precipitation a year, and alder, willow, and cottonwood carpet the adjacent hillsides. It is especially colorful in mid-September when the leaves are turning.

HISTORY

Klondike Gold

An enormous amount of Alaskan history was collapsed into the final decade of the 19th century at Skagway. In August 1896, on the day that George Carmack struck it rich on Bonanza Creek, Skagway consisted of a single cabin, constructed eight years previously by Capt. William Moore, but only occupied sporadically by the transient pioneer. News of the Klondike strike hit Seattle in July 1897; within a month 4,000 people huddled in a haphazard tent city surrounding Moore's lone cabin, and "craft of every description, from ocean-going steamers to little more than floating coffins, were dumping into the makeshift village a crazily mixed mass of humanity." Almost immediately, Frank Reid surveyed and platted the townsite, and the stampeders grabbed 1,000 lots, many within Moore's homestead. There was no law to back up either claims or counterclaims, and reports from the time describe Skagway as "the most outrageously lawless quarter" on the globe.

Into this breach stepped Jefferson Randall Smith, known not as J.R. but as Soapy, Alaska's great bad man. A notorious con artist from Colorado, Soapy Smith oversaw a mind-bogglingly extensive system of fraud, theft, armed robbery, even murder. He had his own spy network, secret police, and army to enforce the strong-arm tactics. Finally, a vigilance committee held a meeting to oppose Soapy. Frank Reid, the surveyor, stood guard. Soapy approached. Guns blazed. Smith, shot in the chest, died instantly, at age 38. Of Soapy, the newspaper reported, "At 9:30 o'clock Friday night the checkered career of 'Soapy' Smith was brought to a sudden end by a 38 calibre bullet from a revolver in the unerring right hand of City surveyor Frank H. Reid. . . ." Reid was shot in the groin, and died in agony a week later. His gravestone reads, "He gave his life for the honor of Skagway."

Up the Chilkoot Trail

Skagway was the jumping-off point for White Pass, which crossed the Coastal Range to Lake Bennett and the Yukon headwaters. This trail, billed as the "horse route," was the choice of prosperous prospectors who could afford pack animals to carry the requisite "ton of goods." But it was false advertising at best, and death-defying at worst. The mountains were so precipitous, the trail so narrow and rough, and the weather so wild that the men turned merciless; all 3,000 horses and mules that stepped onto the trail in 1897-98 were doomed to a proverbial fate worse than death. Indeed, men swore that horses leaped off the cliffs on purpose, committing suicide.

The famous Chilkoot Trail, which started in Dyea (die-EE), 15 miles from Skagway, was the "poor-man's route." Stampeders had to backpack their year's worth of supplies 33 miles to Lake Lindeman, which included 40 trips up and down the 45-degree "Golden Stairs" to the 3,550-foot pass. This scene, recorded in black and white, is one of the most dramatic and enduring photographs of the Days of '98. Into this breach stepped Michael J. Heney, the "Irish Prince." An Irish-Canadian contractor with a genius for vision, fund-raising, management, and commanding the loyalty of his workers, Heney punched through the 110-mile narrow-gauge White Pass and Yukon Route Railway, which connected saltwater Skagway to freshwater Whitehorse. The route, so treacherous to pack animals, was no less malevolent to railroaders. They worked suspended from the steep slopes by ropes, often in 50-below temperatures and raging Arctic blizzards, for $3 a day. The line was completed in just under two years, when the final stake was driven in at Carcross, on July 29, 1900, thus ensuring the constant flow of passengers and freight—as well as Skagway's survival. The train shut down when metal prices plummeted in 1982, but reopened again for excursion travel only in 1988. Ore concentrate from the Yukon's enormous Anvil Range lead-zinc mine is trucked to Skagway for shipment to Japan. The WP&YR is once again Skagway's favorite attraction, and one of the only operating narrow-gauge railroads in North America. Today, more than 110,000 passengers ride the train each summer.

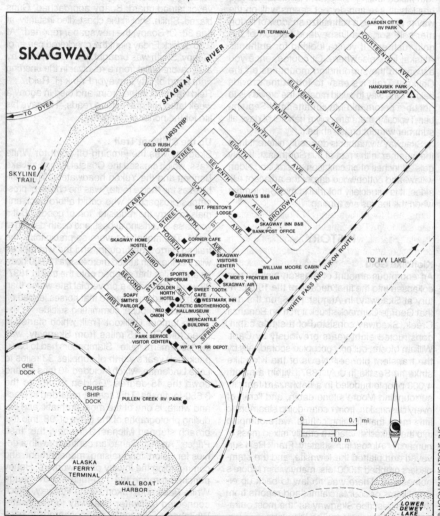

SIGHTS

Downtown Skagway is made up of seven blocks on Broadway, along which are most of the sights. The ferry terminal is at the very bottom of Broadway: a three-minute hike and you're in the heart of beautiful downtown Skagway. Many of the historic buildings are owned and managed by the National Park Service as **Klondike Gold Rush National Historic Park.** Most of the restored structures are leased to private businesses.

On Broadway

The old White Pass & Yukon administration building houses the **National Park Service Visitor Center;** open daily 8 a.m.-7 p.m. in June, July, and August, daily 8 a.m.-6 p.m. in late May and September, and Mon.-Fri. only the rest of the year. Don't miss the excellent "moving slide show" with black-and-white images from the gold rush, shown almost hourly. Narrated by Hal Holbrook, this half-hour show is an articulate and graphic overview of the mad days of the stampede. Other Park Service activities include talks, films, and four-times-a-day 45-minute walking tours of town. Personnel behind the desk have the latest trail, weather, and transportation information, and can probably answer that burning question you've been carrying around all day. Across Broadway on Second is **Soapy Smith's Parlor,** the saloon from where the infamous blackguard supervised his various nefarious offenses. The building is not open to the public.

You can't miss **Arctic Brotherhood (AB) Hall** between Second and Third—the only example of turn-of-the-century Alaska driftwood stick architecture. It has to be the most-photographed building in Alaska. The Brotherhood was organized aboard the vessel *City of Seattle,* which waited out the winter of 1899 in Skagway Harbor. The order spread, and local chapters were established in most Alaskan towns. Dues were paid solely in nuggets.

The **Trail of '98 Museum,** tel. (907) 983-2420, is housed inside the AB Hall, and is open daily 9 a.m.-5 p.m. in the summer; closed the remainder of the year. Check out the old gambling equipment, the "Moorish queen" from the Chicago World's Fair of 1893, the duckskin blanket, the Native artifacts, and the July 15, 1898,

edition of the *Skagway News* with the story of the killing of Soapy. Also here are an amazing salmon-skin parka and an Eskimo mask from Anaktuvuk Pass. Several videos are available if you want to know more about the characters in Skagway's past.

The **Golden North Hotel** at Third and Broadway bills itself as Alaska's oldest, and is filled with antique gold-rush-era furnishings. Ask about the ghost that roams the halls. Duck into the many gift shops in the next few blocks. Many of the furnishings, display cases, and even some of the stuff for sale are worth a look. The National Park Service has restored the historic **Mascot Saloon** at Third and Broadway, with exhibits depicting the saloon and life in the days of '98. **Dedman's Photo Shop,** between Third and Fourth, has a large selection of black-and-white postcards. **Eagle's Hall** on Sixth Ave. houses the "Days of '98 Show" (see "Entertainment" under "Practicalities," below).

Corrington's Museum of Alaskan History, tel. (907) 983-2580, on the corner of Fifth and Broadway, is a combination gift shop and scrimshaw museum ($1). The collection includes 40 exquisitely carved pieces that tell the history of Alaska on walrus ivory. It's well worth a visit. The museum is flanked by a colorful flower garden. At the east end of Fourth Ave. is the **Alaskan Wildlife Adventure & Museum,** Fourth and Spring St., tel. (907) 983-3600, a collection of 70 or so animal mounts from Alaska and the Yukon.

Off Broadway

The original **Capt. William Moore cabin,** which was moved under pressure from the early stampeders to its present location, Fifth and Spring, has been completely refurbished by the Park Service. Its interior walls are papered with newspapers from the 1880s.

The **Gold Rush Cemetery** sits right beside the railroad tracks two miles north of town. The largest monument is Frank Reid's, while Soapy Smith only rates a wooden plank. While you're here, be sure to follow the short trail above the cemetery to scenic **Lower Reid Falls.**

White Pass & Yukon Route Railroad

The narrow gauge White Pass & Yukon Route Railroad runs twice-daily trains from Skagway to White Pass and back (28 miles each way; three hours roundtrip). Trains run from mid-May till late September only. The tracks follow along the east side of the Skagway River, with stunning vistas that get better and better as the train climbs. Tour guides point out the sights, including portions of the Trail of '98. Be sure to sit on the left side from Skagway (right side returning). Excursions leave Skagway at 8:45 a.m. and 1:15 p.m. Get tickets in the restored railroad depot office on Second St. for $75 ($38 for children). Call (800) 343-7373 in the U.S. or (800) 478-7373 in Canada for details. The gracious old steam locomotive no. 73 chugs out of town, with video cameras rolling in all directions. (Note, however, that the steam engine is replaced by a more modern diesel engine on the edge of town to save it from wear and tear on the strenuous climb.) The WP&YR also has a longer six-hour daily roundtrip to Lake Bennett. These trains depart daily at 12:40 p.m. Hikers up the Chilkoot Trail can catch the train back down again (or vice versa) from Lake Bennett.

Through service to Whitehorse ($95 adults or $48 children one-way) departs Skagway at 12:40 p.m., and arrives in Frasier, British Columbia, at 2:40 p.m., where you transfer to buses to Whitehorse, arriving at 6 p.m. The return schedule is: depart Whitehorse at 8:15 a.m. by bus, transfer to the train in Frasier at 10:20 a.m., and arrive in Skagway at noon.

RECREATION

Nearby Hiking

A network of well-marked trails on the slopes just east of town offers excellent day-hikes and a place to warm up for the Chilkoot Trail. Cross the small footbridge and railroad tracks beyond the end of Third and Fourth Aves., then follow the pipeline up the hill. **Lower Dewey Lake** is an easy 20-minute climb. A trail right around the lake branches at the south end off to **Sturgill's Landing** (three miles) on Taiya Inlet. **Upper Dewey Lake** and the **Devil's Punchbowl** are a steep 2.5-mile climb from the north end of the lower lake. Icy Lake is a relatively level two miles from the lower lake, but the trail to **Upper Reid Falls** is steep and hard to follow. A number of clearings with picnic tables surround the lower lake where camping is possible; more are at the other lakes and Sturgill's Landing.

At First Ave. and Alaska St., cross the airstrip and the suspension bridge over Skagway River. A short hike goes left to Yakutania Point and Smugglers Cove. Go right and head out to Dyea Rd.; you'll see the trailhead in a mile up **A.B. Mountain**, named for the Arctic Brotherhood (the letters "AB" are supposedly visible in snow patches each spring). This five-mile jaunt is steep and strenuous; the summit is 5,100 feet above your starting point (sea level) and a five-hour hike.

In 1993, the Forest Service opened a refurbished railroad **caboose** as a public use cabin ($25/night). This attractive old caboose is located six miles north of Skagway near where the railroad crosses the East Fork of the Skagway River. Access is on foot, or the WP&YR train will drop you off for $10. Take your binoculars to scan nearby slopes for mountain goats. The **Denver Glacier Trail** begins right beside the caboose, and climbs five miles and 1,200 feet to Denver Glacier. It's a beautiful hike through subalpine fir, paper birch, cottonwood, spruce, and other trees.

Another excellent hiking option begins at Glacier Station (14 miles north of Skagway).

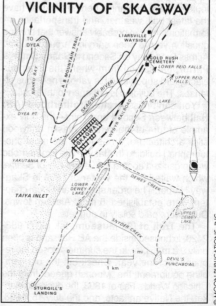

VICINITY OF SKAGWAY

© MOON PUBLICATIONS, INC.

SKAGWAY ACCOMMODATIONS

Note: Skagway adds an eight percent tax to these rates. Places are arranged from least to most expensive.

Skagway Home Hostel; Third and Main; tel. (907) 983-2131; $13 pp; youth hostel

Portland House; Fifth and State; tel. (907) 983-2493; $32 s, $48 d; historic building, shared baths

Miners' Cache Hotel Rooms; Sixth and Broadway; tel. (907) 983-3303 or (800) 764-7670; $45 s, $60 d; historic inn, shared baths

Grammas B&B; Seventh and State; tel. (907) 983-2312; $55 s, $65 d; very nice, open summer only, continental breakfast

Golden North Hotel; Third and Broadway; tel. (907) 983-2451; $60 s, $75 d; oldest in Alaska, private or shared baths

Skagway Inn B&B; Seventh and Broadway; tel. (907) 983-2289 or (800) 478-2290 (in Alaska); $60 s, $75 d; historic bordello and inn, 12 guest rooms, shared baths, full breakfast

Wind Valley Lodge; 22nd and State; tel. (907) 983-2236; $65 s, $75 d; AAA approved

Gold Rush Lodge; Sixth and Alaska; tel. (907) 983-2831; $65-95 s or d

Mile Zero B&B; Ninth and Main; tel. (907) 983-3045; $70 s, $90 d; new B&B, private baths, continental breakfast

Sgt. Preston's Lodge; Sixth and State; tel. (907) 983-2521; $70-80 s, $80-85 d; courtesy van

Cindy's Place; two miles out Dyea Rd.; tel. (907) 983-2674; $74 s, $79 d; modern log cabin in wooded location, hot tub, make-your-own breakfast, bicycle, two night minimum stay

Westmark Inn; Third and Broadway; tel. (907) 983-2291 or (800) 544-0970; $99 s or d; airport shuttle, AAA approved

Have the WP&YR train drop you off here, and then hike up the easy two-mile trail that leads to a Forest Service cabin near **Laughton Glacier** ($25/night). Make cabin reservations for either of these cabins at the Park Service visitor center in Skagway, or from the Forest Service in Juneau. Flag down the train to return.

On the Water

Get guided sea kayak tours from **Klondike Water Adventures,** tel. (907) 983-3769, located in the small boat harbor. **Skagway Float Tours,** tel. (907) 983-3508 or (800) 303-3508, has easy three-hour float trips down the Taiya River for $60 ($25 for kids under 12). More adventurous folks may want to try the two-hour whitewater raft trips for $40 ($25 for kids). The tour company also offers guided hikes and mountain bike trips along the Chilkoot Trail.

PRACTICALITIES

Accommodations

See the "Skagway Accommodations" chart for a complete list of Skagway's lodging options. If you're heading here in midsummer, try to make reservations at least two weeks ahead of time to be sure of a room. Skagway has a comfortable home hostel right in town. Smoking and alcohol are prohibited, and an 11 p.m. curfew may put a crimp in your social life, but the folks here are very friendly and the hostel is open year-round. There's space for only 12, so it's essential to make reservations ahead; call **Skagway Home Hostel** at (907) 983-2131. Register 5-9 p.m. The hostel has cooking space, showers, and laundry machines. They generally accommodate late-arriving ferries. Rates are $13 pp.

Beyond the hostel, there are many choices, but none of them cheap. The least expensive rooms are at Portland House, but the local bed and breakfast places may be a better deal; **Skagway Inn B&B** is especially noteworthy.

Camping

The Park Service maintains a free campground at **Dyea,** northeast of Skagway. It is especially popular with hikers along the Chilkoot Trail. Hitching is possible, or those without wheels can contact one of the local taxi companies for a ride. The rough road to Dyea is not for RVs.

Hanousek Park at 14th and Broadway is the in-town tenters' campground ($6), with flush toilets and showers. The narrow-gauge tracks border the grounds, making this a good place for photo opportunities. **Pullen Creek RV Park,** tel. (907) 983-2768, next to the ferry terminal, has full hookups for $18, and showers for $1. Other RV parks are **Back Track Camper Park** at 12th and Broadway, tel. (907) 983-3333; and **Garden City RV Park,** at 16th Ave. and State St., tel. (907) 983-2378. It's open May-September. Back Track also has space for tents. Quiet, uncrowded campsites are available at **Liarsville,** 2.5 miles out on the Klondike Highway, but there is no water.

Food

With so many visitors coming and going, Skagway's high meal prices should come as no surprise. But at least the variety and quality are considerably higher than what you'll find in Wrangell. **Corner Cafe,** at Fourth Ave. and State St., tel. (907) 983-2155, is the place to go for salmon burgers and reasonably priced breakfasts. Friendly and fast service, too. On Broadway, **Sweet Tooth Cafe,** tel. (907) 983-2405, also serves good breakfasts. You'll find espresso, along with fresh-baked muffins and scones, at **Mabel G. Smith's** on Fifth Ave. between Broadway and State Streets, tel. (907) 983-2609. More fresh baked goods at **Pullen Pantry Bakery,** inside the wildlife museum at Fourth Ave. and Spring St., tel. (907) 983-3600. The tiny **Mrs. Potts Tea Room,** inside the Forget Me Not gift shop on Broadway between Second and Third Aves., is a good place for lunch, with a menu that changes daily.

Pizza seems to be the primary fare of many local eateries. Enjoy pizzas and nachos at the **Red Onion. Northern Lights Cafe,** Fourth Ave. and Broadway, tel. (907) 983-2225, serves Greek, Italian, and Mexican dishes, along with pizzas. **Broadway Bistro,** Third Ave. and Spring St., tel. (907) 983-6000, features delicious pizzas baked in a wood burning oven, plus Italian dishes, espresso, and microbrewed beers on tap. More pizzas, along with focaccia sandwiches are at **Pizzeria Roma II,** Third Ave. and Broadway, tel. (907) 983-3459.

Golden North Hotel is a fine place for dinners, as is the **Chilkoot Room** in the Westmark Hotel. **Lorna's at the Skagway Inn,** Seventh Ave. and Broadway, tel. (907) 983-3161, specializes in inventive French cuisine and Alaskan seafood dinners prepared by a Cordon Bleu-trained chef.

Fairway Market is at Fourth Ave. and State St., tel. (907) 983-2220. Get there on Tuesday for the once-a-week fresh produce delivery. Buy fresh fish from the **Skagway Fish Co.** at the small boat harbor, tel. (907) 893-3474.

Entertainment

The **Red Onion,** Second Ave. and Broadway, is Skagway's well-known establishment, with an occasional local band on stage practicing in public, and red-light mannequins posing in the second-floor windows. But if you want to get down and dirty and start drinking with the locals at 10 a.m., head across the street and up the block to **Moe's Frontier Bar.** Inside the Westmark at Third Ave. and Broadway, **Bonanza Bar & Grill** has pool tables, microbrews, and live music.

The most fun thing to do at night is to attend the **Days of '98 Show** at Sixth Ave. and Broadway. The great-granddaddy of them all, this production is the oldest running theater in Alaska—over 65 years! Check the performance schedules posted around town: matinees (smaller cast) are offered most days at 10:30 a.m. and 2 p.m. (depending upon the ship schedule), and full-production evening performances start at 7:30 p.m. Warm-up gambling with "Soapy money" comes first, then the show goes on at 8:30. Splurge on this one. Call (907) 983-2545 for details. The **Gold Pan Theatre,** Seventh Ave. and Broadway, tel. (907) 983-3177, puts on vaudeville melodramas and free shoot-outs on a daily basis to entertain the cruise ship hordes.

A local character—"Buckwheat" Donahue—recites "The Cremation of Sam McGee" and other ballads from the Robert Service repertoire nightly at 7:30 inside the Mercantile Building on Second Avenue. Shows run from late May to early September and cost $6.

Events

Skagway's first July Fourth in 1898 was celebrated with the outlaw Soapy Smith leading the parade on a white horse; he was dead four days later. **July Fourth** is still a big day, with a huge parade (locals call it the best in Alaska) and other events. The **Klondike Road Relay** takes place every September, with more than a hundred teams composed of 10 runners each competing over a grueling 110-mile course.

The years 1997 and '98 are important for Skagway, with special events to commemorate the heady times a century ago. In July 1997, a special voyage will take descendants of those who sailed south on the SS *Portland* in 1897 on the famous "ton of gold" ship. There will be all sorts of activities in 1998, culminating in the 100th anniversary of the gold rush during the July Fourth festivities.

Information and Services

See "Sights" above for information on the Park Service Visitor Center. The **Skagway Visitor Information Center,** tel. (907) 983-2855, is located just off Broadway on Fifth Ave. near Sockeye Cycle. It's open daily 8 a.m.-5 p.m. May-Sept., and Mon.-Fri. 8 a.m.-noon and 1-5 p.m. the rest of the year. They have a good hiking map and brochure here. Find them on the Internet at http://www.skagway.org.

Sports Emporium on Fourth Ave. between Broadway and State, tel. (907) 983-2480, is the outfitter in town, and sells freeze-dried food for the trail. Books are available at **Skagway News Depot,** tel. (907) 983-3354. Take a **shower** at Pullen Creek RV Park, or at the small boat harbor. National Bank of Alaska, Sixth Ave. and Broadway, changes green dollars into multicolored Canadian dollars, and has an **ATM.** A second cash machine is on Broadway between Second and Third Avenues. The **library** is at Eighth Ave. and State St., tel. (907) 983-2665. Get free reading material on the paperback racks inside (and these aren't all bodice-buster novels either). There is no swimming pool in Skagway.

TRANSPORTATION

On the Water

Skagway is the northern terminus of the ferry system, and ferries arrive daily, sometimes twice, during the summer. The **ferry terminal,** tel. (907) 983-2941, is right next to town. The Juneau-Skagway fare is $26; Skagway-Haines costs $14. The **Haines-Skagway Water Taxi,** tel. (907) 766-3395 (in Haines), offers a break from the ferries. The boat connects Haines and Skagway twice each day in summer, and costs

$18 one-way or $29 roundtrip (half-price for kids, $5 extra for bikes). They also offer a variety of van tours of Haines combined with a roundtrip water taxi ride from Skagway.

Planes, Trains, and Automobiles

See "White Pass & Yukon Route Railroad" under "Sights," above, for Skagway's most distinctive means of transport. You can fly daily from Juneau ($70-80) via **Skagway Air,** tel. (907) 983-2218; **Wings of Alaska,** tel. (907) 983-2442 or (800) 478-9464; **Haines Airways,** tel. (907) 766-2646; and **L.A.B. Flying Service,** tel. (907) 789-9160 or (800) 426-0543. L.A.B. also flies to Haines ($30) and Gustavus ($120). Skagway Air also goes to Gustavus ($81) and Haines ($33). Haines Airways flies between Skagway and Haines for $30. Wings of Alaska flies between Skagway and Haines for $40.

Rent cars from **Avis,** at the Westmark Hotel, tel. (907) 983-2247 or (800) 331-1212; or from **Sourdough Shuttles,** Sixth Ave. and Broadway, tel. (907) 983-2523 or (800) 4878-2529. **ABC Motorhome Rentals,** tel. (907) 983-3222 or (800) 421-7456, rents RVs in Skagway.

Long-Distance Buses

Alaskon Express motorcoaches (Gray Line's public transportation), tel. (800) 544-2206, operate every day from mid-May to mid-September between Skagway and Whitehorse ($54), Anchorage ($205), and Fairbanks ($205). The buses stop for the night in Beaver Creek on their Anchorage or Fairbanks runs, and lodging costs an additional $40 s or $80 d (tiny rooms) unless you camp at Beaver Creek.

Alaska Direct, tel. (907) 277-6652 (in Anchorage) or (800) 780-6652, has bus service between Skagway and Whitehorse ($35), Anchorage ($180), and Fairbanks ($155). Alaska Direct does not stop overnight, so you'll have to sleep on the bus to Anchorage or Fairbanks. Buses run year-round.

Local Tours

Given the influx of tourists to Skagway, it's no surprise that there is a multitude of tour options. The companies seem to change every year, but you're sure to find a way to get around the area. **Gray Line, Atlas Tours,** and the other biggies all do two-hour Skagway tours starting at around $15; you'll see these buses stopped in the middle of downtown streets as the driver rattles on. Local tour and taxi companies, including **Frontier Excursions,** tel. (907) 983-2512; **Goldrush Tours,** tel. (907) 983-2718; **Klondike Tours,** tel. (907) 983-2075; **Southeast Tours,** tel. (907) 983-2990 or (800) 478-2990; and **Skagway White Pass Tours,** tel. (907) 983-2244, will run you around town for $5, or drop you at the Chilkoot trailhead (nine miles away) for $10. Transport from Log Cabin to Skagway costs $20. Or rent a bike from **JD & Paul's Bike** at Fourth Ave. and State St., or from **Sockeye Cycle,** Fifth Ave. near Broadway, tel. (907) 983-2851. The latter offers a speedy ride down White Pass; they drive you up and you roll back down on the bikes. The cost is $65; great fun.

More distinctive tours are aboard the canary-yellow 1930s-era White Motor Company cars run by **Skagway Street Car Company,** tel. (907) 983-2908. The complete two-hour trip (including the multimedia presentation) costs $34, but is generally offered only to cruise ship passengers.

Skagway Air, tel. (907) 983-2218 (907) , does 90-minute Glacier Bay flightseeing trips for $110 pp, and 45-minute gold rush tours (to Lake Bennett) for $55 pp. There are also 50-minute **Temsco Helicopter** tours over the Chilkoot Trail for $142 pp, including a glacier landing.

CHILKOOT TRAIL

One of the best reasons for coming to Skagway is the Chilkoot Trail, an old Indian route from tidewater at Dyea to the headwaters of the Yukon River. A minimum of three days (but preferably four or five) is needed to hike the 32 miles to Bennett over 3,246-foot-high Chilkoot Pass. This is no easy Sunday outing: you must be fit and well prepared. Weather conditions can change quickly on the trail and you should be ready for cold, fog, rain, snow, and wind at all times. The first stretch can be extremely swampy; snowfields linger between Sheep Camp and Happy Camp well into the summer. You will be above the treeline and totally exposed to the weather during the 16 km from Sheep Camp to Deep Lake (the hardest stretch). Nonetheless thousands of people follow the trail of '98 every summer and make fast friends along the way. For scenery and historical value the Chilkoot is unsurpassed in Alaska and western Canada.

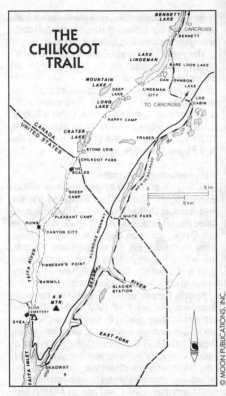

THE CHILKOOT TRAIL

© MOON PUBLICATIONS, INC.

History

It took each would-be miner an average of three months and dozens of trips back and forth from cache to cache to pack his required ton of supplies into Canada. By the spring of 1898, three aerial tramways were operating on the Chilkoot. The thousands of stampeders stopped at Lindeman and Bennett, built boats and rafts, and waited for spring break-up, which would allow them to sail the 900 km to Dawson City along a series of lakes and rivers. When the ice broke up in May 1898, some 7,124 boats and rafts sailed from the shores of Lakes Lindeman and Bennett. Mounted Police records show 28,000 people traveling from Bennett to Dawson in 1898. Ironically, by the time they got to Dawson every claim in the Klondike was already staked. By 1900, Dyea and the Chilkoot Trail were deserted after the railway opened from Skagway to Whitehorse. Today it is possible to follow the gold-rush trail all the way from Seattle to the Klondike in much the same way the stampeders did: ship to Skagway, hike to Bennett, bus or hitch to Whitehorse, canoe to Dawson City.

The Route

The Chilkoot Trail begins just before the bridge over the Taiya River at Dyea, nine miles northwest of Skagway (for transportation, see above). Little remains to be seen at Dyea except for the Slide Cemetery, where 60 men and women killed in the Palm Sunday avalanche of 1898 are buried. The first 12 miles of trail are a gradual climb through the rainforest, followed by a very steep ascent to the pass. At Canyon City, seven miles from the trailhead, a short side trail and a suspension bridge across the Taiya River give access to the remains of one of the villages that sprang up during the rush. The hardest part of the trip is the 30-degree incline from The Scales to the summit. This section was known as the "Golden Stairs," for the steps carved in the ice and the snow. Photos of men going up here in single file are still the best-known images of the gold rush. There is a U.S. park ranger at Sheep Camp and a Canadian park warden at Lindeman City. They recommend that you hike north from Dyea rather than south from Bennett, as this is the historic route, and a descent down the "Golden Stairs" can be dangerous. From Bennett you walk out to the Klondike Highway at Log Cabin and hitch, catch the Alaskon Express bus that stops there every day, or hook up to the White Pass & Yukon Route train (see above).

Flora and Fauna

The vegetation changes from coastal rainforest up the Taiya Valley to alpine tundra as you approach the pass and rise above the 2,700-foot level. On the drier Canadian side you'll find an open boreal forest of alpine fir and lodgepole pine. Although bears are seen along the trail occasionally, there has never been an attack on a hiker. Help keep it this way by storing food and garbage properly.

Practicalities

Camping along the trail is permitted only at designated areas where outhouses are provided. There is a free campground near the trailhead, and a ranger station there could supply a map/brochure if you don't already have one. Backcountry permits are now required, though they are free. Get one here before heading out. Southbound hikers should get permits at the Lindeman Warden Station. Campfires are permitted only at Canyon City and Sheep Camp. There are shelters with woodstoves at Canyon City, Sheep Camp, and Lindeman, but these are for drying out only (not overnighting). You must camp. Some of these sites get very crowded. Sheep Creek has 60 campers on some nights. Because of this popularity, use limits may be imposed in the near future. Boil all drinking water, use a filter, or use purification pills. Everything along the trail dating from the gold rush (even a rusty old tin can) is protected by law, and there are severe penalties for those who damage or remove items. Everyone entering Canada must clear Canadian Customs. If you come in along the Chilkoot Trail and do not speak to an official at either Whitehorse or Fraser, you should report at the first opportunity to either the RCMP in Carcross or the Immigration Office (open Mon.-Fri.) in the Federal Building in Whitehorse.

THE KLONDIKE HIGHWAY

This 157-km road from Skagway to the Alaska Highway 34 km south of Whitehorse closely follows the White Pass & Yukon Route rail line built at the turn of the century. The 105-km stretch north to Carcross was opened in 1981, completing the route started by the U.S. Army in 1942 from the Alaska Highway south to Carcross. The finished highway helped put the railroad out of business, when the large mines in central Yukon began trucking the ore concentrated to Skagway by road, less expensive than freighting them by rail. The road ascends quickly from sea level at Skagway to White Pass at 3,290 feet in 14 miles. Many turnouts provide views across the canyon of the narrow-gauge track, waterfalls, gorges, and long drop-offs—if you're lucky and the weather cooperates. Otherwise, driving over White Pass is like hurtling through space with a small gray box over your head. At the summit, Canadian Customs welcomes you to British Columbia 7 a.m.-11 p.m.; set your watch ahead an hour to Pacific time again on the Canadian side.

Carcross

North of Skagway 105 km, just inside the Yukon Territory, is the revitalizing town of Carcross. Situated at the north end of Lake Bennett, a short shallow stream connects Bennett to Nares Lake, part of the "Southern Lake System" that drains northward (inland) into the Yukon River. A natural fording spot for migrating caribou, the name Carcross is a contraction of "Caribou Crossing." This oft-photographed little settlement (best shots from the shoreline road that passes under the highway bridge before town; walk down the stairs at the south end of the bridge) is chockablock with historical significance. The most impressive evidence is the *Tutshi* (TOO-shy) sternwheeler drydocked on the bank, next to an excellent interpretive center, open daily 9 a.m.-9 p.m. Read the fascinating history of the sternwheelers, and check out the graphic map of the intricate network of lakes that comprises the Yukon River headwaters. The *Tutshi* was one of the largest passenger vessels of the 250 boats that steamed 2,000 miles along the river for 90 years. Here starts one of the recurring themes of travel through the interior of Alaska and Yukon; make sure to visit and compare the sternwheelers in Whitehorse and Dawson, and cruise on one in Fairbanks.

The WP&YR trains crossed the original "swing bridge" in town, built to allow the riverboats to pass; walk across the bridge for a look back through your viewfinder. The golden spike of the WP&YR railroad was laid here on July 29, 1900. A tiny locomotive, the *Duchess,* which

connected with the *Tutshi* and pulled a train over the three km separating Tagish and Atlin Lakes, stands nearby. The old **rail depot** has a gift shop and some wildlife exhibits. To the left are **Mathew Watson General Store** and the **Caribou Hotel,** built in 1911. In the old Carcross **cemetery,** 1.5 km away, rest such stampede-starting notables as Skookum Jim, Tagish Charlie, and Kate Carmack.

Atlin

At Carcross is the turnoff onto Tagish (tahk-LEESH) Rd., which runs 53 km to Jake's Corner on the Alcan. Ninety-three km south of the junction is Atlin, northernmost town in British Columbia, on the shores of Lake Atlin, largest lake in the province. Lucky prospectors discovered a rich vein nearby during the 1898 stampede; within 12 months over 10,000 people had rushed to the area. The Atlin Historical Society keeps photographs from that period. Also in town is the lake boat *Tarahne,* which once connected Atlin to Scotia Bay, on the west side of Atlin Lake, where supplies from Carcross arrived. Today, you can pan for gold on a placer claim set aside by the provincial government 10 km east of Atlin on Spruce Creek. Or drive 16 km south of town on Warm Springs Rd. past McKee Creek mine to a warm springs. At the end of this road just inside Atlin Provincial Park are views of Llewellyn Glacier, at the northern end of an icefield that extends almost to Juneau. Or just taste the cold mineral spring water at the north end of town under the 65-year-old gazebo. The pioneer cemetery is three km east.

GORDY OHLIGER

YUKON TERRITORY

INTRODUCTION

Yukon Territory covers 483,450 square km (208,000 square miles) of northwestern Canada. This represents just under five percent of Canada's total land area; of the country's 10 provinces and two territories, Yukon ranks number eight in size. To put it into an American perspective, Yukon Territory is 25% larger than California. Yet only 32,600 people live here, giving each resident 15 square km. Almost 75% of them live in the capital, Whitehorse. Honors for the second-largest town has seesawed back and forth between Watson Lake and Dawson, but Dawson is now pulling away with more than 2,000 residents, compared to Watson Lake's 1,800. Some 5,000 Yukoners are native Indians, mostly Athabascan.

The name Yukon comes from *yuchoo,* an Indian word for "Big River." The Yukon River, fourth longest in North America at 3,680 km (2,300 miles), was named in 1846 by John Bell, a Hudson's Bay Company trader. Yukon Territory also has the mightiest mountain range in Canada, great herds of caribou and tiny wriggling iceworms, and beautiful wildflowers that paint the landscape bright pink in the summertime.

The Land

Yukon Territory sits like a great upside-down wedge, bordered by Alaska, British Columbia, Northwest Territories, and the Arctic Ocean. The massive St. Elias Mountains pass through the territory's southwest corner, with Canada's highest peak, Mt. Logan (5,950 meters), the world's largest nonpolar icecap (700 meters deep, feeding glaciers 30 km long), and 20 peaks higher than 3,000 meters. The rest of Yukon is a huge expanse of rolling hills, long narrow lakes, and thick forests (except for the tundra above the Arctic Circle), with the mighty Yukon River draining the southwestern section and the Peel and Mackenzie Rivers draining the northeastern. The Dempster Highway runs 726 km north from Dawson City to Inuvik, Northwest Territories, on the Arctic Ocean, making Canada the only contiguous country in the world with road access to three oceans.

Fauna

Yukon's wildlife is similar to Alaska's. Caribou number in the hundreds of thousands (nearly 300,000 total). Moose are also plentiful at 50,000.

Yukon has 10,000 black bears and upwards of 7,000 grizzlies; 22,000 sheep (Dall and Stone) and 2,000 goats; and 4,500 wolves. There's no one best place to see the local fauna, though Kluane National Park offers perhaps the most accessible backcountry. A woman hiker was stalked and killed by a grizzly bear in Kluane during the 1996 season, the first fatality caused by a bear in the park's history.

HISTORY

The most ancient archaeological evidence (50,000 years old) in the Americas was unearthed at Old Crow, establishing Yukon Indians as the earliest residents of North America. According to oral tradition, the Yukon "First Nations" people have lived here since the beginning of time; Natives can be traced back to roughly 10,000 years ago and today they belong to the Athabascan and Tlingit clans.

It wasn't until 1842 that civilization arrived, when Robert Campbell of Hudson's Bay Company opened the first fur-trading post in this uncharted wilderness. Six years later he opened a second, Fort Selkirk, at the confluence of the Yukon and Pelly Rivers, near present-day Pelly Crossing. In 1870 Canada purchased Rupert's Land, of which Yukon was a part, from the Company. The government didn't show much interest in the area until 1887-88, when George Dawson was sent north at the head of the Canadian Yukon Exploration Expedition. By this time, mining had already replaced fur trading as the region's economic lure; the first prospectors, moving continually north ahead of the peaking gold rushes in British Columbia and southeast Alaska, began cresting the Chilkoot Pass and floating down the Yukon River and filtering into the Klondike Valley.

On August 17, 1896, a sourdough named George Carmack and his two Indian brothers-in-law, Skookum Jim and Tagish Charlie, found gold in the Klondike Valley, thanks to a tip from fellow prospector Robert Henderson. This sparked North America's last great gold rush, which saw upwards of 40,000 stampeders from all points of the compass descend on Dawson, having burst through the barrier of this immense wilderness to open the last frontier. Since the

strike, more than $900 million has been recovered from these goldfields. In 1898 Yukon was separated from Canada's Northwest Territories and Dawson City was made the capital.

The Alaska Highway

After 1900, mining went into a slow decline and nobody paid much attention to the territory until early 1942, when an anticipated Japanese invasion of the western Aleutians prompted President Roosevelt to order construction of a military road northwest through Canada to Alaska. By November, a mere eight months later, the road opened in a ceremony at Soldiers' Summit beside Kluane Lake. Upgrading work continued and by the following year all 2,437 km (1,511 miles) from Dawson Creek, B.C., to Fairbanks had been surfaced in gravel and the 130 bridges had been completed. Some 25,000 men labored on the road for 20 months, at a cost to the U.S. of $140 million.

The Alaska Highway (or "Alcan") had an impact on the Yukon equivalent to that of the Klondike gold rush. Whitehorse replaced Dawson City as the capital in 1953. Road improvements began in earnest in the mid-'70s, and today the Alaska Highway is almost completely paved, except where ongoing construction is replacing stretches of cracked, buckled, and patched road. But although the highway, which celebrated its 50th anniversary in 1992, is the vital link Roosevelt foresaw and a highly scenic route in its own right, to discover the Yukon that Robert Service expressed so well you must take to the rivers and trails, where the real country is waiting.

GENERAL INFORMATION

For info concerning crossing the Canadian border, see "Border Crossings" under "Other Practicalities" in the On the Road chapter. For a 100-page booklet on visiting Yukon, contact Tourism Yukon, P.O. Box 2703, Whitehorse, Canada Y1A 2C6, tel. (403) 667-5340. Yukon time is the same as Pacific time, an hour later than Alaska. Beware of arriving in Yukon without enough Canadian currency to tide you over until you can get to a bank. There are no exchange facilities at the borders and businesspeople give discouraging rates. Large banks in America and

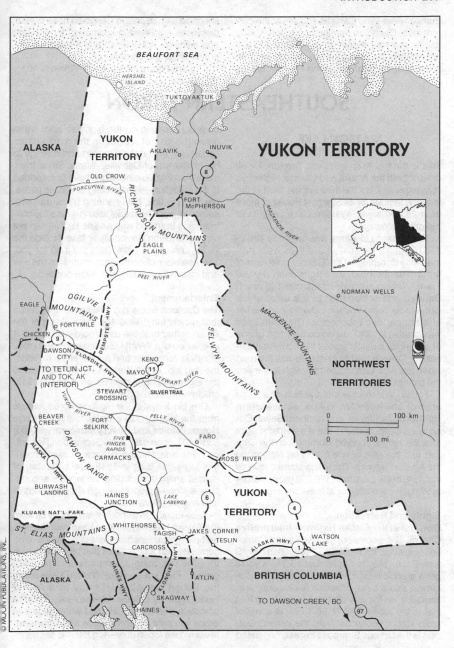

Europe will sell you Canadian dollars at the current rate. Canadian immigration officials may ask to see your money to guarantee you will not compete for scarce jobs or already strained social benefits. All prices in this chapter, unless specified as US$, are in Canadian dollars. Also, distances are listed in kilometers for Canada and miles for Alaska—sorry if it looks schizophrenic near the borders.

The **area code** for the entire Yukon is 403.

SOUTHEASTERN YUKON

WATSON LAKE

This is the first town in Yukon Territory for all drivers: both the Alaska and Cassiar Highways converge here. It's the third-largest town in the territory, famous for its Signpost Forest of more than 25,000 signs. Watson Lake calls itself Yukon's Gateway.

The Watson Lake area was originally inhabited by Kaska Indians, whose lives were permanently disrupted by the Cassiar gold rush of the 1870s. In 1898, an Englishman named Frank Watson abandoned his quest to reach Dawson and settled next to this lake, which came to be called Watson Lake, to lead the life of a trapper and prospector. The town itself was created in 1940, during construction of one of a string of airfields across the northern vastness of Canada, and its existence was ensured when the Alcan was routed through to service the airfield.

Today, Watson Lake is the hub of a large area of southwestern Yukon, southeastern Northwest Territories, and northern British Columbia. Indeed, Watson Lake is a welcome sight after the several hundred kilometers on the Cassiar and the all-day ride from Fort Nelson on the Alaska Highway. The telling statistic reveals that 75% of the more than 175,000 yearly visitors to Watson Lake stay for at least one night.

Sights and Recreation

Stop first at the **Alaska Highway Interpretive Centre,** at the corner of the Alaska and Campbell highways, tel. (403) 536-7469, open daily 9 a.m.-9 p.m. May to September 15. Here you'll get a graphic lesson, via photos, displays, dioramas, and a three-projector audiovisual presentation, on the monumental engineering feat that is the Alcan. CKYN, 96.1 FM, is a visitor radio station broadcast from the center. Outside is the famous **Signpost Forest,** originated by a G.I. working on the highway who, when given the task of repainting the road's directional sign, added the direction and mileage to his hometown of Danville, Illinois. Since then, more than 24,000 other signs have been added to the collection—with town signs, license plates, posters, pie tins, gold-panning pans, mufflers, driftwood, even flywheels stating where the contributor is from and who he/she is. You can put up your addition personally or take it inside the visitor center and have them put it up for you. The chamber of commerce maintains the site and installs new posts as they're needed.

Entertainment

The **Canteen Show** is a musical-comedy revue that recalls the 1940s and the building of the Alcan, rather than the usual gold-rush focus. A re-creation of a WW II USO show, it's performed nightly in June, July, and August at 8 p.m. under the "big top" at the Watson Lake Hotel next to the Signpost Forest. Admission is adults C$17, children under 12 C$8.50.

One block east of the Signpost Forest, across from the Watson Lake Hotel, is the **Heritage House Wildlife and History Museum,** tel. (403) 536-2400, open daily June-September. Reposited in the oldest house in Watson Lake, a beautiful log cabin built in 1948, are a number of stuffed animals, including the world's second-largest stone sheep, plus a gift shop with Native and nugget souvenirs.

Take Eighth Street north a few blocks up from the Alaska Highway to **Wye Lake,** with its park and playground; nature trails encircle the lake, complete with a boardwalk platform from which to view migrating shorebirds and resident grebes. Five km south of Watson Lake along the Robert Campbell Highway (aka Airport Road) is **Lucky Lake,** a day-use recreation area complete with a big S-shaped water slide that drops you right into the shallow and surprisingly warm lake (open June-Aug.); this is the northernmost water slide. There's also a picnic area, a sandy beach, a baseball field, and a five-km hiking trail to Liard River Canyon.

There's a nine-hole par-35 **golf course** nine km north of town, actually west on the Alaska Highway, and a **ski area** with two T-bars north of town off the Robert Campbell Highway, open Dec.-March.

Practicalities

Coming into Watson Lake from the road, you'll be tired and hungry, guaranteed. Half a dozen motels, several campgrounds, and a handful of restaurants are there to serve. The **Cedar Lodge Motel,** tel. (403) 536-7406, charges C$70 for one of its 14 rooms. **Gateway Motor Inn,** tel. (403) 536-7744, also charges C$70 d. **Watson Lake Hotel,** tel. (403) 536-7781, goes up to $95; it has a sauna and some kitchenettes. The **Belvedere Motor Hotel,** tel. (403) 536-7712, has 48 rooms, some with jacuzzis or waterbeds. **Downtown RV Park,** tel. (403) 536-2646, right in the middle of Watson Lake, has full hookups, laundry, showers, and a free car wash with overnight stay; spaces go for $11-18. The **Recreation Park** turnoff is at Km 1025, then

head in three km to the provincial campground: 50 gravel sites, water, pit toilets, C$9.

Both the Belvedere and Watson Lake Hotels have coffee shops and dining rooms. The **Gateway** has the Pizza Palace, serving Italian dishes and pizza. The **Nugget** restaurant serves okay Chinese food at reasonable prices till 10 pm daily. **Country Kitchen** is open for breakfast (from C$4), lunch, and dinner. **Watson Lake Foods** has a bakery and sells groceries Mon.-Sat. 8 a.m.-9 p.m., Sunday 10 a.m.-5 p.m.

TO WHITEHORSE

It's 454 km from Watson Lake to Whitehorse, passing by the Cassiar Mountains. At Km 1043 is the junction with the **Cassiar Highway,** which runs 270 miles down the west side of British Columbia to the Yellowhead Highway. **Junction 37,** tel. (403) 536-2794, is at the intersection, with a Chevron service station, motel, RV park, cafe, and market.

The **Rancheria Motel,** with gas station, restaurant, lounge, groceries, and camping, is at Km 1144, tel. (403) 851-6456. A pullout at Km

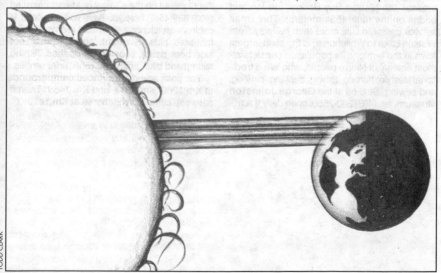

The sun's rays hit the earth at the equator in short, straight, and hot beams; they reach the north country in longer, more angled, and less intense beams. This explains the low rays and golden light of Alaska in summer—a photographer's dream.

1163 marks the **Continental Divide** between rivers that drain (via the Mackenzie system) into the Arctic Ocean and those that empty (via the Yukon) into the Pacific. **Swift River Lodge** at Km 1181, tel. (403) 851-6401, has the usual Alaska Highway set-up: restaurant, gas, repair shop and wrecker service, and souvenirs. As does the **Morley River Lodge,** at Km 1252, tel. (403) 851-6401.

At Km 1282, 11 km south (east) of Teslin, is **Dawson Peaks Northern Resort,** owned and run by David Hett and Carolyn Allen, tel. (403) 390-2310. It's open mid-May through mid-September (when David is on summer vacation from being the principal at Teslin School). The resort, which is right on Teslin Lake, consists of 22 campsites, five cabins, and a sauna, along with one of the best restaurants on the Alaska Highway (steaks, Mexican, fish fry, home baking). You can also rent canoes and boats for the lake, browse the gift shop and bookstore, and arrange for river trips. Be sure to sign the guest book!

Teslin

Coming into Teslin at Km 1,292, the highway crosses the Nisutlin Bay Bridge, the longest bridge on the route (584 meters). This small service center, a little more than halfway from Watson Lake to Whitehorse, is the sixth largest town in the territory. Its population consists almost entirely of Native people, who live a traditional lifestyle: hunting, fishing, trapping, carving, and sewing. Stop off at the **George Johnston Museum,** tel. (403) 390-2550, open daily 9 a.m.-7 p.m. in summer, which has displays of Tlingit culture, Yukon frontier artifacts, and one-of-a-kind photographs taken from 1910 to 1940 by Johnston, a Tlingit hunter, trapper, and photographer and the first car owner in the area.

Teslin has the **Yukon Motel,** tel. (403) 390-2443—cafe, RV park, and boat rentals; **Northlake Motel,** tel. (403) 390-2571—restaurant; and **Halstead's Teslin Lake Resort,** tel. (403) 390-2608—cafe, RV park, and souvenir shop. **Mukluk Annie's Salmon Bake** is 14 km north of Teslin, serving salmon, ribs, steaks, and road food 11 a.m.-9 p.m. daily; take the houseboat ride on the lake after you eat. About two km past Annie's, at Km 1307, is **Teslin Lake Campground,** with 19 sites, pumped water, boat launch, and fishing.

The Rest of the Way to the Big City

Johnson's Crossing is at Km 1346, tel. (403) 390-2607, open May-Sept.: wooded campground (some sites with electricity), Chevron station, groceries, and showers. **Jake's Corner** is next up at Km 1392, tel. (403) 668-2727, with motel, restaurant, and lounge. **Lakeview Resort and Marina** is another 22 km, two km off the highway on the shores of Marsh Lake, tel. (403) 399-4567; here you have your choice of 10 cabins with kitchens, 10 motel rooms, RV and tent sites, plus restaurant, lounge (with an outside beer patio), showers, groceries, fishing, hiking, and bike, boat, and windsurfer rentals.

You pass several **provincial campgrounds** at Km 1366, Km 1432, and Km 1459. Then finally you come to Whitehorse at Km 1470.

GORDY OHLIGER

WHITEHORSE

Windy Whitehorse is a friendly oasis in the heart of an unforgiving land. With 23,000 residents, Whitehorse is the largest city in northern Canada. It squats on the western bank of the Yukon, hemmed in by 60-meter bluffs which create something of a wind tunnel along the river. To the east, the bare rounded hulk of Grey Mountain (1,494 meters) fills the horizon. Whitehorse has its share of gold rush history and nostalgia, but is not dominated by it; as capital of Yukon Territory for the past 44 years, this growing city has a brash, modern frontier energy all its own. It's easy to slip into Whitehorse's strong stream of hustle and bustle, which seems to keep pace with the powerful Yukon itself. Yet the town has a warm, homespun vitality to it, like huddling around the fire on a cold Yukon night.

History
The 25,000 stampeders who braved the Chilkoot or White Pass Trails spent the winter of 1897-98 on the banks of Lindeman or Bennett Lakes, building boats and waiting for break-up. A veritable homemade armada set sail in late May and quickly encountered Miles Canyon and its rapids, some of the roughest waters on the entire Yukon.

The name White Horse was given to the rapids, which reminded miners of the flowing manes of albino Appaloosas. An entry in an early edition of the *Klondike Nugget* described the scene.

Many men who ran these dangerous waters had never handled a boat in their lives until they stopped at Lake Bennett to figure out which end of their oar went into the water. . . . The boats filed into that tremendous first section of the canyon, dodged the whirlpool in the middle, rushed down the second section of the canyon, tossed around for a while in the seething water of the rapids, made that stupendous turn into White Horse, as with rapidly accelerating speed they plunged into the final chaos of angry water. . . .

A few men drowned; many managed to hang onto their lives but lost their boats and grubstakes.

Quickly, the ever-present Mounties instituted some regulations, allowing only expert handlers to pilot the creaky craft through the rapids—Jack London earned $3,000 that summer as a boatman. Undoubtedly, this saved countless lives and supplies from the more than 7,000 boats launched from the lakes after break-up in 1898. Soon after, an eight-kilometer horse-drawn wooden tramway was built around the rapids from Canyon City to the present site of Whitehorse, where goods were reloaded into boats to complete the journey to Dawson City. A tent city sprang up at the tramway's lower end, and Whitehorse was born.

The town's role as a transportation hub began in 1900, when the White Pass & Yukon Route Railroad reached Whitehorse, finally connecting tidewater at Skagway to the Yukon by public transportation. At Whitehorse, passengers and freight transferred to riverboats for the trip down the Yukon River to Dawson City. In 1942-43 this role grew substantially, as did Whitehorse along with it, during the construction of the Alcan Highway; Whitehorse expanded from about 750 people pre-construction to a peak of 40,000 right afterwards. In 1953, Whitehorse eclipsed declining Dawson in population and importance and became the territorial seat of government. Whitehorse today thrives on Alcan traffic, territorial administrative duties, and its function as the main supply center for the mines of Yukon.

SIGHTS

SS *Klondike*
Start your visit with the 25-minute tour of this large sternwheeler, beached at the bottom of Second Avenue. Conducted every half-hour 9-9:30 a.m. and 7 p.m. by extremely knowledgeable and entertaining guides, the tour proceeds from the boiler, freight, and engine deck, up to the dining room and first-class cabins, and finally up to the bridge, one of the highest points in town. Built in 1937, the *Klondike* made 15 roundtrips a season, requiring one and a half days and 40 cords of wood for the downstream trip to Dawson, four and a half days and 120 cords back to Whitehorse. The *Klondike* is beautifully and authentically restored, right down to the 1937 *Life* magazines and the food stains on the waiters' white coats. Bridges erected along the road to Dawson in the mid-1950s blocked the steamers' passage; the last one ran in 1955 and the SS *Klondike* was beached in

Whitehorse in 1960, where it's sat ever since. Admission is $3.25. Don't miss the 20-minute film on the history of riverboats shown in a tent theater next to the *Klondike*.

Town Center
The **chamber of commerce,** 302 Steele St., tel. (403) 667-7545, open daily 8 a.m.-8 p.m., has a ton of brochures about Whitehorse, Dawson, and the rest of the territory, along with the helpful staff you've come to expect in Yukon. A new visitor reception center will open in spring 1997 between Hanson and Lambert and First and Second right across the street from the library.

Walk down Steele St. toward the river for the **MacBride Museum** on First Ave., tel. (403) 667-2709, open daily 10 a.m.-6 p.m. May 15 through September 30, $3. The sod-roofed log cabin contains a large and varied collection including the old government telegraph office, engine no. 51 from the WP&YR, Sam McGee's cabin, a display of stuffed Yukon wildlife, and hundreds of gold-rush photographs. Notice the 1,175-kg copper nugget on the corner of the property.

The **Old Log Church** and rectory (1900) at Third Ave. and Elliot a block from Main have been restored and opened as a museum (C$2) with exhibits on the Native people, early exploration, gold rush, missionary work, and church history. It's open from late May to Labor Day daily 9 a.m.-6 p.m., Sunday 12:30-4 p.m. Nearby, have a look (from the street) at the **log "skyscrapers."**

A couple of blocks away at Second and Hawkins, the big modern **Yukon Government Building** (1976) is worth exploring, open weekdays 9 a.m.-5 p.m. Colorful tapestries and murals interpret the land, history, and people of the Yukon; the acrylic mural on the main floor is 37 meters long, consisting of 24 large panels depicting Yukon history. Downstairs is a good public cafeteria. The library next door has a selection of local books; it's open weekdays 10 a.m.-9 p.m., Saturday 10 a.m.-6 p.m., Sunday 1-9 p.m.

To Miles Canyon
An excellent all-day hike from Whitehorse takes you right around Schwatka Lake, with a number of historical and scenic attractions along the way. Take a lunch. Either set off on your own or contact the Yukon Conservation Society (see "Guided Walks" below) and go on their hike. Begin by

crossing the bridge beside the *Klondike II*. A nature trail leads through the woods on the east bank of the Yukon River, toward the hydro dam (1959) that created Schwatka Lake and tamed the once-feared White Horse Rapids. The world's longest wooden fishway, also built in 1959, allows salmon, grayling, and longnose suckers to get around the dam and up to their spawning grounds upriver. Three underwater windows inside the fishway building give you a good look at the chinook; displays tell the whole story.

Above the dam is a high hill, which the more energetic may want to climb for the view. Go down the other side (or around along the shore) to Chadburn Lake Road. Follow this road south till you see some paths along the lake or river; follow any one for a more enjoyable walk. Above the lake the Yukon River flows through spectacular Miles Canyon. A path along the canyon leads to Lowe Suspension (1923), first bridge across the Yukon, crossing to the west side. The views along here are superb.

Continue 1.5 km beyond the bridge, staying on the east side, to find the site of Canyon City. The opening of the railway in 1900 put an end to river travel above Whitehorse, and Canyon City disappeared. Today, nothing remains at the site but some old tin cans and the gentle grade of the tramway, now a cross-country ski route. Return to the suspension bridge; on the west side, Miles Canyon Rd. runs five km back to Whitehorse.

One km before town, follow the signs to the MV *Schwatka* excursion boat, tel. (403) 668-4716, which leaves from a dock on the lake near the dam for two-hour cruises at 2 and 7 p.m., C$17 adult, C$8.50 child.

Buses (C$1.25) run along South Access Rd. into town every hour until 6:20 p.m. (except Sunday) and will stop to pick you up if you wave. You can also pay for a transfer on Gray Line.

Yukon Gardens

These botanical gardens, the only ones north of Vancouver, encompass 22 acres, with over 1,000 species of plants and 250,000 annuals; 17,000 gallons of water are pumped daily to maintain them. Considering that Whitehorse is limited to 72 frost-free days a year, it should come as no surprise that it took seven years to establish the gardens. (By comparison, Vancouver enjoys 216 frost-free days a year.) Yukon Gardens is located at the intersection of the Alaska Highway and South Access Rd., tel. (403) 668-7972, open daily 9 a.m.-9 p.m., $10 admission; buy some fresh vegetables while you're there.

Yukon Visitor Reception Center

This dramatic visitor center, on the Alaska Highway in front of the airport, tel. (403) 667-2915, open daily 8 a.m.-8 p.m. mid-May to mid-September, opened during the Alaska Highway's 50th-anniversary celebrations in June 1992. The entrance is reminiscent of a tall ship, with large billowing sails and curved beams, and guy wires all around. The first room you come to inside is the Wash Pavilion, where at least a dozen shiny, luxurious, and private bathrooms await your (toilet and sink) pleasure (the mirrors, however, cut off the heads of everyone taller than five-foot-two); it's domed with a simulation of the night sky around a skylight. The Great Hall has the information counter, local displays, a laser-disc video presentation, and a spectacular 12,000-year-old four-meter-tall woolly mammoth skeleton, Yukon's typical ice age mammal. There's also a 200-seat theater where you can relax and try not to fall asleep during the 20-minute moving slide presentation. Aw, what the hell—go ahead and catch 20 winks. It's certainly comfortable enough.

Yukon Transportation Museum

Walk next door to wake up! Inside is one of the finest museums in the north, open daily 11 a.m.-8 p.m., C$3.50 adult, C$2 child, where you could easily spend an entire morning or afternoon examining the many excellent displays and watching the several long historical videos. Here's just a sample: look up to view *Queen of the Yukon*, the first commercial aircraft in the territory, hanging from the ceiling; take the "Golden Stairs" up to the second floor, where murals and artifacts re-create the gold rush from Skagway to Dawson; sit in Lake Annie, a White Pass & Yukon Route railcar, and watch the 30-minute video while the model train circles the track; check out the Alcan room with a fascinating video on the highway's construction, the Canol Road exhibit, the dogsled room with Yukon Quest photos, the winter travel display, the stagecoach, jeeps, dozers, bicycles, mooseskin boots, and the early civilian-travel exhibit (the Alcan was opened to the public in 1948), including the first edition of the venerable *Mile-*

post from 1949. The museum is one of the highlights of Whitehorse, and Yukon—in fact, the whole North Country.

Takhini Hot Springs

These are excellent natural mineral-water hot springs, 36° C (96° F) with no sulphur. The huge pool is filled 8-10 a.m. and drained at 10 p.m. The pool costs C$9 for all day, to camp is C$7, or pay C$14 for both. Lockers are a quarter. If you don't want to pay, follow the overflow "creek" to where the locals have dug out a public pool. The dining facility is more of a snack bar than a bona-fide coffee shop, with C$6 bacon and eggs and burgers, and some of the best chicken soup north of San Francisco; there's a big relief map of the vicinity on the wall, with skiing, hiking, and horse trails outlined (horseback riding available). Go 16 km from Whitehorse to the Klondike Loop Highway, turn right, go five km, turn left at the sign, then go 10 km to Takhini. There's no public transportation, though you could take the Kopper King bus from the depot (see "By Bus" under "Transportation," below) to get close to the junction, then hitch the rest of the way. The 62-km roundtrip would only add $15 to your rental-car bill. A taxi is C$35 one-way. A good way to do it with your own car is to plan on spending the night on the way to and from Dawson. But be sure to get there before around 7 or 8 p.m., or plan to stay into the next morning, so you can have a few hours in the pool.

Guided Walks

A 45-minute walking tour of downtown Whitehorse heritage buildings is led by volunteers from the **Yukon Historical & Museums Association.** It leaves from the Donnenworth House, 3126 Third Ave., tel. (403) 667-4704, 9 a.m.-4 p.m.; C$2. If the tour times don't fit into your plans, stop by the Donnenworth House, pick up the walking tourbook, and take a self-guided tour. The **Yukon Conservation Society,** 302 Hawkins St., tel. (403) 668-5678, leads a variety of hikes, from two to six hours, several times a day in July and August. The hikes are free; bring mosquito repellent, wear sturdy boots, and have a lunch for the longer excursions. You can also buy self-guiding trail booklets at the office and set out on your own.

PRACTICALITIES

Accommodations

Whitehorse has a surprising number of motels and hotels for its size: 22, accounting for nearly 900 rooms. The competition, of course, works to the traveler's advantage, and some of the digs are actually affordable.

Fort Yukon Hotel, Second and Black, tel. (403) 667-2594, has spartan rooms with shared bath for C$40 s and C$45 d, C$47 s and C$49 d private bath. If you don't mind commuting, the **Kopper King Motel,** five km west on the Alaska Highway (Km 1477), tel. (403) 668-2347, has rooms for C$45 s, C$55 d. **Chilkoot Trail Inn** on Fourth Ave. across from Qwanlin Mall, tel. (403) 668-4190, has large pleasant rooms with cooking facilities for C$45 s, C$65 d. **High Country Inn,** 4051 Fourth Ave. across the street from the Klondike, tel. (403) 667-4471, is a large

In 1900, riverboats crowded Whitehorse's bustling waterfront, where goods and supplies, people, and gold were transferred to and from the new White Pass and Yukon Route Railroad, completing the route from tidewater at Skagway to Dawson on the Klondike.

YUKON ARCHIVES

lodging facility with a variety of rooms, starting at C$45 for a small single and going all the way up to C$129 for the fanciest suite. It's right next to the Lion's Swimming Pool.

Six hotels are strung along Main St. between Fifth and First Avenues. They all have interesting lobbies, large dining rooms, comfortable and dark lounges, and individual character. **Gold Rush Inn,** 411 Main, tel. (403) 668-4500, has a big boardwalk along Main, balustrades over the second-story windows, unusual "hardwood carpet" complete with nail heads, and an old-time barber shop and beauty parlor. Some rooms sport jacuzzis, wet bars and kitchenettes, and bunk beds. Rates are C$95 s and C$105 d. The **Town and Mountain (T&M) Hotel** is on the corner of Main and Fourth, tel. (403) 668-7644, C$79 s, C$84 d; it has the largest of the lounges along Main, in modern pastels with a big dance floor. The **Taku Hotel** is right across Fourth, tel. (403) 668-4545, C$75 s, C$84 d; its lounge is also quite expansive and has a large video screen. The **Capital Hotel,** at 103 Main, tel. (403) 667-2565, is the least expensive of the bunch (C$54 s, C$65 d), as well as the most "historical"; it has clean beds with springs, hot baths with soap, whiskey by the shot, and even painted ladies inside. The **Edgewater Hotel** next door, 101 Main, tel. (403) 667-2572, could be the fanciest; it certainly has the fanciest prices: C$110 s C$132 d. It also has two dining rooms (see below).

Robert Service Campground is two km south of town by the river off South Access Rd., tel. (403) 668-3721. For tenters only, it gets very crowded during the summer. The gate is locked midnight-7 a.m., and there are two showers in the bathrooms (no shower curtains). It's C$11 per night per tent. Register at the office, where there's a very useful message board and a pay phone. If the Robert Service is full or you don't want to pay, continue walking south past the dam along the shoreline. Plenty of good places to pitch a tent are found in the woods just above the lake. Other unofficial places to camp are along the top of the bluff above town toward the airport (walk up Cook St. from Qwanlin Mall and along the trails to the top), and on Kishwoot Island. Head west out Second Ave. and look for the big parking lot across from the Chevron station. Walk by the No Camping sign, cross the new suspension bridge, and get lost in the undergrowth. This place is very

convenient to the bus station; you can see the bridge from the depot parking lot. It's not windy, either. But stay well out of sight.

There are a score or two of **bed and breakfasts** in Whitehorse; call the chamber of commerce for the phone numbers of several. Rates start at C$50 s and C$60 d and go up to C$120 s and C$130 d.

Food

Mom's Kitchen, on Second by Fort Yukon Hotel, has filling breakfasts and a local-color setting, open Mon.-Fri. 7 a.m.-8 p.m., Saturday 7 a.m.-3 p.m. **Blues Moose** is the upscale coffee shop at the Yukon Inn, Fourth Ave. across from the bright bright golden arches, serving eggs and meat breakfasts C$6-9, crab and shrimp omelette C$9, a variety of "eggs Benny's," burgers C$6, veggie burger C$7, pizza C$12-18, and burritos C$6-10. Sit on the deck or get entertained by rhythm and blues players while you dine inside (Thurs.-Sat.).

No Pop Sandwich Shop, Fourth and Steele, open Mon.-Thur. 7:30 a.m.-8:30 p.m., Friday till 9:30 p.m., Saturday and Sunday 10 a.m.-8:30 p.m., has the most unassuming appearance in relation to its coffee house coziness on the inside. Breakfast fare includes eggs Benedict, crepes, and omelettes for C$8; good wholesome sandwiches are C$4-6; the fresh bakery products go great with the coffee drinks; you can also get liquor and beer. The **Talisman Cafe,** on Second between Main and Steele, is one of the cultural centers of the capital. The atmosphere is heady, the service is excellent, and the food is, well, see for yourself. Breakfast (6-11 a.m.): one egg and bacon C$6, french toast C$7, omelettes C$6; lunch (11 a.m.-5 p.m.): salads C$4-5, veggie sandwich C$6, veggie burrito C$8, piroshki C$10; dinner (6-10 p.m.): turkey jambalaya C$10, Middle Eastern combo C$9, pesto pasta C$10, kabobs C$11. They serve espresso, beer, wine, and fine desserts. Can't go wrong here.

Next door to the Talisman at the corner of Second and Steele is the **Klondike Rib and Salmon Barbecue,** open Mon.-Fri. 11 a.m.-10 p.m., Saturday noon-10 p.m., and Sunday 4-10 p.m. For lunch try burgers $8, smoked salmon on rye C$9, a small filet C$9, or chicken fingers C$8; dinner choices include salmon steak C$17, halibut C$19, Danish pork ribs half rack C$13, barbecued chicken breast C$13, caribou or musk ox stroganoff C$19, and various combo plates.

Sam and Andy's, Main near Fifth across from Gold Rush Inn, open Mon.-Fri. for lunch 11:30 a.m.-2 p.m. and dinner 4:30-10 p.m., weekends just for dinner, is another Whitehorse cultural phenomenon like the Talisman. Chicken lime soup is C$3.50; seafood chowder C$4.75; nachos C$9; wings C$6; *hamburgesas* C$8; enchiladas, tacos, and tostadas C$10; fajitas C$21; combos for two C$22; specials C$13-18. **Arizona Charlies** in the Westmark Inn, Second Ave. Extension, serves expensive Mexican: quesadillas C$13, fajitas C$14, margaritas C$5.

The **Parthenon,** on Main across from the capitol, serves American, Greek, and Italian for lunch and dinner, open Mon.-Fri. 11 a.m.-2 p.m., and daily 4:30-11 p.m. Try some Greek pizza (C$10-22), souvlaki or moussaka, lasagna, steak, king crab, or salmon, all in the C$13-25 range.

Across the street at the **Edgewater,** you can grab a bargain bite with your booze in the Gallery Lounge, open Mon.-Sat. 2-9 p.m.: prime rib C$13, halibut C$12, chicken schnitzel C$10. The Cellar is the fine dining room, serving appetizers like smoked salmon pate C$7 and oysters casino C$9; Caesar or Greek salad C$7, filet C$26, prime rib C$25, peppercorn steak C$25, and seafood C$22-40.

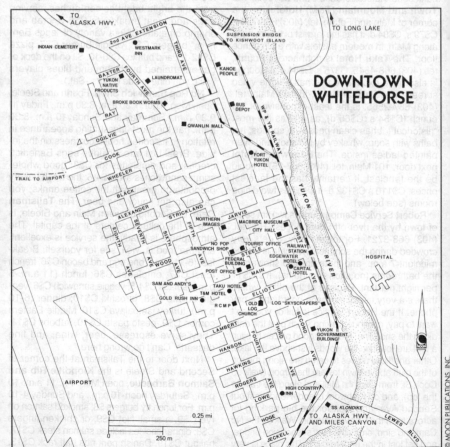

DOWNTOWN WHITEHORSE

Extra Foods in the Qwanlin Mall, Fourth and Ogilvie, sells some bulk food, good produce (for Yukon), and a stunning selection of boxed juices. **Yukon Health Food Centre,** 504 Main, has nuts, dried fruits, energy bars, cereals, etc. **Food For Thought** is the other health-food store, at Fourth and Wood, a block from the No Pop.

The fast food is mostly found on Second St. around the Greyhound bus depot: **Subway, Taco Time,** and **Pizza Hut.** There's another supermarket, **Food Fair,** right across the street from Greyhound.

Entertainment
Kopper King (a.k.a. the KK), five km west of town on the Alcan, hops to live country most nights.

Frantic Follies is one of many vaudeville revues along the route that harken back to the Days of '98 with songs, skits, cancan, and Robert Service recitations. The Follies are performed at the Westmark Whitehorse, Second and Wood, tel. (403) 668-2042, at 7 p.m. and 9:15 p.m. most of the summer, C$17.50 adults, C$8.75 under 12. The **Canteen Show** takes a lighthearted look at the Alaska Highway construction with 1940s nostalgia, music, and comedy. It plays in the Gold Rush Inn; tickets for the 90-minute performance are C$16.50 adult, C$7.50 child.

Twin Cinemas is out by the mall; **Yukon Theatre** is at the corner of Third and Wood, around from the chamber of commerce; call (403) 668-6644 for schedules.

Shopping
An outstanding array of items made by the Indians and Natives of Canada's Northwest Territories is sold at **Northern Images,** Fourth Ave. and Jarvis, tel. (403) 668-5739. This large store is owned by a Native co-op, and all of the articles are handmade. Even if you're not buying, Northern Images is well worth a visit and is better than most museums. Get to know your endangered species! Remember that clothing or souvenirs made from animals considered endangered (including lynx, wolf, grizzly bear, and polar bear) or from marine mammals (whales, porpoises, seals, sea lions, walruses, and otters) are prohibited from entry into the United States, as is ivory. For handicrafts made by Yukon Indians, including mukluks, parkas, and birch-bark and porcupine-quill baskets, visit **Yukon Native Products,** 4330 Fourth Ave., across from McDonald's.

Mac's Fireweed, 203 Main St., is open Mon.-Sat. 9 a.m.-9 p.m., Sunday and holidays 10 a.m.-7 p.m., and has a large selection of local- and general-interest books, children's books, magazines, and sundries. **Broke Book Worms,** right across from the Real Canadian superstore at Qwanlin Mall, tel. (403) 633-6214, open 9 a.m.-9 p.m., is the place to trade in your used paperbacks for other used paperbacks.

TRANSPORTATION

By Air
The airport is right above town on the bluff. Get there by going west out Fourth to the Alaska Highway and take a left, or go east out Second and turn right. On foot, follow the path along the fence around the northwest end of the runway and over to the bluff. A cab costs C$8, or call Yellow Cab to arrange for the airport limo, C$5 pp, which meets all flights. You can't miss the "world's largest weathervane"—the restored DC-3 (mounted on a moveable pedestal) that points its nose into the wind.

Canadian Airlines, tel. (800) 665-1177 or (403) 668-4466, has service to and from Vancouver and Edmonton. **Air North,** tel. (403) 668-2228, flies four times a week to Dawson, Fairbanks, and Juneau, and they have a charter service. **Alcan Air,** tel. (800) 661-0432 or (403) 668-2107, is one of several commuter airlines with scheduled service to places like Inuvik, Old Crow, Mayo, Faro, Ross River, Dawson City, and Watson Lake.

By Bus
The bus depot is on Second Ave. behind the Qwanlin Mall, tel. (403) 668-2223. Whitehorse is the northern terminus for **Greyhound;** none of their buses runs north or west of here. One bus a day departs for points east and south at noon (except Sunday).

Alaskon Express, or Gray Line of Yukon, tel. (403) 668-3225, departs Whitehorse for Fairbanks and Anchorage three-four times a week; these buses overnight in Beaver Creek (lodging not included in price). You can get off and/or transfer in Tok. They also depart for Skagway

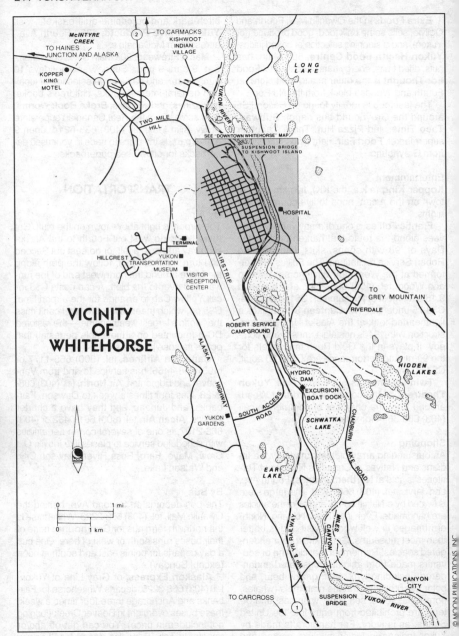

TO CARMACKS
KISHWOOT
INDIAN
VILLAGE

McINTYRE
CREEK
TO HAINES
JUNCTION AND ALASKA

KOPPER
KING
MOTEL

LONG
LAKE

YUKON RIVER

TWO MILE
HILL

SEE "DOWNTOWN WHITEHORSE" MAP

SUSPENSION BRIDGE
TO KISHWOOT ISLAND

HOSPITAL

TERMINAL

HILLCREST

YUKON
TRANSPORTATION
MUSEUM

AIRSTRIP

VISITOR
RECEPTION
CENTER

TO GREY MOUNTAIN

RIVERDALE

VICINITY
OF
WHITEHORSE

ROBERT SERVICE
CAMPGROUND

ALASKA HIGHWAY

HIDDEN
LAKES

HYDRO
DAM

EXCURSION
BOAT DOCK

YUKON
GARDENS

SOUTH ACCESS ROAD

SCHWATKA
LAKE

CHADBURN LAKE ROAD

0   1 mi

0   1 km

EAR
LAKE

WP & YR RAILWAY

MILES CANYON

CANYON
CITY

TO CARCROSS

SUSPENSION
BRIDGE

YUKON RIVER

© MOON PUBLICATIONS, INC.

daily. The buses depart from the bus terminal and the Westmark Whitehorse. Days of departure and fares change annually, so be sure to call for the current schedules.

Alaska Direct, tel. (403) 668-4833, offers regularly scheduled bus service to Anchorage and Fairbanks three times weekly, and to Skagway daily.

Norline Coaches, tel. (403) 668-3355, leaves for Dawson at 9 a.m. from the bus depot Monday, Wednesday, and Friday, arriving at 3:30 p.m. It's recommended to take the northern route—more scenic, more historic—through the Yukon into Alaska, via Dawson, Top of the World Highway, Eagle, and the Taylor Highway. Note, however, that ground connections die in Dawson. Beyond there, you can hitch or fly—your only choices.

By Train
The **White Pass & Yukon Route** trains are happily back on track (a part of it, anyway). Buses leave Whitehorse at 8:30 a.m. and connect to the WP&YR narrow gauge at Fraser, B.C., at 10:20 a.m., arriving in Skagway at noon; US$95. The train depot is right downtown at the corner of First and Main. For reservations, call (403) 668-RAIL.

By Boat
The most authentic way to travel from Whitehorse to Dawson is by canoe in 10-15 days, the way the stampeders did it before the advent of the sternwheelers. This is quite feasible and easily arranged; several outfits in Whitehorse supply everything required at a reasonable price. **Kanoe People** is the least expensive and most

friendly, renting two-person canoes, which come with two life preservers and three paddles. Drop your boat off in Dawson with the Kanoe People agent up there. They also have shorter trips, such as to Carmacks and the Teslin River or the Big Salmon River, and lead guided wilderness trips. Write P.O. Box 5152, Whitehorse, Yukon Y1A 4S3; or call (403) 668-4899.

Or try **Tatshenshini Expediting,** 1602 Alder, Whitehorse, Yukon Y1A 3W8, tel. (403) 633-2742. When checking around, remember to ask about drop-off charges, life preservers, etc. You could also buy a canoe for about C$600 at the Hudson's Bay Co. and paddle yourself right into Alaska, terminating at Eagle, Circle, or the Dalton Highway.

By Thumb
To hitch west take the Porter Creek bus and ask the driver to drop you off as far out as he goes on the Alaska Highway. To hitch east take the Hillcrest bus to the corner of Alaska Highway and South Access Road.

Getting Around
Whitehorse Transit buses (C$1.25) run Mon.-Sat. 6:15 a.m.-7 p.m. (to 10 p.m. on Friday). Pick up a schedule at the visitor center or from the drivers. Day passes are available from drivers for C$3, as are transfers. All routes begin and end beside Hudson's Bay Co. opposite Qwanlin Mall. Bus stops are clearly marked with blue-and-white signs.

Avis, tel. (403) 667-2847; **Budget,** tel. (403) 667-6200; **Rent-A-Wreck,** tel. (403) 668-7554; and **Norcan,** tel. (403) 668-2137, rent cars. All have a desk or a courtesy phone at the airport.

ALASKA HIGHWAY TO BEAVER CREEK

Unless you're in a hurry to reach mainland Alaska, heading specifically to Kluane National Park, or going to Anchorage by public transportation, it's highly recommended to take the Klondike Highway to Dawson, over the Top of the World Highway into Alaska, up to historic Eagle, and down to Tok on the Taylor Highway. This adds only 400 km (250 miles) onto the distance between Whitehorse and Fairbanks or Anchorage on the Alaska Highway (and just 192 km/120 miles if you

bypass Eagle). It also completes the Trail of '98 and includes Dawson, a must-stop on any Northern itinerary. If you do take the "low road" to Alaska, it's 180 km (108 miles) to Haines Junction, 300 km (180 miles) from there to Beaver Creek, and 140 miles (224 km) from there to Tok.

Government campgrounds are found at Km 1543, Km 1602, and Km 1628. Thirteen km west of Whitehorse is the turnoff for Dawson (right) onto the Klondike Loop (see below). At

Km 1568 is **Champagne,** which grew up in the gold rush and is now home to the Champagne Indian Band. The cemetery by the side of the highway is not for public inspection; please respect the private property. A couple of dozen kilometers east of Haines Junction, the Kluane Icefield Ranges and the foothills of the St. Elias Mountains start to dominate the view; when it's clear, Mt. Kennedy and Mt. Hubbard loom high and white.

At Km 1604, just 21 km east of Haines Junction, is a bridge over the Aishihik River at Canyon Creek. The original log bridge, built in the early 1900s, was rebuilt in 1942 during Alcan construction, only to be abandoned when the road was rerouted a year later. Territorial engineers rebuilt the original bridge in 1987. Walk out on the bridge to compare the log action with the steel-supported highway bridge.

HAINES JUNCTION

Sights

Established in 1942 as a base camp for the U.S. Army Corps of Engineers connecting the Alcan with Haines, this town of 800 is the largest between Whitehorse and Tok, and growing. It's the gateway to Kluane National Park, the only national park in Yukon. Stop at the village square near the intersection of the Alaska and Haines Highways, where a grotesque sculpture of mountains, mammals, and humans has been plopped—part, ironically, of a Yukon beautification program. It looks more like a misshapen cupcake with really ugly icing. While there, read the signboards describing the history and attractions of the Haines Junction area and sign the gigantic guest book. Just up the road toward Whitehorse is **Our Lady of the Wake Church,** built in 1954 by a Catholic priest who converted an old Quonset hut by adding a wooden front, a shrine on top, and a steeple with bell in back. **St. Christopher's** log church nearby is also photogenic.

Practicalities

Haines Junction is a convenient rest stop 160 km from Whitehorse, with another 500 miles to go to Fairbanks. It has four motels: **Mountain View Motor Inn,** tel. (403) 634-2646, open year-round; **Gateway Motel,** tel. (403) 643-2371; **Kluane Park Inn,** tel. (403) 634-2261; and **Cozy Corner,** tel. (403) 634-2511. There's also **The Raven,** tel. (403) 634-2500, the newest digs in town, a nonsmoking hotel with 12 rooms, a fine-dining restaurant (room service available and breakfast included), and an art gallery/gift shop. You can't miss it; the Raven looks like a modular mansion, right in the middle of town.

There's one private campground and RV park, **Kluane RV Kampground,** tel. (403) 634-2709, with wooded campsites, excellent showers, gas and diesel, and groceries. Nearest public camping is at **Pine Lake,** seven km east of town on the Alaska Highway—the usual excellent Yukon facility (C$10) with 33 sites, water, firewood, picnic tables, children's playground, and cold swimming in the lake. Or pitch your tent unofficially behind the vehicle way station or just before the bridge on the road to Haines.

The Cozy Corner and Mountain View have restaurants. **Village Bakery,** across the road from the Park Visitor Centre, is a popular hangout; open daily 7:30 a.m.-9 p.m., they sell delicious baked goods and gooeyness, such as muffins, strudels, donuts, and cheese sticks, as well as breads, croissant sandwiches, soups, quiche, lasagna, meat pies, and whatever else the good cooks feel like creating. Perfect for a snack, lunch, or dinner if you can't stand the thought of more road food. If you can, the **Frostee Freez,** open 11 a.m.-11 p.m., has burgers, dogs, fish and chips, shakes, and the like.

Madley's General Store's motto is "We've Got It All," and it's not too far from the truth. Here you can pick up groceries, fruit and meat, sundries, hardware, paint, magazines, lottery tickets, fishing and camping supplies, and more; the bank (open Tuesday and Friday 8-9 a.m. and Mon.-Thurs. 12:30-3:30 p.m., Friday till 4:30 p.m.) and a post office are also inside. Next door is the **Territorial Administration Building,** with the library and a liquor store.

The **community swimming pool** is on Kluane St. (across from the visitor center); check the door for hours. For the Kluane National Park visitor center, see below.

Hitching *to* Alaska, it's rare you'll get stuck at Haines Junction unless your ride is stopping to explore Kluane (in which case do the same!); but most likely your ride won't be getting off the

Alcan to go to Haines. Most hitchhikers get stuck here heading out from Alaska, though you can always change your plans and catch the ferry in Haines Junction if that's where the wheels are heading. Either way, it's not hard to get a ride at the junction, but if your road karma is failing you temporarily, Alaskon motorcoaches pass through Haines Junction on the way to and from Alaska, stopping at the Mountain View Inn on various days of the week. Note that technically you can't buy a ticket from Haines Junction to Whitehorse, since Alaskon Express is not a common carrier within the Yukon—though unofficially it's up to the driver's discretion.

KLUANE NATIONAL PARK

The lofty icecapped mountains of southwest Yukon, overflowing with glaciers and flanked by lower ranges rich in wildlife, have been set aside as Kluane National Park. Although the Alaska and Haines Highways, which run along the fringe of the park, make it accessible, Kluane is a wilderness hardly touched by human hands; once you leave the highways you will see few other people. No roads run into the park itself, so to experience the true magnificence of this wilderness you must embark on an overnight

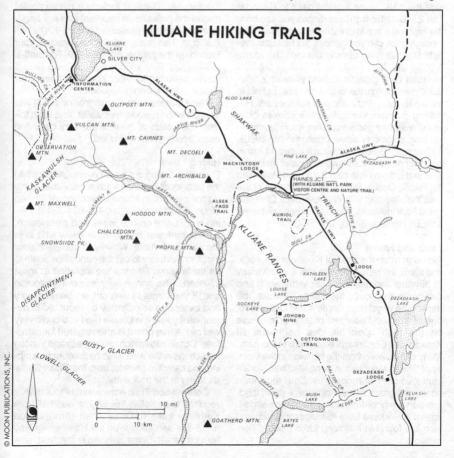
KLUANE HIKING TRAILS

hike. Signposts identify the trailheads, and all the trails offer splendid mountain scenery and a good chance to see wildlife. The fishing (Kluane means "Place of Many Fish") is also superb. Buy a license to fish in Kluane, as well as any national park in Canada (a territorial license is not required).

The Land

The St. Elias Range, running from Alaska through Yukon to British Columbia, is the highest mountain range in North America and the second-highest coastal range in the world (the Andes are first). Mount Logan (5,950 meters), totally inside the park, is the highest peak in Canada. The 2,500-meter-high front ranges you see from the highways are impressive enough, but only through gaps can you glimpse the fantastic Icefield Ranges lying directly behind. The many 5,000-meter-high peaks of this range are surrounded by a gigantic icefield plateau 2,500-3,000 meters high, the largest nonpolar icefield in the world, occupying a little over half the park. Radiating out from the icefield like spokes on a wheel are valley glaciers up to six km wide and 60 km long, some very active. During the late 1960s, for example, Steele Glacier advanced 11 km in only four months. Kaskawulsh Glacier is unusual in that it drains into both the Yukon River and the Pacific Ocean. Such is the importance of the area that, together with Wrangell-Saint Elias National Park in Alaska, Kluane has been declared a World Heritage Site by UNESCO.

Flora and Fauna

Although more than half of Kluane is ice, rock, and snow, the remainder includes a wide variety of climates and habitats, drier in the north and damper in the south; the wetter the area, the denser the vegetation. Some 4,000 Dall sheep, one of the world's largest populations, reside on the high open hillsides northwest of Kaskawulsh Glacier and elsewhere in the park. Many can be seen from the highway in the vicinity of Sheep Mountain. Kluane also has significant numbers of moose, caribou, mountain goats, and grizzly bears. Kokanee, a dwarf landlocked variety of freshwater sockeye salmon, spawn in Sockeye Lake (fishing prohibited) and also are found in Kathleen Lake (fishing permitted).

Flightseeing

Flightseeing over the park is available from the Haines Junction Airport. The one-hour flight (starting at C$90 pp) affords a spectacular view of Mt. Logan plus several glaciers and is highly recommended if you happen to be there on a clear day. Contact **Sifton Air,** tel. (403) 634-2916. You can also take the scenic helicopter flight over the park offered by **Trans North Helicopters,** tel. (403) 634-2242.

Practicalities

The **Kluane National Park Visitor Centre** at Haines Junction is open daily 9 a.m.-9 p.m. in the summer. Displays include a riveting relief map of the park and an excellent free sight-and-sound slide show presented hourly 9:30 a.m.-7:30 p.m. This is a great place to practice your French: all the exhibits are bilingual. The staff is multilingual. Buy a topographical map here if you're planning to hike. You also have your choice of two hiking guidebooks.

The **Kathleen Lake Campground** (C$3) has 41 sites with firewood, well water, and flush toilets. The waters of the lake are very clear and deep, and the fishing is good.

Hiking

Everyone setting out on an overnight hike into the park must register in advance, either at the visitor centers in Haines Junction or Sheep Mountain or by phone (tel. 403-634-2345). Hiking is free and no one is refused permission, but the park wardens want to know who is in the park and where. When you complete your trip, it's mandatory to call the park office again to let them know. Phones are installed at most trailheads. This system is for your own protection and, if you forget to sign out, an unnecessary and expensive search may be mounted to determine if you are in trouble (and you could very well be). A free permit is also required for campfires. Obtain information on the trails and various attractions in the area, plus backcountry camping and campfire permits, from the Parks Canada trailer at the trailheads.

Cottonwood Trail: A minimum of four days is required to complete this 85-km loop trail from Kathleen Lake to Dezadeash (pronounced "DEZ-dee-ash") Lodge on the Haines Highway (or vice versa). Some climbing is involved, several creeks must be waded across, and portions of the trail can be difficult to follow. The dividend is a great variety of plants and wildlife: many ptarmigan can be seen in the alpine areas, and watch for Dall sheep on the steep slopes. This is also prime grizzly habitat. You'll see many signs of old copper and placer gold-mining sites along the way. Primitive campsites are found at Goat Creek and where Dalton Creek crosses Mush Lake Road.

From the Kathleen Lake Campground you follow an old mining road along the south shores of Kathleen and Louise Lakes. Goat and Victoria Creeks must be forded. Beyond Victoria Creek the road continues through the spruce forest, passing the ruins of the Johobo Mine where copper was extracted in the 1960s. From the mine continue along a trail cut through the forest, across some meadows, up a creek bed, then across a long stretch of alpine tundra to Dalton Creek and the Mush Lake Rd., which leads back out to Dezadeash Lodge. The great cheeseburgers with fries (C$4) served at the lodge reward you at the end of the trail.

Auriol Trail: This 19-km loop trail begins six km south of Haines Junction and can be done in a day. There are excellent views from several points and a great variety of plant and animal life. About one km up the trail take the fork to the right, which climbs steeply to the treeline; the left-hand side is more gradual and safer for the descent. The creek, located halfway up both forks of the trail, is narrow and easy to cross. A primitive campground is near the top on the left-hand side of the loop.

Alsek Pass Trail (Dezadeash-Alsek River Valley): This 24-km trail begins near Mackintosh Lodge, 10 km west of Haines Junction, and is relatively flat and easy to follow. The first 21 km take you on an abandoned mining road that ends at a washout; the last three km lead to Sugden Creek. Just 125 years ago this area was submerged under a lake that formed when Lowell Glacier pushed up against the west side of Goatherd Mountain, blocking the Alsek River. The lake, which once extended up the Dezadeash River well beyond Haines Junction and rose as much as 81 meters above present river levels, drained when the glacier receded. Today the old beach line is clearly visible as a sandy strip, complete with driftwood, high along

the hillsides in the Dezadeash, Alsek, and Kaskawulsh river valleys. Also look for the rare plants on the sand dunes at the junction of the Dezadeash and Kaskawulsh Rivers.

Slims River Trail: This is perhaps the best short (24 km one-way) hike in Kluane National Park because it offers old mining relics, excellent wildlife viewing, and a spectacular look at Kaskawulsh Glacier at the base of the St. Elias Mountains. The trail begins near the Sheep Mountain information trailer and leads up the west side of the Slims River. The first nine km are on an old mining road. After the road ends you have to find your way between the hillside and the riverbed. There are three major creeks to cross. The trail ends at Observation Mountain, which should be climbed for the classic view of the Kaskawulsh. Several side trails go off to the right. The first leads up to Sheep Creek Canyon (6.5 km one-way), where abundant wildlife may be found. The second runs into the historic Bullion Creek placer gold-mining area (9.5 km one-way). Another route up the east side of the Slims is often easier due to fewer creek crossings.

THE REST OF THE WAY TO ALASKA

To Beaver Creek

For 250 of the next 300 km to Beaver Creek, you're passing right next to Kluane National Park or Kluane Game Sanctuary—a comparatively well-populated, civilized, and stunningly scenic stretch of the Alaska Highway. There are three provincial campgrounds (Km 1725, Km 1853, and Km 1913), along with three little settlements and a dozen lodges. At **Soldier's Summit,** Km 1707, a sign commemorates the official opening of the Alcan on November 20, 1942, a mere eight months after construction began; an interpretive trail from the parking area leads up to the site of the dedication ceremony.

Destruction Bay is the tiny town at Km 1743. It was named when the original road-construction camp was destroyed by a wind storm in 1942. Destruction Bay has a Chevron station, Talbot Arm Motel (tel. 403-841-4461), a cafeteria and dining room, an RV park, a general store, and a gift shop; there's also a school and a playground, a road-maintenance station, and territorial offices.

Only 16 km west is **Burwash Landing,** tel. (403) 841-4441, where the Destruction Bay residents, it seems, come to play. The Kluane Museum (and handicrafts shop) has a wildlife exhibit, a large model of the area, a mammoth tooth, fossils, and a mineral display. Hotel rooms start at C$60 s and go up to C$80. You can also boat and fish in the lake from here; guides are available. The cafeteria is huge, there's a fine dining room, and the bar gets raucous most nights—check out the back wall papered with money.

Five lodges dot the next 120 km, then it's another 65 km into Beaver Creek.

Beaver Creek

The last place with facilities in the Yukon, Beaver Creek is a tiny town (pop. 145) with a big economy. Canadian Customs is here, as is an Alaska Highway road crew. A **Westmark** hotel and a campground are here, where every Westours tourist between Fairbanks and Whitehorse, and every Alaskon Express passenger between Anchorage or Fairbanks and Whitehorse or Skagway, spends the night. Whether you're staying at the Westmark or not, stop in to see the large

wildlife display behind the gift shop. The dining is cafeteria style, open for breakfast 6-9:30 a.m. and dinner 6-9 p.m.

Ida's, tel. (403) 862-7223, is across the highway in a pink and beige building; there's a bright and airy dining room (bacon and eggs and burgers C$6-7, sandwiches C$5-7) and 20 motel rooms, C$70-80. Up the road is **Beaver Creek Motor Inn,** tel. (403) 862-7600, with a rustic and dark dining room in the log building with a polar bear on the roof. Motel units next door.

Camp free by moseying into the woods nearby, as always.

The **Visitor Reception Center,** tel. (403) 862-7321, is open 9 a.m.-9 p.m. during the summer.

Canadian Customs is three km before town if you're heading east into Canada; U.S. Customs is 22 miles beyond town. Canadian border guards are somewhat sensitive about guns; U.S. Customs officers seem to distrust young travelers, suspecting them to be transient workers or carrying drugs. Extensive searches of cars, backpacks, etc., are not uncommon, especially these days, with drug hysteria and "zero tolerance" rampant among law enforcers.

KLONDIKE LOOP

The Klondike Loop runs 521 km from the junction of the Alaska Highway and the Klondike Highway (30 km northwest of Whitehorse) up to Dawson City, then 105 km on Top of the World Highway to the border with Alaska, then another 109 miles on the Taylor Highway back to the Alaska Highway outside of Tok. The first stretch follows the original overland trail to Dawson; the road is almost completely paved, with just a few gravel breaks. This roadway was laid from Whitehorse to Stewart Crossing in 1950, then it was pushed through to Dawson five years later. That ended the Yukon riverboat era.

Lake Laberge, 62 km from Whitehorse, is famous primarily as the site of the burning of the corpse in Robert Service's immortal "Cremation of Sam McGee." The excellent trout fishing here has also been well known since stampeder days, when the fish were barged to Dawson by the ton. Around 15 km north is **Fox Lake Campground** (19 sites, water). **Little Fox Lake,**

15 minutes up the road, is extremely photogenic; its tiny islands densely covered with spruce seem to smile at the camera. Good camping between Whitehorse and Carmacks—all the territorial campgrounds are right on lakes.

Carmacks

A little more than 190 km from Whitehorse is Carmacks (pop. 470), the first civilization since the capital. This small town on the Yukon is named after George Washington Carmack, credited with the Bonanza Creek strike that touched off the Rush of '98. It grew up as a supply stop for riverboats steaming between between Whitehorse and Dawson; it also served then, as now, as an overnight stop on the overland trail. This locale on the river marks the boundary line between the territories of the Northern and Southern Tutchone First Nations.

Coming into Carmacks, you're greeted by a 48-by-96-meter **mural** painted by local residents.

Called "A Moment at Tantalus Butte," the colorful and detailed rendition of the local sights marks the 100th anniversary (1992) of George Carmack's establishing the first trading post in the area.

Get the lay of town (and the Yukon) by driving down Three Gold Road (at the Carmacks Hotel) to the river. By going left, you drive along the Yukon, passing residences, large trees and a profusion of flowers, municipal buildings, the community center, and a skating rink. Turn around and head back past Three Gold Road, then continue along the river to the public campground (primitive) right on the river. A **two-km boardwalk** installed here in 1995 runs along the river from the campground to a park, complete with a gazebo. There are benches, viewing platforms, and interpretive signs along the way.

Carmacks has two gas stations (Esso and Cheveron), the **Sunset Motel** (tel. 403-863-5266; rooms starting at C$44), the **Tatchun General Store** townside, and **Northern Tutchone Trading Post** across the Yukon, tel. (403) 863-5381, open 8 a.m.-10 p.m. Like Madley's in Haines Junction, the Northern Tutchone contains the bank (open Tuesday and Thursday 11 a.m.-2 p.m.) and the post office.

Hotel Carmacks, tel. (403) 863-5221, rents rooms for C$88 s and C$99 d, and cabins for C$65. A large lounge is attached, sporting a couple of pool tables and an interesting brass railing along the bar, perfect for bellying up to. Part of its restaurant, the **Goldpanner Cafe,** occupies the old Carmacks roadhouse, built in 1903 and the only remaining roadhouse of the 16 that once operated between Whitehorse and Dawson. Bacon and eggs cost C$7, steak and eggs C$11, spaghetti C$13.

Twenty-five km north of Carmacks is a pullout overlooking **Five Finger Rapids,** the halfway point on the river trip from Whitehorse to Dawson. Four rock towers here choke the river, forming five channels through which current rips. According to the *Milepost,* only the eastern right-hand channel is safe for navigation. At **Five Finger Rapids Recreation Site** is a wooden platform overlooking the river; stairs from the platform lead down to a trail that leads to the river. The trail passes through open meadows and wooded groves, with stairs along the more difficult sections. Allow an hour or so for the roundtrip to the river—a nice little walk to break up the drive.

To the Silver Trail

In another 108 km is **Pelly Crossing,** a small Native town (pop. 290). Pelly Crossing is roughly halfway between Whitehorse and Dawson. It has a gas station, a grocery/drug store (open 10 a.m.-7 p.m.), an RCMP station, and a health center. A four-panel signboard stands at the north end of the parking lot, with descriptions of the Selkirk Indians of Pelly Crossing, who moved to this site in the early 1950s after the road was completed. Study the map of the traditional lands of the tribe.

The bridge north of town crosses the Pelly River, discovered and named by Robert Campbell, an explorer for the Hudson's Bay Co. who established Fort Selkirk in 1848 at the junction of the Pelly and Yukon Rivers. From the top of the hill beyond the bridge, you get a good view of the town, the crossing, and the Pelly River.

Stewart Crossing

Seventy-two km north is Stewart Crossing, a small settlement consisting of a Yukon road-maintenance camp, a Chevron station, Stewart Crossing Lodge and cafe (tel. 403-996-2501), and a visitor information center for the Silver Trail, Mayo, and Keno. The Stewart River was discovered in 1849 by James Stewart, Robert Campbell's clerk. The first actual gold struck in Yukon was along the Stewart River in 1883, and three of the earliest sourdough prospectors in the territory, Arthur Harper, Jack McQuesten, and Alfred Mayo, established a trading post at this site in 1886. A roadhouse supplied stampeders during the main gold rush to Dawson, as well as prospectors who filtered up the Stewart River into Keno country in the early 1900s. Jack London's one winter in the Yukon was spent in Stewart, snowbound on his way to the goldfields. He came down with scurvy, and recovered during his short visit to Dawson, before he returned by way of the Yukon to California—where he turned 22. Stewart Crossing also served as a staging area for transporting silver ore from Mayo to smelters in the Lower 48. The bridge across the river was erected in the late 1950s when the Mayo road was built. It's 181 km from here to Dawson; top off your tank so as not to worry.

The Silver Trail

You cross the Yukon River and come to a stop sign. Take a left for Dawson or right for Mayo. It's 51 paved km from the junction of the Klondike Highway and the Silver Trail (Yukon Highway 11) to **Mayo,** a good-size town (pop. 475) on a wide bend of the Stewart River. Mayo grew up as a transshipment center for the ore mined from the Keno silver deposits. The sternwheeler *Keno* (parked now in Dawson) plied the Stewart, bringing supplies for distribution to the miners and picking up the ore to be shipped to smelters in San Francisco.

Be sure to stop off at the **Binet House Interpretive Center,** tel. (403) 996-2317, for a complete rundown of the Mayo District, including historical photos; displays on the geology, minerals, flora, and fauna of the area; and silver samples.

The 12-room **Bedrock Motel,** tel. (403) 996-2290, has rooms starting at C$70, a lounge, lunch and dinner service, and a campground. The **North Star Motel,** tel. (403) 996-2231, has nine rooms with kitchenettes for C$55 s, C$65 d. **Country Charm Bed and Breakfast,** tel. (403)

996-2918, is on a 320-acre historic farm eight km north of Mayo, with plenty of hiking, fishing, and boating; C$50 s, C$55 d.

From Mayo, it's another 45 km on hard-packed gravel to **Elsa,** the site of United Keno Hill Mines, which mined silver continuously for more than 70 years, until it closed in 1989 after the price of silver tanked. In another 14 km is **Keno City** (pop. 55), named after a high-risk casino game familiar to anyone who's ever been to Nevada. Keno Hill grew up as a Yukon boomtown around a major silver deposit unearthed in 1919. In Keno you'll find the **Keno City Mining Museum,** tel. (403) 995-2792, open June-Aug. 10 a.m.-6 p.m., housed in the old Jackson Hall saloon, built in the 1920s. After checking out all the mining exhibits, be sure to ask about Keno's network of hiking trails, some of the best in the Yukon. It's 10 km to the top of Keno Hill. Across the street is the **Keno Snack Bar,** also open 10 a.m.-6 p.m., serving pizza, sandwiches, and snacks. You can stay either at **Keno City Hotel,** tel. (403) 995-2312; or **Keno City Campground,** tel. (403) 995-2792, near Lightning Creek: seven sites, water.

GORDY OHLIGER

DAWSON CITY

Of all the destinations in the North, Dawson has the widest fame and the wildest past: one day after the steamer *Portland* hit San Francisco in August 1897 the entire world equated the name Dawson with a ton of gold. Within a year, 35,000 stampeders (out of an estimated 100,000 who started out) had descended on Dawson, making it the largest Canadian city west of Winnipeg—though 25,000 of its residents were Americans! The city's heyday, however, was as brief as its reputation was beefy, and Dawson quickly declined into another small town on the banks of the Yukon. Today, Dawson's population has grown to 2,000, more than doubling during the last decade, and it is now again the second-largest in the territory, edging out Watson Lake by 200 people. And it's experiencing a second stampede, sparked in part by renewed mining of precious metals but mostly by tourism and its tiny piece of the continent-wide gold rush of the 1990s: casino gambling. The hundreds of thousands in profits from Diamond-Tooth Gertie's are funding the restoration of downtown and beyond; the past eight years have seen more rehabilitation of Dawson than the past 88, the town having geared up for the centennial of the original rush.

There is still, to be sure, a delightful salmagundi of historic facades and abandoned buildings, tiny old cabins and huge new ones, touristy gold panning and bulldozer placer mining, leaving you with the impression that Dawson's many opportunities for adventure and fortune are as authentic and valid as ever. And thousands of hopefuls are again covering the miles from all over North America, sharing on arrival the thrill of the stampeders, and forging a living link with the past that will linger long into the future.

HISTORY

Discovery

The Klondike goldfields cover an area of 2,000 square km southeast of the city. In 1895, Robert Henderson, a prospector from Nova Scotia born with a lust for gold, was grubstaked by Joe Ladue, a trader at the tiny settlement of Ogilvie, 100 km upstream on the Yukon from where it is joined by the Thron-diuck River. Ladue pointed Henderson in the direction of what would come to be called the Klondike, and Henderson prospected for two years, finding color on the creeks, but not the fortune he was looking for. Finally, in spring 1896, he climbed what was later named King Dome and surveyed six creeks radiating out from where he stood like spokes on

Dawson's original red-light district was the alley between Second and Third from King to Queen. As the city became more established, the prositutes were shifted across the Klondike to Lousetown, where they continued to do a brisk business until the respectable ladies of Dawson led a campaign to close the brothels.

YUKON ARCHIVES

a wheel—six of the richest gold-bearing creeks ever known in the world. Sticking his pan into one, he found 20-30 cents' worth of gold in a single wash—four times as much as he was used to—and hurried off to tell the nearest miners about his prospect on his newly named "Gold-Bottom Creek." (Before the rush, the free sharing of information among miners was a code strongly subscribed to in the North, for it occasionally meant the spreading around of fortunes, and often the difference between life and death.)

Henderson and his companions worked Gold-Bottom Creek all that summer. In August 1896 Henderson was returning from Ogilvie with supplies when he had the fateful meeting with "Siwash" George Washington Carmack, who was fishing with his two Athabascan brothers-in-law for salmon at the mouth of the Thron-diuck (Hammer-Water) River, named for the fish-trap stakes hammered into its bed. Invoking the miner's code, Henderson again shared his news of Gold-Bottom Creek, advising Carmack to prospect the Thron-diuck—and send word if he found anything.

On August 17, 1896, Carmack struck gold where Rabbit Creek (soon to be renamed Bonanza) empties into the Klondike, in extraordinary quantities—$3-4 a pan. Barely able to contain their incredulity, he and his partners, Tagish Charlie and Skookum Jim, prospected along the creek, staked three claims, and hurried off to file in Fortymile, the largest supply settlement, a half-day's journey down the Yukon. Carmack

displayed his vial of large new nuggets to everyone he met, and Fortymile was deserted the next day. The news then reached Ogilvie, emptying it immediately; Joe Ladue himself rushed to the Klondike and staked, but he also had the great foresight to establish a sawmill on a wedge of fetid swamp where the Klondike met the Yukon—thus founding Dawson. By fall, the news had spread to Circle City and as far as Juneau, and most of the rich ground had been claimed. Ironically, only Robert Henderson, working his Gold-Bottom Creek a few hours' hike on the other side of the dome, didn't get word; by the time he heard of the Klondike, it was too late to get in on the riches.

Gold Fever

The news of the strike reached the outside world a year later, when a score of prospectors, so loaded down with gold that they couldn't handle it themselves, disembarked in San Francisco and Seattle. The spectacle triggered mass insanity across the continent, immediately launching a rush the likes of which the world had rarely seen before and has not seen since. Clerks, salesmen, streetcar conductors, doctors, preachers, generals, even the mayor of Seattle simply dropped what they were doing and started off "for the Klondike." Mining companies advertising in New York papers for investment capital were inundated with money. Adventurers from Europe, Australia, Mexico, and elsewhere set out to seek the gold. Boatloads of would-be brides sailed around Cape Horn. City dwellers, factory workers, and men who had never climbed a mountain, handled a boat, or even worn a backpack were outfitted in San Francisco, Seattle, Vancouver, and Edmonton, and set out on an incredible journey through an uncharted wilderness with Dawson—a thousand miles from anywhere—as the imagined grand prize.

Meanwhile, the first few hundred lucky stampeders to actually reach Dawson before the rivers froze that winter (1897) found the town in such a panic over food that people were actually fleeing for their lives. At the same time that tens of thousands of stampeders were heading toward Dawson via the Chilkoot and White passes, up the Yukon River, over the Mackenzie, Peace, and Pelly Rivers from Edmonton, over the Valdez Glacier at Prince William Sound and the Malaspina Glacier at Yakutat, and up from the Skeena and Stikine Rivers through interior British Columbia, others passed them on the trails heading the other way, talking of famine. Most hopefuls were caught unprepared in the bitter grip of the seven-month Arctic winter, and many froze to death or died of scurvy, starvation, exhaustion, heartbreak, suicide, or murder. And when the break-up in 1898 finally allowed the remaining hordes to pour into Dawson the next spring, every claim worth working within 150 km had already been staked and filed.

Heyday and Paydirt

That next year, from summer 1898 to summer 1899, was a unique moment in history. As people and supplies started deluging Dawson, all the hundreds of thousands in gold, worthless previously for lack of anything to buy, were spent with a feverish abandon. The richest stampeders established the saloons, dance halls, gambling houses, trading companies, even steamship lines and banks, much easier ways to get the gold than mining it. The casinos and hotels were as opulent as any in Paris. The dance-hall girls charged $5 in gold per minute for dancing (extra for slow dances), the bartenders put stickum on their fingers to poke a little dust during transactions, and the janitors who panned the sawdust on the barroom floors were known to wash out $50 nightly. A pauper could become a millionaire on a roll of the dice, and vice versa. Dawson burned with an intensity born of pure lust, the highlight of the lives of every single person who braved the trails and experienced it.

And then Dawson burned—literally—twice that year, the second time practically to the ground. Only a few diehards had the heart to rebuild the town a third time. Also, word filtered in that gold had been discovered on the beaches of Nome, and just as the Klondike strike had emptied Ogilvie, Fortymile, and Circle, Nome

Miners operating rockers at King Solomon's Hill up Bonanza Creek in 1898. Gravel was shoveled into the wooden boxes, whick were rocked back and forth manually using handles on the sides. Larger particles were screened out on top, while gold, which is twice as heavy as lead, would collect in the bottom after the other material had been removed.

YUKON ARCHIVES

emptied Dawson. By the summer of 1899, as the last bedraggled and tattered stampeders limped into Dawson two years after setting out (mostly overland from Edmonton), the 12-month golden age of Dawson was done.

By far the most comprehensive, colorful, and poetic history of the great gold rush is *The Klondike Fever,* by Pierre Berton (Carrol and Graf, 1958), a well-known and prolific Canadian journalist and editor who grew up in Dawson after his father crossed the Chilkoot in '98. Also, don't miss "City of Gold," a "moving slide show" written and narrated by Berton, shown at the Dawson tourist office.

Modern Times

From an estimated population high of 30,000 (23,000 of whom were Americans) during the summer of 1898, die-hard Dawson residents were down to 3,000 in 1911. This was the era of the dredge and large-scale corporate mining of the Klondike gold; a total of 35 dredges scooped up whole mountains of gravel and silt, operating through 1966. That year Dawson's population hit its 100-year low of 742. But gradually, as the price of gold rose in response to President Nixon's removal of the American dollar from the gold standard, placer mining enjoyed a resurgence; in addition, tourists began to rediscover Dawson's charms, especially after Diamond-Tooth Gertie's casino opened in 1971. By 1989, the population had grown to 1,700 year-round residents and it surpassed 2,000 for the first time in 100 years in 1995.

SIGHTS

Dawson's plentiful free or inexpensive attractions can keep you happily busy for several days. Its expensive nightlife, however, will greedily relieve you of your daytime savings. The excellent campground is no longer free, and staying anywhere indoors, along with the price of most meals, will quickly consume your Canadian dollars. Still, the vibe around this town is *party,* so just accept it and splurge guilt-free on those perennial pleasures of the flesh.

Visitor Reception Centre and Vicinity

As always, start your visit at the visitor center, right in the thick of things at Front and King Sts.,

tel. (403) 993-5566, open daily 9 a.m.-9 p.m., mid-May to mid-September. This center is extremely well organized and prepared for the most common questions from the hordes of hopefuls that are, after all, Dawson's legacy. They stock books of menus, hotel rates, and gift shops; schedules of tours; hours of attractions and movies; prices of showers; and much, much more. Be sure to pick up the requisite slew of informative booklets and flyers. You can also stand and watch a laser video on a variety of local-interest subjects, learn about Yukon gold production, and freshen up in the large restrooms. CKYN, 96.1 on your FM dial, broadcasts visitor programming from here. Leave your pack here for C$1 a day.

One-hour walking tours of the town core leave from the visitor center several times a day; check the schedule of events for times. Recommended. A second guided walk, the Fort Herchmer tour, goes out once a day. *Le tour en Français commence aussi au centre d'information sur demande seulement.*

Across the street from the visitor center is a wooden deck with interpretive signs about what once occupied this prime riverfront property. Next to it is the **Dempster Highway and Northwest Territories Information Centre,** tel. (403) 993-6167, open 9 a.m.-9 p.m. June-September. Like the visitor center, this outpost, in the restored British Yukon Navigation Building, is full of exhibits, media, and information about heading into the really remote backcountry. Stop here before you go up Dempster Highway for current conditions and the ferries situation.

The restored riverboat **SS *Keno,*** built in 1922 in Whitehorse, is beached on Front St. down from the two centers; tours are no longer given. You'll really appreciate the size of Whitehorse's *Klondike* by comparing it to the *Keno,* which once plied the Stewart River, bringing ore concentrates from the mining area around Mayo down to the confluence of the Yukon, where larger riverboats picked them up and transported them upriver to Whitehorse and the railhead. The *Keno* sailed under its own steam to its resting place here in 1960; it's in the process of being turned into a museum.

The exterior of the **Bank of Commerce,** near the *Keno,* hasn't changed much since Robert Service worked here in 1908.

There's a **river walkway** at the top of the dike that extends from south of the bank building to the mouth of the Klondike. Here people stroll, hike, and jog.

Downtown

Parks Canada and the Klondike Visitors Association have been doing an outstanding job bringing the color of life back to town. A number of ramshackle buildings have been spruced up with brightly painted facades and informative window displays, and most of the commercial hotels, gift shops, restaurants, beauty parlors, bed and breakfasts, etc., have followed suit. There are even painted boards around town with holes for you to stick your head through

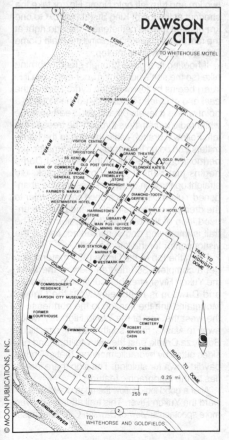

and be photographed as a gambler, a riverboat pilot, a Native sledder, a gold panner, or a dance hall queen and king. Thankfully, much of the semi-ghost town flavor remains, of course—to the continuing livelihood of Mr. Eastman and Mr. Kodak. The KVA has purposefully left alone the most picturesque ruins of permafrost, gravity, and neglect.

On King St., up a block from the visitor center, is the **Palace Grand Theatre,** built in 1899 by "Arizona Charlie" Meadows, the most famous bartender/gunslinger on the Trail of '98. At the time, the Grand was one of the most luxuriously appointed theaters in the west, hosting everything from Wild West shows to opera. The original structure, built from the remnants of two beached sternwheelers, was restored in 1962 by Parks Canada, complete with Klondike Kate's room upstairs. Catch tours of the Palace Grand during the day. At 8 p.m. nightly (except Tuesday) mid-May to mid-September, **Gaslight Follies,** a typical Klondike-style variety show, is performed ($13-16).

On the corner of King and Third across from the Palace Grand is the old **post office,** built in 1900; a clerk at the original window sells postcards, stamps, and commemorative postmarks; a historical brochure on the post office is available at the visitor center. On the opposite corner is **Madame Tremblay's Store** (1899), with a dry-goods window display. The ***Dawson Daily News*** at Third and Queen, **Billy Bigg's blacksmith shop** at Third and Princess, and **William Horkin's library, restaurant, and natatorium** (1902) at King and Second all have interesting window exhibits. Also check out the **bank** at Second and Queen and Parks Canada's photographic exhibit, "Dawson as They Saw It," at **Harrington's Store,** Third and Princess.

The **Firefighters Museum** is at Fifth and King next door to the Dawson City fire hall, open Mon.-Sat. 11 a.m.-5 p.m. A local guide (generally a seasonal college student from B.C.) takes you on a personal tour of the old fire trucks, water pumper, steam engine, and hose reels.

Dawson City Museum

If possible, before you do anything else in town try to visit this excellent and extensive museum and take the tour through the rest of the former Territorial Administration Building (built in 1901 and restored in 1986) on Fifth Ave. and

Church St., tel. (403) 993-5291, open 10 a.m.-6 p.m. Memorial Day through Labor Day, $3.50 adults. The south and north galleries present an enormous amount of history, from fossils and flora and fauna through northern Athabascan lifestyles up to the gold rush and the subsequent white civilization. The museum has a wealth of material to draw from and it's all well-presented, with well-written, interesting, and brief descriptions. The mining-history displays alone, from hand mining to dredges, are worth the price of admission; also check out the display on law and order during the gold rush.

Tours of the building are given at 11 a.m., 1 p.m., and 5 p.m. You're taken upstairs into the old territorial court chambers, which has some original furniture and is still used a few times a year as a circuit court. Then it's on to the resource library with its special Yukon and Dawson collection, open to the public daily. You then are treated to a peek into the Visible Storage area, where about one-fifth of the museum's collection of 30,000 artifacts is housed. Some government offices remain in the building, designed by Thomas Fuller, a grand-style architect.

Finally, you're escorted outside to view the Victory Gardens (1910) beside the building and the two-story brick vault behind, one of the only brick structures in town (impractical due to permafrost), used for fireproof storage.

Several **locomotives** that once ran from town to the goldfields (1906-14) may be seen free in the park adjoining the museum. The outdoor city **pool** is adjacent (C$3.50 adults, including shower; get hours at the visitor center).

Celebrity Cabins

Stroll three blocks uphill from the museum to Eighth Ave. and Hanson to see **Robert Service's log cabin.** Irish actor-director Tom Byrne has been entertaining visitors with Robert Service's life story, famous epics, and obscure ditties for over a decade. Hear how Service, who never took shovel nor pan to earth or water, wound up as a troubador-bank teller in Dawson and made his fame and fortune unexpectedly while living here, penning such classic prose poems as "The Cremation of Sam McGee" and "The Shooting of Dan McGrew." No one has lived in this cabin since Service left Dawson a celebrity in 1912, and people have

been making pilgrimages to it for 75 years. Performances are given daily at 10 a.m. and 3 p.m. (C$3) and the cabin is open 9 a.m.-5 p.m. You can buy tapes of the recitations at the cabin.

Two blocks away at Eighth and Fifth is **Jack London's cabin.** This is a replica of the one from Stewart Crossing, in which the young adventurer spent a Yukon winter; half its logs were used to construct this cabin, the other half a similar cabin in Jack London Square in Oakland, California. Interpretive readings are given at 1 p.m. by Dick North, author of *The Mad Trapper of Rat River.* Admission is free.

Midnight Dome

If you're driving, either take Front St. out of town two km and turn left onto Dome Rd., or take the shortcut at the top of King St. (at Ninth). Go one km up past the old cemeteries, then go right at the fork for another km till joining the main Dome Rd.; it's five km up to the top.

If hoofing it, a good (though steep) morning hike (so the sun's not right in your eyes, like it is later) begins by following the hydro lines at the east end of Queen St. directly up the slope to a point where it levels off and you see two large white radio transmitters through the trees to the left. Follow a branch cable through to the transmitters and go up the dirt road to the smaller, uppermost disk. The trail to the Midnight Dome begins just behind and above this disk. Go straight up through the woods passing the abandoned Yukon Ditch, which once carried water to the dredges on the goldfields, and pass an unused loop of the old road to the summit. The trail is improving and semimarked; ask at the visitor center for the latest details.

From the top of the Dome (885 meters) you get a complete 360-degree view of the area; the Yukon River stretches out in both directions and Dawson is right below you; the Ogilvie Mountains line the horizon to the northeast; to the west the Top of the World Highway winds away to Alaska; to the south you look directly up Bonanza Creek, past the wavy tailings and hillsides pitted by hydraulic monitors that still bring paydirt down for sluicing. The sign there identifies all the topographic features.

After a good look, follow the ridge down west toward the Yukon River. This trail affords an even more spectacular view of Dawson City. After pass-

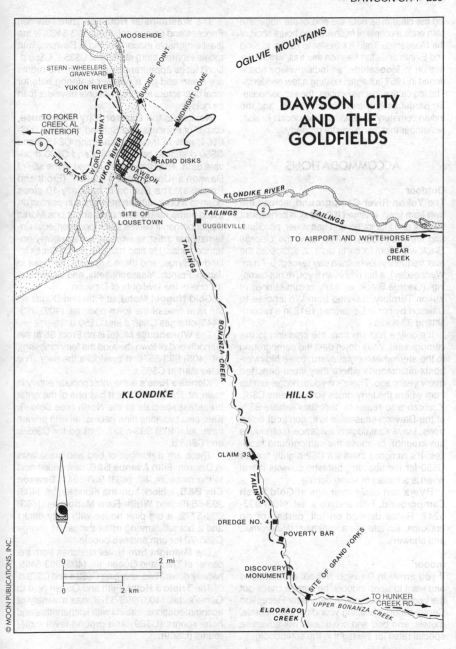

MOOSEHIDE

OGILVIE MOUNTAINS

STERN - WHEELERS
GRAVEYARD

SUICIDE POINT

YUKON RIVER

MIDNIGHT DOME

DAWSON CITY
AND THE
GOLDFIELDS

TO POKER
CREEK, AL
(INTERIOR)

9

TOP OF THE

WORLD HIGHWAY

YUKON RIVER

RADIO DISKS

DAWSON
CITY

KLONDIKE RIVER

2

SITE OF
LOUSETOWN

TAILINGS

TAILINGS

GUGGIEVILLE

TO AIRPORT AND WHITEHORSE

TAILINGS

BEAR
CREEK

BONANZA CREEK

KLONDIKE

HILLS

CLAIM 33

TAILINGS

DREDGE NO. 4

POVERTY BAR

DISCOVERY
MONUMENT

SITE OF GRAND FORKS

TO HUNKER
CREEK RD.

ELDORADO
CREEK

UPPER BONANZA CREEK

0   2 mi

0   2 km

© MOON PUBLICATIONS, INC.

ing the clear area near the end of the ridge, the path ends a couple of bushwacking hours short of the Moosehide Trail. It's easier to return to King and Eighth and start fresh on this trail, which carries on to **Moosehide,** an Indian village abandoned in 1957 but again hosting a few residents. The log cabins, the cache houses, the schoolhouse, St. Barnabas Anglican Church (1908), and the Indian cemetery all remain. If you decide to visit, remember that this is private property.

ACCOMMODATIONS

Outdoor
The **Yukon River Campground,** across the river from town, is large (100 sites), is convenient for cars and foot traffic, and has water, pit toilets, and firewood (C$8). A free ferry, the *George Black,* with room for six to eight cars, crosses the river frequently, 24 hours a day (except 5-7 a.m. Wednesday), a fun ride even if you're not camping. (George Black, an early commissioner of Yukon Territory, traveled from Whitehorse to Dawson by car in December 1912 in a record-setting 33 hours.)

It's only a half-km from the crossing to the campground. Walk down past the campground to the sternwheeler graveyard; three big riverboats disintegrate where they were beached many years ago. There's a youth hostel just up from where the ferry drops you off (tents C$8). You can also repair to "tent flats" where 85% of the Dawson seasonals live; don't cut down trees, leave scatalogical evidence (outhouses are around), or abuse the campground facilities. It's rumored there's a C$2 nightly fee (or C$50 for the season), but who collects it and when is a matter of some debate.

RVers can circle their rigs at **Gold Rush Campground,** Fifth and York, tel. (403) 993-5247. Rates depend on full, partial, or no hookups. On-site are a minimart, laundromat, and showers.

Indoor
If you arrive in Dawson without reservations and want to sleep indoors, be sure to check out the Lodging scrapbook in the Visitor Reception Centre before choosing your digs; often hotels, motels, and bed and breakfasts will advertise special rates for the night in the scrapbook.

The **Westminster Hotel,** on Third between Princess and Queen, tel. (403) 993-5463, is the least expensive indoor lodging in Dawson, with rooms (shared bath) starting at C$35 s, C$55 d. Don't let its appearance put you off: the rooms are clean and it's a popular watering hole for local characters and international travelers (can be noisy).

Next up is the **Dawson City Bunkhouse,** corner of Princess and Second, tel. (403) 993-6164, new in the '90s, charging C$45 s and C$50 d shared bath, C$75 s and C$90 d private bath. The Bunkhouse is next to the site of Dawson's "Underground Station" (Front and Princess). The Station is basically 10 steps down to a door with the midnight sun painted on it and some newspaper clips about one Martin Kippenberger. It seems that Kippenberger, an international artist, is working on a subway-entrance series. He also has one on the Greek island of Syros, and there are plans for more in Japan, France, Massachusetts, and elsewhere. It's one of the lowlights of Dawson.

Gold Nugget Motel, at Fifth and Dugas on the river side of the town pool, tel. (403) 993-5445, charges C$46 s and C$50 d.

The **Whitehouse Motel** is on Front St. at the far north end of town (beyond the ferry crossing), tel. (403) 993-5576. It overlooks the river. The rates start at C$65 s.

Klondike Kate's is the most popular eatery in town, at Third and King; it has one of the great breakfast specials in the North (see below). Kate also provides nine cabins, all with private bath, tel. (403) 993-6527, that go for C$55 s and C$65 d.

There are a number of bed and breakfasts in Dawson: **Fifth Avenue B&B,** new house next to the museum, tel. (403) 993-5941; **Dawson City B&B,** a block from the Klondike, tel. (403) 993-5649; and **White Ram Manor,** tel. (403) 993-5772, a big pink house with cozy decks and a hot tub, among other things. All charge C$65-79 for one and two people.

The **Midnight Sun Hotel** stretches from the corner of Third and Queen, tel. (403) 993-5495, halfway down Third, charging C$69 s and C$79 d.

The **Triple J Hotel,** Fifth and Queen next to Gertie's, tel. (403) 993-5323, has a variety of accommodations: cabins with kitchenettes and hotel rooms (C$89) and ground-level motel rooms (C$69).

FOOD

Dawson is great for eating out, with lots of choices of both palatables and price tags. By studying the menu book at the visitor center closely, you'll be able to ferret out the meal you want at the price you like.

The breakfast special at **Klondike Kate's,** Third and King, open 7 a.m.-11 p.m., is legendary; Las Vegans will get misty-eyed. Bacon and eggs with real live home fries will set you back C$4. It's served 7-11 a.m. Kate also serves the best french fries and gravy in town, C$3. For lunch, try the *tzatziki* dip (yogurt blended with cucumbers, feta, and spices) with pita or the hummus for C$5. Greek and Caesar salads are C$3.95-5.50. The seafood chowder is excellent at C$3.50, as is the falafel, C$5. You can opt for outdoor patio seating. Klondike Kate (Kathleen Rockwell) is the most enduring woman from the early days of Dawson. A chorus girl at 15, she set out for Dawson at 21 and made a name for herself as an entertainer of various kinds. She married several Dawsoners over the years and spent the last half of her life promoting herself as the Klondike Queen. Kate died in 1957 at the age of 81.

M.T. Bellies, in the Chief Isaac Memorial Center next door to the visitor center, also serves a breakfast special till 11 a.m.: two eggs and meat for C$3.99. They also offer burgers C$5-7, sandwiches C$4-8, eggs Benedict C$8, and tacos, fajitas, and burritos C$6-8.

Nancy's, also on Front St. but at the other end of town, open daily 7 a.m.-9 p.m., serves granola and hot cereal for breakfast, good soup (salmon chowder, C$4.50), sandwiches on homemade bread and burgers C$5-7, schnitzel C$15 with a side of sauerkraut C$2.50, and half a baked chicken C$15. Try the banana bread, only 75 cents.

Marina's, Fifth and Princess, open 3 p.m.-1 a.m., is highly touted, and deservedly so, for its pizza (starting at C$14-26) and Italian and Greek dishes C$13-21. The Alaska king crab and top sirloin is C$42.

River West Cafe is the health food store in town on Front St. next to Maximillian's. Open at 7:30 a.m., it has a coffee bar and juice bar and sells bulk foods.

All the hotels have big dining rooms with big menus, and the numbers on the left side of the decimal point aren't too hard to bear. For example, **Belinda's** in the Westmark Inn, open 6 a.m.-10 p.m., serves C$6 waffles, C$7 bacon and eggs, and C$8 omelettes; C$5.50 sandwiches and C$6-7 burgers; as well as chicken, ribs, halibut, and salmon in the C$17-20 range. You can eat outside on a deck overlooking the green, backed by a row of tall and steep or short and squat A-frame cabins. Pleasant.

China Village is the restaurant at the Midnight Sun Hotel, open 6 p.m.-1 a.m., serving typical "frontier Chinese": chop suey, egg foo yung, chow mein, and sweet and sour in the C$11-14 range.

For dessert, try **Madame Zoom's** ice-cream parlor at Second and King, open 11 a.m.-11 p.m.—all kinds of ice cream and frozen yogurt in the C$2-3 range.

Cooking for yourself? Visit **Dawson General Store** on Front Street or **Farmer's Market** on Second near Princess and concoct yourself a campground culinary cudfest.

ENTERTAINMENT

Diamond-Tooth Gertie's

Though casinos were as common as sluice boxes and saloons at the height of the Dawson madness, gambling in the Yukon (and throughout Canada) wasn't formally legalized until 1971. That was the year Diamond-Tooth Gertie's, Canada's first legal casino, opened for business, and Dawson hasn't been the same since. Gert's is the northernmost casino in the world. It's also probably the only nonprofit noncharity casino in the world. At Fourth and Queen, Gertie's is open 7 p.m.-2 a.m. nightly and charges $4.75 admission to the dance hall-casino. (Where I come from, a joint that lifts $4.75 right off the top of your bankroll wouldn't last the night.) But that's just for openers. The games played are as follows: jacks or better video poker (6/5 with a 4,000 flattop, 15 for four of a kind, 40 for a straight flush), deuces wild video poker (20/10/8/4, for a payback percentage in the low 90s), reel slots, blackjack (six decks, double on 10 or 11, no double after split, no insurance), Texas Hold'em (minimum $5), roulette (double 0), and red dog. Drinks are not comped, not even if you're dropping major-league green. The floor show is a half-hour of Geritol oldies and cancan. You have to be 19 to get in.

Needless to say, you don't want to go to Gertie's to try to grind out a little profit from some minor exploitable edge at blackjack or video poker. This joint makes a fortune off every wager laid—what did you think paid for the miraculous restoration of the town? Taxes? Get real. These are the '90s. Casino gambling is the biggest growth industry in North America. And little Diamond-Tooth Gertie's, open only seven hours a day roughly 125 days a year, has hold of a fantastically lucrative monopoly in the Northland.

The dealers and floorpeople will tell you up and down that Gertie's is a "nonprofit establishment," and that much is true. It's run by the Klondike Visitors Association, which uses the net to restore and promote Dawson. But make *no* mistake! In 1995, the table games netted $540,000 and the slots took in $736,000. After expenses, the casino earned $350,000. Gert's loaded.

I'm not saying that you might not experience a positive fluctuation and walk out with a somewhat larger bankroll than you walked in with. But the only way to approach this joint is with the attitude that you're making a donation. And why not? It's a very good cause. The modern history of the Great Land began at this spot. The richness of its legacy not only survives but is being actively revitalized. And a casino is the perfect symbol of both the past and the future of Dawson.

Palace Grand Theatre

Arizona Charlie Meadows was a young impresario and theater builder who arrived in Dawson in 1898. Within a year he erected the Palace Grand Theatre. With its horseshoe balconies and private box seats, the interior was modeled after European opera houses, though the entertainment in this remote boomtown was of a decidedly rustic sort, not unlike the theater's rough-hewn exterior. The building was about to be torn down for scrap lumber in 1960, when the Klondike Visitors Association stepped in and saved it; in 1961 the theatre was turned over to Parks Canada, which painstakingly tore it apart and put it back together again.

Today, the Palace Grand, on King between Second and Third, hosts **Gaslight Follies,** one of the best of the many vaudeville revues in the North Country. Shows are presented at 8 p.m. every night but Tuesday, C$14.50.

SHOPPING AND SERVICES

Gift Shops

Gift and souvenir shops are abundant in touristy Dawson. The biggest is **Flora Dora's,** at the corner of Second and King, in the last dance hall to close in Dawson (1908). **Art's Gallery** is a block up at Third and King; check out the paintings, pottery, jewelry, and books.

Maximillian's Gold Rush Emporium on Front St., open Mon.-Sat. 9 a.m.-8 p.m., Sunday at 10 a.m., has a great selection of paperbacks and books of northern interest, including excellent *The Klondike Fever* by Berton in a couple of different editions; you can also buy cassette tapes, T-shirts, newspapers and magazines, and sundries. **Klondike Nugget and Ivory** on Front St. just across from Maximillian's sells jewelry made from gold nuggets and mammoth-tusk ivory, as well as china, jade, and gifts.

Services and Information

The visitor center is on Front St.; see "Sights," above, for details. It's not difficult to de-dust in Dawson—several establishments provide public showers. Nearest and cheapest are those in the laundromat at the rear of the Chief Isaac Hale building next door to the visitor center: one loonie (C$1 coin) for five minutes (cramped). Somewhat more spacious are the showers at Guggieville (at the junction of Bonanza Creek Rd. and Klondike Highway); buy tokens at the campground store. Guggieville was the center of operations for the huge gold-mining operation run by the Morgan-Guggenheim Syndicate (nine dredges!) after it bought up most of the original individual claims on the Klondike. You can also grab a shower at the city pool.

Change your money at the CIBC bank on Queen between Front and Second. Topographical maps are sold in the mining recorder's office adjoining the main post office, on Fifth between Queen and Princess. They also sell an excellent blueprint map of the Klondike Placer Area showing all the goldfields (for only C$1—a bargain).

The **library** is at Fifth and Queen in the same building as the public school. It's open Tuesday, Wednesday, Friday noon-7 p.m., Thursday till 8 p.m., and Saturday 11 a.m.-5 p.m. Remove your shoes before walking in.

Gold City Travel is on Front St. across from the *Keno,* tel. (403) 993-5175; here you can book sightseeing tours of Dawson, Midnight Dome, and the goldfields, as well as airline and ferry tickets and hotel reservations.

TRANSPORTATION

Norline buses leave for Whitehorse from the Chevron station at Princess and Fifth, tel. (403) 993-6010, three times a week in the afternoon. Beyond returning to Whitehorse and catching a bus to Tok, Fairbanks, or Anchorage, Dawson is the end of the road for buses. You can hitch the 127 km across the border to the junction with the Taylor Highway, then continue the 65 miles up to Eagle or the 96 miles down to Tetlin Junction on the Alaska Highway. **(Note:** Customs at Boundary is only open mid-May to mid-September, 9 a.m.-9 p.m.). Top of the World and Taylor Highways are surprisingly well traveled during the summer; getting a ride shouldn't be too long an ordeal. The extension to Eagle is less so, and depending on karma could be excruciatingly time-consuming. You can try standing at the line-up to the ferry in the morning and asking drivers for a ride; if someone who has room is willing, you could wind up in Tok or Fairbanks or Anchorage by nightfall.

Another option is to fly. **Air North,** tel. (800) 661-0407 in Yukon, flies direct to Fairbanks from Dawson four times a week; you can also fly Air North to Whitehorse and Old Crow from Dawson. Tickets are available at Gold Rush Travel. Dawson's airport is 17 km east of town.

One more possibility is to catch Gray Line's *Yukon Queen* to Eagle. This riverboat plies the Yukon daily between Dawson and Eagle, US$77 one-way, and reports have been unanimous—an excellent crew, a beautiful ride, and a great ship. Buy tickets at Yukon Queen Cruises on the river side of Front St., tel. (403) 993-5599. From Eagle it shouldn't be too hard to hitch a ride down to Tok.

an Inuit mask, carved from a piece of driftwood

DIANA LASICH HARPER

Tours

The *Yukon Lou* does a daily 90-minute cruise to Pleasure Island for an all-Yukon-eat smoked salmon barbecue, leaving from the dock behind the Birch Cabin ticket office just north of the *Keno,* tel. (403) 993-5482.

One local tour company has been doing city, Midnight Dome, and goldfields tours for many years. **Gold City Tours,** on Front St. across from the *Keno,* tel. (403) 993-5175, is highly recommended by everybody. Inquire, too, about their bus service to Inuvik up the Dempster Highway. Charter flightseeing is available through **Bonanza Aviation,** tel. (403) 993-6904. Or hop a chopper operated by **Trans North Air,** tel. (403) 993-5494, for 20-minute rides over the area.

VICINITY OF DAWSON

The Goldfields

For a close-up look at some of the most torn-up country in the North, and for some insight into the gold frenzy that created and continues to stimulate the area, head out on Bonanza Creek Road. The mountains of tailings could cover the entire Yukon Territory with gravel, and the heavy equipment could spread it around and level it off. A monument at Discovery Claim, 16 km southeast of town, marks the spot where George Carmack pulled up $4 in his first pan in 1896. A kilometer beyond the monument is the confluence of Bonanza and Eldorado Creeks, site of the gold-rush town of Grand Forks. Nothing remains at the Forks as the entire area has since been dredged. The Klondike Visitors Association owns a claim here where you may pan for gold as much as you like free of charge (bring your own pan). On the way up from Dawson you pass a commercial panning operation, **Claim 33,** where you pay C$5 for a guaranteed (spiked) pan of gold. Still, it's good fun and practice for your technique.

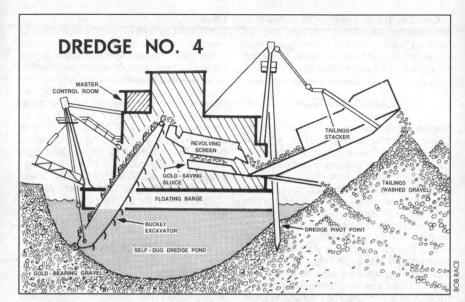

DREDGE NO. 4

MASTER
CONTROL ROOM

TAILINGS
STACKER

REVOLVING
SCREEN

GOLD - SAVING
SLUICE

TAILINGS
(WASHED GRAVEL)

FLOATING BARGE

BUCKET
EXCAVATOR

DREDGE PIVOT POINT

SELF - DUG DREDGE POND

GOLD - BEARING GRAVEL

BOB RACE

The highlight of the trip, however, is **Dredge No. 4,** largest wooden-hulled gold dredge in North America. Built in 1912, this massive machine scooped paydirt from the creek beds right up until 1966. An info trailer has descriptions of the operation. You can walk right up to the control room at the top of the dredge, but that's about all; the rest of the machinery is chicken-wired shut. Wait till you get to the Jack Wade Dredge on the Taylor Highway to really climb on one of these houseboat-cranes.

Four km beyond the dredge, take a left at the fork to Upper Bonanza Creek for miles more of mucking. You can continue along this road (which gets pretty rough in spots) all the way up to King Dome, where Robert Henderson stood, surveyed the land, and chose the wrong creek. You pass a turnoff (left) to Quartz Creek, then shortly another left to Sulphur Creek. This gravel road travels a 100-km loop into some seriously isolated country—you'll probably not see another car. It rejoins Upper Bonanza Rd. (which soon becomes Hunker Creek Rd.) only a bit beyond where it cut out. Then you start to descend along Hunker Creek Rd. for more placer operations, including another small dredge (inaccessible but photographable). Finally you come out (after a 72-km loop) at the glorious pavement of the Klondike Highway about a km on the Dawson side of the airport.

Into Alaska
Top of the World Highway from Dawson to the Taylor Highway in Alaska is one of the best unpaved roads in the North. It's wide, smooth, and *fast*—90 km/h and fourth gear. It's a high road, climbing straight out of Dawson (at just over 333 meters elevation) into the upper taiga and alpine tundra of the lower White Mountains, with vast vistas in which you can see the road running along the ridgetops in the distance.

Civilization along the highway, however, is scanty. You finally come to **Poker Creek, Alaska,** population two, elevation 4,127 feet. This is the northernmost border port in the U.S. Customs firmament. Check in with the stern guards, but hold it in till you get to **Boundary.** This is a tiny mountaintop settlement, with a bunch of log cabins, trailers, fuel tanks, low-flying aircraft, and Boundary Lodge; here you can use the outhouse, grab a microwaved bite, or buy Top o' the World T-shirts and jackets. The landing strip is way out of proportion to the town.

Boundary is 111 km from Dawson. Human habitation is nonexistent till the junction of the Taylor and beyond. Keep a close eye on your gas gauge: the next gas after Boundary is at O'Brien Creek Lodge, 40 miles past Boundary on the Eagle Cutoff; or at Chicken, also 40 long miles on the Taylor. Note, too, that both American and Canadian Customs operate only from mid-May to mid-September, and only 9 a.m.-9 p.m. If you get there at 9:01 p.m., you'll have to wait there until morning, an unpleasant prospect if there ever was one. And don't forget the time change at the border: Alaska time is an hour earlier than Yukon time.

GORDY OHLIGER

GORDY OHLIGER

INTERIOR

Interior Alaska is a great tilted plateau between the crests of the Alaska and Brooks Ranges. The mighty Yukon and Tanana Rivers are the main features of this region, but vast expanses of rolling hills are almost always in view. Interior Alaska has one medium-sized city, Fairbanks, several small towns, and a number of bush villages, the most interesting along the rivers but some beside the highways. Much of the region is expensive or inaccessible to visit without your own vehicle, but great adventures await on the many wild and scenic rivers, in the wildlife refuges, and in spectacular Denali National Park.

EAGLE

Eagle Cutoff
If you're coming from Dawson, hang a right at **Jack Wade Junction,** just a few miles beyond Boundary; it's 65 miles to Eagle on the Eagle Cutoff. This stretch is almost more a trail than a road: very narrow and winding, with steep grades, rough surface, endless hairpin turns, and little traffic—20-30 mph max. For the same

reasons, it's one of the funnest roads in the state, too. Lots of twists and turns, ups and downs, few other cars to worry about—you can really *play* on this one. The scenery is the same Interior hills and spruce trees you've been accustomed to since Whitehorse, so it's not a loss to keep your eyes glued to this road at all times; one glance away and you're driving into a ditch or off a 300-foot cliff. Expect to spend at least two hours for these 65 miles, two hours of white-knuckled, bug-eyed, teeth-chattering thrills and chills—hopefully without the spills.

To Go or Not to Go
More than 160 miles of hard-packed gravel from Tetlin Junction and 145 miles from Dawson, it takes a strong desire and a serious commitment to get to Eagle. Even if you're on the way from Dawson into Alaska, it's 130 miles, at least five anus-clenching hours of driving, from the junction of Top of the World and Taylor Highways to Eagle and back. And gas when you get there is a buck-seventy-five a gallon. Is it worth it?

Consider this. Eagle is a total history lesson. The small photogenic town of 150 may have more square feet of museum space than anywhere else in the state. The moving-right-along walking tour can take up to three hours! Add to that a beautiful free campground, great showers, good food, friendly people, and Yukon River scenery, and Eagle is without hesitation worth the extra time, effort, and expense.

History

In 1881, Francis Mercier, a French-Canadian trader, established a trading post at the site of Eagle to compete with Fort Yukon and Fort Reliance, two Hudson's Bay Co. posts along this eastern stretch of the Yukon River. It was a shrewd choice of location. Just inside the American border, stampeders fed up with Canada's heavy-handed laws and taxes organized a supply town here in spring 1898, naming it Eagle for the profusion of the majestic birds in the area. Also, sitting at the southernmost point on the Yukon in eastern Alaska, Eagle occupied a strategic spot for transportation, communication, and supply routes to the Interior from Valdez at tidewater. Within six months, three large trad-

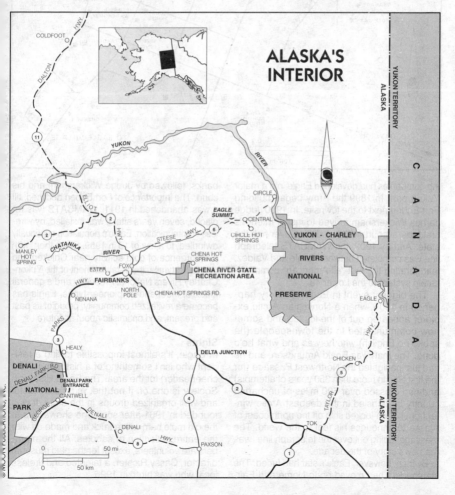

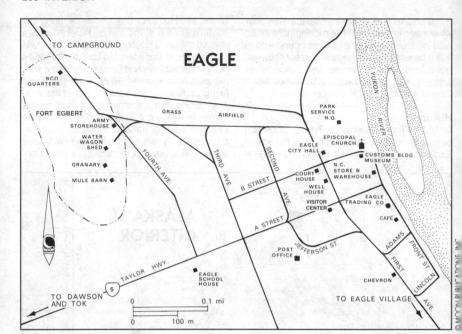

ing companies had developed Eagle into a major Yukon port. In 1899 the Army began building Fort Egbert next to the townsite. In 1900 Judge James Wickersham arrived to install Interior's first federal court, with jurisdiction over half the state. And by 1902, the WAMCATS telegraph line was completed between Eagle and Valdez, inaugurating the first "all-American" communication system to the Lower 48.

The biggest event in Eagle's history happened in 1905, when a Norwegian Arctic explorer appeared out of the icy fog and somehow communicated to the townspeople (he spoke no English) who he was and what he'd done. The man was Roald Amundsen, and he had just navigated the Northwest Passage (for the first time in more than 350 years of attempts) and had crossed over 500 miles of uncharted country by dogsled in the deepest Arctic winter from his ice-locked ship off the north coast of Alaska to announce his feat to the world. The message, going out over the telegraph line, was the news story of the decade.

By then, however, Eagle's star had faded. The stampeders had moved on to Nome and Fair-

banks, followed by Judge Wickersham and his court. The importance of Fort Egbert declined, till it was abandoned in 1911. WAMCATS was replaced, seven years after it was installed, by wireless communication. Eagle's population continually dwindled, to a low of 13 in 1959. Since then, with a resurgence of gold activity near Chicken and on the Fortymile, the establishment of the Yukon-Charley Rivers National Preserve, and a general influx of independent pioneer-types, Eagle has become a revitalized community, proud of its past and present, and optimistic about its future.

Sights
In Eagle, it's almost impossible to find a resident who isn't something of a historian (and a cheerleader) for the area. The Eagle Historical Society is one of, if not the, most successful and well-organized groups in the state. It was founded in 1961 after someone showed up at the old mule barn with a truck and made off with the entire collection of saddles. All the members are volunteers, except for the paid museum director, Cassy Richter, a talented and tireless local who was hired in 1996.

The care, devotion, and thoroughness with which they display Eagle's awe-inspiring array of artifacts is something to see. And their guided tour ($5), which leaves from Judge Wickersham's courthouse steps at 9 a.m. daily Memorial through Labor Days, is really the only way to see it; it's a fun hands-on outing, during which you're encouraged to operate an old peanut-warming machine or tickle the keys of an ancient pump organ. While waiting in the morning, fill up your water containers at the **wellhouse** next door to the court. The well, dug 60 feet deep by hand in 1910, still pumps cold H_2O—delicious; three out of four residents still haul water from this source. Struggle through the three heavy doors and either fill your bottle at the faucet or stretch the gas-pump-type handle to the jugs in your vehicle.

The tour begins appropriately inside the **courthouse**, built in 1901 by Wickersham for $5,000. All four rooms plus the hallway on the ground floor are covered with displays of the Han Indians, geology and archaeology, early pioneers, the telegraph story, etc. Be sure to check out the front page of the December 7, 1905 issue of *The New York Times*, with Amundsen's story, plus the map of the Northwest Passage in the hallway. (A romantic footnote: the intrepid Suzan Amundsen, Roald's great-granddaughter, continues a family tradition by taking a rest at the popular Eagle checkpoint during the Yukon Quest dogsled race.) Don't miss the amazing Nimrod's false teeth (homemade from caribou and bear teeth) and his remarkably accurate relief map of the vicinity (a newspaper papier-mâché printed with moose blood). Upstairs in Wickersham's courtroom is a small gift shop run by the Historical Society—great stuff for a good cause.

Then you mosey down to the **Customs House** on the Yukon waterfront, another two-story museum brimming with history. Study the six dated shots of the freezing of the Yukon River from October 13, 1899, to January 12, 1900, plus the photos upstairs of "wild" animals—Fred Ferwilliger's wolf pups, Mae Collins's pet black bear, and some bewildered-looking moose hitched to wagons and carriages. Sign the original U.S. Customs entry book.

A walk along the town's grassy airstrip leads to to **Fort Egbert**. The restoration of the few remaining fort buildings was sponsored by Sen. Ted Stevens and financed by the BLM from 1975 to 1979. There's a pictorial history of the renovations. The huge old mule barn, at 150 feet long and 30 feet wide one of the largest restored buildings in Alaska, is full of relics from Eagle's past: tools, weapons, uniforms, wagons and tack, dogsleds, boats, a prototype Sears chain saw, an old outboard motor that looks like a cross between an early sewing machine and a Weed Wacker, and much more. Upstairs is the gold-mining exhibit with its own collection of Rube Goldberg equipment.

The newest acquisition on the tour is the **Improved Order of Redmen Building**, a wilderness version of a lodge/benevolent society, ostensibly dedicated to the preservation of the ways and traditions of the area's Native people. Of course, only white guys were allowed to to be members, the humor of which isn't lost on the Historical Society. The building is also now used for local gatherings.

Don't miss this tour: it's the thing to do in Eagle.

Others

For **National Park Service headquarters** info, see "Yukon-Charley Rivers National Preserve," below. Out First Ave. (take a right coming into town) 2.5 miles is **Eagle Village**, a picturesque Indian settlement that predates the white settlers. Fish wheels operate just offshore, and racks of salmon dry under the clouds. The residents are friendly, but please respect their privacy. Back in town read the bulletin board outside the post office to see if anything's going on.

Practicalities

Follow the signs from town left to the free campground just beyond the cemetery (a few old markers; Nimrod's grave is here): big, uncrowded, nice wooded sites, free

GORDY OHLIGER

firewood, vault toilets. There's an easy nature walk between the campground and the airstrip. You can park your RV (hookups) or stay inside at **Eagle Trading Co.** on the riverfront, tel. (907) 547-2220, where rooms with two queens and full bath start at $50, $10 each additional person; all rooms have a view of the river.

For B&Bs, **Falcon Inn,** tel. (907) 547-2254, is a beautiful two-story scribe-log structure with dormers and a lookout tower right on the Yukon. Charley and Marlys House built the Falcon on the site of the Alaska Exploration Co. next to the historic Customs House. Marlys is the local science educator and naturalist; Charley captains the riverboat *Kathleen.* Inn guests are entitled to discount excursions. Rates begin at $65 with private bath and include breakfast.

Another fine bed and breakfast is the **Yukon Adventure,** at the public boat launch on the river, tel. (907) 547-2221. Kay and Darrel Christensen offer rooms for $50-80, all including a sumptuous breakfast; each room has a VCR and videos. It has a big yard with a picnic area and barbecue grill, and downtown Eagle is a short walk.

Next door to Eagle Trading Co. is the **Riverside Café,** open 6:30 a.m.-8 p.m., with burgers and fries at $5.50, and $5 specials. They also have oh-so-fine showers, $4 for 15 minutes, but nobody's counting. The motel is open from mid-April to mid-October, the cafe from mid-May. This is also the place to find someone heading to Dawson, Tok, or Fairbanks if you need a ride. Eagle Trading Company sells gas for around $1.75 a gallon. **Telegraph Hill Service** two miles out of town, and the **Village Store,** tel. (907) 547-2270, also sell gas at the same price—no gas wars here. No crime, either. This is one friendly, peaceful, close-knit community. Village Store also has hardware, propane, and gifts.

A mile down the Eagle cutoff is **Yukon Ron's,** tel. (907) 547-2305, a great little gift shop featuring the carvings, handcrafted on the premises, of owner Ron West. Check out the custom *ulus* made from antique saw blades found in the area. Well worth the stop.

Transportation

No public ground transportation is available to Eagle. It's a good four hours by car from Dawson, and at least another five down to Tetlin

Junction, depending on how long you play in the gold country. **Warbelow's Air Ventures,** tel. (907) 474-0518 or (907) 547-2222, flies daily to and from Fairbanks, $88 one-way—a real bush-pilot trip, the daily mail and supply run. Fly in, take the tour, then sail to Dawson on Westours' *Yukon Queen* riverboat, which leaves Eagle daily at 2 p.m., arriving in Dawson at 7 p.m., $79 one-way, $130 roundtrip. Highly recommended. Warbelow's also offers seats aboard bush-mail planes to outlying villages not accessible by road. If you're entering the U.S. on the Yukon, be sure to stop into Customs at the post office.

YUKON-CHARLEY RIVERS NATIONAL PRESERVE

Eagle itself is pretty far out there, but if you really want to disappear, you can explore Yukon-Charley Rivers National Preserve. This huge, 2.5-million-acre park is primitive, with no facilities or established transportation and a skeleton Park Service staff with headquarters on the Fort Egbert strip at Eagle. The Yukon-Charley Rivers National Preserve Visitor Center on the corner of First and Fort Egbert Ave. has a selection of books and maps on the preserve; the staff will plug in a video on request and can provide advice for those contemplating a trip. HQ is open Mon.-Fri. 8 a.m.-5 p.m. For further info, write to them at P.O. Box 64, Eagle, AK 99738.

The popular raft or canoe trip is from road's end at Eagle down the Yukon to road's end at Circle; allow five to 10 days. Or you can charter a bush plane to drop you and a boat way up around the Charley headwaters and float down to the Yukon. You must be highly experienced, entirely self-sufficient, and have at least a tolerance for, if not a love of, mosquitoes. Check in at HQ for advice, and conditions, and to leave your intended itinerary. For outfitting from Eagle, contact Theresa and Bill Elmore at **Eagle Commercial,** tel. (907) 547-2355. These experienced outdoorspeople rent canoes and 14- and 16-foot rafts, fully outfitted. Their tours are guided and unguided; bush-plane pickups and dropoffs can be arranged. Theresa is the local agent for Warbelow's and Bill is the U.S. Geological Survey map dealer.

TAYLOR HIGHWAY

Coming back down from Eagle south of Jack Wade Junction, the highway remains primitive, pretty, and fun. Have "long eyes" to enjoy the distant vistas. The road itself continues to be rough, especially when it descends, about six miles past the junction, into **Fortymile** country and the old **Jack Wade** mining camp, which consists of many abandoned buildings but modern mining machinery—take care not to trespass.

In another three miles you round a bend, and there, like the biggest jungle gym you've ever seen, is **Dredge no. 1.** Though half the size of dredges no. 4 on Bonanza Creek and no. 8 near Fairbanks, and not in use since 1942, it's still solid as a rock, and you can climb over every inch of it—monkey heaven.

For the next several miles, the rough road, mountains of tailings, and mining equipment will also remind you, on a smaller scale, of Bonanza Creek Road outside of Dawson. It's the Bottom of the World Highway for a while around here. Four miles farther, stop off at the BLM **Walker Fork Campground** to stretch your legs—and maybe soak your feet if it's real hot. In a beautiful site where the South and Walker Forks of the Fortymile meet, a footbridge across the creek leads to a three-minute trail to the top of the limestone wall—nice view of the valley, one of innumerable similar valleys in the immense Interior.

Fortymile Canoe Route

Canoeists frequent this stretch of the road to put in to the Fortymile and its forks. Mile 49 (West Fork bridge), Mile 66 (Mosquito Fork bridge), Mile 69 (Chicken), and Mile 75 (South Fork bridge) are all good places to start, with high enough water levels. Where you take out depends on your time and prior arrangements. O'Brien Creek bridge (Mile 112) is the closest; or float to Clinton Creek in Yukon Territory, which has a 40-km unmaintained road back to the Top of the World Highway; or just keep paddling into the Yukon River and down to Eagle or Circle, or to the bridge at Mile 56 on the Dalton Highway, or all the way to the Bering Sea. Like Yukon Charley, you're entirely on your own out here (except for skeeters so thick they can blot out the sun); help can be days away. The main route (Chicken to Eagle) is rated Class I and II with some Class III rapids and one Class IV. The BLM brochure lists the 20 or so USGS topo maps for the route.

To Tok

Twelve miles south of Walker Fork Campground is **Chicken** (pop. 14), the vernacular name for ptarmigan, which the miners mucking for gold around here in 1895 were unsure how to spell. Anyone who's read *Tisha* by Ann Purdy, the story of a young teacher who overcame enormous local resistance to teach in this neck of the tundra, will be interested to know that the late author made her home here. The original Chicken, an abandoned mining camp, is now on private property. Tours are given at 1 p.m.; the tour leaves from "downtown" Chicken and is led by Sue Wiren who, with her husband Greg, owns the Mercantile, saloon, and cafe.

Goldpanner gift shop, grocery, and gas is right on the highway. **Chicken Mercantile** is down the airport road a piece in "downtown"; here you can get gas and the usual burgers and booze, plus famous T-shirts, copies of *Tisha*, local gold, and Chicken souvenirs. A cafe, bar, and salmon bake are attached.

Before you take off from Chicken, make sure your gas tank and water-jug levels are sufficient: from here down to Tetlin Junction, the Taylor crests some passes, descends into some valleys, and encounters almost no civilization. About 10 miles north of Tetlin Junction, you enter the area burned up in the massive lightning-induced forest fire of 1990. The wildfire, which started in early July, burned nearly 3.2 million acres and cost $36 million to contain, making it the most complex and costly wildfire in Alaska history. A graphic display on "How Tok Was Saved" is exhibited at

GORDY OHLIGER

the Public Lands Information Center in Tok. You follow the blackened forest the rest of the way to Tok.

The road gets progressively smoother, wider, and faster the closer you get to the Alaska Highway, till you cruise down a long hill, come around a corner, and there, like blue velvet after days of sandpaper, is pavement, glorious pavement, your first in 305 miles.

TOK

Twelve miles west of Tetlin Junction, and 96 miles from the border, Tok (pop. 1,300; rhymes with "smoke") considers itself the "gateway to Alaska" and is the service center for several Native villages in the upper Tanana Valley. Where the Tok River empties into the Tanana, the Athabascan tribes once gathered to affirm peace among them, and Tok is usually translated to mean "Peace Crossing." The town itself grew from a mid-1940s highway-construction camp, and is still unincorporated. The turnoff to Anchorage (326 miles) is in the town center; continue straight on the Alaska Highway 101 miles to Delta Junction.

The thing to do in Tok is to visit the Alaska Division of Tourism's **Alaska Public Lands Information Center,** open 8 a.m.-8 p.m. May-Sept., tel. (907) 883-5667. Similar (though smaller) to the Public Lands Information Centers in Fairbanks and Anchorage, this is the place to collect brochures and maps for the whole state, pick the personnel's brains, catch a movie or a slide show, spend some time perusing the exhibits, and freshen up in the large bright bathrooms. There's a map with 20 buttons that illuminate various sites, along with a large collection of taxidermied mammals; a historic timeline; an exhibit on mosquitoes; and an in-depth display of the huge 1990 fire. Read about the miracle that took place after the fire had raged for five days and was about to engulf the town; the loss of houses and private property was slight. The bulletin board outside the johns might have ride info.

Next door to the Public Lands Center is the Tok Chamber of Commerce **Main Street Visitor Center,** tel. (907) 883-5887, open 7 a.m.-9 p.m. It has a nice display of seabirds, lots of brochures, and an informative staff; the Tok library adjoins it.

Mukluk Land is a little amusement park with a kids' igloo for bouncing, skee-ball machines, minigolf, dogsled rides, Alaska's largest mosquito, gold panning with guaranteed color, gardens, videos, a museum, and an occasional performance by Donna Bernhardt, author of *Tent In Tok,* a series of poetry books about life in a tent in Alaskan winters. Mukluk Land is open June-Aug. daily 1-9 p.m. Admission is $5 adults, $2 kids.

You can take in free **dog-team demonstrations** at the Burnt Paw gift shop across the road nightly (except Sunday) at 7:30 p.m. Sign up for the drawing to ride the sled around the track.

Practicalities

Pitch your tent at the good state campground, **Tok River State Recreation Site,** which survived the fire, five miles east of Tok on the Alaska Highway, $10. Several RV parks cluster around the intersection. **Northstar,** tel. (907) 883-4631, is a major complex of RV and tent sites, fuel and car wash, laundromat and showers, restaurant, gift shop, and Western Union office. You get two free showers with a hookup, or you can buy one for $3.25, two for $5. **Sourdough Campground,** tel. (907) 883-5543, is on the other side of the road, with similar facilities, plus a nightly slide show and a locally famous sourdough pancake breakfast (starting at 7 a.m.). You can also park your rig at the **Golden Bear,** on the Tok Cutoff, tel. (907) 883-2561; **Tundra,** tel. (907) 883-7875; **Rita's,** tel. (907) 883-4342, the pinkest RV park in Alaska; **Tok RV Center,** tel. (907) 883-5750, a new center with a full-service RV repair shop; not to be confused with **Tok RV Village,** tel. (907) 883-5877, which features a big gift shop and laundry.

A half-dozen other motels in town start at $60.

Fast Eddy's is Tok's main restaurant action. It's open long hours (6 a.m.-midnight), has good, plentiful, and reasonable diner food (pizza from $9.75, burgers $4.85, hoagies $5.50 plus 50 cents to share, spaghetti, lasagna, steaks, and seafood), a surprisingly well-stocked salad bar ($6 as, $3 with, a meal), and huge pie a la mode for $3.25. If you ask to see Fast Eddy, he won't be around.

A good alternative is the **Gateway Salmon Bake** (you can't miss it), open Mon.-Sat. 11 a.m.-9 p.m., Sunday 4-9 p.m. Cleta Aller takes your order and your money at the check-in booth, and her husband Dave barbecues your buffalo or salmon burger ($7.50), king salmon or halibut slab ($17.95), ribs ($13.95), or reindeer sausage ($12.95), then calls you by name to pick up your chow. The meal includes the usual salad bar, baked beans, sourdough rolls, and lemonade. You can eat out or in the big barn. A very congenial meal!

Young's Cafe at the junction serves breakfast all day. You can also grab something fast at **Tastee-Freez**.

Transportation

For years Tok has had the notoriety of being a hitchhiker's worst nightmare. Legends abound about men growing beards and women going through menopause while standing with their thumbs out at the junction. If only 12 hitchers are in front of you, and you only spend one night on the side of the road, consider yourself lucky.

On the bright side, Tok is a crossroads for **Alaskon Express** buses rolling between Skagway, Whitehorse, Beaver Creek, Fairbanks, and Anchorage, and you can catch the one going in your direction four times a week (ask at either visitor center).

DELTA JUNCTION

The next junction town is another 100 miles northwest, where the Richardson Highway merges with the Alaska Highway, which technically ends. Fairbanks makes a cheap claim to possessing the end of the famous road, a distinction that belongs, without dispute, to Delta: not only does all the historical and current travel literature list the Alaska Highway at 1,422 miles long (as opposed to the 1,520 to Fair-

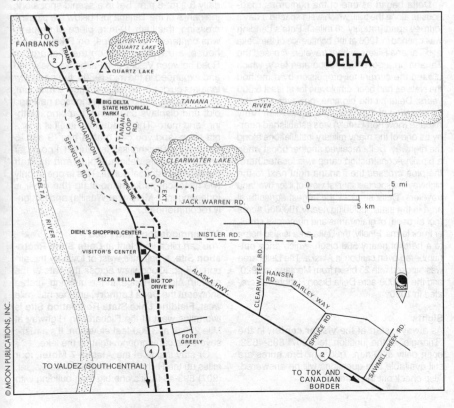

DELTA

TO FAIRBANKS

QUARTZ LAKE

QUARTZ LAKE

BIG DELTA STATE HISTORICAL PARK

TANANA RIVER

RICHARDSON HWY.

ALASKA

TANANA LOOP RD.

T LOOP RD.

SPENGLER RD.

PIPELINE

CLEARWATER LAKE

T LOOP EXT.

JACK WARREN RD.

DELTA RIVER

DIEHL'S SHOPPING CENTER

NISTLER RD.

VISITOR'S CENTER

PIZZA BELLA

BIG TOP DRIVE IN

ALASKA HWY.

CLEARWATER RD.

HANSEN RD.

BARLEY WAY

0   5 mi

0   5 km

MOON

FORT GREELY

SPRUCE RD.

SAWMILL CREEK RD.

TO VALDEZ (SOUTHCENTRAL)

TO TOK AND CANADIAN BORDER

© MOON PUBLICATIONS, INC.

banks), but the mileposts end with finality at the Delta Visitor's Center. The mileposts to Fairbanks then pick up at Mile 266 (the distance from Valdez on the Richardson Highway).

The Richardson was Alaska's first road. The WW II road designers specifically aimed the Alcan to join at Delta, connecting it to both Interior Alaska and tidewater. The Richardson was originally envisioned as an "all-American route" to the goldfields along the Yukon just before the turn of the century, and a trail was constructed in conjunction with the WAMCATS telegraph cable to Eagle. But with the shift of attention to the Fairbanks area in the early 1900s, the trail was redirected there and upgraded to a wagon road in 1907 under the auspices of Wilds P. Richardson, first president of the Alaska Road Commission.

Delta began as one of the numerous roadhouses along the trail, which were spaced a day's journey apart (roughly 30 miles). Bate's Landing was opened in 1906 at the confluence of the Delta and Tanana Rivers, where travelers crossed the Tanana on a government-operated ferry, which utilized the current for propulsion by a method the Natives had been employing for at least 5,000 years. Delta hit the big time, however, with the construction of the Alcan, and when Allen Army Airbase (now Fort Greely) was established nearby as one of the many military installations along the highway. Delta received another boost when a pipeline-construction camp was located here; the pipe crosses the Tanana right next to the highway—a spectacular first view of it for overland travelers. Delta services the largest agricultural area in the state, including nearly 100,000 acres (not all used) of grain farms and numerous smaller truck farms. Finally, the Delta area is also home to a herd of nearly 500 bison, which once outnumbered even caribou in Alaska. The Delta area was stocked with 23 bison from Montana in 1920, and the 70,000-acre Delta Bison Range was created in 1980.

Sights

As always, start at the **visitor center,** in the "Triangle" at the junction, tel. (907) 895-4632, open daily 8:30 a.m.-7:30 p.m. Brochures are still available and questions will be answered. Also check out the garden.

You can take a short loop through the **agricultural area** by heading back down the Alaska Highway eight miles; take a left at Sawmill Creek Rd., another left on Bailey Way, again a left on Hansen Rd., and one more left on Clearwater, which delivers you back to the highway. Good views of the eastern peaks of the Alaska Range from the Clearwater area, if it's clear.

To get the total 360 degrees, though, head down to **Donnelly Dome,** 23 miles south on the Richardson. Go right on the gravel road at Mile 248, continue for a quarter-mile past the second sharp bend; an obvious though unmarked trailhead is at the car park there. Allow a half-day to the dome and back.

But if you only do one thing in Delta, take an enjoyable and educational stroll through history at **Big Delta State Historical Park,** eight miles past town toward Fairbanks, open daily 8 a.m.-8 p.m. Set in a scenic spot along the banks of the Tanana just below the pipeline crossing, this lush 10-acre piece of property was centered, for decades, on Rika's Roadhouse, a travelers' stop on the Richardson Road between Valdez and Fairbanks. Restored and expanded in the mid-1980s, the park now features guides in period costumes, a museum, barns, cabins, signboards, outhouses new and old, and displays on mining, trapping, clothing, and more. The Roadhouse itself is now a gift shop, and you can grab a bite (9 a.m.-5 p.m.) at the Packhouse Restaurant, known far and wide for its delicious pies and its staff dressed in historical outfits. This is one of only two historical parks in the state (the other is Independence Mine near Wasilla) and is highly recommended.

Accommodations and Food

You can pitch your tent at **Delta State Recreation Site,** a half-mile west of town by the airport, $6 pp. Good view across the flats of the eastern Alaska Range. In the morning, grab a shower at the **Delta Laundry,** another half-mile west. **Fielding Lake State Recreation Site** is two miles west of the Richardson Highway at Mile 200.5, at 3,000-feet elevation. It's a rustic seven-site campground, right on the lake.

Or stay inside at the **Alaska 7 Motel,** four miles up the Richardson toward Fairbanks, tel. (907) 895-4848; it's one big long building with red-frame doorways, with rooms starting at $55. **Kelly's Country Inn Motel,** tel. (907) 895-4667, in town has rooms for $55 s and $60 d.

Across from the visitor center on the Rich is venerable **Pizza Bella,** tel. (907) 895-4841, open 10 a.m.-midnight. Across the street from Pizza Bella is **Big Top Drive In** for burgers and shakes.

Or pick up your own supplies at **Diehl's Shopping Center** on the main drag.

FAIRBANKS

Arguably no city in the North is closer to the Edge than Fairbanks. With several hundred miles of subarctic bush surrounding it on all sides, the frontier feeling is pervasive: haphazard layout, constant infrastructure improvements, two military bases, dozens of churches overflowing with large families on Sunday mornings, and a colorful core of hard-drinking, hard-living "pioneers." Second-largest town in the state, it's still no more than a quarter the size of Anchorage, with a compact, convenient, and hospitable hominess that Anchorage has long since forgotten. But it's still one of the largest population centers this far north on earth.

The town itself isn't pretty—barely scenic—but for such an outback, plain, boxy place, Fairbanks, like the rest of Alaska, takes extrovert pride in itself; it has a lot to offer the visitors who stagger in from the bush and want to kick back or live it up for a few days. Plan on at least a couple of days here to dust off from the road and relax in comfort without abandoning the Edge—one of the best places in Alaska to combine all three.

Climate

Fairbanks has one of the widest temperature ranges of any city in the world. The mercury can plummet to -66° F in January and soar to 99° F in July, for a whopping 165-degree differential. In addition, one day in July could be 90° and cloudless, while the next day could be 40° and rainy. Visitors are often taken aback by Fairbanks' occasional sizzling summer days, and scramble for the few air-conditioned hotel rooms. During the mild days, the 21 hours and 47 minutes (on solstice, to be exact) of direct sunlight are a novelty to travelers, but that hot sun beating relentlessly down on residents *all summer long* can make you just as crazy as 18 hours of darkness in December—and it can fry your pineal gland to a crisp!

The seasons here are pronounced. Spring generally occurs around Memorial Day weekend, or sometimes even over a one-day period! A 1986 Weather Service press release cited May 22 as the day "the leaves finally sprouted" in Fairbanks: "The 24-hour transformation of the Fairbanks area from gray to green was quite dramatic." During the 90-day summer the foliage changes from green to yellow, orange, and red. It generally goes brown in early September, sometimes over Labor Day weekend! It can snow and drop into the teens anytime in September, when the first day of winter is still more than three months away. Winter solstice sees a few hours of daylight, and then there's five more months till spring.

HISTORY

E.T. Barnette

In August 1901, E.T. Barnette was traveling up the Tanana River on the *Lavelle Young* with a boatload of supplies bound for Tanacross to set up a trading center on a well-used gold-rush trail. Unable to negotiate some rapids, Capt. Charles Adams turned into the Chena River to try to bypass them but got stuck on the Chena's silt-laden sandbars. Adams refused to go any farther, and Barnette refused to turn back, leaving the two men as stuck on the boat.

Peering through field glasses from a distant hill, Felice Pedroni (Felix Pedro, as he's remembered) watched the boat's progress—or lack thereof—by the smoke from its stacks. A mountain man and prospector extraordinaire, Pedro had been looking for gold in the huge wilderness north of the Tanana and Chena Rivers for several years and had found signs of color on some creeks near where he stood watching the steamer. However, running low on provisions, he was facing a several-hundred-mile roundtrip to Circle to restock, unless. . . .

The Yukon Quest is a 1,000-mile dogsled race between Whitehorse and Fairbanks.

FAIRBANKS CONVENTION AND VISITORS BUREAU, ROXANNE KFNT

Meanwhile, Captain Adams was unceremoniously dumping Barnette, his wife, and their goods on the shore. "We cut some spruce and helped him get his freight off," Adams recalled 30 years later. "We left Barnette furious. His wife was weeping on the bank. They were standing directly in front of the present site of [the heart of downtown Fairbanks]." That's when Pedro showed up, quietly informed Barnette of his prospect, and bought a winter's worth of supplies. Back at his promising creek, Pedro finally hit pay dirt.

News of the strike traveled far and fast. Miners abandoned played-out Klondike and Nome and headed for the tiny outpost on the Chena River, named after Illinois Sen. Charles Fairbanks, who soon became vice president under Teddy Roosevelt. Unfortunately, Barnette wasn't content with his good fortune of owning most of the townsite of rich little Fairbanks. In 1911, he was tried for embezzling funds from his own Washington-Alaska Bank. Though he was acquitted, he left town with his family, never to return. His wife divorced him in 1920 in San Francisco; where he went from there, and when or how he died, are complete mysteries. Only one clear photograph of his face survives today: Barnette standing in a line with several other early Fairbanks bankers. But when the photo was found, old-timers were hard-pressed to identify which one was the town father. In fact, a discrepancy even exists over his first name. In *E.T. Barnette,* Terrence Cole calls him Elbridge,

while *The $200 Million Gold Rush Town,* by Jo Anne Wold, remembers him as Eldridge, and the city fathers commemorated him by naming an elementary school Ebenezer T. Barnette. Whatever his name, possibly no man embodies the boom-bust character of Fairbanks better than its founder, E.T. Barnette.

Gold

The Fairbanks strike differed markedly from the shiny shores of the Klondike and the golden sands of Nome—this gold was buried under frozen muck anywhere from eight to 200 feet deep. Fortune hunters quickly became discouraged and left, which rendered Fairbanks's boom much less explosive than Dawson's or Nome's. But even determined miners eventually reached the limits of both their endurance and the primitive placer-mining technology. After fires and floods, by 1913, when the road from Valdez to Fairbanks was completed, the town was in the midst of a serious bust cycle. But in 1923 the Alaska Railroad reached Fairbanks from Seward and Anchorage, which inaugurated the real Golden Age. Major mining corporations freighted up and installed the mechanical monsters required to uncover the gold, and eventually $200 million worth was dredged from the surrounding area. When the Alcan was pushed through to Delta from Canada in 1942, connecting the Richardson Highway to the outside world, the city's future was assured.

From the Pipeline to Modern Times

A massive flood in the summer of 1967 nearly drowned the town, and the future looked bleak for a while, but in early '68 the Prudhoe Bay strike promised to drown the town *in oil* and Fairbanks's prospects looked bright again. Many local people invested heavily on speculation of a boom around the proposed pipeline; most went bust in the six years it took to start the project. But pipeline construction finally began in 1974, and Fairbanks boomed yet again. Of the 22,000 total pipeline workers, 16,000 were dispatched from Fairbanks's union halls. Suddenly demand far exceeded supply, making it a seller's market for everything from canned food to cocaine, from housing to hookers. In fact, there were so many hookers, and the unions grew so strong, that the hookers themselves sought union representation to get the city council and cops off their backs, so to speak.

So many people poured in with dreams of the big bucks that officials took out ads in Lower 48 newspapers telling everyone to stay away. Only half the job seekers ever got hired, and the lines at the bank were only exceeded in length by those at the unemployment office. For three years you could barely utter or hear a sentence in Fairbanks that didn't contain the word "pipeline." The word itself eventually reached mythical status, with the locals blaming the exploding population, rampant crime, deteriorating social services, long separations from home and family, and every other local problem on it, while the oil companies and workers hailed it as the best thing since J. Edgar Hoover invented the vacuum cleaner. For better or for worse, Fairbanksans mined this vein for three years, and those with enough brains and self-control set themselves up for the bust that was sure to follow. And did. E.T. Barnette would've been proud. Those were the days.

Like the rest of the state, the town has surfed the oil wave for nearly two decades and has survived the peaks and valleys. "Pipeline" seems still to be the magic word, actually. A proposed 769-mile natural-gas pipeline out of Prudhoe Bay seems to have gone the way of 16-cylinder automobiles and first novels, but it still surfaces occasionally. Meanwhile, Fairbanks (50,000 town residents, 85,000 in the borough) prospers on the military payroll, on the summer tourist season, as a supply center for the bush, and on the Fort Knox gold mine up in suburban Fox, which will keep the area flush with gold for years to come.

SIGHTS

The smoothest sight around hard-edged Fairbanks may be the rounded hills that surround the bowl at the bottom of which Fairbanks sits, flat as a mackerel. It's not a particularly colorful town, yet only the savviest tour drivers make the *Solar Borealis* (see below), a psychedelic public-art sculpture at the airport, a stop on their city tour. But the residents do their bit to beautify, and the profusion of potted, planted, and painted

The Trans-Alaska Pipeline snakes above ground through the vast rolling interior.

GORDY OHLIGER

flowers really spruces up the place. Walk around downtown to get the frontier flavor, and be sure to wander through the nearby residential neighborhoods for the flowers, log cabins, and huge heads of cabbage.

Downtown

Start out at the **Fairbanks Convention and Visitors Bureau** (open daily 8 a.m.-8 p.m.) on First Ave. near Cushman, in a sod-roofed log cabin by the Chena River. Load yourself down with a few pounds of paper: be sure to get the excellent, annual, and venerable *Interior and Arctic Alaska Visitors Guide* tabloid published by the Fairbanks *Daily News-Miner;* the annual *Fairbanks Visitor's Guide* magazine, a comprehensive listing of local practicalities; as well as the two excellent handouts, *Fairbanks Walking Tour,* describing almost 50 historical sites within a 10-square-block area downtown, and *Fairbanks Driving Tour.* You can call the Tourist Office at (907) 456-5774 (800-327-5774) or access their recorded "InfoLine" with the day's events at 456-INFO. A cadre of volunteers fluent in a dozen foreign languages is on call to translate for anyone who needs it.

Just outside the log cabin is **Golden Heart Park,** opened in 1987. The centerpiece is a large heroic sculpture of *The First Unknown Family,* created by Malcolm Alexander, who also did *Builders of the Pipeline* in Valdez. The statue's fountain foundation is covered with 36 bronze plaques, some of which describe the growth of the park's large corporate sponsors, while others list the names of sponsoring individuals.

Walk a block up to Cushman and Second Ave., to the storefront of the **Yukon Quest,** tel. (907) 451-8985, open 10 a.m.-5 p.m. The Yukon Quest race was established in 1983 as an alternative to the Iditarod dogsled race from Anchorage to Nome. The first 1,000-mile race from Fairbanks to Whitehorse by way of Circle, Eagle, and Dawson City was run in Feb. 1984 by 26 mushers. The store sells Yukon Quest T-shirts, sweatshirts, and other race souvenirs, along with a handful of books and stuff.

In 1996, the **Dog Mushers Museum,** tel. (907) 456-6874, was upstairs from the Sunshine Co-op mall on Second Ave., but the location for the 1997 season was undecided when

this book went to print. The museum features exhibits of the history, lore, sleds, and gear of dogsledding, along with big-screen videos depicting you-are-there views of the big statewide competitions and profiles of individual mushers. A gift shop sells souvenirs of the sport. Since Fairbanks is the dog-mushing capital of the world and most winners of the sports' biggest races hail from the Interior, it's unlikely this interesting attraction will fade away. Call for the new location; it's well worth the effort to see it.

At the corner of Second Ave. and Lacey St. in the historic Lacey Street Theater is the **Fairbanks Ice Museum,** tel. (907) 451-8222, open 9 a.m.-9 p.m., $6 adults. This is the "coolest show in town," a 25- to 30-minute multi-screen slide show of large ice sculptures created at Ice Art, an international ice-sculpting competition held in Fairbanks each March. There's also an 8,000-cubic-foot walk-in freezer holding 40,000 pounds of sculpted ice on display.

Backtrack to Cushman for the **Alaska Public Lands Information Center,** Third Ave. at Courthouse Square, tel. (907) 456-0527, open daily 9 a.m. to 6 p.m. in summer, 10 a.m.-6 p.m. Tues.-Sat. in winter. A combination museum and information bureau, this excellent facility represents eight state and federal agencies, from the Alaska Division of Tourism to the U.S. Geological Survey. You can easily spend a couple of hours here looking and playing: interesting aerial and relief maps hang on the walls, four-minute videos give thumbnail sketches on different aspects of the six geographical regions of Alaska; old-time stereoscopic viewers show three-dimensional views of historic Alaska; a touch-activated trip-planning computer is programmed with more than 200 public-land sites throughout the state; tasteful displays include photographs, taxidermy, Native artifacts, etc. You can view scheduled films in the comfortable 35-seat theater at 10 a.m., noon, and 4 p.m. The office sells prints, slides, books, and tapes—take advantage of this place. Note: APLIC no longer handles Denali Park reservations for shuttle tours or campgrounds.

Across the River

Visit the **Immaculate Conception Church** (1904), just across the river from the Tourist Office, for its beautiful stained-glass windows. Far-

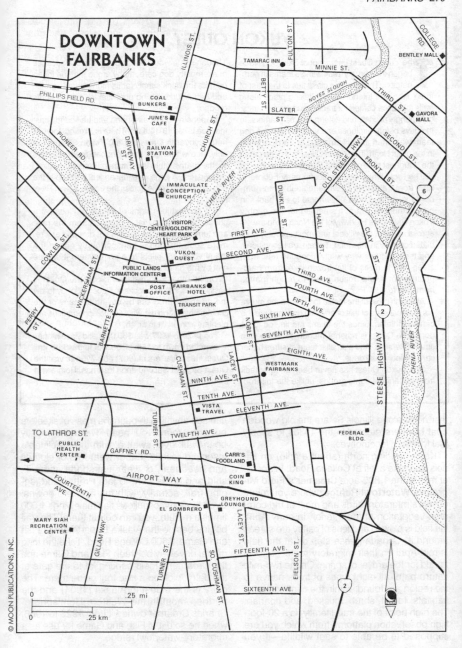

DOWNTOWN FAIRBANKS

COLLEGE RD.

BENTLEY MALL

ILLINOIS ST.

FULTON ST.

TAMARAC INN

MINNIE ST.

BETTY ST.

NOYES SLOUGH

THIRD ST.

SECOND ST.

GAVORA MALL

PHILLIPS FIELD RD.

COAL BUNKERS

SLATER ST.

CHURCH ST.

JUNE'S CAFE

DRIVEWAY

PIONEER RD.

STREET ST.

RAILWAY STATION

CHENA RIVER

OLD STEESE HWY

FRONT ST.

CLAY ST.

6

IMMACULATE CONCEPTION CHURCH

DUNKLE ST.

HALL ST.

VISITOR CENTER/GOLDEN HEART PARK

FIRST AVE.

YUKON QUEST

SECOND AVE.

COWLES ST.

WICKERSHAM ST.

PUBLIC LANDS INFORMATION CENTER

THIRD AVE.

POST OFFICE

FAIRBANKS HOTEL

FOURTH AVE.

FIFTH AVE.

PERRY ST.

TRANSIT PARK

SIXTH AVE.

2

BARNETTE ST.

NOBLE ST.

SEVENTH AVE.

EIGHTH AVE.

CHENA RIVER

CUSHMAN ST.

LACEY ST.

WESTMARK FAIRBANKS

NINTH AVE.

TENTH AVE.

VISTA TRAVEL

ELEVENTH AVE.

TURNER ST.

STEESE HIGHWAY

TO LATHROP ST.

TWELFTH AVE.

FEDERAL BLDG.

PUBLIC HEALTH CENTER

GAFFNEY RD.

CARR'S FOODLAND

AIRPORT WAY

COIN KING

FOURTEENTH AVE.

GREYHOUND LOUNGE

MARY SIAH RECREATION CENTER

GILLAM WAY

EL SOMBRERO

LACEY ST.

FIFTEENTH AVE.

EIELSON ST.

TURNER ST.

SO. CUSHMAN ST.

SIXTEENTH AVE.

2

0   .25 mi

0   .25 km

© MOON PUBLICATIONS, INC.

YUKON QUEST

The Yukon Quest International Sled Dog Race began in February 1984 with 26 teams in competition. The race has close ties to the past of the Yukon and Interior Alaska, taking place along trails that once carried fur traders and missionaries, gold-hungry pilgrims and determined mail carriers. In the days before airplanes and automobiles, the dog team was often the only method of transportation in the great North. The Yukon Quest has been called the "toughest race on earth." For good reason.

The race, which takes place in early February, runs from Fairbanks to Whitehorse in even-numbered years and from Whitehorse to Fairbanks in odd-numbered years. It's named for the mighty Yukon River, "the Highway of the North," and travels across some of the wildest and most sparsely populated country in the world. Terrain, trail conditions, and temperatures vary wildly along the trail, from steep hills to miles of flat frozen lake, from hard-packed snow and frozen rivers to rough gravel, from -80° to +30° F.

Although most of the media focus is on the mushers, the real stars of this or any sled dog race are the canine athletes. Since the teams are limited to 14 dogs, the Quest is musher-friendly to those with smaller kennels. And a smaller team ensures better care for individual dogs.

The Yukon Quest has never been under attack from the animal-rights groups, unlike the Iditarod. Though some would like to believe this is because of exemplary dog care, many argue that the Iditarod gets the flack simply for its higher media profile and better fund-raising potential for animal rights groups.

Depending on weather and and trail conditions, the race takes 10-14 days. There is a mandatory 36-hour layover in Dawson City, Yukon. This is the only stop where dog handlers can feed and care for the teams while the mushers get some much-needed rest. A large veterinarian tent is set up in the dog camp, which lies across the frozen Yukon River from Dawson.

If a dog exhibits signs of fatigue or illness at a checkpoint, the animal is dropped from the race and turned over to the handlers. If dropped at a remote spot, the dog is transported by one of the many volunteer pilots to a point where it can be met by the handlers.

Unlike other long-distance races, the Quest is easily accessible to onlookers. Race fans may follow the mushers' progress by driving to many of the checkpoints along the way. Photo opporutnities are plentiful from start to finish.

Top prize in 1997 was $30,000, and prize money is awarded down to 15th place. For further info, call Quest Headquarters at (907) 452-7954 or visit the Quest Store at Second and Cushman. Both are in Fairbanks.

ther north along Illinois St. are the old wooden **coal bunkers** erected in the 1930s to supply fuel to steam locomotives.

Keep heading north (about a mile) on Illinois and take a left at College Road. In another mile is the 1,800-acre **Creamer's Field Migratory Waterfowl Refuge,** where you might observe migratory birds and most of the common vegetation of the Interior. In early April, the field is plowed and tons of barley are spread around it. Canada geese stop off at the field in mid-April on their migratory route—a local herald for the arrival of spring. On the two-mile nature path, all eight types of trees native to the region are found, within the common local habitats: forest, shrub, muskeg, and riparian. The high point of the trail, literally, is a 20-foot-high observation platform, from which you are supposed to be able to spot wildlife—if you can see anything through the mass of skeeters buzzing around your head. The trail is mostly boardwalk over swamp, with the predictable insectoid results. Either wear lots of clothes and headgear, or wear just shorts and a T-shirt and come here to jog. Pretty good jogging trail, actually, with fun ups and downs. Even though mosquitoes flap their wings 1,000 times a minute, you can outrun them! The trail begins beside the Alaska Department of Fish and Game, 1300 College Road. Take the long gravel driveway between Fish and Game and the Creamer's Field parking lot to the gate at the dairy; pick up a free trail guide there. The dairy is the oldest in Alaska (1904) and the northernmost in the Western Hemisphere. Charles Creamer owned it from 1928 to 1966, when he sold it to Fish and Game for use as a migratory-waterfowl refuge.

To the University

Continue on College Rd. to the **University of Alaska, Fairbanks** (UAF), main educational facility in the state. When it opened in 1917 as Alaska Agricultural College, there were six students and as many faculty; today 8,000 students attend the 2,500-acre campus. This facility is highly regarded for its Arctic research and Alaska Native studies. The bus drops you at the Campus Commuter Terminal. Ask the driver or any student to direct you to the **Wood Campus Center** nearby, where you can pick up a free map of the grounds, check the ride board for people going in your direction, and grab a cheap breakfast or a good lunch in the cafeteria or pub.

A free shuttle bus runs every 15 minutes from the Commuter Terminal around campus; grab it for a ride to the excellent **University Museum,** tel. (907) 474-7505, open 9 a.m.-7 p.m. June, July, and Aug., $5 adults, $4.50 over 60 and under 12. The museum collection is divided according to the state's six geographical areas. The wildlife and gold exhibits are mind-boggling; the Russian artifacts and the permafrost display are exceptional. So is an exhibit dealing with the incarceration of Japanese-Americans during WW II; read the heartbreaking personal letters from the families pleading for compassion. Other highlights include a three-ton copper nugget and 425-pound quartz crystal, a 1905 Sheldon car, an antler couch, a 36,000-year-old bison, polar dinosaur bones, and the aurora video from the university's research center at Poker Flats. The gift shop sells the usual books, prints, and cards, and some unusual items like fish neckties. On a clear day Mt. McKinley, across the broad Tanana Valley, can be seen in all its awesome eminence from the museum hill.

Other activities on campus include daily movies about mining and permafrost (at 11 a.m. in room 204 in the Brooks Building). Tours of the Large Animal Research Station (musk-ox, caribou, and reindeer) are conducted on Tuesday and Saturday at 11 a.m. and 1:30 p.m., Thursday at 1:30 p.m., $5, on Yankovich Rd. a mile off Ballaine Rd., or go anytime and use the viewing stand. The Agricultural and Forestry Experimental Station is below the museum at the west end of campus. Here is grown a large variety of flowers, grains, and vegetables that can withstand the northern rigors. Call (907) 474-7627 for directions and information about the self-guided tour.

Alaskaland

This enjoyable 44-acre theme park, the only one of its kind in the state, occupies the site of the 1967 state centennial celebration. Many of the original buildings from the early days of Fairbanks and various locations around Alaska have been moved here and assembled into a gold-rush-era town. Park HQ is in one such restored building just inside the entrance off Airport Way between Nome and Peger roads. Pick up a map of the park and spend a few hours browsing around the replica Mining Valley and Native Village, with its lifestyle exhibits and performances of authentic dances and songs. The big (227-foot-long) 1933 sternwheeler riverboat, *Nenana,* promises to be fully restored for the 1997 season. There's also a vintage 1915 carousel ride ($1.50), miniature golf, a train ride ($2 adults, $1 children), and the new horse-and-buggy or stagecoach rides of the park, provided by Heavy Horse Farm of Fairbanks. Pulled by huge one-ton Percheron horses (Walter and Wade), a trip around the park behind these two gentle giants is a great way to see the sights ($4 adults, $2 kids). Be sure to see the historic home of the first Territorial Governor, James Wickersham, President Harding's Alaska Railroad car, and the Pioneer Museum (all free). The Pioneer Air Museum has a remarkable display of Alaska's aviation history. The parking lot is open to motor homes at $9 a night (no hook-ups, but potable water and 24-hour restrooms and dump station). Alaskaland is open year-round 11 a.m.-9 p.m., but most of the shops and rides only operate from Memorial Day to Labor Day, admission free. The salmon bake is $8.50 for lunch (noon-2 p.m.) and $18.95 for dinner (5-9 p.m.). A free salmon-bake shuttle bus runs 4-10 p.m. and stops at the major hotels from the Northern Lights Hotel downtown all the way out to Sophies Plaza at University and Airport Way, plus the Norlite Campground. Good free rides. The Blue Line (Airport Way) also passes Alaskaland's gates (hourly on weekdays).

Solar Borealis

Like the *Nimbus* in Juneau, the *Solar Borealis* ("Northern Sun") was built with funds from Alaska's "Percent for Art" program, which earmarks one percent of the state's construction budget for public art. This $107,000 sculpture, selected from over 71 pieces submitted for the site, was created by San Franciscan Robert Behrens and unveiled in June 1985. The welded-steel archway rises 50 feet above the exit from Fairbanks International Airport. Special diffraction tiles attached to the front of the sculpture reflect all shades of the spectrum, depending on what angle you view it from—so long as the sun is shining. Otherwise, the metallic trellis appears stark and silvery-white. Designed specifically for the few hours of potential sunlight during the deepest dark of Fairbanks' long winter night, the best time to view it is on a clear bright day from 10 a.m. to 1 p.m.—guaranteed to give you acid flashbacks, even if you've never taken LSD.

RECREATION

Hiking
For the local trail, see "Across the River," above. Also see "Chena River State Recreation Area" under "Vicinity of Fairbanks," below. Farther afield, for hiking and backpacking opportunities in the White Mountains and in the Pinnell Mountains, see "Pinnell Mountain Trail and Eagle Summit" in the same section.

Biking
Fairbanks has an excellent series of connecting bike routes: from downtown along the river to Alaskaland; from University and Airport out a ways on Chena Pump Rd.; and a great up-and-down route on Farmer's Loop Rd. from the Steese Highway to the university.

Swimming
Three indoor pools are open to the public. You can swim at **Hamme Pool** at Lathrop High School, Airport and Cowles, tel. (907) 456-2969, Tues.-Fri. 2-4 p.m. and 7-9 p.m.; you can also take showers there every day 6 a.m.-9 p.m. Call **Mary Siah Recreation Center,** 1025 14th Ave., tel. (907) 456-6119, for their complete list of hours. **Patty Gym Pool** at UAF, tel. (907) 474-7205, is open Mon.-Sat. 7:30-9 p.m. for $3 per visit.

Ice Skating
No need to wait for winter freeze-up in this town. **Big Dipper Ice Arena,** 19th and Lathrop, tel. (907) 456-6683, is open Mon.-Sat. 11:45 a.m.-1:15 p.m., plus additional odd hours. Admission with skate rental is $2.50.

Fishing
Fishing in the Chena River for grayling is fair; they must be 12 inches or longer to keep. Better grayling fishing is found at the Chatanika River, between miles 30 and 40 on the Steese Highway toward Circle. Chum, silver, and a few kings run up here from mid-July. Chena Lakes Recreation Area has good rainbow-trout fishing. Fish and Game provides a recorded hotline of fishing tips, updated once or twice a week, tel. (907) 452-1525. The *Fairbanks Daily News-Miner* carries fishing updates every Friday in its "Outdoors" section. For guided fishing trips to the Interior, check under "Guide Service" in the Yellow Pages.

ACCOMMODATIONS

Hostels and Camping
Backpackers Hostel is at 2895 Mack Rd. (heading north on College Rd., take a right on Westwood and look for the house with international flags), tel. (907) 479-2034. You can stay here for $15 a night, or pay just $10 for tent space. The hostel provides a kitchen, showers, travel information, and sourdough breakfast ($5), and has the added bonus of a sundeck, a barbecue, volleyball, and basketball.

Grandma Shirley's Hostel, 510 Dunbar St. between E and F streets, tel. (907) 451-9816, is a clean, homey hostel with a nice lounge (cable TV), kitchen, outdoor picnic area, and a garden and greenhouse where you can pick your own salad (as long as you make enough for everyone there). All ages welcome; $15 per bunk.

Tanana Valley Campground at the Fairgrounds on College Rd. at Aurora Drive charges $6 for a biker's or hiker's site (up to four people—two tents), or $15 for RVs with full hookups. Showers are free and campfires are allowed in this natural setting. **Norlite Campground** on Peger Rd. near Alaskaland, tel. (907) 474-0206, has been here for 30 years; the city has grown up around it. They charge tenters $8.50 d, and RVs $15 for full hookup. The campground has its own laundromat, showers (25 cents for five minutes), store, and restaurant. No campfires are permitted, but barbecuing is allowed. Norlite is very convenient to Alaskaland and the salmon-bake bus. Otherwise, get there on the Blue Line; the last bus out leaves at 6:45 p.m. Mon.-Friday.

River's Edge RV Park is a large handy campground on the banks of the Chena River (on Boat St. off Airport Way near University Ave.), tel. (907) 474-0286, charging $15.50 for tenters, $24 for full hookup, with free showers. New in 1997 are 50 cabin units with private baths, queen beds, and riverfront patios. This campground is right on the river bike trail and has a private boat launch. The tent sites near the river are the most relaxing, while those on the edge of the woods are the most private (but for the odd visiting family of mosquitoes).

Chena River State Recreation Site, locally known as Chena Wayside, is a state campground on University Ave. just north of Airport Way (Red or Blue lines if traveling by bus). It has 59 sites, running water but no showers, fireplaces, boat launch, and fishing—a bit high density, but not bad for city camping, if you arrive early enough to get a site; $10 walk-in, $15 drive-in. From May 15 to Aug. 10 there's a 5-night maximum stay.

Rooming Houses

Several houses rent rooms by the night (around $25) or week ($150) near downtown, with shared bath and kitchen. Mostly for men, they're not a bad deal if you don't mind the communal atmosphere. Check the classifieds in the *Daily News-Miner* under "Furnished Rooms."

Moderate

Golden North Motel, 4888 Airport Way, tel. (907) 479-6201, is a little out of town, and the nearest bus (Blue Line) passes about a quarter mile away, but their courtesy van will drop you off and pick you up if you ask nicely. The motel rooms could be larger and fresher but have cable TV; $69 s, $99 for a minisuite with a sitting room. There's a $10 key deposit.

Downtown, the **Alaskan Motor Lodge,** 419 Fourth Ave., tel. (907) 452-4800, charges $70 s, $81 d. The **Fairbanks Hotel,** 517 Third Ave., tel. (907) 456-6440 or (800) FBX-HOTL, is the oldest in town (1941); it's been completely remodeled and is under new management. You'll pay $69-83. With reservations, a free shuttle will fetch you from the airport or the train.

About a mile from downtown, within walking distance of the train depot, the **Tamarac Inn,** 252 Minnie St., tel. (907) 456-6406, charges $64 s, $74 d with shared bath, $74 s, $80 d with private bath. Some rooms have kitchenettes.

The large shopping malls three blocks from the Tamarac make the kitchenettes in each room especially convenient and cost-cutting.

Expensive

The **Westmark Fairbanks,** 813 Noble St., tel. (907) 456-7722, has 238 rooms starting at $180, but try for a corporate, military, or government discount. It has a steakhouse, coffee shop, and lounge. The **Fairbanks Princess Hotel,** 4477 Pikes Landing near the airport, tel. (907) 455-4477, has 200 rooms and a terraced deck right on the river, with rates and discounts similar to the Westmark. It has three restaurants, entertainment, and a health spa. **Sophie Station Hotel,** 1717 University Ave., tel. (907) 479-8888, has suites starting at $160. All rooms have queen beds, kitchenette, bedroom and living room with cable TV. Catering to business people (rather than visitors), big corporate discounts are available. Sophie's is probably the most luxurious digs in town.

Bed and Breakfasts

One might think there's not a single private residence left in Alaska that isn't a B&B. The Fairbanks phone book alone has nearly three pages of listings. Most charge $60-100, with full breakfasts and some transportation provided. They can come and go pretty fast, but the venerable ones (meaning they appeared in the last two editions of this guide) include: **Joan's,** tel. (907) 479-6918; **Fairbanks B&B,** tel. (907) 452-4967; and **Chena River B&B,** tel. (907) 479-2532.

7 Gables Inn, tel. (907) 479-0751, is one of the largest and most spectacular B&Bs in Alaska. Originally a university frat house, the 7 Gables is a 7,000-square-foot custom Tudor house on an acre and a half by the river, complete with seven-foot stained-glass windows, a seven-foot indoor waterfall, and a two-story greenhouse. Breakfasts are "healthy gourmet," such as stuffed french toast, salmon quiche, peach-pecan crepes, cherry-cheese blintzes, with homemade breads, muffins, fruit, herb tea, and specialty coffees. Rates start at $90 for regular rooms and end at $130 for suites. All have private bath, cable TV, VCR, and phones with fax/modem jacks; separate lodging for smokers and non-smokers. Laundry and kitchen available. Hosts Paul and Leicha Welton have been honored by the Visitors Bureau with the Golden Heart Award for exceptional hospitality.

Emergency Accommodations

If you're broke, **Fairbanks Rescue Mission,** tel. (907) 452-6608, next to Foodland, offers a bed for $3 a night or you can work to pay your way. Meals are provided after a Christian service. Check in before 6:30 p.m. and be up by 6 a.m. for breakfast. Because these facilities are provided for locals, use them only if you have to. Freeloading might take a space that could be used by someone truly in need.

FOOD

Breakfast

The **Bakery,** 69 College Rd. near the corner of Illinois, open Mon.-Sat. 6:30 a.m-9 p.m., Sunday 7 a.m.-4 p.m., is highly recommended for any meal, but especially for big breakfasts and fine baked goods. Bacon and eggs are $6; steak and eggs $9.25; six kinds of French toast; burgers $5.25-7; sandwiches $6; cheap dinners 3-9 p.m., like steaks, chicken, and fish $7-14. **Maria's Place Cafe,** downtown at the corner of Fourth and Lacey, has a good breakfast special of eggs, sausage, and pancakes for $4, served all day. **June's Cafe** on Illinois St. at the corner of Phillips Field Rd. has good coffee-shop fare, friendly efficient service, and reasonable prices. Breakfast, lunch, or dinner served all hours. Have breakfast here before catching the train to Denali; open Mon.-Sat. 6 a.m.-7:30 p.m.

Lunch

A good salad bar is in the gourmet/deli section of **Carr's Foodland Supermarket,** corner of Gaffney and Lacey, just south of downtown. Excellent selection of fruit, veggies, salads, soup, taco bar—$3.29 a pound. Pay for your salad at the cashier, then sit and eat in the deli or on the deck outside.

Campus Corner (intersection of University and College) is a good place to head for lunch. **Whole Earth Grocery** sells bulk groceries daily 10 a.m. -7 p.m.; their deli, open Mon.-Sat. 11 a.m.-3 p.m., has great no-bull burgers, tempeh Reubens, falafel, veggie sandwiches, daily specials, and a great salad bar, everything around $6. Highly recommended. Upstairs is **Wok n' Roll** fast-food Chinese, open Mon.-Sat. 11 a.m.-9 p.m.: quick spring rolls ($1.50), hot-and-sour soup ($4.50), fried rice and chop suey ($5.50-8), and flesh dishes ($7.50-9.50). Stroll next door to **Hot Licks,** open weekdays 7 a.m.-11 p.m., Saturday 11 a.m.-11 p.m., Sunday noon-10 p.m., for homemade ice cream, frozen yogurt, and great sherbet, as well as bread, soup, baked goods, and espresso.

Souvlaki, just across the Cushman Street Bridge on Illinois near the *News-Miner,* serves good Greek gyros and salads.

Downtown are two Fairbanks dining institutions. The **Sunshine Diner** on Second Ave. has been in the same location (though in a different part of the building) since the 1930s. This is classic Americana: $5.25 bacon and eggs, $6-8 burgers, $4 chili, plus $4 root beer floats, $4.25 hot fudge sundaes, $6.75 banana splits, and $5-6 triple thick shakes and malts. **Woolworths,** around the corner on Cushman, has a big menu of similar fare that's a little cheaper than the Sunshine: $6-7 for bacon and eggs, burgers, hot turkey and roast beef sanwiches, liver and onions, and the like. Banana splits and fountain treats in the $4 range.

Fast-food row is on Airport Way between Lathrop and Wilbur: Wendy's, McDonald's, Denny's, Pizza Hut, Burger King, etc. **Golden Shanghai,** tel. (907) 451-1100, is a big gaudy Mandarin restaurant, a bit odd-looking on the block, serving a lunch special 11:30 a.m.-3 p.m. Mon.-Sat. for $5.50, and pork, beef, poultry, duck, seafood, moo shu, and noodle dishes for $7-13 till 10 p.m. nightly. The Golden also has Fairbanks' only Mongolian barbecue. A McDonald's and a Wendy's are also in the mall area near the Tamarac Inn. The two **Food Factories,** one at the Bentley Mall and the other on S. Cushman at 17th, seem to enjoy a good reputation around town, even though the prices are pretty high and the food—burgers and subs, mostly—tastes kind of like the name sounds.

Dinner

Try **Pasta Bella,** 706 Second Ave., for fresh pasta, homemade bread, gourmet pizza, and subs. Recommended.

Peking Garden, best Chinese in town, is at 1101 Noble St. at 12th, serving Mandarin and Szechuan in the $8-10 range, plus a daily all-you-can-eat lunch buffet, $6.95. Locals are enthusiastic about the **Thai House,** at 526 Fifth Ave. downtown.

Heading south out of town on S. Cushman you'll find two Mexican restaurants: **El Sombrero** (corner Airport Way next to the **Drop In Cafe,** which is the oldest restaurant in Fairbanks— opened in 1950) and **Los Amigos** (28th Ave.), which is the better. If you're looking to get out of all that sun, Los Amigos gives the best dark in town.

If you're not sick of salmon bakes by now, try the one at Alaskaland (see "Alaskaland," above, for hours and prices) The salmon is superb— kings caught around Sitka and flown in fresh daily. The owner grew up in Juneau where his father was a commercial fisherman, so he knows his fish. The big $13.95 **buffet** at Ester Gold Camp (see "Ester" under "Vicinity of Fairbanks," below) includes Dungeness crab for $18.50.

For some alfresco dining on the river, head for **Pike's Landing,** out Airport Rd., tel. (907) 479-6500, open daily 11:30 a.m. to 11 p.m. Lloyd Pike opened his log bar at this site in 1969; since then, the Landing has expanded into a 130-seat dining room and a 100-seat sports bar (12- to 27-inch TV sets scattered around), with a massive 11,000-square-foot wood deck (accommodates 500 diners) and dock. Pike's serves burgers for $6.75, sandwiches (Reuben, hot turkey) $8, clams linguine $8.50, crab-stuffed chicken $22, king salmon $24, king crab $32. Great desserts: key lime pie $4, baked Alaska $5. Or just get some finger food in the bar or on the deck.

The fanciest rooms in town are the **Bear and Seal** at the Westmark Fairbanks (one of the only restaurants in Alaska that doesn't publish prices on the menu) and the **Turtle Club,** 10 Mile Old Steese in Fox. For the **Pump House,** see "Entertainment," below.

ENTERTAINMENT

Drinkin' and Dancin'
For the best view in town, have a drink (but skip the food) at **Ravens Nest,** top of the Northern Lights Hotel (formerly the Captain Hook, before that the Polaris), corner of Lacey and First Avenue. For a nice riverside drink and hors d'oeuvres, head out to the **Pumphouse,** 1.3 Mile Chena Pump Rd., tel. (907) 479-8452. A National Historical Monument, the Pumphouse was built in 1933 to pump water up Chena Ridge to provide pressure for the hydraulic "giants" used in gold dredging. Renovated in 1978, the restaurant/bar has a fascinating interior of mining and pumping artifacts. Good food, too: lunch

$7-10 (steak, chicken, seafood, burgers), and dinner $15-28 (salmon, peppersteak, king crab).

Don't be put off by the weird exterior of the **Greyhound Lounge,** corner of Airport and Cushman, tel. (907) 452-7977. It's walkable from downtown, the room is large and comfortable, the dance floor is huge, and if the band is halfway decent, you've got it made.

But if you wanna *rock,* head straight for the **Howling Dog Saloon,** 11 Mile Old Steese Highway in Fox, Alaska, which advertises itself as "the Farthest Northern Rock 'N Roll Bar in the World." The house band is usually the hottest around and will get you jumping up and down, becoming one with the music, all night long. Note the steel pipeline weld-ring hanging over the bar; when a local or two who shall remain nameless get to feeling frisky, a hammer taken to the ring produces a sound that easily overpowers the band's wall of amplifiers, and the vibrations are picked up on the university's seismograph. Also check out the flags from around the world.

Movies
The nine-screen **Goldstream Cinema** is on Airport Way at Lathrop, tel. (907) 456-5113. Movies might also be showing at **Alaskaland Civic Center** Mon.-Wed. at 8 p.m., $4. Finally, don't forget about the 30 free documentaries at the **Alaska Public Lands Information Center,** Third and Cushman.

Saloon Theaters
The **Palace Saloon** at Alaskaland, tel. (907) 456-5960, offers a musical-comedy revue nightly all summer, written and performed by Jim Bell, in his third decade at the Palace. The show, "Golden Heart Revue," changes a little every year; it goes on at 8 p.m., $11. The **Malemute Saloon** in Ester, 10 miles south of Fairbanks, tel. (907) 479-2500, has been a local institution since 1958, putting on a musical revue and Robert Service recitations nightly at 9 p.m., $11 adults, $5 under 12. You sit at plywood and beer-barrel tables; the pitchers keep coming and the peanut shells mingle with the two-inch-deep sawdust. (For other entertainment in Ester, see "Ester" under "Vicinity of Fairbanks.")

Baseball
One local "rookie" team, the Alaska Goldpanners, plays against teams from throughout Alaska,

Hawaii, and the West Coast. The games are played at Growden Field, Second and Wilbur, behind Alaskaland, starting at 7:30 p.m. The famous Midnight Sun game, played around the summer solstice, starts at 10:15 p.m. and goes nine innings without using the field's artificial lights.

Events

Fairbanksans have roughly 90 days a year to get their fill of outdoor extravaganzas—without having to worry about frostbite, that is—and they go at it with a vengeance. The first big event of the season is the summer solstice's **Midnight Madness** (June 20-21), another excuse for department-store sales. Next comes **Golden Days,** between the second and third weekends in July—a weeklong party culminating in The Grand Parade. The whole town turns out, and if you happen to be there, even without your camera, you won't forget it. Next comes the **World Eskimo-Indian Olympics,** a 29-year-old event featuring Alaska Native athletic games, dance, and art. This three-day event, held at the Big Dipper Recreation Arena at 19th and Lathrop, tel. (907) 456-6683, includes such unusual competitions as the Ear Pull, Greased Pole Walk, Kneel Jump, Knuckle Hop, Seal Skin, Toe Kick, and Blanket Toss. It could be one of the most exotic and memorable events in Alaska. Finally, the **Tanana Valley State Fair** takes place at the Fairgrounds, College Rd., the second and third weeks of August. Dress warmly.

SHOPPING AND SERVICES

Gift shops abound downtown; **Arctic Travelers** at 201 Cushman (and Alaskaland) is the biggest. Next door is **Alaska Rare Coins,** selling rare coins, rare license plates, and out-of-print books about Northland—a classic old store. At 537 Second Ave. is Native-owned **Beads and Things,** selling handmade gifts and curios.

If you're looking for gold nuggets fresh from Alaskan streams at "spot" prices, go to **Oxford Assaying,** 748 Gaffney Rd., tel. (907) 456-3967; they have all sizes of nuggets at all prices—great to take home as authentic souvenirs or to bring to a jeweler to be made into rings, necklaces, or earrings. Look around at gold nugget jewelry in the gift shops, then go to Oxford to pick out the nuggets to design your own.

For groceries go to **Carr's Foodland,** Lacey and Gaffney; the two **Super-Value** stores, at the Gavora and Shoppers Forum malls, could have better (though more expensive) produce.

The **Great Alaskan Bowl Company,** 4630 Old Airport Rd. (take a left off Airport onto Sportsman between the Castle and Fred Meyers and follow it around to the right), tel. (907) 474-9663, sells a variety of birch hardwood bowls, all fashioned from a single split log. Four inch bowls $48, two 9-inch bowls $38, three 11-inch bowls $99, matching sets of seven-, nine-, and 11-inch bowls $99, add a 13-incher for $180. A window overlooks the wood shop; the wood shavings are used for packing material and decoration in the showroom.

Services

The **post office** is right downtown between Third and Fourth Avenues. The most convenient **laundromat** is Coin King, across from Foodland. But bring your bankroll—$3 a load to wash and dry. Next door to Coin King is a do-it-yourself **car wash;** again, bring your quarters in a wheelbarrow: 25 cents for 40 seconds of hot water. To wash your own self, **B&C Laundromat,** Campus Corner Mall (on College at University Ave.), has public showers: $2.50 for 15 minutes. Or shower then swim at **Mary Siah Recreation Center,** open weekdays 8 a.m. to 9 p.m., Saturday 8 a.m. to 4 p.m., $2.

Vista Travel, 1211 Cushman, tel. (907) 456-7888, is the Fairbanks agent for the state ferry system and will happily and helpfully sell you tickets for any other kind of transportation. If you'd like some film developed quickly, head to **Photo Express** in the Bentley Mall Annex. If you need a doctor, the **Fairbanks Public Health Center** is at 800 Airport Way (corner of Gillam), tel. (907) 452-1776, or look up "Health and Social Services" under State Government Offices in the blue pages of the phone book. If they can't help try the **Fairbanks Clinic,** 1867 Airport at Wilbur, tel. (907) 452-1761—$80 to see a doctor. For emergencies, drag yourself to **Memorial Hospital** at 1650 Cowles, tel. (907) 452-8181.

INFORMATION

For the **Fairbanks Visitors Bureau** and the **Alaska Public Lands Information Center,** see

"Sights," above. Topographical maps of all of Alaska are sold in Room 126 in the Federal Building, 101 12th Ave. (open Mon.-Fri. 9 a.m.-4:30 p.m.).

Noel Wien Library

The Noel Wien Library, corner of Airport Way and Cowles, is a very comfortable and complete facility. One look inside tells you a lot about Fairbanks' nine months of winter. Over 60% of borough residents hold library cards, compared to an average of 15-25% nationally. Odd hours; call (907) 452-5177 for info. Noel Wien was a pioneer bush pilot who, with his two brothers, founded Wien Airlines. The library was built in 1977 on the site of Weeks Field, the first airport in Fairbanks.

Bookstores

Waldenbooks is in the Bentley Mall, College Rd. and Steese Hwy., tel. (907) 456-8088, open mall hours. **Baker and Baker** is now in the University Center at Airport and University, open weekdays 10 a.m. to 8 p.m., weekends 10 a.m. to 6 p.m. **Gulliver's Books,** at Campus Corner on College Rd. and University Ave., is an Alaskan used-bookstore chain. Good bargains here.

TRANSPORTATION

By Air

Fairbanks International Airport (FAI) is six miles southwest of downtown. The second floor houses a gift shop, a snack shop, and a lounge. On the first floor are an unmanned info booth with a bunch of brochures, a few stuffed animals, and the Curtiss JN-4D "Jenny" biplane used by Carl Ben Eielson, one of the earliest and most famous bush pilots from the area.

Alaska Airlines, tel. (907) 452-1661, flies between Fairbanks and Anchorage nine times daily. **Delta Airlines,** tel. (800) 221-1212, flies once a day. **Air North Canada,** tel. (800) 764-0407 (Alaska) and (800) 661-0407 (Canada), flies to Dawson Tuesday, Friday, and Sunday; be sure to take proof of citizenship when you fly into Canada. **Warbelows,** tel. (907) 474-0518, flies out of Fairbanks to places varied and sundry; see the "Eagle" section for details.

There is no city bus service out to the airport; transfers are provided by **Prestige Limo,** tel. (907) 479-2036, $5, or **King Cab** limo service,

tel. (907) 456-5464, $5. **G.O. Shuttle,** tel. (907) 474-3847, charges $5 from Fairbanks and also does transfers from North Pole ($25) and Eielson AFB ($40).

By Train

Alaska Railroad departs Fairbanks daily between mid-May and mid-Sept. at 8:30 a.m., arriving at Denali at 12:30 p.m. ($50) and Anchorage at 8:30 p.m. ($135). The northbound train departs Anchorage daily at 8:30 a.m. and is scheduled to arrive at Denali Park at 3:50 p.m. ($95) and in Fairbanks at 8:30 p.m.; the train leaves Denali for Fairbanks at 4 p.m.; $50 one-way, bicycle $2 extra. Tour-bus fares to Denali and Anchorage are comparable to those of the train, though minivan fares are much cheaper. But the train is a more comfortable, enjoyable, and historical way to see this part of Alaska.

If you want to go in luxury, however, buy a ticket for the superdome vistacruisers hooked onto the end of the train, run by Tour Alaska and Westours. The train depot is at 280 N. Cushman, tel. (907) 456-4155, only a five-minute walk to downtown, 10 minutes to the local transit terminal.

By Bus

From Fairbanks, bus transportation southbound is good. **Denali Express,** a company run by young locals that's been around an unusually long time (about seven years), had the least expensive deal to Denali ($25) and Anchorage ($100) in a 14-seat minivan; that was in 1994, but nobody answered their phone or returned calls in 1996. You can try calling them at (800) 327-7651, or in Anchorage at (907) 274-8539.

Gray Line/Westours, tel. (907) 452-2843, no longer offers bus service to Denali or Anchorage from Fairbanks.

Eastbound, Gray Line runs **Alaskon Express** from Fairbanks to Whitehorse, overnighting at the Westmark Inn in Beaver Creek, Yukon, near the border, for $165 one-way. The coaches depart from the Westmark Fairbanks and Westmark Inn at 8 a.m. Sunday, Tuesday, and Friday. Show up half an hour early and check in with the red-vested expeditors. You can book a room in Beaver Creek for $40 pp double occupancy; tel. (907) 452-2843 for reservations. Also ask about the 10- and 14-day **Alaskon Pass.**

Getting Around

Fairbanks' public bus system, Metropolitan Area Commuter Service (MACS) is just that: a commuter service that runs weekdays roughly 6:30 a.m.-7 p.m. After that, the lines run infrequently till around 9:30 p.m.; Saturday has very limited service, and Sunday has none. The routes are color-coded, and you can pick up folded timetables of individual routes at all the info centers, travel desks, and the central Transit Park (where all routes begin and end) on Cushman and Fifth Avenue. The fare is $1.50, 75 cents for seniors. A good deal is either a $3 all-day pass or racks of five tokens for $5. Bus drivers are extremely helpful; don't hesitate to ask them anything. Or call MACS Transit Hotline at (907) 459-1011.

To get around town at your pace, **G.O. Shuttle,** tel. (907) 474-3847, is a good bet for a personal tour at your own speed. For $25 per person, you can visit most of the major attractions around Fairbanks by calling in advance with time and destination. They do limit the pickups to two or more, but this is a great way to design your own daily tour.

Taxis charge $1.50 for the flag drop and $1.60 per mile thereafter. Most drivers are locals who speak pretty good "guide."

Car Rentals

Rent-A-Wreck has a branch in Fairbanks at 2105 Cushman, tel. (907) 452-1606 or (907) 456-8459; cheapest rates in town for not-too-badly beat-up cars, vans, and trucks. **Arctic Rent-a-Car** at the airport, tel. (907) 479-8044, also has good rates, but ask if you can take the cars into Canada. Surprisingly, **Avis,** tel. (907) 474-0900, had the best rate, with unlimited mileage, in Alaska in 1993. To rent 4WD vehicles, call the specialists at **Affordable Car Rental,** tel. (907) 452-7341. And if you want to tool around in an RV, contact **Fireweed RV**

Rentals, tel. (907) 474-3742; they rent 21- and 27-footers from $125 a day, along with extras such as housekeeping and linen packages, barbecues, and lawn chairs.

Hitchhiking

First, get as far out of town as possible on MACS, then pick a good spot on the highway. For Delta Junction and the Richardson or Alaska highways, catch the Green Line out to North Pole. For Denali and Anchorage on the George Parks Highway, take the Red Line to the corner of Geist Rd. and Fairbanks St., then walk the half-mile to the highway, or take the Blue Line to the corner of Geist and Chena Pump Rd. and stand right there with the other hitchhikers.

Tours by Bus

Gray Line has a travel desk in the lobby of the Westmark Fairbanks, Noble and Eighth, tel. (907) 452-2843. Book a city tour, a gold-dredge tour, or a riverboat cruise, and catch the bus in back of the hotel. Princess Tours, tel. (907) 479-9640, does the same, from their new hotel out near the airport.

The Binkley family, now in its third (soon to be fourth) generation of riverboat pilots, runs **Discovery Riverboat Cruises,** tel. (907) 479-6673. This four-hour 20-mile cruise on the Chena and Tanana rivers is a bargain at $37. This is the only operating paddlewheeler outfit in Alaska, with three riverboats in the fleet. In 1987, *Discovery III,* designed by the Binkleys and built in Seattle, chugged into Fairbanks after a 1,000-mile voyage—the first sternwheeler to make the trip up the Yukon River from St. Mary's in more than 30 years. The cruises depart from the dock at the end of Dale Rd. out by the airport at 8:45 a.m. and 2 p.m. Some evening cruises are available, but call for scheduling. If you need a ride, try the tour companies, taxis, or limos.

DIANA LASICH HARPER

SUBURBS OF FAIRBANKS

NORTH POLE

In 1949, Con Miller was cleaning out the Fairbanks trading post he'd just bought and found a Santa Claus suit. He liked it so much that he took to wearing it during his trips to the Interior to buy furs and sell supplies. The costume made a big impression on the Native children. A few years later, when he moved 12 miles southeast of Fairbanks near Eielson Air Force Base, he built a new trading post and called it Santa Claus House. Miller and his neighbors chose the name

North Pole for their new town, reportedly to attract a toy manufacturer to the area (none arrived).

Today, Santa Claus House, right on the Richardson Highway, is the largest and tackiest gift shop in the state. North Pole is a large suburb of Fairbanks (pop. 1,550), with street names like St. Nicholas and Kris Kringle Drives and Santa Claus and Mistletoe Lanes, business names such as Santaland RV Park and Elf's Den Diner, and a 50,000-watt Christian radio station KJNP (King Jesus of North Pole). Twenty-three churches are in the area, including St.

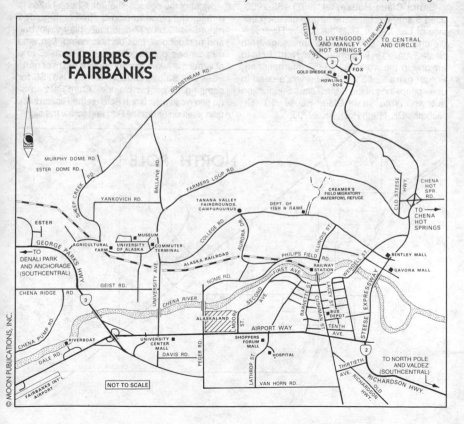

Nicholas Church, and Santa Claus House has a 40-foot Santa figure out front.

The North Pole **Visitor Log Cabin** is just off the Richardson Highway (corner of Mission Rd.), tel. (907) 488-2242, open daily June, July, and August 8 a.m.-7 p.m. There's a **campground** on Fifth Ave., and Chena Lakes Recreation Area (see below) is nearby. But the big thrill here is to get your letters postmarked "North Pole, Alaska." Post them from the Santa Claus House or the post office on Fifth Avenue. Throughout December, this post office is deluged with letters and cards from people wanting a North Pole postmark—the stacks can be piled 10 feet high. And that's *not* including the estimated 10,000 letters to Santa Claus himself, which are all answered by students at North Pole Middle School.

Santa Claus House, tel. (907) 488-2200, open 8 a.m.-8 p.m., is the largest gift shop this side of Las Vegas. Ride the Snowy River kiddie choo-choo. Buy a "holiday message from Santa," mailed in December from North Pole to anyone in the world, $2.50 ($3 international). For an extra $2.50 they'll send you a deed to one square inch of the Santa Claus Subdivision in town. Write Santa Claus House, 101 St. Nicholas Dr., North Pole, AK 99705.

Chena Lakes Recreation Area

In mid-Aug., 1967, it rained seven inches in seven days, and the Chena River overflowed its banks, inundating low-lying Fairbanks under five feet of floodwaters. Half the town's residents were evacuated; damage neared $200 million. The task of preventing a similar disaster in the future fell to the Army Corps of Engineers, which mucked around for 15 years, building a dam at Moose Creek, a levee and spillway into the Tanana River, and this 2,000-acre park of man-made lakes and recreational facilities. The recreation area contains the nearest beach to Fairbanks, and on hot weekends the exodus is not unlike that of Bostonians fleeing to Cape Cod—you might be able to wedge a dishtowel onto some sand and swim in place.

Most of the season, though, Chena Lakes is a delightful place to picnic, stroll (self-guided nature trail), bike (7-mile trail), play volleyball and horseshoes, pick berries, camp, fish, and rent canoes, paddleboats, and sailboats. Camp at either the lakes campground or the river park. Fees are $3 per carload for day use, $6 for camping, $1 per bicycle rider. From Fairbanks, go five miles past North Pole on the Richardson, take a left on Laurance Rd., and follow the signs.

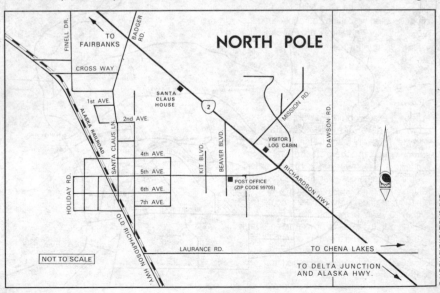

NORTH POLE

NOT TO SCALE

© MOON PUBLICATIONS, INC.

Santa is larger than life in North Pole.

Or catch the Green Line from town and have the driver drop you off on Laurance Road. Or call (907) 452-3279 and ask if the Fairbanks transit system is running a special bus to the recreation area.

FOX

In 1901, Felice Pedroni (Felix Pedro) found color on what is now Pedro Creek and was credited with the discovery of the Cleary and Goldstream veins, which touched off the rush from the Klondike and Nome to the Fairbanks area. However, the gold here was anything but easy for the taking: this gold-laden bedrock was normally 80-100 feet under gravel, muck, and permafrost. Within 20 years of the find, the rich creeks were worked out, the shallow, low-grade ground was exhausted, and most miners couldn't afford the expense of working the deep claims. In 1923, however, the railroad was finished from Seward to Fairbanks and brought with it the feasibility of large-scale gold production. Hydraulic giants,

monster dredges, miles of tailings, and businessmen in three-piece suits replaced the lone prospector with his hammer and bucket. This second—corporate—gold rush to Fairbanks eventually produced almost $200 million worth of the precious heavy metal.

A ride 10 miles up the Steese Highway from Fairbanks to and around Fox clearly reveals the impact of this second boom (as well as the third—you pass the pipeline on the way). Huge cleared fields and stripped hillsides trace the progress of the giants and dredges, and the tailings lie in the snaking mounds they were spit into 50 years ago. Marble, gravel, and sand are for sale along the roadside. Heavy machinery dots the land with the bovine patience of metal and rubber.

Fox boasts the **Fox Roadhouse,** one of the most popular local steak-and-seafood houses (best prime rib in the Interior), tel. (907) 457-7461 for reservations. The famous **Howling Dog Saloon** (see "Entertainment" under Fairbanks) is across the highway. Up the road a hair is the **Turtle Club,** tel. (907) 457-3883: prime rib $17-26, along with halibut, prawns, lobster, and king crab in the $15-25 range.

Continue another 15 miles past town for the monument to Felice Pedroni, who started it all rolling at the turn of the century. Across the road is Pedro Creek; try your hand at panning for a little dust, and note the unnatural look of a creek played for gold for most of the century.

Gold Dredge No. 8

Local placer gold derives from ancient quartz veins once exposed in creek beds, now buried up to 100 feet below the surface. To get to it, first you hose off the surface layer down to two feet with hydraulic cannons or "giants," then down another few feet as the exposed frozen gravel thaws on its own. The deeper frozen muck and rock is thawed over a year or so by water pumped through pipes from the surface to bedrock, supplied by monumental aqueducts such as the Davidson Ditch. Once the earth down to bedrock is diggable, a gold dredge is brought in.

The dredge dwarfs even the most giant machine in this land of giant machines. It's a true Alaskan-size contraption that looks like a cartoon cross between a houseboat and a crane. An endless circular conveyor of up to 100 steel buckets scoops up the gravel, conveys it·to the top end of a revolving screen, and dumps it. The screen separates the larger rocks, shunting them off to the tailing piles, from the golden gravel, which is sifted from the screen to riffles, where quicksilver (mercury) gleans the gold, forming an amalgam. The riffles are cleaned every couple of weeks, then the gold is further processed and assayed. In the old days during the height of production, the gold would next be shipped to the mint, where it earned $35 per troy ounce (the price hovers around $400 today).

Gold Dredge No. 8, the only National Historic Mechanical Engineering Landmark in Alaska, is just a little larger than its official designation. One of Alaska's first steel-hulled bucketline dredges, it was installed in 1928—five stories tall, 250 feet long, weighing over 1,000 tons. The tour, $10, lasting around a half-hour, starts every 45 minutes from 9 a.m. to 6 p.m. After the tour you can pan for gold—and keep what you find—for as long as you like. The grounds also contain a restaurant, a bar, a small hotel, and a gift shop. Open daily, tel. (907) 457-6058. To get there, drive or hitch eight miles up the Steese Highway toward Fox, take a left on Goldstream Rd. and another left on the Old Steese. No public transportation nears the place, but Gray Line leaves from the major hotels at 6:30 and 7:30 p.m.

ESTER

Like Fox, Ester had a two-boom gold rush: panning and placer mining in the early 1900s, then dredging by the Fairbanks Exploration Co. from the mid-1920s to the late '50s. Today, Ester, which is ten miles south of Fairbanks on the Parks Highway, has a few buildings that remain from the once-booming mining days, now housing a hotel, a gift shop, a gallery, and the famous Malemute Saloon. Since 1958 the Hotel Cripple Creek, now **Ester Gold Camp,** tel. (907) 479-2500, has been in operation here, in a refurbished bunkhouse. The rooms are plain but functional and a real bargain at $48 s (shared bath)—making Ester Gold Camp an attractive alternative to pricey Fairbanks if you have a car. Free continental breakfast is served in the mess hall downstairs, which also spreads out an all-you-can-eat buffet with broasted chicken, reindeer stew, and halibut daily 5-9 p.m., $14.95; you can also partake of all-you-can-eat Dungeness crab for an extra $7.

Top off the evening with the Robert Service musical extravaganza at the **Malemute Saloon** (see "Entertainment" under Fairbanks), or take in the "Crown of Light" photosymphony ($5, daily 7 and 8 p.m.) at the Firehouse Theater just up the road. This 45-minute musically accompanied slide show of the northern lights on a curved 30-foot screen (affectionately known as **"Aurorarama"**) is decidedly more high-tech than most attractions in Alaska, and wonderfully dark. The shots are individually pretty, but on the whole the show is slow-changing and ponderous.

By car, head down the George Parks Highway toward Denali 10 miles, then follow the signs for Ester and Ester Gold Camp. All the tour companies offer packages with roundtrip transportation and the saloon show, but the resort company has its own shuttle bus, leaving around 6:15 and 7:30 p.m. from the major hotels in town. Call (907) 479-2500 (907) to arrange pickup, $4.

VICINITY OF FAIRBANKS

The vicinity of Fairbanks offers three outstanding opportunities to explore and experience the land and waterways, and then to luxuriate in hot springs that have soothed and refreshed travelers for a century. With the Interior's predictable good weather, the long days and low lighting, and the humbling power of this vast humanless wilderness, you'll return from any of these trips knowing a lot more about Alaska, and yourself. **Chena Hot Springs Road** boasts three exciting hiking trails, two stunning campgrounds, a choice of canoe routes and fishing spots, and a large pool resort, all within an hour's drive of town on a good paved road. The **Steese Highway** has five campgrounds, abundant canoeing and fishing, a high-country backpack that rivals much of Denali, and the fascinating evidence of gold fever—past and present. And the pool waiting at Arctic Circle Hot Springs is about as close as you'll come to hedonist heaven in central Alaska. The **Elliott Highway** is the longest, roughest, and most primitive ride of the three. Along it is one long trail close to Fairbanks, no campgrounds to speak of, and no facilities of any kind, all of which make the small pool and hot tubs at the road's end in friendly Manley all the more rewarding.

And for a real road adventure, one that's rivaled only by the Dempster Highway in Yukon and Northwest Territories, you can head up the Dalton Highway, which begins at Mile 73 on the Elliott Highway and continues 414 miles all the way to Deadhorse, a few miles south of Prudhoe Bay.

CHENA HOT SPRINGS ROAD

Depending on whom you believe, either Felix Pedro (1903) or the U.S. Geological Survey (1907) discovered the hot springs off the north fork of the Chena River. Shortly after, the land was homesteaded by George Wilson, who built a lodge and cabins and enclosed the springs in a pool. The 55-mile road from Fairbanks was completed in 1967, only to be wiped out a few weeks later by the great flood. It was finally rebuilt and completely paved by 1983. From Mile 26 to Mile 51 is Chena River State Recreation Area, a well-developed and beautiful playground in Fairbanks's backyard, where numerous trails, river access, picnic areas, and two campgrounds are within an easy hour's drive from town. You could easily fill up three or four days camping, hiking, backpacking, and canoeing (all free), and then satisfy the creature-comfort yearnings you accumulated in the backcountry with a soak in the pool and a drink at the resort at the end of the road.

By car, take the Steese Highway just north of town to the exit to Chena Hot Springs Road. It's well trafficked, so hitching shouldn't be too time-consuming. The road starts out somewhat roller-coasterish from frost heaves, but the scenery is pleasing—rolling green hills dotted by small verdant farms.

Tack's General Store

The essence of one-stop shopping, Alaska-style. The giant greenhouse is warm and beautiful and will satisfy all the craving for color you've been having in this rather monochromatic environ-ment. The cafe serves breakfast all day, reasonably priced sandwiches on homemade bread, and your choice of at least two dozen pies—biggest slice you've ever seen for $3.25. The two-story general store houses everything from a post office to pipe fittings to the latest videos. Open daily 8 a.m.-8 p.m., tel. (907) 488-3242.

Chena River State Recreation Area

At 254,000 acres, this is Alaska's largest state recreation *area;* only Denali, Chugach, and Kachemak Bay *parks* are larger. Chena River SRA boasts luxurious campgrounds, excellent outdoor recreational opportunities, lush greenery, towering trees (for Interior Alaska), rolling hills, the curvy Chena River, and best of all, no crowds. When town becomes oppressive, head a half-hour east to some of the best that Interior has to offer. For information, contact the Alaska Department of Natural Resources in Fairbanks at (907) 451-2700.

The **Granite Tors** loop trail starts at Mile 39, on the righthand side just before the bridge just before the second campground. Constructed by the YCC in 1980-82, this well-maintained trail is a 15-mile, six-hour roundtrip. The first mile or so is on boardwalk over muskeg; the first tors (strange granite sculptures thrust to near the surface, then exposed when the surrounding earth eroded away) are around six miles from the trailhead on both the north and south forks of the trail.

Angel Rocks trail begins at Mile 49 just beyond a pullout right before the fourth bridge over the Chena. It's only three miles or so, though the first couple are uphill. The rock outcroppings in the high country are worth the huff. Allow three to four hours.

For the **Chena Dome** trail, take the northern trailhead, which starts at Mile 50.5, a half-mile past Angel Creek on the left side of the road; it's a three-day, 29-mile loop trail mostly along ridgetops marked by cairns—great views. A quarter-mile up the trail is the sign for Chena Dome (nine miles); after a short boardwalk you start to climb and leave the mosquitoes and heat behind. One mile up the trail is a good viewpoint.

The road parallels the river all the way to the hot springs and crosses it four times, at Miles 37, 40, 44, and 49. Numerous well-marked pullouts give easy river access and your choice of the

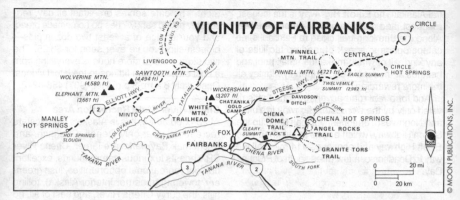

VICINITY OF FAIRBANKS

© MOON PUBLICATIONS, INC.

length of a canoe trip. A good place to put in is at the Mile 44 bridge—a little faster and more fun than downriver. Watch for sweepers, dead-heads, shallows, and especially the many impassable sloughs—stagnant, stinking, and mosquito-ridden.

Grayling fishing is great on this river, especially in July and August. You'll throw most back in, but you'll usually keep a half-dozen 12-to-15-inchers. If you see salmon migrating up-river, enjoy the view; you're not allowed to catch them in the SRA. Four small lakes (Miles 30, 43, 46, and 48) are also well stocked with grayling and trout.

Rosehip Campground, Mile 27, right at the entrance to the recreation area, is as big and lush a campground as you could ever want, only a half-hour from town. The level gravel pull-outs are big enough for 40-foot RVs, and you can put up a tent in one site and not see the tent in the next, almost. The river is never more than a two-minute walk away. There are 25 sites, pit toilets, water pumps, and numerous signboards with info about trails, wildlife, canoe routes; $8 pp. **Tors Trail Campground,** Mile 39, is a little less woodsy and inviting than the Rosehip, but it has the same excellent elbow room, facilities, and river, and the Granite Tors trailhead is right across the road. Less crowded, 18 sites, $8 pp.

Chena Hot Springs

At Mile 57, the road ends at this sprawling resort. Along with the hot-spring-fed swimming pools and hot tub, it offers hotel rooms and honeymoon suites ($70-115, depending on the room

and the season), four sizes of cabins ($40-110), RV parking (dry $10, hookups $12; dump station, showers $2); camping (secluded and quiet if a little mucky; $10 per site a night), and numerous activities: volleyball, croquet, badminton, billiards, cookouts, hiking, mountain biking, gold panning, horseback riding ($15-60), and massage; and skiing, snowmobiling, sleigh rides, ice-fishing, and snowshoeing in winter.

The lodge is worth exploring for its neat little dining rooms, beautiful woodwork and furniture, and relaxing couches and library. Prices at the restaurant in the lodge are reasonable. The geothermal facilities are modern by Lower 48 standards. The solarium features pools, hot tubs, and a giant redwood deck. The water comes out of the spring at nearly 160° F, and is a little under 110° in the pools.

For information and reservations, call (907) 452-7867 or (800) 478-4681 in Alaska only. You can also write at Box 73440, Fairbanks, AK 99707.

STEESE HIGHWAY AND CIRCLE HOT SPRINGS

Gold is the color of this country: the precious metal wrested with brute force from the reluctant earth, the golden-green panoramas of the alpine tundra, the golden light sparkling through the plumes of dust-fog along the road, and the pot of gold of the hot springs at the end of its own rainbow.

Other than the drive itself and the unlimited fishing and canoeing on the Chatanika River and Birch Creek, the excitement on the Steese can be found at the **Davidson Ditch,** on the challenging **Pinnell Mountain Trail,** and at **Circle Hot Springs** resort. The Davidson Ditch was one of the first miracle-of-engineering pipelines in this country, and unlike the oil pipeline, you can play on it! The Pinnell Trail is a three-day stroll along the windswept ridges of the White Mountains, with distant jagged horizons for the long-eyed, and stunning alpine wildflowers for the short. And after you've reached the limits of backcountry endurance, only 20 miles up the road is the biggest, deepest, hottest pool in Alaska, with not only all the conveniences and sociability you've been missing, but budget accommodations as well.

The Road

Named for Army general James G. Steese, president of the Alaska Road Commission 1920-27 who oversaw its entire construction, the Steese Highway parallels the original Fairbanks-Circle Trail. Thousands of fortune seekers floated up and down the Yukon to Circle, hit the trail after news of Felix Pedro's strike spread, and helped open up the Interior in the early 20th century. The road was completed in 1928 and paved for the first 44 miles in the early '50s.

Starting from Fairbanks, the highway immediately climbs into the gold-bearing hills, with a great viewpoint overlooking the Tanana Valley on the left at Hagelbarger Road. On a clear day, turn around to see if the Alaska Range is "out"—stunning panorama from Mt. McKinley to the eastern peaks of Deborah, Hess, and Hayes. Just up the road is a pullout to view the pipeline, which runs aboveground here, and an informative sign. Don't climb on this pipe. In a few miles

you come to the Goldstream dredge and Fox; note the extensive tailings in the area. Stop in at the **Fox General Store** and say hi to owner Lisa Kavanagh; the Fox Roadhouse, Turtle Club, and Howling Dog Saloon are covered under "Food" and "Entertainment" under "Fairbanks," above.

At the junction with the Elliott Highway (Route 2), take a right for the Steese (Route 6). At Mile 16 is a turnout with a plaque mounted on a stone monument to Felix Pedro; walk across the road to Pedro Creek, whose golden sands infected the stampeders with Fairbanks fever.

Fairbanks Exploration Company/Poker Flat

From Pedro Creek the frost-heaved pavement climbs quickly to the Cleary Summit (elevation 2,233 feet) ski hill. The road twists and turns down to **Chatanika;** at Mile 28, take a hard right and climb to the site of the Fairbanks Exploration Company Gold Camp. After the completion of the Alaska Railroad in 1923, the U.S. Smelting, Refining, and Mining Co. began acquiring and consolidating many of the placer properties around Fairbanks. By 1938, the subsidiary F.E. Co. had three dredges operating between Chatanika and Ester, had installed the Davidson Ditch (see below), and fueled the entire operation with its own power plant in Fairbanks. In its 30 years of production, F.E. Co. took out nearly $100 million in gold—and that was at no more than $35 per troy ounce, less than 10% of what it's worth today. The grounds are covered with vintage equipment and 15 restored buildings that are still maintained by machinery used during the '40s.

The **Chatanika Old F.E. Gold Camp** resort is open year-round, tel. (907) 389-2414. It's chock full of early Alaska memorabilia and mining artifacts. Rooms start at $50, suites go for $150. The restaurant serves three meals, an all-you-can-eat afternoon buffet, and Sunday brunch. The Sourdough Saloon serves the usual; the gift shop specializes in photos and posters of the aurora borealis.

A mile up the road is the **Chatanika Lodge,** tel. (907) 389-2164. Rooms here go for $45-50; a good special is dinner, breakfast, and room for two for $90. The restaurant is open daily (year-round) 9 a.m.-10 p.m. Check out the videos about the aurora and gold dredging on the big-screen TV. The large bar and dance floor look

GORDY OHLIGER

like they can handle just about anything. The Lodge also hosts the **Chatanika Days Outhouse Races** each March. Five-person outhouse teams race a one-mile course, with four pushing and one riding in the specially built "racing outhouses." Winners of the two-day event win cash, prizes, and trophies (with a miniature gold-plated outhouse on top). Needless to say, competition is tough!

At Poker Flat, two miles farther, the **Geophysical Institute** of UAF studies the aurora and the upper atmosphere. When it was constructed in the late 1960s, Poker Flat took its name from a Bret Harte short story, *The Outcasts of Poker Flat,* about a gambler and a prostitute who were banished from a mythical California gold-rush town in the winter and eventually froze to death. The construction crew building the rocket range for the Geophysical Institute considered itself similarly outcast. This is the only rocket range owned by a university in the world. Suborbital rockets are launched here; nearly 250 large and 1,500 small rockets have been sent up since 1969. The Alaska Aerospace Development Corporation, created in the early 1990s, is attempting to attract space-related industry to Alaska, which is well-situated to launch low-polar orbit satellites for telecommunications and research. Poker Flats is off-limits to the public, but tours can be arranged by calling (907) 474-7634.

Upper Chatanika River
State Recreation Site—Mile 39
Another excellent state facility, this campground has 28 sites, pit toilets, a water pump at the entrance, and plentiful river access for fishing (grayling) and boating, $8 pp. Head around to the back of the grounds and try for a campsite right on the river. Bring an inner tube and ride from the bridge down to your tent.

Davidson Ditch
The pavement ends at Mile 44, and the next 15 miles are rough—washboard shaky and deep gravel, slippery when dry. Take heart, though; it gets much smoother along the way. At Mile 57 are a side road and a pullout (left). The side road leads seven miles to **Nome Creek,** a historic mining area with a designated area for recreational gold panning. The pullout is for a long stretch of pipe, a remnant of the Davidson

Ditch, the amazing engineering feat (1925) that slaked the F.E. Co. dredges' enormous thirst for water (the dredges floated on man-made ponds so they could be moved). Starting at a dam on the upper Chatanika River, the 12-foot-wide, four-foot-deep, 83-mile-long ditch, along with nearly seven miles of 48-inch pipe and a combined mile of tunnels, crossed 90 miles of hilly wilderness, directing 56,000 gallons of water per minute to the goldfields. Notice the expansion or "slip" joint in the middle of the level section of the pipe here, and the wooden saddle below it. The pipe was drained in the winter but the cold still took its toll: note the bulge in the pipe where it cuts uphill, and the repair job on the joint.

This is one of several views of the ditch in the next 10 miles, standing in mute testimony to the struggle of rugged miners against rugged terrain and harsh elements in the quest for gold. You can't help but be amazed by this project, especially when you consider that the road was barely built, the machinery was primitive, and the land unyielding. F.E. Co.'s contract did not require the removal of the pipe when gold production ceased, so here it still sits—either a blight on the landscape or evidence of the colorful history of this land, depending on your perspective. Whichever it is, watch your footing as you monkey around on the pipe.

Cripple Creek Campground and Beyond
This BLM facility at Mile 60 consists of an inner loop for pickups and RVs and a walk-in section. Either take a site with the RV crowd or park in the walk-in lot by the toilets, head to the back of the campground, and pitch your tent right by the river. The water pump is at the start of the inner loop; a signboard, a nature trail, and toilets are at the other end. The mosquitoes are fierce in mosquito season.

The road out here gets smoother, wider, less slippery. From the back of a large pullout (right) at Mile 62 is another view of the pipe disappearing into a tunnel; it's an easy thrash through the brush to play on it. At Mile 81, natural spring water gushes cold and delicious from an open spigot, about five gallons a minute. While you've got the Davidson Ditch on your mind, multiply the pressure of the water from the spigot by a factor of 10,000 for an idea of the force with which the ditch moved its H_2O.

Pinnell Mountain Trail and Eagle Summit

The first trailhead leaves the Steese at Mile 85 at Twelve-Mile Summit (elevation 2,982 feet); the second rejoins the highway near Eagle Summit (Mile 107). A short access road (right) at the first trailhead leads past a signposted section of the Fairbanks-Circle Trail to a small mountain pond— nice spot for a picnic. The trail follows a boardwalk for the first-quarter mile, then climbs steadily for a long time. Most hikers prefer to start at the second trailhead, 700 feet higher, which has a great signboard full of fascinating information. This beautiful 27.3-mile, three-day trail through alpine tundra along White Mountain ridgelines is famous for its views of the Alaska and Brooks Ranges and the midnight sun on solstice, plus the incomparable wildflowers (especially the state flower, forget-me-not—striking blue dots on the tundra), which also peak in mid-June. This rolling, treeless high country, with long-distance views in all directions, makes you want to stop, get out, and book all the way to the Edge. Be prepared for wind! Get info and a trail map at the Public Lands Info Center in Fairbanks.

Eagle Summit, at 3,624 feet, is the highest point on the road, a popular destination for Fairbanksans and travelers around solstice time to watch the sun skirt the horizon, never setting. If the sun is *shining,* that is. It's been known to snow up here on solstice, or you could be socked in by clouds or fog. In fact, you might wish for a nice blizzard to hold down the skeeters, so thick and ferocious that they've been rumored to pick up men—large men— and carry them off. The mile-long access road to the summit is particularly steep and rocky; alternatively, walk up or drive a couple of miles past the turnoff just past Mile 109 and hike up the back side to save wear and tear on your vehicle. If you drive up and down the access road, though, when you get back to the Steese it feels like pavement!

To Central

At Mile 94 a road to the right leads to undeveloped camping and the launching point for the popular **Birchcreek Canoe Trail.** Coming down from the summit, there are gorgeous views of the current gold-mining activities on the valley floor, along Mammoth and Mastodon Creeks, so named for the frozen remains of large Alaskan mammals uncovered by strip mining. The tusks

on display at the UAF Museum came from here. Make sure to stop at 101 Gas to check out the ancient gas pump, which pumped its last gas(p) in the past. Take a left at Mile 119 and go straight at the fork for **Bedrock Creek Campground** (BLM); though it's now "closed," or unmaintained, you can certainly camp here if you want. It'd be just you and the skeeters.

Central

Ten miles farther is Central, whose year-round population of 150 triples in the summer due to the influx of miners. Passions run high around here about the right of individuals to mine their claims. **Witt's End,** tel. (907) 520-5115, has a gas station, a general store, clean rooms ($45 d), showers ($3), and free camping. **The Circle District Museum** in the log cabin in town has mining and mushing artifacts from the early days and a good wildflower photo display; $1, usually open daily noon-5 p.m. Walk around back to see the wagon-wheel camper. **Central Motor Inn and Campground,** tel. (907) 520-5228, rents trailer rooms for $40 s, $45 d, and serves meals in a small cafe.

Circle Hot Springs Resort

Hang a right on Hot Springs Rd. in central Central; in eight miles is the hot springs resort, tel. (907) 520-5113. This water is hot! It bubbles out of the ground at a rate of 386 gallons a minute and at a temperature of 139° F. Some of it fills an Olympic-size swimming pool; the water is completely exchanged every 18 hours. It also runs through pipes to keep the lodge at a tropical 72° F when it's 72° below outside, and has been irrigating sumptuous vegetable gardens in the area since 1905. Even if you don't get out of the car between Fairbanks and here, this pool is worth the trip. The water is much hotter than the pool at Manley, and the sulphur is nowhere near as strong as at Chena; $8 to swim all day.

This large family resort also has a well-stocked general store and an ice-cream parlor, as well as a gift shop, a bar, a restaurant, and a lodge. Rooms in the lodge, romantically furnished with brass beds and individually color-coordinated, cost $45 s, $65 d, or $90 for a deluxe suite with jacuzzi. Furnished cabins with kitchenettes, linens, and Porta Potti portable toilets start at $60, $15 each additional person. An inexpensive deal is the hostel rooms on the fourth floor. For $20, you crawl through the three-quarter-size door and under the attic eaves, where you sleep on your own bedding; bathroom down the hall. All rates include use of pool facilities. Or just camp for free at **Ketchum Creek Campground** (BLM) three miles before the hot springs: again, it's closed, unmaintained, but campable still.

Circle
Erroneously named by miners who thought the townsite was close to the Arctic Circle (which is actually 50 miles north), Circle is a long 34 miles beyond Central. The road is in good condition, just quite winding; the last 11 miles are a rally-car driver's dream. Gold was discovered on nearby Birch Creek in 1893, and Circle was a boomtown with two dozen saloons, a library, a hospital, even an opera house, long before anyone had heard of the Klondike. When the miners did hear of the Klondike a few weeks after the strike, Circle immediately lost half its population. The town gradually declined as a supply center for the big Circle Mining District, largest in Alaska, after the Steese Highway hooked up to Fairbanks.

Today, with a population of just under 100, Circle is typical of end-of-the-road Alaska—a couple of streets, lots of cars (mostly junked). The main attraction is the mighty Yukon. Pitch your tent at the denuded campground (free) on the banks and watch the river flow. The **Yukon Trading Post**, tel. (907) 773-1217, has a cafe, a bar, gasoline, motel rooms (from $60 d), a post office, and free camping. **H.C. Company Store** sells gas, repairs tires, and has groceries, gold pans, and gifts. Get directions here to the **Pioneer Cemetery. Warbelow's Air Ventures**, tel. (907) 474-0518 in Fairbanks, flies to Central and Circle.

THE ELLIOTT HIGHWAY AND MANLEY HOT SPRINGS

The Elliott Highway, named after Maj. Malcolm Elliott, president of the Alaska Railroad Commission 1927-32 (following George Steese), begins at the junction with the Steese Highway in Fox, 11 miles north of Fairbanks. The road is paved to Mile 28 (but watch for frost heaves), then turns into a very wide, occasionally smooth two-lane gravel road until the junction with the Dalton, when it narrows to a one-and-a-half-lane rough hard-dirt ribbon through total wilderness. Because of this abrupt transition at the Dalton, the Elliott could almost, ironically, be considered an extension of the old Haul Road. (The highway department certainly is aware of which side its bread is buttered on!)

Other than the BLM White Mountain Trail at Mile 28, and gorgeous views in several spots on the road (especially Miles 95-96), there's little on the way to Manley Hot Springs, a small town at the end of the highway, 152 long miles from Fox. In fact, there's only one facility between the Hilltop Truck Stop, just outside of Fox, tel. (907) 389-7600, and Manley; it's the **Wildwood General Store** at Mile 49.5. Most of the road is in the 40- to 50-mph range, with a few 20- to 30-mph stretches, totaling four to five hours one-way from Fairbanks.

Between Fox and the Dalton Highway junction, huge supply trucks to and from Prudhoe barrel along, raising blinding clouds of dust; by the time you get back to Fairbanks from Manley, a fine layer of dust will have settled over everything you've got, including your entire respiratory tract. It's essential to have *plenty* of water along for this ride. Also take food, as there's no Denny's at the next exit, since there aren't any exits. And don't forget your bathing suit.

To the White Mountain Trail
The road climbs quickly out of Fox, with good views of the Interior's rolling hills. One mile north of the abandoned railroad and mining town of **Olnes**, just before the Mile 11 bridge over the Chatanika River, a large gravel road on the left goes a mile in to Chatanika Pond, part of the **Chatanika River State Recreation Site:** no facilities, but fair fishing and camping. On the other side of the Mile 11 bridge is the rest of the recreation site: camping ($8), picnicking, pit toilets, fishing for grayling in the summer, and for whitefish (spearfishing) in the fall.

At Mile 28 on the right are a parking area and the trailheads for myriad trails through the White Mountains. Read the information board carefully. Most trails are for winter use and are not maintained during the summer for hiking. The Summit Trail starts from the trailhead on the left and is designated for summer use. This 21-mile trail (one-way), mostly along alpine ridgetops through the foothills of the White Mountains, ends at Beaver Creek. Across the creek is the Borealis-LeFavre Cabin, which can be reserved through the BLM, 1150 University Ave., Fairbanks, AK 99709, tel. (907) 474-2350.

As for hiking, you start out high up to begin with, and the first mile or so of the Wickersham Creek Trail takes you out of the taiga and onto a ridgetop, with a beautiful 300-degree view of the Tanana Valley, Alaska Range, and gigantic sky. Even if you're not hiking all the way, it's worth it to do this mile for the view.

Bye Bye Pavement
The pavement ends 100 yards from the trailhead. Enjoy this wide gravel stretch while you've got it! Nice views of the pipeline here—shining in the sunlight, twisting through the tundra, suddenly disappearing underground and surfacing again. At Mile 49.5 is **Wildwood General Store,** tel. (907) 322-2602, where you can get groceries, gas, and gifts, and pick up fishing and hunting licenses. A half-mile beyond the store is Northern Lights School, a two-room schoolhouse with an enrollment of 23.

At Mile 57 is the only official campground on the Elliott, nicknamed **Mosquito Creek Campground.** Unless you want to donate a few pints of life's precious fluid (per minute) to the local bloodsucking population, do not camp, do not get out of your car, don't even stop.

At Mile 71 is the two-mile access road to **Livengood,** a tiny mining center that flourished briefly as a pipeline construction camp. It now has a population of seven (though there are about 100 people in the area). Two miles farther is Mile 0 of the Dalton Highway (see below). Take a left to stay on the Elliott.

To Manley
A bit past the junction, right after the bridge over the Tolovana River, is a little pullout (left), a nice spot for a picnic, camping, fishing, or even swimming (no facilities). Here the road narrows considerably, and you follow the two tire-packed stripes down the middle of it, hoping nobody is coming in the other direction. At Miles 95-96 is a fantastic view overlooking the Minto Flats, the Tanana River, and the foothills of the Alaska Range. If you're very lucky and have charmed cloud karma, you'll get a breathtaking view of Mt. McKinley and the accompanying snowcapped peaks to its right and left, jutting straight up like a big militant fist from the lowlands. Even though the range is more than 100 miles due south, the possibility of seeing it is worth the whole ride—even the dust. From here to Manley are some fun roller-coaster humps and curves; watch for porcupines, foxes, snowshoe hares, tree squirrels, hawks, and other cars.

Manley Hot Springs
This relaxing and friendly town (pop. 90) is a couple of miles this side of the end of the Elliott at the Tanana River. Like many Interior villages, Manley Hot Springs had its heyday in the early 1900s during the peak activity of nearby mines. The U.S. Army Signal Corps set up a telegraph station here in 1903, and Frank Manley built the town's first resort in 1907. Because of the geothermal activity, Manley boasts agricultural features uncommon for Interior—rich warm soil, a long growing season, even earthworms—and is known for its abundant produce. Manley also has a resort, a roadhouse, a popular landing strip, wilderness tours, and more ATVs than cars. A lot more. Best of all, the hot springs have no sulphur, so you can enjoy the soak without the stench.

Just as you come into town, take a right into **Manley Hot Springs Resort,** tel. (907) 672-3611. For $5, you can swim all day in their pool. Rent towels and suits for a buck apiece. The lodge has a bar ($2.50 for beers), a restaurant ($5.75 for burgers), a giant pool table, and a beautiful jade fireplace. The jade came from a single nugget, weighing more than a ton. Hotel rooms in a long double-wide trailer cost $60 d with toilet, $75 d with shower, $90 d with jacuzzi; dry cabins go for $50 per night. If you're interested in a fishing trip, ask here for guide Frank Gurtler, who charges $30 an hour.

Continue toward town and take the next right to the large greenhouse, and look around for Chuck or Gladys Dart. These long-time Manley residents (the school is named after Gladys) are friendly Alaskan farmers who use the hot springs bubbling up on their property to grow tomatoes, cucumbers, and other vegetables, which they sell to local residents and passersby. Inside the first greenhouse are four square concrete hot tubs with 108° spring water. After an hour's soak ($5), buy some produce, add your favorite dressing for some zing, and you'll have a true Manley experience.

Keep going toward town and park by the bridge over Hot Springs Slough. Go right just before the bridge and walk a half-mile to the first road to the right. The first part of the trail past the cabins is private property. Then it's three miles to the tower, and two more up to Bean Ridge. Great views and camping up there.

The public campground below the bridge on the other side of Hot Springs Slough in the middle of town has toilets, picnic tables, and cinder-block barbecues, $5 a night—handy to everything. The campground is maintained by the Manley Hot Springs Park Association; pay at the Roadhouse.

The **Roadhouse,** tel. (907) 672-3161, was built in 1906 and is a popular meeting place for local miners, trappers, and dog mushers. It has many prehistoric and historic artifacts on display, collected from around the area, along with the usual bar, restaurant, friendly atmosphere, and rooms ($45 s, $60 d, cabins $70).

The Elliott Highway continues past the landing strip and trading post 2.5 miles to the end of the road at the mighty Tanana River. Here it's scenic and breezy, and you could camp here in a pinch.

DALTON HIGHWAY

Before pipeline days, the Elliott Highway ran from just outside of Fairbanks to Livengood, where a 56-mile spur road cut north to the Yukon River. The Dalton Highway began as the "Haul Road" in 1974, constructed to run parallel to the Alaska pipeline from the Yukon River to Deadhorse, a small oil settlement on Prudhoe Bay.

The Dalton Highway, more popularly known as the Haul Road, on which materials for the North Slope oilfields were transported during the mid-'70s, was constructed beyond the Elliott. In 1981, the spur road and the Haul Road, a total of 414 miles, were renamed the Dalton Highway after James Dalton, who pioneered early oil exploration efforts on the North Slope (and not Bill Dalton, who pioneered Moon Publications). This long road traverses some of the most spectacular and remote land accessible by road in Alaska (and therefore in the country), through taiga and tundra, over the Arctic Circle, past towering snowcapped peaks, through the Brooks Range, and within a mile of Gates of the Arctic National Park. Wildlife is abundant: caribou, Dall sheep, and wolves can be seen if you look real sharp.

The road is still primarily a truck-supply route and is fairly wide, but it can become very dusty or slippery depending on recent weather. Until 1994, a permit was required to travel past Mile 211, but now you can drive right up to Deadhorse without any legal limits. Make no mistake: this is a somewhat excruciating seven to 11 hours on a tire-eating, bone-jarring, teeth-grinding, anus-clenching "highway." A trip up the Dalton is not to be taken lightly.

There are only two service stations along the way, which charge $35 just to hop into the tow truck, another $35 to back it out of the garage, and $5 a mile each way. Always travel with plenty of water, your headlights on, and two spare tires, and *watch for trucks*. In most cases, you can see them coming from a fur piece, ahead as well as behind, thanks to the dust trails they raise. Be prepared for all that dust to come your way.

Hitching is conceivable in the summer, since a steady trickle of hardy travelers braves this highway. The trucks, of course, won't stop for you. Not all car-rental agencies allow their vehicles on the Dalton, so ask first. **Northern Alaska Tour Company,** tel. (907) 474-8600, offers a few different tours to the Arctic Circle and Prudhoe Bay, leaving from Alaskaland in Fairbanks at various times and days. The overnight tour goes up the highway, spends the night in Coldfoot, tours the oilfields, and flies back, for $159.

To Coldfoot

Mile 0 of the Dalton is 73 miles north of Fairbanks, accessed by the Elliott. From here it's 56 miles to the Yukon River, with sweeping views of the undulating landscape and good glimpses of the pipeline. No developed campgrounds are maintained along the Dalton, but the first of many undeveloped areas is at **Hess Creek,** Mile 24. A 2,290-foot wooden-deck bridge crosses the mighty Yukon at Mile 56. On the northern side is **Yukon Ventures Alaska,** tel. (907) 655-9001, the only service facility before Coldfoot, with gas, tire repair, a restaurant open 7 a.m.-9 p.m., and 40 motel rooms ($50 pp). An interesting pipeline interpretive display is beside the road, and the BLM's **Yukon Crossing Visitor Station** is open seven days a week June-August. Cross the road and drive under the pipeline for an undeveloped camping area.

Isolated granite tors are visible to the northeast at Mile 86, and at Mile 98 are excellent views of the mountains across the tundra before the road descends again to travel along the valley floor. At Mile 115 is the Arctic Circle: latitude 66°, 33 minutes. A huge sign proclaims the location. A road behind the sign leads a half-mile to camping.

At Mile 132 are **Gobbler's Knob** and the first views of the Brooks Range on the distant northern horizon. The road winds past Pump Station 5, over numerous rivers and creeks, and by great fishing; at Mile 175 it rolls into Coldfoot.

Coldfoot

Gold was discovered at Tramway Bar in the upper reaches of the Koyukuk River in 1893, attracting enough prospectors and miners to found the town of Coldfoot. Still, the town reportedly received its sobriquet when most of them got cold feet at the onset of the first winter and left the country. Two of the original mining cabins are still in the bush at the northern end of the airstrip.

It's no wonder the old miners' feet became frosty. In January 1989, Coldfoot recorded a temperature of -82° F, and for 17 days the mercury refused to rise above 62° below. Then, that summer, it got up to three degrees below 100°—the 179-degree differential broke all North American records.

A **visitor center** puts on a daily presentation on Gates of the Arctic and the Brooks Range. **Coldfoot Services,** tel. (907) 678-5201, calls itself the "world's northernmost truck stop." Its cafe meals are comparable price-wise to Denny's, gas goes for $1.80 a gallon, and rooms range from $95 s with shared bath to $125 d with private bath. The Coldfoot post office and a gift shop are also here. You can arrange 4WD trips and mining excursions in the summer and dogsledding and snowmachining in the winter. Top off your tank; the next gas is 239 miles away at Deadhorse.

The owners of Coldfoot Services recently acquired the **Wiseman Trading Company,** at Mile 185 and three miles down a spur road. It's an old gold-mining store-turned-gift shop, though it's more of a museum than anything else. Two dozen people live in and around Wiseman, a mining village that dates back to 1910.

And Beyond

Undeveloped camping is found at Marion Creek at Mile 180. Views across the Koyukuk River take in Wiseman, a historic mining town, and fantastic mountain scenery; the road runs parallel to the Koyukuk for the next 20 miles or so. Gates of the Arctic National Park boundary are high up on the slopes to the west, and at Mile 194 are the first views of Sukakpak Mountain. The road passes along the base of this rugged peak, and a trail at Mile 203 leads a half-mile right to the base. The strange-looking mounds between the road and the mountain are "palsas" formed by ice beneath the soil pushing upwards.

Mile 211, Disaster Creek, was the point where, before December 1994, all vehicles without travel permits had to turn around and go back down the way they came. From here the road climbs quickly up to Chandalar Shelf, a huge basin with a healthy population of grizzlies, then over Atigun Pass at Mile 244, the highest highway pass in Alaska (4,800 feet). The road winds quickly down through the Atigun Valley and onto the North Slope. At Mile 414 is **Deadhorse,** the town built to service the Prudhoe Bay oilfields. There are three lodging houses, all of which have dining rooms, and two gas stations. Alaska Airlines, 40-Mile Air, and ERA Helicopters service Deadhorse. As many as 8,000 workers make up the area population.

The only way to get to the Arctic Ocean is on a tour. The local Native corporation, NANA, operates **Tour Arctic,** out of the Arctic Caribou Inn in Deadhorse. They offer a one-hour Arctic Ocean tour and a four-hour oilfield tour (including the Oilfield Visitor Center and a stop at the Arctic Ocean). Call (907) 659-2360 for prices, time, and reservations.

TO DENALI

George Parks Highway

Completed in 1971, the George Parks Highway (Rt. 3) is named for George Parks, an early territorial governor. It's not named, as is commonly believed, for Denali National and State parks. Running 359 miles from Fairbanks to Anchorage, the stretch of road between Ester and Nenana is one of the few places in Alaska where you can legally drive 65 miles per hour. Live it up! The highway winds through the Tanana Hills south of Fairbanks (good views of the Alaska Range to the east) and passes **Skinny Dick's Halfway Inn** (it *is* halfway between Fairbanks and Nenana, which makes it an even better pun and T-shirts of it are available in every imaginable color—call (907) 452-0304 to order), several fireworks stands, and the **Monderosa,** just north of Nenana, whose "best burger in Alaska" is in fact a great deal—one fills up two. A large steel bridge crosses the Tanana River (pronounced "TA-na-naw"); notice the Nenana River (pronounced "nee-NA-na") emptying into it on the right.

NENANA

Nenana (pop. 542) was an Athabascan Indian village at the confluence of the two rivers (*na* in Athabascan means "river"; Nenana means "Camping Spot at Two Rivers") until it mushroomed into a town of 5,000 in 1916 as a base for construction on the northern leg of the Alaska Railroad. At the north end of the 700-foot railroad bridge spanning the Tanana, Warren G. Harding, first president to visit Alaska, drove in the golden spike, marking the completion of the line on July 15, 1923.

Harding's visit was the culmination of a long train tour across the country, on which he attempted to rally support for his flagging administration, which was dogged by suspicions of high-level corruption. Prior to his trip, Harding had supported exploitation of Alaska's resources, but the firsthand experience changed his mind. Returning from Alaska to Seattle, he made a speech calling for more roads and agriculture and conservation of lumber, fish, and mineral resources. "We must regard life in lovely, wonderful Alaska as an end and not a means, and reject the policy of turning Alaska over to the exploiters." Unfortunately, Harding died a week later, under extremely mysterious circumstances; his new vision was buried with him.

Nenana is famous for its yearly **Ice Classic,** "Alaska's Biggest Guessing Game." It all started in 1917, when Alaska Railroad workers started a pool for the exact time the ice on the Tanana River would break up; the payoff was $800. Now in its 80th year, the prize has grown to $330,000, which is 50% of the gross (meaning the Ice Classic has an edge of 50%). The rest goes to taxes, salaries, promotion, and the town till. Tens of thousands of Alaskans and Outsiders place $2 bets on the day, hour, and minute of the break-up. A four-legged tripod (the town's symbol) is set up on the river ice in

Ice Classic tripod on Tanana River

GORDY OHLIGER

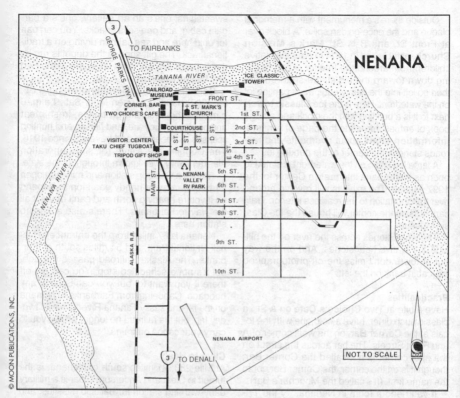

February, with a cable running to a clock tower on the river bank. When the ice moves, the cable stops the clock, recording the official time. Earliest break-up was April 20, in 1940; latest was May 20, in 1964. Pick up entry forms ($2) at the visitor center or the Tripod Gift Shop and enter before the April 1 deadline.

The Ice Classic and the town's active waterfront, where freight and supplies are loaded onto barges for bush towns strung along the Tanana and Yukon Rivers, make Nenana a prosperous, photogenic, and friendly little place—great for a leisurely stroll to break up (sorry) the trip from Fairbanks to Denali.

Sights

Stop off at the log-and-sod **visitor center** at the bottom of the bridge, corner of the Parks Highway and A St., tel. (907) 832-9953, open daily 8 a.m.-6 p.m. Behind the cabin is the *Taku Chief,* the last

commercial wooden tugboat to ply the Yukon and Tanana Rivers, till it was condemned in 1978 in Nenana, where it still sits. Unfortunately you can't climb on it. Between the visitor center and the tugboat is a large cinder-block restroom, the most convenient toilets on the Parks Highway.

Walk up A St. toward the river. Go right on Front St. and enter the old depot. Inside is the **Alaska State Railroad Museum,** tel. (907) 832-5500, open daily 9 a.m.-6 p.m., free. This is a wonderful little museum, full of information, photographs, and artifacts from planning, construction, and maintenance of the Alaska Railroad. Be sure to read the railroad bridge-building history, and flip through the log books on the stationmaster's counter. Don't miss this one. The big gift shop next door, Tripod II, is worth a stroll; you can buy the fine historical video on the railroad. Upstairs is the Bed and Maybe Breakfast; see below.

Outside there's a monument with a memorial plaque and the once-golden spike. A block over at Front St. and B is **St. Mark's Mission Church,** established in 1904 to educate Native children from around the Interior. Keep heading down toward the big single-span bridge, then go left into the heavy-equipment parking lot on the waterfront. Here is the **Ice Classic tower;** next to it is a building with the clock and a huge book of entries, turned to the page of winners. **Information signs** about riverboats and railroads stand in the center of the parking lot.

A large log cabin on the waterfront is slated to open as the Nenana Interpretive Center for the 1997 season. The exhibits will revolve around river transportation to the roadless Interior. Train cars outside the center will house the Ice Classic Museum.

The white stones across the river on the hillside are Native headstones. And on the way out of town, don't miss the oft-photographed log-cabin bank on the left.

Practicalities

Have a bite at **Two Choice's Cafe** on A St., a classic bush diner; have a cold one with the locals at the **Corner Bar,** on the west corner of A and Front Streets. The bar across the street on the east corner is not called the Corner Bar, though it is on the corner; the Corner Bar got to the name first. (It's called the Moocher's Bar).

If you need a room in Nenana, try the **Tripod Motel** on the highway, tel. (907) 832-5590; or **Nenana Inn,** Second and A, tel. (907) 832-5238. You can pull your camper to a hookup at **Nenana Valley RV Park** between Fourth and Fifth and B and C Streets., tel. (907) 832-5431; $17 d full hookups, $10 for tent camping, $1 each additional person. The **Bed and Maybe Breakfast** is upstairs from the Railroad Museum in the depot, tel. (907) 832-5272; this could be the most historic B&B in the state.

Several gift shops line A Street. The **Tripod Gift Shop** is across from the visitor center, open 8 a.m.-7 p.m., tel. (907) 832-5272. The Tripod is perhaps the most extensive gift shop in Alaska. There's the main log cabin, jammed to the rafters with sundry souvenirs (check out the collection of Alaska playing cards); then four cabins line the boardwalk between the big tripod and the working fishwheel: one sells XXXL T-shirts and sweatshirts, one's an art gallery, one's a bargain cabin, and one sells snacks. You can pan for gold here and see salmon drying on a traditional rack. The gift shop in the depot is run by the Tripod folks, who also take care of the Bed and Maybe Breakfast.

Coghill's General Merchandise, on A St., tel. (907) 832-5422, open Mon.-Sat. 9 a.m.-6 p.m., has been selling groceries, fresh meat and produce, hardware, and fishing and hunting licenses to Nenanans and travelers since 1916. The Coghills are a five (or six) generation Alaskan family, well-known throughout the state.

There's a Chevron station and minimart open 24 hours a day, a handy gas stop to depend on if you're heading north and can't make it all the way to Fairbanks. There's also a Tesoro station here.

Nenana is 67 miles from the entrance to Denali National Park, and 54 miles south of Fairbanks. The Alaska Railroad passes through, but it's not a scheduled stop. You can get off there if you want to, but you can't check any baggage. Canoeing from Fairbanks to Nenana on the fat and sassy Tanana River is a wild two-day trip, but the railroad no longer allows you to carry your canoe on trains.

Clear to Healy

At Mile 283, 21 miles south of Nenana, is the turnoff to Clear and Anderson. Clear is a military early-warning station for ballistic missiles, and not surprisingly, entry is prohibited. Six miles down the Clear road is the little settlement of Anderson on the Tanana River. At Mile 280 is **Clear Sky Lodge,** tel. (907) 582-2251, with gas, a steakhouse (open 11 a.m.-11 p.m.), a lounge, and a liquor store. Four miles south of there is the popular **Tatlanika Trading Company,** Mile 276, tel. (907) 582-2341, where the Gray Line and Princess buses take a rest stop on their way between Denali and Fairbanks. This big shop has a major selection of Alaskan arts and crafts, worth a stop to browse.

At Mile 249, you come into the town of **Healy** (pop. 600). Healy has grown up around the coal mining that has taken place here for the past 70-odd years. Usibelli Coal Mine is the largest in Alaska, which isn't saying much, since it's Alaska's *only* commercial coal mine. However, its nearly one million tons of coal mined a year *does* say something: a four-million-pound "walking dragline" digs 1,000 cubic yards of overburden every hour, exposing the seams. Some coal is shipped to Korea, some to Fairbanks, and some to the Golden Valley Electric Association power plant, the largest coal-fired electrical-generating plant in Alaska. The power supplies the Tanana Valley and Fairbanks. Thanks to the mine and power plant, little Healy has the highest per-capita income in Alaska, which makes it one of the richest places in the whole United States.

The historical **Stampede Lodge** at Mile 248, tel. (907) 683-2242 or (800) 478-2370, was built in 1946 to house local Alaska Railroad workers and coal miners and served as the commu-nity center. The Railroad sold the hotel in 1985, when it was restored for the first time; it was re-modeled again in 1995. The lobby is about as homey as can be. There are 29 rooms, going for $70 d; the Bushmaster Grill restaurant is open daily 6 a.m.-10 p.m.

The **Totem Inn,** on the other side of Healy Spur Rd., tel. (907) 683-2420, has 36 rooms for $70 s or d, and a restaurant that's popular with park employees when they want to get away from it all. On the other side of the Parks Highway is sprawling **Denali North Star Inn,** tel. (800) 684-4026.

McKinley KOA is a few blocks south of the intersection, tel. (907) 683-2379.

GORDY OHLIGER

DENALI

INTRODUCTION

Denali National Park is now Alaska's number-two tourist attraction (the first is Portage Glacier). Denali attracts more visitors during its 114-day season than the entire state has residents. Most travelers come to see Mt. McKinley, highest peak in North America (20,320 feet), which towers above the surrounding lowlands and 14,000- to 17,000-foot peaks. Although it's visible only one day in three, and often shrouded for a week or more at a time, those who get lucky and see The Mountain experience a thrill equivalent to its majesty and grandeur. Those who don't are usually consoled by lower snowcapped mountains and attending glaciers, high passes and adrenaline-pumping drops off the road, tundra vistas and "drunken forests," and an incredible abundance of wildlife, including the Big Four: caribou, moose, sheep, and bear. But even if The Mountain's socked in, the grizzlies are hiding, and the shuttle-bus windows are fogged up, you're still smack in the middle of some of the most spectacular and accessible wilderness

in the world. It was the call of the wild that brought you out here in the first place. And all you have to do is step outside and answer.

The Land and Climate

The Alaska Range is a U-shaped chain that extends roughly 600 miles from the top of the Alaska Peninsula (at the head of the Aleutians) up through the Park and down to south of Tok. It's only a small part, however, of the coastal mountains that include California's Sierra Nevada, the Northwest's Cascades, the Coast Mountains of B.C., Yukon's St. Elias Range, and eastern Alaska's Wrangell Range. The Park road starts out a bit north of the Alaska Range and follows the "U" 90 miles southwest toward its heart—Mt. McKinley. One thing that makes The Mountain so spectacular is that the surrounding lowlands are so low: the Park hotel sits at 1,700 feet, and the highest point on the road, Thoroughfare Pass, is just under 4,000. The base of Mt. McKinley is at 2,000 feet, and the north face rises at a 60-degree angle straight up to 20,000 feet—highest vertical rise in the world.

Weather patterns here differ between the south side of the range (wetter, cooler) and the north. During the summer, the prevailing winds come from the south, carrying warm moisture from the Pacific. When they run smack into the icy rock wall of the Alaska Range, they climb, the moisture condenses, and depending on the amount of moisture and altitude, it either rains or snows. A lot. On top of that whole system sits mighty Mt. McKinley—very high, very cold, and very alone. So alone that The Mountain has its own relationship to the weather. The combination of wind, wet, cold, and height creates weather extremely localized around McKinley, which can get violent. Storms can blow in within an hour and last weeks, dumping 10 feet of snow. Winds scream in at up to 80 mph. The mercury drops below zero in mid-July. Some of the worst weather in the world swirls around up there. But when The Mountain emerges bright white against bright blue, and you're craning your neck to see the top, it's an unforgettable sight worth waiting around for—even in the rain.

Flora and Fauna

From sea level to around 2,300 feet is the habitat for the **boreal forest,** in which the black spruce, with its somber foliage and clusters of tawny cones, is the climax tree. Younger white spruce, along with deciduous aspen, birch, and cottonwood, grow near the streams and the road and in recently burned areas. Climbing out of the forest, above 2,300 feet you enter the **taiga,** a Russian word meaning "land of twigs." This transition zone (between the forest below and tundra above) accommodates no deciduous trees; the spruce are thinned out and runty (though they can be over 60 years old), and a green shag carpet of bush, mostly dwarf willow, layers the floor. Sitka spruce is the state tree because of its size, grandeur, and commercial value, but it's the willow that vegetates Alaska. And it has endless uses. Before synthetics like nylon, the bark was stripped, split, and braided, and made into rope, bows, wicker baskets, snowshoes, fishnets, and small game and bird snares and traps. The inner bark is sweet; the sap is very sweet. Young buds and shoots are edible and nourishing, and willows are the nearly exclusive staple of the moose diet. The taiga also hosts a variety of berries: blueberries and lowbush cranberries by the ton, crowberries, bearberries, soap and salmon berries, raspberries.

Above 2,500 feet is the **tundra,** its name a Lapp word meaning "vast, rolling, treeless plain." There are two types of tundra: the moist, or Alaskan, tundra is characterized by the taiga's dwarf shrubbery, high grasses, and berries, but no trees; the alpine tundra, the highest zone, has grasses, moss, lichens, and small, hardy wildflowers, including the stunning forget-me-not, Alaska's state flower.

The animal life varies with the vegetation. In the forest, look for moose, porcupine, snowshoe hare, marten, lynx, two kinds of weasels, red or tree squirrels, and several varieties of small rodents. On the taiga—or in both the forest and the tundra—you might see coyote, wolf, fox, grizzly, and ground squirrel. In the tundra, keep an eye out for caribou, wolverine, Dall sheep, marmot, vole, lemming, and shrew.

LOUISE FOOTE

somber black spruce limbs

COEXISTING WITH THE BEARS

Bears seem to bring out conflicting emotions in most people. The first is a gut reaction of fear and trepidation: what if the bear attacks me? But then comes that other urge: what will my friends say when they see these great bear photos? Both of these reactions can lead to a multitude of problems in bear country (which includes most of Alaska). Though "bearanoia" is a justifiable fear, it can easily be taken to extremes such as avoiding going outdoors at all. On the other hand, the "I want to get close-up shots of that bear and her cubs" attitude can lead to a bear attack. The middle ground incorporates knowledge of and respect for bears, with a sense of caution that keeps you alert to danger without letting it rule your travels in the wild. Nothing is ever completely safe in this world, but with care you can avoid most of the common pitfalls that lead to unwanted bear encounters.

Bears are beautiful, eminently fascinating, and surprisingly intelligent animals. They can be funny, playful and inquisitive, vicious or protective, and unpredictable. The more you watch bears in the wild, the more complex their lives seem, and the more they become individual animals, not simply the big and bad. One thing to remember about bears is how variable their behavior can be. You don't expect all dogs to behave the same way, nor should you expect bears to. They have bad days sometimes, and when the salmon stop running in the fall, bears can get irritable.

Entering Bear Country

Enter bear country with respect but not fear. Know that bears rarely attack humans; you're a thousand times more likely to be injured in a highway accident than by a bear. In fact, more people are hurt each year by moose than by bears. Contrary to the stories you often hear, bears have surprisingly good eyesight, but they depend more upon their excellent senses of smell and hearing. A bear can tell who has walked through an area, and how recently, with just a quick sniff of the air.

Avoid unexpected encounters with bears by letting them know you're there. If you walk with a breeze hitting your back, any bears ahead of you will know you are coming. If you're unable to see everything around you for at least 50 yards, warn any hidden animals by talking, singing, clapping your hands, tapping a cup, rattling a can of pebbles, or wearing a bell. Be especially wary when traveling through thick brush or high grass, into the wind, along streams, or at twilight. If you think the bears might not be able to hear you, don't be shy, yell! It might seem a bit foolish, but yelling might also prevent an encounter of the furry kind. Safety can also be found in numbers: the more of you hiking in a group, the more likely a bear is to sense you and stay away.

At the Campsite

When choosing a campsite, avoid places like salmon streams, ground-squirrel mounds, berry patches, or game trails. Watch for fresh signs of bears (droppings, tracks, diggings). If possible, camp near a climbable tree. Keep your campsite clean! Avoid smelly foods such as fish, fresh meat, cheese, sausage, or bacon; freeze-dried food is light and relatively odorless. Keep food in airtight containers or several layers of plastic bags. Your cooking, eating, and food-storage area should be at least 50 yards away from your tent. Wash up after eating. Burying garbage is useless, as animals soon dig it up. Instead, burn what garbage you can, and wash and flatten tin cans. Store unburnable garbage, and the clothes you were wearing while cooking, in the same place.

Put your food, toothpaste, and soap in a plastic bag inside a stuff sack and suspend it from a branch or between two trees, at least 12 feet off the ground. Tie two cups or pots to it so you will hear if it's moved. In the absence of trees, store food well downwind of your tent. Some campgrounds provide handy bear-proof metal food caches. Perfumes, deodorants, and sexual smells are all thought to attract bears. Women should be especially cautious during their periods. Used tampons should be stored in airtight containers and packed out with all other garbage.

BOB RACE

Avoiding Bear Hugs

Hunters and photographers are the main recipients of bear hugs. Never, under any circumstances, approach a bear, even if it appears to be asleep. Move off quickly if you see bear cubs, especially if one comes toward you; the mother is always close by. Dogs create dangerous situations by barking and exciting bears—leave yours at home. And, of course, never leave food around for bears. Not only is this illegal, it also trains the bears to associate people with free food. Fed bears become garbage bears, and wildlife officials are eventually forced to destroy them. Remember, bears are dangerous wild animals which may be encountered anywhere in the North. This is *their* country, not a zoo. By going in you accept the risk—and thrill—of meeting a bear.

Encounters of the Furry Kind

If you do happen to encounter a bear and it sees you, try to stay calm and not make any sudden moves. Do not run—you cannot possibly outrun a bear; they can exceed 40 mph for short distances. If a good-sized tree is nearby, climb it as high as you safely can and stay there until you're certain that the bear has left the area. If no tree is close, your best bet is to back slowly away. Sometimes dropping an item such as a hat or a jacket will distract the bear, and talking also seems to have some value in convincing bears that you're a human. If the bear sniffs the air or stands on its hind legs it is probably trying to identify you. When it does, it will usually run away. If a bear woofs and postures, don't imitate, as this is a challenge. Keep retreating! Most bear charges are also a bluff; the bear will often stop short and amble off.

If a *grizzly* bear does attack, curl face-down on the ground in a fetal position with your hands wrapped behind your neck and your elbows tucked over your face. Your backpack may help protect you somewhat. Remain still even if you are attacked, since sudden movements may incite further attacks. It takes a lot of courage to do this, but often a bear will only sniff or nip you and leave. The injury you might sustain would be far less than if you had tried to resist.

Many authorities now recommend against dropping to the ground if you are attacked by a *black* bear, since they tend to be more aggressive in those situations. You're better off fighting back with whatever weapons are at hand if attacked by a black bear. (This, of course, assumes you can tell black bears from brown bears. If you can't, have someone who knows—such as a park ranger—explain the differences before heading into the backcountry.)

Protecting Yourself

Many Alaskan guides and others working for extended times in bear country carry weapons of some sort; 12-gauge shotguns are a common choice. Visitors to Alaska are unlikely to carry such weapons, and even less likely to know when to use one even if you have one along. As an occasional hiker or even a veteran backpacker, if you feel the need to carry a gun for protection, it's better you stay out of the wilderness. You have plenty of alternative places to go; the bears do not.

Recently, cayenne pepper sprays such as "Counter Assault" (Bushwacker Backpack & Supply Co., P.O. Box 4721, Missoula, MT 59806) have proven useful in fending off bear attacks. These "bear mace" sprays are effective only at close range but are not a replacement for being careful in bear country. This is particularly true in the tundra, where winds quickly disperse the spray or may blow it back in your own face. Another real problem with bear mace is that you cannot carry it aboard commercial jets, and most air taxis do not allow it inside an aircraft, due to the obvious dangers should a canister explode. Most floatplane pilots will, however, carry the sprays in the storage compartments of the floats. But be sure to let the pilot know that you have it with you on the flight.

Every Northerner has a bear story. Listen to them, but take them with a grain of salt. If you see a bear yourself it will probably be the most memorable event of your trip, and the one you'll talk about most to the folks back home. Let's hope the great bears always remain an intriguing part of the northern wilderness.

HISTORY

William Dickey

In 1896, a prospector named Bill Dickey was tramping around interior Alaska looking for gold. Like everyone who sees it, Dickey was captivated by the size and magnificence of the mountain that was then variously known as Tenada, Denali, Densmore's Mountain, Traleika, and Bulshaia. Dickey was from Ohio, William McKinley's home state, and a Princeton graduate in economics.

When he came out of the Bush and heard that McKinley had been nominated for president, he promptly renamed the mountain "McKinley," wrote numerous articles for stateside magazines, and lobbied in Washington, D.C., in support of adoption of the name, which finally caught on after President McKinley was assassinated in 1901.

Harry P. Karstens

Karstens reached the Klondike in 1898 when he was 19, bored by Chicago and attracted by adventure and gold. Within a year he'd crossed over into American territory and wound up at Seventymile, 20 miles south of Eagle. When the local mail carrier lost everything one night in a card game and committed suicide, Karstens took his place. He became proficient in dog mushing and trail blazing and within a few years was delivering mail on a primitive trail between Eagle and Valdez, a 900-mile roundtrip every month (the Richardson Highway follows the same route). Later he moved on to Fairbanks and began delivering mail to Kantishna, the mining town on what is now the west end of the Park, growing very fond of and familiar with the north side of the Alaska Range. So when a naturalist from the East Coast, Charles Sheldon, arrived in 1906 to study Dall sheep in the area, Karstens guided him around Mt. McKinley's northern foothills, delineating the habitat of the sheep. Karstens was also the co-leader of the four-man expedition that was the first party to successfully climb the true peak of Mt. McKinley, the south summit, in 1913.

OF WOLVES AND WORDS

If societies are judged by their systems of order, justice, land rights, and family, the kingdom of the wolf is one of the most sophisticated. Few creatures, two-legged or four, honor a hierarchical system with such respect, teach and nurture their young with such diligence, defend their territories with such passion, and hunt and fight for survival with such dogged ferocity.

—Editors,
Alaska magazine, May 1991

Meanwhile, Charles Sheldon was back in Washington, lobbying for national-park status for the Dall sheep habitat, and when Mt. McKinley National Park was created in 1917, Karstens was the obvious choice to become the first park superintendent. He held that post from 1921 to 1928, patrolling the Park boundaries by dogsled. He died in 1955 in Fairbanks, at age 76.

Pioneer Climbs

Many pioneers and prospectors had seen The Mountain and approached it, but Alfred Brooks, a member of the first U.S. Geological Survey expedition in Alaska (1902), first set foot on it. He approached it from the south and reached an elevation of 7,500 feet before running out of time. He published an article in the January 1903 issue of *National Geographic,* in which he recommended approaching The Mountain from the north. Following that suggestion, the next attempt was from the north, led by James Wickersham, U.S. district judge for Alaska. Judge Wickersham was sent from Seattle to bring law and order to Eagle in 1900; he moved to Fairbanks in 1903. That summer, he had a spare couple of months and set out to climb The Mountain, traveling more than 100 miles overland and reaching the 7,000-foot level of the north face, later named Wickersham Wall in honor of His Honor.

That same summer, Dr. Frederick Cook, who'd been with Peary's first party to attempt the North Pole (1891) and Amundsen's Antarctic expedition (1897), also attempted to climb The Mountain from the north and reached 11,300 feet. In 1906, Cook returned to attempt McKinley from the south but failed to get near it. His party broke up and went their separate directions, and a month later, Cook sent a telegram to New York claiming he'd reached the peak. This was immediately doubted by the members of his party, who challenged his photographic and cartographic "evidence." But through public lectures and articles, Cook's reputation as the first man to reach the peak grew. Two years later, he claimed to have reached the North Pole several months ahead of another Peary expedition, and Cook began to enjoy a cult status in the public consciousness. Simultaneously, however, his credibility among fellow explorers rapidly declined, and Cook vanished from sight. This further fueled the controversy and led to the Sourdough Expedition of 1910.

WALTZING AT TERROR LAKE

Kodiak has a higher population density of brown bears than anywhere else on the planet, about 3,000 of them—that's a bear for every five people. Arguably, one bear is as good as five people, as they've been known to stand over 10 feet tall and weigh up to 1,500 pounds. So when 500 construction workers were building a dam and power plant at Terror Lake in the Kodiak National Wildlife Refuge in 1982-85, it provided Alaska Fish and Game an excellent opportunity to observe the man-bear choreography. Workers were trained how to behave around bears, there were no garbage dumps nearby, and only supervisors and remote crews carried firearms. Huge bears were encountered continually, but during the course of the study, no bears or men killed or even injured each other. Only a small fraction of the local bear population was attracted to the garbage cans. A minimum of bear activity was disturbed by the blasting, building, and general bedlam. It was reported that the bears "even became somewhat accustomed to helicopters." Bears scratched their backs on power poles while crews strung wire nearby. The major impact, of course, was the shrinking of the brown-bear habitat. But it's clear that brown bears and humans can learn to dance.

Four sourdoughs in Fairbanks simply decided to climb The Mountain to validate or eviscerate Cook's published description of his route. They left town in December and, climbed to the north peak in early April. Then the three members who'd actually reached the peak stayed in Kantishna to take care of business, while the fourth member, Tom Lloyd, who hadn't reached the peak, returned to Fairbanks and lied that he had. By the time the other three returned to town in June, Lloyd's story had already been published and widely discredited. So nobody believed the other three—*especially* when they claimed they'd climbed up to the north peak and down to their base camp at 11,000 feet in 18 hours, with a thermos of hot chocolate, four doughnuts, and dragging a 14-foot spruce log that they planted up top and claimed was still there! Finally, in 1913, the Hudson Stuck/Harry Karstens expedition reached the true summit,

the south peak, and could prove that they'd done so beyond a shadow of a doubt. Only then was the Sourdough Expedition vindicated: all four members of the Stuck party saw the spruce pole still standing on the north peak!

Since then, nearly 3,000 people have reached the south peak, the youngest being 16, the oldest 70. For the full story on the early attempts, read the excellent *Mt. McKinley: The Pioneer Climbs* by Terris Moore. For the report on the subsequent explorations, mapping expeditions, and scientific excursions on The Mountain, read *A Tourist Guide to Mt. McKinley* by Bradford Washburn.

Created, Expanded, and Developed
Woodrow Wilson signed the bill that created Mount McKinley National Park, Alaska's first, in 1917. The Park road, begun five years later, was completed to Kantishna in 1940. In 1980, with the passage of the Alaska National Interest Lands Conservation Act (ANILCA), with its famous section d2, McKinley Park was renamed Denali National Park and Preserve and expanded to nearly six million acres, or roughly the size of Vermont.

In 1978, development at McKinley Park consisted only of the Park Hotel. It had 200 rooms, a dining room, a snack bar, a bar, and a gift shop. A small lodge at the south entrance of the park, McKinley Village, accommodated the overflow. Little more than 120 employees handled all the visitors that passed through. That same year the McKinley Chalet was born, three miles north of the park's north entrance; by 1983, it had 160 rooms, a dining room, bar, and gift shop. The Chalet marked the beginning of an eruption of commercial development along the Parks Highway; today, there are seven hotels and motels, ten restaurants, four raft companies, three flightseeing operations, five gift shops, a couple of grocery stores, and a gas station. No other place in Alaska has weathered such explosive growth over the past dozen or so years as the north entrance of Denali National Park.

WHAT TO TAKE

Because of the lack of affordable indoor accommodations, the rainy and cool nature of the Park summer, the crowded conditions of the backcountry, and the small selection at the grocery stores, it's essential to be well pre-pared if you're planning to hang around these parts for any length of time. Experienced back-packers should have no problem making them-selves at home at Denali for a week or more, but even novice campers, with the proper equipment, can be comfortable in the worst weather. If you've made it to the middle of Alas-ka without a tent, beg, borrow, or buy one. It's the only thing that stands between you and cold, wet nights (and possible hypothermia), other than $100 or more to sleep inside. And a good sleeping bag is worth its weight in warmth and comfort.

Competition has brought the cost of snack bar food down over the years, so beefless burgers won't bludgeon your budget as bloodless as be-fore, bubba. Still, you might want to bring as much food as you can carry—there are only three small grocery stores around here. Raw and de-hydrated foods, along with the old standbys of nuts, seeds, and dried fruits, will see you through a minimalist Park experience. But with a small backpacking stove, freeze-dried and instant foods, along with grains and beans (sprouting for a few days diminishes cooking time and fuel) are convenient, filling, and sometimes even tasty. A little flour, dried milk, and cheese can be the basis for numerous sauces and stews. You might consider bringing extra fuel along for security, and don't forget matches. Layers of clothing (T-shirt or thermals, wool shirt, down vest or parka, etc.) are as useful here as everywhere else in Alaska, and hiking boots are imperative. A sponge is a handy item to have along, as are extra plastic bags (and don't forget the wire ties). For more helpful hints, see "What to Take" under "Other Practicalities" in the On the Road chapter.

PARK ENTRANCE

Visitor Access Center
Make sure to stop off at this visitor center near the beginning of the Park road. The center opens on April 27, 10 a.m.-4 p.m.; on May 24 the hours extend, 7 a.m.-8 p.m. This $3.2 million facility opened in May '90. In 1991, the park fi-nally began charging "admission": $5 for visi-tors between 16 and 62, $10 per family. This pass is good for seven days only, or buy an an-

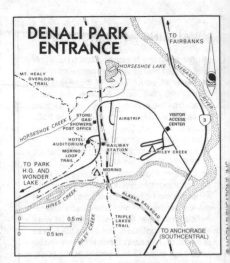

nual permit for $20. You'll need it if you intend to travel beyond Checkpoint Charlie at the Sav-age River Bridge on a shuttle bus or a mountain bike, but don't bother if you're just stopping off to see what's around the entrance.

The Visitor Access Center has a general in-formation desk, the backcountry-permit desk (see "Recreation"), the camping-permit desk (see "Camping Inside the Park"), and the shuttle-bus coupon desk (see "Getting Around" under "Transportation" under "Accommodations"). There's also a backcountry simulator that fea-tures interactive videos concerning bear en-counters, stream crossing, food preparation, etc. A 12-minute slide show on the park is pre-sented once an hour 7:30 a.m.- 5:30 p.m., and orientation programs take place regularly throughout the day. The Alaska Natural History Association has a major selection of books, maps, posters, postcards, and guides to the park. Pick up a copy of *Denali Alpenglow,* the park newspaper, and check the bulletin board for a schedule of daily naturalist programs—guided walks, talks, slide shows, kids' programs, etc.

Denali Park Hotel
The original Lodge had 84 rooms, tennis courts, a badminton room, and a cigar counter; ac-cording to *McKay's Guide to Alaska,* published in 1959, a double with bath went for $17. It

burned down on Labor Day 1972—the same year that the George Parks Highway opened, the shuttle system began, and visitors doubled. In order to be ready to open the next May, construction continued all winter on a new hotel, with three wings of modular units and a dozen Pullman sleeper and dining cars rolled in on tracks laid by the Alaska Railroad. This "emergency" accommodation still stands today, 25 years later, with the train cars in front (which never fail to confuse most tourists who pull up from the train depot!), though the Park Service has since judged them not fit for human habitation. The lobby is dark and congenial, a good place to watch the action, meet other travelers, and succumb to your Big Mac attack (at the snack shop) or craving for a cold beer (at the Golden Spike Saloon). The gift shop has a large selection of the usual; Denali Park T-shirts and sweatshirts are the hot-selling items.

The Park Service auditorium in back of the hotel hosts varying interpretive programs on a wide range of topics about Denali Park, daily at 1:30 and 8 p.m.

Park Headquarters

One of the highlights of the Park is the Sled Dog Demonstration at the kennels behind headquarters. The dogs are beautiful and accessible (the ones not behind fences are chosen for friendliness and patience with people), and the anxious collective howl they orchestrate when the lucky six dogs are selected to run is something to hear. Naturalists give a talk about the current and historical uses of dogs in the Park, their breeding and training, different commands for controlling them, and sometimes the fascinating statistics of maintaining a working kennel in a national park. Then certain dogs, according to a rotating schedule, are taken from their cages or houses, hitched up to a wheel sled, and run around a gravel track. The enthusiasm of the dogs to get off the chain and into the harness is an eyebrow-raising glimpse into the consciousness of Alaskan sled dogs—they live to run.

Demonstrations are given daily at 10 a.m. and 2 and 4 p.m. A free shuttle bus leaves the Visitor Access Center, the Park Hotel's front dock, and the Riley Creek bus shelter 30 minutes prior to the demos. Don't miss this one.

ALONG THE ROAD

A few miles beyond headquarters the road climbs out of the boreal forest, levels off, and travels due west through a good example of taiga. The ridgeline to the north (right) of the road is known as the **Outer Range**, foothills of the massive Alaska Range to the south (left).

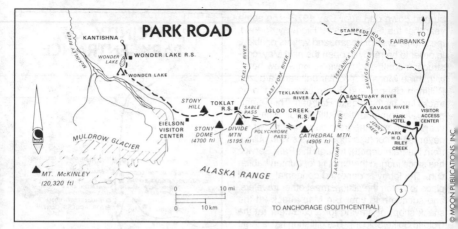

PARK ROAD

KANTISHNA

MCKINLEY RIVER

WONDER LAKE

WONDER LAKE R.S.

WONDER LAKE

STONY HILL

TOKLAT R.S.

SABLE PASS

IGLOO CREEK R.S.

EAST FORK RIVER

TOKLAT RIVER

TEKLANIKA RIVER

TEKLANIKA RIVER

STAMPEDE ROAD

TO FAIRBANKS

SANCTUARY RIVER

SAVAGE RIVER

SAVAGE RIVER

PARK HOTEL

VISITOR ACCESS CENTER

JENNY CREEK

PARK H.Q. RILEY CREEK

EIELSON VISITOR CENTER

STONY DOME (4700 ft)

DIVIDE MTN (5195 ft)

POLYCHROME PASS

CATHEDRAL MTN (4905 ft)

CATHEDRAL MTN.

SANCTUARY RIVER

MULDROW GLACIER

MT. McKINLEY (20,320 ft)

ALASKA RANGE

0   10 mi

0   10 km

TO ANCHORAGE (SOUTHCENTRAL)

3

© MOON PUBLICATIONS, INC.

The Outer Range is much older, of different geological origins, and much more rounded and eroded than the jagged Alaska Range. First view of The Mountain comes up at Mile 9; look southwest. The day has to be nearly perfectly clear to see McKinley from here: you're at around 2,400 feet and The Mountain is at 20,000 feet, which leaves nearly 18 grand spread over 70-odd miles of potential cloud cover. That's a lot of potential.

Next you pass Checkpoint Charlie and the **Savage River Campground,** then wind down to the river valley and cross the bridge. From the bridge, look upriver (left) and notice the broad, U-shaped, glacial valley with large gravel deposits forming braids or channels, then look right to compare the V-shaped valley obviously cut by running water. The Savage Glacier petered out right where the bridge is now around 15,000 years ago during the last Ice Age. Here you also kiss the pavement goodbye, then start climbing Primrose Ridge, which offers excellent hiking, especially in June and early July when the wildflowers are in full bloom. Turn around and look back at the Savage bridge; the stark rock outcropping just up from it has a distinct resemblance to an Indian's facial bone structure, which is how the Savage got its name. Just up the road is a pullout—if The Mountain's out, the driver should stop for the clear shot.

McKinley disappears behind jagged lower peaks as the road descends into the broad, glacial **Sanctuary River** valley. Watch for moose,

caribou, fox, lynx, waterfowl, and eagles along here. Right on the other side of the Sanctuary is a good view down at a "drunken forest," one effect that permafrost has on the vegetation. Notice how many of the trees are leaning at bizarre and precarious angles, with some of them down entirely. As an adaptation to the permafrost, these spruce trees have evolved a root system that spreads horizontally across the surface soil; there's no tap root to speak of. So the taller a tree grows around here, the less support it maintains, and the more susceptible it is to falling over. When the surface soil becomes saturated (due to lack of absorption over the permafrost), it sometimes shifts, either spontaneously or due to slight tremors (a major fault runs through here), taking the trees with it.

Next you descend into the broad **Teklanika River** valley, with a good view across the river of the three vegetation zones on the mountain slopes: forest, taiga, and tundra. You pass a number of small ponds in this area, known as "kettles," usually formed when a retreating glacier drops off a large block of ice, which melts, leaves a depression, and fills with rainwater. The stagnant water is very rich in nutrients and provides excellent hatching grounds for Alaska's famous mosquitoes, and as such the ponts are good feeding spots for ducks and shorebirds. Look for mergansers, goldeneyes, sandpipers, buffleheads, and phalaropes in these ponds. And in some of the higher, smaller, more private kettles, look for hikers and Park employees with no clothes on . . . maybe even join them, if you care to brave the skeeters, which have been known to show up on Park Service radar screens.

Cross the river and enter **Igloo Canyon,** where you turn almost due south. The mountain on the right is Igloo (4,800 feet); the one on the left is Cathedral (4,905 feet). Igloo is in the Outer Range, Cathedral in the Alaska Range. Closest distance between the two ranges, the canyon is right on the migration route of the Dall sheep and a great place to view the white dots on the slopes. Or climb either mountain to get close.

Sable Pass is next, at 3,900 feet the second-highest point on the road. This area is closed to hiking and photography due to the large grizzly population. Keep your eyes peeled. Also, the next good views of The Mountain are from these highlands.

Once you cross the **East Fork River** (great hiking out onto the flats from here), you begin your ascent of Polychrome Pass, one of the most spectacular and sphincter-clamping sections of the road. If you're scared of heights or become frightened at the 1,000-foot drop-offs, just do what the driver does—close your eyes. These rocks have a high iron content; the rate of oxidation and the combination of the iron with other minerals determines the different shades of rust, orange, red, and purple. Look and listen for hoary marmots in the nearby rocks, and from here almost the rest of the way to Eielson Visitor Center, watch for caribou and wolves; these are the Murie flats, where wildlife biologist Adolph Murie studied the lifestyle of *Canis lupus.*

Descend to the **Toklat River,** the last and largest you cross before Eielson. This is the terminus of the wildlife tour, but the shuttle buses continue on to Eielson and Wonder Lake. The Toklat's source is the Sunrise Glacier, just around the bend upriver (left). You can see from the size of the river how big the glacier was 20,000 years ago. Great hiking up into the Alaska Range from here. Next you climb up **Stony Hill,** and if the weather is cooperating, when you crest the ridge you're in for the thrill of a lifetime: Denali, The Great One, in all its immense, majestic glory. You can't believe that The Mountain is still 40 miles away! But wait, you get another five miles closer, crossing **Thorofare Pass,** highest elevation on the road (3,950 feet). Finally you arrive at Eielson Visitor Center.

Eielson Visitor Center

Open daily 9 a.m.-7 p.m., Eielson is four hours from the Visitor Access Center. The view from here, weather cooperating, is unforgettable. Even if you can only see the bottom 12,000 or 14,000 feet, have a naturalist or your driver point to where the top of Mt. McKinley is, and visualize it in your mind's eye. Also, things change fast around here, so keep an eye out for the peak popping out of the clouds as a surprise just for you. The visitor center has running water and flush toilets; sells film, maps, and books; and has a nice display delineating the peaks and features in the cloudless view. Naturalists lead 30-minute "Tundra Walks" daily at 1:30 p.m. The excellent backpacking zones in this area are usually the first to fill up.

To Wonder Lake

Half the buses turn around at Eielson and travel back the same 62 miles; the other half go on another 25 miles to Wonder Lake. The road comes within 25 miles of The Mountain, passing **Muldrow Glacier,** which is covered by a thick black layer of glacial till and vegetation. From Wonder Lake, the **Wickersham Wall** rises magnificently above the intervening plains, with the whole Alaska Range stretching out on each side. In addition, the reflection from the lake doubles your pleasure and doubles your fun, from which even the mosquitoes here, some of the most savage, bloodthirsty, insatiable beasts of the realm, cannot detract.

RECREATION

Touring the Park

If you just want to ride in to Eielson or Wonder Lake and back out again, you can get a seat on the shuttle buses at the Visitor Access Center or on the Wildlife Tour (see "Transportation," below for info on both).

Hiking around the Hotel

Horseshoe Lake Trail starts behind the McKinley Mercantile and parallels the road till the railroad crossing (this is where the shuttle buses drop you off); then it descends to the lake, where you might see waterfowl and beaver. It's 1.5 miles roundtrip and moderately strenuous. **Morino Loop Trail** goes through the forest between the Park Hotel and the tenters' campground; 1.3 miles roundtrip, easy. Hiking the five-mile roundtrip **Mount Healy Overlook Trail** is a great way to get the lay of the land, see The Mountain if it's out, quickly leave the crowds behind, and get your heart pumping. Pick up the trail near the top of the parking lot behind the Park Hotel, or have an employee point you in the right direction. Once at the overlook, keep climbing the ridges for another several hours to get to the peak of Mt. Healy (5,200 feet).

Hiking in the Park

Grab a window seat on the left side of the shuttle bus and ride until you get stiff, sore, or inspired. Or ask at the backcountry desk at the Access Center, or any hotel employee or local you run across, where the best hiking is found. Popular areas include up the Savage River toward Fang Mountain; down the far side of Cathedral Mountain toward Calico Creek (get off the bus just before the Sable Pass closure); up Tatler Creek a little past Igloo Mountain; anywhere on the East Fork flats below Polychrome toward the Alaska Range; anywhere around Stony Hill; and the circumnavigation of Mt. Eielson (get off five to six miles past the visitor center, cross the hundred braids of the Thorofare River, and walk around the mountain, coming back up to the visitor center). There are backcountry description guides at the backcountry desk. You can also read *Backcountry Companion* for ideas.

You can get off the outbound bus, explore to your heart's content, then get back on an inbound bus, if space is available. Consult with the driver and study the bus schedule closely; the camper buses usually have space coming back.

Large as it is, it's nearly impossible to get lost in the Park—you're either north or south of the road. And since the road travels mostly through open alpine tundra, there aren't any man-made trails to follow—just pick a direction and book. Usually you'll want to make for higher ground in order to: a) get out of the knee- to hip-high dwarf shrubbery of the moist tundra and onto the easy hiking of the alpine, b) get to where the breeze will keep the skeeters at bay, and c) see more. Or walk along the gravel riverbars into the mountains, though depending on the size of the gravel, it can be ankle-twisting. Hiking boots are a must, and carry food, water, compass, binoculars, maps, raingear, and litter bag. And keep your eyes and ears wide open for wildlife that you don't want to get close to, sneak up on, or be surprised by.

Backpacking

You need a permit (free) to spend the night in the backcountry. Permits are issued one day in advance; reservations are not accepted. Check the big maps at the backcountry desk; you'll see 43 quota units, where a limited number of backpackers are allowed. Now check the quota board to find the vacancies in the units. Make sure the unit is open (some are always closed; others periodically due to overcrowding or wildlife situations) and that there are enough vacancies to accommodate your whole party. Then get the permit from the ranger. You might have to wait a few days for openings in your chosen area, or have a plan B or C in mind. Finally, reserve a seat on one of the camper buses ($15) to get you and your gear into the park. Or drive over to Wrangell-St. Elias National Park where you'll have the whole place to yourself.

Rafting

Four raft companies run the Nenana, from two-hour canyon trips (12 miles, $40) to four-hour long-distance floats (22 miles, $60). All provide raingear, boots, and life jackets, plus transportation to and from the hotels. Pick up the different brochures, decide, and book at any of the travel desks. **Alaska Raft Adventures,** tel. (907) 683-2215, is run by the Park Hotel concession. **Denali Outdoor Center,** tel. (907) 683-1925; **McKinley Raft Tours,** tel. (907) 683-2392; and **Denali Raft Adventures,** tel. (907) 683-2234, are competitive.

Flightseeing

If The Mountain is out and there's room on the plane, this is the time to hand over a couple of those precious $100 traveler's checks or pull out the credit card. These one-hour flights around McKinley will leave you flying high for days. Book at the travel desks or at the office of Denali Air across the tracks from the train depot, tel. (907) 683-2261. You can also contact **Fly Denali,** tel. (907) 683-2889, run by long-time Park residents Jim Trumbull and Tom Klein, both of whom have decades of experience in wildlife management; prices start at $65 and take off from there. Or try **Denali Wings,** tel. (907) 683-2245.

You can go for a helicopter ride on ubiquitous ERA, tel. (907) 683-2574; flights last 55 minutes for $175.

ATVs, Llamas, Horses, Mountain Bikes Ridge Riders, tel. (907) 683-2580, takes you into the backcountry aboard low-impact eight-wheel ARGO all-terrain vehicles; $60-175 for three- to six-hour guided tours. **McKinley Llamas,** tel. (907) 683-2864, does two-and-a-half-hour ($45) and overnight ($150) guided pack trips into the Alaska Range foothills on gentle llamas bred in Southeast Alaska. Call (907) 683-2402 for **wilderness trail rides** on horseback, and (907) 452-0580 to rent **mountain bikes** or take guided bike tours.

ACCOMMODATIONS

Indoors

Denali Hostel, tel. (907) 683-1295, provides co-ed bunk accommodations in a log house with blue trim. It's 10 miles north, but the proprietors will pick you up (at 5 or 9 p.m.) and drop you back off in the morning at the Visitor Access Center. The hostel has kitchen facilities, showers, and a laundry; check in 5:30-10 p.m. It's $22 for a bed for the night.

The next cheapest place to stay inside is at the Denali Salmon Bake in the **tent cabins,** starting at $65. This is half as much as the next highest room rate and it's right there in the thick of things near the park entrance. The tent cabins have wood walls, screened windows, electric heat, and shared bath. Call (907) 683-2733 for reservations.

Some motel-type digs have sprung up over the past few years. **Sourdough Cabins,** down the bluff below Lynx Creek store, tel. (907) 683-2773, charges $124; **River View Inn,** up on the road just south of Princess Lodge, tel. (907) 683-2663, charges $129, as does **Mt. McKinley Motor Lodge** nearby, tel. (907) 683-1240.

At the south entrance, eight miles south of the turnoff into the park, you'll find **Denali River Cabins** in a great location right on the Nenana, with large sundecks and a hot tub and sauna, tel. (907) 683-2500, $140 off-river, $150 on-river. Across the street is **Grizzly Bear Campground and Cabins,** tel. (907) 683-2696, with a variety of cabins, from tent cabins ($21.50) up to

sleep-six log cabins ($99); campsites are $16. A little south of there at Mile 229 is **Denali Cabins,** tel. (907) 683-2643, charging $93-149.

Otherwise, you can stay at the Denali Park Hotel, Denali Princess Lodge, Denali Bluffs Hotel, or McKinley Chalet, which charge $155-180. The best deal is at the **McKinley Chalet,** tel. (907) 276-7234 year-round. You've got to call and book amazingly early to get one; most are automatically blocked for the tour companies. The two-room suites go for $180 after June 5, but can sleep four comfortably, five with a rollaway, and you get the use of the recreation center: pool, sauna, jacuzzi, weight room. This is the only indoor pool within 125 miles! The 350 local K-12 kids learn to swim here during the summer. The Chalet is not a bad deal if you can get a reservation and stuff several bodies in.

Camping inside the Park

Inside the Park seven campgrounds offer a total of 228 sites. To get a site, sign up at the Visitor Access Center as soon as you arrive. During peak season all the sites are filled the day before. It's best to get to the VAC as early as possible and hope for some space somewhere the next day, or the next. You can camp for 14 days. Sites at Riley Creek, Savage River, Teklanika River, and Wonder Lake (all with water) go for $12 a night (no refunds). Sites at waterless Igloo and Sanctuary are $6. More than 100 of the 228 sites are at **Riley Creek** at the Park entrance, which has flush toilets and a dump station. This campground is mostly for RVs and car campers. **Morino Campground,** for tents only, is next to the depot, a short walk from the hotel. It's officially listed at 10 sites, but you can usually find a patch of ground for your tent, $6. Rangers regularly comb the nearby woods looking for squatters.

You can drive to **Savage River Campground,** with 34 sites, so it fills up fast. The **Wonder Lake Campground** is also extremely popular for hiking and the potential to see The Mountain, especially around sunset and sunrise, when the alpenglow turns it purple and pink and you'll expose every frame of film you have, plus make a permanent imprint on your retina.

Camping outside the Park

The closest camping to the Park entrance is one mile north at **Lynx Creek,** tel. (907) 683-2215, with 42 sites at $20 apiece ($25 with electricity).

You can usually find a space here if you show up early enough (before noon). The camping site comes with a token for a shower; they're not open to the public. **KOA Kampground,** tel. (907) 683-2379, is 10 minutes north of the Park at Healy, charging $21 d for one of 88 sites; it's a somewhat wooded area but right next to the road. **Grizzly Bear Campground,** eight miles south of the turnoff into Denali at the southern entrance, tel. (907) 683-2696, has 59 sites that go for $16 each.

West End

The latest boom neighborhood near Denali Park, the town of **Kantishna,** 85 miles west of the Park entrance at the western end of the Park road, now has four roadhouses and several in the planning stages. The Kantishna area has been settled since 1905, when several thousand miners rushed to the foothills just north of Mt. McKinley to mine, as of 1978, 55,000 ounces of gold, 265,000 ounces of silver, plus millions of pounds of lead, zinc, and antimony. After 1980 and the Alaska National Interest Lands Conservation Act, which expanded Denali Park's boundaries, Kantishna found itself inside the Park, and in 1985, mining was halted by court order. Without their traditional livelihood, some of the property owners have gone into the tourism business.

You take private buses through the park to get to and from the following facilities. **Kantishna Roadhouse,** tel. (907) 733-2535 or (907) 683-2710, is highly recommended for comfort, service, and friendliness, along with a restaurant, a bar, and gold panning. Rates are $123 s, $155 pp with meals. At **Camp Denali** and **North Face Lodge,** P.O. Box 67, Denali, AK 99755, tel. (907) 683-2290, rates start at $120 s and go up to $220 pp including meals and transportation. Similar is **Denali Backcountry Lodge,** tel. (907) 683-2594 or (800) 841-0692.

OTHER PRACTICALITIES

Food

In the snack bar department, you've got the **Whistle Stop Snack Shop** in the lobby of the main Park Hotel, where you can get $6-7 sandwiches and $7.50 burgers. The **Chalet Center Cafe** in the rec building at the McKinley Chalet opens at 5 a.m. and serves scambled eggs alone for $2.25 and an "express breakfast" for

$9; sandwiches with your choice of turkey, ham, roast beef, or tuna, along with choice of cheeses and breads for $6.50; half a sandwich and soup $6.50; burgers $6.50; rotisserie chicken quarter $3.75, half $6.75, and whole $11.50. The **snack bar** next to the Cruiser Bar at the Princess Lodge has a good daily special (such as a half pastrami on rye $4.95), or sandwiches $4.50-6.50, chili $3.25, halibut and chips $7.95, and a chicken burger $7.50.

On the highway just north of the entrance is the **Denali Smoke Shack,** serving "real Alaskan barbecue": veggie dinners $10, fajitas $13, chicken $13, teriyaki $13, grilled salmon $15, barbecue and Cajun sandwiches $8, burgers $6.50, hot dogs $3.50.

Lynx Creek, at Mile 238, a mile north of the Park entrance, serves Mexican food: nachos $4 and $8.50, burritos $8.25, tostadas $8.25, quesadillas $7; pizza slices $3.25, small $10, large combo $22.50; Häagen-Dasz single-scoop $2.75, double-scoop $3.75.

Across the street is the **Denali Salmon Bake.** For breakfast (opens at 5 a.m.), get one egg, meat, and juice $7.45; otherwise, tuck into some king salmon, for $15-18, halibut $16-18.50, barbecue spare ribs $15-17.50, combo plate $17.45-20. They also serve steaks and fried chicken $13-19, burgers $8, and sandwiches $7. Read the menu outside the front door, pay as you walk in, then help yourself to a ton of food.

A different kind of salmon bake is at **Alaska Cabin Night** at the McKinley Chalet. This is all-you-can-eat, and a rip-roaring half-hour musical comedy comes with the food. It's corny but fun; seatings are at 5:30, 7, and 8:30 p.m., $35 pp.

For fancy dining, the room of choice is at the **Princess Lodge.** They have a good $17.95 trio: roast turkey dinner, pot roast, or rib platter. Also good are the Alaska salmon $21, king crab $28.50, smoked salmon fettucine $19.50, halibut and prawns $22, steak and lobster $42, 10-ounce filet $24, New York strip $23, or top sirloin $18.

Sentimental favorite is the original **Denali Dining Room** at the Park Hotel, once the only restaurant in the area. With the profusion of other hotels and restaurants, the DDR tends to get a little left behind, so you can almost always walk right in and sit right down. Good food too, at slightly less expensive prices than the other fancy hotel dining rooms: bacon and eggs or french toast $6, seafood omelet $8, lox and onion bagel $8.50; burgers $7, sandwiches $7-8; blackened salmon Caesar salad $10.25, coconut salmon $7, reindeer sausage $6, breaded pork chops $12, roast turkey $13.50, halibut piccata $17.50, charbroiled brochettes of shrimp $15, Alaska crab cakes $13, salmon $17.50, top sirloin $18.

Crow's Nest has a bar, a steakhouse (expensive: $15 burgers!), and a great view from the deck. The **Denali Fruit Express,** a step van outfitted like a catering truck, stops at the Park post office every Thursday between 7:30 and 8:30 p.m., or check the bulletin boards for current schedule.

Entertainment
The Park Service puts on talks, walks, slide shows, movies, kids' programs, etc. Check the bulletin boards at the Visitor Access Center and the Hotel Auditorium, and *Denali Alpenglow.* You can catch the **Aurorarama,** the northern lights photosymphony, frequently during the day in the Northern Lights Auditorium, in back of the Northern Lights Gift Shop across from the McKinley Chalets ($6.50; see description under "Ester" in the "Suburbs of Fairbanks" section this chapter). Robert Service readings are also performed here ($4).

A good place to hang out with the locals is at the Burgermeister Bar at **McKinley Village Lodge,** at the south entrance to the Park, eight miles south of the Park road. It's low key and congenial, with two pool tables and Alaskan Beer on tap. There are also bars and lounges at the Park Hotel, the Chalet, Crow's Nest, the Princess Lodge, and Lynx Creek.

Shopping and Services
The gift shop at the **Chalet** is one of the best around. Here you'll find unusual things for sale: laser totemic signs on cedar, glass plates and sculptures, candleholders, Siberian Yup'ik masks, dolls, ceramics, crystal villages, amphora raku bowls and pots, a whole cabinet full of McKinley cups, and Christmas tree ornaments, along with the usual T-shirts and sweatshirts, postcards, posters, jewelry, and knick-knacks. It's also the only place around to buy the *Anchorage Daily News, New York Times, Wall Street Journal,* and *USA Today.* The **Northern Lights Gift Shop** in the big log cabin across from the Chalet is owned by longtime locals Karen and Ford Reeves. They sell a lot of clothing, from Patagonia to Native beachwear, from Big Dipper sweatshirts to silk totem hankies. The outdoor clothes are no more expensive than at Beaver Sports in Fairbanks. They also sell posters, postcards, kids' stuff, windsocks, and jewelry. The "husband's waiting bench" is handy outside the front door.

You can buy the necessities at one of three grocery stores, **McKinley Mercantile** next to the Park Hotel, **Lynx Creek** at Mile 238, or **Denali General Store** across the highway from there. Lynx Creek also sells gas and has a sizable selection (for the area) of beer and alcohol.

Coin-operated showers ($2, no time limit) are in a small bathhouse behind McKinley Mercantile, open 7 a.m.-10 p.m.; pay at the Mercantile. The showers and laundry rooms in the dormitory right behind the hotel and at the bottom of the road that comes up from the lower Chalets are for employees only. The closest official medical aid is a physician's assistant in Healy, 11 miles north of the Park, tel. (907) 683-2211. The hotel company hires a nurse or even a doctor to fill one of its positions; ask around. Any emergencies should be reported immediately to the Park Service, tel. (907) 683-9100.

Miscellaneous Information
The Park is open year-round, though the facilities only do business from mid-May to mid-September. A skeleton winter Park Service crew patrols the Park by dogsled and hauls out the season's garbage. After the first heavy snowfall, the Park road is plowed only to headquarters, but many locals run dogs and snowshoe. The wildflowers peak around summer solstice (as do the mosquitoes); the berries, rose hips, and mushrooms are best in mid-August (as are the no-see-ums). The fall colors on the tundra are gorgeous around Labor Day weekend, the crowds start to thin out, and the northern lights start to appear, but it can get very cold. Most questions can be answered at the visitor center at the Park entrance, but if you have an especially esoteric, academic, theoretic, or thermodynamic matter on your mind, try the staff or the small library at Park Headquarters. For brochures and general info, write Denali National Park, P.O. Box 9, Denali Park, AK 99701; or call (907) 683-2295.

TRANSPORTATION

Getting To and From

By **train,** Alaska Railroad leaves Fairbanks at 8:30 a.m. and arrives at Denali at 12:30 p.m., $50 one-way; it departs Anchorage at 8:30 a.m., arriving Denali at 3:45 p.m., $95. Inside the Park depot is a railroad gift shop, storage lockers, and a big board of brochures. The train leaves the Park northbound at 3:55 p.m., southbound at 12:45 p.m.

Vans travel between Anchorage and Fairbanks and stop at Denali. Cheapest is Denali Express, tel. (907) 274-8539 in Anchorage, $35 to Fairbanks, $85 to Anchorage.

Getting Around

In 1971, before the George Parks Highway connected McKinley Park to Fairbanks (125 miles) and Anchorage (245 miles), you had to take the train, or from Fairbanks you had to drive down to Delta Junction, take the Richardson Highway to Paxson, the Denali Highway to Cantwell, then the Parks Highway up to the Park entrance, for a grand total of 340 miles. From Anchorage you had to drive to Glennallen, then up the Richardson to Paxson, over to Cantwell, etc., for 440 miles. That year, nearly 45,000 visitors passed through the Park. In 1972, when the George Parks Highway radically reduced driving times from both main urban centers, almost 90,000 visitors came. In anticipation of the huge jump in tourism, the Park Service initiated the shuttle system of school buses running a regularly scheduled service along the Park road.

There's no question that the shuttle system is highly beneficial to the Park experience: the road is tricky and dangerous, crowds are much more easily controlled, there's much less impact on the wildlife (which take the buses for granted), and it's much easier to see wildlife when 40 passengers have eyeballs, binoculars, spotting scopes, and telephotos trained on the tundra.

You can reserve tickets in advance, starting on the last Monday in February and ending up to five days ahead of the day you want, by calling (800) 622-7275, or in Alaska (907) 272-7275. Forty percent of the available tickets are sold in advance; the other 60% are sold only at the Visitor Access Center. Fares vary, anywhere from free (for backpackers 12 and under) to $40 (six-trip pass). If you're 17 or over, you'll pay $12 to Polychrome/Toklat, $20 to Eielson, $26 to Wonder Lake, and $30 to Kantishna. Backpackers pay $15 to anywhere in the park on the camper bus. Fares do not include entrance fees. One out of three of the shuttle buses is accessible for people with disabilities.

Buses for Eielson begin departing from the Visitor Access Center at 5 a.m. and continue roughly every 30 minutes through 3:30 p.m. Other buses depart during the day for Polychrome/Toklat and Wonder Lake. The Riley Creek loop bus runs 5:30 a.m.-9:30 p.m., stopping at the Horseshoe Lake trailhead, Park Hotel, and train depot before heading back to the visitor center, every half-hour. Shuttle buses also run between the visitor center/Park Hotel and Denali Bluffs Hotel, Princess Lodge, McKinley Village, and Denali Hostel.

It's recommended that you try to get on an early-morning bus into the Park: better chance to see wildlife and The Mountain in the cool of the morning, and more time to get off the bus and fool around in the backcountry.

You can get off the bus and flag it down to get back on (if there's room; the buses leave with a few seats empty to pick up day-hikers in the park) anywhere along the road. Many riders never get off the bus at all and just stay on for the entire roundtrip. Schedules are readily available at the visitor centers and hotels. Take everything you need, as nothing (except books) is for sale inside the Park.

Tours

The park Wildlife Tours leave from the hotels throughout the day. You can take a three-hour Natural History Tour ($30) to Primrose Ridge (17 miles one-way), where you walk around with the driver/naturalist; or take the seven-hour Wildlife Tour ($54) to Toklat (53 miles one-way). More than 150,000 people take these tours annually, and they fill up fast with package travelers, so you need to make your reservations as far in advance as possible, tel. (907) 276-7234 or (800) 276-7234.

DENALI HIGHWAY

The Denali Highway, which stretches 136 miles east-west across the waist of mainland Alaska from Cantwell, 30 miles south of Denali Park, to Paxson at Mile 122 of the Richardson Highway, may be the best-kept secret in Alaska. Originally the only road into Denali National Park, this beautiful side trip has been largely ignored by visitors since the opening of the George Parks Highway in 1971. Denali Highway is paved for 21 miles on the east end of the road, from Paxson to Tangle Lakes, the rest well-maintained gravel, which has received an undeserved bad rap—usually from folks hoping to set world land-speed records on their Alaska vacation.

Rumor has it that work will begin in spring 1997 to pave the rest of the Denali Highway. This same rumor has reared its head from time to time since the first 21 miles were paved years ago. That first year, the state road crew completed its work before snowfall and left, promising to return each spring and pave 20 miles a year until it was done. They haven't been seen or heard from since. Every couple of years or so, however, the state throws a bunch of money at a new survey crew to spend the summer measuring and photographing the same hundred miles of road. So who knows, this could be the year!

The Denali Highway began as a "cat" track in the early 1950s when a man named Earl Butcher first established a hunting camp at Tangle Lakes. Known for years as Butcher's Camp, it's now the site of Tangle Lakes Lodge. The back rooms of the present lodge were the original structure of Butcher's Camp.

About the same time, Chalmer Johnson established a camp at Round Tangle Lake. Now known as the Tangle River Inn, this lodge is still operated by the Johnson family, Chalmer's son Jack and Jack's wife Naidine. The oldest known structure in the area is probably Whitey's Cabin at the Maclaren River Lodge. Built during the mid-'40s as a private residence, this old cabin serves as a rental unit at the lodge.

The Denali Highway offers a varied selection of outstanding scenery and wildlife-viewing op-

portunities. Much of the route punches through the foothills of the magnificent Alaska Range. This area is part of the home range of the huge Nelchina caribou herd (50,000 strong). In the fall they begin to group in the greatest numbers—sightings of several hundred caribou are not unusual.

The Denali Highway is closed from October through mid-May, but in the winter it becomes a popular trail for snowmachiners, dog mushers, and cross-country skiers. Die-hard Alaskans also use this trail in the winter months for access to unparalleled ice-fishing and caribou and ptarmigan hunting.

As always, travelers on the Denali Highway should be prepared for emergencies. Always carry a spare tire and tire-changing tools, water, some snacks, and warm clothing. Towing is available from Paxson, Gracious House, and Cantwell. But it ain't cheap, so take your time and be safe.

Cantwell

Cantwell is a small town (pop. 240) just under 30 miles south of Denali Park. An old railroad town, it's at the west end of the Denali Highway, two miles west of the Parks Highway; the railroad tracks run right through the middle of it. **Cantwell Lodge,** tel. (907) 768-2300 or (800) 768-5522, is the main action, with rooms, cafe, bar, liquor store, RV parking, camping, laundry, and showers. **Cantwell RV Park,** tel. (907) 768-2210 or (800) 940-2210, lies a third of a mile west of the junction with the Parks Highway.

Heading East

About three miles in from the Denali Highway/Parks Highway junction is a turnout with a view of Cantwell and Mt. McKinley, if it's out. There's another potential view of The Mountain at Mile 13, then in another five miles the highway runs parallel to the Nenana River. The headwaters of the Nenana emanate from a western digit of the icefields atop the Alaska Range trio of Mounts: Deborah (on the left at 12,339 feet), Hess (in the middle at 11,940 feet) and Hayes (on the right at 13,832 feet).

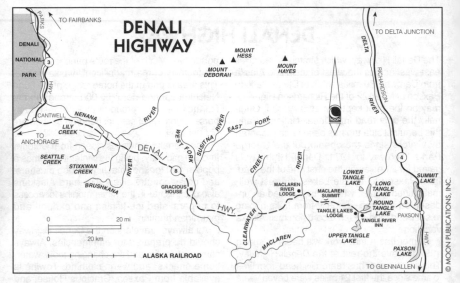

Over the next 10 miles the road crosses Lily Creek, Seattle Creek, and Stixkwan Creek; throw in a line and pull up some grayling or Dolly Varden. At Mile 30 you come to the Brushkana River, where the BLM has a good 12-site campground right on the river, with picnic tables, firepits, water pumps, and pit toilets. Over the next 10 miles you get some great views of the three prominent peaks, along with the West Fork Glacier. The southern glaciers off Deborah, Hess, and Hayes feed the Susitna River, which travels west (to the Parks Highway), then south, and empties into the Cook Inlet across from Anchorage.

Gracious House Lodge and Beyond

Fifty-one miles from the junction of the Parks and Denali Highways is **Gracious House Lodge,** tel. (907) 333-3148 (message phone) or (907) 822-7307 (this is a radio phone: let it ring!). This lodge has 16 cabins/motel rooms, most with private baths, starting at $45 s, and campsites for tents and self-contained RVs. Minor tire and mechanical repairs are done on the premises, and towing is available. You can also arrange for an air taxi and guide services.

In five miles you cross the single-lane 1,000-foot-long Susitna River bridge. Farther south, the Susitna is a popular river to float, but passage between here and there is considered im-

possible, due to the impassable Devil's Canyon just downriver from the bridge.

At Mile 79, the highway crosses Clearwater Creek; there are pit toilets at a rest stop here. In six miles is a turnout with a view of numerous lakes and ponds that provide a staging area for waterfowl; look for ducks, cranes, geese, trumpeter swans, and migrating shorebirds.

Maclaren

At Mile 93 out of Cantwell, the road crosses the Maclaren River, a tributary of the Susitna, flowing from the southern icefields of mighty Mt. Hayes. From here to the other end of Denali Highway, you get occasional views of the three Alaska Range peaks. A mile before the bridge is Maclaren River Road; turn left and follow it 12 miles north to Maclaren Glacier.

Just before the bridge crossing is **Maclaren River Lodge,** tel. (907) 822-7105. This is a year-round facility catering to hikers, hunters, anglers, and sightseers in the summer, and snowmachiners and dog mushers in the winter. You can stay overnight in motel rooms, intimate cabins, or the bunkhouse ($35). The lodge has a restaurant and bar, with a pretty good selection of beer, a pool table, and satellite TV. If you want a kick, ask Mike, your host, what his Indian name means.

In another seven miles is Maclaren Summit, at 4,080 feet the second highest road pass in Alaska. It provides breathtaking views of Mt. Hayes and the Maclaren Glacier. Peer through binoculars at the plains below to spot wildlife. Up at the summit you might see rock ptarmigan.

East End

At Mile 113 is **Tangle Lakes Lodge,** tel. (907) 688-9173 or (907) 822-7302. The lodge has canoes, fishing charters and gear, log cabins ($45), fine dining, a bar, showers, and a sauna. Fly-fishing is spoken fluently here; the "Tangle Lakes Teaser" dry fly is a grayling-getter. This is also a good place to get a look at some of the Nelchina caribou herd. But it's one of the best places in Alaska to birdwatch; the hosts, Rich and Linda Holmstrom, are avid birders and can answer any questions about our fine feathered friends. Once you arrive at Tangle Lakes Lodge, you're only a mile from the pavement.

The Tangle Lakes BLM campground is just up the road, with water pumps, pit toilets, blueberries in season, and a boat launch for extended canoe trips into the "tangle" (or maze) of lakes and ponds and creeks in the neighborhood. A 1.5-mile portage leads to the Gulkana River drainage and the trip to Sourdough on the Richardson Highway. This trip takes about a week and has class IV rapids. The boat launch is also the put-in point for a popular float trip along the Delta National Wild and Scenic River, a 35-mile three-day float that requires a half-mile portage around a set of waterfalls. It ends at Mile 212 on the Richardson Highway, north of Summit Lake. Although most of the trip is a slow float, there are a couple of swift rocky sections, often well-marked by aluminum canoes twisted artistically around stubborn boulders. Check with the BLM office in Glennallen for maps and information, tel. (907) 822-3217.

Two miles east of the campground is **Tangle River Inn,** tel. (907) 822-7304. Jack and Naidine Johnson have owned this place for nearly three decades. The Johnsons sell gas, liquor, and gifts, and offer good home cooking, lodging (from $45), RV hookups, camping sites, canoes, and fishing gear. The bar provides the nightlife in the area: nightly karaoke-style sing-alongs. Some of the locals can really belt out the tunes (Naidine, for one!). Some fine storytellers are found around here, too.

Nearby is **Denali Highland Adventures,** tel. (907) 479-0765 or (800) 895-4281. The Yates family provides 4WD rentals, canoes, home-cooked meals, and guided package tours of one to five days of hiking, boating, camping, and fishing for salmon, burbot, lake trout, rainbows, and grayling.

The Tangle Lakes Archaeological District begins at Mile 120 and extends back to Crazy Notch at Mile 90. A wealth of evidence of prehistoric peoples is contained in this area. To protect the land for further study, offroad vehicle travel is limited to designated trails. A short hike from the highway to any given promontory along this 30-mile stretch could have you standing at an ancient Athabascan hunting camp where no human footprints have been made for thousands of years. Even the most intrepid explorer will find this somewhat humbling.

At Mile 122, there's a viewpoint from the summit that looks south over a great tundra plain. The three most prominent peaks of the Wrangell Mountains are visible from here: Mt. Sanford on the left, Mt. Drum on the right, and Mt. Wrangell in the middle. Look for steam rising from Mt. Wrangell, as it smokes earth's crustal cigarette.

At Mile 125 is a paved turnout with a view of Ten Mile Lake. A short trail leads down to the lake, where you can fish for grayling and trout. A turnout at Mile 129 affords a spectacular view of the Alaska Range to the north. The Gulkana and Gakona Glaciers can be seen from this point.

Paxson

Paxson is a tiny settlement at Mile 185.5 of the Richardson Highway and at Mile 136 (from Cantwell, or Mile 0) of the Denali Highway. There's a 3,000-foot airstrip, a modern lodge, and a backcountry guide company. **Paxson Lodge,** tel. (907) 822-3330, offers gas, gifts, food, lodging, and a liquor store. Summer hours are 8 a.m.-11 p.m. Meals are served till 10 p.m., the cocktail lounge is open till midnight. This is the local post office and the gathering place for the far-flung Paxson community (population around 33) on Tuesday and Thursday when the mail is trucked in. **Paxson Alpine Tours,** tel. (907) 479-0765, provides wildlife tours, float trips on the Gulkana and Delta Rivers, or birding, fishing, and hiking trips (with llamas).

GORDY OHLIGER

SOUTHCENTRAL ALASKA

Southcentral Alaska is a land of short rivers, long mountain ranges, and wide valleys, that extends north from the Gulf of Alaska to the crest of the Alaska Range. The Kenai and Chugach Mountains are a rugged strip 60 miles wide that swings northeast along the Gulf, from Cook Inlet to the Yukon border. To the north lie the Matanuska and Susitna valleys, with Mt. McKinley visible beyond. Much of the area around Prince William Sound and on the Kenai Peninsula falls within the Chugach National Forest. In many ways, Southcentral is the rich heartland of Alaska, with one big metropolis (Anchorage) and many picturesque small towns, the main agricultural region of the state, and some of the state's finest scenery and best hiking and camping opportunities. Getting around is easy by road, and a variety of public transportation, including an efficient ferry system, brings the best within reach. Southcentral Alaska offers something for everyone.

DENALI STATE PARK

Another superlative state facility, Denali State Park is actually a continuation of Denali National Park, sharing its southeast border, at Mile 169 on the George Parks Highway. Its 324,240 acres, half the size of Rhode Island, provide an excellent alternative wilderness experience to the crowds and hassles of its federal next-door neighbor. The Mountain is visible from all over the park, bears are abundant, and you won't need to stand in line for a permit to hike or camp while you wait for McKinley's mighty south face to show itself. Several trails offer a variety of hiking experiences and spectacular views. However, the park is accessible only by car, and it's imperative to be super prepared—the nearest grocery store is 50 miles away.

Sights

If The Mountain or even "just" some of the lower peaks of the Alaska Range are out, you won't need to read the next sentence to know what or where the sights are. The best viewpoint along the highway in the park is at the large pullout at Mile 135, a half-mile north of Mary's McKinley View Lodge. Set up your tripod and shoot shoot shoot. A signboard here identifies the glaciers and peaks. Other unforgettable viewpoints are at Miles 147, 158, and 162. The **Alaska Veterans Memorial,** within walking distance of Byers Lake Campground, is a shrine consisting of five monumental concrete blocks with stars carved out, commemorating the enormous contribution the armed forces have made to Alaska since its purchase by the U.S. in 1867. As usual, the state planners chose and developed this spot with care and respect. Turn your back to the monument, and if you're lucky, there's blue-white McKinley, perfectly framed by tall spruce trees.

Trails

Little Coal Creek trailhead is at Mile 164, five miles south of the park's northern boundary. This is the park's gentlest climb to the alpine tundra—five miles east up the trail by Little Coal Creek, then you cut southwest along Kesugi Ridge with amazing views of the Range and glaciers; flags and cairns delineate the trail. Watch for bears! The trail goes 27.5 miles till it hooks up with Troublesome Creek Trail just up from Byers Lake Campground. About halfway there, **Ermine Lake Trail** cuts back down to the highway, an escape route in case of really foul weather. Ermine Lake Trail is not quite completed, but it is flagged well enough to follow.

Troublesome Creek Trail is so named because of frequent bear encounters; in fact, Troublesome Creek Trail is frequently closed in late summer and early fall because of the abun-

SOUTHCENTRAL ALASKA

© MOON PUBLICATIONS, INC.

dance of bears. It has two trailheads, one at the northeast tip of Byers Lake (Mile 147), the other at Mile 138. The park brochure describes this 15-mile hike along Troublesome Creek as moderate. It connects with Kesugi Ridge Trail just up from Byers Lake or descends to the easy five-mile **Byers Lake Loop Trail,** which brings you around to both campgrounds. Just down and across the road from the Byers Lake turnoff is a family day-hike along Lower Troublesome Creek—a gentle mile.

Camping
Byers Lake Campground (73 sites, $12) offers the usual state accommodations—huge, gorgeous, uncrowded. It has abundant outhouses, water, interpretive signs, large well-maintained sites, and beautiful Byers Lake a stone's throw down the road. Just under two miles along the Loop Trail from here, or across the lake by boat, is the **Lakeshore Campground,** with six sites, outhouses, no water, but unimpeded views of The Mountain and Range from your tent flap. Across the road and a quarter-mile south, **Lower Troublesome Creek Campground** has 20 sites and all the amenities of Byers Lake, $6.

Other Practicalities
Only two commercial facilities are within park boundaries. **Mary's McKinley View Lodge** at the southern entrance (Mile 134), tel. (907) 733-1555, has a restaurant, a lodge, great views of The Mountain out the big picture windows, and a chance to visit with Mary Carey, one of the most prolific and renowned Alaskan authors—incredible life story. You can buy autographed copies of her dozen books, including her most famous, *Alaska, Not For A Woman.* Mary's daughter, Jean Richardson, is also a writer, but of children's books. Check out her *Tag-Along Timothy* and *Dingbat Cat* series, as well as *Courage Seed,* a fourth grade textbook that's distributed nationally.

Chulitna River Lodge and Café, Mile 156, tel. (907) 733-2521, is 13 miles from the north entrance, with cabins, a small menu off the grill, gas, and gifts; it's now open year-round. Otherwise, the nearest civilization is 69 miles north of the northern boundary of the state park at the entrance to Denali National Park, and 48 miles south of the southern boundary at Talkeetna.

Neither Denali Express nor Gray Line lists a stop at this state park, but you could probably make arrangements with them to deliver and later collect you there for the price of a one-way through ticket.

The junction of the Parks Highway and the 14-mile spur road to Talkeetna is at Mile 98.

TALKEETNA

Two closely related phenomena dominate this small Bush community: The Mountain, and flying to and climbing on The Mountain. On a clear day, from the overlook a mile out on the spur road, Mt. McKinley and the accompanying Alaska Range scrape the sky like a jagged white wall. Though still 60 miles northwest, you actually have to crane your neck to see the summit of the highest peak in North America. Also on a clear day, the four flightseeing and air-taxi companies take off in a continuous parade to circle McKinley, buzz up long glaciers or even land on them for a champagne lunch, then return to Talkeetna's busy airport to drop off passengers whose wide eyes, broad smiles, and shaky knees attest to the excitement of this once-in-a-lifetime thrill. In May and June, mostly, these same special "wheel-and-ski" planes might be delivering an American, European, Japanese, or even African climbing expedition to the Kahiltna Glacier (elevation 7,000 feet), from where—if they're lucky—they inch

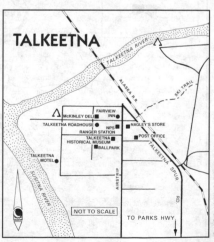

their way up the popular West Buttress route 13,000 feet to the peak. On a clear day, if you're anywhere within striking distance, make a beeline for Talkeetna and be whisked away to some of the most stunning and alien scenery you'll ever see.

Sights and Hikes

Talkeetna (Where the Rivers Meet), nesting at the confluence of the Talkeetna, Chulitna, and Susitna Rivers, was originally settled by trappers and prospectors who paddled up the Susitna River to gain access to rich silver, coal, and fur country around the Talkeetna Mountains. The settlement got a boost when the railroad was pushed through in the early 1920s and still remains a popular stop on the route. In 1965 the spur road from the Parks Highway to Talkeetna was completed, providing further access to the town.

At the intersection of the Parks Highway and the spur road is a privately owned visitor center. Covering the area from Willow (south) to Healy (north), the **Talkeetna/Denali Visitor Center,** tel. (907) 733-2688 or (800) 660-2688 (907-733-2599 off-season), is staffed May-Sept. 8 a.m.-8 p.m. by friendly and informative local residents. They can book flightseeing trips, fishing expeditions, guided hikes, and rooms at hotels and B&Bs, or just supply brochures and info on the area.

A mile off the Parks Highway is **Mary's Fiddlehead Fern Farm Gift Shop,** tel. (907) 733-2428, the other Mary Carey gift shop (see above). This facility hosts the world's only fiddlehead fern farm, selling gourmet ferns pickled, frozen, and fresh, along with a fern cookbook. The gift shop also stocks rocks, crafts, burls, souvenirs, and autographed copies of the many fine books written by Mary and her daughter Jean Richardson.

Turn off onto gravel roads at Miles 3 and 12 for out-of-the-way lakes and camping spots. At Mile 13 is the big turnout with an interpretive sign on the Alaska Range and heart-stopping views—if the clouds are cooperating. Then you head right into Talkeetna (pop. 450).

For a graphic and detailed look at the history of the town and its connection to The Mountain, check out the excellent **Talkeetna Historical Museum.** Take a left after Nagley's Store, which you can read all about in the museum; the museum is a half-block down the side street on the right in an old red schoolhouse, open daily 10 a.m.-5 p.m., $1. Housing hundreds of historical articles, including an eclectic library in the back room with eyebrow-raising old magazines and scrapbooks of newspaper clippings, the museum is dedicated to Don Sheldon and Ray Genet, hometown boys who were two of Alaska's most heroic figures. Sheldon was the honorary guiding light of Alaska's elite fraternity of bush pilots until his untimely death from cancer in 1975 at the age of 56; Genet was the all-time record-holder for climbs on McKinley and other Alaska Range peaks until his untimely death at 27,000 feet on Mt. Everest in 1979 at the age of 48. Separately and together, they pulled off some of the most daredevil rescues imaginable, and Sheldon's exploits have been immortalized in *Wager With The Wind.* Reading the displays devoted to these giants of northern lore will give you an idea of the kind of people who gravitate to Talkeetna. Also check out the original railroad depot with its restored ticket office, Ole Dahl's trapper cabin, and an old railroad section house.

Next door to the museum is a funky little cabin that houses the National Park Service ranger. Ask about wuh thappening on The Mountain, or just pull up a chair and thumb through the beat-up bookshelf copy of *Wager With The Wind* and eavesdrop on the ranger and the radio! For sale are some books on mountaineering. Better yet, walk out to the airport to watch the different bush planes take off and land; strike up a conversation with a pilot or a mechanic about flying conditions around The Weathermaker.

The **Museum of Northern Adventure,** right on Main St., tel. (907) 733-3999, open daily 10 a.m.-6 p.m., has 24 life-size dioramas with wax figures on the history and lifestyles of the North Country, including cabin fever, fishing, and even the cremation of Sam McGee; $2.50 adults, $1.50 children.

The ski trail signposted at the back of the small park as you enter town is hikable in summer, though it'll probably be extremely muddy. To stretch your legs and keep your feet dry, saunter along the railroad tracks in either direction: graded, cleared, scenic.

Flightseeing

Best of all, get on one of the planes and see for yourself. The flight services in town offer a bewildering array of possibilities, including short scenic flights, glacier landings, drop-off hiking or fishing, wildlife viewing, overnight trips, and flights to, around, and even over the top of The Mountain. Rates vary according to the type of airplane, length of the flight, and how many people there are in your group. Most outfits will try to match you up with other folks to maximize your flightseeing dollar. Expect to be flexible in your plans, since weather is infinitely variable and is always the most important consideration when it comes to flying you safely to see the sights. Prices range from $37 pp, for a party of three for a half-hour ride without glacier landing, on up. As always, reservations are recommended, but not always necessary. Note that the climbing season on Mt. McKinley runs from early spring until mid or late June, and the flight services are busiest then.

Five charter companies provide service to Mt. McKinley: **Hudson Air Service,** tel. (907) 733-2321 or (800) 478-2321; **Doug Geeting Aviation,** tel. (907) 733-2366 or (800) 770-2366; **K2 Aviation,** tel. (907) 733-2291 or (800) 764-2291; **Talkeetna Air Taxi,** tel. (907) 733-2218; and **McKinley Air Service,** (907) 733-1765 or (800) 564-1765.

Fishing
The fishing in Talkeetna is excellent, with one species of fish or another available May-September. Rainbow trout, grayling, Dolly Varden, and all five species of Pacific salmon are there for the catching. Local riverboat services can drop you off along the river for the day or overnight, supply you with a fishing guide, or arrange a scenic float trip if you just want to ride the river without fishing. Contact **Mahay's,** tel. (907) 733-2223; **Talkeetna Riverboat Service,** tel. (907) 733-2281; **Talkeetna River Guides,** tel. (907) 733-2677; or **Tri-River Charters,** tel. (907) 733-2400.

Practicalities
Camping at the River Park is officially discouraged—signs warn of its illegality, but they're often

You'll stay high long after you touch back down in Talkeetna from your flightseeing trip around the Great One.

BOB RACE

ignored and/or torn down. For hassle-free camping, go to the new camping park, **Talkeetna River Adventures, Boat Landing & Campground** (great name if you're a sign painter paid by the letter!) at the boat-launch site near the airport. By 1997, they expect to have 60 campsites, 20 with electricity, plus showers and a laundromat. Beautiful downtown Talkeetna is a mere quarter-mile walk through the woods from the campground.

The historic **Fairview Inn** (1923) has the best prices of the five lodging houses—$40 s, $50 d—but their six rooms fill up fast. Take your chances and register at the bar, or write ahead to P.O. Box 645, Talkeetna, AK 99676, or call (907) 733-2423. **Talkeetna Roadhouse,** tel. (907) 733-2341, has rooms for $45 s, $60 d; a cabin available for $75 d; and a four-bed co-ed bunkhouse for $21 per bed. At **Talkeetna Motel,** tel. (907) 733-2323, rooms run from $65 s up to $100 q. The place is newly refurbished and all rooms have private baths and color TV.

The **Classy Shack B&B,** tel. (907) 733-1234, is beautifully finished and trimmed with local wood. The $140 price includes a hot tub, VCR and movie rentals, fresh flowers, and a selection of fresh-baked goods for breakfast. Check with Dave at the McKinley Deli for details. **Swiss-Alaska Inn,** tel. (907) 733-2424, has rooms with private bath ($70 s, $80 d) and a restaurant, books local services, and will pack your lunch for fishing trips and even cook your catch. **Talkeetna Camp & Canoe,** tel. (907) 733-2267, rents cabins on walk-in lakes in the area for $64 or $74 per night (the $64 cabin is a few minutes farther away), sleeping four in queen-size bunk beds. The cabins have outhouses, propane lights, heat, cook stoves, and cooking utensils. They also rent canoes for $35 per day. Talkeetna has turned into quite the spot for good, inexpensive food, a definite rarity on the Alaska road system. At the **McKin-**

ley Deli, a mini-cheese pizza is $7, a Large McKinley goes for $20.50, and they've got an extensive sandwich menu. Their sidewalk grill features sausages, burgers, ribeye steaks, and king salmon or halibut; prices range from $3.95-13.95. Dinner selections include lasagna, spaghetti, barbecue ribs, and a huge chef salad. **Talkeetna Roadhouse** serves family-style dinners 5:30-9 p.m.; breakfast starts at 6:30 a.m., and they now have a bakery and a beer and wine license. The restaurant at **Talkeetna Motel** is recommended: massive amounts of good food, reasonable prices, and relaxing surroundings. Try breakfast here, or the dinner special. It's open 7 a.m.-9 p.m. seven days a week year-round. The **Fairview** has a beer garden; for lunch or dinner, try the Fairview Pantry, serving inexpensive and tasty fare. **Sparky's** is a fast-food walk-up take-out on the left as you enter town. The **pay phone** in town is on the campground side of the Talkeetna Roadhouse.

Getting There

The turnoff to Talkeetna is 100 miles north of Anchorage on the George Parks Highway. The spur road is a little more than 14 miles. Several van services provide transportation between Talkeetna and Anchorage, two based in Talkeetna and catering mostly to the climbing crowd, one based in Anchorage. **Denali Overland Transportation,** tel. (907) 733-2384, charges $45 pp for a group of four, one-way to or from Anchorage (or $60 pp for three, $90 pp for two, $180 for one). **Talkeetna Shuttle Service,** tel. (907) 733-2222, charges $40 pp for four ($60/$90 for three/two). If you don't have enough people to fill a van, they'll try to match you up with other small groups traveling at about the same time. **Alaska Backpacker Shuttle,** tel. (907) 344-8774 or (800) 266-8625, charges $30 one-way and $55 roundtrip, $5 extra for gear, $10 for bikes. Their vans leave from the Youth Hostel in Anchorage, 700 H St., at 10 a.m., arriving in Talkeetna at 1 p.m. All services require reservations and deposits.

The **Alaska Railroad,** tel. (800) 544-0552, does a special roundtrip to Talkeetna for $90, leaving you five hours to explore the town. The train leaves Anchorage every morning at 8:30, arrives in Talkeetna at 11:20, and leaves for the return trip at 4:30. If you want to spend more time in Talkeetna, you can lay over for no extra charge.

CONTINUING SOUTH

On the 45 miles from the Talkeetna cutoff to Willow, the next town, are half a dozen restaurants and gas stations and two state campgrounds. **Montana Creek campground,** Mile 97, is now operated by a private company. Rates are $10 per night for camping, $5 for day use. It's a large, attractive campground, with 89 sites, chemical toilets, water, a few short trails, and good salmon fishing in season. Two miles east of the Parks Highway on Hatcher Pass Rd. (Mile 71) is **Deception Creek;** there are seven campsites, but no water. Next up is **Willow Creek State Recreation Area,** four miles down the Susitna River access road. There are 145 sites at $10 per night, but don't expect a quiet night's repose in the wilderness here if the salmon are running, which they do for most of the summer. The boat launch attracts fishing parties at all hours of the day and night, as well as lots of RVs with their inevitable generator noise. Still, it's a pretty and handy place to spend the night if it's getting late and you plan to travel Hatcher Pass Rd. to Independence Mine State Historical Park and Wasilla or Palmer (see below).

At Mile 69 is **Willow** (pop. around 500), a roadside town with gas, grocery, hardware, cafe, and air service that you'll miss if you sneeze. Fifteen years ago, however, Alaskans voted to move the state capital here; if it'd happened, Willow today would be the Brasilia (an overnight pre-fab metropolis in the middle of nowhere) of Alaska, a bureaucrat's instant wet-dream on the tundra. A multibillion-dollar city was planned, and real estate speculation went wild. However, when a second election was held in 1982 to decide whether to actually *spend* the billions, the plan was soundly defeated. For a fascinating look at this bit of Alaskan lore, read John McPhee's renowned *Coming Into The Country.* Also check out the "Capital Move Cabin" in back of the Wasilla Museum.

Nancy Lake State Recreation Area

Sixth largest in the system, this state park has unusual topography compared with what you've become accustomed to in Interior: flat, heavily forested terrain, dotted with over 100 lakes, some interconnected by creeks. As you might imagine, the popular activities here are fishing, boating, and canoeing, plus there are a very comfortable campground and a couple of hiking trails. As you might also imagine, the skeeters here are thick.

Heading south on the Parks Highway, turn right onto a wide gravel road at Mile 67. A little more than a mile in stands a fee kiosk; parking is $3 per day, campsites at the South Rolly Lake Campground $10. A half-mile past the kiosk is the trailhead to the public-use cabins, which can be reserved at the Mat-Su State Parks office at Mile 0.7, Bogard Rd. in Wasilla, tel. (907) 745-3975; or at the Dept. of Natural Resources office in Anchorage at 3601 C St., Suite 200, tel. (907) 269-8400. Cost is $35 per night. The cabins are very popular, so unless you've planned well ahead, chances of reserving one are slim. However, there are often vacancies in mid-week, and it never hurts to check.

Just under a mile beyond this trailhead is the **Tulik Nature Trail,** an easy walk that takes about an hour. A self-guiding brochure, wonderfully written and illustrated by creative YCC teenagers, identifies ferns, shrubs, grasses, and trees, and includes some nice legends, descriptions, and suggestions for enjoying yourself. Keep an eye out for loons, beavers, and terns, and watch for that prickly devil's club! The thorns can cause nasty infections.

The **Lynx Lake Canoe Route** begins at Tanaina Lake Canoe Trailhead at Mile 4.5, Nancy Lakes Parkway. This leisurely 12-mile, two-day trip hits 14 lakes, between most of which are well-marked portages, some upgraded with boardwalks over the muskeg. Hunker down for the night at any one of 10 primitive campsites (campfires in fireplaces only!). Another possibility, though requiring a long portage, is to put into the Little Susitna River at Mile 57 on the Parks Highway and portage to Skeetna Lake, where you connect up to the southern leg of the loop trail.

Tippecanoe, tel. (907) 495-6688, at Mile 66.6 of the Parks Highway, rents canoes for the Nancy Lake canoe trails. They'll also take you on guided tours of the lakes. The Cry of the Loon tour costs $35 for the six- to eight-hour trip. Daily rental for canoes or kayaks is $22, with discounts for longer terms or for renting three or more boats. They also rent equipment for unguided float trips down local streams and can arrange for fly-in trips.

Nancy Lake Resort, tel. (907) 495-6284 at Mile 64.5, also rents canoes, boats and/or motors, pedal boats, cabins, fishing tackle, etc., and even has gas for your airplane. One- to two-hour trips aboard their restored sternwheel boat are available for under $10.

At the end of the road is **South Rolly Lake Campground,** with 98 sites and the usual excellent state amenities. An easy three-mile roundtrip trail leads to an overlook above Red Shirt Lake. Continue on this trail all the way to the lake.

HATCHER PASS ROAD

It's a boring 25 miles from Nancy Lake State Recreation Area to Wasilla on the Parks Highway. But a highly recommended side trip is the 50-mile road from Mile 71 of the Parks, two miles north of Willow, over Hatcher Pass (3,886 feet), taking in the Independence Mine State Historical Park on the way. The first 10 miles off the highway are paved, and the next 15 gravel miles are quite smooth and scenic, through beautiful forest, following Willow Creek and the route of a wagon trail built to service the gold mines along the creek. Then the road climbs four miles on rough gravel up to Summit Lake and Hatcher Pass, an area of vast vistas, high tundra, excellent hiking (and cross-country skiing), and backcountry camping. Another two miles brings you to Independence Mine.

Independence Mine State Historical Park

It's hard to imagine a park that better combines the elements of the Alaska experience: scenery, history and lore, and that noble yellow metal, gold. And it's free. This mine is very different from the panning, sluicing, deep-placer, and dredging operations seen in Yukon and Interior. This was "hard-rock" mining, with an intricate 21-mile network of tunnels under Granite Mountain. The miners drilled into the rock, inserted explosives (which they set off at the end of shifts to give the fumes time to dissipate before the next crew went in), then "mucked" the debris out by hand, to be sorted, crushed, amalgamated, assayed, etc., a process similar to the finish operations up north.

Hard-rock or "lode" mining is often preceded by panning and placer mining. Prospectors

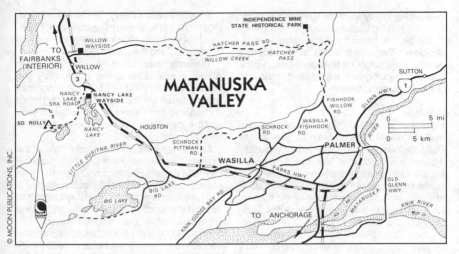

who first took gold from Grubstake Gulch, a tributary of Willow Creek, in 1897 noticed the gold's rough, unweathered nature, which indicated a possible lode of unexposed gold nearby. In 1906, Robert Lee Hatcher staked the first lode claim, and his Alaska Free Gold Mine operated till 1924. In 1908, the Independence Mine opened on the mountain's east slope, and over the next 25 years it produced several million dollars' worth. In 1937, the two mines merged into the Alaska Pacific Consolidated Mining Company, which operated Independence Mine at peak production through 1942, when WW II shut it down. A series of private sales, and public deals with the Alaska Division of Parks, culminated in 1980, leaving the state with 271 acres, including the whole mining camp, and deeding 1,000 acres to the Coronado Mining Corporation, which has active operations in the area.

A couple of dozen camp buildings are in various stages of ruin and refurbishing. Start at the visitor center in the rehabilitated house of the camp manager, Walter Stoll. Take some time to enjoy the excellent displays: historic charts, gold-mining overview, "touch tunnel" complete with sound effects, and wage summaries of workers and management. Don't miss the spinning board that points to old black-and-white snapshots and displays vignettes about the people and scenes. Guided walks are given several times daily by park personnel ($3), but you're free to wander the whole site on your own; interpretive signs in front of most buildings describe their purpose. Independence Mine State Historical Park is a must-see on any Alaskan itinerary.

WASILLA

In 1977, Wasilla consisted of a landing strip and a grocery store, which advertised the convenience of flying in from the Bush, buying Matanuska Valley produce, and flying out again—without the hassles of Anchorage. Then, when the capital looked like it might be moved to Willow, 25 miles up the highway, Anchoragites began to discover Wasilla's quiet, beauty, and affordable land, and contractors took advantage of the town's lax restrictions on development. And develop it did, with a vengeance. During 1980-82, the town's population of 1,200 doubled, then doubled again from '82 to '84. Stores, malls, and fast-food chains popped up faster than you could say "We do chicken right." Teeland's General Store was jacked up, moved from the corner it had sat on for over 60 years, and unceremoniously dumped in a parking lot around the block to make way for a 7-Eleven. The original airstrip, which had kept Wasilla on the map for so long, was moved out from the middle of all the hustle and bustle of town. Dozens of strip-type buildings line the highway. Driving south into and through Wasilla on the Parks Highway is like passing through a space warp and reemerging in any southern California suburb. Even the parking lots are paved!

The fact that it's such a shock, however, is instructive either way you look at it: rendering Wasilla surprisingly exotic in an Alaskan context, or enhancing your appreciation of the rest of Alaska by comparison.

Sights

Make sure to visit **Dorothy G. Page Museum and Historical Park** on Main St. just off the Parks Highway, tel. (907) 373-9071, open daily 9 a.m.-6 p.m. in summer, 10 a.m.-5 p.m. in winter, $3. Get the eager staff-on-hand to tell the stories behind any of the museum's hundreds of artifacts, including a collection of old lenses, Mr. Herning's (a town pioneer from the '20s) original radio, and the excellent 20-year-old relief map. Downstairs through the "mining tunnel" are more displays, including an entire early dentist's office. Walk out the back door to the little settlement, with a schoolhouse, a bunkhouse, a smokehouse, a steam bath, and a cache.

DAVID STANLEY

famous Alaska-size cabbage at the Matanuska Experimental Farm near Wasilla

Wasilla Public Library, 391 N. Main St., tel. (907) 376-5913, is open Tuesday and Thursday 10 a.m.-8 p.m., Wednesday and Friday 10 a.m.-6 p.m., and Saturday 1-5 p.m.

Teelands Store, one of the oldest buildings in Alaska, is now at the corner of Boundary and Heiring, tel. (907) 373-9071. In the process of being refurbished, the upstairs is turning into a coffeehouse and library with live entertainment, and the lower floor is being leased to local artisans and craftspeople.

Lakeshore Park at Wasilla Lake right off the highway has swimming (not too cold), picnic tables, and a view of the craggy Chugach—great place to set up your tripod. A less crowded day-use lake area is at **Kepler-Bradley Lakes** just beyond the junction of the Parks and Glenn Highways, on the Glenn toward Palmer.

About 1,000 feet before that same intersection, take a left onto Trunk Rd. and climb the hill to the University of Alaska's **Agricultural Experimental Station.** Founded in 1917 by the U.S. Dept. of Agriculture, this 960-acre farm was deeded to the university in 1931. Agricultural information collected here was the contributing factor in colonizing this valley with Midwestern farmers in 1935. The large cabbages, giant begonias, and scores of flowers will add some vibrant color to your day. Free tours of the facility, given 8 a.m.-4:30 p.m., last about an hour and include the grounds, the dairy, and the lab building. Walk into the main building across from the gardens and go left on the ground floor to the tour guide's office, tel. (907) 745-3257.

Wasilla is the headquarters for the 1,049-mile **Iditarod Sled Dog Race** from Anchorage to Nome. At the company offices is a museum housing a large display of race memorabilia, Native artifacts, videos, and pioneer and dog-mushing equipment. It's at Mile 2.2 Knik Rd., open daily 8 a.m.-5 p.m. Call (907) 376-5115 for directions. Admission is free, though a fee is charged to go for a ride on a wheeled dogsled.

About four miles north of town at Mile 46.5, take a left at the sign and head a half-mile down to the **Museum of Alaska Transportation and Industry,** tel. (907) 376-1211, open daily 9 a.m.-6 p.m., admission $5. This museum has an extensive collection of antiques relating to Alaskan aviation, railroading, fishing, mining, and road transportation.

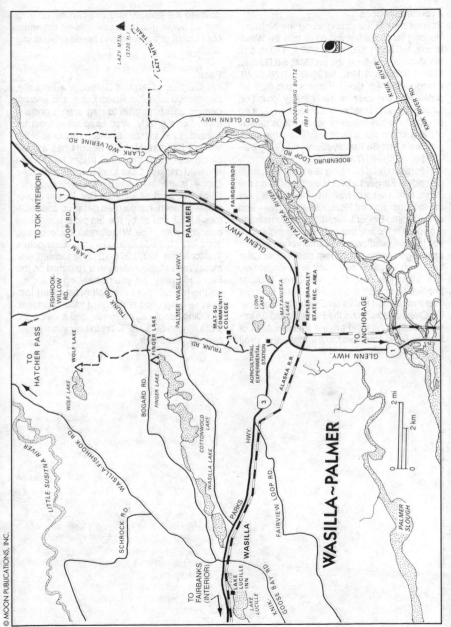

© MOON PUBLICATIONS, INC.

WASILLA~PALMER

PALMER

WASILLA

TO TOK (INTERIOR)

TO HATCHER PASS

TO FAIRBANKS (INTERIOR)

TO ANCHORAGE

GLENN HWY.

GLENN HWY.

OLD GLENN HWY.

KNIK RIVER RD.

CLARK WOLVERINE RD.

BODENBURG LOOP RD.

BODENBURG BUTTE
1881 ft.

LAZY MTN.
13720 ft.

LAZY MTN. TRAIL

FAIRGROUNDS

MATANUSKA RIVER

KNIK RIVER

FISHHOOK-WILLOW RD.

FARM LOOP RD.

TRUNK RD.

TRUNK RD.

WOLF LAKE

WOLF LAKE

FINGER LAKE

BOGARD RD.

PALMER WASILLA HWY.

MAT-SU COMMUNITY COLLEGE

LONG LAKE

MATANUSKA LAKE

KEPLER-BRADLEY STATE REC. AREA

AGRICULTURAL EXPERIMENTAL STATION

ALASKA R.R.

COTTONWOOD LAKE

WASILLA LAKE

WASILLA FISHHOOK RD.

SCHROCK RD.

LITTLE SUSITNA RIVER

FINGER LAKE

PARKS HWY

FAIRVIEW LOOP RD.

KNIK-GOOSE BAY RD.

GOOSE BAY RD.

LAKE LUCILLE INN

LAKE LUCILLE

PALMER SLOUGH

3

3

1

1

2 mi

2 km

0

0

Accommodations

Several motels are strung along the highway. Heading south, the first you come to is the **Windbreak,** tel. (907) 376-4484, $65 s, $70 d, $10 key deposit, register at the bar. **Mat-Su Resort,** Mile 1.3 Bogard Rd., tel. (907) 376-3228, charges $85 for deluxe rooms and $95 for suites. Heading south on the highway, go left on Crucey by McDonald's for a mile, then right on Bogard for a half-mile. For reservations for any of the accommodations or activities in the area, call **Dee's Mat-Su Reservations,** tel. (907) 745-7373 or (800) 731-7374.

Nearest official camping is at a state campground on **Finger Lake.** Heading south on the Parks, take a left onto Main St., then bear right at the fork onto Bogard Road. Go a few miles and turn right into Finger Lake, 42 sites, sometimes crowded. If it's full, the map on the signboard points to an overflow state campground at **Wolf Lake**—go another 1,000 feet past Finger Lake turnoff on Bogard, take a left onto Engstrom, and follow it to the left to Wolf Lake. Closest *unofficial* camping is on Lake Lucille. Go right over the railroad tracks on Snyder across from the Chevron station on the Parks. Make an immediate left and wind around to the bottom of Snyder Park. Park next to the gate and stroll down to the lake, where you can set up your tent on some grassy areas right on the water out of sight of the road and houses. Good in a pinch.

Food

Wasilla has a Carrs, a Safeway, a Shoprite, health-food stores, a Roadhouse, and enough generic galloping grub to gag even a gorging glutton of a grizzly. Also keep an eye out for roadside produce stands to sample some of the valley's harvest. **Mat-Su Resort** has a good dining room with the usual prices for burgers and fried chicken. **Lake Lucille Inn,** on W. Lake Lucille Dr. at Mile 43.5 of the Parks Highway, replaced the landmark Hallea Bar. Dinner is prohibitively steep, but you can get soup and steak fries for $3 and sit by the big picture windows over the lake. The **Windbreak Cafe** serves good-value breakfasts and lunches. **Evangelo's Trattoria,** tel. (907) 376-1212, is located, like most Wasilla businesses, in a strip mall on the Parks Highway. As you're heading south, it's on the left just past the defunct Kashim Inn. They've got a good selection of Italian standard, including spaghetti, calzones, and scampi; the pizza ranges $9.50-$26. Try the excellent Italian sausage sandwich.

DIANA LASICH HARPER

ANCHORAGE

Texas always seemed so big,
but you know you're in the largest state
in the Union
when you're anchored down in
Anchorage. . . .

—from "Anchored Down in Anchorage"
by Michelle Shocked

It's hard to arrive in Anchorage (pop. 240,000)—especially if you've been traveling around the state for a while—without some strong preconceived notions of what to expect from the place. Generally, Alaskans either love or hate Anchorage, their degree of affection or distaste usually revealed by their chosen proximity to the city. You'll certainly have heard, from well-meaning Juneau, Fairbanks, and Bush dwellers, of Anchorage's unplanned urban sprawl, its traffic jams, sprouting trailer parks and condos, corporate skyscrapers, yuppie bars, airplane noise, mall mania, fast-food frenzy, crime, and air pollution; in other words, that it's the antithesis of every virtue and value that God-fearing, law-abiding, and patriotic Alaskans hold sacred. And you've probably heard the old joke

about being "able to see Alaska from Anchorage," and heard it called "Los Anchorage." You might also have heard that Anchorage has nothing to see or do, that all the ostensible attractions are either a joke or a scam, and that if you're looking for a true *Alaskan* experience, you should avoid the city altogether. Don't believe everything you hear; Anchorage has much to offer.

As a traveler you'll find yourself in Anchorage at least once on your Alaska itinerary, and all the city's drawbacks notwithstanding, you'll more than likely be very pleasantly surprised by your visit. The fact is, Anchorage can be an eminently enjoyable *and* affordable place in which to hang out. And it certainly has one of the most flower-filled downtowns of any American city; visitors are always impressed with the late summer bounty of blooms. You can easily fill a whole day touring downtown, another exploring its far-flung corners by bike or bus, another researching the many places to go from Anchorage and the best ways to get there, and another just lying around a downtown park for the one day in four that the sun shines. There are good reasons so many people live here!

Anchorage's highlights include its Museum of History and Art, the Alaska Heritage Library-Museum, the Aviation Heritage Museum, and more than 100 miles of world-class biking and hiking trails, along with an abundance of good restaurants, hip coffeehouses, hopping bars, two minor league baseball teams, and places to outfit yourself for the Alaskan outdoors. And for the budget traveler, inexpensive flights to the Lower 48, the youth hostel two blocks from the Transit Center, and the extensive People Mover bus system are real boons. The natural beauty of the surroundings helps lend Anchorage an Alaskan air; if the city becomes at all oppressive, just lengthen your gaze to the Chugach Mountains, the Alaska Range, and either arm of the Cook Inlet (where beluga whales are frequently seen on summer days). Anchorage is within easy striking distance of some of the most exciting and extensive hiking, climbing, fishing, kayaking, flightseeing, and wilderness areas that Alaska has to offer.

Of course, if you can't overcome the idea that "Alaska population center" is a contradiction in terms, you can simply breeze into town, make your connection, and quickly "get back to Alaska." But if you want a fully rounded experience of the 49th state, get to know Anchorage, *urban* Alaska, and come to your own conclusions.

Climate

Two of the deciding factors in choosing Anchorage as a main construction camp for the Alaska Railroad were mild winters and comparatively low precipitation. The towering Alaska Range shelters Southcentral in general and the Cook Inlet Basin in particular from the frigid winter breath of the Arctic northerlies; the Kenai and Chugach Mountains cast a rain shadow over the Basin, allowing only 15-20% of the annual precipitation in communities on the windward side of the ranges. Anchorage receives at most 20 inches of annual precipitation (10-12 inches of rain, 60-70 inches of snow), while Whittier, 40 miles away on the Gulf side of the Chugach, gets 175 inches. Anchorage's winter temperatures rarely drop below 0° F, with only an occasional cold streak, compared with Fairbanks's frequent -40°; its summer temperatures rarely rise above 65° F, compared with Fairbanks's 80s and 90s.

HISTORY

Beginnings

In June 1778, Capt. James Cook sailed up what's now Turnagain Arm in Cook Inlet, reaching another dead end on his amazing search for the Northwest Passage. But he did dispatch William Bligh (of HMS *Bounty* fame) to explore, and he saw some Tanaina Indians in rich otter skins. George Vancouver, who'd also been on Cook's ship, returned in 1794 and noted Russian settlers in the area. A century later, prospectors began landing in the area and heading north to Southcentral's gold country, and in 1902 Alfred Brooks began mapping the Cook Inlet for the U.S. Geological Survey. In 1913, five settlers occupied Ship Creek, the point on the inlet where Anchorage now stands.

The stunning Chugach Mountains backdrop Anchorage, urban Alaska.

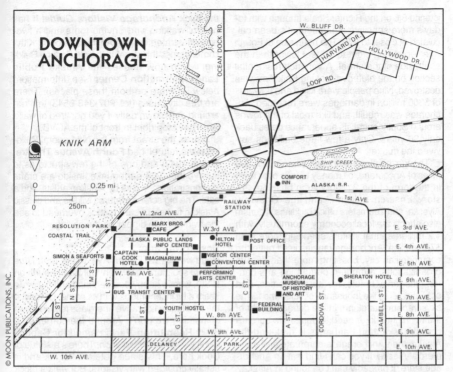

DOWNTOWN ANCHORAGE

KNIK ARM

W. BLUFF DR.

HARVARD DR.

HOLLYWOOD DR.

LOOP RD.

OCEAN DOCK RD.

SHIP CREEK

COMFORT INN

ALASKA R.R.

E. 1st AVE.

RAILWAY STATION

W. 2nd AVE.

E. 3rd AVE.

MARX BROS. CAFE

RESOLUTION PARK

COASTAL TRAIL

W.3rd AVE.

POST OFFICE

E. 4th AVE.

ALASKA PUBLIC LANDS INFO CENTER

HILTON HOTEL

SIMON & SEAFORTS

CAPTAIN COOK HOTEL

IMAGINARIUM

VISITOR CENTER

CONVENTION CENTER

E. 5th AVE.

W. 5th AVE.

PERFORMING ARTS CENTER

ANCHORAGE MUSEUM OF HISTORY AND ART

SHERATON HOTEL

E. 6th AVE.

BUS TRANSIT CENTER

E. 7th AVE.

YOUTH HOSTEL

W. 8th AVE.

FEDERAL BUILDING

E. 8th AVE.

W. 9th AVE.

E. 9th AVE.

DELANEY PARK

E. 10th AVE.

W. 10th AVE.

0   0.25 mi

0   250m

© MOON PUBLICATIONS, INC.

A year later, Congress passed the Alaska Railroad Act and in April 1915, the route for the federally financed railroad from Seward to Fairbanks was made official: it would pass through Ship Creek, where a major staging area for workers and supplies would be located. This news traveled fast, and within a month a ramshackle tent city of nearly 2,000 railroad job seekers had sprung up. Things developed so quickly that in July, the U.S. Land Office auctioned off 650 parcels at the new townsite. The settlement, renamed Anchorage, grew quickly, with water, telephone and power lines, sidewalks, and schools in place within a year.

Slumps and Spurts

Railroad laborers, earning 37 cents an hour (low for Alaska), struck in 1916, after which the minimum wage was raised to 45 cents an hour. The population continued to boom, topping out at around 7,000 in 1917. With WW I and completion of the southern portion of the railroad, the number of people dropped below 2,000 in 1920, when the town incorporated, electing its first mayor and city council. Through the 1930s, Anchorage held steady at 3,000-4,000 people, but WW II changed that in a hurry. The town's strategic location led to a huge influx of military personnel, when the Army's Fort Richardson and Air Force's Elmendorf Field were constructed outside of town. By 1950, Anchorage was a prosperous small city of over 11,000. In the following decade Anchorage also experienced the post-war boom, with the attending shortages of housing and modern conveniences, which created its own construction miniboom. In 1957, when Richfield Oil discovered black gold on the Kenai Peninsula, the oil companies started opening office buildings in the city, and the economy stabilized.

Since Statehood

Much of Anchorage collapsed in the incredible **Good Friday earthquake** of March 27, 1964, which lasted an interminable five minutes, registering 8.6 on the Richter Scale (though with to-day's more sensitive equipment, it's been cal-culated at closer to 9.2). The north side of Fourth Ave. wound up eight to 10 feet lower than the south side of the street. A very rich residential section on the bluff overlooking Knik Arm was destroyed. Nine people were killed and upwards of $300 million in damages were recorded. An-chorage was rebuilt, and like most of the towns around Southcentral, its appearance dates back only 30 years. Only a few large buildings sur-vived the quake.

Though the pipeline doesn't come within 300 miles of Anchorage, oil money towers over town in the form of the 21-story Arco building, 20-story Enserch building, and the Chevron, Alyeska, and Teamsters office buildings. Tourism also affects the local economy enormously, with 1.2 million annual visitors spending more than $700 million. Anchorage fancies itself quite the cosmopolitan city, boasting more than 75 arts organizations, a modern performing arts cen-ter, plus fancy hotels, restaurants, cafes, and bars to cater to the thousands of suits who fill the skyscrapers that gleam in the diffracted light of the midnight sun. Indeed, if Juneau is bureau-cratic Alaska, and Fairbanks is rank-and-file Alaska, then Anchorage is corporate and com-mercial Alaska. If you can't find it at an Anchor-age store, it probably can't be found in Alaska.

SIGHTS

Anchorage is an easy town to get the hang of quickly. The blocks are square, with the lettered streets (A through L) going north-south and the numbered avenues (starting at Second Ave. just up the hill from the tracks) running east-west. Once you get east of the lettered streets they start over again with alphabetized names (Bar-row, Cordova, Denali, Eagle, Fairbanks. . .).

Starting Out

Start your tour of downtown at the **Anchorage Convention and Visitors Bureau** (ACVB) log cabin on the corner of Fourth Ave. and F St., tel. (907) 274-3531. It's open daily 7:30 a.m.-7 p.m. in June, July, and August; 8:30 a.m.-6 p.m. May and September; and 9 a.m.-4 p.m. the rest of the year. Stock up on any of the brochures that interest you, and be sure to take a copy of

the thick **Anchorage Visitors Guide.** It has helpful walking and driving tours and a two-page illustrated map of Anchorage bowl. Kitty-corner across the street is the old Federal Build-ing, which now houses the **Alaska Public Lands Information Center** (see "Information" below for more on both these places). There are free city buses (tel. 907-343-6543) that run around downtown daily if you get tired of walk-ing. They stop right in front of the ACVB.

Across the street from the old Federal Build-ing is the refurbished **Fourth Avenue Theatre,** built in 1947, and one of the few structures to survive the 1964 earthquake. Inside are crafts demonstrations, works by Alaskan artists, and a cafe. The big screen features wildlife and classic Alaskan flicks. Be sure to look overhead to see the twinkling big dipper on the ceiling.

Downtown Parks

Head west down Fourth Ave. to the **Last Blue Whale** sculpture (between Third and Fourth on K St.), whose happy countenance and big smile seem a bit incongruous with its name. Or maybe the felicitously figurative fiberglass fellow knows something we don't. Around the corner on L St. is **Resolution Park,** named for Captain Cook's ship, the *Resolution.* There's a statue of Cook here. This place gets a lot of ink and is usually crowded with visitors. But walk a block to Fifth, and down the hill to **Elderberry Park**— larger, more comfortable, and frequented by Anchorage families. At the bottom of the park is one of the historical signposts that stand in a dozen locations around downtown; this one is all about pioneer aviation, early-day Anchorage, and the **Oscar Anderson** house which is next door. This refurbished little house—built in 1915—is the oldest frame residence in this young city. Open Mon.-Fri. 11 a.m.-4 p.m. and Sat.-Sun. 1-4 p.m. in the summer; $3 for adults, $2 for seniors, $1 for ages five to 12, and free for children under five. Call (907) 274-2336 for details.

Also here is convenient access to the **Tony Knowles Coastal Trail,** a 10-mile-long asphalt track that wends its way along the Knik Arm from downtown past the airport to Kincaid Park at Point Campbell, where the Knik and Turna-gain Arms meet. Stroll the trail a ways—at least through the tunnel, beyond which you leave downtown behind and emerge into a new world:

the grand sweep of the Arm, tidal flats, rock wall up to the trail, railroad tracks, and a sparsely populated residential neighborhood on the hill. On nice summer weekends this trail is more like a freeway, with people on every kind of wheels imaginable: bike and unicycle riders, roller skaters and bladers, skateboarders, and babies in carriages. The Coastal Trail gets especially crowded around duck-filled Westchester Lagoon, a mile south of downtown.

Stop awhile to enjoy the mountainscape. **Mount McKinley** stands far to the north, and the mountain just northwest across Cook Inlet is aptly named **Sleeping Lady** (the maps call it Mt. Susitna). Behind it, and just a bit south, stand several active volcanos, including **Mount Spurr** (it dumped ash on Anchorage three times in 1992) and **Mount Redoubt** (it last erupted in 1989) to the southwest. If you have eagle eyes and crystalline weather, you might pick out a third volcano, **Mount Iliamna** (it began showing seismic activity in 1996), far to the southwest. Out of sight is yet a fourth volcano, **Mount Augustine,** which last spewed ash in 1986.

Enjoyable **Delaney Park** runs between Ninth and 10th Aves. from L St. to Barrow. Known as the "park strip," early in Anchorage's history it marked the boundary where the town stopped and the wilderness started, and in 1923 the strip where the park is today was cleared as a fire break. Since then it has served as a golf course, and airstrip, and now hosts half a dozen softball games every night of summer, tennis and basketball courts, and large grassy sections for Frisbee, hackey sack, tai chi, sunbathing, or people-watching.

Ten blocks farther south is another park strip, along **Chester Creek,** with very popular bike and jogging trails. Chester Creek flows into **Westchester Lagoon,** a favorite place to feed the ducks on a summer evening, or to skate away a winter night. This path connects with the Tony Knowles Coastal Trail (described above) at the mouth of the lagoon.

Alaska Experience

Across the street from the People Mover Transit Center at Sixth and G is the Alaska Experience. If you get dizzy spells or motion sickness easily, skip this 40-minute film, shown on the hour 10 a.m.-9 p.m., tel. (907) 276-3730. Admission is $7

for adults, $4 for kids. The half-dome screen and special 180-degree fish-eye cinematography create a perspective so big, so melodramatic, and so off that it actually dwarfs even the vast panoramas it strives to capture, and gets quickly tiresome. They also have a separate 15-minute earthquake film/shaker ($3 extra for this).

Architectural Anchorage

Anchorage's central focal point is the **Performing Arts Center** (PAC), an unusual brick and glass building with colorful Olympic-like rings of light ringing the top. Find it at Fifth Ave. and G Street. Inside are three auditoriums with wonderful acoustics and horrific carpeting; wags say it looks like a pepperoni pizza. Hold the anchovies! Tours (tel. 907-263-2900) are offered on Monday, Wednesday, Friday, and Saturday at 1 p.m. The front lawn of the PAC comprises **Town Square,** a fine, flower-filled field of fecundity. **Egan Civic & Convention Center** is right across Fifth Avenue.

A block back on G between Sixth and Seventh is the **Arco Building,** tallest in Anchorage. Arco puts on a free 12-minute oil history or Native arts film daily at 2 and 3 p.m. in the auditorium off the lobby. The building walls are lined with more artwork.

Anchorage Museum of History and Art

Located on Seventh Ave. between C and A Sts., tel. (907) 343-6173, this is the highlight of downtown Anchorage, open daily 9 a.m.-6 p.m. in the summer, or Tues.-Sat. 10 a.m.-6 p.m., and Sunday 1-5 p.m. the rest of the year. Entrance is $5 for adults, $4.50 for seniors, free for kids under 18. Plan to linger awhile in the permanent wing; the Cook Inlet collection is outstanding. The historical art section is fascinating, especially the paintings by Sydney Laurence, one of Alaska's most famous and prolific artists; his six- by 10-foot oil of Mt. McKinley is the centerpiece. Upstairs is the extraordinary Alaska Gallery, with Alaska-size dioramas chronicling a spectacular journey from prehistoric archaeology all the way up to the pipeline. The library, with a collection of over 150,000 historical photographs, is open Tues.-Fri. 10 a.m.-noon. Free documentaries are shown in the comfortable auditorium at 3 p.m., and excellent tours are given daily in the summer at 10 a.m., 11 a.m., 1 p.m., and 2 p.m. The cafe serves light meals.

More Museums

The **Imaginarium,** Fifth Ave. and G streets, tel. (907) 276-3179, open Mon.-Sat. 11 a.m.-5 p.m., $5 adults, $4 children and seniors, is a fun place if you've got young ones in tow. "Measure up" against moose, polar bears, and king salmon; learn all about Arctic ecology, rainforests, human ears and eyes, seismics, mega-bubbles, and much, much more.

The **Reeve Aviation Picture Museum,** in the Reeve offices at 343 W. Sixth Ave., tel. (907) 272-9426, has more than a thousand historic photos of Alaska's aviation history, from bush pilots to military jets. It's open Mon.-Fri. 9 a.m.-5 p.m.

The **Alaska Heritage Library-Museum,** housed in the lobby of the National Bank of Alaska corporate offices on the corner of Northern Lights Blvd. and C St., is open Mon.-Fri. noon-5 p.m. summers (Mon.-Fri. noon-4 p.m. the rest of the year), free; call (907) 265-2834 for tours. This is one of the state's largest privately owned collections of Alaskana artifacts and books, and will keep you spellbound for hours, if you have the time. Only a handful of the highlights include: parkas made from bird skins and walrus intestines, Sydney Laurence's "Cave Woman" and other jaw-dropping paintings, Nome and Fairbanks newspapers from the early 1900s, stunning black-and-white photos made from the original glass plates of gold rush scenes, and two walls of beautiful bookcases filled with rare books and maps. This little gem of a museum is not to be missed.

Alaska Aviation Heritage Museum, 4721 Aircraft Dr. (take the Lake Hood exit off International Airport Rd.), tel. (907) 248-5325, is open daily 9 a.m.-6 p.m. May-Sept., and Mon.-Sat. 10 a.m.-4 p.m. the rest of the year. Entrance costs $5.75 for adults, $4.50 for seniors, $2.75 for ages six to 12, and free for kids under six. This unusual museum displays 21 vintage aircraft—including a 1936 Stinson A Trimotor. Also here are Japanese artifacts from the WW II Aleutian Island battles, flight uniforms and jackets, and historical photos. The theater shows 30-minute movies on early aviation in Alaska, early Alaska Airlines footage, and recovery operations. The museum faces out over **Lake Hood,** where floatplanes take off and land almost constantly in the summer. This is the world's largest floatplane base. One of the nation's busiest airfields is **Mer-**rill Field,** on the east side of town along the Glenn Highway. There are more than 230,000 takeoffs and landings each year here; overall, Alaska has 16 times as many aircraft per capita as the Lower 48 states!

Farther Afield

The **St. Innocent Russian Orthodox Church,** 6724 E. Fourth Ave., is one of the most dramatic churches in Alaska. Check out the 12 onion-shaped domes, or attend a Sunday service to view the interior. **Earthquake Park,** out Northern Lights Blvd. near the airport, has an interpretive sign about the Big One on Good Friday, 1964. Also here are an okay view of the skyline and Cook Inlet, but the view is better from **Point Woronzof,** another mile or so out. The Coastal Trail (described above under "Downtown Parks") parallels the coast along here, making a far more interesting way to explore this area; it continues from downtown all the way south to Kincaid Park.

Alaska Zoo

Located at 4731 O'Malley Rd., two miles east of New Seward Highway, tel. (907) 346-3242, the zoo is open daily 9 a.m.-6 p.m. in the summer and Wed.-Mon. 10 a.m.-5 p.m. the rest of the year; $6 for adults, $5 for seniors, $4 for ages 12-18, $3 for ages three to 12, free for tots. The zoo is also connected by a special hourly bus from the Transit Center. It is not too bad from a human standpoint—nice grounds, enjoyable shady paths, bridges over creeks—and all the Alaskan animals, plus elephants, cougars, etc., but no monkeys. From the animals' perspective, however, this—like most zoos—is a pretty sad place. Anyone who has watched bears in the wild will cringe at the sight of one pacing from one end of the pen to another, or at the mountain lion being taunted by obnoxious people. A cage is a cage is a cage. If you've got kids, they'll enjoy it, especially **Annabelle,** the elephant who paints ($225 for an original oil), and the playful river otters. Instead of visiting the zoo, continue out O'Malley Rd. to nearby Chugach State Park, where you can see wildlife in the wild.

Military Bases

Since WW II, Anchorage has thrived on military spending, as a visit to the largest of the installations, **Elmendorf Air Force Base** just north of downtown, will illustrate. The summer-only weekly free tour (Wednesday 2:30-5 p.m.) of the base is highly recommended, but call (907) 552-8151 a week ahead for reservations. The tour bus always fills up. The highlight of the tour is a visit to a hangar to see an F-15 and talk to the pilot. The size and sophistication of this giant fighter-bomber base is mind-boggling; the way tourists are allowed to wander around will startle visitors from abroad. Even if you can't get on the tour, the **Wildlife Museum** (tel. 907-552-2282, open Mon.-Sat. 10 a.m.-2 p.m.; admission free) on base is worth visiting. Entrance is through the Boniface Parkway gate.

Fort Richardson Army Base, seven miles north of Anchorage on the Glenn Highway, has self-guided tours available of the base, fish hatchery, national cemetery, and small wildlife museum. Get a pass at the gatehouse, or call (907) 384-0431 for details.

Midtown
Anchorage's Anytown, USA, commercial strip is known as Midtown, and is encompassed by Northern Lights and Benson Blvds. between Minnesota Dr. and Old Seward Highway. Here you'll find all the malls, shopping centers, supermarkets, fast food, and other stores you could possibly need. It's only a 20-minute walk from downtown to Midtown, and almost any southbound bus gets you there in 10 minutes. It isn't exactly a tourist attraction, but this, along with shopping malls on the south and east end of town, is where Anchoragites spend their cash.

SUMMER RECREATION

Hiking and Floating
For a complete description of all the hiking trails around Anchorage and vicinity, see "Chugach State Park" under "Vicinity of Anchorage" below. The University of Alaska's (UAA) outstanding Wilderness Studies program offers classes in camping, backpacking, natural history, mountaineering, climbing, skiing, and many other subjects throughout the year for reasonable prices. Most of these involve expeditions to various parts of Alaska, some right next door, others as far away as the Brooks Range. Call (907) 786-1468, or stop by the **Alaska Wilderness Studies** office on the UAA campus for details.

Check with **Eagle River Raft Trips,** tel. (907) 333-3001, for six-hour float trips down the Eagle River. Another company with similar offerings is **Alaska Whitewater,** tel. (907) 337-7238.

The **Alaska Mountaineering Club** holds monthly meetings at 7:30 p.m. on the third Wednesday of each month at the Pioneer Schoolhouse, Third Ave. and Eagle Street. Visitors are welcome to enjoy the various slide shows, and it only costs $10 to join the club and go along on any of their frequent outings. For more information, call the Alaska Mountaineering & Hiking store at (907) 272-1811.

Rock-Climbing
Climbing walls are located at **Alaska Rock Gym,** 4840 Fairbanks St., tel. (907) 562-7265, with a considerably smaller version at **Alaska Pacific University,** tel. (907) 564-8308. The Rock Gym has classes, a pro shop, locker rooms, and a weight room. Quite impressive. For the real thing, most folks head south to Turnagain Arm or north to Hatcher Pass. For specifics, check with folks at AMH or REI (see "Shopping" below). Turnagain Arm is also extremely popular with ice climbers in the winter months.

Flightseeing
The best way to get a bird's-eye view of the Anchorage area is from a bird's-eye vantage point: in an airplane. Anchorage has a large number of companies offering flightseeing; see the Yellow Pages under "Aircraft Charter" for the full list. Some of the larger and more established include the following Lake Hood operations: **Rust's Flying Service,** tel. (907) 243-1595; **Regal Air,** tel. (907) 243-8535; and **Ketchum Air Service,** tel. (907) 243-5525, or (800) 433-9114. The following established companies fly out of Merrill Field: **Airlift Alaska,** tel. (907) 276-3809; **Jayhawk Air,** tel. (907) 276-4404; and **VernAir,** tel. (907) 258-7822 or (800) 478-7822. **Alaska Bush Carrier,** tel. (907) 243-3127, flies out of the airport, as does **Era Helicopters,** tel. (907) 248-4422 or (800) 843-1947.

Many operators have the following standard flights: 90-minute flight over the Chugach Mountains and Knik Glacier for $140-155 pp; three-hour flight over Prince William Sound and Columbia Glacier for $200 pp (including a stop on the water); and three-hour flight over Mt. McKin-

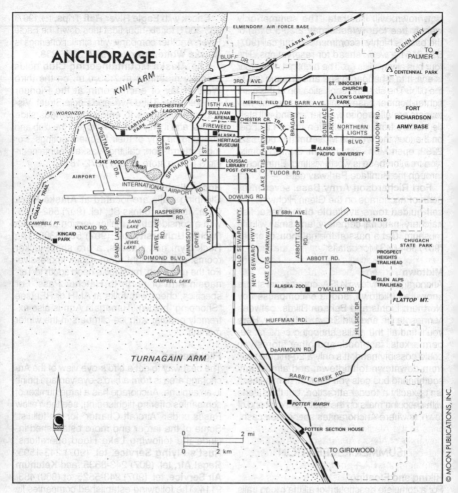

ANCHORAGE

ELMENDORF AIR FORCE BASE

ALASKA R.R.

GLENN HWY

TO PALMER

CENTENNIAL PARK

KNIK ARM

BLUFF DR

3RD. AVE.

ST. INNOCENT CHURCH

LION'S CAMPER PARK

FORT RICHARDSON ARMY BASE

PT. WORONZOF

WESTCHESTER LAGOON

15TH AVE.

MERRILL FIELD

DE BARR AVE.

EARTHQUAKE PARK

SULLIVAN ARENA

CHESTER CR. TRAIL

BRAGAW ST.

BONIFACE PARKWAY

NORTHERN LIGHTS BLVD.

MULDOON RD.

WISCONSIN ST.

FIREWEED

ALASKA HERITAGE MUSEUM

C ST.

LAKE OTIS PARKWAY

UAA

ALASKA PACIFIC UNIVERSITY

POSTMARK DR.

LAKE HOOD

AIRPORT

SPENARD RD.

LOUSSAC LIBRARY / POST OFFICE

TUDOR RD.

COASTAL TRAIL

INTERNATIONAL AIRPORT RD.

DOWLING RD.

CAMPBELL PT.

RASPBERRY RD.

E 68TH AVE.

CAMPBELL FIELD

KINCAID PARK

KINCAID RD.

SAND LAKE RD.

SAND LAKE

JEWEL LAKE RD.

JEWEL LAKE

MINNESOTA DRIVE

ARCTIC BLVD.

NEW SEWARD HWY.

OLD SEWARD HWY.

ABBOTT LOOP RD.

CHUGACH STATE PARK

DIMOND BLVD.

PROSPECT HEIGHTS TRAILHEAD

ABBOTT RD.

CAMPBELL LAKE

ALASKA ZOO

LAKE OTIS PARKWAY

O'MALLEY RD.

GLEN ALPS TRAILHEAD

FLATTOP MT.

HUFFMAN RD.

HILLSIDE DR

TURNAGAIN ARM

DeARMOUN RD.

RABBIT CREEK RD.

© MOON PUBLICATIONS, INC.

POTTER MARSH

POTTER SECTION HOUSE

0   2 mi
0   2 km

TO GIRDWOOD

ley for $200 pp (including a stop at a lake). Day-trips to Brooks Camp in Katmai National Park are around $500 pp. The air taxis also feature fly-in fishing trips, primarily to the Susitna River area. Expect to pay $150-165 pp for a drop-off and same-day pickup, or $185-270 pp for an overnight trip to a lakeside cabin. The latter fee includes the cabin use, along with a skiff and outboard. Rust's Flying Service has a large number of such cabins available.

Charter service may be the way to go if you have a group of four or more people and a spe-cific destination, such as a public cabin ($25/night) in Chugach National Forest. Rates are generally around $210/hour for a Cessna 185 (up to four people), or $280/hour for a Beaver (up to seven people).

Boating and Fishing

So many charter companies, sportfishing ex-cursions, pilot guides, fly-in lodges, cruise op-tions, and rentals are based in Anchorage that you'll wind up with a dozen brochures even if you're an inveterate landlubber who gets seasick on a waterbed. Also consult the *Visitors Guide* for listings and advertisements, and the Yellow Pages under any of the above categories. To figure out where the fish are running and when, or what the local regulations are, call Fish and Game at (907) 344-0541 (recorded message at 907-349-4687) or visit the Public Lands Information Center downtown.

Increasingly popular are fly-in fishing trips that start as low as $125 pp roundtrip. All the local air taxi services offer guided or unguided trips to nearby rivers and lakes for world-class salmon fishing. See "Flightseeing" above for a list of companies.

Swimming

If you're lucky enough to be in Anchorage during a hot spell and want to cool off under the bright blue sky, head out to **Lake Spenard, Lake Hood** down Spenard Rd. toward the airport, then right on Lakeshore Drive. **Jewel Lake** also has swimming, on Dimond Blvd. between Jewel Lake and Sand Lake Rds. in the southwest corner of the city. The most developed outdoor swimming is at **Goose Lake,** out Northern Lights between Lake Otis and Bragaw near UAA, on the bike trail, with basketball courts, pit toilets, and a snack bar.

If you're in the mood for a swim anytime, Anchorage is a good place to experience Alaska's love affair with Olympic-size indoor pools. There are seven to choose from—five at the high schools ($4.25 for adults, or $2.75 for kids; call (907) 343-4474 for locations and times), plus ones at the Alaska Pacific University and the University of Alaska Anchorage (UAA). With its high ceiling, taut diving boards, and hard-body swimmers, the **UAA pool,** tel. (907) 786-1231, is easily the finest in Alaska. The cost is $4 for adults or $2.50 for kids under 12. For the same price you get access to the other facilities here, including a fine ice rink, weight room, saunas, racquetball courts, and gym.

Ice-Skating

Anchorage is wild about ice-skating and ice hockey. The **UAA Seawolves,** tel. (907) 786-1293, and semi-pro **Anchorage Aces,** tel. (907) 258-2237, attract standing-room-only crowds all season, and the area has five indoor rinks. All are open year-round and offer skate rentals as well as

instruction: **Ben Boeke Ice Arena,** in the Sullivan Arena at 334 E. 16th, tel. (907) 274-2767; **Dempsey Anderson Ice Arena,** 1741 W. Northern Lights Blvd., tel. (907) 277-7571; **Fire Lake Recreation Center,** Eagle River, tel. (907) 688-4641; **UAA Sports Center,** 2801 Providence Dr., tel. (907) 786-1233; and **Dimond Ice Chalet,** in the Dimond Mall at 800 E. Dimond, tel. (907) 344-1212. Two of these—Ben Boeke and Fire Lake—are Olympic-sized hockey rinks.

Golf

There are four Anchorage-area golf courses: **O'Malley,** tel. (907) 522-3322; **Russian Jack Springs,** tel. (907) 333-8338; **Eagleglen,** tel. (907) 522-2773; and **Moose Run,** tel. (907) 428-0056. The last two of these are on military bases, but are open to the general public as well.

WINTER RECREATION

Contrary to popular belief, Alaska—and Anchorage in particular—does not go into hibernation for the long months of winter. Instead, many Anchoragites look forward to the cold and snow because of the wonderful outdoor activities they bring. Anchorage is a national center for cross-country skiing, dogsledding, skijoring (skiing behind a dog), hockey, and all sorts of other winter fun. Visitors soon discover what the residents already know—the city is blessed with excellent facilities for all of these. There are dogsled race tracks; dozens of miles of free, groomed ski trails; several excellent ice rinks; and three downhill ski areas, including the state's best resort—Alyeska. Add in such events as the Iditarod and Fur Rendezvous, the college and semi-pro hockey games, and the World Masters Cross-Country Skiing Championships, and it's easy to see why more and more visitors are arriving in the winter months.

Downhill Skiing

Alpine skiers (along with telemarkers and snowboarders) head to **Alyeska** (see "Girdwood" under "Girdwood to Whittier," below) for the finest skiing to be found, and some of the deepest snow at any American resort. **Hilltop Ski Area,** tel. (907) 346-1407 or (907) 346-1446, is right on the edge of town at Abbott Rd. near Hillside Dr.,

SAFETY IN AVALANCHE COUNTRY

Backcountry skiing is becoming increasingly popular in Alaska's limitless backcountry. Unfortunately, many skiers fail to take the necessary precautions before heading out. Given the enormous snowfalls that occur, the steep slopes the snow piles up on, and the high winds that accompany many storms, it should come as no surprise that avalanches are a real danger. Nearly all avalances are triggered by the victims. If you really want to avoid avalanches, ski only on groomed ski trails or "bombproof" slopes that, because of aspect, shape, and slope angle, never seem to slide. Unfortunately, this isn't always possible, so backcountry skiers need to understand the conditions that lead to avalanches. The best way to learn is from a class such as the backcountry and avalanche programs taught by **Alaska Wilderness Studies** at the University of Alaska at Anchorage, tel. (907) 786-1468. Failing that, you can help protect yourself by following these precautions when you head into the backcountry:

• Be sure to carry extra warm clothes, water, high-energy snacks, a dual-frequency avalanche transceiver (and know how to use it!), a lightweight snow shovel (for digging snow pits, or emergency snow shelters, or for excavating avalanche victims), first-aid supplies, a Swiss Army knife, a topographic map, an extra plastic ski tip, a flashlight, matches, and a compass. Many skiers also carry that cure-all, duct tape, wrapped around a ski pole. Let someone know exactly where you are going and when you expect to return. It's also a good idea to carry special ski poles that extend into probes in case of an avalanche.

• Carry an avalanche transceiver, and make sure it's turned on.

• Check the angle of an area before you ski through it; slopes of 30-45 degrees are the most dangerous, while lesser slopes do not slide as frequently.

• Watch the weather; winds over 15 mph can pile snow much more deeply on lee slopes, causing dangerous loading on the snowpack. Especially avoid skiing on or below cornices.

• Avoid the leeward side (the side facing into the wind) of ridges, where snow loading can be greatest.

• Be aware of gullies and bowls; they're more likely to slip than flat open slopes or ridgetops. Stay out of gullies at the bottom of wide bowls; these are natural avalanche chutes.

• Look out for cracks in the snow, and listen for hollow snow underfoot. These are strong signs of dangerous conditions.

• Look at the trees. Smaller trees may indicate that avalanches rip through an area frequently, knocking over the larger trees. (Avalanches can, however, also run through forested areas.)

• Know how much new snow has fallen recently. Heavy new snow over older weak snow layers is a sure sign of extreme danger on potential avalanche slopes. Most avalanches slip during or immediately after a storm.

• Learn how to dig a snow pit and how to read the various snow layers. Particularly important are the very weak layers of depth hoar or surface hoar that have been buried under heavy new snow.

---

and consists of a small chairlift and a rope tow. It has lights for night skiing, and is a favorite place to learn skiing or to play around without having to suffer the 45-minute drive to Alyeska. Tickets cost $16-18 for adults, $14-16 for students, $10 for kids under five. Open daily till 10 p.m.

A bit farther afield is **Alpenglow at Arctic Valley,** tel. (907) 428-1208 or (907) 563-2524. Call (907) 249-9292 for recorded snow conditions. Rates are $22 for adults, $15 for seniors and kids. Night skiing costs $12 for adults, $10 for seniors and kids. There are three chairlifts and a poma, providing a wide range of slopes and conditions. The "Military Lift" (it's on Army land) is a bit down the hill from the other lifts, but is also open to the public. More adventurous skiers turn left from the uppermost lift (chair three) and ski into often-untracked powder in the upper bowls. Arctic Valley is also open Wed.-Sun. nights, with lighted runs on three of the lifts. **Sledders** of all ages play on the steep powerline slope that cuts along the road up to Arctic Valley, with parents taking kids back uphill in their cars. Downhill skis can be rented from REI, tel. (907) 272-4565; the Rental Room, tel. (907) 562-2866; and the various ski areas.

Cross-Country Skiing

Any Anchoragite over the age of four seems to be involved in cross-country skiing in one form or another. The city is laced with trails that serve as summertime cycling and jogging paths and wintertime ski routes. They are all groomed, with both set tracks for traditional cross-country skiers and a wider surface for the skate-skiing crowd. Skate-skiing is getting more popular each year, and skijorers are also often seen on these tracks in this dog-happy town.

The best-known cross-country area is **Kincaid Park,** where a convoluted maze of paths cover the rolling terrain, offering fun for all levels of ability. Kincaid is considered one of the top three competitive ski venues in America; the 1994 U.S. Olympic cross-country ski trials were held here. You can warm up inside the chalet and enjoy the vistas of Sleeping Lady and Mt. McKinley. Also in Kincaid near the chalet is a very popular sledding hill. Another great sledding hill (600-foot run) is in Centennial Park. **Russian Jack Springs Park,** near Debarr Rd. and Boniface Pkwy., has many more groomed ski trails, as well as a small rope tow ($3) and a warming house.

Several more miles of groomed trails await at **Hillside Park** off Abbot Rd. next to Hilltop Ski Area; watch out for the moose here. All these trails are groomed for both traditional cross-country and the faster skate skis, which are becoming increasingly popular. Rent cross-country skis from REI, tel. (907) 272-4565; the Rental Room, tel. (907) 562-2866; AMH, tel. (907) 272-1811; and Adventures & Delights, tel. (907) 276-8282 or (800) 288-3134.

Backcountry Skiing

If you're more ambitious—and have the wheels to get there—you'll find incredible backcountry skiing all around Anchorage. The Chugach Mountains offer an endless choice of skiing options that last from mid-October all the way into late June in some places. These areas are *not* for novices, so don't head out without knowing about and being prepared for such dangers as avalanches and hypothermia. Quite a number of skiers have died in the mountain avalanches near Anchorage—including some with years of backcountry experience. Even such favorites as the nearby summit of Flattop Mountain have taken a high human toll over the years.

The best-known backcountry areas are in Chugach State Park, and at Turnagain Pass and Hatcher Pass. Access to **Chugach State Park** is the same as in the summer (see "Vicinity of Anchorage" below); get a winter routes map from the state park office in the Frontier Building at 36th and C Street. **Turnagain Pass** is 60 miles southwest of Anchorage on the way to Seward. The west side of the road is open to snowmachiners, but Tele-skiers avoid them by heading to the east side. There's a big parking lot, and from here you can head up into the open meadows or high into the mountains for deep untracked powder.

Hatcher Pass is a favorite backcountry area, and the fall training area for the U.S. National Cross-Country Ski Team. The long drive from Anchorage (70 miles) takes you up a gorgeous canyon due north of Palmer. The road can sometimes be a bit treacherous if you don't have studded tires, so be sure to call ahead for road conditions (tel. 907-745-2827 or 907-745-3975). The road isn't plowed beyond the historic buildings at Independence Mine State Park but you can park here to play on 10 km of groomed trails ($5) or to ski up the steeper (and more avalanche-prone) slopes that rise on three sides. After skiing, be sure to stop by **Hatcher Pass Lodge,** tel. (907) 745-5897 (the A-frame building) for a pizza and beer, plus a sunset view to die for. Cozy cabins are $110 d, complete with sauna and a continental breakfast. Fantastic fondues, pastas, and pies too. The lodge is only open Fri.-Sun. in the winter.

See "Skiing Events" below for several very popular cross-country events in Anchorage. Check at REI in Anchorage for cross-country and telemark clinics. A popular weekend retreat for skiers is **Sheep Mountain Lodge,** tel. (907) 745-5121, at Mile 114 of the Glenn Highway. In addition to accommodations, the lodge has groomed ski trails, a sauna and a hot tub. Fantastic views from here, or you can explore the surrounding country of Matanuska Glacier and the Chugach Mountains.

Dog Mushing

There are all sorts of dogsled races in Anchorage each winter, all the way up to the world-famous Iditarod each March. If you want to try it on your own, several local operators offer sled tours. A few even let you drive a small team of dogs; trying to control a full team of eight or more huskies requires a pro. Anchorage-area mushers to contact include: **Mush-A-Dog Team** in Chugiak, tel. (907) 688-1391; **Birch Trails Sled Dog Tours** in Chugiak, tel. (907) 688-5713; **Hatcher Pass Sled Dog Tours** in Wasil-

THE IDITAROD

The most Alaskan of all Alaskan events is the Iditarod Trail Sled Dog Race from Anchorage to Nome. The "Last Great Race" is run each March, attracting 60 or so of the world's best mushers, each with a team of up to 20 dogs. With a top prize of $50,000, and a $400,000 purse for the top 20 teams, the race has become an event with an international following.

History

Today's Iditarod Trail Sled Dog Race is run on the historic Iditarod Trail, a path that had its origins in the 1908 discovery of gold along a river the Ingalik Indians called "Hidedhod," meaning "Distant Place." Thousands of miners flooded into the area following the find, and trails were cut from Seward to the new boomtown of Iditarod so that mail and supplies could be brought in and gold shipped out. Once the gold ran out after a few years, the miners gradually gave up and left, and the old town began a long, slow return to quietude. But other events would eventually bring Iditarod back to life in a new form.

During the winter of 1925, a diphtheria epidemic broke out in Nome, and the territorial governor hurriedly dispatched a 20-pound package of life-saving antitoxin serum to halt the disease's spread. Regular boat mail would take 25 days, and the only two airplanes in Alaska were open cockpit biplanes. With temperatures far below zero, and only a few hours of light each day (it was mid-January), that option was impossible. Instead, the package was sent by train from Seward to Nenana, where mushers and their dogs waited to carry the antitoxin on to Nome. What happened next is hard to believe: a Herculean relay effort by 20 different mushers and their dogs brought the vaccine to Nome in just six days. They somehow managed to cover the 674 miles in conditions that included whiteout blizzards, 80 mph winds, and temperatures down to -64 °F! The event gained national attention, and President Coolidge thanked the mushers, presenting each with a medal and 50 cents for each mile traveled.

Long after this heroic effort, two more people entered the picture: Dorothy Page and Joe Redington, Sr. ("Father of the Iditarod"). In 1967, the two organized a commemorative Iditarod race over a small portion of the trail. Six years later they set up a full-blown dogsled race from Anchorage to Nome, a distance in excess of 1,100 miles. It took winner

DON PITCHER

la, tel. (907) 373-5617; **Happy Husky Kennels** in Wasilla, tel. (907) 373-5399; **Lucky Husky Racing Kennel** in Willow, tel. (907) 495-6471; and **Snow-Trek Mushing Adventures** in Willow, tel. (907) 495-6743.

ACCOMMODATIONS AND CAMPING

As might be expected in a city of more than a quarter-million people, Anchorage has a wide range of lodging options. Unfortunately, most of these are also priced at Alaskan standards. The only real exceptions are the hostels and the dorms at Alaska Pacific University. For couples, the many local bed and breakfasts offer a fine option. If you plan to stay longer than a few days, check out the "For Rent, Rooms" classified section of the *Anchorage Daily News,* or look under "Boarding Houses" or "Rooming Houses" in the Yellow Pages. The "Anchorage Accommodations" chart has a complete listing of Anchorage motels, hotels, and other lodging. Be sure to make reservations far ahead for July and August.

Dick Wilmarth 20 days, 49 minutes, and 49 seconds to make it under the Nome archway. At the finish line, Wilmarth lost his lead dog, Hot Foot. Fourteen days later the dog wandered into his master's home in Red Devil—500 miles from Nome.

Over the years the race has become more professional and far faster. The record run of nine days, two hours, 42 minutes, and 19 seconds was set by Doug Swingley in 1995 (the 1996 race winner, Jeff King, came in three hours slower). And this was even with two mandatory layovers of 10 hours along the way. The Iditarod is certainly one of the most strenuous events in the world; a recent *Outside Magazine* article rated it the third most harrowing contest on the planet. With below zero temperatures, fierce winds, and all the hazards that go with crossing the most remote parts of Alaska in winter, the race is certainly not for everyone. Despite this, the Iditarod has gained a measure of fame as one where women are equally likely to win as men. Between 1985 and 1993, five of the nine winners were female, and Susan Butcher won four of these races. (After Butcher won the race three consecutive years, T-shirts began appearing in local stores saying "Alaska: where men are men, and women win the Iditarod.")

In recent years, the Iditarod has been plagued by claims from animal rights groups that the race is inhumane because dogs occasionally die from overexertion. Their efforts led major sponsors to drop funding for the race, but support remains very strong in Alaska. Most Alaskans view animal rights activists as know-nothing outsiders with no understanding of how much mushers care for their animals. And anyone who has ever watched a dog team in full stride will instantly realize how the dogs love to run.

The Race

The Iditarod has not one, but two actual starts. The official start is from Fourth Ave. in downtown Anchorage, where several thousand onlookers cheer each team that leaves the starting line. The mushers and dogs run as far as Eagle River, where they load into trucks and drive on up to the "restart" in Wasilla. (This is to avoid having to sled over the thin snow conditions around Palmer and open water of Knik River.) At the restart, the fastest teams into Eagle River leave first, creating often chaotic conditions when several 20-dog teams are pulling to the start at once. The last stop on the road system is 14 miles away in the town of Knik; from here on, it's a thousand miles of wilderness.

The top mushers today are professional racers who spend much of their time training or caring for their dogs. Top competitors often spend $70,000 or more just to get their dogs into the race, and a lead dog can sell for over $8,000.

The **Iditarod Trail Committee** has its headquarters at Mile 2.2 Knik Rd., in Wasilla, tel. (907) 376-5155. There are official Iditarod gift shops in Anchorage's Fifth Avenue Mall (downtown), tel. (907) 276-2350; and Northway Mall (near Airport Heights and Glenn Hwy.), tel. (907) 276-7533; or call (800) 545-6874 for a mail order catalog of Iditarod trinkets. In recent years, there has also been a proliferation of me-too Iditarod races: Iditaski, Iditabike, and the Iron Dog Classic (snowmachine) along the Iditarod trail each winter.

Hostels and Dorms

The saving grace of accommodations for shoestring travelers is the **Anchorage Youth Hostel** at 700 H St., between Seventh and Eighth, two blocks south of the Transit Center, tel. (907) 276-3635. The 100-bed facility is open for check-in from 7:30 to noon and 2 p.m. to midnight, but you can't stay here between noon and 5 p.m. At $15 for AYH members and $18 for nonmembers, it fills up *fast* in the summer, though they can direct you to a couple of unofficial hostels elsewhere in town. A couples' dorm has larger beds (same rates), and a few private couples' rooms are available at $40 d for members, or $46 d for nonmembers. Reservations are strongly advised for the summer, and the peak season may fill up many weeks ahead. Make reservations by sending one-night's fee deposit per person, and let them know if you are a member. There's a four-night maximum stay in summer, and you must be out by noon after completing a chore. Curfew is 1 a.m. The hostel has a kitchen, common rooms, washers ($1), and dryers ($1). Men and women sleep in segregated rooms. Store extra baggage for $1 per day per item if you have a future reservation with them. Bring your sleeping bag or rent linen for $1. The hostel also has reasonable wintertime long-term lodging rates.

Another cheap option is the **Spenard Hostel,** 2845 W. 42nd Place, tel. (907) 248-5036, where dorm spaces are $15 pp. Things are less restrictive than at the youth hostel; no curfew. Spenard Hostel also has a full kitchen, and

ANCHORAGE ACCOMMODATIONS

Note: The city of Anchorage adds an eight percent bed tax to all motel lodging rates. See the text for details on local B&Bs. The lodging places are listed from least to most expensive.

International Backpackers Inn; 3601 Peterkin, Unit A; tel. (907) 274-3870; $12-15 pp in dorms; full kitchens, weekly rates available

Spenard Hostel; 2845 W. 42nd Place; tel. (907) 248-5036; $15 pp; dorm rooms, full kitchen, weekly rates available

Anchorage Youth Hostel; 700 H St.; tel. (907) 276-3635; $15-18 pp in dorms, $40-46 d for private rooms; central location, full kitchens, closed noon-5 p.m.

Alaska Pacific University; 4101 University Dr.; tel. (907) 564-8238; $25 pp; dorm rooms, open mid-May to early August

Thrift Motel; 606 W. Northern Lights; tel. (907) 561-3005; $40 s or d; mainly long-term tenants and often booked up, see rooms first

AAA Mexico Hotel; 3903 Spenard Rd.; tel. (907) 248-4848; $45 s, $65 d; microwaves and fridges, see rooms first, marginal place

Alaska Budget Motel; 545 E. Fourth Ave.; tel. (907) 277-0088; $49 s or d; kitchenettes $10 extra, very plain rooms, marginal neighborhood

John's Motel and RV Park; 3543 Mt. View Dr.; tel. (907) 277-4332 or (800) 278-4332; $50 s, $55 d; $60 s, $65 d for kitchenettes; marginal neighborhood

Spenard Motel; 3960 Spenard Rd.; tel. (907) 243-6917; $55 s, $65 d; $69 s, $79 d for kitchenettes; free airport transport, plain rooms

Arctic Tern Inn; 5000 Taku Dr.; tel. (907) 337-1544; $55 s or d; $75 s or d for kitchenettes; free shuttle service

Big Timber Motel; 2037 E. Fifth; tel. (907) 272-2541; $60 s or d; busy location, jacuzzi, free airport transport

Inlet Inn; 539 H St.; tel. (907) 277-5541; $60 s or d

Al's Alaskan Inn; 7830 Old Seward Hwy.; tel. (907) 344-6223; $60 s $65-70 d; kitchenettes

Woods Motel; 2005 E. Fourth Ave.; tel. (907) 274-1566; $60 s, $70 d

Midtown Lodge; 604 W. 26th Ave.; tel. (907) 258-7778; $60 s, $75 d; bath down the hall, plain small rooms, continental breakfast, free airport shuttle, refrigerators

Southseas Hotel; 3001 Spenard Rd.; tel. (907) 561-3001; $65 s or d; free airport transport, see rooms first

Kobuk Motel; 1104 E. Fifth Ave.; tel. (907) 274-1650; $65 s, $75 d; kitchenettes for $75 s, $85 d; busy street, marginal neighborhood

Mush Inn Motel; 333 Concrete St.; tel. (907) 277-4554 or (800) 478-4554; $65-120 s or d; large and well-maintained, kitchenettes, free airport transport

Hillside Motel; 2150 Gambell St.; tel. (907) 258-6006 or (800) 478-6008; $69 s or d; kitchenettes for $90 s or d

Arctic Inn Motel; 842 W. International Airport Dr.; tel. (907) 561-1328; $69 s, $79 d; kitchenettes

Red Ram Motor Lodge; 642 E. Fifth Ave.; tel. (907) 274-1515; $70 s, $80 d; free airport transport, busy street, community kitchen

Black Angus Inn; 1430 Gambell St.; tel. (907) 272-7503 or (800) 770-0707; $70-75 s or d; busy location, free airport transport, kitchenettes available

Alaskan Samovar Inn; 720 Gambell St.; tel. (907) 277-1511 or (800) 478-1511; $70 s, $85 d; busy location

Snowshoe Inn; 826 K St.; tel. (907) 258-7669; $75 s, $80 d with shared bath; $85-95 s, $90-100 d with private bath; very clean, free continental breakfast, recommended place

Anchor Arms Motel; 433 Eagle St.; tel. (907) 272-9619; $79 s or d; marginal neighborhood, kitchenettes, free airport transport

Royal Suite Lodge; 3811 Minnesota Dr.; tel. (907) 563-3114; $79 s, $89 d for studios; $89 s, $99 d for one-bedroom suites; kitchenettes, free airport transport

Anchorage Uptown Hotel; 2509 Fairbanks St.; tel. (907) 279-4232 or (800) 478-4232; $80 s or d; kitchens

Bonanza Lodge; 4455 Juneau St.; tel. (907) 563-3590 or (800) 478-3590; $80-90 s or d; kitchenettes in all rooms

Merrill Field Motel; 420 Sitka St.; tel. (907) 276-4547; $85 s or d; $108 s or d for kitchenettes; well maintained, free airport transport, AAA approved

Tudor Motel; 4423 Lake Otis Pkwy.; tel. (907) 561-2234; $89 s or d; free airport transport, kitchenettes

Lakeshore Motel; 3009 Lakeshore Dr.; tel. (907) 248-3485 or (800) 770-3000; $94 s, $104-114 d; $134-155 for suites; kitchenettes available, near airport

Nelchina Point Suites; 1601 Nelchina St.; tel. (907) 279-1601; $94-124 s or d; one-or two-bedroom apartments with kitchens

Puffin Inn; 4400 Spenard Rd.; tel. (907) 243-4044 or (800) 478-3346; $96 s, $106 d; free continental breakfast, free airport transport

Super 8 Motel; 3501 Minnesota Dr.; tel. (907) 276-8884 or (800) 800-8000; $99 s, $108 d; free airport transport

Chelsea Inn Hotel; 3836 Spenard Rd.; tel. (907) 276-5002 or (800) 770-5002; $95 s, $105 d; free airport transport

Copper Whale Inn; 440 L St.; tel. (907) 258-7999; $100 s or d with shared bath, $145 s or d private bath; very nice, continental breakfast, historic building, fine views

Eagle Nest Hotel; 4110 Spenard Rd.; tel. (907) 243-3433 or (800) 848-7852; $105-170 s or d; overpriced, studio units to two-bedroom suites with kitchenettes, free airport transport

Puffin Place Suites; 1058 W. 27th Ave.; tel. (907) 279-1058 or (800) 478-3346; $116 s, $126 d; one-bedroom suites, kitchenettes, free continental breakfast, free airport transport

Best Western Golden Lion Hotel; 1000 E. 36th Ave.; tel. (907) 561-1522 or (800) 528-1234; $116-126 s, $122-132 d

Eighth Avenue Hotel; 630 W. Eighth Ave.; tel. (907) 274-6213 or (800) 274-6213; $120-145 s or d; overpriced, see rooms first, AAA approved

Sourdough Motel; 801 Erickson St.; tel. (907) 279-4148; $121 s or d for one-bedroom suites; $138 s or d for two-bedroom suites; kitchens, free airport transport

Voyager Hotel; 501 K St.; tel. (907) 277-9501 or (800) 247-9070; $129 s, $149 d; kitchenettes, AAA approved

Executive Suite Hotel; 4360 Spenard Rd.; tel. (907) 243-6366 or (800) 770-6366; $129-219 s or d; studio units to two-bedroom suites with kitchenettes, free continental breakfast

Inlet Tower Suites; 1200 L St.; tel. (907) 276-0110 or (800) 544-0786; $130-190 s or d; tall apartment building, kitchenettes, free airport transport, AAA approved

Holiday Inn; 39 W. Fourth Ave.; tel. (907) 279-8671 or (800) 465-4329; $135 s, $155 d; indoor pool, sauna, free airport shuttle, AAA approved

Northwoods Guest House; 2300 W. Tudor Rd.; tel. (907) 243-3249; $135 for up to four ($10 extra pp for additional guests); three-bedroom suites, quiet location near park, full kitchen, weekly rates available

Best Western Barratt Inn; 4616 Spenard Rd.; tel. (907) 243-3131 or (800) 221-7550; $141-156 s, $151-166 d; free airport transport, kitchenettes available, exercise facility, AAA approved

Westcoast International Inn; 3333 W. International Airport Rd.; tel. (907) 243-2233 or (800) 544-0986; $144 s, $154 d; $233-248 s or d for suites with kitchenettes; sauna, health club, free airport transport

Comfort Inn; 111 W Ship Creek Ave.; tel. (907) 277-6887 or (800) 362-6887; $145-165 s, $155-175 d; $210 d for suites with kitchenettes; free continental breakfast, indoor pool, jacuzzi, AAA approved

Days Inn; 321 E. Fifth Ave.; tel. (907) 276-7226 or (800) 222-3297; $149 s or d; free airport transport, AAA approved

(continues on next page)

ANCHORAGE ACCOMMODATIONS
(continued)

Ramada Northern Lights Inn; 598 W. Northern Lights; tel. (907) 561-5200 or (800) 272-6232; $154 s, $164 d; free airport transport

Westmark Anchorage; 720 W. Fifth Ave.; tel. (907) 276-7676 or (800) 478-1111; $172 s or d

Anchorage Hotel; 330 E St.; tel. (907) 272-4553 or (800) 544-0988; $179-199 s or d; kitchenettes available, AAA approved

Sheraton Anchorage Hotel; 401 E. Sixth Ave.; tel. (907) 276-8700 or (800) 325-3535; $200 s, $210 d; sauna, health club, AAA approved

Regal Alaskan Hotel; 4800 Spenard Rd.; tel. (907) 243-2300 or (800) 544-0553; $220-235 s, $235-250 d; sauna, exercise room, free airport transport, AAA approved

Hotel Captain Cook; Fifth Ave. and K St.; tel. (907) 276-6000 or (800) 478-3100; $230 s, $240 d, $245-1,500 d for suites; athletic club, jacuzzi, sauna, indoor pool

Anchorage Hilton Hotel; 500 W. Third Ave.; tel. (907) 272-7411 or (800) 445-8667; $240-285 s, $260-305 d; largest hotel in Alaska, indoor pool, sauna, jacuzzi, health club, AAA approved

weekly rates are available. The managers at **International Backpackers Inn,** tel. (907) 274-3870, maintain five houses on the northeast side of Anchorage in the Mountain View area. These contain coed or same-sex dorm rooms for $12-15 pp, including a full kitchen. No curfew, private rooms, or alcohol. Tent spaces may also be available during the summer, along with short-term storage of bags. Backpackers Inn is popular with workers who need a place for phone and fax messages (free local calls) and an official address while looking for a summer job. The location (3601 Peterkin, Unit A) is not as central as the AYH hostel, but is an easy bus ride from downtown. One major drawback is that Mountain View is the most crime-ridden section of Anchorage, though the Backpackers Inn is in one of the better parts of the neighborhood. Not everyone is comfortable staying in this area, but the inn is well-maintained.

Between mid-May and early August, travelers can stay in the dormitory at **Alaska Pacific University,** tel. (907) 564-8238. The charge is $25 pp for twin beds in double rooms. Reserve ahead to be sure of a space, but don't call before mid-April. There is often room even if you call the same day. Some kitchenettes are available, or you can eat in the APU cafeteria when it's open (not every day in the summer).

Bed and Breakfasts
Anchorage had over 125 B&Bs at last count, including luxurious hillside homes with spectacular vistas, cozy older homes downtown, and rent-out-the-spare-room suburban houses. Several booking agencies can help you find a place. Contact **AAA-Anchorage Adventures & Accommodations,** tel. (907) 344-4676; **Accommodations in Alaska,** tel. (907) 345-4279; **Alaska Private Lodgings,** tel. (907) 258-1717; **Alaska Sourdough B&B Association,** tel. (907) 563-6244; and **B&B Hotline,** tel. (907) 272-5909. See the *Anchorage Visitors Guide* (available from ACVB's Visitor Information Center downtown) for a complete listing of local and regional B&Bs, or take a look at the blizzard of B&B brochures filling the visitor center's racks.

The following are a few recommended B&Bs in the $60-75 d range: **A View with a Room B&B,** tel. (907) 345-2781; **Arctic Feather B&B,** tel. (907) 277-3862; **Arctic Loon B&B,** tel. (907) 345-4935; **Bonnie's B&B,** tel. (907) 345-4671; **Country Garden B&B,** tel. (907) 344-0636; **Gallery B&B, tel. (907) 274-2567;** Green Bough B&B, tel. (907) 562-4636; **Heidi's B&B,** tel. (907) 563-8517; **Mullen House B&B,** tel. (907) 562-4155 or (907) 258-9260; and **Valley of the Moon B&B,** tel. (907) 279-7755.

More expensive B&Bs ($80-125 d) with additional amenities (some have hot tubs) and full breakfasts: **Alaskan Frontier Gardens B&B,** tel. (907) 345-6556; **All the Comforts of Home B&B,** tel. (907) 345-4279; **Always Paradise B&B,** tel. (907) 345-2973; **Arctic Fox B&B,** tel. (907) 272-4818; **Arctic Pines B&B,** tel. (907) 278-6841; **Aurora Winds B&B,** tel. (907) 346-2533; **Camai B&B,** tel. (907) 333-2219 or (800) 659-8763; **Country Garden B&B,** tel. (907)

344-0636; **De Veaux's Contemporary B&B,** tel. (907) 349-8910; **English Country B&B,** tel. (907) 344-0646; **Glacier Bear B&B,** tel. (907) 243-8818; **Little Rabbit Creek B&B,** tel. (907) 345-8183; **Lynn's Pine Point B&B,** tel. (907) 333-2244; **Snowline B&B,** tel. (907) 346-1631; and **Swan House B&B,** tel. (907) 346-3033 or (800) 921-1900.

Camping

Two city parks offer camping May-September. **Lion's Camper Park,** tel. (907) 333-9711, has space for both tents and RVs, and costs $13 per site with a seven-day limit. Take Boniface Parkway south from the Glenn Highway and go a half-mile. The campground, in Russian Jack Springs city park, is marked by two small entrance and exit signs. Or take bus routes 5 or 8 to E. Sixth and Boniface, and walk south a thousand feet.

Centennial Park, tel. (907) 333-9711, has the same prices and facilities, but is roomier and a bit farther out the Glenn Highway from town. Take Muldoon Rd. south from the Glenn, hang your first left onto Boundary, then the next left onto the highway frontage road for a half-mile to the campground. Bus routes 3 and 75 stop at the corner of Boundary and Muldoon.

Local RV parking lot "campgrounds" include: **Golden Nuggett Camper Park,** 4100 DeBarr Rd., tel. (907) 333-5311 or (800) 449-2012; **Highlander Camper Park,** 2706 Fairbanks, tel. (907) 277-2407; **Hillside Motel & RV Park,** 2150 Gambell, tel. (907) 258-6006; **John's Motel and RV Park,** 3543 Mountain View Dr., tel. (907) 277-4332; **Polar Bear Inn,** 4332 Spenard Rd., tel. (907) 243-0533; and **Ship Creek Landing RV Park,** Ship Creek, tel. (907) 277-0877. Expect to pay around $20-25 with full hookups. Some travelers park RVs in the Wal-Mart and Kmart parking lots; the store managers don't care.

FOOD

Anchorage's size and diverse population are mirrored in a wide range of eating places, from grab-a-bite fast-food joints to high-class (and high-priced) gourmet restaurants. To reach many of the best places, you'll need a vehicle or a knowledge of the bus schedule, but there are a number of good restaurants right in down-

town. Another option is **Takeout Taxi,** tel. (907) 562-8150, with deliveries from nearly 30 local restaurants for an extra $4.50.

Cheap Eats

One place in Anchorage has Lower 48 prices for food: the cafeteria in the **Federal Building,** Eighth Ave. and D St., open Mon.-Fri. 7 a.m.-3:30 p.m. Several vendors have carts in the center of town right in front of the old Federal Building at Fourth Avenue. The best—look for the long line—is the bratwurst-and-grilled-onions vendor on the corner of Fourth Ave. and G Street. For fast food downtown, head to the **food court** on the fourth floor of the Fifth Avenue Mall at Fifth Ave. and C Street. Inside are fast food eateries of all persuasions, offering Thai, Chinese, deli sandwiches, seafood, frozen yogurt, burritos, and pizza. Also here are Kentucky Fried Chicken, Mrs. Fields cookies, Burger King, and Arby's outlets. A veritable feast of finger food. Get more cheap grub at **Subway,** 508 W. Sixth Avenue. Many more gut-busters are strung out the east end of town along Sixth Ave., and in Midtown along Benson and Northern Lights. For far better burgers—at reasonable prices—head to **Arctic Roadrunner,** 2477 Arctic Blvd., tel. (907) 279-7311; or **Hamburger Heaven,** 716 Muldoon Rd., tel. (907) 337-6141.

Breakfast

Given the abundance of fine eating places in Anchorage, the lack of a really great breakfast joint comes as a disappointment. **Hogg Bros. Cafe,** 1049 W. Northern Lights Blvd., tel. (907) 276-9649, serves gigantic breakfasts and burgers, and has a rather impressive collection of pig trinkets. Not surprisingly, the menu is heavy on the fat. For somewhat lighter fare, **Roosevelt Cafe,** 2419 Spenard Rd., tel. (907) 272-2416, serves breakfasts and lunches in a spaciously frumpy setting with mismatched chairs and tables. The menu is limited, but quite good; try the very tasty spinach quesadilla. **Gwennie's Old Alaska Restaurant,** 4333 Spenard, tel. (907) 243-2090, makes the best sourdough pancakes and reindeer sausage in town, and serves breakfast all day. **Roscoe's Skyline Restaurant,** 601 Hollywood Dr., tel. (907) 276-5879, is Anchorage's soul-food eatery, with catfish and grits for breakfast, along with great BBQ ribs and chicken for dinner, complete with collard greens. For dessert, order a slice of peach pie. It's on Government Hill, on the north side of the railroad tracks. Two good places for a Sunday brunch splurge are the **Crow's Nest** atop the Captain Cook Hotel at Fourth Ave. and K St., tel. (907) 276-6000; and the **Regal Alaskan Hotel,** 4800 Spenard Rd., tel. (907) 243-2300. The Regal's outside deck faces scenic Lake Hood, where you can watch floatplanes take off.

Lunch Fare

Downtown Deli, 525 W. Fourth Ave., tel. (907) 278-7314, is an Anchorage institution. Not especially budget, but with all the bagels and lox, blintzes, and pastrami sandwiches, you might think you went into a time warp and landed back on the planet near Delancey St. in Manhattan. Owner Tony Knowles also happens to be Alaska's governor, elected in 1994.

Sacks Cafe, 625 W. Fifth, tel. (907) 276-3546, is another popular downtown lunch place with all sorts of yuppie fare. The Thai chicken sandwich is especially notable. **Dianne's,** in the Enserch Building at 550 W. Seventh Ave., tel. (907) 279-7243, has wonderful soups, fresh-baked breads, and lots of vegetarian fare, including a veggie chef salad. **Wings 'N Things,** 529 I St., tel. (907) 277-9464, makes tasty fried chicken. **Mike and Sara's Deli-Cafe,** 809 E. Loop Rd., tel. (907) 277-1445, is up on Government Hill (north of the railroad tracks), with wonderful sub sandwiches and Philly cheese steaks.

Several Midtown eateries offer quick lunch meal deals. **The Bagel Factory,** 136 W. 34th, tel. (907) 561-8871, has fresh and delicious bagel sandwiches and other light meals; very popular with nearby office workers. Try their bagel chips. **California Roll,** on the corner of Benson Blvd. and C St., tel. (907) 563-8896, has the standard fast food menu with a few noteworthy twists, including a spicy Cajun chicken sandwich. Also in Midtown, **Crazy Croissants,** 1406 W. 31st, tel. (907) 278-8787, can be a bit hard to find since 31st Ave. is really just an alleyway off Minnesota Dr., but inside you'll find authentic French baked goods and excellent lunches. Two outstanding places for sandwiches are **Atlasta Deli,** 701 W. 36th Ave., tel. (907) 563-3354; and **Europa Bakery,** a short distance away at 601 W. 36th Ave., tel. (907) 563-5704. You won't be disappointed at either place. And don't miss the ever-crowded **L'Aroma Bakery & Deli,** 3700 Old Seward Hwy., tel. (907) 562-9797, for sandwiches, small pizzas baked in a wood-fired oven, and wonderful pastries. L'Aroma is inside the same building as two other gourmet favorites: a Kaladi Brothers Coffee shop; and **New Sagaya,** tel. (907) 561-5173, where the Asian deli has fill-your-plate specials for under $6, along with fresh sushi. All the local **Carrs** stores have similar delis with tasty and cheap Asian food, plus sandwiches and salad bars.

Pizza and Italian

Anchorage has all the pizza chains—Chuck E. Cheese, Domino's, Godfather's, Pizza Hut, and Round Table—and the "Pizza" listing in the Yellow Pages includes some 60 different places. Out of these, **Pizza Olympia,** 2809 Spenard Rd. (across from REI), tel. (907) 561-5264, is a personal favorite. The owners are Greek, and roll out such unique offerings as garlic and feta cheese pizzas. Good Greek food, too. Other very good places for pizza are **Sorrento's,** 610 E. Fireweed, tel. (907) 278-3439 (best southern Italian food in Anchorage); and **Fletcher's,** in the Hotel Captain Cook at Fifth Ave. and K St., tel. (907) 276-6000, where Anchorage waiters and cooks go after work. Another recommended pizza house is **Today's Pizza,** 4608 Spenard Rd., tel. (907) 248-6660. They also have very good Italian food. Pizzas are also served up at **Moose's Tooth Pub and Pizzeria** (see "Brewpubs" below). For delicious northern Italian dinners with a nouvelle-Alaskan twist, visit the small **Campobello Bistro,** 601 W. 36th Ave., tel. (907) 563-2040. Recommended but pricey, and the salads are extra.

L'Aroma Bakery & Deli, 3700 Old Seward Hwy., tel. (907) 562-9797, is next to the popular New Sagaya Asian grocery store and deli, and cranks out wonderful pizzas baked in a wood-fired brick oven. The atmosphere is very casual, with tables used by both latte drinkers from the adjacent Kaladi Brothers and folks from New Sagaya with plates piled high. Always crowded.

Chinese Food

No great downtown Chinese restaurants, but *do* head out to **Twin Dragon Mongolian Barbeque,** 612 E. 15th Ave., tel. (907) 276-7535. Lunch is just $6 for a fill-it-up plate of stir-fry veggies and meat, along with soup, appetizer, tea, and rice. You choose what goes in and then watch as the chef provides the show. In the evening, all-you-can-eat dinners are $10. Great fun. **Golden Pond Restaurant,** 300 W. 36th, tel. (907) 563-5525, has an excellent all-you-can-eat Chinese buffet for lunch or dinner. **Yen King Restaurant,** 3501 Old Seward Hwy., tel. (907) 563-2627, is another place with a good all-you-can-eat lunch buffet plus free delivery if you don't want to eat out. **Chinese Kitchen,** 2904 Spenard Rd., tel. (907) 279-2222, is a great little family eatery with lunchtime specials and friendly owners. If you're adventurous, ask about the menu items listed only in Chinese. Another recommended Chinese place is **Ding How Restaurant,** 1301 E. Huffman Rd., tel. (907) 345-0033. Be sure to try the sizzling rice soup and Chinese noodles with spicy black bean sauce.

Thai Restaurants

Anchorage now has quite a number of Thai restaurants—seven at last count. None of these measures up to what you'd find in Thailand, but several are well worth a visit. The best-known and most central is **Thai Cuisine,** 444 H St., tel. (907) 277-8424. Lunch is a good bargain, which means that the place gets packed with the office crowd then. But hip locals know that the most authentic Thai food is **Thai Kitchen,** 3405 E. Tudor, tel. (907) 561-0082, in the back of a small Asian grocery within a strip shopping mall on Tudor near Bragaw. Be sure to try the Popeye chicken or any of the spicy soups. Thai Kitchen's half-dozen tables fill up fast on weekend nights. It's open for lunch and dinner on weekdays, but dinners only on weekends. Get there early since they close at 9 p.m. Another fun place (housed in an old Dairy Queen) is **Thai House Restaurant,** 860 E. 36th Ave., tel. (907) 563-8616. Excellent service, and everything is made fresh while you wait. **Thai Village,** 954 Muldoon, tel. (907) 337-9559, emphasizes vegetarian dishes, brown rice, and no MSG.

Other Asian Restaurants

Maharaja's, Fourth and K, tel. (907) 272-2233, serves a decent Indian lunch buffet ($8) and a more diverse dinner menu. Get fresh sushi, tempura, and teriyaki at **Yamota Ya,** 3700 Old Seward Hwy. (next to New Sagaya), tel. (907) 561-2128. Another good place is **Ichiban,** a Japanese restaurant and sushi bar, 2488 E. Tudor

Rd., tel. (907) 563-6333. **Sushi Garden,** 1120 E. Huffman Rd., tel. (907) 345-4686, claims to have the best sushi in town. Local Carrs supermarkets also have fresh sushi in their delis, as does New Sagaya. Get Vietnamese meals from **Saigon Restaurant,** 3561 E. Tudor Rd., tel. (907) 563-2515.

Mexican

A longtime favorite—it's the oldest Mexican restaurant in Alaska—is **La Cabaña,** 312 E. Fourth Ave., tel. (907) 272-0135. This is a great place for lunch, with notable halibut fajitas. Two **La Mex** restaurants (900 W. 6th, tel. (907) 274-7678, and 2552 Spenard Rd., tel. (907) 274-7511), are very popular places for evening nachos and margaritas, or for full meals. The steaks aren't bad, either. **Mexico in Alaska,** 7305 Old Seward Hwy., tel. (907) 349-1528, is one of the best local south-of-the-border spots, but it's a long ways out. Another place worth trying is **Garcia's Mexican Restaurant,** 4140 B St., tel. (907) 561-4476.

If you're looking for the quick version, **Taco King,** 112 W. Northern Lights Blvd., tel. (907) 276-7387, serves very good burritos and tacos. They have a second outlet at 126 E. Eighth Ave., tel. (907) 274-3777.

Vegetarian

Vegetarians are probably best off heading to one of Anchorage's Thai or Indian restaurants, but the macrobiotic crowd often prefers the two organic food cafes run by **Enzyme Express.** Their downtown shop is across from Cyrano's at 402 D St., tel. (907) 272-1879, with a second cafe in Midtown at 2604 Fairbanks, tel. (907) 272-5433. The lunch specials are not bad; try the big bowl of soup or the smoothies. Add 25 cents for a tablespoon of "Intesticlense" to cleanse your intestines, or a dose of Klamath Lake algae (who comes up with these things?). More adventurous types may want to risk a shot of wheatgrass juice; sort of like drinking lawn clippings that someone threw in the blender. **Natural Pantry,** 300 W. 36th, tel. (907) 563-2727, is extremely popular for lunch, and almost always has quiche specials. The **Middle Way Cafe,** 1200 W. Northern Lights Blvd., tel. (907) 272-6433, has outstanding vegetarian sandwiches, fruit smoothies, baked goods, espresso drinks, teas, and other light fare. Recommended. Other places (listed elsewhere in this section) serving vegetarian fare include L'Aroma Bakery & Deli, Europa Bakery, Dianne's, and Sacks.

Salmon Bake

Sourdough Mining Company, 5200 Juneau, tel. (907) 563-2272, has an all-you-can-eat $20 buffet all summer long. In addition to broiled salmon, you can choose halibut, ribs, chicken, corn on the cob, salads, sourdough rolls, carrot cake, and soft drinks. Call in the afternoon to get picked up on their free shuttle service from downtown. The buffet is open daily 5-11 p.m. **Phyllis' Cafe,** 436 D St., tel. (907) 274-6576, has an off-the-menu salmon and halibut bake with all the fixins for $17. It's served outside, but is not an all-you-can-eat buffet.

For a Splash

Several downtown restaurants offer delightful inlet views and fine dining. **Simon & Seaforts,** 420 L. St., tel. (907) 274-3502, has an eclectic menu, excellent food and service, and splendid views. This also happens to be one of the most financially successful restaurants on the West Coast! Simon's serves daily fresh fish specials; wonderful cracked wheat sourdough bread comes with each meal. Expect to pay $25-30 for dinner. Lunch is considerably less expensive. If you don't have restaurant dinner reservations, head to the bar, where a cheaper menu is also available; lunchtime sandwiches here start at $6. If you're in the bar for a drink and the view, be sure to try the brandy ice, a blend of ice cream, Kahlúa, brandy, and creme de cacao. For more traditional all-American fare—including Anchorage's juiciest steaks—take the side trip to the **Black Angus Meat Market Restaurant,** 1101 W. Fireweed Lane, tel. (907) 279-3122.

A much smaller and quieter place than Simon's, the elegant **Marx Bros. Cafe,** Third Ave. and I St., tel. (907) 278-2133, is open Mon.-Sat. 6-9:30 p.m., with $7-12 hors d'oeuvres and $18-30 dinners. The Caesar salad—made at your table—is especially notable. The menu changes daily, but it's always creative, and the big wine list and good dessert selection complement the meal. Highly recommended if you can afford it, but reservations are essential. Last, but not least, is the **Top of the World,** high atop the Anchorage Hilton, tel. (907) 265-7111. The food rivals the dramatic vistas over Cook Inlet and north to Mt. McKinley. Outstanding desserts, too. Expect to pay $35 and up. Get here early for an outside seat where you can watch the constant show of F-15 jets landing at Elmendorf Air Force Base.

Brewpubs

In 1996, Anchorage went from no brewpubs to five, all offering food and fresh-brewed beer. Their longevity is tenuous at best, but they've certainly greatly improved the city's food-and-booze scene. Fanciest of the lot is **Railway Brewing Co.,** tel. (907) 277-1996, housed in the spacious railroad depot building at 412 W. First Avenue. The yupscale lunch and dinner menu emphasizes distinctive sandwiches, seafood, chicken, and unusual pizzas. Right downtown, **Glacier Brewhouse,** 737 W. Fifth Ave., tel. (907) 274-2739, also appeals to a similar professional crowd, though the food can be a bit uneven at times.

Also in town is **Snow Goose Restaurant and Sleeping Lady Brewery,** 717 W. Third Ave., tel. (907) 277-7727. Open for lunch and dinner Mon.-Sat., it features sandwiches and pasta for lunch, and seafood, poultry, and beef for dinner ($14-19 entrees). The real treat is the upstairs pub with an outdoor patio overlooking Cook Inlet. Snow Goose always has a half-dozen homebrews on tap, as well as a big wine selection. **Cusack's Brewpub & Roaster,** 598 W. Northern Lights Blvd., tel. (907) 278-2739, is housed inside the Ramada Inn in Midtown. It features a light menu of steamed clams, salads, and soups, along with five fresh brews on tap. **Moose's Tooth Pub and Pizzeria,** 3300 Old Seward Hwy., tel. (907) 258-2537, is the most laidback of the city's breweries, with a pizza and salad menu and a friendly atmosphere.

As of this writing the various brewmasters were still tinkering and learning on the job to some extent, but any of them beat mass-produced swill. Some of the pubs have live music several nights a week.

More Pub Grub

You won't go wrong by eating at **F Street Station,** 325 F St., tel. (907) 272-5196, where there are always reasonably priced daily specials. The beer-batter halibut is guaranteed to please. Besides, this is a great place to hang out in the evening with the downtown white-collar crowd.

Humpy's Great Alaskan Ale House, 610 W. 6th Ave., tel. (907) 276-2337, attracts a younger college-age crowd with many microbrews on tap and a dependable pub menu of halibut burgers, salads, pastas, and other light fare. Live bands play most nights in this very popular hangout. Another place with great beer bites is the **Peanut Farm,** 5227 Old Seward Hwy., tel. (907) 563-3283, where the draft beer and bulging burgers (served on an outdoor deck in the summer) attract both locals and visitors. But don't confuse the Peanut Farm with the strip joint next door! **Harry's Restaurant & Bar,** in Midtown at 101 W. Benson Blvd., tel. (907) 561-5317, specializes in fresh seafood, and has an outstanding choice of draught microbrews—more than 20 on tap at any time.

Grocers

Those new to Alaska may be surprised that the major grocery stores look pretty much like those in the Lower 48, and have just as much (or more) to choose from. True, the prices are a bit higher, but not nearly as high as out in the Bush. The biggest and best grocery stores—by far—are the **Carrs Supermarkets.** Their mega-marts are found all over Anchorage and the Valley, but none are particularly near downtown. The most impressive Carrs stores are on the corner of Northern Lights and Minnesota, and at Huffman and New Seward Highway. Most Carrs have very good delis and salad bars, and the larger ones even make fresh sushi and U-bake pizzas. (Note, however, that the one inferior Carrs also happens to be the closest to downtown, at 13th and Ingra.)

A distinctive grocer and Asian market is **New Sagaya,** 3700 Old Seward Hwy., tel. (907) 561-5173. The store sells all sorts of Asian supplies—tea sets, spices, noodles, 50-pound sacks of rice, sushi and potstickers to go, and exotic produce; plus live crabs, clams, and mussels. Stop off here just for a visit, but be warned that the prices for this exotic fare are Alaska-sized. **Natural Pantry,** 300 W. 36th, tel. (907) 563-2727, is the place to go for overpriced organic and natural foods. You'd do better to head to the **Saturday Market,** held at the parking lot on Third Ave. and E St. every summer Saturday 10 a.m.-6 p.m. By August, they'll have all sorts of fresh organic produce from the Matanuska Valley. Get there early for the best selection. The

best places to find fresh seafood are **Tenth & M Seafoods,** 1020 M St., tel. (907) 272-6013; **Alaskan Gourmet Seafoods,** 1020 W. International Airport Rd., tel. (907) 563-3752; and the previously mentioned New Sagaya and Carrs stores.

Bakeries and Sweets

Fresh-baked goods are available from all the Carrs stores, but some of the best breads and pastries come from **Europa Bakery,** 601 W. 36th, tel. (907) 563-5704. Their rustic breads compare favorably to anything you might find in Seattle, San Francisco, or Europe. **Great Harvest Bread Co.,** 570 E. Benson Blvd., tel. (907) 274-3331, is certainly the most distinctive bakery in town, with hefty two-pound loaves for an equally hefty price ($4-7). Stop by for a free sample slice of the day's best, including cookies and sweets. Great Harvest is in a small mall across the street from the Sears Mall in Midtown. Also in this mall are Metro Music and Books and **Cafe Amsterdam,** 530 E. Benson, tel. (907) 274-1072, with Dutch sweets. **L'Aroma Bakery & Deli** 3700 Old Seward Hwy., tel. (907) 562-9797, bakes wonderful Italian pastries. **Crazy Croissants,** 1406 W. 31st, tel. (907) 278-8787, has a stupid name that you might expect in a shopping mall outlet, but the French pastries are authentic, as are the French owners. **The Bagel Factory,** 136 W. 34th, tel. (907) 561-8871, makes the finest Anchorage bagels. **Alaska Wild Berry Products** has a 20,000-square-foot chocolate factory and gift shop on Juneau St. near the corner of Old Seward Hwy. and International Airport Road. This is a fun place for chocoholics; there's even a 20-foot waterfall of melted chocolate; free taste samples too.

COFFEEHOUSES

Several years ago Anchorage saw a renaissance of sorts as dozens of espresso coffee places popped up all over town. Tucked away in a Midtown shopping mall, **Cafe del Mundo** at 341 E. Benson, tel. (907) 274-0026, is very popular with the lawyer/Volvo crowd, and is a fine place to while away a morning. Downtown's **Sorella's,** 1001 W. Fourth Ave., tel. (907) 274-0070, has a warm atmosphere, good coffee, and tasty lunch sandwiches. Friendly **Cyrano's**

Cafe, 413 D St., tel. (907) 274-1173, is also downtown, next to the bookstore of the same name. **Cafe Fonte** has several Anchorage locations, including 510 L St., tel. (907) 272-1701, and in Dover Center at 36th Ave. and C St., tel. (907) 562-1702. The **Middle Way Cafe,** 1200 W. Northern Lights Blvd., tel. (907) 272-6433, is a surprising little coffeehouse with delicious lunches, tucked inside a shopping mall next to REI.

Bear Paw Coffee Company, 646 F St., tel. (907) 279-3665, is a classy small place that has much more than espresso coffees. Their pies, pastries, biscotti, and chocolate truffles are some of the best in Anchorage. Great waffles for breakfast and panini sandwiches for lunch. **Adventures & Delights,** 414 K St., tel. (907) 276-8282, or (800) 288-3134, has a small coffee shop. Stop in to peruse the many travel books and maps, to enjoy one of the Wednesday evening slide shows, or to sign up for outdoor classes and trips.

A personal favorite is **Kaladi Brothers,** 6921 Brayton, tel. (907) 344-5483. If you don't have a vehicle, don't even attempt to get here, since it's hidden on a frontage road along New Seward Highway. If you do have wheels, head south on the highway to Diamond, turn left and go under the highway, turn left again onto Frontage Rd., and continue a half-mile north to the Brayton Mall where Kaladi is located. The atmosphere is California laid-back. Upstairs, you can watch folk musicians most days and access the Internet from their free computer terminal. They make the best mochas in town here, and also sell fresh-roasted coffee. Most of the other Anchorage shops where you're likely to find espresso buy their beans from Kaladi Brothers. **Barnes & Noble Bookseller** at 200 E. Northern Lights Blvd., tel. (907) 279-7323 or (888) 279-7323, also houses a cafe and is the first place in Alaska to offer Starbucks coffee.

All Anchorage coffeehouses prohibit smoking.

ENTERTAINMENT

Performing Arts
Anchorage's active cultural scene centers on the downtown **Performing Arts Center.** There are events throughout the year, including modern dance, ballet, comedy troupes, opera, concerts by nationally known artists, and performances by the Anchorage Symphony Orchestra. Call (907) 272-1471 for more information on the performing arts, or check the Friday "Calendar" section of the *Daily News* for upcoming events. Check with **Anchorage Community Theater,** 1133 E. 70th Ave., tel. (907) 344-4713; **Toast Theatre,** 710 Orca, tel. (907) 258-6278; and **Out North Theatre,** tel. (907) 279-8099, for live productions. (Out North is Alaska's only gay and lesbian theatrical group.)

Movies
Free documentary flicks are shown several times a day at the **Public Lands Information Center** (see below) and the **Museum of History and Art** (see above). **Denali Theater,** 1230 W. 27th at Spenard Rd., tel. (907) 279-2332, shows double features for $1—easily the best deal in town. The movies are mostly second-run, but at two for a buck, you could stand seeing them again. Take bus routes 7 or 9. Watch foreign films and off-beat flicks at **Capri Cinema,** 3425 E. Tudor (near Bragaw), tel. (907) 561-0064. **Loussac Library** also has foreign films on some Friday nights; call (907) 261-2844 for upcoming movies. The other cinemas are all multitheater places, showing first-run single features that, at $7, you can either do without or wait for the video. But if you're craving a big-screen experience, there should be something playing at one of the multiplex places: **Totem Theatre,** 3101 Muldoon, tel. (907) 275-3188; **Fireweed Theatre,** Fireweed and New Seward, tel. (907) 277-3139; and **University Cinemas,** 3109 Old Seward Hwy., tel. (907) 562-1250.

DRINKING AND DANCING

The best sources for Anchortown action are the Friday "Calendar" and "8" sections of the *Anchorage Daily News.* With dozens of listings from coffeehouse folk guitarists to the "Young at Heart" big band that livens up the senior center on Friday nights, there's something to satiate even the most bored visitor. The newspaper's pithy descriptions of Anchorage's nightclubs and coffeehouses are a big help in making your evening plans.

Spenard

Joe Spenard, one of Anchorage's more colorful pioneers, owned one of the first automobiles in the new town, which he put to work as City Express, a taxi, delivery, and emergency service. He also opened a roadhouse and beach resort on Jeter Lake, which he renamed Lake Spenard, at that time several miles south of town. For many years, Spenard Rd. was the undisputed vice district of Anchorage, where most of society's fringe element decamped to, after revitalization desleazed downtown. Today the "Mischief Mile" between Northern Lights Blvd. and International Airport Rd. has been cleaned up, but still has its share of pawn shops, liquor stores, rough-and-tumble bars, adult bookstores, and escort services. There are also, of course, lots of less sleazy places, including several of the city's finest motels, along with some of the most popular Anchorage nightclubs: Chilkoot Charlie's, The Wave, Firehouse Cafe, Buckaroo Club, and Fly By Night Club.

Neighborhood Bars

Anchorage is a "Cheers"-type town, with lots of corner bars and local pubs tucked away. Downtown, a popular place is **F Street Station** between Third and Fourth next to the Hilton, which also serves good-value lunches. Also, **Darwin's Theory** on G between Fourth and Fifth attracts a good after-work crowd. Free hot pepper schnapps—if you can stomach it—when the bartender rings the bell (quite often some evenings). A very friendly neighborhood pub in Midtown is the **Cheechako Bar,** 317 W. Fireweed, tel. (907) 276-9490. The owner is Irish, so the crowd packs in here on St. Patrick's Day. They also have a great jukebox. The four best sports bars in town are: **Peanut Farm,** 5227 Old Seward Hwy., tel. (907) 563-3283; **Sports Edition Bar** (17 TV screens) in the Anchorage Hilton at 500 W. Third, tel. (907) 272-7411; **Crossroads Lounge,** 1402 Gambell, tel. (907) 276-9014; and **Legends** in the Anchorage Sheraton at 401 E. 6th Ave., tel. (907) 276-8700. **Harry's Restaurant & Bar,** in Midtown at 101 W. Benson Blvd., tel. (907) 561-5317, has more than 20 draught beers on tap, including lots of microbrews.

Rockin' Out

Anchorage's most popular downtown bar is **Humpy's Great Alaskan Ale House,** 610 W. 6th Ave., tel. (907) 276-2337. Drop by on a Friday night to rub shoulders (arms, legs, and other body parts—it gets mighty crowded) with a hip and raucous young crowd. The bar has microbrews on tap, and the kitchen cranks out reasonably good pub grub. Live bands play most nights. Humpy's is a must-see place if you're staying downtown.

Chilkoot Charlies, 2435 Spenard Rd. just south of Fireweed, is a ramshackle building where you can do some serious jumping up and down to real rock 'n' roll, play horseshoes out back, and generally have a night of good raunchy fun—so long as you don't ask the wrong guy's girl (or the wrong girl's guy) to dance. There are two separate dance floors, and three different bands on weekends (the third is generally of the one-woman-with-guitar variety in the no-smoking section). 'Koots is a love-it or hate-it sort of place; if you aren't into the bar cruisin' and pickup scene, try elsewhere. But you should at least go here to say you didn't miss the most famous place in town. 'Koots gets extremely crowded on weekend nights, so you may have to wait quite a while to get in if you come after 10 p.m. There's always a cover charge on weekends.

A dressier crowd heads to **Hot Rods,** 4848 Old Seward Hwy., tel. (907) 562-5701, where there's even valet parking. The decor is what you might expect, with '50s and '60s cars as the centerpiece. No live bands at Hot Rods, but lots of dancing to old rock 'n' roll discs. (Listen to several of the commercial FM radio stations in Anchorage and you'd think it was still 1969!) Downstairs in Hot Rods, you'll find a fine **billiards room** with 16 antique tables, certainly the classiest pool joint in the state; it's been rated one of the best billiard rooms in the nation.

Don't miss Anchorage's most distinctive bar: Mr. Whitekey's **Fly By Night Club** at 3300 Spenard, tel. (907) 279-SPAM. The "Gormay Kweezeen" menu explains the phone number: it features delicacies such as Spam with Nachos and Cajun Spam (with "Paul Prudhomme's own spices"). Anything with Spam is half price when ordered with champagne, and free with Dom Perignon. (In case you didn't know, Spam is an old Alaskan Bush standby, and remains very popular today.) There's also a 50-cent "Budweiser tax"—for all the nitwits who *still* want Bud in spite of the huge selection of imported and microbrewed beers. Mr. Whitekey's **"Whale Fat Follies"**—put on most weeknights in the summer—is a hilarious send-up of everything Alaskan, including spawning salmon, duct tape, and Skinny Dick's Halfway Inn. Newcomers to Alaska may be a bit baffled by the political humor and inside jokes, but the more time you've spent here, the funnier it is. Beware, however, the humor gets pretty raunchy at times. There's a no-smoking show on Tuesday nights. After the Follies, Mr. Whitekey and his Fabulous Spamtones continue with a tight rock/blues/jazz band. Fly By Night is closed Jan.-March.

Chef's Inn, 825 W. Northern Lights Blvd., tel. (907) 272-1341, is Anchorage's "Blues Central," with live blues bands Wed.-Sat. nights. The bar attracts leather-clad chain-smoking bikers and others. Good food and great blues bands, but bring a gas mask. More blues at **Alaska Blues,** 530 E. Fifth Ave., tel. (907) 279-2583. Downtown's **Rumrunners,** 330 E St., tel. (907) 278-4493, mixes R&B with rock tunes on weekends, and has a big dance floor for trying your steps to DJ tunes other nights.

Lost Abby/Thirsty Monk Cafe, 2520 E. Tudor Rd., tel. (907) 563-8194, is an all-ages club with alternative bands four nights a week. **Gig's Music Theatre,** 140 E. Fourth Ave., tel. (907) 278-4447, also attracts the young set, with a no-alcohol policy and Seattle-sound bands.

Date Bars

Several Anchorage bars offer a quiet and romantic atmosphere; see also "Coffeehouses" above. **Bernie's Bar & Grill** in the Sears Mall (Northern Lights and New Seward Hwy.), tel. (907) 272-3223, has piano jazz on Friday and Saturday nights. If you luck into a clear evening, have packed something a little dressy, and don't mind blowing two-days' budget on a beer, head up to the **Crow's Nest** atop the Captain Cook Hotel at Fourth and K, tel. (907) 276-6000—the view is worth the effort. The **Regal Alaskan Hotel,** 4800 Spenard, tel. (907) 243-2300, has a yuppie bar overlooking Lake Hood, within a lodge-type atmosphere complete with taxidermy and a huge cozy fireplace.

And if your boyfriend happens to be of the same sex as you, head for **The Wave,** a big club at 3103 Spenard Rd., tel. (907) 561-9283. This is the center of Anchorage's surprisingly active homosexual scene, with female imper-

sonators Wednesday nights, DJ tunes and country line dancing other evenings.

Cowboy Bars

Country and western bands can be found at a number of Anchorage saloons. The biggest places are **Buckaroo Club,** 2811 Spenard Rd., tel. (907) 561-9251; **The A-K Korral Saloon,** 2421 E. Tudor Rd., tel. (907) 562-6552; and **The Last Frontier Bar,** 369 Muldoon Rd., tel. (907) 338-9922. The A-K has one of the largest dance floors around. All three of these offer free country dance or line dance lessons on certain weeknights.

The Wilder Side

It's not surprising Anchorage now has a **Hooters Restaurant** 701 E. Tudor, tel. 907-563-5653, where busty waitresses with skimpy outfits are the main attraction, as it is one of the few places in America where strip joints are not only tolerated, but are a featured attraction. Perhaps it's because of the military bases or all the lonely single men who arrive from the Bush looking for a chance to see women again. The most famous place is the **Great Alaskan Bush Company,** 631 E. International Airport Rd., where strippers perform at eye level for the price of a beer. Amazingly enough, it's tastefully designed, with high-powered ventilation and beautiful bodies—about as unsleazy as a strip joint could be. Other popular strip joints are **Crazy Horse,** 16th and Gambell; **Crazy Horse Too,** 156 Muldoon Rd.; and **PJ's,** 3608 Spenard. Crazy Horse is known for bringing in "name" acts with names like "Nikki Knockers." **Showboat,** at International and Old Seward, is an equal-opportunity strip club: male strippers downstairs, female strippers upstairs. The *real* action takes place in the red light district behind Chilkoot Charlie's off Spenard, and at the massage parlors, one of which is right next door to a police substation on 36th near Spenard! You can't miss the New Lovely International Hostesses sign out front.

EVENTS

Summer Events

Winter is the time for Anchorage's best-known events (the Iditarod and Fur Rendezvous), but the city is certainly full of life in the summer. The most popular ongoing event is the **Saturday**

Market, which takes place at the parking lot on Third Ave. and E St. on Saturday 10 a.m.-6 p.m. It features fresh produce and quality arts and crafts. Every Friday at noon, head downtown to Fourth Avenue for a free **concert on the lawn** next to the visitor center.

Anchorage has not just one, but two different semi-pro baseball teams—the **Anchorage Bucs,** tel. (907) 272-2827; and the **Glacier Pilots,** tel. (907) 274-3627—so there's almost always a game worth watching between June and early August. Past players have included such pro stars as Reggie Jackson and Dave Winfield. The **Elmendorf Open House and Air Show** at Elmendorf Air Force Base comes around in early June, and generally includes a stunning performance by the Air Force's Thunderbirds. **The Taste of Anchorage** is a fun early June event held on the Delaney Park Strip. It features food booths from a number of local restaurants, plus live music and entertainment. Then comes the **Anchorage Festival of Music,** with classical concerts at the Performing Arts Center the last half of June.

There's a **July Fourth** parade downtown, but when the fireworks show starts at midnight the sky still isn't very dark! Don't miss Mr. Whitekey's Alaskan spoof, the **"Whale Fat Follies"** (described above) at the Fly By Night Club all summer. He puts on similar shows such as "Freeze-up Follies" or "Springtime in Spenard" at other times of the year.

Other fun Anchorage events include the **Three Barons Renaissance Faire** in early June—where the crowd gets into the act by pelting bad actors with rotten tomatoes—plus the **Scottish Highland Games** in mid-June, and the **Spenard Solstice Street Party.** Several of the biggest "local" events—the State Fair in Palmer, the Girdwood Forest Faire, the Talkeetna Bluegrass Festival, and the KBBI Concert on the Lawn in Homer—are not in Anchorage. But, if you're around when any of these are happening, get out of Anchorage to where the fun really is!

Winter Events

In recent years, tourism to Alaska has increased in the winter months as visitors discover what Alaskans already know—that winter opens up a panoply of outdoor options. Several companies specialize in winter tours and activities; see the visitor center for their brochures. The one Alaskan event that always attracts national attention is the **Iditarod Dogsled Race** from Anchorage to Nome. The start is in downtown Anchorage in early March. (See the special topic "The Iditarod" for more on this fascinating and historic dogsled race.) After the Iditarod, **Fur Rendezvous** is Anchorage's biggest annual event. Because it comes in mid-February, many of the participants are locals. There are all sorts of activities during this 10-day-long festival. A carnival packs a downtown lot with rides of all sorts, and there are car races, fireworks, snow sculpture contests, dress balls, concerts, ski races, dog pulling contests, and—most exciting of all—the world championship sled dog race. Lots of fun. Another very popular event is the **Great Alaska Shootout** basketball tournament that takes place in Sullivan Arena each November, and features eight top college teams. This one gets national media attention because it is so early in the year.

Skiing Events

If you're in Anchorage the latter half of February, be sure to sign up for the **Grandview Ski Train,** sponsored by the Nordic Skiing Club. The train leaves Anchorage for an all-day trip to the Grandview area between Portage and Seward. There are glaciers to explore, plus steep mountain slopes in all directions. Hundreds of cross-country skiers of all types and abilities pack the train on two weekends and are treated to a you-have-to-see-it-to-believe-it polka slamdance in the baggage car on the return trip. Call well in advance to be sure of a ticket. Expect to pay approximately $60 roundtrip (including membership in the club). The Nordic Skiing Club, tel. (907) 561-3141, is a great organization that keeps hundreds of miles of local trails groomed, and puts on lots of other events such as the **Tour of Anchorage** in late February and a 21-mile ski over **Hatcher Pass** in late March.

Another unique ski event is put on by the Alaska Mountaineering Club. On Super Bowl Sunday each January, the club leads a free ski trip from the Portage Visitor Center over Portage Pass to Whittier. Once in Whittier, everyone warms up in the bars as they watch the football game, then they catch the train back to their cars on the Anchorage side of the tunnel. For more information, call Alaska Mountaineering & Hiking at (907) 272-1811.

SHOPPING

Although big-city folks sometimes complain that Anchorage doesn't have the fancy boutiques they're accustomed to finding, it *does* have just about every other sort of place—from Costco to Nordstrom. The city is a car haven, so many of these stores are scattered in the various shopping malls that help give Anchorage its "charming" urban sprawl. The largest are **Northway Mall** on the east end of town, and **Dimond Center** on the south side. In the last couple of years things have gotten worse with the arrival of Kmart, Wal-Mart, Fred Meyer, Costco, and other mega-marts. Much of downtown is given over to shops selling tourist doo-dads. Downtown Anchorage's **Fifth Avenue Mall** includes two big stores—JCPenny and Nordstrom—along with a couple dozen storefronts.

As might be expected in a city of this size, ATMs can now be found practically anywhere, including most banks around town and many grocery stores. Change foreign bills at **Thomas Cook Foreign Exchange,** 311 F St., tel. (907) 278-2822 or **American Express,** 5011 Jewel Lake Rd., tel. (907) 266-6622.

Gift Shops and Galleries
Downtown, Third and Fourth Aves. are lined with gift shops selling an enormous selection of Alaskan arts and crafts—everything from $2 trinkets to a $20,000 jade sculpture. In an hour or two of strolling up Third and back down Fourth, you can shop for ceramics, clocks, belt buckles, dishes and cups, pendants, placemats, posters, slides, T-shirts, stuffed animals, candles, notecards, postcards, videotapes, wall hangings, and a score of other souvenirs—all with Alaska shapes, scenes, graphics, and typography, all for under $25. From there, you can work your way up through Native commercial and fine art: ivory, jade, and soapstone carvings; scrimshaw, totems, *ulu* knives, masks, dolls, weaving, and jewelry, which can max out your credit line in a single bound. If you've been traveling around the state for a while, you might have an idea of what you'd like to buy, and here in the big city you'll probably come close to what you're looking for, though the prices are inflated to help the storekeepers meet the high overhead. If you're a cheechako, look, shop, com-pare, and wait. Either you'll find what you like cheaper elsewhere, or you'll pass through Anchortown again for a second look.

Three of the finest places to purchase original artwork in Anchorage are **Artique, Ltd.,** 314 G St., tel. (907) 277-1663; **Stonington Gallery,** behind the visitor center at 428 G St., tel. (907) 272-1489; and **Aurora Fine Arts Gallery,** 713 W. Fifth Ave., tel. (907) 274-0234. Tourists often stop in to see the photos at Myron Rosenberg's Gallery, at Fourth Ave. and D Street. Despite the quality work, Myron's abrasive personality means few Anchoragites shop here. A much better option is the **Saturday Market,** held at the parking lot on Third Ave. and E St. every summer Saturday 10 a.m.-6 p.m. In addition to local produce, the market has arts and crafts, food booths, and entertainers. Recommended.

Native Crafts
Some Anchorage dealers in Native arts and crafts are less than trustworthy, but the following places offer authentic works. An unusual and very expensive purchase to consider is qiviut: caps, scarves, shawls, sweaters, or baby booties, hand-knitted by Natives from the wool of domestic musk ox (the musk ox farm is outside of Palmer). Supposedly many times warmer and lighter than down, these fine knits can be seen and salivated over at **Oomingmak Co-op,** 609 H St., tel. (907) 272-9225. Two of the finest Native crafts shops are **Tahita Arts,** 605 A St., tel. (907) 272-5829; and the new **Alaska Native Medical Center Gift Shop,** 4315 Diplomacy Dr. (off E. Tudor Rd.), tel. (907) 257-1150. Excellent grass baskets, dolls, masks, yo-yos, and more are sold on consignment at the Medical Center. Another shop with fair prices is **Alaska Native Arts and Crafts,** near Fourth and C in the Post Office Mall, tel. (907) 274-2932. Anyone looking for a traditional Alaskan parka should be sure to stop by **Laura Wright Alaskan Parkys,** 343 W. Fifth Ave., tel. (907) 274-4215.

Outfitting for the Outdoors
Anchorage is an excellent place to get stocked up on outdoor gear before heading into the Bush. The biggest place to shop—and one of the best—is **Recreation Equipment Inc. (REI),** on the corner of Northern Lights and Spenard,

tel. (907) 272-4565. Anyone from the West Coast already knows about this Seattle-based cooperative where members get an end-of-the-year dividend on their purchases (generally around 10%). The staff is highly knowledgeable, and includes lots of climbers, skiers, mountain bikers, kayakers, and other enthusiasts. They offer free clinics and talks of all sorts throughout the year, and the bulletin board upstairs is a good place to look for used equipment or travel partners. You can also rent canoes, kayaks, tents, backpacks, skis, snowshoes, and other outdoor equipment from REI.

Another good place to rent kayaks, bear-proof canisters, tents, sleeping bags, lanterns, and other stuff is **Adventures & Delights,** 414 K St., tel. (907) 276-8282 or (800) 288-3134. Be sure to ask about guided sea kayaking tours to Prince William Sound and Kenai Fjords National Park while here. They also offer sea kayaking classes, and in winter have ski and ice-climbing classes.

An excellent outdoor store with a technically adept staff is **Alaska Mountaineering & Hiking**—better known as AMH—just a block away from REI at 2633 Spenard, tel. (907) 272-1811. AMH is much smaller than REI, but often has equipment unavailable elsewhere. Check their bulletin board for used gear. Across the street is **Play it Again Sports,** tel. (907) 278-7529, where used equipment of all sorts is available, from backpacks and tents to baseball gloves and fishing poles. They also buy used equipment if you need a little cash on your way out of town. The same building houses **Alaska Aquarium,** tel. (907) 258-7921, a fun place to explore. Packed with fish and other critters.

Downtown shoppers head to the **Army Navy Store,** 320 W. Fourth Ave., tel. (907) 279-2401, for more traditional Alaskan outdoor clothing and boots. High quality gear here, too. Also downtown is **Skinny Raven Sports,** 800 H St., tel. (907) 274-7222, the city's premier running store, with cross-country skis for when the snow flies. **Mountain View Sports,** 3838 Old Seward Hwy., tel. (907) 563-8600, is another large camping goods store, and a good place to purchase fishing gear. **B&J Commercial,** 2749 C St., tel. (907) 274-6113, is a surprising place, with a downstairs packed with sport and commercial fishing supplies. This is where you'll find the really heavy-duty clothing and equipment. Fair prices too. In general, Anchorage's best-known outdoors store—**Gary King's**—is to be avoided. The sales staff works on a commission basis, and it shows.

Secondhand Stores

Anchorage is a great place to buy used clothes and gear of all sorts. The largest secondhand stores are **Bishop's Attic,** 11th and Gambell, tel. (907) 279-6328; and **Value Village,** 5437 E. Northern Lights Blvd., tel. (907) 337-2184, and 501 E. Dimond, tel. (907) 522-9090. The latter stores have an enormous selection of good quality clothing—arranged by color! On the unique side is **The Second Chance,** 3106 Spenard, tel. (907) 277-2748. It's a pigsty with junk all over the yard, basement, and roof—a great place to buy used bunny boots. The owner often prices things according to how feisty you are in return.

Bookstores

Anchorage's book scene has changed dramatically in the last few years, with the arrival of the superstores and disappearance of several long-established smaller bookstores. **Borders Books & Music,** 1100 E. Dimond Blvd., tel. (907) 344-4099, is out next to Kmart on the south end of town, and has a huge selection of books and CDs, plus an espresso cafe. Even bigger (and more centrally located) is **Barnes & Noble Bookseller,** 200 E. Northern Lights Blvd., tel. (907) 279-7323 or (888) 279-7323. Inside, in addition to books and CDs, you'll find a huge magazine selection, and the first Alaskan cafe to sell Starbucks coffee. Another place with tons of magazines is **Sourdough News & Tobacco,** 735 W. Fourth Ave., tel. (907) 274-6397.

The city's largest independent is **Metro Music and Books,** in Midtown at 530 E. Benson Blvd., tel. (907) 279-8622. In addition to books, the store has thousands of CDs and tapes, and will even let you listen to CDs before you decide to buy anything. A fine downtown store is **Cook Inlet Book Company,** 415 W. Fifth Ave., tel. (907) 258-4544 or (800) 240-4148, with a big selection of Alaskan titles. Not far away is **Cyrano's,** 413 D St., tel. (907) 274-2599, a small bookstore that was once the center of the city's literary culture, but has seen hard times since the big players moved into town. It still has a coffeehouse and Cyrano's Off Center Playhouse next door. **Waldenbooks** is in four local malls: Fifth Avenue Mall, Dimond Center, Northway Mall, and University Center.

Get used books at the spacious and well-organized **Title Wave Used Books,** 1068 W. Fireweed, tel. (907) 278-9283; and tarot cards from **Source Metaphysical Book Store,** 329 E. Fifth, tel. (907) 274-5850. The latter is Anchorage's only "headshop." More groovy stuff at **Light in Motion Crystals,** 579 W. Ninth, tel. (907) 279-7825.

INFORMATION

One of the best things about Anchorage is how easy it is to collect all the information you could possibly need, not just for the city but also for much of the state. Two stops near the corner of Fourth Ave. and F St. downtown can supply you with a ton of fliers, brochures, booklets, guides, schedules, and maps, plus the synthesizing expertise of the extremely solicitous and knowledgeable staffs who can help you make sense of it all. For info about the Municipality of Anchorage, stop in at the Anchorage Convention and Visitors Bureau; and for all state and national parks, preserves, and other public lands, hit the Alaska Public Lands Information Center.

Anchorage Convention and Visitors Bureau
A small log cabin with a sod roof houses the ACVB's Visitor Information Center, at Fourth and F, tel. (907) 274-3531. The center is open 7:30 a.m.-7 p.m. June-August, 8:30 a.m.-6 p.m. May and September, and 9 a.m.-4 p.m. the rest of the year. Pick up a copy of *Anchorage Visitors Guide* magazine, which includes a downtown walking tour and an Anchorage-area driving tour, plus numerous listings of practicalities. You can also call their Info line at (907) 276-3200 for a recorded message on special events, or call (907) 276-4118 to receive assistance in any one of 20 foreign tongues. Ask at the desk for the bike trail map of Anchorage. The ACVB maintains the visitor centers at the airport terminals: one in the domestic terminal and the other in the international. The ACVB's Internet address is http://www.ci.anchorage.ak.us. It includes everything from bus schedules to upcoming events and details on moving to Anchorage.

Alaska Public Lands Information Center
This excellent facility, corner of Fourth and F, tel. (907) 271-2737, open daily 9 a.m.-7 p.m., combines the resources of eight federal and state land and water management agencies. This center has videotapes, computers, and exhibits, including taxidermy and relief maps. The Alaska Natural History Association's bookstore here sells topographic maps from the Anchorage area, and the large auditorium shows free documentaries on the Great Land. You can also make reservations for Chugach and Tongass National Forest cabins at the center.

GORDY OHLIGER

For the more obscure topographic maps, you'll need to get out to the **U.S. Geological Survey** at 4230 University Dr., tel. (907) 786-7010. A store selling topographic and many other types of cartography is **The Maps Place,** 113 W. Northern Lights Blvd., tel. (907) 562-6277.

Get info on Alaska state parks—including details on the many public-use cabins ($35/night) scattered throughout the state—from the Dept. of Natural Resources office in the Frontier Building at 3601 C St., Suite 200, tel. (907) 269-8400 open Mon.-Fri. 11 a.m.-5 p.m.

Libraries

The **Z.J. Loussac Library** is a gorgeous facility out in Midtown at 36th and Denali, tel. (907) 261-2975. It's open Mon.-Thurs. 11 a.m.-9 p.m., Fri.-Sat. 10 a.m.-6 p.m. (closed Sunday). Named after a pioneer pharmacist, politician, and philanthropist who made his fortune selling drugs to early Alaskans, it can make you easily lose an afternoon just wandering among the stacks, enjoying the cozy sitting room on Level 3, studying the huge relief map of the state, browsing among the paintings hanging on the walls, or picking a book at random from the large Alaskana collection and filling yourself up with arcane information that will no doubt color the rest of your trip. Getting to the Alaskana section is an adventure in its own right—the architects did everything they could to make it difficult to reach: up two flights of stairs, across a long connecting walkway, and then back down two levels. And it's back out the same way, since there is no exit here! Other Anchorage libraries are the **Muldoon Branch Library** at 7731 E. Northern Lights, tel. (907) 337-2223; the **Samson/Dimond Branch Library** in the Dimond Center Mall at Dimond Blvd. and Old Seward Hwy., tel. (907) 349-4629; and the **University Library** on the UAA campus, tel. (907) 786-1871.

GETTING THERE AND AWAY

Anchorage International Airport

For many years Anchorage styled itself "air crossroads of the world," with over-the-pole flights stopping to refuel on their way to Tokyo, London, or New York. The advent of jets able to travel longer distances without refueling, and the opening up of Russian airspace, have greatly reduced the number of international connections. Anchorage remains, however, a vital link for the air cargo companies; both Federal Express and UPS have major international terminals at the airport.

Almost everybody who flies into Alaska from the Lower 48 lands at Anchorage, even if just to connect to other carriers around the state. While waiting for your luggage, take a look at the collection of stuffed Alaskan animals and fish on the upper level. The city skyline and Chugach Mountains are visible from up here; go out, breathe the air, dig the view, and indulge in a private smile—you finally made it to Alaska.

Anchorage International Airport is six miles southwest of downtown. An information booth (open daily 9 a.m.-5 p.m.) is located near the baggage area; if they're closed, check the racks for free brochures. You can store luggage nearby for $2-5/day, depending upon the size, tel. (907) 248-0373. People Mover bus route 6 ($1) runs from the lower level into downtown Anchorage every hour Mon.-Fri. 6 a.m.-10 p.m., every two hours 8 a.m.-8 p.m. on Saturday; no service on Sunday or holidays. Taxi fare is approximately $12 to or from downtown, and there's always a line of cabs waiting out front.

Airlines

Many of the big domestic carriers fly into and out of Anchorage—including **Alaska,** tel. (800) 426-0333; **America West,** tel. (800) 235-9292; **American,** tel. (800) 433-7300; **Continental,** tel. (800) 523-3273; **Delta,** tel. (800) 221-1212; **Northwest,** tel. (800) 225-2525; **Reno Air,** tel. (800) 736-6247; and **United,** tel. (800) 241-6522—so your flying options are great. Most of these arrive via Seattle, but Northwest also has direct flights from Minneapolis-St. Paul. In the last few years, competition has helped keep prices low between Seattle and Anchorage, sometimes dipping to $80 one-way. Check with any travel agent for the best deals. Alaska Airlines now offers service from Anchorage to eastern Russia—Magadan, Khabarovsk, Vladivostok, and Petropavlovsk-Kamchatski—during the summer. **Aeroflot,** tel. (907) 248-8400, also has service to Russia's far east, if you dare fly with them. In addition, **Korean Air,** tel. (800) 438-5000, provides direct connections between Anchorage and Asia, often for excellent rates.

Alaska's larger regional airlines are: **Reeve Aleutian Airways,** tel. (800) 544-2248; **Era Aviation,** tel. (907) 243-3322 or (800) 866-8394; **PenAir,** tel. (907) 243-2323 or (800) 448-4226; and **SouthCentral Air,** tel. (907) 283-3926 or (800) 478-2550. All offer daily service to cities and villages in other parts of Alaska. Reeve Aleutian is an old company with an excellent reputation and classy planes.

If you're looking to save money on airfares, check the "Travel-Transportation" section of the classifieds in the *Anchorage Daily News;* several local travel agencies always have discount fares listed, sometimes with rates lower than you might find from Lower 48 travel agents.

Alaska Railroad

The daily express to Fairbanks on Alaska Railroad, First Ave., tel. (907) 265-2494 or (800) 544-0552, has prices comparable to those of the tour buses but is a much more comfortable, historical, enjoyable, and leisurely ride. The express departs Anchorage mid-May through mid-September at 8:30 a.m. for **Denali** (arriving around 4 p.m., $95 one-way) and **Fairbanks** (arriving 8:30 p.m., $135 one-way). The express also stops in Wasilla, Talkeetna, and Nenana, and you can hop off there, but you're not allowed to check any luggage—only what you can carry on.

The local service (self-propelled rail diesel car) departs Anchorage on Sunday, Wednesday, and Saturday for Hurricane Gulch (south side of Broad Pass *before* Denali), and costs just $88 roundtrip. This is flag-stop service; a good way to meet rural Alaskans. A variety of possible rail/lodging and rail/lodging/air options are listed in Alaska Railroad's brochure.

Princess Tours, tel. (800) 835-8907; and **Gray Line,** tel. (907) 277-5581 or (800) 544-2206, hook their superdome cars to the back of the express for an old-fashioned luxury rail experience. These are mostly for the cruise ship crowd, but they also sell seats to independent travelers. Be ready to plunk down $343 pp for an Anchorage-Denali-Anchorage trip that includes an overnight at a hotel near the park; or $280 from Anchorage to Fairbanks for a trip that includes an overnight near Denali.

Take the Alaska Railroad to **Seward** for a fantastic over-the-top voyage across the Kenai Peninsula. The route diverges from the highway near Portage, and then winds steeply into the Kenai Mountains past several glaciers. Daily train service costs $50 one-way or $80 roundtrip. See "Transportation" under "Whittier" for details of **Portage-to-Whittier** train service, another unique and interesting ride.

Buses

There is no central station for longhaul buses in Anchorage, and schedules and prices change frequently. The companies themselves seem to change almost as rapidly, so use the information below only as a guide. Many of these companies will take bikes along for an extra $10 or so.

Alaskon Express buses (Gray Line's public transportation), tel. (800) 544-2206, depart for Haines ($185), Whitehorse ($190), and Skagway ($205) every Sunday, Tuesday, and Friday at 7 a.m. All these runs overnight at Beaver Creek in the Yukon. Lodging ($40 s or $80 d in thin-walled rooms) and food are extra. These buses only run between mid-May and mid-September.

Alaska Direct, tel. (907) 277-6652, or (800) 770-6652, has year-round van service to Fairbanks ($65), Denali National Park ($45), Whitehorse ($145), and Skagway ($180). **Seward Bus Lines,** tel. (907) 278-0800, runs daily vans year-round to Girdwood ($21) and Seward ($30). **Homer Stage Line,** tel. (907) 272-8644, runs to Cooper Landing ($35), Soldotna ($40), and Homer ($45)—summers only. **Alaska Backpacker Shuttle,** tel. (907) 344-8775 or (800) 266-8625, heads to Denali ($35), Talkeetna ($30), and Portage ($20) from mid-May to mid-September. **Alaska Transportation Moon Bay Express,** tel. (907) 274-6454, has summertime vans to Denali for $35.

GETTING AROUND

City Bus

People Mover, Anchorage's public bus system, covers the entire sprawling Anchorage Basin. Because it is mostly a commuter line, weekday service is extensive, with all 23 routes operating 6 a.m.-10 p.m. On Saturday, most lines run 8 a.m.-8 p.m., but 90% of the company rests on Sunday. The **Transit Center** is at Sixth and G, where you can pick up a "Ride Guide" timetable of all routes for $1. The Transit Center is open Mon.-Fri. 7 a.m.-6 p.m.; or call (907) 343-6543 for specific instructions on where and when to catch the People Mover to your destination. Store bags in the lockers here for $2 per day. Exact fare ($1 for adults, or 50 cents for children) is required, and transfers (10 cents) are valid only on a different bus traveling in the same direction within two hours of the time of receipt. People Mover buses are free all day in the downtown area; just get onboard and ride.

Cycling

Anchorage is wild about bicycles. The city has 200 miles of urban cycling/jogging trails; get bike trail maps at the ACVB. A great ride goes 10 miles from the west end of Third Ave. along the **Coastal Trail,** past Westchester Lagoon, Earthquake Park, and Point Woronzof, and then all the way to Kincaid Park at Point Campbell, out on the western tip of the city. The **Chester Creek Trail** meets the Coastal Trail at Westchester Lagoon and takes you almost five miles to Goose Lake, where you can take a dip if you're hot. Another popular ride is to get on C St. heading south to Dimond Blvd., then head west (right) along Campbell Creek to Campbell Lake. Or just bomb around to wherever the wind blows you. For mountain bike rentals, try **Anchorage Coastal Bicycle Rentals,** tel. (907) 279-1999; **Bicycle Shop,** 1035 W. Northern Lights Blvd., tel. (907) 272-5219; **Downtown Bicycle Rental,** 145 W. Sixth Ave., tel. (907) 279-5293 (fun T-shirts here too); **Midtown Bicycle Rentals,** 1317 W. Northern Lights Blvd., tel. (907) 258-6100; and **Sunshine Sports,** 1231 W. Northern Lights Blvd., tel. (907) 272-6444. Bike tours into outlying areas are offered by **Birch Bark Mountain Biking Adventures,** tel. (907) 345-9055; and **Alaska Two-Wheel Tours,** tel. (907) 522-1430.

Taxis

Taxis are expensive: most charge about $2 flag drop and $1.50 per mile thereafter. The companies include: **Alaska Cab,** tel. (907) 563-5353; **Anchorage Taxicab,** tel. (907) 278-8000; **Yellow Cab,** tel. (907) 272-2422; and **Checker Cab,** tel. (907) 276-1234. Common fares are: around downtown $4; downtown to Midtown $7; downtown to the airport $12. There's always a line of waiting cabs outside the airport if you are just arriving and need a way into Anchorage.

Rental Cars

Anchorage is a car-happy city, so rental cars can be very hard to come by during the summer. Making car reservations just a few days in advance comes in handy, but as much as two months can be needed to be sure of a car in the peak season. All the major car rental companies (Affordable, Dollar, Hertz, Avis, National, Payless, Budget, Rent A Wreck, Thrifty, etc.) operate from Anchorage, offering rates starting around $40/day with unlimited mileage. The best rates are frequently through Budget, tel. (907) 561-0350 or (800) 722-6484; and **Denali Car Rental,** tel. (907) 276-1230 or (800) 757-1230. Many of these companies also rent 4WD vehicles and vans. See the Yellow Pages for a complete listing of local car rental companies and their 800 numbers. Don't even think of renting a car and leaving it elsewhere in Alaska; the charges are sky-high for this luxury. Try not to take the first price car rental places quote. Be sure to mention it if you have an AAA card or are a member of Costco; you can often save substantially on the rates.

Several places let you borrow honkin' Alaska-size RV land yachts—the ones you sit behind for miles as they waddle down the road at 30 mph and four miles to the gallon. Two of the better companies are **Clippership Motorhome Rentals,** tel. (907) 562-7051; and **Alaska Economy RVs,** tel. (907) 248-7723. Check the Yellow Pages under "Recreational Vehicles—Renting & Leasing" for others, priced around $125-150/day in the summer. Recreational vehicles may be of some value for groups of six or more but are completely unnecessary for smaller groups. Avoid RVs if at all possible; the state already has far too many folks driving them.

TOURS

By Foot
Anchorage Historic Properties, tel. (907) 274-3600, leads hour-long summertime walking tours of downtown for $5 ($4 for seniors, $1 for kids). They begin from old city hall at 524 W. Fourth Avenue. Several companies offer day-hikes into the country around Anchorage; pick up their brochures from the ACVB or call one of the following for specifics: **Alaska Trail & Sail,** tel. (907) 346-1234; **Chugach Hiking Tours,** tel. (907) 278-4453; and **Alpina Tours,** tel. (907) 783-2482.

By Bus
At least a half-dozen tour companies are happy to sell you bus tours of Anchorage and the surrounding area. Unless you're very short on time and long on tender, skip the city tour. Besides, half the fun of cities is finding your own way around. For the canned version, hop on the red **Anchorage City Trolleys** in front of the Fourth Avenue Theater, tel. (907) 257-5603. These operate daily May-Oct., and cost $10 for an hour-long tour through town. Other companies offer longer versions that include a visit to the museum. Mainly for cruise ship folks, these cost $25. For more adventure, plunk down $55 for a bus-and-boat trip to Portage Glacier, or $74 for

a too-quick combination city and glacier tour. Stop by the ACVB for brochures from the various tour bus operators, or wander along Fourth and Fifth Aves. where most of them have their offices. The larger companies—Gray Line/Westours, Alaska Sightseeing/Cruise West, and Princess—also offer a wide range of other package trips on land, sea, or air throughout Alaska.

By Boat
Although there are no boat tours out of Anchorage, it *is* a good place to check out the different boat trips across Prince William Sound. Several tour companies—including **Gray Line, Alaska Sightseeing/Cruise West,** and **Phillips**—offer trips that include a bus from Anchorage to Portage, train to Whittier, boat across the Sound, and flight or bus ride back to Anchorage. Or get to Whittier on your own and hop on one of these tour boats; see "Whittier" below for specifics.

Alaska Marine Highway's southwest ferry routes do not reach Anchorage, but you can connect up with the system in Whittier or Seward via the Alaska Railroad. The ferry to Valdez passes within sight of massive Columbia Glacier, the budget way to see the Sound; continue on to Cordova, Seward, Homer, Kodiak, etc., or take the bus back to Anchorage via the magnificent Richardson Highway. Call (800) 642-0066 for ferry schedule or prices. The ferry has an Anchorage office inside the Alaska Public Lands Information Center at Fourth and F, tel. (907) 272-7116 (general), or (907) 272-4482 (arrival and departure times). The Alaska Marine Highway's toll-free number is (800) 642-0066.

GORDY OHLIGER

VICINITY OF ANCHORAGE

CHUGACH STATE PARK

Alaska's second-largest chunk of state-owned land, Chugach State Park encompasses nearly half a million acres—half the size of Delaware. The park covers the entire Chugach Range from Eagle River, 25 miles north of Anchorage, to Girdwood, 35 miles south. It could take a committed hiker years to explore all its trails, ridges, peaks, and passes. From the easy 3.5-mile roundtrip hike to Flattop Mountain in Anchorage, to the 25-mile trek from the Eagle River Visitor Center over Crow Pass down to Girdwood, you have a wide range of trails to choose from, each varying in length, elevation, difficulty, access, and congestion. See Jenny Zimmerman's *A Naturalist's Guide to Chugach State Park, Alaska* for the full story.

Pick up hiking brochures at the Alaska Public Lands Information Center in Anchorage, decide on a trail, then dress for rain! The clouds often sit down on these city-surrounding mountaintops and when it's sunny and hot in Anchorage, it could be hailing only a few minutes away on the trails. But don't let that stop you. This whole park is within a few miles of the largest city north of Vancouver and west of Edmonton, where over 60% of Alaska's population huddles, but up in these mountains it's easy to pretend you're a hundred years behind the crowds, and all the hustle and bustle on the Inlet flats is far in the future.

Practicalities

Developed **campgrounds** are found at Eklutna Lake and Eagle River north of Anchorage, and at Bird Creek to the south. The latter two are almost always filled to capacity; all three have four-day limits, outhouses, and water. They are generally open May-September. Rates run $10 at Eklutna Lake, $10 at Bird Creek, and $15 at Eagle River. Or plunk down $150 ($75 for Alaskan residents) for a season pass, good for a full year of camping privileges in any of Alaska's state parks. Call (907) 345-5014 for details. A wonderful cabin ($35/night) can be rented on the shore of Eklutna Lake; call (907) 269-8400 for details.

The **Chugach State Park Visitor Center** sits at the end of 11-mile Eagle River Rd., which leaves the Glenn Highway 13 miles north of Anchorage. For a 24-hour recorded message about naturalist programs, guided hikes, and trail conditions, call (907) 694-6391. To file a trip plan with the main office of Chugach rangers, call (907) 345-5014.

Activities

Hiking is the main one, with about a dozen well-maintained, well-used, moderate-to-difficult trails. You share this wilderness with the usual land and air creatures; photography and wildlife-watching go hand in hand with hiking. Rock-climbing is poor due to the sedimentary and metamorphic composition of the mountains, but snow-and ice-climbing are possible year-round, with permanent freezing conditions above the 6,000-foot level. Boating is popular at Eklutna Lake, and rafters and kayakers on Class II Eagle River can put in at two access points (Miles 7.5 and 9) on Eagle River Road.

NORTH OF ANCHORAGE

Arctic Valley

Six miles north along the Glenn Highway is the exit to Arctic Valley Rd., which climbs seven steep miles to the parking lot at the Alpenglow ski area (see "Downhill Skiing" under "Winter Recreation" in the Anchorage section). A trailhead about a mile before road's end leads to long **Ship Creek Trail,** which with a little cross-country hiking hooks up with Bird Creek and Indian Creek Trails via the passes of the same names. It's 22 miles from Arctic Valley to Indian Creek Trailhead. Plan on two or three days to do this traverse. From the Alpenglow parking lot a two-mile trail goes up to **Rendezvous Peak,** an easy hike with great views of the city, inlet, and even Mt. McKinley if you're lucky.

A dozen miles up the Glenn from Anchorage is the Hiland Rd. exit that takes you 1.5 miles to **Eagle River Campground,** $15. Get here early

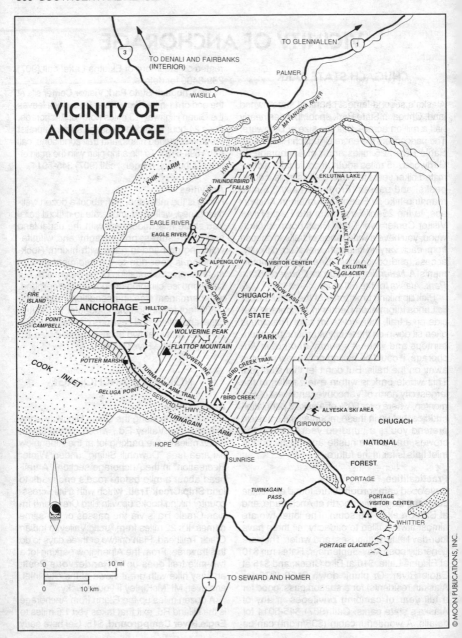

VICINITY OF
ANCHORAGE

© MOON PUBLICATIONS, INC.

in the day to claim a spot in this too popular camping spot on the south side of Eagle River.

Eagle River Area

Take the Eagle River exit at Mile 13 of the Glenn, then your first right onto Eagle River Rd., a dazzling, paved, 11-mile ride right into the heart of the Chugach. The road ends at the parking lot to the **Chugach State Park Visitor Center,** which features a "close-up corner" with furs and a track book, as well as an aurora display, and T-shirts and postcards for sale. The center is open Fri.-Mon. 11 a.m.-7 p.m. in the summer, and is staffed by state park rangers, tel. (907) 694-2108. The **Rodak Nature Trail** is a wide gravel route, a half-mile roundtrip, with informative signs on snow, glaciers, forest, the sun, etc. It's 15 minutes well spent. For a longer walk, take the seven-mile **River Trail** along the Eagle River.

For one of the longest and most scenic hikes in the park, get on 25-mile-long **Crow Pass Trail.** This trail (also known as the Historic Iditarod Trail) provided a turn-of-the-century overland route from Seward through the Chugach to the Interior gold mining town of Iditarod. The gradual climb to Crow Pass fords several streams, including Eagle River midway along the trail. It might be wise to camp overnight and cross the river in the morning, when the glacial runoff is lower. Raven Glacier and Crystal Lake are scenic highlights near Crow Pass, where you leave Chugach State Park and continue in immense Chugach National Forest. The Forest Service has a very popular A-frame **cabin** on the summit that you can rent for $25/night. Call (907) 271-2500 for details. From here it's four miles down to the trailhead on rough Crow Creek Rd., then another five miles to the Alyeska Ski Resort access road. Experienced skiers sometimes use the Iditarod/Crow Pass Trails for a winter traverse of the mountains, but be aware that avalanche danger can be very high.

Eklutna Village

This is one of those surprising discoveries just off the Glenn Highway. Take the Eklutna Rd. exit (26 miles northeast of Anchorage), and cross back over the highway to **St. Nicholas Russian Orthodox Church** and the **Tanaina "Spirit Houses."** From this point, at the site of the first Tanaina (a branch of Athabascan) settlement

on the Inlet, down through the western Kenai Peninsula, Kodiak, and the Aleutians, Russian Orthodoxy is strongly overlaid on the Native culture. The ancestors of most of these Indians were converted by Russian missionaries, and the church—dating from the 1830s—is the oldest building in the Anchorage area. The miniature log chapel, set against a backdrop of colorful "spirit-house" headstones, is one of the most photographed in Alaska. Half-hour tours ($3.50) are offered daily 8 a.m.-6 p.m. mid-May to mid-September; the rest of the year you'll have to look in from the picket fence. There's also a small gift shop. Call (907) 696-2828 for details.

Eklutna Lake Area

On the opposite side of the highway, Eklutna Rd. follows Eklutna River 10 miles to Eklutna Lake. A pleasant, small campground ($10) is at the lake at the end of the road, with outhouses and a large picnic area. The 14-mile **Lakeside Trail-Eklutna Glacier Trail** skirts the west side of Eklutna Lake and then climbs to this very scenic glacier. Three side trails lead off the main route to Twin Peaks, Bold Ridge, and East Fork of Eklutna River. This is an outstanding mountain biking area in summer, or wintertime ski/snow-machine trail. Most of the route is also open to ATVs Sun.-Wed., so you may not have peace and quiet. Experienced skiers may want to continue beyond Eklutna Glacier via a multiglacier traverse that takes them 31 miles to Crow Pass. The Alaska Mountaineering Club (P.O. Box 102037, Anchorage, AK 99510) has three huts along the way. Call the Alaska Mountaineering & Hiking store at (907) 272-1811 for details.

From the Eklutna exit, you can follow the access road a mile south to **Thunderbird Falls** (if you're heading north from Anchorage, there's a marked Thunderbird Falls exit before you reach the Eklutna exit). The trail takes you on an easy mile hike up Thunderbird Creek. From there follow your ears to the falls.

EAST OF ANCHORAGE

Four trailheads on the city's southeastern outskirts give access to a network of crisscrossing and connecting trails in the section of the range that hems in Anchorage Bowl. They're all off

MT. GORDON LYON   HURDY GURDY MTN.   TIKISHLA MTN.   TEMPTATION PEAK   WOLVERINE PE

Hillside Dr., which skirts a suburb of sparkling glass houses and gorgeous views of the skyline, inlet, and Mt. Susitna to the west. Route 92 buses stop at the corner of DeArmoun Rd. and Hillside Drive. From there, continue on Hillside Dr. uphill till you come to Upper Huffman Rd., and go right. In a half-mile, go right again onto aptly named Toilsome Hill Drive. Toil uphill for 2.5 miles to get to the **Glen Alps Trailhead.** Take a look from the overlook near the parking lot, and then head up the **Flattop Mountain Trail** for even better looks. This extremely popular 3.5-mile roundtrip hike gains 1,500 feet and is very steep near the top as you scramble through the boulders. Also from the Glen Alps Trailhead are several moderate and very scenic hikes: **Little O'Malley Peak,** 7 1/2 miles roundtrip; the **Ramp and Wedge,** 11 miles roundtrip; and **Williwaw Lakes,** 13 miles roundtrip. A great mountain bike route is the 11-mile (one-way) **Powerline Trail** that also takes off from the Glen Alps Trailhead and goes over 3,550-foot Powerline Pass all the way to the Indian Creek Trailhead on Turnagain Arm.

Continue north on Hillside past Upper Huffman Rd. and take a right on Upper O'Malley Road. The second left leads to **Prospect Heights Trailhead,** where the **Wolverine Peak Trail** leads to the top of this 4,455-foot mountain (11 miles roundtrip). You'll discover great views of the Alaska Range and Anchorage, but go in late summer when the snow has melted.

SOUTH OF ANCHORAGE

Potter Marsh Area

Potter Marsh is on the south end of Anchorage, with a boardwalk over the edge of the marsh. This is a good spot to look for over 80 kinds of waterfowl, including Canada geese, trumpeter swans, and even the flyin'-fool Arctic terns. Bring binoculars. This marsh was created when the railroad builders installed an embankment to protect the track from Turnagain Arm's giant tides, which dammed the freshwater drainage from the mountains.

A mile south on the other side of the highway is the **Potter Section House,** a small railroad museum of interpretive displays and signs outside, and inside, the restored original "section" house. This is also headquarters for Chugach State Park; get brochures on local trails here. Check out the nine-foot rotary snowplow (to clear avalanches), the track display, and an excellent signboard on Alaska Railroad's use of high-tech: microwave repeaters, solar crossing guards, electromagnetic tampers, and articulated flatcars. A small gift shop sells railroad memorabilia and books. Open Mon.-Fri. 8 a.m.-4:30 p.m. year-round.

Turnagain Arm Trail

Across the highway from Potter Section House is the parking lot for **Potter Creek Trailhead,** the first access to the Turnagain Arm Trail, which parallels the highway for over nine miles. The

NAINA PEAK — O'MALLEY PEAK — FLATTOP MTN. — MT. WILLIWAW — PTARMIGAN MTN. — SUICIDE PEAK — McHUGH PEAK

trail began as a turn-of-the-century wagon road built to transport railroad workers and supplies. This is a very popular early-summer path since its south-facing slopes lose the snow early. In three miles is McHugh Creek Picnic Area, a day-use area and trailhead for the seven-mile hike up to **Rabbit Lake**. You can continue south on Turnagain Arm Trail past three more trailheads all the way to **Windy Corner Trailhead** nine miles from your starting point, and not far from Beluga Point.

Beluga Point

Twenty miles south of Anchorage is Beluga Point, a good place to see these small white whales cavorting in Turnagain Arm in late May and late August (they follow salmon into these shallow waters). Look behind you for the **Dall sheep** that often wander close to the highway in this area. Or just have a picnic and wait for the Cook Inlet's famous **bore tides.** The tides here, at 30 feet, are among the world's highest, and the lead breaker can be up to eight feet high, and a half-mile across, and can move at over 10 miles per hour. This is the only bore tide in the U.S., created when a large body of water (Cook Inlet) is forced by strong tidal action into a narrow shallow one (Turnagain Arm). Look for a series of small swells (two to three feet high, larger depending on the wind) that crash against the rocks and send up a mighty spray. You won't soon forget the roar of the bore, which goes by Beluga Point roughly two hours after low tide

in Anchorage—check the tide tables in the daily newspapers. One warning: do not go out on the mudflats at any time. The mixture of glacial silt and mud creates quicksand; a number of people have drowned after getting their feet stuck in the mud and being inundated by the incoming tide. Don't take a chance!

Indian and Bird Creeks

Twenty-five miles south of Anchorage, and right before Turnagain House Restaurant in Indian (an old gold town), take a left on the gravel road and head 1.5 miles through Indian Valley to the **Indian Creek Trailhead.** This trail, which follows Indian Creek over Indian Pass (especially rewarding during Indian summer), is six miles of easy walking on a well-maintained path. You can then continue for several miles of undeveloped hiking till you hook up with the Ship Creek Trail, which runs 22 miles to Arctic Valley north of Anchorage. The Powerline Pass Trail (see above) goes 11 miles from the Glenn Alps trailhead and also nearly reaches Indian Creek Trail; you cross-country hike about a quarter-mile on the ridge to hook up.

Two miles down the highway from the turnoff to Indian Creek is the Bird Creek area. It features two trails, the first up the ridge and the second along Bird Creek to Bird Pass. Also here is the **Bird Creek Campground** ($10). This thickly forested campground is almost always full of anglers working Bird Creek. A bike trail runs right through the middle of it.

GIRDWOOD TO WHITTIER

At Mile 90 of the Seward Highway, you leave Chugach State Park and cross into immense Chugach National Forest. Covering nearly six million acres, this national forest encompasses the entire Prince William Sound area, plus part of the Kenai Peninsula. From here to Seward, the land and all its facilities are managed by the U.S. Forest Service. Two towns—Girdwood and Whittier—are outposts of civilization surrounded by this, the nation's second-largest national forest.

GIRDWOOD

Go left at Girdwood Station (Mile 90), site of the town before it was leveled by the earthquake. The access road runs three miles to new Girdwood and **Alyeska Ski Resort.** Only 40 scenic miles from 240,000 people, this winter resort even in summer is a favorite destination for Anchoragites, package tourists, unsuspecting travelers, and the occasional backpacker who likes a quick ride to the alpine tundra. Don't mistake the end of the road for a tour-bus convention—it's okay to park your car here, too.

First check out the resort itself, a classic Alaskan tourist trap. If you're still solvent after the food, dessert, T-shirts, souvenirs, etc., fork over $16 to ride the six-minute **tram** up Mt. Alyeska (2,300 feet). On top are two restaurants, and what *Condé Nast Traveler* rated the best view of any American ski resort. The two 60-passenger tram cars started running in 1993 and are entirely wheelchair accessible. Follow the well-marked trail to the alpine overlook onto cute Alyeska Glacier. If you have reservations to dine at Seven Glaciers restaurant, the tram ride is a mere $6.

Finally, stop off at the **Candle Factory,** on the access road a half-mile from Seward Highway, tel. (907) 346-1920. The candles they sell are not only unique and inexpensive souvenirs or gift items, they also burn till the cows come home without smoke or odor. The candlemakers start with a soapstone sculpture of a wildlife image from which they form a silicone mold. Then they pour in a mixture of paraffin, stearic acid, Alaska crude, and seal-oil by-product, heat at 200° for seven hours, *et voilà!* Small candles start at $3, large guys go for around $12. Don't miss the Candle Factory.

Crow Creek Mine, three miles out Crow Creek Rd., tel. (907) 278-8060, open daily 9 a.m.-6 p.m. May 15-September 15, is the site of one of the earliest gold strikes in Alaska (1896). Eight of the original mine buildings are been restored and are open; $3 entrance charge, or drop another $2 to pan for gold. Overnight campsites are available for $5. There's a gift shop on-site. It's a pretty place.

Activities

A mile before the resort is a gravel access road (six miles) to **Crow Pass Trailhead.** It's 3.5 miles to the pass, with a 2,000-foot elevation gain. You pass old mining ruins and a Forest Service cabin; a half-mile beyond the pass is Raven Glacier, where you enter Chugach State Park (see above). **Alpine Air,** tel. (907) 783-2360, offers a one-hour flight with a glacier landing for $99 pp. They also do floatplane tours of Prince William Sound, drop-off fishing flights, and statewide charters year-round.

Skiing

Alyeska Resort is at the center of winter activity in Southcentral Alaska. Over the last few years the resort has undergone a $70 million expansion that added several lifts and new runs, a 60-passenger aerial tram, six restaurants (including the Pond Cafe for breakfast, lunch, and dinner, the Katsura Teppanyaki Japanese steakhouse at the hotel level, and the Seven Glaciers and the Glacier Express self-service restaurants at the top of the mountain), and an elaborate hotel complex. The resort now covers 500 skiable acres and has 60 trails, a tram, seven chair lifts, and two pony lifts. Most of the ski runs are at the intermediate or advanced level. In addition to abundant natural snowfall (depths generally exceed 10 feet), there is snowmaking capability on the lower slopes.

Alyeska Resort generally opens for skiing in mid-November and closes the end of April. Hours are daily 10:30 a.m.-5:30 p.m., with night skiing till Wed.-Sat. till 9:30 p.m. ($10 extra); reduced hours early and late in the season. A shuttle bus connects the main ski area with the new Alyeska Prince Hotel (where the tram departs).

Adult lift tickets cost $38 full day, $26 half-day; on Friday and Saturday there's night skiing. A half-day ticket plus night skiing will run you $31. There are discounts for children, students, and multiday passes. Skis, snowshoes, snowboards, and ice skates (for use on their skating pond) can be rented in the daylodge, where you can also get expensive cafeteria food and check out the latest in Alaskan ski fashions. More cafeteria fare, along with an elaborate restaurant and lounge, is on top of the mountain. Ski classes at all levels are available. Traffic between Anchorage and Girdwood can back up on winter weekends, so head out early, or leave the driving to the Alaska Railroad or one of the bus companies listed under "Transportation," below. Call (907) 754-1111 for more information on Alyeska. Phone (907) 754-7669 for the latest snow conditions (24 hours).

Accommodations
Heading toward the resort on the access road, go right on Timberline, pass gorgeous ski chalets, then turn right again on Alpina. Around a couple of curves is the **Alyeska Home Hostel,** tel. (907) 783-2099. This is a great place, with eight beds in the sleeping loft, a kitchen and a bathroom downstairs, and a wood-burning sauna out back (no shower); $10 pp. Make reservations (required) at the Anchorage hostel, tel. (907) 276-3635. Other Girdwood lodging places are **Alyeska View B&B,** tel. (907) 783-2747; and **Alyeska Accommodations,** tel. (907) 783-2010. The sparkling 307-room **Westin Alyeska Prince,** tel. (907) 754-1111 or (800) 880-3880, opened in late 1994 and offers some of the fanciest lodging in Alaska. The eight-story hotel features four restaurants, a fitness center, an indoor swimming pool, and a whirlpool to work all that food off. The tram to the top of Mt. Alyeska is right out the back door. The Japanese investors who own Alyeska did this one right.

Food
At the intersection of the Girdwood Spur Rd. and Seward Highway is a strip mall with a variety of services. There's a gas station and 7-Eleven (open 24 hours), a video store, Glacier Gifts, the Taco's restaurant, even a chiropractor to ease the pain of those long car rides. The **Alpine Diner & Bakery,** tel. (907) 783-2550, serves breakfast, lunch, and dinner, and has fresh-baked treats, espresso drinks, and ice cream. Meals include sandwiches, burgers, seafood, pizza, and Italian dinners $9-14. **Taco's** has very good Tex-Mex food, reasonably priced.

At the Alyeska resort is the **Bake Shop,** a good spot for lunch. Homemade sourdough bread, breakfast, soups and stews, sandwiches, ice cream, and pizza fill out the menu.

Up top, **Seven Glaciers Restaurant,** billed as casual fine dining, offers excellent food with one of the best views you're ever likely to get while dining. Sitting on a crag at 2,303 feet above sea level, you can see the valley below, across to the Crow Pass area, and up Turnagain Arm. Main courses run $18-$24, desserts are spectacular, and if you're feeling especially flush, you can top off your meal with a $100 snifter of cognac. *Trés élégante,* but not at all stuffy or pretentious. The seven-minute tram ride gives you the chance to survey the area, and if you've got dinner reservations, you get a break on the price of the ride.

Girdwood itself, on the other side of the access road, has several restaurants, a post office, and a laundromat with showers ($1.50). **Girdwood Griddle** is the local coffee shop.

The famous **Double Musky Inn,** tel. (907) 783-2822, is a quarter-mile up Crow Creek Rd. on the left, open Tues.-Thurs. 4:30-10 p.m., and Fri.-Sun. 4-10 p.m., no reservations taken. Owned by Bob and Deanna Persons, this 100-seat restaurant serves 300 dinners on a typical night—in other words, crowded and loud, with long waits and brief visits from your server. But as soon as the food comes, none of that makes any difference. No need to sample the appetizers, unusual though they may be; save *all* your room for dinner. Cajun shrimp, scallops, halibut, or salmon dishes go for $20, chicken is $16, steaks from $20; all come with vegetables, potatoes, and trendy rolls. The house specialty is French Pepper Steak, $22, which is the biggest, juiciest, and tastiest slab you've ever been served. One diner had managed to polish off a good third of it when his tipsy Scottish companion looked over and exclaimed, "Have you not *started* your steak yet?" Light eaters can get dinner and five sandwiches out of it.

Transportation

Two companies offer bus service to Girdwood from Anchorage and on south to Seward or Homer: **Seward Bus Lines,** tel. (907) 563-0800 in Anchorage and (907) 224-3608 in Seward, charges $21 one-way Anchorage to Girdwood. **Alaskon Express,** tel. (907) 277-5581, charges $25 to Alyeska Resort. **Alaska Railroad,** tel. (907) 265-2494 or (800) 544-0552, offers a wintertime ski train between Anchorage and Girdwood. Otherwise, it should be an easy hitchhike down the Seward Highway.

PORTAGE GLACIER

At Mile 79 of the Seward Highway (48 miles south of Anchorage) is the staging and loading facility for the Alaska Railroad to Whittier (see "Transportation" under "Whittier" below). One mile farther is the 5.5-mile access road through Portage Valley to Portage Glacier. A town that stood on this corner was destroyed when the 1964 earthquake dropped the land six to 10

feet. Salt water from Turnagain Arm inundated the area, killing the still-standing trees. Portage Glacier is the number-one tourist attraction in Alaska, with roughly 700,000 visitors each year. If you're here on a clear weekend day, you might think that all 700,000 of them are here with you.

Seeing the Glacier

The Forest Service's **Begich, Boggs Visitor Center** is a beautiful facility named after Nicholas Begich (U.S. representative from Alaska) and Hale Boggs (majority leader of the U.S. Senate), whose plane disappeared in the area in 1972; they were never found. The center, tel. (907) 783-3242, is open daily 9 a.m.-7 p.m. in summer, and Thurs.-Mon. 10 a.m.-5 p.m. the rest of the year. No charge. The visitor center and Portage Glacier are now the most popular stopping places for tourists in all of Alaska. A large picture window overlooks the narrow outlet of Portage Lake, where icebergs jam up after floating down from Portage Glacier. Note, however, that the glacier itself is on the opposite side of the lake. You'll need to get much closer to appreciate its magnitude.

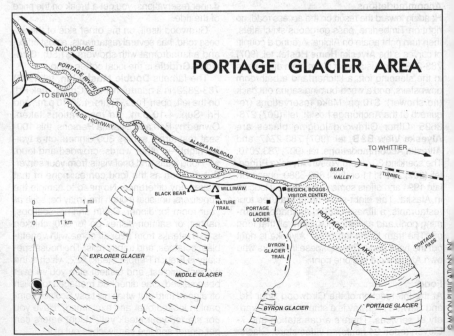

PORTAGE GLACIER AREA

The visitor center boasts an amazing array of displays, including an ice cave, a "live" iceberg hauled in from the lake, an engrossing relief map of local icefields, and everything you ever wanted to know about glaciers, including moving displays on glacial motion and crevasses. Don't miss the vial of tiny iceworms, which inhabit the surfaces of glaciers, feeding on pollen grains and red algae and surviving within a very delicate near-freezing temperature range. There's also good footage on iceworms in the 20-minute movie, *Voices From the Ice,* shown every 45 minutes 9:30 a.m.-5:30 p.m.; $1 suggested donation. During the summer, Forest Service naturalists lead half-mile **"iceworm safaris"** from the Byron Glacier Trailhead at 7 p.m. Tuesday and Friday evenings. They also put on **campfire programs** five nights a week at the Williwaw Campground. Get to the glacier itself on a Westours boat (see "Practicalities," below). There's also an **observation platform** near the Williwaw Campground where you can see spawning red and chum salmon in late summer.

Hiking

Two hikes are within walking distance of the visitor center. The **Moraine Loop Trail,** accessible from the path to the lodge, is a five-minute stroll through typical moraine vegetation; Portage Glacier occupied this ground only 100 years ago. Interpretive signs explain some of the vegetation, and there's an awesome overlook of the parking lot. Follow the access road past the visitor center (south) just under a mile. At the back of the parking lot starts the **Byron Glacier Trail,** an easy three-quarter-mile walk along the runoff stream to below this hanging glacier.

Practicalities

Two Forest Service **campgrounds** along the access road contain 50 sites: large, woodsy, water, toilets. Black Bear campground is $9, Williwaw Creek $10. These campgrounds, like many of the USFS sites on the Kenai, are managed by Facilities Management Incorporated, an independent concessionaire. You can make reservations for several of the campgrounds, including Williwaw Creek, by calling (800) 280-2267. **Portage Glacier Lodge,** across the way from the visitor center, tel. (907) 783-3117, has a cafeteria with surprisingly reasonable prices; try the cross-cut fries for your crunch craving.

To get to Portage Glacier, take the **Seward Bus Lines** van, tel. (907) 563-0800 (in Anchorage), or take the $40 day-trip offered by all the package-tour companies from Anchorage. The Anchorage visitor center has their brochures.

Westours/Gray Line operates the 200-passenger *Ptarmigan* tour boat on Portage Lake; catch it at the dock near the visitor center. These one-hour cruises cost $21 for adults or $10.50 for kids and start at 10:30 a.m., with the last tour at 4:30 p.m. Call (907) 277-5581 or (800) 544-2206 for more info. This boat tour, plus roundtrip bus transportation from Anchorage (stops at Alyeska) costs $57 pp on Gray Line.

WHITTIER

Thousands of tourists pass through this tiny town (pop. 330) every week, transferring from ferries and tour boats to the Alaska Railroad between Anchorage and Prince William Sound. But possibly only a dozen ever *see* Whittier. The vast majority step off the boat right onto the train and miss one of the strangest and friendliest places in Alaska. Since at least five train trips daily hook up to Portage or Anchorage, it's a simple matter to catch the early or late train and avail yourself of Whittier's unique charm. After all, this has to be the only Alaskan town named for a poet (John Greenleaf Whittier).

History

While less well known than the Alaska Highway, the construction of the railway to Whittier was one of the great engineering feats of WW II. Two tunnels, 1,497 and 3,990 yards long, were carved through the Chugach Mountains to link the military bases in Anchorage and Fairbanks to a secret saltwater port. Seward, the main ice-free port in Southcentral Alaska at that time, was considered too vulnerable to Japanese attack, so from 1941 to 1943 the Army blasted through the mountains and laid the tracks that would ensure the flow of supplies for the defense of Alaska. After the defeat of Japan, the military pulled out of Whittier, but a year later they were back as the Cold War began with the Soviet Union. Whittier became a permanent base, and large concrete buildings were built at that time. The 14-story Begich Tower (completed in 1954), an unlikely skyscraper in this small village, is near another

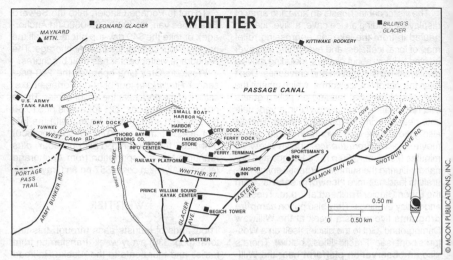

© MOON PUBLICATIONS, INC.

anomaly, the "City Under One Roof," which once housed 1,000 men and was the largest building in Alaska. Why build high-rises? To lessen the need for snow removal in a place where the snow sometimes tops 14 feet.

The base was deactivated in 1960 and the buildings were heavily damaged in the 1964 earthquake. One of them is still vacant, but Begich Tower has been restored and converted into condos. A third high-rise, Whittier Manor, was privately built in the 1950s and later turned into more condos. The military presence today is limited to an oil pipeline that supplies military installations in Anchorage. Until 1992, Whittier was an extremely popular docking place for cruise ships. Deteriorating docking facilities and a four percent sales tax combined to push the ships to Seward. Independent travelers will be able to enjoy Whittier without the hordes of cruise-ship passengers found in most Alaskan port towns.

Sights
Most travelers never get farther than the tourist action on the waterfront, but the town of Whittier is worth exploring. Stop off first at the railroad car that houses the **visitor center,** open daily 11 a.m.-noon and 1-6 p.m. (summers only). Pick up train and charter boat info here. The **Small Boat Harbor** across the road is a misnomer—this large facility has some very big boats.

Follow the signs for Whittier down past the dry dock, then go left across the tracks onto Whittier Street. Take a right on Glacier Ave. to the **Begich Tower.** In its 198 condos live most of the town's population; the rest reside in the 70 condos at **Whittier Manor** (a.k.a. Sportsman's Inn). Your typical three-bedroom sells for less than $20,000 (some for well under $15,000), or rents for $500 a month. Many are owned by Anchoragites who use them as weekend and summer getaways, boosting Whittier's summer population to nearly 1,000.

In room 107 of Begich Tower is the town **museum,** tel. (907) 472-2321, housing one of the state's wildest and most eclectic collections of artifacts. Open daily 11 a.m.-5 p.m., (with luck) you'll almost always have the volunteer staff member entirely to yourself. Check out the Alaskan white, brown, and black coral; the shellfish display preserved by Babs Reynolds (owner of Hobo Bay; see below); the teeth of the wolf fish; the 1951 photo of Whittier; Russian coins; and sealskin etchings. Marvel over the walrus-jaw bootjack, the two-by-eight board punched clean through a 22-inch truck tire by the 1964 tidal wave, and Lori Simonds's collection of Alaska matchbooks. Leave a donation on your way out.

Continue a quarter-mile out Eastern Ave. to quiet, scenic **Smitty's Cove,** where one of Whittier's very few private residences sits. Here you'll discover a great view across Passage Canal of waterfalls, a kittiwake rookery, and giant Billing's Glacier.

Hikes

In back of Begich Tower is a road up a ways to Whittier Creek; from the end of the road at the creek you could bushwack up to the waterfall and close to Whittier Glacier. But the popular trail is up to **Portage Pass.** In the early days when gold was discovered around Hope on the Kenai Peninsula, Hope-bound hopefuls would boat to this harbor, portage their supplies over the glacier pass, and float down Turnagain Arm to their destination. This highly recommended day-hike from Whittier affords splendid views of Passage Canal, Portage Glacier, and the Chugach Mountains. On a clear day the views of the glacier from the Portage Pass area are far superior to those from the Portage Visitor Center, which is accessible by road from Anchorage.

From Whittier station, walk back a mile along the road beside the railway line to the oil tanks and tunnel at the foot of Maynard Mountain. Cross the tracks on the dirt road to the left, but do not cross the river. Take the road to the right and climb southwest along the flank of the mountain up a wide, easy track. If you walk briskly, you can be at Portage Pass (elevation 700 feet) in less than an hour. There are places to camp beside Divide Lake, but beware of strong winds at the pass. From the lake follow the stream down toward the glacier, then find a way via a tributary on the right up onto one of the bluffs for a view of Portage Lake. Deep crevasses in the blue glacial ice are clearly visible from here. **Portage Glacier** has receded far enough that the gold-rush route is no longer traversable, due to the lake, unless you're packing an inflatable raft. You must go back the way you came. This hike is highly recommended; allow a minimum of three hours roundtrip. Note that there is no clear trail beyond Divide Lake; you must find your own way. Do not attempt to walk on the glacier itself, as the crevasses can be deadly.

Sea Kayaking

Prince William Sound Kayak Center, a block in front of Begich Tower, tel. (907) 472-2452 or (907) 562-2866, mainly rents kayaks but also offers instruction and guided tours. For charters and tour-boat rides, see "Tours," below.

Accommodations and Camping

Sportsman's Inn out on Eastern Ave., tel. (907) 472-2352, has large hotel rooms for $65 s, $70 d; **Anchor Inn,** tel. (907) 472-2354, charges the same. The Sportsman's Inn's shuttle bus to the dock is big and brown; the Anchor Inn's is small and yellow. Both have restaurants and bars, though at Anchor Inn the two are combined and you eat among drinkers and pool shooters, with the TV or jukebox on. Another option is **June's B&B,** tel. (907) 472-2396. Condo rooms go for $60 s or $75 d, or $90 with an ocean view, $80 mountain view; all include breakfast.

Designated **camping** behind Begich Tower is good and plentiful, with secluded spots, clearings for tents, and a shelter for cooking and socializing in the rain. You can use the bathrooms on the first floor of Begich Tower if the outdoor pit toilet is uncouth.

Food

Hobo Bay Trading Company on the waterfront is open for lunch and dinner: fresh fish, burgers, burritos, good pies. Something busily local is usually happening here; for a long story, ask Babs how she preserved the shellfish at the museum. **Tsunami Trading Co. Restaurant,** tel. (907) 472-2462, open daily 11 a.m.-9 p.m., bakes wonderful fresh breads and also serves pizza and burgers, while **Cafe Orca** has gourmet coffees and bagels. **Irma's Outpost** serves burgers, deli food, and seafood, and has a liquor store on the premises. The menu at the **Anchor Inn** is the most extensive in town. They serve typical breakfasts and lunches, and seafood, steaks, and pizza for dinner.

Other Practicalities

Both the hotels have small grocery stores, but don't miss the classic **Harbor Store,** a combination grocery/dry goods/clothing/sporting goods/laundromat/hardware/bait-and-tackle/supermarket/department store—all in an ATCO trailer. Not to mention their RV park next door.

BOB RACE

Look out, Wal-Mart! The **post office** is on the first floor of Begich Tower; the **library** is in the firehall. Get **showered** ($3.50) at the Harbor Office, next to Hobo Bay. **Log Cabin Gifts,** tel. (907) 472-2501, features arts and crafts items, locally made mostly by the owner, Wilma Buethe Wilcox. She also carries natural gifts from the wildflower garden, and you can pet, photograph, and even feed the two pet reindeer.

The main Whittier events—other than the rain in summer and snow in winter—are a **sailing regatta** in early May and a summer-long **halibut and salmon derby.**

Transportation

Almost everybody comes in by boat and leaves by train, or vice versa. There are no roads from Whittier to the rest of Alaska, though cars are carried on the train. The MV *Bartlett* connects Whittier to Valdez ($58) most days in the summer. Logistics for taking a vehicle aboard differ from those in Valdez and Cordova. Due to the way the docking facilites are built in Whittier, the ferry comes in bow first, and the entire forward section lifts up and out of the way for loading and unloading. When traveling to and from Whittier, the drill is first on, first off when driving; thus it pays to get to the front of the line so you can get on and off first and secure good seats once you're aboard. The Monday sailing to Cordova is the only trip that doesn't pass Columbia Glacier. See "Tours," below, for other watery options across the Sound.

The **Alaska Railroad** train to Whittier runs under the Chugach Mountains through two three-mile tunnels. You line up by the tracks, drive up the ramp onto flatcars, and ride the train behind your steering wheel. Try to get toward the back for less diesel fumes in the long eerie tunnel. There are also standard railcars for walk-on passengers. This makes an excellent day-trip from the city. A trivia note: The route to Whittier was used in scenes from the 1986 film *Runaway Train.*

Alaska Railroad (tel. 907-265-2607) makes several roundtrips a day between Portage and Whittier, 12 miles, 30 minutes, $13 pp one-way, or $70 roundtrip for car and driver. Portage is 47 highway miles south of Anchorage; it now has a depot housing a ticket office, a gift shop, and offices for a couple of the tour companies that operate out of Whittier. Get here from Anchorage

by driving, hitching, or catching the **Alaska Backpacker Shuttle,** tel. (907) 344-8774 or (800) 266-8625. They charge $20 one-way, $35 roundtrip, and their van meets the trains in Portage. (There is no train service between Anchorage and Portage.)

Tours

The big Alaskan tour operators all run boats between Whittier and Valdez during the summer. There are many options, including day-trips out of Anchorage, overnight trips that include a night in Valdez, or simple one-way crossings with close-up visits to the glaciers.

Phillips Tours and Cruises, 509 Fourth Ave., Anchorage, tel. (907) 276-8023 or (800) 544-0529, operates the 26 Glacier Cruise for $120 (cruise alone), $136 from Portage (includes train fare), or $180 from Anchorage (includes motorcoach ride to and from the big city and train fare). Though the trip aboard the 30-meter high-speed catamaran covers a lot of ground, it still allows plenty of time to linger at the faces of several glaciers, waiting for big things to happen. A hot lunch is included, there's a bar onboard, and the lounges are spacious, providing plenty of room inside should the weather be less than perfect. You can even visit the wheelhouse and see the Sound from the skipper's perspective.

Gray Line of Alaska, 745 W. Fourth Ave., tel. (907) 277-5581 or (800) 544-2206, runs the *Nunatak* right up to Columbia Glacier on its bus-train-boat-hotel-bus tour that goes Anchorage-Whittier-Valdez-Anchorage for $293 pp (two days and one night), or a one-day fly/cruise that features a Whittier-Valdez cruise followed by a flight back to Anchorage for $275 pp.

Renown Charters and Tours, tel. (907) 272-1961 or (800) 655-3806, runs a three-hour cruise out of Whittier for $59 (doesn't include transportation from Anchorage or Portage). They run a morning and an afternoon cruise, with box lunches available for an additional $6, or you can buy snacks onboard.

In addition to these big operators with their mega-boats that hold up to 300 passengers, a number of locals offer trips into Prince William Sound. The prices may be a bit higher, but you get a far more personal trip. See the visitor center for a list of local charter boats. One recommended company for sightseeing, fishing, and kayak drop-offs is **Honey Charters,** tel. (907) 344-3340. Other local operators of cruise/sightseeing/water taxi/charter fishing boats include: **Lazy Otter Charters,** tel. (907) 345-1175; **Sound Eco Adventures,** tel. (907) 333-8209; **Alexandra Inc.,** tel. (907) 272-8989; **Alaska Trail & Sail,** tel. (907) 346-1234; and **Captain Ron,** tel. (907) 235-4368.

PALMER TO VALDEZ

Glenn Highway

Named for Capt. Edwin Glenn, an early Army explorer of the area, this road (Route 1) stretches 328 miles from downtown Anchorage to Tok, where it joins the Alaska Highway. Most of the Glenn was built during the corridor-construction craze of 1942, first from Tok to Gulkana, where it joins the Richardson Highway, then from Glennallen, where it leaves the Richardson, and finally to Palmer. Palmer was already connected to Anchorage by rail; the final 42 miles of road were completed a few years later. Head out Sixth Ave. from downtown Anchortown, past Merrill Field, the Northway Mall, and Fort Richardson, and onto the highway. In 10 miles you pass the exit for Eagle River and the northern section of Chugach State Park. At Mile 29, take a right onto the Old Glenn Highway, the scenic alternate route to Palmer.

PALMER

For its first 20 years, Palmer (pop. 3,500) was little more than a railway depot for Alaska Railroad's Matanuska branch. Then in May 1935, during the height of both the Depression and a severe drought in the Midwest, the Federal Emergency Relief Administration of Pres. Franklin D. Roosevelt's New Deal selected 200 farming families from the relief rolls of northern Michigan, Minnesota, and Wisconsin, and shipped them here to colonize the Matanuska Valley. Starting out in tent cabins, the colonists cleared the dense virgin forest, built houses and barns, and planted crops pioneered at the University of Alaska's Agricultural Experimental Station in Wasilla. These hardy transplanted farmers endured the inevitable first-year hardships, including disease, homesickness, mismanagement, floods, and just plain bad luck. But by the fall of 1936, the misfits had been weeded out, 120 babies had been born in the colony, fertile fields and long summer days were filling barns with crops, and the colonists celebrated with a three-day harvest festival, the forerunner of the big state fair. In a few more years, Palmer had become not only a flourishing town but also the center of a bucolic and beautiful agricultural valley that was and still remains unique in Alaska. The 125-pound pumpkins, 75-pound cabbages, 10-pound onions, and two-pound radishes you might have heard about come from here.

Sights

Driving into Palmer from Wasilla along the Palmer-Wasilla Highway is a lot like driving into Wasilla from the bush on the Parks Highway—time warp. The contrast between Palmer, a 60-year-old farming community, and Wasilla, with its spontaneous combustion of helter-skelter development, is startling. Suffice it to say, Palmer is more conducive to sightseeing.

Start your visit at the **Palmer Visitor Information Center, Museum, and Gift Shop,** 723 S. Valley Way at the corner of E. Fireweed, tel. (907) 745-2880, open daily 8 a.m.-6 p.m. in summer (brochures in a rack outside if it's after hours). Outside is a signpost with distances from Palmer to all over the world: 3,061 road miles to Elko, Nevada; 10,446 air miles to the South Pole, etc. Inside, load up with brochures and visit the small museum downstairs depicting the colonists' lifestyle. Don't miss the framed front page of the June 30, 1958 *Anchorage Daily Times* featuring the story of Alaska being voted into the Union. The **Palmer Library** is across the street at 655 S. Valley Way, tel. (907) 745-4690, open Monday and Wednesday noon-8 p.m., Tuesday noon-6 p.m., Thurs.-Fri. 10 a.m.-6 p.m., Saturday 10 a.m.-2 p.m.

Walk two blocks east on E. Elmwood to visit the **Church of a Thousand Logs,** built by the colonists in 1936-37.

Another block east brings you to the **Agricultural Experimental Station** headquarters, where you can check out the greenhouses and arboretum across the street.

TO MATANUSKA GLACIER AND GLENNALLEN

PIONEER MOTEL

W. ARCTIC AVE. E. ARCTIC AVE. (OLD GLENN HWY.)

MATANUSKA RIVER PARK

TO LAZY MOUNTAIN AND BODENBERG BUTTE (SCENIC RT. TO ANCHORAGE)

PALMER

LAUNDROMAT

S. COBB
S. BAILEY
S. ALASKA ST.
S. COLONY WAY
S. VALLEY WAY
S. DENALI

E. COTTONWOOD

POST OFFICE

E. DAHLIA

CARRS MALL

VALLEY HOTEL

LIBRARY E. ELMWOOD

PALMER-WASILLA HWY.

W. EVERGREEN E. EVERGREEN

KLONDIKE MIKE'S

INFO. CENTER

CHURCH OF 1,000 LOGS

E. FIREWEED

AG. EXP. STATION H.Q.

GLENN HWY.

ALASKA R.R.

TO WASILLA AND DENALI (INTERIOR)

PARKS HWY.

AIRPORT RD.

AIRPORT

ALASKA STATE FAIRGROUNDS

TO ANCHORAGE

NOT TO SCALE

© MOON PUBLICATIONS, INC.

About a mile south of town down the Glenn Highway is the **Alaska State Fairgrounds;** the fair is held from the last week in August through Labor Day. At the fairgrounds is **Colony Village,** which preserves some of Palmer's early buildings, including houses (one built in 1917 in Anchorage), several barns (including one that serves as the Colony Theater), a church, and a post office. The Village is free, open Mon.-Sat. 10 a.m.-4 p.m.

Farms

While in Palmer, take the opportunity to visit the world's only domestic **musk ox farm** and

see these prehistoric Arctic creatures up close. During the 30-minute tour ($7), you learn that, among other things, these exotic animals were hunted nearly to extinction around the turn of the century. The musk ox wool is combed out here, shipped back east to be spun, then distributed to Native villages to be woven into qiviut wool products. Qiviut is eight times warmer than sheep's wool and much softer and finer than even cashmere. Scarves, stoles, caps, and tunics are sold in the showroom ($165-425); don't miss the display of little squares of qiviut, cashmere, alpaca, and wool from sheep, camel, and llama to compare the softness. The farm is open daily 10 a.m.-6 p.m. from the second Sunday in May through September, take the Glenn Highway north of town to Mile 50 and turn left on Archie Rd. (first left past Fishhook Rd.).

After communing with the musk ox, continue another mile to **Wolf Country USA,** Mile 51.8, tel. (907) 745-0144, open daily 9 a.m.-8 p.m., $3. See the hybrid wolves and maybe even buy a hybrid wolf cub.

Heading north through downtown, take a right on Arctic Ave., which turns into the Old Glenn Highway. Go about four miles to Bodenberg Loop Rd., a five-mile Sunday drive through some of the most gorgeous farmland in the valley, with the Chugach's Pioneer Peak towering over it. You'll hardly know you're in Alaska. To see some of the original colonial farms, head east out the Glenn Highway nine miles to Farm Loop Road.

Hiking

Two excellent hikes are accessible off the Old Glenn Highway east of Palmer. Heading north from downtown, go right on Arctic Ave., which becomes the Old Glenn. Just beyond the bridge across the Matanuska River, go left onto Clark-Wolverine Rd., then continue about a mile till the next junction. Take a right on Huntley Rd., go about a mile and bear right at the fork, then drive past the caretaker's cabin to the large gravel parking lot. The trailhead is not marked, but it's obvious at the upper end of the lot. It's two hours to the top of **Lazy Mountain** (3,270 feet). A better view and a shorter hike are from the top of **Bodenberg Butte** (881 feet). Keep going south on the Old Glenn, pass the first right onto the Loop Rd., and take the second right. In a quarter-mile, just beyond a gravel pit, is a steep unmarked trail (you'll see it), eroded from the traffic of horses. A 40-minute huff rewards you with a 360-degree view of the valley, Chugach, Talkeetnas, Knik Glacier, and some of the uncleared forest, which graphically illustrates what the colonists confronted in "clearing the land."

Accommodations

Palmer has one of the most luxurious city campgrounds in Alaska. **Matanuska River Park,** on E. Arctic Ave. (or Mile 17, Old Glenn Highway) about a half-mile east of town, occupies a lush site full of big old cottonwoods and wild roses. There's lots of space between the 80 campsites (20 of them oversized for RVs, but no hookups), which are usually uncrowded (except at state-fair time), $10 per site per night. Surrounding the campground is a day-use area, complete with picnic area, softball and volleyball, horseshoe pits, and a nature trail around the ponds. The park also has coin-operated showers ($2 for 10 minutes), firewood for sale, trails, river access, and an observation deck. Call Mat-Su Parks and Recreation at (907) 745-9631 for more info.

To stay indoors, the **Pioneer Motel,** 124 W. Arctic, tel. (907) 745-3425, rents rooms with cable starting at $45 s, $55 d; the singles go fast, then you pay for a double, even if you're alone. The **Valley Hotel,** 606 S. Alaska St., tel. (907) 745-3330, is the big action in town, with 34 rooms going for $55 s or d, a 24-hour coffee shop, plus a lounge and a liquor store. The **Colony Inn,** 325 E. Elmwood Ave., tel. (907) 745-3330, has all nonsmoking rooms for $75-100. It's operated by the Valley Hotel folks. **Pollen's B&B,** tel. (907) 745-8920, charges $63-69 in the summer, $50 in the winter.

Wash Day Too, 127 S. Alaska, tel. (907) 746-4141, is open 7:30 a.m.-9 p.m.; showers are $3, $3.50 with towel.

Food and Entertainment

The **Round House Café** coffee shop at the Valley Hotel is open 24 hours, serving bacon and eggs $5.95, burgers $5-7, a good halibut sandwich for $7, and halibut, chicken, pork, steak, scallop, and pasta dinners $9-15. **Klondike Mike's Saloon** has live rock 'n' roll Wed.-Sat. starting at 9:30 p.m.

Transportation

Gray Line's **Alaskon Express** buses run through Palmer four days a week on their way to Haines; they leave Anchorage at 7:30 a.m. Sunday, Tuesday, and Friday and arrive in Palmer at 8:30 a.m.; the fare is $59. Call (907) 277-5581 in Anchorage or (800) 544-2206. **Alaska Direct** buses run through Palmer on Sunday, Wednesday, and Friday at 7 a.m. on their way to Whitehorse, $15 from Anchorage. **Alaska Railroad** only runs to Palmer during the state fair. For tours of the Matanuska Valley out of Anchorage, see "Tours" under "Anchorage."

TO GLENNALLEN

Just outside of Palmer, the Glenn enters some hilly forested wilderness. Only 12 miles from town, at Mile 54, is **Moose Creek Campground,** a small but useful overnight alternative if Palmer is too crowded or expensive for your taste; $10. At Mile 76 is **King Mountain Wayside,** a large, beautiful campground with water, outhouses, and choice spots right on the Matanuska River (though the interior loop might be less windy); $10 The site faces King Mountain across the river—a perfect triangular peak. **King Mountain Lodge** is only 100 yards up the road. You could easily spend an idyllic day and night simply enjoying this spot. Or you can stop off at **Long Lake State Recreation Site,** Mile 85, to stretch your legs; no camping. But if you're looking for easy access to the Matanuska Glacier, the highlight of this highway, pitch your tent at the **Matanuska Glacier State Recreation Site,** at Mile 101 on a hillside overlooking the ice giant, with the usual excellent state facilities, and the usual $10 charge.

Matanuska Glacier and Beyond

This glacier is so close, safe, and spectacular that it's worth the price of admission. Admission? To a glacier? That's right, folks. For a low, low $6.50—cheaper than a movie or even a paperback these days—you can be the first on your block to get muddy on the Matanuska Glacier. This unique concept combines homesteading, sightseeing, and conservation, all in the same neat package. John Kimball homesteaded 400 acres from near the highway up to the face of the glacier in 1966, then spent two years and a considerable bankroll building a road and bridges to a bluff overlooking the ice. Since 1968, Kimball has "managed" the glacier with foresight and care.

Take a right at the colorful sign to Glacier Park Resort at Mile 102, then drop down a wide well-graded gravel road to river level and continue on to the lodge, tel. (907) 745-2534. Stop in and have a drink and a burger, or just pay the toll. You can camp anywhere on the property ($6), but the official campground is right there at the entrance. Also here, you can book a one-hour $85 flightseeing trip.

The gate is raised and you drive another two miles on an okay gravel road (rough at the end) to the parking lot. Today, this glacier is 27 miles long and four miles wide; 8,000 years ago it reached to where the lodge is, and 18,000 years ago it occupied Palmer, but it hasn't done much in the last 400 years. The terminal moraine is mostly solid, though some spots are quicksandy—wear hiking boots and expect to get a bit muddy. You can muck around right to the face, though the closer you get, the slicker it gets. Bring black-and-white film and a polarizing lens. Bring a hammer, a chisel, and a plastic bag to chop off a chunk of muddy ice. Wash it off as best you can and put it in your cooler; it'll keep your milk cold and fresh for two or three days.

It's another 85 miles to Glennallen and the intersection of the Glenn and Richardson Highways. If you have a chance to make this drive in late August or September, by all means, do it. The acres of aspen trees along this route turn a brilliant gold, and the contrasting dark green spruce, combined with the backdrop of glaciers and snowcapped peaks, make for some extraordinary photo ops. You ll be tempted to pull off at every twist in the road to burn film and drink in the surroundings.

At Mile 98, look to the mountainside to the north for scattered bunches of white dots—Dall sheep like to congregate here, apparently for a mineral lick on the hillside. The **Long Rifle Lodge** at Mile 102.2, tel. (907) 745-5151, features home-made baked goods along with fairly typical Alaska road food. However, the real reason to stop here is the view from the dining room of the nearby glacier and valleys—it's hard to keep your eyes on your plate with this mountain panorama in front of you.

When you get past Eureka Summit, you're in caribou country, so scan the open ground everywhere for members of the local Nelchina herd. From Eureka to Glennallen, and then north on the Richardson Highway toward Tok, it's possible to spot caribou almost anywhere. Also as you approach Glennallen, if the weather's clear, there's a great view of the Wrangells: Mt. Drum is the beautiful snowcapped peak right in the middle of the view at 12,010 feet elevation, Mt. Sanford is just to the south (right) of it at 16,237 feet, and Mt. Wrangell is to the north at 14,163 feet.

GLENNALLEN

At Mile 187 of the Glenn, just before the junction with the Richardson Highway, is this small service town, named for both Edwin Glenn (see above) and Henry Allen, leader of the first expedition up the Copper River. Strung along both sides of the road, Glennallen (pop. 900) is the gateway to the big Copper River Valley country and Wrangell St. Elias National Park.

First stop in at the **Copper River Valley Visitor Center,** a log cabin with a sod roof right on the corner of the highways, tel. (907) 822-5555, open daily 8 a.m.-7 p.m. May 15 to September 15, to pick up the requisite load of brochures and tabloids with information about every place between Tok and Cordova, watch whatever video is playing, and talk to the friendly staff member.

Northern Lights Campground is just a little in from the intersection on the Glenn, with tent and RV camping, a gift shop, and firewood. The state campground, **Dry Creek,** is five miles north of the junction: 58 sites, pit toilets, unfriendly mosquitoes, $10. Or go a half-mile west of Caribou Cafe, turn north at the library, and go an eighth of a mile to the baseball fields. The woods, tables, and pit toilets would make an adequate unofficial campsite in a pinch.

Otherwise, stay at the **Caribou Hotel,** tel. (907) 822-3302, a lodge built in 1991, with 45 rooms starting at $95 s, $109 d, $132 for a room with a hot tub, and $187 furnished two-bedroom suite. **Caribou Restaurant** out front, open 7 a.m.-11 p.m., serves bacon and eggs for $6.50, burgers and sandwiches for $5-8, "favorite" dinner specials for $9, and steaks for $12-15. Read the Official Caribou Glossary on the back of the menu. Get road food at the **Tastee-Freez,** tel. (907) 822-3923, open 10 a.m.-11 p.m., serving Glennallen for the last 20 years. The **Hitching Post Restaurant,** tel. (907) 822-3338, across the street from the Park's Place Grocery (which now features an espresso bar, like every other wide spot in the road throughout the state), specializes in good, reasonably priced, basic Mexican dishes like burritos and both hard and soft tacos. They also serve basic American road food and have a great selection of hot sauces, a taste and temperature for every occasion. Glennallen also has three gas stations, Pardner's

general store, Park's Place Supermarket, and a laundromat.

Backcountry Connection is the latest in a *long* line of scheduled van-touring services out of Glennallen, but this one's lasted half a decde now. BC offers roundtrip fully guided tours from Glennallen to McCarthy, lunch included, for $99, or shuttle trips in a 15-passenger van for $70 roundtrip same-day travel, $88 if you go out and back on different days, or $49 one-way. From Chitina, the prices are $60, $70 and $35, respectively. Trips operate every day except Sunday, and reservations are recommended. Call (907) 822-5292 for further information and reservations.

Hitchhiking to Valdez usually isn't a problem— 115 miles on one road. But northbound thumbists should try using a destination sign for the first day or two, then bite the bullet on one of the many buses that pass through here. The Alaskon Express bus stop is at the Caribou Cafe. Call or stop in for the latest schedules and prices; public bus systems around here change faster than Dolly Parton's costumes. Good luck.

RICHARDSON HIGHWAY SOUTH

These 115 miles, running between the rugged Chugach (on the right, or west) and the massive Wrangell (on the left, or east), are so chock full of history, scenery, wilderness, and fish that you could easily spend your entire Alaskan experience between Glennallen and Valdez. This route—the oldest road in Alaska—was blazed during the stampede of 1898 and has since been used as a footpath, a telegraph right-of-way, a wagon trail, and an auto thoroughfare. It provides access to Wrangell-St. Elias, largest national park in the country. The Edgerton Highway (Route 10) goes 96 miles from the Richardson through Chitina, which boasts superb salmon fishing on the Copper River, to McCarthy and the Kennecott copper mines, deep in the heart of the national park. Finally, the last 25-mile stretch to Valdez ranks in the top three of the most scenically varied and spectacular roads in the North—right up there with the Denali Park road around Eielson and the Icefields Parkway between Lake Louise and Jasper. And that's not all. Read on.

Copper Center

Copper Center (pop. 400) is 15 miles south of Glennallen at Mile 100 on the Richardson. Settled in 1896, this was the first non-Native town in the interior of Southcentral, opened up by all the explorations on the mighty Copper River. This was also the point where the perilous trail over Valdez Glacier came down from the mountains. When the stampeders arrived, they found a score of tents, several log cabins, a post office, and the Blix Roadhouse, built in 1898 for $15,000, with spring beds and modern bath. **Copper Center Lodge,** tel. (907) 822-3245, which replaced the roadhouse in 1932, rents rooms with prices starting at $75 s and shared bath. They also rent a cabin for $125 per night for up to six people, and a cottage for $135 for up to eight. The restaurant hours are 7 a.m.-9 p.m., serving burgers, sandwiches, seafood, and steaks, with homemade baked goods and desserts. The bar is no longer in operation. Backcountry Connection will pick you up here and take you to McCarthy, if you so desire.

The **Ashby Museum** collection traces the history of the Copper River Valley, including Athabascan Indian and early-settler artifacts. Gold rush and pioneer days are remembered with photographs, tools used to develop the area, and old Sears catalogs, the only way the local inhabitants could procure many necessary supplies from Outside. The museum has recently added a second building and is open Mon.-Sat. 1-5 p.m. Across the highway, **Chapel on the Hill,** the oldest log chapel in the Copper River Basin, was built by Army volunteers in 1942. A slide show on Copper River Country is shown on request for no charge. If the chapel isn't open, go to the trailer on the grounds and knock on the door—the caretakers will open the place for you.

Edgerton Highway to Chitina—and Beyond

At Mile 82, 18 miles south of Copper Center, is the turnoff of Route 10 to Chitina and on to McCarthy. The Edgerton, named after yet another Alaska road commissioner, is a 33-mile highway, the first 20 miles paved. It ends in Chitina (pronounced "CHIT-nuh," from the Athabascan *chiti* meaning "copper," and *na,* meaning "river"). The Chitina Indians used copper tools to hammer copper nuggets into plates, which they traded with the Tlingits; someone who owned five or

six plates was considered very rich. Chitina became an important junction in 1909, when the Copper River and Northwest Railroad arrived; a spur road connected the track to the original Richardson wagon trail to Fairbanks. The town began its decline in 1938 when the railroad shut down, and its future was further eroded by the Good Friday earthquake of 1964, which knocked out several bridges on the Copper River Highway. The highway project to link Cordova and Chitina was abandoned at that time.

Chitina (pop. 50) is famous for its dipnetting season in June, when Alaskan residents converge on the confluence of the Copper and Chitina Rivers, "dip" 35-gallon nets on 10-foot-long aluminum poles into the water, and lift out eight-pound reds and 25-pound kings by the score. Chitina has one motel, a gas station, a pay phone, a Park Service station, and a couple of restaurants. The nearest official camping is at BLM's **Liberty Falls** campground 10 miles before town, but tents spring up around Town Lake and along the three-mile appendage road south of town.

McCarthy Road

This could be the longest 60-mile road in the North—plan on at least four hours, several more if it's clear and you stop for the views of the Wrangells. At Mile 16 get ready for an adrenaline-pumping drive across the Kuskulana River on a narrow three-span bridge built in 1910 by the railroad and improved in 1988 (when guardrails were added—if you can imagine that!). The bridge is nearly 600 feet long and sits almost 400 feet above the water—perfect, in other words, for bungee jumping! A handful of underground entrepreneurs have lately tried to get away with some commercial jumping (first jump $50) behind the state's back; the state, in turn, has threatened them with trespassing charges. They might (but probably won't) be there when you are. Just before the end of the road is a spectacular overlook of McCarthy, the surrounding mountains, and the Kennicott and Root Glaciers.

Backcountry Connection, tel. (907) 822-5292, does the roundtrip between Glennallen and McCarthy (see "Glennallen" above). McCarthy Air, tel. (800) 245-6909, will fly three people from Glennallen to McCarthy for $300, $50 pp up to five, one-way. From Chitina the rate is $180 for two, $20 pp up to five. They also offer flightseeing and backcountry drop-offs. **Elias Air Taxi,** tel. (907) 822-3368, will fly you from Gulkana to McCarthy for $61 one-way, $110 roundtrip, departing daily at 10 a.m. Or you can leave from Anchorage for $177 one-way, $330 roundtrip. Reports from readers are that hitchhiking to and from McCarthy is not only easy but memorable.

The road ends on the wrong side of the Kennicott River. Residents built a kind of tram in 1983 (upgraded in 1988), where you climb up on an open platform and pull yourself the length of a football field, hand over hand, to get to the other side. It's tough going, especially during the uphill part! It's a lot easier for someone at either end to pull you across; return the favor for the other person. Hang backpacks and bikes on the brackets on the outside of the car. Once across, walk up the road; the right fork takes you a mile to McCarthy, the left fork nearly five miles to Kennicott.

McCarthy

This beautiful little settlement (pop. 25) was another boomtown from the early 1900s till 1939, serving the copper workers at Kennecott mines and the railroad workers on the Copper River and Northwestern. The mines, in their nearly 30 years of operation, eventually extracted $220 million in rich ore, nearly 70% copper and a little silver and gold on the side. The Alaska Syndicate (owned by J.P. Morgan and Daniel Guggenheim) held the controlling interest; it also owned the CR&NW railroad, which freighted the ore to tidewater, plus the Alaska Steamship Co., which shipped the ore to various smelters. The mines shut down in 1938 when world copper prices dropped and the cost of production became prohibitive. The semi-ghost town of Kennicott (pop. 10) and mines of Kennecott (the town was named after an early Alaskan explorer named Robert Kennicott; the original misspelling of the mines was never corrected) are a long day-hike or an easy overnight trip from McCarthy (or pay $5 for a ride with Wrangell Mountain Shuttle Service; it runs back and forth all day).

The McCarthy-Kennicott area is a private island surrounded by the vast Wrangell-St. Elias National Park, so camping is a bit problematic; you won't find any developed campgrounds,

but camping places do exist. Be sure to ask first. In McCarthy, stay at the historic (built in 1916) **McCarthy Lodge,** tel. (907) 554-4402. Rooms are available at rates of $95 s, $105 d, and $125 t. Package deals include breakfast, dinner, and transportation from Kennicott for $125 s, $180 d, and $225 t. The lodge also houses the Bear Den, the only bar within 60 miles.

Kennicott Glacier Lodge, tel. (907) 554-4477 to talk to someone at the lodge, or (800) 582-5128 for recorded info, offers vacation package rates for rooms, which include three meals, transportation to and from McCarthy, and a tour of the ghost town for $120 pp double occupancy, $70 more for each additional person, $35 for children four to 12. The a la carte rate (rooms and tour only) is $169 d, $199 t, and $229 q. Rooms with a view of the mountains instead of the glacier are $10 less.

The restaurant serves breakfast, lunch, and a one-seating family-style dinner at 7 p.m., menu and price varying.

Wrangell-St. Elias National Park

Though somewhat less accessible than Denali, this park is an excellent alternative to the crowds, clouds, wows, and crying-out-louds. The mountains (Chugach, Wrangells, and St. Elias) are incredible, and Mt. Wrangell (14,163 feet), highest volcano in Alaska, usually puffs away on earth's crustal cigarette. In fact, of the 16 tallest mountains in North America, nine are in this park! The icefields are world class, and their glacial tentacles rival any in the state. The Copper River can provide weeks-long raft or canoe rides, with all the fish you can stand. The wildlife is as abundant and visible as Denali's, and this park even has beaches on the Gulf of Alaska. Two roads plunge deep into the park's wildlands, and bus and plane service are available. This is the largest national park in the country (larger than southern New England), with 12.2 million acres (8.4 million park, 4.8 million preserve); along with Kluane National Park across the Canadian border, the whole area was the first designated U.N. World Heritage Site. Finally, you don't need backcountry permits to traipse around or camp on this federal land—just pick a direction and backpack till you crack.

Ground access is via the Edgerton Highway-McCarthy Rd., which cuts off from the Richardson at Mile 82 and runs almost 100 miles into the heart of the park, and the 43-mile road from Slana at Mile 65 of the Tok Cutoff (Glenn Highway) to the abandoned mining town of Nabesna. Air taxis and charter services can drop you off anywhere in the park; check around Glennallen or Cordova.

Park HQ is in Glennallen: write Superintendent, P.O. Box 29, Glennallen, AK 99588, tel. (907) 822-5234. The visitor center is at Mile 105 on the Richardson, 23 miles south of the Edgerton Cutoff. It's open 9 a.m.-6 p.m. during the season; the rangers can help you with trip planning, sell you USGS topo maps, and record your proposed itinerary in case of emergency. You can also buy books, posters, and postcards and view a 10-minute video. Small ranger stations are also located at Slana, Chitina, and Yakutat.

To Valdez

The next 75 miles are a wonderful drive through green forested hillsides along surging creeks with countless waterfalls emanating from ice patches and small glaciers atop the jagged Chugach. If you're terminally enchanted by this stretch of road and want to linger, two state recreation sites offer camping: **Squirrel Creek** at Mile 79 and **Little Tonsina** at Mile 65. The Tonsina site is a bit noisy, being a half-mile from pipeline pump station number 12, which, run by jet aircraft turbines, sounds like a plane perpetually taking off. Signboards across the highway from the pump station (Mile 65) describe pipeline history, oil spills, communications, the turbines, and the pump station (which propels 1.6 million barrels daily over Thompson Pass 45 miles south—that's 1,200 barrels a minute, or 50,000 gallons).

At Mile 56, the **Tiekel River Lodge,** tel. (907) 822-3259, has food, gas, rooms, campsites, and a gift shop. Lodging prices vary from $5 for tent sites up to $75 for a motel room with bath. Good food, friendly staff, and year-round activities make it a worthwhile stop on the road to Valdez.

Near Mile 33, you come around a bend, unsuspecting, and the **Worthington Glacier** looms into view, its three fingers creeping out of Girls Mountain like a grotesque hand in a horror movie. Contrary to popular misconception, this glacier is not named after Cal Worthington,

largest automobile franchiser on the West Coast.

In another few miles is the turnoff to the state recreation site, on a very rough road about a quarter-mile to the overlook parking lot. There's no established campground here, only an open cinder-block shelter with interpretive signs and a view down on the longest glacial finger. Trails cover the short distance to the glacier.

It gets better. A mere three miles down (or more accurately, *up*) the road is **Thompson Pass,** elevation 2,771 feet. A long row of serrated peaks, like a cosmic cross-cut saw with only a few dull or missing teeth, lines the high horizon. Blueberry and Summit Lakes are accessible by a loop road about a mile on the Valdez side of the pass; the small campground at Blueberry is beautiful—though it's exposed, especially if Thompson Pass is in the process of maintaining its record-setting precipitation levels. Confirming that this is one of the snowiest spots on earth are 15-foot-tall right-angle orange poles that show snowplow drivers the edge of the road. Contrary to general misconception, Thompson Pass is not named after Hunter S. Thompson.

It gets better still. In about seven miles, you drop from the pass to **Keystone Canyon,** one of the most gorgeous sights in Alaska, even in the rain. This four-mile section is steeped in gold-rush and copper-frenzy history. At the height of Klondicitis, accounts of the heavy tax and strict regulations that Canadian authorities imposed on the stampeders (which saved countless lives) were passed down the coast, and rumors of an old Indian-Russian trail from Valdez to the Yukon circulated simultaneously. The vague story of an "all-American route" to the gold sent 4,000 would-be prospectors headlong to Valdez—a measure of the madness that gripped the land. Suicidally unprepared, like lemmings they attempted to cross the brutal Valdez Glacier. Also responding to the rumors, the U.S. Army dispatched Capt. William Abercrombie in 1898 to find or blaze a route from Valdez to the Interior. Abercrombie had been on the original American expedition to Copper River country in 1884. He *knew* the land and the conditions; when he crossed Valdez Glacier in 1898, he postponed his trail-blazing assignment in order to deal with the horror that he found (see "Valdez" for the rest of this tragedy). Abercrombie returned in 1899 and thoroughly explored and mapped the whole area, locating and naming the Lowe River, Keystone Canyon, and the Thompson Pass route to the Interior.

Then in 1906, during the often violent race to build a railroad from tidewater to the Kennecott copper mines, two of the competing construction companies clashed over the right-of-way through Keystone Canyon; one man was killed. The ensuing murder trial further fanned the flames, and the "Shoot-out at Keystone Canyon" became a great issue between the op-posing sides. All this is highly dramatized in Rex Beach's novel, *The Iron Trail*.

Today, you drive along the raging Lowe River, at the bottom of nearly perpendicular 300-foot cliffs. The entire canyon is a psychedelic green; every crack and crevice in the sheer walls is overgrown with bright lime moss. Waterfalls tumble over the walls to the river below, spraying the road with a fine mist. Bridal Veil and Horsetail Falls live up to their names. And now you're ready to enter Valdez.

VALDEZ

At the end of Valdez Arm and completely surrounded by snowcapped peaks, Valdez (pronounced "val-DEEZ," pop. 4,000) is not only one of the most picturesque towns in Alaska, but it's also one of the most prosperous, having hosted the pipeline terminal for the past 20 years. In addition, it's one of the most progressive, the city leaders planning ahead for when the oil money inevitably stops flowing and Valdez reverts to Anytown, Alaska. Valdez's $50 million floating container dock is the largest of its kind in the world. The Copper Valley hydroelectric plant supplies power for distant towns (the power lines along the Richardson all the way to Glennallen emanate from here). Its tailing waters are used by Solomon Gulch Hatchery, working to ensure large runs of salmon for the future. Valdez is proud of its $3 million Civic Center, $1.3 million teen center, $1.5 million softball and recreation complex, library, hospital, pioneer home, mushrooming community college, and other civic projects. Finally, with year-round access by road, ferry, and air, and with well-developed tourist facilities, charter-fishing opportunities, tour-boat cruises to popular Columbia Glacier, and seemingly endless wilderness around it, Valdez's pivotal place in Alaska's future is well assured.

History

Captain James Cook sailed into and named Prince William Sound in 1778; Spanish explorer Don Salvador Fidalgo entered "Puerto de Valdez" in 1790, naming it after Spain's Marine Minister. In 1898, Valdez was a tent city of stampeders similar to Skagway—except for one critical detail: no trail to the Interior. Still, between 4,000 and 6,000 death-defying cheechakos crossed the Valdez Glacier that year. Army Capt. William Abercrombie described the foolhardy newcomers as "terrifyingly incompetent . . . wholly unprepared physically and morally for what they would face." They barely knew how to strap packs on their backs, and few thought to carry the two basic necessities: water and wood. Many were blinded by the sun's reflection off the ice. Many got lost in howling storms, in which it was impossible to see or hear the man ahead. Of those who managed to reach the summit, many lost their loads and lives on slick downhill slides into oblivion. And those who actually got off the glacier intact had to contend with the fast cold waters of the runoff. Many men with heavy packs lost their footing and drowned in knee-deep water. Some attempted to build boats and float down the Klutina River to Copper Center; few made it. And those stuck between the glacier and the river had nothing.

In the final count, all but 300 (and the countless dead) of those who'd set out from Valdez during the spring and summer of '98 returned to Valdez the way they came by fall. Abercrombie found them destitute and broken. Many had gone mad, some had scurvy, most had frostbitten hands, feet, faces. Facilities were squalid. And there was no food. Abercrombie postponed his orders to blaze a trail into the Interior for six months to feed, clothe, house, and arrange transportation home for the survivors.

But the town of Valdez was growing up around them. Only four or five years later, a corporate copper rush kicked off a fierce competition among Valdez, Cordova, and a town called Katalla, all vying to be selected as the tidewater terminus of the proposed railway to the copper mines of what's now Kennecott. A dozen projects were conceived, and one was even begun out of Valdez (see "To Valdez," above), but Cordova won out in the end. For the next 60 years, Valdez was a sleepy fishing and shipping port, competing with Seward, and later Whittier, to provide access for freight to the Interior. Then in 1964 the Good Friday earthquake struck, wiping out the entire old town, which was rebuilt four miles inland on property donated by a local. Finally, in 1974, civic leaders sold the virtues of Valdez—its ice-free port, 800-foot-deep harbor, and proximity to the Interior—to the pipeline planners, who chose the town as their terminus.

Everything went along miraculously smoothly and without serious incident until March 29, 1989, almost 25 years to the day after the Good Friday earthquake, when the *Exxon Valdez* ran aground on Bligh Reef a few hours after leaving the pipeline terminal in Valdez, dumping 11 million gallons of North Slope crude into Prince William Sound. The unthinkable had happened. In the mad summer of 1989, Valdez was turned on its head by the "Exxon Economy." The lives and livelihoods of the residents have since returned to normal.

SIGHTS

Downtown
For its size, **Valdez Museum,** right in the middle of town on Egan, open 8 a.m.-8 p.m., tel. (907) 835-2764, $3, has an extraordinary amount of comprehensive displays. Check out the fascinating photo display on the pipeline's impact, and the early black-and-whites, especially one of a steamship at the Columbia Glacier in 1928. Some rare early maps and charts include a Russian one from 1737; look for the beautiful engraving by Webber, Cook's prolific ship's artist. Informative displays illustrate Indian, mining, and telegraph history; the 1840 lighthouse lens and the 1907 Ahrens steam engine are the highlights. Spend some time reading the descriptions of the earthquake—unbelievable. And if you have any grief and amazement to spare after that, read about Valdez's namesake supertanker.

Up Meals Ave. toward the mountains is **Prince William Sound Community College;** a number of wooden sculptures by Peter Toth dot the grounds, including one magnificent Indian head. Down Meals Ave. by the harbor, bear left onto Clifton and go up past Coast Guard HQ to the **Civic Center.** An interpretive signboard describes the pipeline terminal across the bay. Climb the steep stairs up to **Point of View Park** for the good view of town.

Out of Town
Crooked Creek spawning area is out the Richardson about a half-mile from town. In late summer, walk out on the boardwalk and watch the salmon go through the final act of their incredible life cycle; cross the road to see what happens to them after they spawn. Continue out the Rich about 3.5 miles to where a historical sign points to Old Valdez. The only thing left of the old townsite besides the post office foundation and memorial plaque are the mileposts on the Rich: zero still starts here. In another three miles, turn right onto Dayville Rd.; in several miles you come to the hydroelectric plant and the salmon hatchery. Pause here to see the powerful falls at Solomon Gulch, take the brief self-guided tour around the hatchery (staff will usually answer your questions), and hike the steep 2.5-mile roundtrip Solomon Gulch Trail up to the dam and the lake. The trailhead is about 150 yards east of the plant (to the left if you're facing the plant).

Continue two miles to the front gate of the pipeline terminal. The sculpture is by Malcolm Alexander, who did the similar one at Fairbanks's Golden Heart Park. The information center moved from the gate out to the airport for security reasons during an unfortunate episode in which Americans, fighting a "virtual war," slaughtered roughly 150,000 Iraqi soldiers and civilians in the winter of 1991; it remains at the airport as of this writing. The center has a row of signboards explaining everything from the history of Valdez to pipeline "pigs"—capsule-type rotors sent through the pipe periodically to scrape the waxy yellow buildup on the inner walls. Check out the graphic comparison between a *Bartlett*-size ferry and a two-million-barrel oil tanker, one of four that the terminal docks can accommodate. For a point of reference, the *Valdez* was Exxon's largest super-

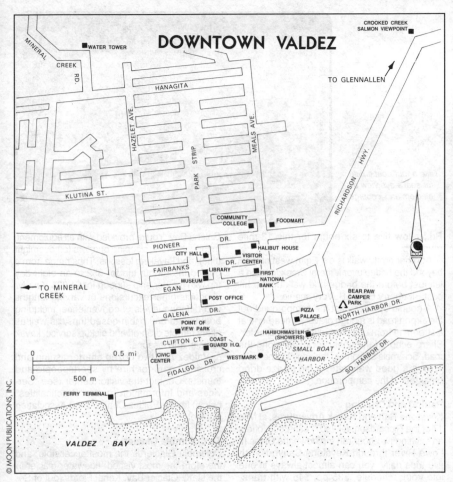

DOWNTOWN VALDEZ

tanker. The center itself basically only sells T-shirts and souvenir gimcracks; the proceeds help the Alyeska consortium meet the payroll. Alyeska sponsors a free bus tour through the pipeline terminal four times a day. It leaves from the visitor center at 9 and 11:30 a.m., 1:30 and 4 p.m., stops at the gate for a security check, allows you to get out of the bus at two designated viewing areas, and provides, as a reader put it, "A good and painful way to be exposed to some heavy oil-company propaganda." Call (907) 835-2686 for reservations; the tours fill up fast.

RECREATION

Hiking

A good walk is out beautiful **Mineral Creek Road**—a stunning canyon leading to a turn-of-the-century stamp mill. The 5.5-mile road is very narrow and bumpy, better used as a trail; a mile beyond the end is Smith Stamp Mill, which crushed ore from mines up the mountain to process through sluice boxes. Go up Hazelet to Hanagita, turn left, then right on Mineral Creek

Take a tour boat cruise for seal's-eye view of glaciers and icebergs.

GORDY OHLIGER

Rd.; allow five to six hours for this 13-mile roundtrip.

Another pretty walk is out Egan west of town beyond the bridge over Mineral Creek; or take a left just before the bridge and walk up the hill past Blueberry Hill B&B. Very scenic.

A couple of miles past the campground out the airport road is a huge gravel-pit dead-end at a stream in front of the deadly **Valdez Glacier.** Sharp echo off the sheer rock wall along the road. Scramble straight up the ridge for the view. This is a good walk after a big freeze-dried breakfast at the campground.

Rafting and Cruising

Keystone Raft and Kayak Adventures, at Mile 17 of the Richardson, tel. (907) 835-2606, offers an exciting two-hour raft trip down the Class III Lowe River through Keystone Canyon. With five trips daily, you can almost always fit one into your schedule, $35 pp, $45 with transportation from town. Rain suits, life jackets, and rubber boots are provided. Keystone also does a half-day trip on the Tsaina River for $70, a four-hour trip that includes transportation from Valdez. Also ask about their charter trips around the Interior and Copper River country.

If you've always wanted to learn how to kayak, or if you know how and want to explore Prince William Sound around Valdez in style, contact Hedy Sarney of **Anadyr Adventures,** tel. (907) 835-2814. You cross open water in their charter vessel, then put in single or double kayaks at places like Shoup and Columbia Glaciers or

Galena Bay. You're provided with all equipment, meals, showers, sleeping quarters (on overnight trips), and kayaking lessons. Trips range from a guided three-hour trip for $52 to an eight-day trip with mother-ship support for $1,925. Anadyr conducts other excursions of varying lengths and differing levels of convenience, including boat-based and cabin-based trips, as well as offers remote drop-off and pickup service, kayak rentals, and lessons.

Valdez has two dozen charter fishing and cruising boats for hire by sportspeople and tourists. Contact the visitor center (see "Services and Information" under "Practicalities" below) for the Valdez Charter Boat Association Booklet.

To Columbia Glacier

Columbia Glacier is the most accessible, and therefore the most visited, tidewater glacier in the state. Glacier Bay, Kenai Fjords (out of Seward), and College Fjords (out of Whittier) are also popular, but to see them it's necessary to take private, fairly expensive cruises. Columbia is the only glacier passed so closely by the state ferry, from which most people view this stunning grandfather of glaciers in Prince William Sound. Covering about 440 square miles, Columbia Glacier is 42 miles long and more than three miles wide at its face, which rises up to 300 feet above the water and plunges an incredible 2,000 feet below. Although it's the second largest of its kind in Alaska and still extends 32 miles out into its ancestral fjord, Columbia Glacier is but a minor remnant of the vast glacier that only a few thousand years ago filled Prince William Sound; its face reached a height of 4,000 feet.

Since 1982, the glacier has been in rapid retreat, at a rate averaging a half-mile per year. This rapid retreat has filled Columbia Bay with icebergs, and tour boats can no longer get within five miles of the face. Ice in the the bay has also caused navigational hazards in Prince William Sound, and it was to avoid ice that the *Exxon Valdez* took its fateful shortcut near, and onto, Bligh Reef. Scientists speculate that by the time the glacier stops its current rate of backward movement, a new fjord 25 miles long will be exposed, into which several calving glaciers will flow.

Only 25 air miles from Valdez, the state ferry *Bartlett* pauses on its trip between Valdez and Whittier to view the Columbia. At least four tour boats cruise the bay left by the receding glacier. However, because of the glacier's recent movement back up the bay, boats can only get to within about six miles of the face. This changes, but does not diminish, the experience, as the boats cruise through and over the fields of drifting ice towering above the deck to see the glacier as more huge chunks shear off and drop into the bay.

Trips come in many combinations, including plane-boat, bus-boat, train-boat, or just the roundtrip cruise from Valdez. **Stan Stephens Charters,** tel. (907) 835-4731 or (800) 992-1297, runs the *Glacier Spirit;* the eight-and-a-half-hour cruise to and from the glacier includes a seafood lunch at Growler Island for $94 adults, $64.50 kids; or stay overnight in tent cabins for $189 adults, $161 kids. **Glacier Charter Service,** tel. (907) 835-5141, runs the luxurious *Lu-Lu Belle,* the "limousine" of Prince William Sound: eight-to-eight-and-a-half-hour wildlife cruises take in a sea lion rookery, seabirds, and whale watching. The $115 cruise includes a hot meal, and the boat spends an hour at the calving face of Meares Glacier.

PRACTICALITIES

Accommodations

Creative camping is the name of this game. RV parks abound right in town, mostly along the waterfront. **Bear Paw Camper Park** on N. Har-

bor Dr., tel. (907) 835-2530, charges $15 per tent, $20-22 full hookup, including unlimited hot showers. But the closest official campground is five miles away. Go back out the Richardson, turn left toward the airport, and continue another mile past it to the **Valdez Glacier Campground,** tel. (907) 835-2282. This huge 100-site campground ($10) has picnic and barbecue areas, outhouses, and water, and is quite scenic, though barely accessible to people on foot. **Allison Point Campground** is on Dayville Rd. near the Alyeska oil terminal. It's run by the same folks who operate Valdez Glacier Campground; rates and facilities are similar in both locations. Allison Point has 68 sites and good fishing from shore nearby.

Otherwise, to camp free, walk around the corner from the ferry terminal and take a left on Egan Dr.; a quarter-mile out will hide you in the trees. You can also pitch your tent on the grassy area across from the parking lot around the bend from the ferry, though it's exposed and close to the canneries. Or disappear on the hill behind the waterfront. Or head halfway around Harbor Drive; on the left is a large city park with good views and lots of seasonals. You can camp here for $6.

All hotel rooms in Valdez cost well over $100. True to recent Alaskan form, the Valdez "Facilities and Services" brochure lists 52 bed and breakfasts. Contact the visitor center (see below) for the list. For quick and easy reservations at B&Bs, hotels, charter-boat fishing companies, etc., call Cathy at **One Call Does It All** reservation service, tel. (907) 835-4988. She can describe all the B&Bs in town and provide a map to the place when you reserve through her service, all at no charge.

Food

Lots of choices here. The **Totem Inn,** Pt. 5 Richardson Hwy., tel. (907) 835-4443, gets crowded with locals at breakfast time in the big dark dining room with aquariums, wildlife displays, and big-screen video. **Alaska Halibut House** on appropriately named Meals Ave. across from the college, tel. (907) 835-2788, has good local fast-food fish, such as a halibut basket for $5.85, as well as $6 burgers and $15 fish dinners. It also has a good salad bar. To get there, go out N. Harbor Dr. past Bear Paw and around the bends.

VICINITY OF VALDEZ

TO GOLD MINING AREA

MINERAL CREEK RD.

MINERAL CREEK

CROOKED CREEK SALMON SPAWNING VIEWING & HATCHERY

RICHARDSON HWY.

VALDEZ GLACIER

TO VALDEZ GLACIER

HAZELET AVE.

MEALS AVE.

HANAGITA

KLUTINA ST.

TIDAL FLATS

VALDEZ GLACIER

MINERAL CREEK LOOP RD.

AIRPORT

VALDEZ AIRPORT RD.

VALDEZ

FERRY

SMALL BOAT HARBOR

FLOATING DOCK

McKINLEY ST.

ALASKA AVE.

OLD VALDEZ TOWNSITE & MONUMENT

NOT TO SCALE

PORT   VALDEZ   BAY

VALDEZ GOLD FIELDS SOFTBALL COMPLEX

ROBE LAKE

ROBE LAKE RD.

TO KEYSTONE CANYON

SAW ISLAND

ALYESKA TERMINAL SECURITY GATE

ALLISON POINT

SOLOMON GULCH FISH HATCHERY

DAYVILLE RD.

BALLAST WATER TREATMENT PLANT

ALLISON POINT

SOLOMON GULCH

HYDROELECTRIC PLANT

W. TANK FARM

E. TANK FARM

© MOON PUBLICATIONS, INC.

The **Pizza Palace,** also on N. Harbor, is extremely popular for pizza and Italian food. The **Cafe Valdez** next door to the Village Inn serves tasty Mexican food, with a number of dishes that take advantage of local seafood; great salsa and chips and a good selection of Mexican beers. **Fu Kung** Chinese is in a Quonset hut on Kobuk behind the Totem Inn. The **Pipeline Club,** attached to the Valdez Motel, is similar to the Totem Inn, and the **Westmark Valdez** has the usual hotel-restaurant food.

Services and Information
The **public showers** are at the harbormaster's office, corner of Meals Ave. and Harbor Dr. across from the chamber of commerce; buy your tokens ($3) upstairs in the office, then take your showers in the dungeon (no electrical outlets).

The **visitor center** is across from City Hall at 200 Chenega St., tel. (907) 835-2984, open daily 8 a.m.-8 p.m. This is often a crowded little store, especially when a cruise ship is in port; the center handles 45,000 people a year, most during the season, and 100,000 written inquiries. This visitor center has even more paper than usual, with lots of written fact sheets about Valdez, the oil spill, free activities, sport fish, and more. Check out the stuffed salmon, ptarmigan, big brown bear, and antlers, as well as the big map with pins representing visitor places of origin. A 45-minute documentary about the earthquake is shown on demand ($3).

The **Valdez Consortium Library,** on Fairbanks St., tel. (907) 835-4632, is open Tuesday, Wednesday, Thursday 10 a.m.-8 p.m., Monday and Friday 10 a.m.-6 p.m., and Saturday noon-5 p.m. A 30-minute video on Valdez is shown at 11 a.m. and 4 p.m.—very slick.

Bingo happens every Friday and Saturday at the Royal Center Building, 310 Egan Dr., put on by the Valdez Native Association. Doors open at 6 p.m., games begin at 7 p.m.

Transportation

Valdez is 366 miles from Fairbanks on the Richardson; from Anchorage it's 189 miles on the Glenn Highway to Glennallen, then another 115 on the Richardson. **Alaskon Express,** tel. (907) 835-2357 (Valdez), (907) 277-5581 (Anchorage), or (800) 544-2206, leaves Valdez from the Westmark Valdez daily at 8 a.m., arriving in Anchorage at 6 p.m., $65 one-way; their buses also leave Anchorage at 8 a.m. from the Hilton and arrive in Valdez around 6 p.m.

ERA Aviation flies turboprop airplanes between Valdez and Anchorage, with one-way costs running $74-99 and roundtrip from $129, depending on advance purchase, restrictions, etc. The airport is four miles outside of town; a Yellow cab, tel. (907) 835-2500, runs around $5.

Avis, tel. (907) 835-4774 or (800) 331-1212, rents cars for $52-65 per day, unlimited mileage. Reservations for rental cars are always recommended, especially in smaller towns. One good-sized cruise ship can eat up the available inventory of rental cars, so when at all possible, plan ahead.

Alaska Marine Highway's *E.L. Bartlett* runs between Valdez and Whittier (days and times change every year; check the latest ferry schedule); around $60. It also runs between Whittier and Cordova and Valdez and Cordova. Note that the *Bartlett* is the only state ferry *without* showers—painful. The *Tustumena* departs from Valdez a couple days a week on its way around Prince William Sound and over to Seward,

Homer, and Kodiak, but different weeks have different times; check the schedule and prices carefully.

A few tactical suggestions for ferry travelers. The ferry service advises you to check in at the office one hour before departure. But if you're a foot passenger, you should get there much sooner if you want to secure a spot in line for the initial dash onboard to get good seating. The *Bartlett* has a spacious lounge area that provides a wide view forward and to both sides, but the seating isn't all that comfortable. There's a TV monitor where movies are shown, and lots of young and old passengers milling around. Another smaller seating area has 17 airliner-style seats on the port side. The views aren't as all-encompassing, but there's definitely less commotion and the seats are much more conducive to resting and reading. Take the companionway down just aft of the men's room near the purser's station on the weather (main) deck.

If you're driving, the *Bartlett* is a first-on, last-off vessel. If you want to beat the rest of the drivers to good seating, get in line several hours before departure. However, if for some reason you'll be in a hurry to get off quickly, stay toward the back of the line.

Beaver Sports, 316 Galena, down from the post office, tel. (907) 835-4727, rents Trek mountain bikes for $9 an hour. They're open Mon.-Fri. 10 a.m.-7 p.m., Saturday 9 a.m.-6 p.m., and Sunday 1-6 p.m.

GORDY OHLIGER

CORDOVA

Cordova (pop. 2,000) is noticeably less populated, less prosperous, and less accessible than its big-sister city Valdez—and most people like it that way. Though only a six-hour ferry ride away, its setting is its own, its climate is milder and wetter, and its vibration is nothing like Valdez's. Cordova might feel more at home somewhere between Petersburg and Juneau: connected only by boat and plane, with a large commercial fishing fleet, lush forests, small islands, and snowcapped peaks. Many travelers, especially those who gravitate to the coast, use Cordova as the stepping-stone from Southeast to Southcentral and the mainland, bypassing the hundreds of miles of overland travel through Yukon and Interior.

But Cordova is more than just the coast; it's also Chugach National Forest, Prince William Sound, and their abundant outdoor recreation; the Copper River and its wild rides and massive delta; railroad history and the Million Dollar Bridge. Amidst all of this is a bustling little community bursting at its seams during the summer fishing season, but also glued together by the magic of the fishing lifestyle. Drift over to Cordova and spend a couple of days exploring this special corner of Alaska—you'll be glad you did.

History

In 1884, Army captain William Abercrombie surveyed the Copper River delta, which made the area known to a few hardy prospectors. The crazed stampede of 1897-98 opened up the area to settlement. Still, in 1905, Cordova was little more than a couple of canneries processing the pinks and silvers from the Sound. Then Michael J. Heney showed up. After years of surveying rights-of-way, watching railroad ventures to the rich coal and copper mines nearby start and fold, and failing to convince the Morgan-Guggenheim Alaska Syndicate not to start their road from Katalla, Heney invested his entire savings and in 1907 began laying track from Cordova toward Kennecott Mines. After the Katalla facilities were destroyed by a storm, the Syndicate purchased the Copper River and Northwest line from Heney and completed it in 1911 at a total cost of $23 million; by 1917 it had hauled over $100 million in ore to Cordova for transshipment to smelters. Cordova was a boomtown till the Kennecott Mines closed in 1938. Since then the town's economy has reverted to fishing and canning. The year-round population doubles in the summer, and in good years there's plenty of work.

SIGHTS

The **Cordova Museum** is in the Centennial Building at First and Adams, adjoining the library, tel. (907) 424-6665, open Mon.-Sat. 10 a.m.-6 p.m. (and Sunday 2-4 p.m. if enough volunteers can be rounded up), free. This museum is small but packed with artifacts, including an old Linotype, an ancient slot machine, a three-seat *baidarka,* and an amusing exhibit on

Cordova's world-famous Iceworm Festival (held each February). Look for the aerial views of earthquake damage to the Million Dollar Bridge. The 30-minute *Story of Cordova* is shown daily at 3 p.m. The **library** is open Tues.-Saturday 1-8 p.m. This is a good place to read, rest, even sleep, and meet fellow travelers while waiting for the ferry.

Many buildings around town were built during Cordova's original construction in 1908, including (all on First St.) the Alaskan and Cordova

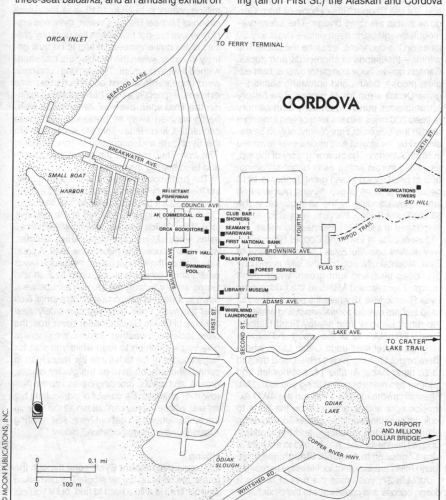

Hotels, the Ambrosia Pizza building, and the Red Dragon, oldest building in town, which served weekdays as a rowdy clubhouse but on Sundays turned into a church when the altar was let down by ropes from the beams. Pick up the historic walking-tour map at the museum for a complete list of the old buildings.

Million Dollar Bridge

There aren't enough superlatives in the English language to describe adequately the 50-mile ride out the Copper River Highway from Cordova to this amazing bridge. The scenery—mountains, glaciers, river, delta—rivals any 50 miles on the continent, let alone the state. The wildlife—thousands of shorebirds and ducks, Canada geese, huge trumpeter swans, bald eagles, moose, bears, and spawning salmon—gives Denali a run for its money. The history encompasses punching an early-20th-century railroad 200 miles into the Interior and starting a road in the '60s on its right-of-way, only to be destroyed by the largest earthquake ever recorded in North America. The crowning glory of the trip, as visible in rain or fog as in bright sunshine, built at great expense and great danger in 1910 between the faces of two moving glaciers and left mostly standing by the earthquake, is the Million Dollar Bridge, the vista from which is unsurpassed in a land of unsurpassed vistas.

Just outside of town, the Copper River Highway passes beautiful Eyak Lake at the base of Eyak Mountain. Notice how the lake is two colors, deep blue and light green, which don't merge. From around Mile 6 at the bridge over Eyak River to Mile 12 where the pavement ends, keep a sharp eye out for waterfowl and wildlife in the runoff sloughs from nearby Scott Glacier. Take a left at Mile 12 for the airport and follow a two-mile gravel road up to Cabin Lake, where there're trout fishing, picnic tables, and trails to three other lakes. At Mile 14, another left and another two miles of gravel bring you to the Mt. Sheridan trailhead; hike a mile on the 4WD extension spur and scramble up on the ridge to look out over the two-finger glacier flowing down either side of the mountain, and the iceberg-clogged lake at its face. A side road to the right at Mile 17 goes off to **Alaganik Slough;** the three rough miles are excellent for viewing shorebirds.

At Mile 27, you cross the first of nearly a dozen bridges and causeways to the other "side"

of the Copper River, more than 10 miles distant—it might remind you of the south Florida Keys. Long Island, from Mile 28 to Mile 33.5, sits smack in the middle of the mighty river delta. Good canoeing in the ponds along here, which connect up with a minimum of portage. Out here you can understand why, out of 196 miles of track from Cordova to Kennicott, 96 miles were built over bridges or trestles.

Finally, at Mile 48, you arrive at Million Dollar Bridge. This bridge, which cost a little over a million dollars to build in 1910, was the culmination of Michael Heney's vision, faith, and employee loyalty—not to mention the uncanny abilities of his civil engineers. It had to be built entirely in winter, when the two glaciers that sandwiched it were dormant. The working conditions were unbearable at best and the danger was extreme, especially as the builders raced to finish the final span even as its supports were being washed away by break-up. But it *was* completed, and Heney sold the whole show to the Syndicate and, according to Rex Beach in *The Iron Trail,* married the girl of his dreams and lived happily ever after.

The north span collapsed in the earthquake, but the state jury-rigged a ramp down to the abutment, and it's a fun little joyride to the other side. On the bridge, look to your left at the massive face of the **Childs Glacier;** look right about three miles across Miles Lake to the **Miles Glacier,** which has receded two miles since 1910. A short side road on the left just before the bridge leads past a small concrete shack, used by Fish and Game while counting the salmon escapement, down to a viewing pavilion set up on a small bluff over the river. From here you can safely view the face of Childs Glacier, under cover from the often inclement weather. Informative displays give you something to read while you wait for huge chunks of ice to fall into the river. Plan to spend all afternoon here as the glacier creaks, groans, and cracks, dropping calves into the narrow river channel. *Be careful* of particularly big calves, whose waves can splash all the way up the embankment. To get out here, see "Getting Around" under "Transportation," below.

Hiking

Two trails climb **Mount Eyak**—one through the forest, the other up the ski slope. The unmarked **Tripod Trail** is a little hard to find, but if you cut to the right between a cabin and a driveway near the end of Fifth St., you'll see the trailhead. This is a pretty hike through forest primeval, with salmonberries (a little bitter but juicy) ripe for the picking in August. Otherwise, head straight up Council Ave., bear left onto Sixth, and follow it around the Alascom communications apparatus. You can start right up the mountain from there, and you don't have to go far to get a great view of the town and harbor. You could camp around here in a pinch.

The excellent **Crater Lake Trail** begins opposite Skaters Cabin on Eyak Lake, two miles from town beyond the old cemetery, the seaplane base, and the municipal airstrip. The trail climbs 1,500 feet in two miles through a beautiful forest, with panoramic views near the top of Eyak Lake and the Heney Range. The terrain around Crater Lake is fairly open and it would be easy to scale the surrounding summits, if you have the time and energy. Allow a minimum of two hours roundtrip from the road to the lake. The trail is solid and very easy to follow; even if a wet wind is blowing, it will be relatively still in the forest, but be careful not to slip. Don't miss this one.

At the end of Power Creek Rd., six miles from town, a trail leads about a mile up to Ohman Falls—and when you see it you'll definitely say, "Oh man!"

The Forest Service maintains the **Lydick Slough Trail** (3.2 miles), starting at Mile 7 of the Copper River Highway; the **Lake Elsner Trail** (four miles), from the end of Cabin Lake Rd.; the **Pipeline** (two miles) and **McKinley Lake** (two miles) trails, both from Mile 19.8 of the highway; and the **Mount Sheridan Trail** (two miles), from the end of Glacier Road. The **Haystack Trail** at mile 19 is a little under a mile, mostly uphill over boardwalks and through second-growth forest. It terminates at a wonderful overlook spot, affording sweeping views of the delta, well worth the short trek. Pick up a photocopied handout on these hikes at the Forest Service office (see "Services and Information" under "Practicalities," below).

Recreation Cabins

Over a dozen Forest Service cabins are available for rent ($25) in the Cordova area; all but three are accessible only by plane or boat. There are cabins at both ends of the McKinley Lake Trail. If you've never seen one, hike for 75 yards up the McKinley Lake Trail (Mile 19.8) and peer in the windows. Readers report that staying here is quiet (except for the spawning salmon), secluded, and beautiful. To reserve, go to the Forest Service office on Second Ave. (see below).

PRACTICALITIES

Accommodations

One motel and two hotels are on First St., the main drag, all above or connected to bars. Least expensive is the **Alaskan Hotel,** above the Alaska Bar, tel. (907) 424-3288, charging $35 s or d without bath, $55 with. Next door, the **Cordova Hotel,** above the Cordova Bar, tel. (907) 424-3388, charges $30 s without bath, $40 d with bath, no credit cards accepted. Check into both at the bars downstairs. The **Prince William Motel,** behind the Club Bar and Cafe, tel. (907) 424-3201, charges $70 s, $80 d. The **Reluctant Fisherman** down on Railroad Ave., (907) 424-3272, is the classy joint—rooms cost $115 mountain view, $135 harbor view, if you can get one; special rates for winter and for corporate and government travelers.

The **Northern Nights Inn,** tel. (907) 424-5356, has four rooms with private baths, kitchens, phones, cable TV, and VCRs (but no breakfast) in a beautiful old home. It's close to downtown and overlooks the harbor. Room rates run $50-65. Owner Becky Chapek operates an informal B&B booking service and will help you find a room if her place is full. Becky also meets every ferry that comes into Cordova and provides free rides into town. Look for a van marked Footloose Tours or Copper River & Northwest Tours. For $35, she'll take you on a guided tour across the Copper River delta to the Million Dollar Bridge, gourmet lunch included. This is an excellent deal for a highly recommended tour. It's the thing to do in Cordova.

The **Cordova Rose Lodge,** tel. (907) 424-7673, will put you up in a room on their converted landlocked barge for $69.50 s (shared shower) or $79.50 private, $10 for each additional person.

A municipal parking area for RVs is a half-mile out Whitshed Rd. beside what was once the city dump. Camping on this gravel-surfaced area overlooking Orca Inlet is $5; showers are available to noncampers.

Camping in Cordova has been a problem, but is becoming less so with the building of a couple of municipal campsites. One is on Fleming Spit, just 700 yards north of the ferry terminal, and the spaces for 50 RVs and 20 tents are due to be completed by August 1997. In the works is another site at the base of the ski hill, also for both RVs and tents. Plopping down your tent close to town is a problem, since almost all of the land is owned by individuals or by a Native corporation. If you've got wheels, head out of town towards the Million Dollar Bridge, and as soon as you pass Mile 17, there's a sign indicating that you're on Forest Service land. You can theoretically camp anywhere after this point, but the most comfortable places are at the roadside picnic area at Mile 22, or at the parking area of Alaganik Slough. There aren't any developed campsites at these places, but camping is allowed. There's picnic tables, outhouses, and fire pits, but you'll need to supply your own water, so carry plenty or boil water from the nearby streams.

Food

Two coffee shops open at 6 a.m., giving you someplace to go when you arrive on the early ferry. The **Club**, behind the Club Bar on First Ave., serves the usual bacon and eggs for $6; the **Reluctant Fisherman** coffee shop is similar. Both stay open till 9 p.m. A great place to eat brunch or lunch is the **Killer Whale Cafe** in the Orca Bookstore on First Avenue. Wholesome West Coast-type breakfast fare starts at $4; sit upstairs for the view of the harbor (or the store). They also serve unusual combination sandwiches, such as teriyaki chicken, ham, and pineapple for lunch ($5.50), and excellent bakery goods till 4 p.m. **Ambrosia Pizza** and **OK Chinese Restaurant** are also on First Avenue. **Powder House,** out a mile on the highway, does a thriving business in soup and sandwiches; sit on the deck overlooking the lake.

Alaska Commercial Co. on Nickoloff Rd. is the larger supermarket in town. **Davis Foods** is the smaller one, right on First Avenue.

Entertainment

Don't come to Cordova for the nightlife; other than drinking with the seafood folks, it's strictly make-your-own. The **Club Bar** has live music most nights, dancing some nights when someone wild instigates it. The **Alaskan** and **Cordova** bars, next to each other on First Ave., and the **Anchor Bar** on Breakwater Ave., are hard-core. The best view is from the bar at the **Reluctant Fisherman,** with prices to match. At the **Powder House** a mile out the Copper River Highway, you can have a drink on the deck on Eyak Lake.

Services and Information

Showers are available at the harbormaster's office. Get tokens at City Hall/police department if it's after business hours. Or plan to get to the community pool on Railroad Ave. at the appropriate public hours; $4 first half-hour, $1 each additional hour. You can also shower at the RV area on Whitshed Road. Anything you want to know about the business side of Cordova you can find out at the **chamber of commerce,** in the Union Hall Building at 510 First St., tel. (907) 424-2759; it's open Mon.-Fri. 8 a.m.-4 p.m. Also stop at the **USFS** office, on the third floor of the old post office building on Second Ave., tel. (907) 424-7661. Big maps on the wall, plus local maps, handouts, info on cabins; ask for the 21-page handout on the many trails in the area. Open Mon.-Fri. 8 a.m.-5 p.m.

TRANSPORTATION

By Ferry

The **MV** *Bartlett* services Cordova three times a week in the summer, leaving Valdez twice a week and Whittier (not via Columbia Glacier) once. Since the days, times, and fares change every year, check the latest schedule. The **MV** *Tustumena* does a run from Valdez to Cordova one day a week. The *Tustumena* has showers; the *Bartlett* doesn't. It's a 20-minute walk from the Cordova ferry terminal to town; take a right at the fork onto Railroad Ave. to avoid the First Ave. hill, then walk up Council Ave. from the Reluctant Fisherman. Becky Chapek also picks people up at the ferry and drops them in town for free, as an opportunity to plug her tour; see below.

By Air

Alaska Airlines flies into Cordova once daily (twice on Friday and Sunday) on its way to and from Juneau, $170 one-way. Although expensive, this is how you can hop over from Southeast to Southcentral, connecting up from the one ferry to the other, while skipping the long distances overland. **ERA** flies a turboprop twice daily between Cordova and Anchorage, and Alaska Airlines flies jets, one to Anchorage and one to Fairbanks, daily.

The airport is 12 miles from town out the Copper River Highway. A van service meets every incoming flight, and a ride to town costs $9 one-way, $15 roundtrip. The van makes several stops in town before heading out to the airport; call **Copper River & Northwest Tours** at tel. (907) 424-5356 to arrange pickup or for info on where to meet the van.

Getting Around
If you want to get out to the glaciers or Million Dollar Bridge, you have a number of options. You can ferry your own car across from Valdez for $128 roundtrip (make reservations far in advance). If that sounds steep, compare it to renting a car from the Reluctant Fisherman: $55 a day ($75 daily for a van), 25 cents a mile, plus insurance, plus gas, plus city tax. Without even trying you can rack up $125 for the day. **Imperial Car Rental,** tel. (907) 424-5982 or (907) 424-7440 after hours, rents cars, pickups, and vans for $55 per day with unlimited mileage.

Luckily, there's an alternative. Becky Chapek's **Footloose Tours/Copper River & Northwest Tours,** tel. (907) 424-5356, operates a six-hour van tour out to the bridge and back for $35 pp (minimum four), gourmet lunch included.

Hitchhiking is possible, especially on a fair day when an occasional local might pick you up on his or her joyride; visitors' vehicles tend to be crowded with travelers sharing expenses. Or you could grab an airporter van out to the end of the pavement and try hitching from there; if you don't get picked up, you don't have that far to come back.

KENAI PENINSULA

The Kenai Peninsula is like a mini-Alaska, compressing all of the state's features—mountains, icefields and glaciers, fjords and offshore islands, large fish-filled rivers and lakes, swampy plains, varied climate and precipitation, a few scattered port towns and a sprawling population center—into an area roughly one-thirty-fifth the size of the state. The outdoor recreational opportunities are practically inexhaustible, with innumerable choices of every pedestrian, pedaled, paddled, piloted, port-holed, piscatory, predatory, and picaresque particular you could ever ponder—just you and 300,000 other folks from the neighborhood. The Kenai is the major playground for Anchoragites and travelers, and it's possibly the most popular all-around destination for all Alaskans. But don't let that deter you. The resources are abundant, well-developed, and often isolated. And besides, what's wrong with a little company along the trail or under sail?

The Land
At 16,056 square miles, Kenai Peninsula is a little smaller than Vermont and New Hampshire combined. The Kenai Mountains form the Peninsula's backbone, with massive Harding Icefield dominating the lower lumbar. The east side,

facing Prince William Sound, hosts a spur of the Kenai Mountains, with the glimmering Sargent Icefields; the west side, facing Cook Inlet, is outwash plain, sparkling with low-lying swamp, lakes, and rivers. The icefields, glaciers, and plains are all a result of ice sculpting over the million-year course of the Pleistocene, with its five major glacial periods. During the last, the Wisconsin Period, Portage Glacier filled the entire Turnagain Arm, 50 miles long and a half-mile high. Portage stopped just short—10,000 years ago—of carving a fjord between Prince William Sound and Turnagain Arm; otherwise, Kenai Peninsula would've been Kenai Island. Still, this peninsula is so digitated with peninsulettes that it has more than 1,000 miles of coastline. The land is almost completely controlled by the feds; Chugach National Forest, Kenai National Wildlife Refuge, and Kenai Fjords National Park account for nearly 85% of the peninsula.

The Kenai Peninsula has 18 Forest Service public **recreation cabins** ($25/night). These are mostly pan-abode log structures that sleep four and have wood or oil stoves. Those along lakes have rowboats. For reservations, maps, and a brochure describing the various cabins, contact **Alaska Public Lands Information Center,** 605 W. Fourth Ave., Anchorage, AK 99501, tel. (907)

KENAI PENINSULA

Areas labeled on map: COOK INLET, ANCHORAGE, CROW CREEK MINE, MT. ALYESKA, HOPE, PAYSTREKE, PORTAGE, WHITTIER, PORTAGE GLACIER, NORTH KENAI, KENAI, MOOSE RIVER, KENAI RIVER, STERLING, COOPER LANDING, MOOSE PASS, SOLDOTNA, SKILAK LAKE, RUSSIAN RIVER, KENAI LAKE, KALGIN ISLAND, KASILOF, ALASKA RAILROAD, CLAM GULCH, LAKE TUSTEMENA, STERLING HWY, NINILCHIK, SEWARD, KENAI MOUNTAINS, ANCHOR POINT, HOMER, KENAI, SELDOVIA, GULF OF ALASKA, ALASKA STATE FERRY

0   20 mi
0   20 km

© MOON PUBLICATIONS, INC.

271-2599; or stop by Forest Service offices in Anchorage, Girdwood, or Seward. Because of their high popularity, it's a good idea to reserve well ahead of your visit. You can do so up to six months in advance. The Park Service also has five new cabins available for $20/night; see "Kenai Fjords National Park" below for specifics.

History

You begin to feel the Russian influence strongly in this neck of the woods. Baranov's first shipyard was located somewhere along Resurrection Bay down from present-day Seward. Rus-

sians built a stockade near Kasilof in 1786 and a fort at Kenai in 1791. Other than these brief incursions, the land belonged to the Kenai Indians, part of the great Athabascan tribe, till the gold rush, when color was uncovered around Hope and Sunrise on Turnagain Arm, and at Moose Creek halfway to Seward. First trails ran between the mining communities, then wagon roads and finally the railroad pushed from Seward through Anchorage to Fairbanks in the early 1920s. The Seward and Sterling Highways were completed in 1952, opening the Kenai's western frontier. When Atlantic Richfield tapped into oil (1957) and gas (1962) off the west coast, the Peninsula's economic star began to twinkle. And today, the Kenai Peninsula Borough's 40,000 people are occupied with fishing, outfitting, tourism, and services.

TO HOPE

Five miles south of Portage, the Seward Highway starts climbing into the Kenai Mountains. Don't despair or do anything rash if you get stuck behind a rental RV fishtailing along at 30 mph; a passing lane arrives just in time. You'll enter Kenai Peninsula Borough at **Turnagain Pass** (Mile 69, elevation 988 feet), where both sides of the road have rest areas. Stop and stretch in this pretty alpine area. In 2.5 miles at Mile 65 is **Bertha Creek Campground,** 12 sites, $6. At Mile 64 is the northern trailhead to **Johnson Pass Trail,** which goes 23 miles over relatively level terrain and emerges at Mile 33 of the Seward.

To Hope, bear right just beyond Mile 57 onto the Hope Highway. This road is sparsely trafficked, especially compared to the Seward. It follows Sixmile Creek north back up to Turnagain Arm; pan for gold along the first five miles of the crick. The entire 16.5 miles to Hope is pavement, divine pavement.

There are several unofficial campsites along this stretch of road, with a few good ones at Mile 13. Stop at one of the paved turnouts to look for beluga whales in Turnagain Arm, then rotate 180 degrees and search the cliffs for mountain goats high up in the crags. Goats can be distinguished from the more common Dall sheep by their longer, shaggier fur and by their distinctive body shape. Sheep look sleek and trim, while goats look almost rectangular when viewed from the side. Goats also live in higher, rougher country than sheep, although in the summer their ranges often overlap.

Hope

Gold was discovered on Resurrection Creek in 1888, and by 1896 3,000 people inhabited this boom neighborhood, between Hope and Sunrise on Sixmile Creek. Many came by way of the Passage Canal where Whittier now squats, portaging their watercraft over the Chugach glacial pass to Turnagain Arm, which is how Portage Glacier got its name. Large-scale mining

prospered into the '40s, but then Sunrise was abandoned and left to the ghosts, and Hope hangs on today with minor mining and logging supporting the town's 225 people. Turn right off the highway into downtown Hope. Take a quick left for old Hope to see the photogenic **Social Hall**—the original Alaska Commercial Co. store—and the tidal flats (caused by the earth sinking seven feet in the '64 quake); they're dangerous—don't walk on them! Go back and turn left for new Hope, with its post office, its red schoolhouse, and beautiful new and old log cabins.

At the end of Hope Highway is **Porcupine Campground,** featuring an uncommon paved loop road, 24 sites, and red raspberry hors d'oeuvres ($6). Across the road is unique **Davidson Grocery Store,** with its all-glass front. The unmarked **Mount Baldy Trail** is a cat track just beyond the end of the guard rail at the head of the campground. Walk along Porcupine Creek for a quarter-mile, then head up to a knob overlooking the Arm. From here you can hike forever on the ridgeline. Another trail starts at the far end of the campground and parallels the shoreline of Turnagain Arm. It's an easy stroll out to Gull Rock, and although you don't get the sweeping views that a ridgeline hike offers, if the tide is high and the beluga whales are feeding in the Arm, you can sometimes get very close to them.

The **Seaview,** tel. (907) 782-3364 in old Hope, has rooms for rent, campsites for RVs, a bar, a cafe, even a towing service should you have car trouble when you're in the area. **Bear Creek Lodge** at Mile 15.9 of the Hope Highway, tel. (907) 782-3141, has a restaurant and several log cabins clustered around a pond, complete with woodstoves and separate baths for $75 per night summer, $65 in the winter. **Henry's One Stop,** tel. (907) 782-3222, has motel rooms for $50, showers, a laundromat, a small grocery store, and spots for RV hookups.

Resurrection Pass Trail

Head out the highway and go right on Palmer Creek Road. In three-quarters of a mile is a fork: go straight for seven long miles to **Coeur D'Alene Campground** (no charge to camp here), or go right on Resurrection Pass Road. In just under four rough miles is the trailhead with parking, information signboard, and a fun bridge across the crick. This popular backpack trip leads 38 miles down to Cooper Landing on the Sterling

Highway, or you can cut across on **Devil's Pass Trail** to Mile 39 on the Seward. Eight USFS cabins ($20/night—just as easy to camp) are spaced along the route, but most people do the trip in four or five nights. You could also walk right onto **Russian Lakes Trail** on the other side of the Sterling at Cooper Landing, which goes 16 miles to the Resurrection River Trail, and hike another 16 miles to Exit Glacier Road outside of Seward. This 12-day hike covers the Peninsula from head to toe. Recreational miners pan for gold between the bridge at this trailhead and Paystreke, a half-mile upstream. Contact the Forest Service in Seward, Girdwood, or Anchorage for more detailed trail information and to make cabin reservations (necessary in the summer). For more information on the Resurrection Pass Trail, see the special topic this section.

TO SEWARD

A wide road with passing lanes heads up to scenic Summit Lake. At Mile 46 is **Tenderfoot Creek Campground,** in a beautiful area on the shores of this alpine water. Next to it is the incomparable **Summit Lake Lodge,** open year-round. Cozy and well placed, it has consistently recommendable food. Breakfast is served till 2 p.m., after which you have your choice of burgers, salads, entrées, or a Garbage Grinder or Miss Piggy. Be advised, however, that the restaurant only accepts cash and traveler's checks. Lack of phone service precludes them from accepting personal checks or credit cards. There's also a small motel and a gift/ice cream/espresso shop on-site. The original lodge was built in 1953;

RESURRECTION PASS TRAIL

The Resurrection Pass Trail covers 38 miles between the towns of Hope and Cooper Landing, with two side trails leading off to trailheads on the Seward Highway. A series of cabins maintained and rented out by the U.S. Forest Service make this one of the most popular hiking destinations in Southcentral Alaska. The trail winds through spruce forests and tops out in tundra, affording opportunities to see a variety of habitats. Wildlife, wildflowers, and wild fish in the lakes and streams add to the trail's appeal.

The nine cabins along the trail, one of which can only be reached via afloatplane, provide a welcome respite from the often inclement weather. They're very basic, each consisting of wooden bunks, a table and benches, a countertop for cooking, an outhouse, and a heating stove for warmth. There's no electricity, running water, cooking utensils, bedding, etc.—you provide all of that.

The cabins must be reserved in advance and paid for at the current rate of $25 per night. They're very popular, and the farther in advance you can make plans, the more likely you are to secure a reservation. Call (907) 271-2599 in Anchorage for additional reservation information.

If you can't secure cabins, there are plenty of spots to camp for the night, some of them official campsites, others just flat spots big enough for a tent. Be very careful with campfires or, better yet, use a camp stove for cooking. Also treat all drinking water with filters, with chemicals, or by boiling. The streams and lakes may look pristine, but gastrointestinal nasties are an ever-present possibility.

The high point of the main trail is Resurrection Pass at 2,600 feet. However, even at this comparatively low elevation, the snows of winter can linger well into June. Postholing through thigh-deep snow can dampen the enthusiasm of even the most jolly of hikers. If you're thinking of an early-season hike, check with the forest service office in Anchorage (tel. 907-271-2500) or the Seward Ranger District (tel. 907-224-3374) for trail conditions.

Local wildlife includes moose, bears both black and brown, wolves, mountain goats, Dall sheep, and even a local caribou herd. The caribou are scattered and often hard to spot in the summer, but if you look up high in the Resurrection Pass and Devil's Pass areas, maybe you'll get lucky. They often like to bed down in snow patches during the heat of the day, so look for dark spots in the snow near ridgelines.

Loop trips are possible, and you can do the Devil's Pass trailhead-Devil's Pass cabin-Cooper Landing trip (27 miles) in three relatively easy days. Hitchhiking to pick up your car is possible, but the Hope trailhead is well off the beaten path for most car traffic.

A continuation of the trail goes from Cooper Landing to Exit Glacier near Seward, but severe flooding in 1995 wiped out most of the bridges and several sections of trail down there, and whether those repairs will be undertaken is still undecided. Call the Seward Ranger District for updates.

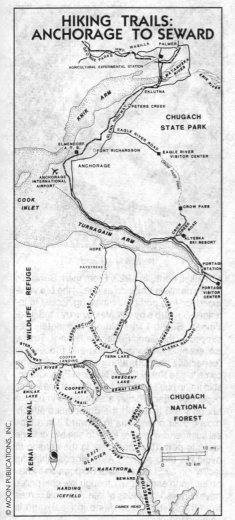

HIKING TRAILS:
ANCHORAGE TO SEWARD

© MOON PUBLICATIONS, INC.

the big fireplace and chimney are the only parts of the building that survived the '64 quake. The new building is constructed of local logs.

Just after Mile 40 and a mile before the Seward-Sterling junction is **Devil's Pass Trailhead;** this trail leads nine miles to the pass, then another mile to where it joins the Resurrection Pass Trail. An alpine cabin ($25/night) sits on the pass. Devil's Pass trailhead is very poorly marked—be prepared.

The **Carter Lake Trail** leaves the highway at Mile 33, climbs 1,000 feet in just over two miles to Carter Lake, and continues another mile around Carter Lake to Crescent Lake. This route gets you into the alpine fast and can be used to loop back to the highway on the Crescent Lake and Crescent Creek Trails. There's a public-use cabin ($25/night) on the south shore of Crescent Lake.

A half-mile beyond the Carter Lake trailhead is the southern trailhead to **Johnson Pass Trail** (whose northern trailhead is at Mile 64). And just beyond that is **Trail Lakes Fish Hatchery,** open 8 a.m.-4:30 p.m., which has a fascinating annotated color-photo display about spawning and stocking salmon.

At Mile 30 you slow down for **Moose Pass,** a town slightly larger than Hope, famous for Ed Estes's waterwheel and for its wild solstice celebrations. Continue six miles to the turnoff for **Trail River Campground,** just over a mile off the highway: large, empty, $6, with some choice sites on the lakeshore loop. Next up on the left at Mile 23 is **Ptarmigan Creek Campground,** 25 sites, $6. The **Ptarmigan Creek Trail** climbs 3.5 miles along the creek to Ptarmigan Lake where there's good fishing for grayling. **Kenai Lake** comes into view just south of here: huge, beautiful, blue-green, with snowcapped peaks all around. Breathe deeply. Three-mile **Victor Creek Trail** starts at Mile 20; in three miles is the turnoff to **Primrose Campground,** a mile from the Seward on Kenai Lake, 10 sites, $6.

Primrose Trail climbs 1,500 feet in eight miles to Lost Lake, where you can hook up to **Lost Lake Trail** and come out at Mile 5 near Seward. Or, if you planned far enough ahead and made a reservation, you can stay at the Clemens cabin, rented out by the Forest Service offices in Seward, Anchorage, or Girdwood. It's the same as the other cabins as far as price ($25/night) and reservation procedures are concerned, but this one has propane appliances and relatively plush furnishings. It was built by a local snowmachine club, then donated to the Forest Service. On clear days, you get a magnificent view of Resurrection Bay and on out to the Gulf of Alaska.

Beautiful Porcupine Creek Falls is three miles in on the Primrose Trail and is a favorite day-hike. From the lake, there are dramatic alpine views, and the chance to explore this high and mighty landscape. This is one of the most popular loop trails in the area, though there have been some problems with the southern end of the trail where it crosses private property. Check with the Forest Service in Seward for the latest on access to this end of the trail. **Grayling Lake, Golden Fin,** and **Lost Lake** Trails complete your journey from Portage—if you've hiked all the trails, overnighted at all the campgrounds, talked to all the townspeople, and kept Kodak and Fuji in business—to Seward, two months later.

SEWARD

Seward (pop. 2,700) is another pocket-size port town on a sparkling bay surrounded by snow-capped peaks, the only large town on the east side of the Kenai Peninsula. It's hooked up by bus, ferry, and plane, and has a maritime climate and a large seafood industry, just like a half-dozen other places you've visited so far—but with a difference: Seward is right on the doorstep of Kenai Fjords National Park. This pup of a park, still in its formative years, contains some of the most inhospitable visitable country in the state. Its Harding Icefield, a prehistoric frozen giant with three dozen frigid digits, rivals Glacier Bay for scenery and wildlife but is decidedly less expensive to visit. Combine this with Seward's convenient camping, good food, excellent access via public transportation, and more bars on Main Street than in any other town in Alaska, and you've got all the elements for a wild time in this old town.

History
In 1791, Baranov, on a return voyage to Kodiak from around his Alaskan domain, waited out a storm in this bay on Sunday of Resurrection, a Russian holiday. The sheltered waters of Resurrection Bay prompted Baranov to install a shipyard. One hundred ten years later, surveyors for the Alaska Central Railroad laid out the townsite for their port. This private enterprise, financed by Seattle businessmen, established Seward, laid 50 miles of track, and went broke. In 1911, Alaska Northern Railroad extended the track almost to present-day Girdwood. In 1912, the U.S. government began financing the completion of this line, which reached Fairbanks,

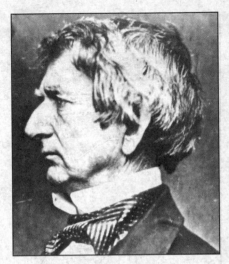

William H. Seward

470 miles north, in 1923. From then, Seward's history parallels Valdez's as one of the two year-round ice-free ports with shipping access to Interior—Seward's by rail, Valdez's by road. Like Valdez, Seward was almost completely destroyed by the Good Friday earthquake. Today, the economy runs on fishing and processing (especially halibut), along with travelers who come to see Kenai Fjords National Park. Cruise-ship traffic has skyrocketed in the last few years, especially after Whittier attempted to impose a tax on them in 1992; the companies simply moved their operations to Seward. On a typical summer day, you're likely to see two or three ships in port. (Get here late in the season to avoid the mob scene.) A major coal shipping facility run by Suneel Alaska Corporation stands on the north end of town, though low coal prices have curtailed business of late. The coal comes from the Usibelli Coal Mine in Healy and is shipped to Korea.

Sights
The most popular sights around Seward are within Kenai Fjords National Park, especially Exit Glacier. For details on visiting the park by foot or on the water, see "Hiking" and "On the Water," below. **Seward Museum,** at Jefferson and Third, tel. (907) 224-3902, is open daily 10

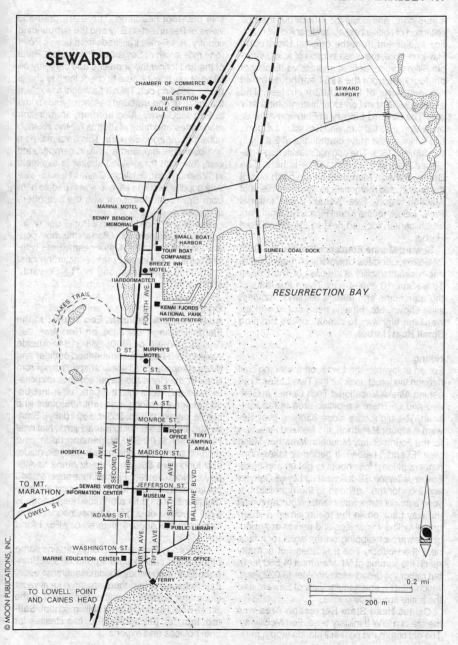

SEWARD

CHAMBER OF COMMERCE

BUS STATION

EAGLE CENTER

SEWARD AIRPORT

MARINA MOTEL

BENNY BENSON MEMORIAL

SMALL BOAT HARBOR

TOUR BOAT COMPANIES

SUNEEL COAL DOCK

BREEZE INN MOTEL

HARBORMASTER

RESURRECTION BAY

2 LAKES TRAIL

KENAI FJORDS NATIONAL PARK VISITOR CENTER

D ST.

MURPHY'S MOTEL

C ST.

B ST.

A ST.

MONROE ST.

POST OFFICE

TENT CAMPING AREA

MADISON ST.

HOSPITAL

JEFFERSON ST.

TO MT. MARATHON

SEWARD VISITOR INFORMATION CENTER

LOWELL ST.

MUSEUM

ADAMS ST.

PUBLIC LIBRARY

WASHINGTON ST.

MARINE EDUCATION CENTER

FERRY OFFICE

FOURTH AVE.

FIFTH AVE.

BALLAINE BLVD.

SIXTH AVE.

FIRST AVE.

SECOND AVE.

THIRD AVE.

FOURTH AVE.

TO LOWELL POINT AND CAINES HEAD

FERRY

© MOON PUBLICATIONS, INC.

0   0.2 mi

0   200 m

a.m.-5 p.m., and costs $2. Check out the fine collection of Native baskets and carved ivory, office equipment from the original Brown and Hawkins store, the cross-section of a 350-year-old Sitka spruce, and an impressive display of photographs from the 1964 earthquake that dropped parts of this country six feet. The evening slide show on local history starts at 7 p.m. The **Seward Library** at Fifth and Adams, open Mon.-Fri. 1-8 p.m. and Saturday 1-6 p.m., has a film on the 1964 earthquake at 2 p.m. in the summer ($2). The original Alaska flag—designed by a local boy in 1927—is here. The **Benny Benson Memorial** on the north end of the lagoon also memorializes this trivial piece of Alaskan history. See "Kenai Fjords National Park," below, for the Kenai Fjords National Park visitor center, located next to the Small Boat Harbor.

Seward Marine Education Center, tel. (907) 224-5261, operates University of Alaska's marine-research facility at the base of Third, open Tues.-Sun. 10 a.m.-4 p.m. There are tours of the aquariums and marine displays, movies, slide shows, etc. Finally, head out Fourth toward the highway to check out the bustling **Small Boat Harbor.**

Hiking

For an enjoyable short walk on a winding trail through the forest, look for the **Two Lakes Trail** behind Alaska Vocational Tech Center at Second and C. There's a picnic area at the trailhead. The high, bare slope hanging over Seward is **Mount Marathon,** the featured attraction for the Fourth of July Mountain Marathon Race (see "Events," below). It generally takes nonrunners at least four hours to get up and back. Follow Jefferson St. due west up Lowell Canyon and look for the trailhead to the right just beyond a pair of large water tanks. You can run all the way back down the mountain on a steep gravel incline if your legs and nerves are good, but beware of slipping on the solid rock face near the bottom. The trail does not actually reach the summit of Mt. Marathon (4,560 feet), but rather the broad east shoulder (3,022 feet), which offers a spectacular view of Seward and the entire surrounding area.

Caines Head State Recreation Area was the site of a WW II military base, Fort McGilvray. The old command post still stands atop a mas-

sive 650-foot headland. There are dramatic views of Resurrection Bay and the surrounding country. A 4.5-mile trail leads from Lowell Point (one mile south of Seward) to the old fort. Parts of the trail follow the shoreline and can only be hiked at low tide; be sure to check the tide charts before heading out. Take a flashlight to explore the maze of underground passages and rooms at Fort McGilvray. Also here are ammunition magazines and firing platforms for the six-inch guns that guarded Seward. This area makes a fine overnight trip, and a walk-in campground complete with three-sided shelter is available at Tonsina Point, a mile in. Caines Head is also very popular with sea kayakers who paddle here from Seward to hang out with the sea otters and seals.

See "Kenai Fjords National Park," below, for details on trails near Exit Glacier, the most popular local hiking paths. Other nearby trails within Chugach National Forest—including Lost Lake Trail—are described in "To Seward," above.

On the Water

Adventures & Delights Eco Tours, at the Fjords Trading Post Bldg. on Port Ave., tel. (907) 224-3960 or (800) 288-3134 (outside Alaska), is a highly recommended outfitter and guide company for all sorts of expeditions. From Seward, they lead sea-kayak voyages and one-to three-day treks into the park, offer instruction in sea kayaking, and rent fiberglass and plastic kayaks ($30 s, $55 d, $80 t daily). Shuttle service by boat out to Kenai Fjords National Park costs $100-300, depending upon your drop-off point. Day-trips including kayak, guide, and lunch are $95 pp. Five-day trips to Ailik Bay or Northwestern Fjord start around $1,140 pp, including a water taxi from Seward. A three-day tour to Kenai Fjords Wilderness Lodge is $795. If you're looking for a honeymoon splurge, be sure to ask about their three-day Fox Island trips ($795 pp).

Sailors say Resurrection Bay contains some of the finest sailing waters north of San Francisco Bay, with windy conditions almost every day. Because of this, there are three local yacht clubs and dozens of sailboats berthed in the Small Boat Harbor. A local sailing school, **Sailing, Inc.,** tel. (907) 224-3160, has classes for both novices and experts.

Accommodations

Seward has plenty of expensive indoor digs, starting with the **Best Western Hotel Seward,** 221 Fifth Ave., tel. (907) 224-2378 or (800) 528-1234, charging $168 s, $178 d. The **Marina Motel,** 1603 Seward Hwy., tel. (907) 224-5518, is a bit less expensive at $105 s and $120 d; they provide a shuttle service around town. **Breeze Inn Motel,** Small Boat Harbor, tel. (907) 224-5237, charges $95 s and $105 d; it's very convenient to restaurants and Kenai Fjords boat tours. The **New Seward Hotel,** 217 Fifth Ave., tel. (907) 224-8001, has rooms for $86 s, $96 d. Least expensive in town is **Murphy's Motel,** 911 Fourth Ave., tel. (907) 224-8090, at $75 s or $90 d.

The Visitor Information Center has a listing of 25 different bed and breakfasts, along with brochures from many of the places. Recommended B&Bs include: **Alaska Nellie's B&B,** tel. (907) 288-3124; **Bay Vista B&B,** tel. (907) 224-5880; **Bearpaw Cove B&B,** tel. (907) 224-5441; and **Stoney Creek Inn B&B,** tel. (907) 224-3940. In addition, **Creekside B&B,** tel. (907) 224-3834, has cabins for a real Alaskan experience. Expect to pay around $70 s or $95 d for rooms in Seward bed and breakfasts.

There's a lovely **Seward Hostel** 16 miles north of Seward, and one mile south of Primrose Campground. It's convenient to hikers coming off the Lost Lake Trail. Inside are 14 beds, two baths, kitchen, and common room; $10 for members of AYH, or $13 for nonmembers. The office is open 8-10 a.m. and 5-10 p.m., with a midnight curfew. Reservations are highly recommended in midsummer. Write Seward Hostel, P.O. Box 425, Seward, AK 99664 for reservations. It is open year-round. No telephone at the hostel, but you can call the Anchorage Hostel (907-276-3635) for information.

There's also a new Seward Hostel, 430 Third Ave., tel. (907) 224-7072. It's got 18 beds, kitchen facilities, and bath and shower for $16.50 pp. Private rooms with kitchenettes go for $60 and $65 per night.

Camping

City officials have seen fit to provide a fine stretch of "campground" along the shore across from Ballaine Blvd., with outhouse, picnic shelter, beautiful view, lots of company, and $6 for tents if anyone shows up to collect. RVs pay $8 (no hookups). You can also camp at the other city grounds at Mile 2 out the Seward—large trees, some highway noise, $4.25. Or pitch your tent in the small **Kenai Fjords National Park Campground** at Exit Glacier. It has only 10 sites and a small parking lot. There's water at the entrance; otherwise, this is minimalist camping on strange moraine terrain. RVers looking for full hookups head to **Bear Creek RV Park** seven miles north of Seward, tel. (907) 224-5725; **Kenai Fjords RV Park** at the Small Boat Harbor, tel. (907) 224-8779; or **Olson's Trailer Park** three miles north of Seward, tel. (907) 224-3233.

Food

Walk up and down Fourth Ave. and read the menus to see what stirs your fancy. Probably the cheapest eats are from **Prospero's,** a van on the corner of Adams and Fourth that serves burritos ($3.50 and up), enchiladas, and tacos. **Peking Chinese Cuisine,** 338 Fourth Ave., is open till 10:30 p.m.; try their kung pao halibut ($7.50). They also have lunch specials for $6.50. The other Chinese eatery is **Paradise,** across from the boat harbor. The food is inexpensive and not bad for fast food. Not far away is **Breeze Inn,** with the best breakfasts in town, and a lunch buffet in summer. **Pristine Seafoods** in the same area sells fresh fish. Try **The Depot Restaurant** on the north end of town near the visitor center for sub sandwiches, greasy-spoon burgers, BBQ ribs, and halibut.

If you have a bit more cash, three local places—Ray's, Harbor Dinner Club, and Apollo—all have great fresh-fish specials. The best halibut fish and chips are at **Harbor Dinner Club** ($8.50). **Ray's** at the Small Boat Harbor is especially convenient for grabbing a bite while you wait for your tour boat (or for a hot drink when you get back), and a great place to have dinner. The walls of Ray's are lined with all sorts of trophy fish, and the picture windows look out over the harbor. They also serve big breakfasts with lots of food. **Apollo Restaurant** on Fourth Ave. is the place to go for the biggest variety of food in town: pizza, pasta, and Mexican fare. **Niko's** pizza is also reasonable.

Get groceries and deli sandwiches at **Eagle Quality Center** on the north end of town. **Resurrect Art Coffeehouse Gallery,** on Fourth between Jefferson and Adams, is housed in an old Lutheran church. This is a wonderful place to hang out over an espresso coffee on a rainy day, or listen to musicians most evenings.

Entertainment
Every other storefront on Fourth is a bar. There's the **Yukon, Tony's,** the **Pioneer,** the **Showcase,** and **DJ's**—take your pick. The Yukon and Tony's both have rock 'n' roll on weekends; DJ's features an unusual right-angled billiard table that makes for strange bounces. **Liberty Theater** on Adams shows movies.

Events
January kicks off in Seward with the **Polar Bear Jump-Off,** a leap of faith into the frigid 39° F water of Resurrection Bay. All sorts of costumed jumpers join the fray. Every July Fourth there's a foot race up and down **Mount Marathon**— the 3,022-foot summit that rises behind Seward. Many runners do it in under an hour but end up with bruises and bloody knees to show for the torture—the record is 43 minutes. It has been run since 1915. This event draws hundreds of runners and onlookers and fills the bars and campgrounds. Also in Seward is the **Silver Salmon Derby** in August. With a $10,000 prize, this is one of Alaska's richest fishing derbies (the Homer Halibut Derby is considerably bigger, with a $30,000 first prize in 1995).

Information and Services
For Seward maps and brochures, start out at the **Visitor Information Center** in the Seward Rail Car on Third St. at Jefferson, tel. (907) 224-3094, open daily 11 a.m.-5 p.m. in the summer (closed in winter). Pick up the *Visitors Guide,* which has a walking tour and some interesting history. The rail car served as a club car on the Alaska Railroad between 1936 and 1960. The **Seward Chamber of Commerce** office, two miles north of town, tel. (907) 224-3046, is open daily 9 a.m.-6 p.m. in the summer and Mon.-Fri. 9 a.m.-5 p.m. the rest of the year. It's one of the first places you pass on your way into Seward from the north. The **Kenai Fjords National Park Visitor Center** at 1212 Fourth Ave. (next to the harbormaster), tel. (907) 224-3175, is open daily 8 a.m.-7 p.m. in the summer, and Mon.-Fri. 8 a.m.-5 p.m. the rest of the year, tel. (907) 224-3175. See "Kenai Fjords National Park" for more on this popular national park.

The **Forest Service office** is on Fourth near Jefferson, open Mon.-Fri. 8 a.m.-5 p.m., tel. (907) 224-3374. They can tell you about all the hikes and cabins, but they can't make up your mind which of the dozen and a half to choose. Soap and rinse your entire naked body in the large locker-room-type facility at the **harbormaster,** open 8 a.m.-10 p.m., $1 for five minutes; or head to **Seward Laundry,** where $3 buys 20 minutes. There's a **swimming pool** at the high school where they throw in a free swim with your shower; call (907) 224-3900 for hours. **Reader's Delight,** 222 Fourth Ave., tel. (907) 224-2665, has books for sale.

Transportation
An **Alaska Railroad** train leaves Anchorage daily during the summer at 6:45 a.m. and arrives in Seward at 11 a.m., then returns to Anchorage at 6 p.m., arriving at 10 p.m., $50 one-way or $80 roundtrip. Note that the train does not stop at Portage to pick up or drop off foot passengers for Whittier. If you are trying to get to Seward from Portage, you have to take a bus to Anchorage and catch the Seward train there or get on the Seward Bus Line van in Portage. The railroad also does not offer Anchorage-Seward passenger service between September 27 and May 22. Call (800) 478-2467 for reservations.

Alaska Marine Highway's trusty MV *Tustumena* calls in at its home port of Seward four times a week at all different hours of the day and night, on its way to and from Homer ($96), Seldovia ($100), Kodiak ($54), and Dutch Harbor ($250). Call (907) 224-5485 for arrival and departure times, or (800) 642-0066 for reservations. For a complete listing, see the chart "Southcentral and Southwest Alaska Ferry Passenger Fares," in the Southwest Alaska chapter.

The Seward airport is three miles north of town. **F.S. Air Service,** tel. (800) 478-9595, has three flights weekdays, two on Saturday, and one on Sunday between Anchorage and Seward for $65. **Bear Lake Guide Service,** tel. (907) 224-5985, offers flightseeing trips and courtesy van service from Seward. A 45-minute to one-hour flight runs $99. Reservations aren't necessary, but they are recommended.

A **trolley** runs around Seward frequently and charges $1 per ride or $3 for all day. **Seward Bus Lines,** tel. (907) 224-3608 (Seward) or (907) 278-0800 (Anchorage), leaves Seward at

all-encompassing view from the shoulder of Mt. Marathon

9 a.m., arriving in Anchorage at noon, then leaves Anchorage (Seventh and Gambell) at 2:30 p.m., arriving at 5:30 p.m., $30 one-way. They also offer bus service to Homer; call them for specifics.

Car rental is available from **Hertz,** tel. (907) 224-6097. Local rentals run $55-63 a day; renting one-way to Anchorage be prepared for hefty drop-off fees (in the neighborhood of $100!).

You can rent mountain bikes for $32/day from **Grizzly Bicycle Rentals,** at Adventures & Delights Eco Tours, tel. (907) 224-3960. See "On the Water," above, for kayak rentals in Seward. Mary Thompson of **Kenai Peninsula Guided Hikes,** tel. (907) 288-3141, leads day-hikes in the Seward area for $25 pp. See below for boat tours of Kenai Fjords National Park.

KENAI FJORDS NATIONAL PARK

Kenai Fjords National Park covers 580,000 acres of ice, rock, and rugged coastline on the southern end of Kenai Peninsula. The centerpiece of this magnificent national park is the Harding Icefield, a massive expanse of ice and snow broken only by "nunataks"—the peaks of high, rocky mountains. The icefield pushes out in all directions in the form of more than 30 named glaciers. Along the coast, eight of these glaciers reach the sea, creating a thundering display of calving icebergs. Kenai Fjords has only been a national park since 1980 but is today one of the most popular attractions in Alaska. Many visitors come to ride the tour boats past teeming bird colonies or up to tidewater glaciers; many others hike to scenic Exit Glacier or up a steep path to the edge of Harding Icefield itself.

Kenai Fjords National Park Visitor Center is in Seward at 1212 Fourth Ave. (next to the Harbormaster) and is open daily 8 a.m.-7 p.m. from Memorial Day to Labor Day, Mon.-Fri. 8 a.m.-5 p.m. the rest of the year, tel. (907) 224-3175. Inside are excellent exhibits on Harding Icefield and little-known sights within the park. They also show videos of the park and sell maps and publications of local interest, including *Guide to Alaska's Kenai Fjords,* by David Miller. Also here is a fine waterproof hiking map to the park published by Trails Illustrated ($8).

Exit Glacier Area
This is the only part of the park that is accessible by road. Get to Exit Glacier by heading four miles north from Seward and turning left at the sign. The ranger station/visitor center is nine miles out this rough gravel road, and a short ways beyond the small walk-in **campground** (no charge). Inside the **Exit Glacier Visitor Center,** a spectacular satellite photo shows what a tiny fraction of the Harding Icefield Exit Glacier is. A dozen taped-together topographic maps create a giant image of the Peninsula. The rangers give programs and lead one-hour

KENAI PENINSULA RECREATION

© MOON PUBLICATIONS, INC.

nature walks daily 10 a.m. and 2 p.m., with a longer trip to the icefield at 8 a.m. on Saturday. Check the board for other activities.

A three-quarter-mile roundtrip **nature trail** offers an easy, quiet forest walk. The **Lower Loop Trail** goes a half-mile, crosses a creek, then climbs a steep quarter-mile up to the 150-foot face of Exit Glacier. The steep and winding **Upper Trail** continues another quarter-mile, of-fering views across the glacier and of several ice caves (don't go into these).

Harding Icefield Trail, 4.5 miles, forks off just after the bridge over the creek and climbs to 3,500 feet and the Icefield. Plan on at least four hours for this far more difficult hike. Check at the ranger station for current trail conditions. Deep snow may block this route till midsum-mer. Skilled skiers may want to carry cross-country skis and slide around on the crevasse-free icefield. In the wintertime, the road into Exit Glacier is not plowed but is very popular with skiers and snowmobilers.

The 16-mile **Resurrection River Trail** starts at Mile 8 of the Exit Glacier Road. This is the southern end of the 74-mile, three-trail system from Kenai's top to bottom. Resurrection River Trail leads to the 16-mile Russian Lakes Trail, which hooks up near Cooper Landing to the 38-mile Resurrection Pass Trail to Hope. A Forest Service cabin ($20/night) is six miles from the trailhead; check with the USFS office in Seward (see above) for availability. Note that the Res-urrection River Trail can become quite a quag-mire when it rains. The trail is popular with cross-country skiers in wintertime because of its low avalanche danger.

ALASKA SALMON

Five species of salmon are found in Alaskan waters. All are anadromous, spending time in both fresh and salt water. All five species also have at least two common names, making them confusing to newcomers. The yearly return of adult salmon is a major event for wildlife in many parts of Alaska, as quiet little streams suddenly erupt in a frenzy of life and death. Commercial fishermen search out the migrating schools in the ocean as they prepare to head up rivers and creeks to spawn. Anglers line the river banks, hoping to catch a big king or coho. Bears pace the creeks, ready to pounce on salmon in the shallow water. Foxes, eagles, ravens, gulls, and magpies wait for the salmon to weaken or die before feeding on them. Smaller birds such as dippers eat the eggs, as do such fish as Dolly Varden and rainbow trout. Crab and halibut move into the areas near creek mouths, eating salmon carcasses that wash downstream.

Female salmon spawn in creeks and rivers during late summer throughout much of Alaska, digging holes ("redds") in the gravel with their tails before laying hundreds of small red eggs. The males fight for position to fertilize the eggs as soon as they're laid. Shortly after spawning the salmon die, and their carcasses create a stench that permeates late summer evenings. But these carcasses also add important nutrients to the system, nutrients that are used by the plankton that form the basis of the food chain. The plankton in turn are eaten by the young salmon fry that emerge from the eggs, thus helping to complete this never-ending cycle of life and death.

Catching Salmon

When salmon move from the ocean into their spawning streams, their bodies undergo rapid changes that reduce the quality of the meat. The freshest and brightest salmon are found in the ocean or lower reaches of the rivers, rather than farther upstream. If you want to try your luck at fishing, purchase a 14-day nonresident fishing license for $30, or a three-day nonresident license for $15. Licenses are available in sporting goods stores throughout Alaska, or by writing to the Dept. of Revenue, Fish and Game Licensing, 1111 W. Eighth St., Juneau, AK 99801. Before heading out, pick up a copy of the latest fishing regulations. Many backpackers carry a small collapsible fishing pole for

their trips out of town. These work well with trout and smaller salmon, but may not survive an encounter with a 10-pound silver, and certainly won't handle a 35-pound king.

DIANA LASICH HARPER/3

King (Chinook) Salmon
The largest of all Pacific salmon, the king commonly exceeds 30 pounds (the record is 126 pounds), and is the most highly prized and one of the best-tasting sport fish in Alaska. The most famous place to catch kings is the Kenai River in Southcentral Alaska.

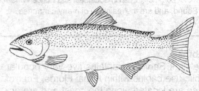

Sockeye (Red) Salmon
Much smaller (six to 10 pounds), and difficult to catch on spinning rods, sockeye are considered the best-tasting salmon. They turn bright red with an olive-green head when ready to spawn. Sockeye are the most important fish in the Bristol Bay and Kodiak areas.

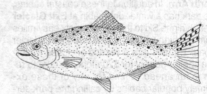

Coho (Silver) Salmon
The silvery cohos generally weigh seven to 10 pounds and are a beautiful and powerful fish that can be caught in both fresh and salt water. They are another favorite of anglers, and have a more delicate flavor. *(continues on next page)*

ALASKA SALMON
(continued)

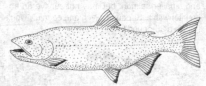
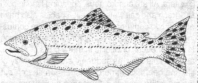

DIANA LASICH HARPER/2

Pink (Humpback) Salmon
The smallest (three to four pounds) and most abundant salmon in Alaska are the pinks. "Humpie" runs sometimes turn creeks into a seething mass of spawning fish. They are considered a "trash fish" by many Alaskans, but are fine to eat when caught in salt water before they have started to change. Once they reach fresh water, however, they develop prominently humped backs and grotesque jaws. Pinks are the major commercial fish in Southeast and Prince William Sound, and are the mainstay of many canneries.

Chum (Dog) Salmon
Chum are also quite large (five to 15 pounds) but are not considered as tasty as kings, sockeye, or coho. Spawning time turns them into grotesque monsters with huge dog like teeth. The name dog salmon may also refer to their use as food for dogsled teams in central Alaska. Chum are a very important food source in villages along the Yukon River.

Cabins
The Park Service maintains five very popular public-use cabins within Kenai Fjords. Four of these are located along the coast and are accessible only by boat or floatplane from Seward. These cabins are open June-Labor Day and cost $25/night. Each has its own treat—a pleasant beach walk at **Aialik Bay,** good fishing at **Delight Creek,** thunderous calving glaciers at **Holgate Arm,** and an old-growth rainforest at **North Arm.** In addition to these coastal cabins, the park has a winter-only cabin at **Exit Glacier** for $25/night. Ski to this cabin the six easy miles from the highway along unplowed Exit Glacier Road. There is also a second enclosed winter-use shelter nearby for $20/night. Be sure to reserve far ahead of time for any of these extremely popular cabins by calling the park service at (907) 224-3175.

Boat Tours
The most exciting thing to do in Seward is to get on a tour boat out into Resurrection Bay or into some nearby fjords. This is *the* cruise for seeing marine wildlife. On a good day, you could see three kinds of whales—including humpbacks and orcas—plus porpoises, seals, sea otters, sea lions, hundreds of puffins, kittiwakes, auklets, and the occasional bald eagle and oystercatcher. Half-a-dozen different tour companies offer cruises with knowledgeable guides. Half-day trips take you around nearby Resurrection Bay and out as far as Rugged Island, while longer voyages include Aialik Bay, Holgate Glacier (calving icebergs), and the Chiswell Islands (a Steller's sea lion rookery and nesting seabirds—most notably puffins). The latter is a far more interesting trip and actually goes inside the park rather than to its edge.

Kenai Fjord Tours, tel. (907) 224-8068 or (800) 478-8068 (in Alaska), offers a variety of cruises into the park from a four-hour Resurrection Bay tour ($49) up to a nine-hour Northwestern Glacier Tour ($129). Other tour companies offer similar sightseeing cruises, including overnight trips, complete packages with transportation to and from Anchorage, side trips to Exit Glacier, etc. **Kenai Coastal Tours,** tel. (907) 224-8068 or (800) 770-9119, charges $95 for an all-day tour (including lunch). **Major Marine Tours,** tel. (907) 224-8030 or (800) 764-7300, offers a half-day dinner cruise (all-you-can-eat crab and shrimp) for $74 pp. These three companies all run large boats that hold 100-plus passengers and are more stable when the sea is rough. Three local companies have smaller boats for a more personal trip: **Alaska Renown Charters,** tel. (907) 224-3806, charges $35 pp ($20 for kids) for short two-and-a-half-hour trips; **Fresh Aire Charters,** tel. (907) 272-2755, charges $70 pp (including lunch) for half-day cruises; while **Mariah Charters & Tours,** tel. (907) 224-8623, charges $50 pp for half-day trips, or $80 pp for all-day voyages (food additional). Mariah was recommended by a number of locals as offering an especially good tour. On Fridays, they go to Harris Bay—where few other tour boats stray.

These tour boats operate between mid-April and mid-September only. If you get here early or late in the season, you're likely to find lower prices and fewer people onboard. Most of the tour companies have booths on the dock behind the harbormaster's office on Fourth Avenue. Binoculars and telephoto lenses are handy, and seven layers of overclothes are imperative. If you get seasick easy, take along medication, especially on the all-day voyages that go into more exposed waters. You may want to wait if the marine weather report predicts rough seas. This trip is guaranteed to be one of the highlights of your Alaskan visit.

Adventures & Delights Eco Tours, tel. (907) 224-3960 or (800) 288-3134 (outside Alaska), leads sea-kayak voyages into the park and rents kayaks. See "On the Water" in the Seward section, above, for details.

WESTERN KENAI PENINSULA

TO SOLDOTNA/KENAI

The junction with the **Sterling Highway** is at Mile 37 of the Seward Highway; the mileposts along the Sterling also start counting at 37 from this point. Between the junction and Cooper Landing (Mile 49) are three USFS campgrounds: **Tern Lake** (25 sites, water, $6); **Quartz Creek** (paved loop road, 32 sites, flush toilets, boat ramp, a beautiful site right on Kenai Lake, $7); and **Crescent Creek** (three miles down Crescent Creek Rd., nine sites, $6). A 6.5-mile trail climbs 1,000 feet from the Crescent Creek parking lot to Crescent Lake.

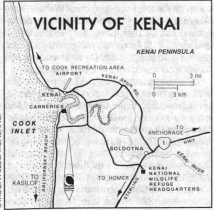

VICINITY OF KENAI

KENAI PENINSULA

TO COOK RECREATION AREA
AIRPORT

KENAI SPUR RD.

0   3 mi

0   3 km

KENAI
CANNERIES

COOK
INLET

TO
ANCHORAGE

SOLDOTNA

1   HWY

KENAI RIVER

KALIFORNSKY BEACH

TO
KASILOF

TO HOMER

KENAI
NATIONAL
WILDLIFE
REFUGE
HEADQUARTERS

STERLING

MOON

© MOON PUBLICATIONS, INC.

Kenai Princess Lodge

Princess Tours out of Seattle, one of the two top Alaska packagers, built this small, beautiful lodge overlooking the roiling turquoise water of the Kenai River in 1989. The lobby, lounge, dining room, conference room, and tour desk are in the main lodge building, built from Alaska pine, with a big stone fireplace, antler chandeliers, and a big outside deck. There are also a separate gift shop and health spa, a half-mile and one-mile nature walk (pick up a brochure at the front desk), an RV park and general store (with showers), and 50 rooms. Each room has a woodstove (and electric heat), two full-sized beds, a sitting area, a TV with remote, and a deck. The lodge is open year-round; summer rates are $175 for a double room and $210 for a suite. September-Dec. and March-May the rates are $79 Sun.-Thurs., $99 Friday and Saturday, $129 for a suite. For details, write P.O. Box 676, Cooper Landing, AK 99572, or call (907) 595-1425. To get there, bear right off the Sterling just before you cross the Kenai River and continue two miles past the school, the library-community center, and the cemetery on a graded gravel road, then bear left at the sign to the lodge.

Cooper Landing

This is the first of the service centers that cling to both sides of the Sterling Highway from here to the town of Kenai. Clumped together in central Cooper Landing are three motels, a couple of restaurants, a Chevron station, and hardware, grocery, and tackle shops. The main attraction in Cooper Landing is the raft trip down the Kenai River. Several raft companies offer this 14-mile ride to Jim's Landing, which includes some Class II rapids at Schooner Bend. **Alaska Wildland Adventures,** tel. (907) 595-1279 or (800) 478-4100, does three two-hour trips daily at 9:30 a.m., and 1 and 5 p.m., $42 adults, $29 kids. The full day Kenai Canyon Raft Trip leaves at 11 a.m., $95 and $55. Guided sportfishing trips on the Kenai will run you $185 full day including lunch, or $125 half-day. Five-dollar coupons can be found in ads in the Kenai visitors guides. **Osprey Alaska Inc.,** just over the Kenai bridge on the left, tel. (907) 595-1265 or (800) 533-5364, offers four-hour scenic floats for $45, or the full-day Kenai Canyon trip for $100 adults, $49 children under 12. Guided sportfishing trips go for $175 full day including a hot shore lunch, or $100 half-day. **Alaska Rivers Co.,** tel. (907) 595-1226, offers half-day scenic river trips for $39, full-day Kenai Canyon trips for $80. Guided fishing trips are $110 and $75 full and half day, or you can fish the Kenai Canyon area on a full-day trip for $150. They also offer guided hiking trips to the Russian River Falls (a real natural phenomenon when the red salmon are running in June and July) for $35, and halibut charters out of Seward for $150. Except for the halibut trips, they reduce the rates by half for kids 12 and under.

Just beyond Cooper Landing is **Cooper Creek Campground,** with 26 sites ($9) on both sides of the road. A mile and a half past that is the large **Russian River Campground,** one of the best places in the state to catch sockeye salmon when they're running (generally mid-June and mid-July). Sites are strung along the two-mile paved road; $11 for one of 85 large, well-spaced sites. Park in the lot ($5) if you just want to hike on the 21-mile **Russian Lakes Trail** or take the "fisherman's path" along the river to Russian River Falls, where salmon leap. The Russian River runs into the Kenai River near the entrance station. The **Resurrection Pass Trail** crosses the Sterling Highway at Mile 53.

Another very popular salmon-fishing area is a couple of miles past the USFS campground, at the U.S. Fish and Wildlife Service **Kenai-Russian Rivers Campground,** Mile 55, $7, where a privately operated, cable-guided, current-powered ferry shuttles anglers between the campground and the sockeye-rich opposite bank.

Kenai National Wildlife Refuge

This large habitat supports so many moose, Dall sheep, bear, salmon, and other wildlife that it was designated a refuge by President Roosevelt in 1941. The Alaska National Interest Lands Act (1980) changed the name from Kenai National Moose Range and expanded the refuge to its present two-million-plus acres, managed by the federal Fish and Wildlife Service. An information cabin is at Mile 58, right at the junction of the Sterling and the rough and dusty 20-mile **Skilak Lake Loop Road.**

From here to Sterling (town) on the Sterling (highway) is a quick 25-mile ride, with a handful of small campgrounds on lakes with fishing and picnicking. The big action in this neck of the woods is on the Loop Road—so many campgrounds, trailheads, lakes, creeks, and accompanying recreational opportunities that even listing them is beyond the scope of this edition. For more information about the seven free campgrounds, more than a dozen trails, and hundreds of miles of boating and fishing lanes, inquire at the USF&WS greeting cabin or the HQ in Soldotna (see below), or use the excellent *Guide to the Kenai Peninsula* booklet and the useful book *55 Ways to the Wilderness in Southcentral Alaska.*

Sterling

You'll know you're in salmon country in Sterling (pop. 1,800), Mile 83, where the widening Kenai River merges with the Moose River, and the fish-hook frenzy pervades all your senses (especially the olfactory). The height of the activity is on either side of the bridge, with a private fish camp on the west side and **Izaak Walton State Recreation Site** on the east. This pretty campground has 38 sites, paved loop roads, toilets, and water, $10. Archaeological excavations conducted here suggest that Natives occupied this fish-rich confluence up to 2,000 years ago.

Oil was discovered in 1957 in the northern wilderness near the Swanson River; the 18-mile gravel road built to the oilfields also opened up this lake-studded lowlands. Two canoe routes, **Swanson River Route** (80 miles, 40 lakes) and **Swan Lake Route** (60 miles, 30 lakes), are accessible by Swanson River Rd., a right turn off the Sterling at Mile 84 by the old log school. Also, 13 miles in on Swanson River Rd. is **Dolly Varden Lake Campground:** free, uncrowded, nice views, right on the lake, frequent moose visits. Pick up the USF&WS brochure *Canoeing in the Kenai National Wildlife Refuge* for detailed info.

The 13-mile stretch from Sterling to Soldotna bristles with guides and outfitters, fish camps, fish exchanges and markets, bait and tackle shops, charters, marine stores, boat rentals, boat engine sales and repairs, propeller-sharpening shops, etc.—essential infrastructure in the eternal struggle between sportsmen and salmon. You'll be in either angler ecstasy or claustrophobia central.

SOLDOTNA

If Kenai is a mini-Alaska, Soldotna (pop. 3,600) is a mini-Anchorage. Just as Anchorage was established as a supply center for the railroad, Soldotna grew up in the 1940s around the junction of the Sterling Highway and Kenai Spur Road. It's still supported by the same Cook Inlet oil money that stabilized Anchorage's economic base. And the sprawling suburban burgh is the seat of the borough government, has a branch of the University of Alaska, and has been mauled by malls, festooned by fast food, and fashioned by fish—it's got everything but the skyscrapers.

Sights
Kenai Peninsula Visitor Information Center is on Sterling Highway just south of the bridge, tel. (907) 262-9814, open daily 9 a.m.-7 p.m. Stop by to gather up information and to see the great wildlife photography and the 94-pound king salmon, one of the largest salmon ever caught by a sport fisherman. The chamber of commerce is in the same building next door.

For the **Kenai National Wildlife Refuge Visitor Center,** take a left at Kalifornsky, then an immediate right, and go a mile up Ski Hill Rd.; tel. (907) 262-7021, open Mon.-Fri. 8 a.m.-4:30 p.m., weekends 10 a.m.-5 p.m. Buy books and posters, and see their 15-minute video hourly noon-4 p.m. weekdays, or free wildlife documentaries noon-5 p.m. weekends. Stroll the mile-long nature trail and climb the observation tower.

Soldotna Historical Society Museum is a collection of log cabins on the way into Centennial Park; it's open Tues.-Fri. 10 a.m.-4 p.m. and Saturday and Sunday noon-4 p.m.

Accommodations
All the action is found either on Sterling Highway in town or on Kalifornsky Beach Rd. (named for an early settler from California), which crosses the Kenai River one more time right at its mouth just before Kenai town. **Centennial Park City Campground** charges $8 a night to camp, $3 a day to park and fish on the river; cross the bridge on the Sterling, take a right at the light onto Kalifornsky, then another immediate right into the campground. This is a big city park with nice wooded sites (some right on the river), picnic tables, fire pits, water, telephones, and a boat-launching ramp. Identical rates apply at **Swiftwater Campground,** also run by the city of Soldotna, on East Redoubt St., Mile 96.1 of the Sterling Highway.

Another two miles out Kalifornsky is **Duck Inn,** tel. (907) 262-1849, which has small rooms with one double bed, which is why they're so reasonably priced (for Alaska, of course) at $79. See the bartender to check in.

Soldotna Bed & Breakfast is a handsome building, sort of a cross between a European chalet and a motel, with 16 rooms; 399 Lovers Lane (off Sterling Highway at the Dairy Queen), tel. (907) 262-4779; $120-140 for rooms during the summer.

Kenai River Lodge on the highway on the north side of the bridge, tel. (907) 262-4292, charges $99-110 for a double room depending on the season; rooms overlook the river.

Food, Entertainment, and Services
A great place to eat, drink, relax, and commune with Soldotna is at the **Tide's Inn Supper Club and Lounge** across the highway from the Kenai River Lodge overlooking the water, tel. (907) 262-1906. This restaurant presents a plain facade—its back side—to the road but is elegant inside and out front. The dining room serves burgers and sandwiches for lunch for $6-8, and the usual Alaskan prime rib, filet mignon, veal oscar, surf and turf, sesame chicken, scallops, salmon, halibut, and king crab in the $15-35 range. The lounge is oh so comfortable and there's a big dance floor for live entertainment—recommended.

There's a restaurant next door to the Duck Inn on Kalifornsky about three miles west of Soldotna: they serve breakfast and lunch ($6-7) and the usual steak, seafood, and poultry dinners starting at $18 and topping out at $30 for king crab or surf and turf. They also make great homemade pizza. Open 7 a.m.-11 p.m.

Klondike City, at the corner of the highway and Lovers Lane across from the Dairy Queen, tel. (907) 262-2220, is a small themed shopping center with a bowling alley ($6 an hour per lane; includes shoes), a roller rink, a pawn shop, a print shop, and Sal's Klondike Diner (open 24 hours), where you can get typical road food and untypically big pieces of pie.

Take your pick of rapid rations in Soldotna. **Grand Burrito,** open 11 a.m.-9 p.m., will fill you up for under $4; the veggie burrito is the best deal. An Armenian bakery is connected.

The bar and lounge at **Kenai River Lodge** are comfortable and scenic: they're on the second floor with big picture windows overlooking the river. Great service, too, as well as very friendly people.

Grab a shower at **Alpine Laundromat** on the highway right next door to Dairy Queen; it's open long hours from early morning to late evening, and charges $3 for showers, 25 cents for towels.

KENAI

The town of Kenai (pop. 6,300) sits on a bluff above the mouth of the Kenai River overlooking Cook Inlet. Across the inlet to the southwest rise Redoubt and Iliamna, active volcanos at the head of the Aleutian Range. The Alaska Range is visible to the northwest. Great white beluga whales enter the mouth of the river on the incoming tides to look for fish. Kenai is the second-oldest permanent settlement in Alaska, founded by Russian fur traders who built St. Nicholas Redoubt in 1791. The U.S. Army built its own fort, Kenay, in 1869, two years after the Great Land changed hands. Oil was discovered in 1957 offshore, and now Kenai is the largest and most industrial city on the Peninsula.

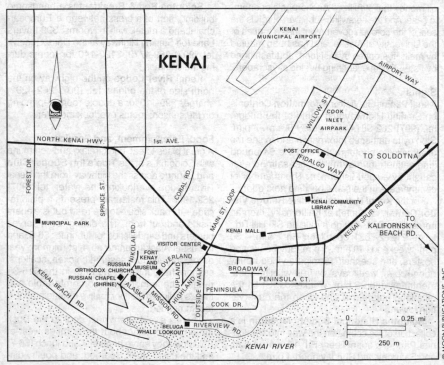

Sights

All the sights of Kenai are in one small area, which you can tour on foot in 90 minutes. Start at the **Kenai Bicentennial Visitor and Cultural Center,** right at the corner of Main St. and Kenai Spur Rd., tel. (907) 283-1991, open weekdays 9 a.m.-8 p.m., Saturday and Sunday 10 a.m.-7 p.m. Here you'll find a complete and well-organized selection of brochures and information sheets about the area. Their museum collection is quite impressive, with cultural artifacts from the local Native peoples, a permanent exhibit of local historical lore and natural history, and temporary exhibits of interest, as well as the inevitable Alaska videos.

Next, walk down toward the bluff on Overland Ave. to the replica of **Fort Kenay,** built in 1967 for the Alaska Centennial. Next door is **Holy Assumption Russian Orthodox Church,** built in 1896 and now the second-oldest Russian Orthodox Church in the state (the oldest is on Kodiak). It's a working church with regular services; tours are available on request, or peek through the windows at the painted altar and brass chandelier. **Saint Nicholas Memorial Chapel** (1906) nearby, built over the grave of Kenai's first priest, also reflects the traditional Russian Orthodox architectural style. Walk east on Mission Rd. for two viewpoints over the bluff; from the first, look out over the riverside canneries, with the Kenai Mountains behind and the Aleutian and Alaska Ranges strung out across the inlet. The second has an interpretive sign about beluga whales.

Accommodations and Food

There is no public camping in Kenai. **Overland RV Park** sort of surrounds the visitor center on three sides, tel. (907) 283-4512; you can pitch a tent or hook up your motorhome and help yourself to the showers and laundry facilities.

Stay indoors at the **Uptown Motel,** on the Spur Rd. in the middle of town, tel. (907) 283-3660, $115 s, $125 d (plus 17% room tax!). Check out the 100-year-old gold-plated cash register behind the front desk. **Kenai Merit Inn,** tel. (907) 283-6131 or (800) 227-6131; and **Kenai Kings Inn,** tel. (907) 283-6060, are on the Soldotna side of the Spur Rd., with rooms and rates similar to the Uptown's.

One classy place to eat in Kenai is **Paradisos,** on the Spur Rd. a block east of the visitor center, tel. (907) 283-2222, serving lunch and dinner to locals and visitors since 1971. The big big menu features Italian, Mexican, and Greek food. Lunch is meatball sandwiches, gyros, and Greek burgers $6-7, along with Mexican plates from $5 (taco, rice, and beans) to $14 (sauteed shrimp); dinner is pasta ($9-13), steak and seafood ($14-20), chicken and veal ($13-14), and Greek ($6-13).

The other classy place in town is **Louis',** attached to the Uptown Motel, serving the usual meat and fish for lunch and dinner for $12-24.

You'll also find Arby's, Dairy Queen, McDonald's, and several pizza places and diners in Kenai. If you're just passing through in a hurry, stop off at Carrs and grab a quick soup-and-salad bar.

TO HOMER

From Kenai, backtrack on Kalifornsky over the Kenai River and go right at the fork to the coast; this spur road joins the Sterling at Mile 109 at **Kasilof** (ka-SEE-loff), gateway to huge Tustumena Lake, whose turnoff is at Mile 110. At Mile 117 is the turnoff for **Clam Gulch State Recreation Area,** a two-mile gravel road down to the campground and clamgrounds. The campground has 116 campsites going for $8/night. Make sure you have a sportfishing license (nonresidents: $10 for one day, $15 for three days, $30/14 days, $50/annual), a shovel, a bucket, and gloves before you dig in the cold sand for the razor-sharp clams; 60 clam limit, best during low low tide in early summer, but possible anytime April-September. Watch how the pros first spot the small hole in the sand, then dig a few shovelsful and reach fast for the escaping clams. If you'd rather get formal instruction, stop at **Ipswich Plaza,** Mile 118, for a guided dig; if you don't feel like digging at all, eat at **Clam Shell Lodge** nearby and pay the price. Clamming is excellent from here all the way down to Anchor Point.

This next 40-mile stretch of the Sterling gives you yet another impression of Alaska's incredible diversity: except for a few back lanes in Southeast, this is the state's only extended coastal road. The view across the Cook Inlet is of the Aleutian crown, Mt. Redoubt (10,197 feet) to the north and Mt. Iliamna (10,016 feet) to the south—both within rhyming Lake Clark National Park. On a very clear day you can also see active Mt. Augustine, a solitary volcanic island with a well-defined cone at the bottom of the Inlet.

Ninilchik

This small town, located where the Ninilchik River empties into the Inlet, has a long history. Settled at the turn of the 19th century by retired Russian-America Company workers who took Native wives, the old village is down a short side road off the Sterling. In old downtown are **Village Arts and Crafts, Beachcomber Motel**

DIANA LASICH HARPER

(tel. 907-567-3417; $60 s or d), and some classic water's-edge houses. Follow the road that follows the Ninilchik River around toward the "spit"; you wind up on the other side of the river and village on the hardpan inlet beach. To the left is a state camping area (generally full of RVs), $6; to the right is the small-boat harbor.

The modern town (pop. 750) is strung along the highway: Ninilchik Corners (laundromat, showers, store, RV park), Ninilchik General Store, Chevron, several motels, restaurants, and charter companies. Stop at the **library**, open weekdays 11 a.m.-4 p.m., tel. (907) 567-3333, and pick up the excellent *Tour of Ninilchik Village*. A dozen historical buildings and signs are along the way; a short footpath leads up to the **Russian Orthodox Church**, built on an overlook in 1900. **Kenai State Fairgrounds** hosts a large fair on the third weekend in August.

On the hill just before you come into town is **North River Campground**. It's big, woodsy, and uncrowded, with water and outhouses; $8. Just before town is **Ninilchik State Recreation Site**, with 35 sites, water, and toilets; $8-10. On a bluff a few hundred feet above the beach, this facility, like **Stariski State Recreation Site** at Mile 152 (13 sites, $10), has one of the best views of any state campground.

HOMER

Homer has a dazzling reputation for some of the finest scenery, the mildest climate, heaviest halibut, biggest bays, longest spits, coolest people, and best quality of life, not only in the state but also beyond. And the truth is, Homer is one of Alaska's peerless towns. It has an undeniably beautiful setting, with the unruly coastline, lingulate fjords, and cavalcading Kenai Mountains across magnificent Kachemak Bay. The temperatures are generally mild—for Alaska. The halibut often tip the scales at over 200 pounds, and for about a hundred bucks you can try your luck with a line. An abundance of fine artists and craftspeople call Homer home, selling their wares at small galleries full of rare and tempting stuff. And some of the state's best fishing, boating, hiking, kayaking, natural history, artists' colonies, wildlife, and photo ops revolve around Homer in Kachemak Bay. So the bottom line is: Homer distinctly deserves its reputation.

CLAMMING

Opinions vary as to the best method to go after a clam. Some clammers say one should place his back to the ocean with his shovel in front of the clam's depression. Others maintain you should start on the side, and still others center the shovel so the first scoop lifts away the dimple. My wife Lacey prefers the "Safeway Method," and buys her clams for 98 cents a can.

The best digging is in muddy sand. Once the vibrations start from above, the razor clam takes the fast elevator down. I have my most consistent success by taking three fast scoops directly over the dimple, then throwing my shovel aside and plunging into the hole with both arms. Though some feel throwing the shovel is optional, it is not. The distance of the toss is a barometer of enthusiasm and a signal to the body that more adrenaline is needed. A good shovel toss can accelerate the capture of a clam by as much as 30 seconds. Sometimes, also, if one does not maintain an awareness of his proximity to the sea, it serves as an offering to the god, Neptune.

Once the arms are buried to the elbows in a wet clam hole, the main thing to remember is you must get as dirty as possible. This is the fun part. A razor clam is evidently awed by an individual who is not afraid to lie on his side in the sand and muck, and extend his arm past the clavicle, fingers groping for its shell. Sometimes, the mollusk will stop its own excavating just to get a good look at its gutsy pursuer. If this should occur and something hard is touched, one must refrain from prematurely making the triumphant announcement that "I've got one!" It may be a clam, but it may also be a rock or the distributor cap to a '49 Ford. It is unnecessary to provide veteran diggers with the stimulus for additional mirth.

Razor clams should be cleaned as soon after the capture as possible, preferably by someone else. The process requires a surgeon's understanding of anatomy, and it often takes longer than the pursuit. The neck is tough, and best saved for chowder and erasers, but the body and "foot" are tender and delicious.

When I figure gas, towing, and dry cleaning, my razor clams cost more than 50 bucks a pound.

—Alan Liere,
Alaska magazine, Sept. 1988

History

The Russians knew of the limitless coal in this area in the early 1800s, and Americans were mining the seams only a decade after the Alaska Purchase. The gold rush began delivering men and supplies to the small port at the end of the Spit on their way to the goldfields at Hope and Sunrise up the Inlet in the mid-1890s. One of the most flamboyant prospectors to pass through, Homer Pennock, left his name on the settlement. Mining the hundreds of millions of tons of accessible bituminous fuel continued until 1907, when a combination of fire in Homer, federal policy, and falling prices burned out the market. Slowly, the inevitable fishermen and homesteaders began settling in during the 1920s, and they found a lifetime supply of home-heating fuel free for the taking right on the beach. Homer remained a small fishing and canning port till the early '50s, when the Sterling Highway finally connected the town with the rest of the continent. Since then, the population has steadily grown to just over 4,000 today, with seafood processing, shipping, and tourism supporting the economy, the Bradley Lake hydroelectric project across the bay making slow progress, and the possibility of oil drilling in the future around the lower Cook Inlet.

Around Town

Start out at **Pratt Museum,** at 3779 Bartlett just up from the corner of Pioneer, tel. (907) 235-8635, open daily 10 a.m.-6 p.m., $3, which was an excellent local museum until it was completely reorganized in 1989 and is now even better. The historical, lifestyle, industry, and artifact displays will engross you for hours, the Russian exhibit is fascinating, and the collection of flora and fauna is one of the state's most outstanding. The beaked whale skeleton extends nearly the length of one room; follow the story of how it was shot and washed up onto a Homer beach, then was taken apart and put back together piece by piece. Some fantastic ivory model boats sport baleen sails. The rest of the fish, shellfish, otter, shorebirds, and aquarium displays fill the Marine Gallery. The Pratt's Exxon oil-spill exhibit is superb, though it might be traveling around the country when you visit. The gift shop features Alaska-made crafts, along with books, cards, and gift items.

Downtown Homer boasts half a dozen or so art galleries; see "Galleries and Shopping," below, for details.

The Alaska Maritime National Wildlife Refuge was created by the Alaska National Interest Lands Act (ANILCA) of 1980, by combining 11 pre-existing refuges with new public lands. The refuge is 3.5 million acres, encompassing 2,500 islands that stretch from Forrester Island in southern Southeast Alaska up through coastal Kenai and Kodiak, the Alaska Peninsula, the Aleutians, the Pribilofs, and along the west coast of the mainland all the way up to Barrow. The refuge protects 40 million seabirds from 30 different species; 200 other species rest and feed in the refuge on their long migrations. Headquarters is in Homer; there's also a visitor center at 509 Homer Bypass Rd. (near the Pioneer Ave. intersection), tel. (907) 235-6546, open weekdays 8:30 a.m.-5 p.m., weekends 10 a.m.-5 p.m. They have an exhibit of marine fauna, including an enormous bald eagle and nest, information on wildlife viewing around Homer, and local-interest books for sale; they also sponsor wildlife programs.

The Spit

This tenuous four-mile finger of real estate jutting boldly into the bounteous and tolerant bay has seen several docks come and go, a railroad and roundhouse, a shipwreck, a fire, a drought, and an earthquake that lowered the land six feet. Today, the Spit hosts the Small Boat Har-

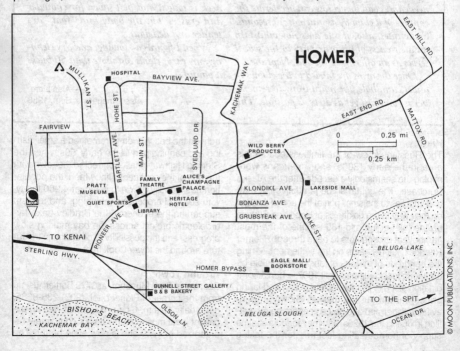

GORDY OHLIGER

Homer Spit juts into Kachemak Bay.

bor, canneries, two touristy boardwalks, the renowned Salty Dawg Saloon, beautiful Land's End Hotel, public camping, the Alaska Marine Highway terminals, and lazy beachcombing with an incomparable view. If you haven't been to town or if the chamber of commerce is closed, be sure to stop in at the **Info Center** here, the first storefront you see (on the right) as you're driving out the Spit (across from the fishing hole).

For details on all the practicalities and activities, see the specific sections below.

Scenic Drives
Head back out the Sterling and take a right on West Hill Rd.; just after the pavement ends, go right at the fork (a left puts you on Diamond Ridge Rd., which drops you back down to the Sterling) onto **Skyline Drive.** You climb pretty high, among expensive homes, till you see the famous view of the Spit, the bay, and the march of mountains on the southern coast, all framed by fireweed. Continue on Skyline Dr. and go left on Ohlson Mountain Rd., till it ends at Ohlson Peak (1,513 feet).

Pioneer Ave. through town turns into **East End Road,** which also has beautiful homes and great views of the Spit and the bay, and it's paved for 12 miles. Out here is a suburb of Homer, with Fritz Creek General Store, the Homestead (entertainment weekends), and increasingly jaw-dropping views of the bay, glaciers, and the Bradley Lake project. The road ends at the school bus turnaround, 20 miles from town. If you don't want to drive all that way, take a hard right onto Kachemak Dr. only a few miles out of town and head back down to the Spit.

But the best views from up on the hill here are from **East Hill Road,** which is a left turn one mile out East End Road. The pavement ends, and then it turns into Skyline, which continues up to an unsigned intersection. Get to Ohlson Mountain by the road on the left. It's another three miles from there to the end of Skyline Drive. Unsurpassed views all the way.

Halibut Cove
Even if you only have two days in Homer, spend half of one visiting this enchanted village (pop. 50 year-round). In an unbelievably beautiful and lush setting, you can stroll the boardwalks, visit two galleries, dine on the deck of the famous **Saltry,** or hike into the surrounding jungle. The fishing-boat ferry, *Danny J*, departs from behind the Salty Dawg at noon and 5 p.m., $36 roundtrip. The noon trip cruises up to Gull Island bird sanctuary, which Alfred Hitchcock should've known about; wear a hat and breathe through your mouth! The 5 p.m. cruise ($18) is only for Cove residents, or visitors with dinner or lodging reservations. The cabins are high up on a hill, with sleeping lofts, kichenettes, and wood-burning stoves. The return trips are at 4 and 9 p.m. Call (907) 235-7847 for information and reservations.

Seldovia
Another sleepy fishing village (pop. 400 or so), Seldovia (from the Russian for "herring") was once the bustling metropolis that Homer is now. The road, the earthquake, and fate exchanged their roles. On the same latitude as Oslo, Norway, Seldovia was first settled by Russians in the

SELDOVIA

OUTSIDE BEACH

WILDERNESS PARK

TO JAKALOF BAY

LAGOON

CAMEL ROCK

CEMETERY

ANDERSON

OTTERBAHN TRAILHEAD

WINIFRED

AIRPORT

SPRUCE

INLET

YOUNG

SHORELINE DR.

SELDOVIA SLOUGH

FERRY DOCK

PARK

SUSAN LAKE

ALDER

MAIN

HARBORVIEW

CEDAR

FULMORE

AIRPORT AVE.

FISH CREEK

SELDOVIA BOARDWALK HOTEL

KACHEMAK KAFE

SYNERGY ART SHOP

CENTURION

NATIVE ASSN.

BOAT HARBOR

TO HARMONY POINT WILDERNESS LODGE

ROCKY ST.

NOT TO SCALE

DANCING EAGLES

BOARDWALK

© MOON PUBLICATIONS, INC.

early 1800s and became an active fur-trading post. Through the years, Seldovia has had many ocean-oriented industries, from the short-lived herring boom to salmon, king crab, and tanner.

Seldovia is a convenient place for really getting away from it all. Catch a ride over from Homer on the state ferry once a week, or on the tour boats; the tour boats give you two hours to visit, just enough time to wander around town and maybe get to the Otterbahn Trailhead.

Start out by strolling along Main, the only paved street in town. Interpretive signs every block or so describe Alaska's Russian history, commercial fishing, the earthquake, etc. Stop off at **Synergy Art Shop** to see the local crafts; the racks on the back wall are stocked with visitor information. Make sure you grab a map of Seldovia and the Otterbahn Hiking Trail. The Russian Orthodox Church might be open for an hour in the early afternoon. Walk along the last remaining section of original boardwalk (the rest was wiped out in the earthquake) just up from the small-boat harbor. Rent a bike from Annie MacKenzie's and pedal out Seldovia St. to Outside Beach or Jakalof Bay. The **Rocky River Road Trail** at the end of Jakalof Bay Rd. is a local favorite. The well-marked **Otterbahn Trail** leads 1.5 miles from the schoolgrounds around the headland to Outside Beach.

Seldovia boasts two hotels and seven bed and breakfasts. **Seldovia Boardwalk Hotel,** tel. (907) 234-7816, is right on the harbor; the back porch is one of the finest places in town to hang out. Rooms are $79-120. The hotel offers a cruise-stay-fly package from $119. **Dancing Eagles B&B,** tel. (907) 234-7627, is another good choice: also right on the water (front porch), full breakfasts, hot tub $45 pp, $125 for the chalet cabin. (Don Pitcher spent part of his honeymoon here—and *that's* a recommendation.) Or camp for free at Outside Beach, a short hike out Jakalof Bay Rd. no running water.

Grab some lunch at **Kachemak Kafe,** a cozy eight-table diner serving bacon and eggs, burgers, and sandwiches for $6-7. **Centurion Restaurant** also has sandwiches and burgers ($6-8) and fish and chips ($11). You can also buy groceries (pricey—peaches at $4 a pound) at **Stampers Family Market.**

The Boardwalk Hotel rents **bicycles** (and does repairs and sells parts) for $2 an hour or $15 a day. Dancing Eagles might or might not be renting mountain bikes and kayaks when you get there; inquire. But be sure to find someone renting bikes; the best thing to do in Seldovia is pedal out the road to the quiet sandy beaches and savor the great views of Kachemak Bay.

The *Tustumena* sails over to Seldovia from Homer three times a week, taking 90 minutes and laying over for an hour or two, then returning to Homer, $18 each way, reservations required, tel. (907) 235-8449. At least three companies offer natural-history and sightseeing cruises across Kachemak Bay, with two-hour layovers in Seldovia. The *Endeavor* departs daily from the Spit at midday, $35 roundtrip. Purchase tickets at the Homer Spit Campground, tel. (907) 235-8206, by 11 a.m. **Rainbow Tours** offers the same basic cruise for a couple more bucks. Make arrangements at their office on Cannery Row on the Spit, or call (907) 235-7272. A few local bush-plane companies also do the roundtrip. **Southcentral Air,** tel. (907) 235-6172, charges $49 roundtrip. **Homer Air,** tel. (907) 235-8591, charges $50 roundtrip.

Others across the Bay

If you have three days in Homer (or two and skip Seldovia), spend one of them on the Kachemak Bay **Natural History Tour,** with the Center for Alaskan Coastal Studies at China Poot Bay. Local naturalists guide you around rookeries, tidepools, rainforest, and prehistoric sites, and give you an appreciation for the marine world that you'll carry for life. The nine-hour experience costs $49, a bargain, which includes the ride across with Rainbow Tours. Bring your own lunch, raingear, rubber boots (some are available at the center), binoculars, camera, etc. For reservations, call Rainbow Tours, (907) 235-7272; for more info, call China Poot Bay Society, tel. (907) 235-6667.

Saint Augustine Charters, tel. (907) 235-7847 (Central Booking Agency), does tours of the bay on their 38-foot wooden cutter sailboat, *St. Augustine's Fire.* Their two-hour evening sail costs $35; the two-hour Marine Wildlife Cruise is $32 (aboard a water taxi). The water taxi also services hikers, campers, birdwatchers, and kayakers.

There are at least two dozen tour, ferry, and taxi boats floating around Homer; many can be booked through the **Central Booking Agency,** tel. (907) 235-7847.

Kayaking and Fishing

True North Kayak Adventures, on a protected island adjacent to Kachemak Bay State Park, tel. (907) 235-0708 (or Central Charters at 907-235-7847), guides intimate encounters with the wild beauty of Kachemak Bay in stable sea kayaks. You paddle around deep fjords, rocky islands, old-growth forests, even caves and arches, viewing sea otters, sea lions, porpoises, eagles, puffins, and the occasional orca or humpback whale. Trip participants are kept to a minimum for a highly personalized experience. Guided day-trips start at $100 (includes lunch and a water taxi to True North); you can rent kayaks for $35 s or $65 d.

Charters run $100-150 for an all-day trip, with tackle and bait supplied. Some companies include a box lunch; most don't. When comparing prices, make sure that cleaning and processing your catch is included, unless you plan to do it yourself. Some companies charge extra (by the pound) for the service, and the fees can get hefty if you catch a "barn-door" halibut. Wear warm, layered clothing topped by raingear, and wear soft-soled shoes. Binoculars are a definite plus, since seabirds and marine mammals are almost always viewable. You can have your catch vacuum-packed, frozen, and shipped home for additional fees.

Whatever you do, don't forget to enter the Homer Halibut derby if you go fishing. First prize is usually more than $30,000, with additional monthly prizes awarded for big fish, and every year sob stories abound of people who saved five bucks by not entering, then caught potential prize-winning sea monsters. Don't let this happen to you!

Homer has at least a dozen fishing charter outfits to help you go out and bag yourself a big halibut. Easiest is to contact **Central Charter Booking Agency,** tel. (907) 235-7847, to make your special arrangements.

But if you just want to drive into town and cast a line in the water, head out to the "fishing hole" on the Spit, across from Glacier Drive-In and Kachemak Gear Shed. Fish and Game stocks this little pond with salmon, which return in such big numbers that the place is occasionally opened up to snagging. Classic roadside fishing stop for RVers, kids, lazy locals, and the like. On a busy day, you might be able to squeeze in at water's edge, if you don't mind using a little elbow grease.

Accommodations

Ocean Shores Motel, 3500 Crittendon just below Homer Junior High, tel. (907) 235-7775, has rooms with and without kitchenettes; $60-120. **Heritage Hotel,** on Pioneer next to Alice's, tel. (907) 235-7787, charges $79 s, $10 each additional person. **Driftwood Inn,** down on Bishop's Beach, tel. (907) 235-8019, charges $50-120 s for their variety of accommodations. Each has its own charm. The Heritage, rooming lodgers since 1948, has cozy rooms and comfortable baths. The Driftwood is right on the water (coming into town on the Sterling, pass Pioneer Ave. on the left and take the next right onto the dirt road), and you can stuff four bodies into all their rooms for the same bill.

Typically, at least 30 bed and breakfasts are at your disposal in Homer, most in the $50-60 range. **Pioneer,** tel. (907) 235-5670, is right downtown on Pioneer Ave.; the **Lily Pad,** tel. (907) 235-6630, is run by the Gjosund family, who've lived in Homer since 1944; **Jelly Bean B&B,** tel. (907) 235-8720, run by Tim and Toni Bean, provide free jelly beans; **Brass Ring B&B,** tel. (907) 235-5450, features an outdoor hot tub and a naturalist host. For additional B&B rooms, call the **Homer Referral Agency** at tel. (907) 235-8996. They can also book fishing charters, flightseeing, etc.

Tutka Bay Lodge is a remote and intimate wilderness lodge on the south shore of Kachemak Bay between Halibut Cove and Seldovia, nine water miles from the spit. Hosts Jon and Nelda Osgood, who'll remind you of your favorite aunt and uncle, cater to nature lovers, photographers, birders, and anglers. Activities include beachcombing, clam digging, hiking, and wildlife viewing (free), plus mountain biking, sea kayaking, sportfishing, and flightseeing (fee).

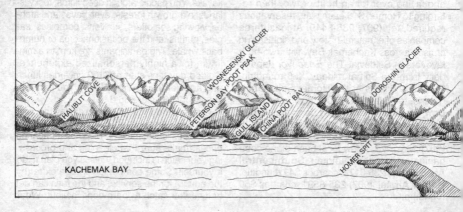

Accommodations are provided in a guesthouse, a cabin, and a duplex; two-night minimum stays cost in the $500 range and include roundtrip transportation from Homer and family-style meals. For details, write P.O. Box 960, Homer, AK 99603, tel. (907) 235-3905.

Camping on the Spit is what most budget travelers and backpackers do, though it's no picnic. It's within spitting distance of the road, and it's barren, windy, and high-density—food rip-offs and late-night rowdiness are not uncommon. Don't say you weren't warned. The oceanside beach has a 14-day limit; at other designated areas you can camp all summer with the cannery workers. For Spit camping, stop at the store on the left side of the road as you drive down. Sites are $7/night, and RV sites can be rented for 14 days for $75. The store also has showers ($3.50 for 20 minutes), laundry facilities, and visitor info, and rents bikes, fishing tackle and clam shovels. It's open 7 a.m.-10 p.m. in the summer.

Another (nicer, quieter, more protected) city campground is near downtown on Mulligan; heading up from the Sterling on Pioneer, go left on Bartlett, left on Fairview, then right on Mulligan, $7.

Food

In town are a couple of excellent places to eat breakfast. You can't miss **Cafe Cups:** four Alaska-size teacups hang atop the front of the converted house on Pioneer Dr. across from the library, tel. (907) 235-8330, open daily 7 a.m.-10 p.m. Try eggs Benedict, Florentine, Wildwood, Sonoran, or ranchero ($4-7.50), or bagels and lox ($7.50). Cups also serves unusual lunch and dinner dishes, and sports big art on the walls along with old books in the cases. Every single table and chair is different. Recommended. If you eat breakfast at Cups, be sure to stop for lunch or dinner at the **Neon Coyote Cafe,** just down the street at 435 Pioneer, tel. (907) 235-6226, open Mon.-Sat. 11 a.m-10 p.m. The Coyote serves great breakfasts all day long, plus an exotic brand of Hawaiian-Chinese nouvelle cuisine (with a little Mexican and hippie thrown in). These guys try real hard to put out a good healthy meal and succeed, and prices are as low as they go in Homer.

On the Spit, consider breakfast at **Land's End,** the hotel at the tip. The prices are competitive, the portions are large, the food is delicious, and the view is—well, words fail. Otherwise, you can't go wrong at **Fresh Sourdough Express Bakery,** a little ways up Ocean Dr. from the Spit, open 7 a.m.-10 p.m. (till 5 p.m. in the winter, no dinner). They serve omeletes, scrambles, yogurt, muffins, pastries, puddings, and cereal for breakfast ($6-8); croissants, veggie stuffs, hot sandwiches, and hoagies for lunch ($5-7.50); and some vegetarian meals for dinner, but also plenty of protein acceptable to carnivores. Fresh-baked bread and goods, espresso drinks, organic coffees, etc., round out the menu, and they'll pack you a box lunch to take on your halibut charter as well.

Alaska Italian Bistro is open noon-11:30 p.m. or so, serving wonderful Mediterranean

seafood, pasta, meat and poultry dinners, and pizza. Dinners run $11-24, and the smell alone is worth the trip to Homer.

Boardwalk Fish and Chips, across from the harbormaster and Salty Dawg, is open daily 11:30 a.m.-9 p.m.; their scallop basket ($7.50) and halibut fish and chips ($5.25) will have you smackin' your chops.

Smoky Bay Cooperative, at the corner of Pioneer and Bartlett across from the museum, open Mon.-Sat. 8 a.m.-8 p.m., Saturday 8 a.m.-7 p.m., Sunday 10 a.m.-6 p.m., has wholesome and bulk food, plus a deli, open 11 a.m.-3 p.m., serving black-bean burritos, twice-baked potatoes, falafels, and salads all in the $5 range, and big.

Two Sisters Espresso and Bakery is one of the finest little coffee joints in Homer. Combine some strong coffee and big muffins or fresh cheesecake with a visit to the Bunnell Street Gallery; you can even stay upstairs in Mabel's Suite, Rose's Room, or Arthur's Study at the bed and breakfast. It all takes place in old downtown Homer, the commercial center of Bishop's Beach, in the old Inlet Trading Post, corner of Main and Bunnell Sts. just south of Homer Bypass Road.

Entertainment

Alice's Champagne Palace next to Heritage Hotel downtown rocks all night, even on Mondays. If you just want to drink, cross the street to **Hobo Jim's Alaska Bar.** Two miles east of town on East End Rd. is **Down East Saloon,** which also has dancing nightly. **Family Theatre,** Pioneer and Main, shows movies; $5, tel. (907) 235-6728.

The **Salty Dawg Saloon** out near the end of the Spit could be Homer's most famous landmark. The original building dates from 1897, the second building from 1909, and the tower from the mid-'60s. Each building housed 12 different companies in eight different locations before settling down here on the Spit. Open from 11 a.m. till the last patron staggers out the door; have a beer for the experience.

Homer has a high proportion of talent, and some of the performers who've been shining for years in the spotlights of Christmas variety shows and springtime cabin-fever talent shows have gotten together to do **Pier One Theater,** across from Glacier Drive-In on the Spit. What-

ever is playing is guaranteed to be one of the finest theater experiences in the state. Also, keep your ears open for **Fresh Produce,** a local improvisational group that performs occasionally.

Galleries and Shopping

Speaking of artists, a few local showcases are must-sees on any Homer itinerary. The most eclectic and endlessly inspiring collection is exhibited at **Ptarmigan Arts** on Pioneer across from Wild Berry Products. Here you might see anything from crystal and alabaster sculpture to shoji screens, windsock banners to wooden toys, notecards to hand-knit sweaters. Next door is **Studio One,** with good-looking local sculpture and pottery, along with some T-shirts and other stuff. Also check out **Homer Artists,** in the Mariner Mini-Mall next to Wild Berry Products, open Tues.-Sat. 10 a.m.-6 p.m., for watercolors, prints, cards, woodwork, and art supplies.

Bunnell Street Gallery is worth a detour to visit, not only for the fine art (acrylics, baskets, ceramics, metalwork, oils, stained glass, T-shirts, watercolors), but also to check out the revitalization of old downtown Homer. The gallery is in the old Inlet Trading Post, built in 1937 in the middle of what used to be the main commercial district of Homer just up from Bishop's Beach (heading out to the Spit on Homer Bypass Rd., take a right on Main St. and go two blocks). Local artists began renovating the trading post in 1989, and it now also houses Two Sisters Bakery and a B&B upstairs.

Halibut Cove Artists is on the boardwalk at Halibut Cove. Diana Tillion's octopus-ink paintings are something to see. **Pratt Museum** also has rotating exhibits of local artwork.

Wild Berry Products, 523 East Pioneer Ave. (you can't miss it) is Homer's classic Alaskan tourist trap. The collection of trinkets, knick-knacks, souvenirs, jewelry, and T-shirts would make any Las Vegas Strip gift shop jealous; they also make candy, jellies, and jams, and sell gift packs of berry products, fudge, and canned salmon.

The **Eagle Mall,** on Homer Bypass heading toward the Spit, opened in April 1989. Step into the **Eagle supermarket** and it's like you never left Anchorage. **The Bookstore** is next door, open Mon.-Sat. 10 a.m.-7 p.m., Sunday noon-5 p.m. Here you'll find all of local celebrity Tom Bodett's books and tapes, along with works of

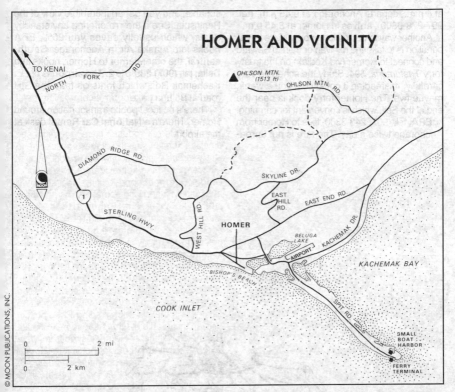

HOMER AND VICINITY

other local authors, a big Alaskana section, field guides, and other kinds of books too.

Services and Information

The **chamber of commerce** itself is now at 1213 Ocean Dr., tel. (907) 235-7740, open Mon.-Fri. 9 a.m.-5 p.m. The chamber's Visitor Information Center is the first building on the right as you drive out the Spit, full of—you guessed it—visitor information. **Central Charter Booking Agency** can book almost anything there is to do in Homer—a good place to call first, tel. (907) 235-7847.

The Homer Public Library is at 141 Pioneer Ave., tel. (907) 235-3180, open Tuesday and Thursday 10 a.m.-8 p.m., Wednesday, Friday, and Saturday 10 a.m.-6 p.m.

For clean underwear and underarms, go to **Washboard Laundromat,** tel. (907) 235-6781, open 8 a.m.-9 p.m., up from Sourdough Bakery on Ocean Drive. This sparkling facility is

enormously appreciated by travelers and locals alike; $3.50 to shower in bright rooms, 30-minute time limit; they also have a message and mail service, and tanning booths. For the same price you can stand under the blessed hot water at Homer Spit Campground.

The **post office** is now on Ocean Dr. at Waddell—notice the eagle done by a stained-glass class at the community college. In fact, the college, the Kachemak Bay Campus of Kenai Peninsula College of the University of Alaska, occupies the old post-office building on Pioneer. It's up to 600 students these days and is growing fast.

Getting Around

Seward and Homer Bus Lines, tel. (907) 235-8280, has service between Homer and Anchorage for $50 ($80 roundtrip), stopping in Soldotna and Kenai along the way. It departs Homer daily at 10 a.m., arrives in Anchorage at 4 p.m., departs Anchorage at 9:45 a.m. (tel. 907-278-0800), arrives in Homer at 3:45 p.m.

Another way to get to Homer by surface transportation is to take the minivan or train to Seward and connect to Homer (via Kodiak) on the trusty ferry *Tustumena,* $94. Study the schedule very carefully; misreading it could cost you a week, maybe two. The Homer ferry dock is near the end of the Spit, which is convenient for camping.

ERA, tel. (907) 243-3300, flies to Homer from Anchorage twice a day. The fare is not unrea-

sonable, and you get an incredible view of the Peninsula. See if they're offering any standby deals, which usually saves you 20%. ERA hooks into Alaska Air in Anchorage. **Southcentral,** the other carrier to Homer, hooks into Delta, tel. (907) 235-6172. The **airport** is out E. Kachemak Rd., which forks off from the Spit road at Beluga Lake.

There's no local public transportation around Homer. There's a **National Car Rental** desk at the airport.

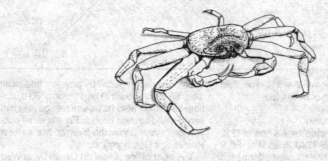

GORDY CHILGER

SOUTHWEST ALASKA

Southwest Alaska includes the Kodiak Island group, the Alaska Peninsula, and the barren, windswept Aleutian and Pribilof Islands. This part of the state contains world-famous brown bear viewing opportunities at Kodiak Island National Wildlife Refuge, Katmai National Park, and McNeil River State Game Sanctuary. In addition, it includes Lake Clark National Park, Aniakchak National Monument, and the Alaska Maritime National Wildlife Refuge. Fur seals, sea otters, walrus, and other marine animals abound around the Aleutians and Pribilofs; the islands are also a birdwatcher's paradise. Due to climatic conditions there are no forests west of northern Kodiak Island and the adjacent mainland; most of the Alaska Peninsula and all the Aleutians are open tundra.

The largest settlements in Southwest Alaska are Kodiak and Unalaska/Dutch Harbor, but many smaller fishing towns and Native villages are sprinkled over this remote landscape. Only Kodiak is fairly reasonable to visit; other places will require considerable outlays of cash.

Geography
From Denali National Park the Alaska Range swings southwest to become the Aleutian Range, marching right into the North Pacific as the Alaska Peninsula and Aleutian Islands. This 1,500-mile arc from the northern end of the Alaska Peninsula to the western tip of the Aleutians is an area of extraordinary volcanic and seismic activity, accounting for an amazing 10% of the world's earthquakes. Kodiak Island sits uneasily on the edge of the Aleutian Trench; Kodiak is nonvolcanic, yet bears the brunt of its fiery neighbors. Great collapsed craters at Katmai and Aniakchak are now administered by the National Park Service, and the 50-60 volcanos along the archipelago comprise the longest and straightest line of smoke-belchers and ash-spewers anywhere on earth.

The vegetation of Southwest Alaska is a thick, luxurious shag carpet of grass and brush; you can travel for hundreds of miles here without seeing a single tree. The climate, however, is particularly disagreeable—fog, rain, snow, wind.

SOUTHWEST ALASKA

© MOON PUBLICATIONS, INC.

Getting There

With ferry service from Homer and Seward three times a week, Kodiak is the only easily accessible place in Southwest Alaska. The trusty *Tustumena* sails out as far as Dutch Harbor once a month, but only in summer. Reeve Aleut-ian Airlines and Peninsula Airways connect Anchorage to many of the small towns, mostly occupied by Aleuts and Yup'ik Eskimos. Access to the remote backcountry areas is by small float-planes that land on the myriad of lakes and ponds.

KODIAK ISLAND

Kodiak Island is an unlikely land of superlatives. At 60 by 100 miles, it is the largest island in Alaska, and second-largest in the U.S. (after Hawaii's Big Island). Kodiak has the world's biggest brown bears; Alaska's longest history, and second largest fishing fleet; and the country's largest Coast Guard station, third-highest grossing port, most expensive bridge to nowhere, and weirdest golf tournament. Besides, what other town has chewing tobacco named for it or a dump voted the nation's "most scenic"? The island is home to nearly 15,000 people, of whom 10,000 live in and around the city of Kodiak.

Kodiak sits on the island's northeast side in St. Paul Harbor, protected from the wild Gulf of Alaska by the photogenic wooded islands in Chiniak Bay. Kodiak town is an exciting place to visit even when it's totally fogged in and the fishing fleet is out. It's clear that the dangerous but romantic lifestyle of commercial fishing in one of the world's richest and roughest fisheries is the only common denominator a community could ever need. It's also clear, even if you don't like fish, that Kodiak's livelihood is one of the most appropriate manifestations of the mystique of the Alaskan experience. Only 250 air miles from Anchorage or 84 nautical miles from Homer, Kodiak is a highly accessible and pleasurable place to visit.

The Land

The Kodiak Island group, an extension of the Chugach-Kenai Ranges, was once possibly connected to the mainland but is now separated by the "entrances" to Cook Inlet and Shelikof Strait. The group perches on the continental shelf, right on the edge of the Aleutian Trench. This makes it highly susceptible to the after-effects of volcanic and seismic activity, such as the ash of Novarupta and the tsunamis of the 1964 earthquake. However, glaciation, not volcanism, has been the primary agent in the shaping of Kodiak's geologic features. Snow and ice almost completely covered the group during the last ice age, and the alpine is chiseled roughly— steep slopes, short fast runoff streams, and rounded kettles. In addition, Kodiak's coastline is so characterized by long fjords that even with a maximum width of 60 miles, no point on the island is over 20 miles from tidewater. Kodiak is also the northwestern front of the spruce forest, and you can see from the intense green of the understory why Kodiak is nicknamed "The Emerald Isle."

Climate

Expect cool, wet, and windy weather. The average temperature in August, the "hottest" month, is 54° F. Kodiak's record high is 86, but most years only half a dozen summer days even exceed 70. Kodiak receives 75 inches of rain a year, of which 12 inches fall June-September. Locals claim that some sun shines one out of every three days—but it can be clear or partly clear for three glorious days, then soupy for nine in a row! Dress warm, and if you intend to explore the backcountry, bring raingear and rubber boots.

HISTORY

Russian America
Russian fur trader Glotoff "discovered" Kodiak in 1763 and told Grigori Sheilikhov (Shelikof) about the abundant sea otters there. The island's second-highest peak (4,450 feet) was named for Glotoff. Shelikof is remembered as the founder of the Russian America Company and the first European settlement in Alaska, at Three Saints Bay, Kodiak, in 1784. This is the site of present-day Old Harbor and had long been an important Koniag village. To gain the site, Shelikof ordered his men to massacre hundreds of the Koniag on the rock where they had taken refuge. Native leaders refer to the battle as "Wounded Knee of Alaska." This slaughter broke the back of Native resistance to Russian rule.

Alexander Baranof arrived in 1791 to manage the company and colony; he promptly relocated the whole settlement to St. Paul's Harbor (present-day Kodiak town) after a tsunami nearly wiped out the previous town. The Eskimo-related Koniag population wasn't sorry to see the Russians and their Aleut slaves move again, in 1800, to New Archangel (Sitka)—except that the sea otters in the vicinity had been almost completely eradicated and, as happened in the Queen Charlottes, the 20,000 Native inhabitants were decimated to 1,500 in a couple of decades, due to war and introduced diseases like smallpox.

Later Years
Kodiak survived the 19th century by fur trading, whaling, fishing, and even ice-making (Russian die-hards began producing ice in the 1850s to supply California gold rush boom towns; they introduced the first horses and built the first roads in Alaska). Salmon fishing really caught on in the early 1900s, and the living was easy until the awesome explosion of Novarupta on Katmai across the strait in 1912. It showered ash down on the town, blanketing fields and villages, crushing roofs, and changing the green island into a gray-brown desert overnight. After 48 hours of total blackness and gasping for air, 450 residents were evacuated by a U.S. revenue cutter in a daring rescue. It took over two years for life to return to normal, and the deep ash layer can still be seen on stream cutbanks throughout the island.

Kodiak, like the rest of Alaska, was mobilized during WW II, but the fortifications here had a more urgent quality: forts, gun emplacements, submarine bases, and command centers were installed to protect the island from Japanese invasion and to manage the Aleutian campaign. Thousands of servicemen left a large economic legacy as well. The major economic boom for the island came later, in the form of the famous Kodiak king crab, harvested by the hundreds of millions of pounds in the early '60s. Then the Good Friday earthquake struck in 1964, quaking the earth for over five minutes, then flooding the town for the next 12 hours with several "waves," that first sucked the tidewater out, exposing the harbor bottom, then swept half the town from its moorings with swells up to 35 feet high. For a gripping description of that terrible night (and a fascinating first-hand look at the Kodiak fishing life) read *Highliners*, by William B. McKloskey.

Kodiak Today
Since the earthquake, Kodiak has rebuilt and retooled for the harvesting of salmon, halibut, shrimp, herring, and bottom fish (king crab were nearly fished out by 1983). The bottom-fishing industry—pollock, rock fish, cod, among others—is one of the fastest growing in Alaska; these "junk fish" are processed into *surimi*, imitation crab and shrimp meat that tastes like salted cardboard. Today, Kodiak consistently ranks near the top of U.S. ports in value of fish landed. There are a dozen different canneries around the city.

A 1993 *National Geographic* article noted that "Kodiak's the kind of town where you think the municipal emblem ought to be a red pickup hauling a golden retriever, with the truck shaking to a country tune like 'Achy Breaky Heart.'" Despite this impression, visitors to modern-day Kodiak may be surprised to see how diverse the population actually is. Many of the taxi drivers, cannery workers, and other blue-collar employees are of Filipino, Mexican, or Latin American heritage. You'll hear more Spanish spoken here than almost anywhere else in Alaska.

SIGHTS

Baranof Museum

Several downtown buildings are reminders of Kodiak's strong Russian heritage. The Baranof Museum, housed in the oldest Russian building in North America, was built around 1808 as a storehouse for sea otter pelts. It's open Mon.-

Fri. 10 a.m.-4 p.m., Sat.-Sun. noon-4 p.m. in the summer; and Mon.-Wed. and Friday 11 a.m.-3 p.m. and Saturday noon-3 p.m. in the winter (closed February); tel. (907) 486-5920. Admission is $2, free for kids under 12. Displays include an impressive Russian samovar collection, along with other artifacts, such as a 10-kopek note printed on sealskin; it's from Alexander Baranof's time. Also here are Koniag and Aleut items such as a remarkable old three-person kayak, a *barabara* diorama, and a grotesque wooden mask found in 1958 on Cape Douglas. The photos from the 1964 tsunami

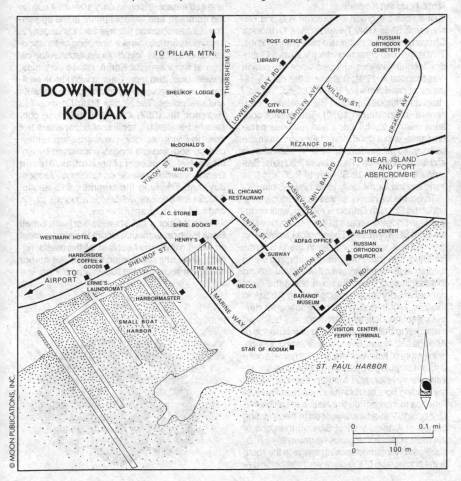

DOWNTOWN KODIAK

are hard to believe: boats were strewn throughout downtown. Out front are several large whale bones. The small **gift shop**—perhaps the best in Alaska—sells authentic trade beads, painted Ukrainian Easter eggs, and Russian nesting dolls ($7-800). If you have the money, take a look at the gorgeous Russian samovars that start around $800. This is the only place in Alaska where you can buy samovars. Not far from the museum is a small tank farm notable for the letters "PMS" boldly emblazoned on the sides of the tanks. Lots of jokes about this one.

More Russian Kodiak

Just across the green on Mission Rd. and Kashevaroff St. is **Holy Resurrection Orthodox Church,** under the distinctive blue onion domes. This is the third church in which Kodiak's Orthodox faithful have worshipped since the parish was founded in 1794; it shelters the earthly remains of St. Herman of Spruce Island, the only Russian Orthodox saint in the Western Hemisphere (canonized in 1970). The interior contains many colorful icons and religious paraphernalia, with a good view of the room from the balcony. To get inside, either put on clean clothes and attend a service (Thursday at 7:30 p.m., Saturday at 6:30 p.m., or Sunday at 9:30 a.m.), or hang around for the daily tours ($1) 1-3 p.m.

To get the full history as well as the modern flavor of the Russian Orthodox religion, walk up toward the bridge overpass to the Veniaminov Museum at **St. Herman's Theological Seminary,** one of three such seminaries in the U.S. Look for Oleg, the museum curator, librarian, and teacher at the seminary, who'll show you around this fascinating room. Ask him about the eight original missionaries working around Kodiak in the late 1700s, and you'll hear how only Herman, through total faith, devotion, and holiness, managed to build up a following of thousands of Koniags and Aleuts. Even more amazing, though, is the story of Ivan Veniaminov—physical scientist, anthropologist, ethnographer, linguist, inveterate traveler, and modern administrator—the guiding light behind the crusade in Russian America to incorporate the Native societies into Orthodoxy. Veniaminov went on to become first bishop of Alaska, then of Siberia, then one of the most important religious figures in all of Russia. Possibly the most moving image in the room is the photograph of the seminary membership—

Natives, Russians, children, all dressed up in religious garb. Notice the antique Bibles—the right-hand pages in Russian, the left-hand pages in Aleut. Russian Orthodoxy is not just history, but a living, breathing, dynamic religious organization, with 85 churches and roughly 20,000 members in Alaska. Don't miss St. Herman's, open daily 1-4:30 p.m. It's a real education.

Other Downtown Sights

The **Aleutiq Center,** 215 Mission Rd., tel. (907) 486-7018, opened in Kodiak in 1995 funded by a $1.5 million grant from the *Exxon Valdez* spill settlement. It's open daily 10 a.m.-4 p.m. in the summer, and variable hours in the off-season. Entrance costs $2; free for kids under 12. This museum contains a sampling of the thousands of artifacts found during archaeological digs at the village of Karluk (stone oil lamps, knives, *ulus*, and more), along with kayak replicas and other items such as spruce baskets and seal pokes. The Kodiak Tribal Council, 713 Rezanof, tel. (907) 486-4449, has also constructed a life-size replica of a *barabara* out near the high school; *barabaras* are underground sod-and-log lodges once used by Kodiak's Native people. The **Kodiak Aleutiq Dancers** perform inside on Monday, Wednesday, and Friday in the summer; $15 adults, $12.50 for seniors, $7.50 for ages six to 12, and free for children under six.

Wander along the shore to Kodiak's **Small Boat Harbor,** without a doubt the state's most crowded. When the fleet is in, all the masts, rigging, and fishing equipment make the harbor an almost impenetrable thicket. The danger in a

BOB RACE

seafarer's life is revealed by the small monument in front of the harbormaster's office. The plaque lists the names of 79 men and women lost at sea. On Marine Way, stop at **National Bank of Alaska,** known as the "Crab Bank," for the display of the king crab life cycle in the entry way. **First National Bank of Anchorage,** around the corner on Center St., is known as the "Bear Bank" for the huge stuffed brown bear in the lobby. Anatomically correct, too. There's another deceased bruin—it weighed 1,400 lbs—in the Alaska Airlines terminal at the airport. Up Mission Rd. and across from the Russian Orthodox church is the **Alaska Department of Fish and Game** office, where you'll find displays of monster king crab, fish, and other sealife. There's even a giant lobster. A $15-million "bridge to nowhere" links Kodiak with nearby Near Island, home to the **Fishery Industrial Technology Center,** tel. (907) 486-1500. This facility is where researchers attempt to develop new seafood products for restaurants and stores. A second building, the Near Island Research Facility, is expected to open in 1998, and will be used for marine biology, marine mammals, and fisheries research by the National Marine Fisheries Service and other government agencies. Near Island is also where floatplanes now land.

Continue left down Shelikof St. to "cannery row," where sea lions are often just off the docks. Additional canneries line the shore on either side of the ferry terminal. Certainly the hardest cannery to miss is the ship-ashore *Star of Kodiak.* Originally christened the *Albert M. Boe,* this was the last Liberty Ship built. It was launched in 1945 as a troop ship, but was towed up from the "mothball" fleet after the 1964 tsunami wiped out other canneries in Kodiak. Today it's an All Alaska Seafoods plant, and is owned by a fishermen's cooperative. Three of the other plants—International Seafoods, Eagle Fisheries, and Pac Pearl—are owned by the controversial Unification Church (otherwise known as the "Moonies"). They also own several commercial fishing boats, a large group house/day care center in town, and a new lodge along the Ayakulik River. Even the Reverend Mr. Moon himself has come here several summers—along with several thousand followers—to sportfish for salmon. They call it "an activity of religious significance."

The *Kalakala*

Continue west out Rezanof Dr.; in about a mile you pass the land-locked *Kalakala,* the world's first streamlined modernistic ferry. The ferry began life as the *Paralta,* and was used in San Francisco Bay from 1927 to 1933. After a to-the-waterline fire, the hull was towed to Seattle to be overhauled by the Boeing Company. Instead of following traditional ferry designs, the new superstructure was streamlined into a silvery blimplike shape. (Some said it looked like a whale with its mouth open.) Newly christened the *Kalakala,* the ferry was put to work plying the waters of Puget Sound. She was a favorite of passengers until 1967, when newer and larger ferries arrived and the *Kalakala* was auctioned off. The new owners towed her to Alaska to be used as the "world's first streamlined floating cannery" at Dutch Harbor. After several more years, the *Kalakala* ended up in Kodiak, used as a seafood processing plant. Veteran commuters from Bremerton will grow misty-eyed here from more than the weather.

Toward the Airport

Kodiak National Wildlife Refuge has a visitor center three miles out of town. See the section below for details on the center and the refuge. **Buskin State Recreation Site** is down the access road on the Buskin River; great fishing here in late summer, especially for Dolly Varden and coho.

Cruise by the airport to the overlook of the **Coast Guard Station.** Largest in the U.S. (21,000 acres), this support center is home to four large cutters and almost 2,500 personnel. Main activities include patrolling the 200-mile fishing zone for illegal fishing (offenders are mostly Japanese and Russian trawlers) and drug trafficking, as well as search and rescue for disabled, distressed, or disappeared local fishing boats.

Right between the visitor center and airport is the turnoff to beautiful **Anton Larsen Bay,** on the island's northwest tip. This 12-mile gravel road goes by a huge crab-pot storage area, overgrown WW II bunkers, communications apparatus, golf course, trailheads to pointy Pyramid Peak, and finally the boat launching area on this scenic protected fjord. The drive is worth the time, even if it's foggy or raining, to see this part of the Emerald Isle.

Fort Abercrombie State Park

Five miles northeast of town out Mill Bay Rd. or Rezanof Dr. East is this state historical and recreational site. The peninsula supports an incredible rainforest of huge Sitka spruce thriving on the volcanic ash from Novarupta. Thick chartreuse moss clings to these stately trees. Check out the gun emplacements on the cliff above the bay—ancient cannons that could never have hit the broad side of any Japanese (floating) barn. From this overlook, watch for puffins (one of the few places in Alaska where they can readily be seen from the shore), whales, sea otters, sea lions, and cormorants. This park is a beautiful, evocative place.

Scenic Drives

A good road climbs right up to the top of **Pillar Mountain,** from which all the overviews of Kodiak town are photographed. Start out at Thorsheim St. and go as far as Maple, where you turn left and go up Pillar Mountain Road. The route can be confusing as it passes through a subdivision, so ask someone along the way for directions. Or you can scramble up the front of the mountain from Rezanof Dr. (west of town)—steep, but much faster than walking up the road.

The Pillar Mountain Golf Tournament is held on the side of this mountain on the spring equinox, in March (see "Events" under "Practicalities," later in this chapter).

All told, Kodiak Island has nearly 100 miles of road (14 paved, one traffic light—and it only flashes): up to Anton Larsen Bay (see above), around Monashka Bay from Abercrombie State Park, over to Cape Chiniak on the island's eastern tip, and all the way down to the Pasagshak Bay and State Park in the southeast. The fossil-filled cliffs, all-encompassing vistas, and grazing buffalo at the south end of the road system near **Pasagshak Bay** are worth the 47-mile drive from town. (Kodiak has several large cattle ranches.) A detailed mileage guide for all the roads is found in the "Kodiak Island Visitors Guide."

Hiking

Many hikes are available around Kodiak; see the visitor center for a map showing the more popular routes. Pillar Mountain is described above. **Pyramid Peak** has two trailheads off Anton Larsen Bay Rd. that climb this steep, 2,400-foot mountain just west of town. Start near the ski lift approximately 1.5 miles past the golf course. Great vistas from the summit.

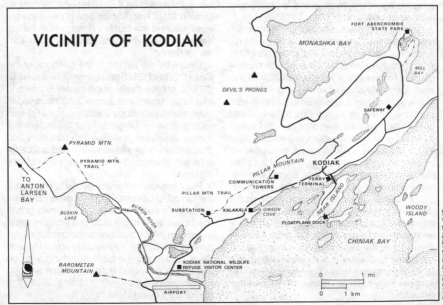

VICINITY OF KODIAK

© MOON PUBLICATIONS, INC.

Barometer Mountain Trail is a steep five-mile hike to the 2,500-foot peak. It starts at an unmarked (but recognizable) trailhead on the first road to the right past the airport runway out Rezanof Dr. West. This is one of the most popular local hikes. **Fort Abercrombie** (described above) has a network of trails around the edge of the peninsula. You'll discover all sorts of WW II detritus on your wanderings here. Before you set out on a hike around Kodiak, be sure to talk over any of these hikes with personnel at the visitor center, or with the park rangers at Fort Abercrombie.

Shuyak Island State Park
Shuyak Island is 50 miles and a 40-minute floatplane flight north of Kodiak (or south from Homer); a flight that takes you to another world. The 11,000-acre park contains virgin Sitka spruce forests and a gorgeous coastline pockmarked with small islands. It's perfect for sea kayaking, and the state maintains four public use cabins available for $50/night. There are only a few hiking trails, and the dense devils club makes bushwhacking very difficult; it is possible to hike along the shore at low tide if you don't have a kayak. Make cabin reservations by calling Alaska State Parks, tel. (907) 486-6339 (Kodiak), or tel. (907) 762-2261 (Anchorage). The cabins are generally available, but reserve well ahead for the silver salmon run in September.

Afognak Island
This large island lies 30 miles north of Kodiak Island, but is vastly different from its neighbor. Afognak is—or rather was—covered with a luxuriant, dense spruce forest. Unfortunately, much of this spectacular country has been logged over in recent years by the local Native corporation. **Afognak Island State Park** covers 43,000 acres of the island, which is accessed by floatplane or boat. Located on the east end of Afognak, **Pillar Lake Cabin** has space for up to seven people and costs $25/night, tel. (907) 486-6339 in Kodiak, or (907) 762-2261 in Anchorage. Floatplanes can land at the lake, but it is small and nearby saltwater is usually too rough. Be sure to talk with the air taxi operators to make sure they are willing and able to land there. The U.S. Fish and Wildlife Service, tel. (907) 487-2600, also has a cabin ($20/night) in remote Bluefox Bay.

Another area that managed to escape the chain saw is the property that surrounds **Afognak Wilderness Lodge,** run by Roy and Shannon Randall, tel. (907) 486-6442 or (800) 478-6442. Anyone willing to part with $400 pp/day (including three meals) will find some of the finest old-time accommodations in Alaska. For cheaper and less elaborate lodging, rent a lakeside cabin from **Afognak Native Corporation,** tel. (907) 486-6014 or (800) 770-6014. Also ask about their expeditions to ongoing archaeological excavations. And while you're at it, ask how they're managing their lands, and why they seem so determined to cut every tree on the island.

Port Lions
The small community of Port Lions (pop. 260) came into existence after the 1964 earthquake and tsunami destroyed the nearby village of Afognak. Port Lions was named to honor the funding and support from the Lions International Club that led to its establishment. The town has a strong commercial fishing base and also has a handful of lodges, eating places, and local stores. The state ferry stops here, and there is air taxi service to the surrounding country (see "Transportation" below). Pete Squartsoff, tel. (907) 454-2333, has five cabins for rent, one of which sits on nearby Whale Island, where visitors will be able to see whales, sea otters, and a kittiwake bird rookery.

PRACTICALITIES

Accommodations and Camping
See the chart for all the expensive lodging options in Kodiak; there are no hostels here. Your best bets are probably the various B&Bs in town.

The closest official campground **Buskin River State Recreation Site,** four miles south of town on Buskin Beach Rd. next to the airport. Hitching shouldn't be a problem. This is an okay site on the water, with shelters, pit toilets, trails, and runways in your ear ($10, seven-day limit). A cannery-workers campground at Gibson Cove, just south of town, is open during the summer, and may have space for other campers. It's best to camp at **Fort Abercrombie State Park,** on the eastern tip of town, five miles away. Even if all 14 sites are occupied, you can pitch your tent somewhere close. It's worth the hitch, bike

KODIAK ACCOMMODATIONS

Note: The city of Kodiak adds a 10% bed tax to local lodging rates.

MOTELS

Shelikof Lodge; 211 Thorsheim; tel. (907) 486-4141; $60 s, $65 d

Inlet Guest Rooms; 1315 Mill Bay Rd.; tel. (907) 486-4004 or (800) 478-4005; $65 s or d; airport transport, six guest rooms with fridge and microwave

Russian Heritage Inn; 119 Yukon St.; tel. (907) 486-5657; $65 s or d; kitchenettes $85 s or d

Kalsin Bay Inn; 30 miles south; tel. (907) 486-2659; $65 s, $75 d

Buskin River Inn; 1395 Airport Way; tel. (907) 487-2700 or (800) 544-2202; $105 s or d; AAA approved

Westmark Kodiak; 236 Rezanof West; tel. (907) 486-5712 or (800) 478-1111; $131 s or d

BED AND BREAKFASTS

Lakeview Terrace B&B; 2426 Spruce Cape Rd.; tel. (907) 486-5135; $45 s, $55 d; one guest room, full breakfast

Wintel's B&B; 1723 Mission Rd.; tel. (907) 486-6935; $50-90 s or d; three guest rooms and one suite, full breakfast

Ocean Side B&B; 3010 Spruce Cape Rd.; tel. (907) 486-5835; $55 s, $65 d; private suite, full breakfast

Star House B&B; 1612 Mission Rd.; tel. (907) 486-8823 or (800) 337-4123; $55 s, $70 d; two guest rooms, continental breakfast

Berry Patch B&B; 1616 Selief Lane; tel. (907) 486-6593; $55-65 s or d; two guest rooms, full breakfast

Otter Crest B&B; 1814 Rezanof Dr.; tel. (907) 486-4650; $55-75 s or d; three guest rooms, full breakfast

St. Herman's Theological Seminary B&B; 414 Mission Rd.; tel. (907) 486-3521; $55-75 s or d; 10 rooms, full breakfast, available June-Aug.

The Teal House B&B; 374 Teal Way; tel. (907) 486-3369; $55-75 s or d; two guest rooms, full breakfast

Country B&B; 1415 Zentner Ave.; tel. (907) 486-5162; $55-80 s or d; four guest rooms, full breakfast

Shahafka Cove B&B; 1812 Mission Rd.; tel. (907) 486-2409; $55-95 s or d; three guest rooms, full breakfast

Russian River B&B; 11572 S. Russian Creek Rd.; tel. (907) 487-4301; $55 s, $110 d; three guest rooms, continental breakfast

Luanne's Emerald Isle B&B; 1214 Madsen St.; tel. (907) 486-4893; $60-70 s or d; two guest rooms, continental breakfast

Kodiak B&B; 308 Cope St.; tel. (907) 486-5367; $60 s, $72 d; three guest rooms, full breakfast

Lotus Inn B&B; 304 Wilson St.; tel. (907) 486-4962; $60-72 s or d; two guest rooms, continental breakfast

Abby's Loft B&B, 426 Teal Way; tel. (907) 486-3615; $60-75; two guest rooms, full breakfast

Bear and the Bay B&B; 216 Rezanof Dr. E; tel. (907) 486-6154; $80-85 s or d; two guest rooms, private baths, continental breakfast

Bay View B&B; 3481 Eider St.; tel. (907) 486-4890; $100 s or d; deck overlooking Mill Bay, private suite, bath, kitchen, continental breakfast

Larch Tree Inn; 720 Larch St.; tel. (907) 486-1706; $110 s or d; private suite on Lilly Lake with kitchen, full breakfast, available May-Sept.

---

ride, or extra miles on the rental car—this is a magical place to pass your nights on Kodiak; ($10/night). Park RVs at **VFW RV Park,** tel. (907) 486-3195, seven miles out Monashka Bay Rd. (north of town).

Pasagshak River State Recreation Site, 45 miles south of town at the very end of the road, also has good camping (no charge). It's il-

legal to camp in town, but in a pinch you could walk across "the bridge to nowhere" (Near Island) and lose yourself in the woods of this city-owned land.

Food

Kodiak's favorite hangout is **Harborside Coffee & Goods** at 216 Shelikof, tel. (907) 486-5862, with lattes, pastries, and amazing espresso shakes. A great place to relax on a rainy day. **El Chicano,** 103 Center St., tel. (907) 486-6116, has unexpectedly authentic Mexican food, with chiles rellenos, tasty homemade tamales, *chorizo con huevos,* and even a little *menudo* for your hangover. Fair prices, too. In the same building is an espresso cart. The **Shelikof Lodge Restaurant,** 211 Thorsheim St., tel. (907) 486-4300, has good dinner specials. Get chicken at **Kentucky Fried Chicken,** next to the Safeway store out Mill Bay Road. A **Burger King** is located inside the downtown A.C. store, and **McDonald's** sits at the main intersection of Rezanof Dr. and Center Street. Directly across the street is **Eugene's Restaurant,** tel. (907) 486-2625, where you can croon Karaoke Elvis tunes to your dish of moo shu pork.

Probably the most popular place for a quick meal is the **Subway** shop, 326 Center, tel. (907) 486-7676. Open till midnight in the summer. **Beryl's Sweet Shop,** 202 Center St., tel. (907) 486-3323, makes tasty sandwiches, burgers, dogs, and steaming espresso coffees. **Mimi's Deli,** 3420 Rezanof Dr. E, tel. (907) 486-2886, is east of town on the way to Fort Abercrombie, and makes the best deli sandwiches on the island.

The lunch specials are a good bet at **Pizza Hut,** 2625 Mill Bay Rd., tel. (907) 486-5454; but get better pizzas from **Mr. Pizza,** 1941 Mill Bay Rd., tel. (907) 486-1778. Locals looking for the best burgers and other dense American grub head to **King's Diner,** beside Lilly Lake at 1941 Mill Bay Rd., tel. (907) 486-4100. Recommended. For vegetarian fare—mainly juice drinks and sandwiches—visit **Cactus Flats,** 338 Mission Rd., tel. (907) 486-4677. And if you have the dough, head to **Buskin River Inn,** near the airport, tel. (907) 487-2700, where they offer prime rib and seafood that can't be beat.

Most visitors to Kodiak buy their groceries at the two downtown stores: **A.C. Store** and **City Market.** The best selection can be found at **Safeway,** two miles out Mill Bay Road. It's said to be the largest Safeway in the western United States.

Entertainment

You'd expect a town whose inhabitants live close to the "edge" to party hearty, and Kodiak definitely won't disappoint you. You don't even have to venture any farther than the Mall downtown, whose dozen or so storefronts are half occupied by bars, big bars. (Following a big salmon opener, a beer can thrown in any direction would hit a drunk fisherman.) The **Mecca** has a popular dance floor; this place competes with the ocean for rockin' and rollin'! For hard drinking with the highliners, sit down at **Ship's Tavern, Breakers Bar, The Village,** or **Tony's.** Tony's advertises itself as the "biggest navigational hazard on Kodiak" and simultaneously "a friendly neighborhood bar with over 3,000,000 drinks spilled." **Tropic Lounge** is a huge bar where some people go bowling. For TV sports, a big choice of draught beers, and good pub-grub (including pasta, burgers, and fish & chips), head to **Henry's Great Alaskan Restaurant,** 512 Marine Way, tel. (907) 486-3313. The decor includes a gorgeous Chilkat robe and other Alaskan pieces of the past. Also check **Shelikof Lodge** for live music. Otherwise, take in a flick at **Orpheum Theater** on Center Street. Wednesday is cheap night: $2.50 tickets.

Events

The infamous **Pillar Mountain Golf Classic,** on the last day of March, is a deranged, par-70, one-hole tournament up the side of this 1,400-foot mountain behind town. The course, cleared by spotters with machetes, runs all the way to the peak, where a bucket in the snow serves as the hole and lime Jello as the green. No power tools allowed, so leave your chain saw at home. The big summertime event on Kodiak is the **Crab Festival,** held on Memorial Day weekend. There's a big parade, survival suit races, a blessing of the fleet ceremony, and various concerts. Lots of fun. In mid-July, the **Kodiak Bear Country Music Festival** brings a mix of sounds—country, rock, blues, and bluegrass—to Kodiak. The **Kodiak State Fair and Rodeo** comes around on Labor Day weekend, and features everything from crafts demonstrations, stock car races, and a rodeo, though the cowboys who compete here would be laughable by Wyoming standards. **St. Herman's Day** is August 9 each year and honors the canonization of the only Russian Orthodox saint from the Americas. The day features a pilgrimage to his old homesite on nearby Woody Island.

Information

The **Visitor Information Center** shares the same building with the ferry office on Marine Way and Center St., tel. (907) 486-4070, and is open summers, Sunday 1-9 p.m., Mon.-Fri. 8 a.m.-5 p.m., and Saturday 10 a.m.-2 p.m., plus evenings when the ferry is in port. The rest of the year, they're open Mon.-Fri. 8 a.m.-5 p.m. Pick up the "Kodiak Island Map" and their "Visitors Guide," and take a gander at the nine-and-a-half-foot bearskin on the wall. They'll also hold your backpack if you want to scout around a little. See "Kodiak National Wildlife Refuge" below for the other local visitor center, out by the airport.

Shopping and Services

For an indoor shower, head straight to **Ernie's Laundromat,** across the street from the main ramp down to the Small Boat Harbor on Shelikof. Another place to shower is **The Wash Tub,** 330 Shelikof Avenue. At either place, $3 buys 20 minutes of blessed steaming, thundering hot water; a mere 50 cents avails you of a dry towel. The **library** on Mill Bay Rd. downtown has an enormous collection of books on Alaskan history, open weekdays 10 a.m.-9 p.m., weekends 10 a.m.-5 p.m. **Shire Books** at 104 Center Ave., tel. (907) 486-5001, is a good place to pick up *Highliners* and immerse yourself in local lore.

TRANSPORTATION

On the Water

If you have time and want to save a bundle on transportation, catch the trusty *Tustumena* in Homer, arriving in Kodiak 12 hours later, and with only $48 less cash in your stash. Or get on at Seward for $54. This is a great, relaxing way to reach Kodiak, but take seasickness pills

SOUTHCENTRAL AND SOUTHWEST ALASKA FERRY PASSENGER FARES (SUMMER 1997 RATES)

	Unalaska	Akutan	False Pass	Cold Bay	King Cove	Sand Point	Chignik	Kodiak	Port Lions	Seldovia	Homer	Seward	Whittier	Valdez
Akutan	16													
False Pass	46	34												
Cold Bay	62	50	18											
King Cove	74	66	34	18										
Sand Point	98	90	58	42	32									
Chignik	132	124	92	76	66	42								
Kodiak	202	194	162	146	136	112	76							
Port Lions	202	194	162	146	136	112	76	20						
Seldovia	246	240	208	192	180	156	122	52	52					
Homer	242	236	204	188	176	152	118	48	48	18				
Seward	250	242	210	194	184	160	124	54	54	100	96			
Whittier	316	308	276	260	250	226	190	120	120	166	162	—		
Valdez	292	296	254	238	226	202	168	98	98	142	138	58	58	
Cordova	292	286	254	238	226	202	168	98	98	142	138	58	58	30

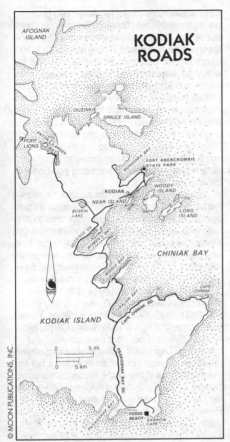

KODIAK ROADS

AFOGNAK ISLAND

OUZINKIE
SPRUCE ISLAND

PORT LIONS
ANTON LARSEN

MONASHKA BAY
FORT ABERCROMBIE STATE PARK

KODIAK
WOODY ISLAND
NEAR ISLAND
BUSKIN LAKE
BELLS FLATS DR
WOMENS BAY
LONG ISLAND

CHINIAK BAY

MIDDLE BAY

KODIAK ISLAND
CAPE CHINIAK
CAPE CHINIAK RD.

PASAGSHAK BAY RD

0   5 mi
0   5 km

FOSSIL BEACH
NARROW CAPE

© MOON PUBLICATIONS, INC.

upon boarding—you may need them! The downtown Kodiak **ferry terminal** is open Mon.-Fri. 8 a.m.-5 p.m., tel. (907) 486-3800. The ferry also stops in the Kodiak Island community of Port Lions along the way. A **water taxi**, tel. (907) 454-2418, connects Port Lions to Kodiak or Anton Larsen Bay.

Wavetamer Kayaking, tel. (907) 486-2604, has a variety of sea kayaking trips around Kodiak, ranging from introductory classes to half-day visits to Anton Larsen Bay and Woody Island. This is a fine way to see sea otters, seals, and puffins. Rent double fiberglass kayaks or folding kayaks from **Backcountry Rentals**, tel. (907) 486-2722 (great if you're flying out to a cabin in the wildlife refuge).

Airlines
PenAir, tel. (907) 487-4014 or (800) 448-4226; **Era Aviation,** tel. (800) 866-8394; and **Alaska Airlines,** tel. (800) 426-0333, offer daily flights from Anchorage, with prices commonly around $215 roundtrip. PenAir also has summertime service between Kodiak and King Salmon. If you're a little short on time and don't want to ride the ferry, this is the way to experience Kodiak.

On the way down, if you're very lucky and it's clear, sit on the right side of the plane for a view of Mounts McKinley and Foraker, down to Mounts Spurr, Redoubt, Illiamna, and even Augustine—nearly 500 miles of spectacular peaks with just a slight twist of your head. You'll also see enormous swaths of clearcut Native land on Afognak Island. On the way back, also sit on the right to see the vast Harding Icefield and Kenai Mountains. The airport is five miles from Kodiak town. A shuttle bus into town ($5) meets most flights; check wall signs for the phone number. Hitching is fairly easy, or catch a cab if you're feeling flush with cash.

Air Taxis
A number of companies have floatplane flights to various parts of Kodiak from the floatplane dock on Near Island. The larger ones are **Sea Hawk Air,** tel. (907) 486-8282 or (800) 770-4295; **Island Air Service,** tel. (907) 486-6196; **Uyak Air Service,** tel. (907) 486-3407 or (800) 303-3407; **PenAir,** tel. (907) 486-4014 or (800) 448-4226; and **Wilderness Air,** tel. (907) 486-8101 or (800) 556-8101. PenAir has daily service to **Akhiok** ($75), **Karluk** ($75), **Larsen Bay** ($60), **Old Harbor** ($50), and **Port Lions** ($30). They can often also do drop-offs along the routes (including Fish and Wildlife Service cabins), saving you a bundle over charter rates. But if you want to fly with one of the best pilots in Alaska, ask for Rolan Ruoss at Sea Hawk Air. Charter rates are generally around $270/hour for a Cessna 206 or $370/hour for a Beaver. Uyak Air, Wilderness Air, and Island Air all offer "guaranteed bear viewing" flights around Kodiak and to the Alaska Peninsula. Expect to pay around $400 pp for a four-hour flight.

Tours and Getting Around
Island Terrific Tours, tel. (907) 486-4777; **Custom Tours of Kodiak,** tel. (907) 486-4997; and **Kodiak Tours,** tel. (907) 486-5989 or (800) 762-

5634, offer all-day van tours of the Kodiak area for $60-70 pp. See the visitor center for a listing of local fishing and sightseeing charter boats.

Several car rental companies have desks at the airport. They include: **Avis,** tel. (907) 487-2264 or (800) 478-2847; Budget, tel. (907) 486-5815 or (800) 248-0150; **Hertz,** tel. (907) 487-2261 or (800) 654-3131; **National,** tel. (907) 487-4435 or (800) 227-7368; and **Rent A Heap,** tel. (907) 486-5200. Or rent a mountain bike from **Elkay Bicycle Shop,** at 104 Rezanof, tel. (907) 486-4219. But don't even think about getting a cab—$3 flag drop and $2.50 per mile, or a whopping $13 out to Fort Abercrombie.

KODIAK NATIONAL
WILDLIFE REFUGE

The 1.9 million-acre Kodiak National Wildlife Refuge was established in 1941 to preserve brown bear habitat on Kodiak. It covers the southwestern two-thirds of the island, along with Uganik Island, Ban Island, and a small portion of Afognak Island. The **U.S. Fish and Wildlife Service Visitor Center** (and headquarters for the refuge) is open Mon.-Fri. 8 a.m.-4:30 p.m., and Saturday noon-4:30 p.m., June-Sept.; and Mon.-Fri. noon-4:30 p.m. the rest of the year. Call (907) 487-2600 for more info. Inside, find a fine relief map of the island, a "please touch" exhibit of furs, and a 15-minute video about bears and the incredible life cycle of salmon—stunning footage, don't miss it. There are more free films on weekends; check with the center for what's coming up. They also sell books and have handouts on animals, birds, and cabins in the wildlife refuge.

Kodiak National Wildlife Refuge itself begins 25 miles southwest of refuge headquarters and is accessible only by floatplane (unless you have a boat or are willing to do some major-league hiking). Most visitors to the refuge fly to one of the lakes and stay in a Fish and Wildlife Service cabin or camp. Many others stay at one of the expensive ($2,000 pp/week) fishing lodges around the island; see the city visitor center for a complete listing—if you have this kind of money.

Bear Watching
Kodiak is world famous for its enormous brown bears. The largest reach 10 feet tall when standing and approach weights of 1,500 pounds;

most adult males (boars) average 800 pounds, adult females (sows) average 550 pounds. Eight out of the 10 largest brown bears killed were taken on Kodiak Island. There are some 2,500 bears on the island, or an average of one for every 1.5 square miles! Visitors often come to watch or photograph these magnificent animals. Unfortunately, quite a few hunters come to kill them as well. Anyone who has spent time around Kodiak bears quickly gains an appreciation for their beauty, and a respect for their intelligence. Hunting for food is justifiable; how someone could kill such an animal to just mount as a trophy—often in a menacing position—is beyond me.

Assuming that you're on Kodiak to see—rather than kill—the bears, several local air taxi operators will fly you on four-hour trips to the Katmai coast or Kodiak Island (depending upon where the bears are) for a hefty $400 pp. The companies include **Sea Hawk Air,** tel. (907) 486-8282 or (800) 770-4295; **Island Air Service,** tel. (907) 486-6196; **Uyak Air Service,** tel. (907) 486-3407 or (800) 303-3407; and **Wilderness Air,** tel. (907) 486-8101 or (800) 556-8101. Wilderness Air also manages a bear viewing program on Koniag Native Corporation land at O'Malley Lake near the southwest end of the island. Day use is outrageously expensive ($680 pp for eight hours), so most folks opt for overnight stays in one of the corporation's three cabins on Camp Island. Guides take you by skiff and foot to the viewing area along Thumb River and back for meals and sleeping. The price is an astounding $799 pp for one night, $1,299 pp for two nights, or $1,699 for three nights, with three meals included. The cabins have hot showers and sleeping bags. Clint Hlebechuck of **Kodiak-Katmai Outdoors, Inc.,** tel. (907) 486-2628 or (800) 762-5634 (outside Alaska), offers bear viewing trips to Hallow Bay on the outer coast of Katmai National Park. Contact the Fish and Wildlife Service for a listing of guides who can take you to other bear viewing camps where you'll get a real taste of the wilderness.

These places are not, of course, the only places to see brown bears on Kodiak Island. They are present along all the salmon streams in midsummer (best time to view them is July), especially where there are major runs of sockeye or king salmon. Ask at the visitor center for your best viewing opportunities. In late summer the bears tend to move up to the smaller spawning streams and into berry patches where they are less visible. Note that you aren't likely to see a brown bear from the Kodiak road system; most of the bears were shot long ago, and the rest tend to stay out of sight in the day. It will almost certainly cost you an airplane trip into the backcountry to see a Kodiak brown bear.

Cabins

The wildlife refuge maintains rustic cabins ($20/night) at seven different locations around Kodiak and Afognak Islands. These are a wonderful way to see the wilderness up-close and personal. You will need to bring fuel oil for the heater, plus all the standard camping supplies. And don't forget to bring insect repellent and headnets for the abundant and pesky no-see-ums. Because of their popularity, drawings are held for the cabins. Apply before January for the months of April-June, and before April for the months of July-September. The most popular time is July. Because of cancellations, the cabins sometimes become open; call the refuge at (907) 487-2600 if you decide to go at the last minute.

Anyone interested in bear viewing may want to check out the cabins at South Frazer Lake or Uganik Lake. It's very helpful to have an inflatable boat or folding kayak to get around these lakes; some air taxi operators rent them for their clients. It is also possible to camp out anywhere on the refuge without a permit. The abundance of both bears and rain can make this a less enjoyable experience, but experienced backcountry travelers will enjoy the chance to savor an untouched landscape.

Hiking and Rafting

The vast Kodiak National Wildlife Refuge is essentially undeveloped country. Despite a paucity of trails, it is relatively easy to hike since there are almost no trees on the southern three-fourths of the island. The best time to hike here is early in summer after the snow is gone and before the grass and brush get too dense; by mid-August hiking can be a struggle. Besides, it's a bit more risky hiking in bear country when the willow thickets are too dense to see the bears! Once you get above the brush line (approximately 2,000 feet in elevation) the hiking gets very easy even in late summer.

There is only one true trail within the refuge; it leads from Larsen Bay to the Karluk River, four miles away. This almost-level path is used by the hundreds of rafters who float down the Karluk during the peak of the king salmon run (mainly July). Rafts can be rented from most of the air taxi operators for $45/day. Rafters put in where the trail reaches the river and float to the village of Karluk, 25 miles away. There is daily plane service ($75 one-way) back to Kodiak from Karluk. The Koniag Native Corporation, tel. (907) 561-2668 (in Anchorage), levies a $100 "trespass fee" (locals use the term extortion) on everyone who floats the river and camps; get forms at Mack's Sporting Goods in Kodiak or from the air taxi operators. **Uyak Air Service,** tel. (907) 486-3407 or (800) 303-3407, maintains four cabins at Portage and a fifth one at the outlet of Karluk Lake ($80/day d up to $165/day for six people). If you fly in to the river at Portage, expect to pay around $350 pp for charter flights; scheduled service to nearby Larson Bay is just $60 pp.

Tiny **Karluk** (pop. 70) has a beautiful old Russian Orthodox church (built in 1888) with a spectacular cliff-and-ocean backdrop. There is also a small store, along with a couple of fishing lodges. The Fish and Game fish weir a mile above the village is Alaska's oldest and one of the largest (320 feet wide). The Karluk River, Ayakulik River, and several others on Kodiak are world famous for their king, sockeye, and silver salmon runs, but also have impressive runs of pink and chum salmon, along with Dolly Varden, steelhead, and rainbow trout. At the turn of the century—before seven local canneries wiped the salmon out and then went out of business—the Karluk River had runs of up to 10 million red salmon. It has taken decades of careful Fish and Game management for the populations to recover, but today this is some of the finest fishing anywhere on the planet.

ALASKA PENINSULA

LAKE CLARK NATIONAL PARK

This 3.6-million-acre national park reaches from the western shore of Cook Inlet and across the Chigmit Mountains to enclose 50-mile-long Lake Clark. The park was established in 1980. Although there are scattered lodges and cabins, the only developed site within the park is **Port Alsworth** (pop. 50) on Lake Clark. Despite the name, Port Alsworth is *not* a port, since the ocean is 50 miles away. Because of the park's ocean-to-mountaintop coverage, it includes a diversity of ecosystems, from dense spruce forests along the coast to active volcanoes (Iliamna and Redoubt). The western flank of the Chigmit Mountains is covered with tundra and boreal forests. Just south of the park is huge Iliamna Lake, the largest lake in Alaska. (The town of Iliamna on its shores has a store with limited supplies.)

Once you get away from the scattering of lodges, Lake Clark National Park is a vast, undeveloped wilderness without roads, trails, or other facilities. Those not staying in the lodges come here to boat and fish on the lake, or to backpack in the mountains. The western foothills have open, dry tundra that's perfect for hiking. Floating down the various rivers that lead westward from the park is another popular activity. Wildlife viewing can be impressive, since you can find caribou, moose, wolves, brown and black bears, and Dall sheep, among other mammals.

Practicalities

Lake Clark National Park headquarters are in Anchorage at 4230 University Dr., tel. (907) 271-3751. They also have a ranger station in Port Alsworth. There are no stores in Port Alsworth, but boats can be rented from local lodges. There is a pretty waterfall on the Tanalian River near town, and if you keep your eyes open you might meet former Republican governor Jay Hammond—certainly the most respected politician the state has seen for several decades. (He and his wife live in a log cabin along Lake Clark.)

Expensive accommodations are available from more than a dozen fishing lodges along the shores of Lake Clark. The Park Service has a listing of lodges. **Lake Clark Air**, tel. (907) 278-2054 (in Anchorage) has daily service between Anchorage and Port Alsworth for $275 roundtrip. A number of companies offer flight-seeing over the park from here; see the Park Service for specifics.

KATMAI NATIONAL PARK

Katmai National Park occupies a large chunk of the Alaska Peninsula, over four million acres (roughly the size of Connecticut and Rhode Island), just northwest of Kodiak Island across Shelikof Strait. Several features attract visitors to Katmai: its wild volcanic landscape, outstanding salmon fishing in a world-class setting, and the opportunity to see brown bears up close. The bears are the big attraction nowadays; they're big, they're bad, and they're ubiquitous, thanks to the million-plus salmon that run up the Naknek River drainage system from Bristol Bay each year. Dozens of other mammal, bird, and fish species thrive in the park.

Novarupta Erupts

In June 1912, one of the great cataclysms of modern history took place here as Mt. Novarupta blew its top, violently spewing volcanic glass, ash, and sulfurous fumes for three days. One of the explosions was heard in Ketchikan, 860 miles away. The fallout choked Kodiak, whose 450 inhabitants were evacuated in a daring marine rescue, but nobody is known to have been killed. Hot ash and pumice piled up 700 feet deep over a 40-square-mile area, and acid rain destroyed clothing hanging on clotheslines in Vancouver. Massive amounts of dust cloaked the vicinity in pitch blackness for 60 hours and circulated in the upper atmosphere for two years, changing weather patterns worldwide. Scientists say this was the second largest blast in recorded history, exceeded only by the eruption of Greece's Santorini in 1500 B.C. By way of comparison, the

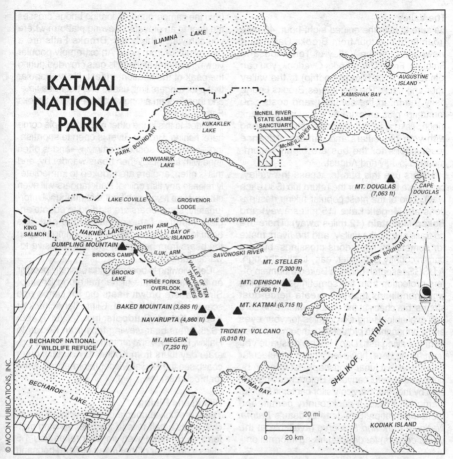

KATMAI
NATIONAL
PARK

ILIAMNA LAKE

AUGUSTINE ISLAND

KAMISHAK BAY

KUKAKLEK LAKE

McNEIL RIVER STATE GAME SANCTUARY

McNEIL RIVER

PARK BOUNDARY

NONVIANUK LAKE

MT. DOUGLAS (7,063 ft)

CAPE DOUGLAS

LAKE COVILLE

GROSVENOR LODGE

LAKE GROSVENOR

KING SALMON

NAKNEK LAKE

NORTH ARM

BAY OF ISLANDS

DUMPLING MOUNTAIN

BROOKS CAMP

ILUK ARM

SAVONOSKI RIVER

PARK BOUNDARY

BROOKS LAKE

THREE FORKS OVERLOOK

VALLEY OF TEN THOUSAND SMOKES

MT. STELLER (7,300 ft)

MT. DENISON (7,606 ft)

BAKED MOUNTAIN (3,685 ft)

MT. KATMAI (6,715 ft)

NAVARUPTA (4,860 ft)

TRIDENT VOLCANO (6,010 ft)

BECHAROF NATIONAL WILDLIFE REFUGE

MT. MEGEIK (7,250 ft)

SHELIKOF STRAIT

BECHAROF LAKE

KATMAI BAY

© MOON PUBLICATIONS, INC.

0   20 mi

0   20 km

KODIAK ISLAND

1883 eruption of Krakatoa in Indonesia was only half as large (though it killed 35,000 people).

Robert Griggs, a botanist sent by the National Geographic Society, discovered in 1916 the nearby **Valley of Ten Thousand Smokes,** where hot gases surfaced via tens of thousands of holes and cracks when the hot ash contacted buried rivers and springs. He reported, "The whole valley as far as the eye could reach was full of hundreds, no thousands—literally, tens of thousands—of smokes curling up from its fissured floor." The area has gradually cooled, and only a few fumaroles remain today. A national monument was created here in 1918; it has since been expanded five times to encompass the large brown bear and salmon habitat. In 1980, under the Alaska National Interest Lands Conservation Act (ANILCA), it was declared a national park.

It's been more than 75 years since the "Noveruption," but volcanologists are still studying this unique phenomenon—a young, intact volcano created by a single event—to determine the hazards from future eruptions. Novarupta, however, is only one of 15 active volcanos monitored within Katmai National Park. The last to spew was Trident Volcano in 1968, but steam plumes occasionally rise from Megeik and Martin Volcanos as well.

The Valley

Be sure to take the guided eight-hour, 46-mile (roundtrip) bus tour from Brooks Camp to a viewpoint over the Valley of Ten Thousand Smokes. From Three Forks Overlook, you can join a three-mile hike (roundtrip) to the valley floor and back. The bus leaves Brooks Lodge daily 9 a.m. in the summer, and costs $50 roundtrip, plus an extra $7 if you want a sack lunch. Take warm clothing and raingear, along with your binoculars and camera. Advance reservations for the bus are highly recommended in July and August.

Hikers use this bus to access the valley, catching a later bus for the return trip ($30 each way). Two of the most popular hiking destinations are **Megeik Lake** (15 miles away) and **Baked Mountain** (12 miles away). There are no trails across the valley, and the rivers make for sometimes hazardous crossings, but the barren country is relatively easy to hike through. A USGS research cabin at Baked Mountain offers protection from the sometimes harrowing wind conditions that can create fierce dust storms, but check at the visitor center to be sure it is available. Bring ski goggles for your eyes and a bandanna to protect your mouth and nose from the flying ash. Don't let this dissuade you from hiking here, however. This is spectacular country, with a lunar landscape cut through by deep and colorful canyons. Before heading out, stop by the Park Service visitor center in Brooks Camp for a map, a backcountry permit, and more information. See Jean Bodeau's *Katmai National Park and Preserve* (available at the visitor centers) for detailed hiking information.

Bear Viewing

Until recently, most visitors to Katmai came to explore the volcanic devastation or to fish for salmon, but more and more are attracted by the chance to view and photograph brown bears as they catch salmon. A spate of national publicity has led to skyrocketing use, with over 350 visitors crowding the Brooks Camp area on a typical July day. As of this writing, park policy was in flux, and management may be turned over to a concessionaire. Call (907) 246-3305 for the latest information.

Bear activity centers on the Brooks River, which flows into Naknek Lake just a half-mile from the campground. A floating bridge crosses the river to an elevated viewing platform where you can watch the bears. **Brooks Falls** are a half-mile hike from here. An extremely popular viewing platform at the falls gets crowded during the peak of the season. In fact, it's so popular that park rangers limit use to one hour at a time, and there's often a long wait to get to the Brooks Falls platform.

Added to this is the other reason people come here: fishing. Brooks River is open to sportfishing—mainly for sockeye salmon—and is often lined with anglers. When bears wander by, and this is often, anglers are required to immediately release any fish online. Park rangers will even cut your line if you don't act fast enough. Unfortunately, some bears are starting to equate anglers with free fish; sometimes the park has been forced to close the river to fishing to keep the bears from becoming more aggressive towards humans.

Bear viewing is becoming increasingly popular on the eastern side of Katmai along Shelikof Strait, where brown bears dig for clams and scavenge for other food. Clint Hlebechuck of **Kodiak-Katmai Outdoors, Inc.,** tel. (907) 486-2628, offers bear viewing trips from Kodiak to Hallow Bay. Several air taxi operators also operate day tours from Kodiak to Katmai's outer coast; see the Kodiak Visitor Information Center for brochures.

Hiking and Biking

There are only a couple of trails within Katmai. One leads a half-mile to the bear viewing platform on Brooks River; another takes you 1.5 miles to the floor of the Valley of Ten Thousand Smokes. Both paths are described above. The **Dumpling Mountain Trail** leaves from Brooks Camp and climbs four miles to the top of this 2,440-foot peak. You'll discover outstanding panoramic vistas from the summit across the surrounding lake-filled, volcano-crowned country.

Life Time Adventures, tel. (907) 746-4644 or (800) 952-8624, leads guided hiking and mountain bike trips in the park, and rents bikes ($30/day) for do-it-yourselfers. The 23-mile dirt road to the Valley of Ten Thousand Smokes is a fine place to ride bikes; the views get more dramatic as you go. Some folks who can't get a space in the Brooks campground rent bikes and head five miles up the road (the minimum required distance) to find a place.

On the Water
Savonoski Loop is a favorite backcountry canoe or kayak trip. Boaters start in Brooks Camp, head up the north arm of Naknek Lake, portage a mile to Lake Grosvenor, float down the Grosvenor and Savonoski Rivers, and paddle across the Iluk Arm of Naknek Lake back to Brooks Camp. Be ready for a four- to 10-day trip, and be sure to talk with Park Service rangers for precautions and backcountry permits before heading out. Canoes and kayaks can be rented from Brooks Lake Lodge or **Life Time Adventures,** tel. (907) 746-4644 or (800) 952-8624. Life Time also offers guided kayak trips ($1,100 for a six-day trip from Anchorage), as well as kayak drop-offs throughout Naknek Lake. **Bristol Bay Charter Adventures,** tel. (907) 246-3750, also does kayak drop-offs. Several companies offer motorboat rentals on Naknek Lake; see the King Salmon visitor center, tel. (907) 246-4250, for a listing. The visitor center can also provide a list of guided sportfishing outfitters and boat tours.

Accommodations
If you want to stay the night at famous **Brooks Lodge,** tel. (800) 544-0551, be prepared to shell out wads of cash. During July (peak season), a package trip that includes roundtrip airfare from Anchorage to Brooks Lodge plus three nights of lodging will set you back $807 pp, d. Stuff-yourself buffet meals are extra: $10 for breakfast, $12 for lunch, and $22 for dinner. The bar here serves mixed drinks. If you're willing to share a cabin with another couple or arrive sometime other than July, your overall cost will be somewhat lower. Brooks Lodge fills up fast, so make reservations in January to be sure of a place in midsummer.

A tiny gift shop at the lodge sells snacks, film, T-shirts and other tourist trinkets, and you can also rent canoes, fishing poles, and hip waders. Lodging and restaurants are also in King Salmon (see below). Five other fishing lodges are on other lakes within the park. They are even more expensive than Brooks Lodge, but are far from the hubbub: **Grosvenor Lodge** charges $1,625

pp for airfare and three nights' lodging. Note that the lodges, along with services such as the bus tours, operate only from the first of June to mid-September. After that, you're on your own.

King Salmon and Naknek
The town of King Salmon is a gateway to Katmai National Park. Travelers who are unable to get a lodge or campground space at Brooks Camp often stay here and make day-trips into the park. Naknek is 15 miles west of King Salmon by road, and is a major fishing port. Both towns have food and lodging, and taxi service connects the two. The towns represent an odd clash between the yupscale tourists out to see Katmai bears and grubby commercial fishermen out to make a buck (or several thousand bucks).

Several places in King Salmon offer lodging: **Bristol Bay B&B,** tel. (907) 246-7570 ($70 pp); **Bristol Bay Charter Adventures,** tel. (907) 246-3750 ($150 d in a cabin); **The Guest House,** tel. (907) 246-7425 ($80-120 s or d); **King Ko Inn,** tel. (907) 246-3377 ($153 s, $178 d in new cabins); **Ponderosa Inn,** tel. (907) 246-3444 ($90 s, $160 d); and the fanciest place in town, **Quinnat Landing Hotel** tel. (907) 246-3000 or (800) 770-3474 ($180 s, $205 d). You can usually pitch a tent for a few bucks next to Dave's World, near the Katmai Air office.

Lodging prices are lower in Naknek, but you'll need to pay $14 each way for the taxi fare, so this may wipe out any savings. Easily the cheapest is **Chulyen Roost,** tel. (907) 246-4458, with $25 bunks in dorms; private rooms are $50 s, $75 d. Very friendly folks keep the place spotlessly clean, and they serve a full breakfast. Recommended. Other places in Naknek are: **Al-Lou's B&B,** tel. (907) 246-4270 ($60 s, $75 d); **Leader Creek Inn,** tel. (907) 246-4415 ($50 s, $60 d); **Naknek Hotel,** tel. (907) 246-4430 ($50 s, $70 d); and **Red Dog Inn,** tel. (907) 246-4213 ($70 s, $80 d).

The modern **King Ko Grill** in King Salmon, tel. (907) 246-3377, serves three dependably good meals a day, with fresh seafood, pizzas (pricey at $20), burgers, and other faves. They also have a big bar with live music on summer weekends. Meals are also available at **Quinnat Landing Hotel,** and you can get groceries, sporting goods, and even espresso from **City Market** in King Salmon.

Camping

The campground at **Brooks Camp** is just a short distance from the lodge and has potable water. It's extremely popular and the spaces fill up fast, so reservations should be made far ahead of your visit; tel. (907) 246-3305. In the past, the campground has been booked for the month of July within three hours after reservations opened in late January! There is no charge for reservations, and you are limited to a maximum of seven nights all summer. Don't bring your kitchen sink along on this trip; you'll have to carry it a quarter-mile from the float-plane dock to the campground, and the bear-proof caches don't have room for a sink anyway. (The Park Service has wheeled carts to make this easier.) This is the only developed campground in Katmai, and backcountry camping is not allowed within five miles of Brooks Camp, so don't come here without a reservation unless you're willing to hike. In the past, no-shows have created openings at the campground even when it was officially full, but it's pretty risky to arrive in Brooks Camp without a place reserved. Campers can purchase meals at Brooks Lodge or take showers there for $4 (with towel). Katmai experiences weather similar to that of the rest of the Aleutian arc—cool, wet, and wildly windy; so come prepared to get wet!

Information and Services

There is a very helpful **visitor center,** tel. (907) 246-4250, at the King Salmon airport that is open Sunday 9 a.m.-5 p.m., and Mon.-Sat. 8 a.m.-5 p.m. in the summer. A second visitor center, run by the Park Service, is in Brooks Camp. The Park Service has free afternoon **nature walks** and evening programs at Brooks Camp daily throughout the summer; check the bulletin boards at the visitor center, campground, and lodge. For more on Katmai, contact the National Park Service at Box 7, King Salmon, AK 99613, tel. (907) 246-3305. You can also pick up a map of the park and a copy of the informative park paper, *The Bear Facts,* at the Alaska Public Lands Information Center in Anchorage at Fourth and E, tel. (907) 271-2737. **Dave's World** in King Salmon, tel. (907) 246-3353, has tents for rent. The National Bank of Alaska in King Salmon has a 24-hour **ATM.**

Getting There

Getting to Katmai isn't cheap. First, fly from Anchorage to King Salmon on **Alaska Airlines,** tel. (800) 426-0333; **Reeve Aleutian Airways,** tel. (907) 246-7686 or (800) 544-2248; or **PenAir,** tel. (907) 246-3373 or (800) 448-4226, for around $375 roundtrip. PenAir also has summertime flights from Kodiak to King Salmon. From King Salmon, **Katmai Air,** tel. (907) 246-3079 or (800) 544-0551, has scheduled service to Brooks Camp for another $120 roundtrip. Other local air taxi operators that fly on a daily basis include **Egli Air Haul,** tel. (907) 246-6119; **C-Air,** tel. (907) 246-6318; and **Branch River Air Service,** tel. (907) 246-3437. All of these also offer flightseeing and trips to nearby McNeil River (see below). A more leisurely option is to take the boat service from **Quinnat Landing Hotel** in King Salmon, tel. (907) 246-3000 or (800) 770-3474 . This is primarily for those staying at the hotel, but is available for the general public as well. The cost is $125 roundtrip. **Bristol Bay Charter Adventure,** tel. (907) 246-3750, has a similar service for $115 roundtrip. One warning: The weather in King Salmon is often bad, so weather-related flight cancellations are not uncommon. People get stuck here often.

MCNEIL RIVER STATE GAME SANCTUARY

Wedged above the northeast corner of Katmai, this state sanctuary is where many of the famous photographs of brown bears, salmon, and gulls (in the same frame) are taken. In fact, during the salmon runs, more brown bears congregate here than in any other single site on earth. Recently, 130 were counted in one day! And when you place 10 or so people observing the action up close, you have an apt symbol for wild Alaska.

National Geographic photographer Cecil Rhode first published frames of McNeil River—without identifying it—in 1954, right after which the federal government closed the area to hunters. It became a state game sanctuary in 1967, and the limited permit system was installed in '73. And in 1979, the river was completely closed to sportfishing. Even with the number of visitors increasing (from 110 in 1980 to 310 in 1988), the number of bears has also grown (from 60 in 1980 to 125 in 1989), yet there have been no casualties among the people or the bears.

Getting In

Each year, more than 1,500 applications to visit McNeil River and nearby Mikfik Creek are received by the Alaska Department of Fish and Game; only 250 or so are granted (including standby permits). Your chances of winning a regular permit are approximately one in 10; worse if you are traveling to McNeil with a group. To get into the select group of those allowed to visit, contact Alaska Dept. of Fish and Game, 333 Raspberry St., Anchorage, AK 99502, tel. (907) 344-0541, for an application. Fill it out, enclose a nonrefundable $20 pp, and mail it back by March 1 at the latest. A lottery is held on March 15 to select the lucky 10 visitors a day who are taken up to the falls (prime habitat) by sanctuary manager Larry Aumiller. Those who are selected pay an additional $250 pp for the actual permit ($100 pp for Alaskan residents). This is in addition to the $20 pp deposit, and all your transportation, food, and other expenses. Bring lots of film to make this worth your while! The permit cannot be transferred. Visitors need to be in good physical condition since it's a 1.5-mile hike to the falls, and if the weather is bad (a common situation) it's easy to get cold while sitting in the rain for hours. A note to professional photographers: because so many people have photographed bears at McNeil for so long, the market for bear pics from here is flooded. Try somewhere else if you want a shot that stands out from the crowd.

In June, sockeye salmon run up Mikfik Creek, attracting a couple dozen bears; visitors are guided here in June and to McNeil River later in the summer. The best time to go bear watching is mid-July to early August, when the chum salmon are running, but it's also the time that most people apply to visit. Second choice is as close to peak as possible on the earlier side; later the excitement tapers off. You're given four days at the sanctuary—take them all.

As a backup, applicants should also apply for a standby permit (it doesn't cost any extra). A separate lottery is held for these openings; the cost is $125 for nonresidents and $50 for Alaskans. Up to five people a day are allowed these permits, and the winners wait for a no-show or (more likely) for a day when the regular permit holders decide to sit in camp instead. This typically happens when the weather is bad, so even if you're lucky enough to get in, you may need to deal with marginal photographic conditions. This policy is currently in flux, so check with Fish and Game for the latest rules. Note that you'll need to supply all your own camping gear and food, and will need hip boots to wade the creeks.

Transportation

Many air taxis provide transport to McNeil from Homer, King Salmon, Kodiak, or Anchorage. Expect to pay around $270 roundtrip from Homer, the primary departure point. **Kachemak Air Service** in Homer, tel. (907) 235-8924, is a friendly flying service that has been doing the trip daily across the Inlet for 20 years.

THE ALEUTIAN ISLANDS

From the tip of the Alaska Peninsula, an arc of 200 islands curves 1,050 miles southwest to Attu Island, separating the North Pacific Ocean from the Bering Sea. The Aleutian Islands are part of the circum-Pacific "ring of fire," one of the most geologically unsettled regions on earth. The titanic tectonic forces clash as the Pacific plate pushes under the North American plate at the deep Aleutian Trench, making the earth rumble, quake, and spew. The 14 large and 65 smaller islands (plus countless tiny islets) are all windswept northern

Pacific outposts. The meeting of the mild Japanese Current with the icy Bering Sea causes a climate of much fog, rain, and wind, but little sun. Compounding this is a meteorological phenomenon known as the "Aleutian low," a low-pressure atmospheric valley that funnels a number of intense storms east into North America. In short—it's not the greatest place to get a tan.

High peaks drop abruptly to the sea. There is no permafrost, but the constant strong winds inhibit tree growth; only tundra and brushy vegetation survive. Frequent storms blow through (Unalaska experiences almost 250 rainy days a year), but due to the warm currents the sea never freezes. Given these extreme climatic conditions, it's perhaps surprising that, prior to the arrival of the Russians, every island was inhabited by Aleut people, (close relatives to the Eskimo). On the other hand, given the abundance of the ocean, the Aleut were skillful hunters who lived in balance with the fish, marine mammals, and birds of their islands. The Russians enslaved and slaughtered the Aleut, and their numbers plummeted from approximately 25,000 in 1741 approximately 2,000 a century later. The Russians also hunted the sea otters and fur seals of the islands to near extinction, and the single-minded exploitation of the islands' resources continues even today. The U.S. Coast Guard must keep a careful watch for plunderers, as Asian and Russian fishing boats steal in during the most extreme weather conditions (when they know the patrol planes will be grounded) and sweep the sea clean of fish.

WAR IN THE ALEUTIANS

The Japanese Challenge
During the spring of 1942, Japan was sweeping triumphantly across the Pacific to the gates of Australia and Hawaii. However, the strength of the U.S. aircraft carriers—none of which had been lost at Pearl Harbor—worried Fleet Adm. Isoroku Yamamoto, commander-in-chief of the

Japanese navy. He knew that time was on the side of the United States. To win, he would have to draw the American carriers into a great naval battle where his superior forces could crush them and end the war. His target was Midway, a tiny island at the end of the Hawaiian chain, where the U.S. had recently built a base. But to first split the American forces, Yamamoto ordered a diversionary thrust at the Aleutians. In June 1942, Japanese carrier-based planes struck twice at Dutch Harbor, a large new U.S. naval base in Unalaska Bay, but inflicted only slight damage; the base continued to function. Meanwhile, at Midway, the U.S. had broken the Japanese naval code, and Yamamoto's plans were falling apart. Their own strength divided, one Japanese carrier after another sank before American momentum. As a face-saving move, the retiring Japanese occupied undefended Attu and Kiska at the west end of the Aleutians in the hope that bases on these islands would shield northern Japan and drive a wedge between the U.S. and Russia.

The Struggle for the Islands
In August 1942, the U.S. Navy occupied Adak Island and built an airfield from which to attack nearby Attu and Kiska. In January 1943, the Navy leapfrogged to Amchitka Island, right next door to Kiska, to provide an advance base. Continuous bombing and a naval blockade weakened Japanese resistance and on May 11, 1943, 16,000 U.S. troops landed on Attu. Of these, 549 Americans were killed before the 2,650 Japanese troops entrenched in the mountains

A string of volcanos from the Alaska Peninsula to the edge of the Aleutians is an active part of the circum-Pacific "Ring of Fire."

NAVAL HISTORICAL CENTER, WASHINGTON D.C., HOWARD W. CURTIS

were overcome. On May 29 about 800 remaining Japanese staged a banzai charge. At first they overran the American lines but their thrust was finally quelled by reserve forces. Only 28 Japanese prisoners were taken, and the 6,000 Japanese on Kiska seemed to face a similar fate.

Late in July, however, Japanese destroyers slipped through the U.S. blockade in dense fog and evacuated their soldiers. On August 15 some 34,000 U.S. and Canadian troops landed, unopposed, on Kiska. Though there was no one to attack and rout, incredibly, they suffered a shocking 99 dead and 74 wounded through landing mishaps and other accidents. Writing in the January 1988 issue of *Alaska Magazine,* Irving Payne described the scene: "The American and Canadian troops [coming in from two directions] mistook each other for the enemy and opened fire. Everything left by the Japanese was booby-trapped." With their masterful evacuation, the Japanese had ended the Aleutian campaign.

The Islands Today

Of the 80 named Aleutian Islands, only eight are occupied by humans. Sea otters are making a strong comeback from the edge of extinction. The rich variety of other marine mammals and seabirds is protected within the Aleutian Islands National Wildlife Refuge, particularly the black brant in Izembek Refuge near Cold Bay at the tip of the Alaska Peninsula.

UNALASKA/DUTCH HARBOR

Located about 800 miles southwest of Anchorage, Unalaska Bay cuts into the north side of mountainous Unalaska Island, creating the finest and most sheltered ice-free harbor in the Aleutians. On a clear day you can see the sometimes-smoking 6,680-foot cone of **Makushin Volcano** rising to the west. The city of Unalaska (pop. 4,000) spreads across both Unalaska Island and the much smaller Amaknak Island. A 500-foot bridge officially named "Bridge from the Other Side" links the two islands.

Although often called Dutch Harbor, this name actually refers to the protected harbor rather than the town itself. Longtime Unalaskans take umbrage at the suggestion that they live in Dutch

THE ALEUTIAN ISLANDS

© MOON PUBLICATIONS, INC.

CHIGNIK
SAND POINT
SHUMAGIN ISLANDS
UNGA ISLAND
KING COVE
COLD BAY
FALSE PASS
UNIMAK ISLAND
SHISHALDIN VOLCANO
ALASKA PENINSULA
AKUTAN
UNALASKA
DUTCH HARBOR
UNALASKA ISLAND
NIKOLSKI
UMNAK ISLAND
YUNASKA ISLAND
SEGUAM ISLAND
ATKA
AMILA ISLAND
ATKA ISLAND
ADAK
ADAK ISLAND
TANAGA ISLAND
KANAGA ISLAND
KISKA ISLAND
AMCHITKA ISLAND
SHEMYA ISLAND
AGATTU ISLAND
ATTU ISLAND
ATTU

PACIFIC OCEAN
BRISTOL BAY
PRIBILOF ISLANDS
ST. PAUL ISLAND
ST. GEORGE ISLAND
BERING SEA

100 mi
100 km
0
0

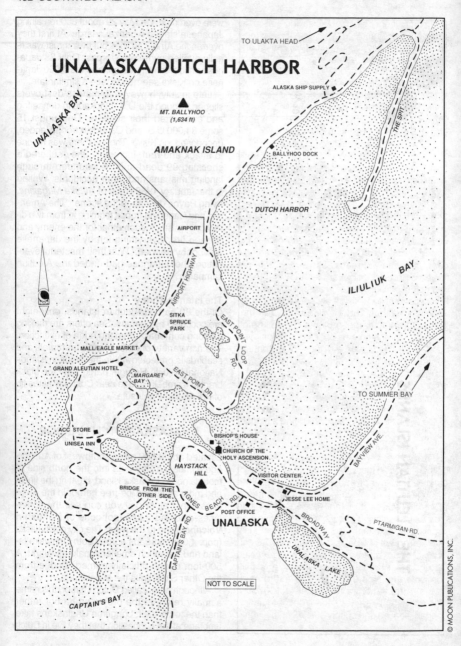

UNALASKA/DUTCH HARBOR

TO ULAKTA HEAD

ALASKA SHIP SUPPLY

UNALASKA BAY

MT. BALLYHOO
(1,634 ft)

AMAKNAK ISLAND

BALLYHOO DOCK

DUTCH HARBOR

AIRPORT

ILIULIUK BAY

AIRPORT HIGHWAY

SITKA
SPRUCE
PARK

EAST POINT LOOP RD.

MALL/EAGLE MARKET

GRAND ALEUTIAN HOTEL

MARGARET
BAY

EAST POINT DR.

TO SUMMER BAY

ACC STORE

BISHOP'S HOUSE

UNISEA INN

CHURCH OF THE
HOLY ASCENSION

HAYSTACK
HILL

VISITOR CENTER

BAYVIEW AVE.

BRIDGE FROM THE
OTHER SIDE

JESSE LEE HOME

AGNES BEACH RD.

CAPTAIN'S BAY RD.

POST OFFICE

BROADWAY

UNALASKA

PTARMIGAN RD.

UNALASKA
LAKE

CAPTAIN'S BAY

NOT TO SCALE

© MOON PUBLICATIONS, INC.

Harbor; to them it's sort of like saying "Frisco" instead of San Francisco. That doesn't stop most folks—especially the transient fishermen and cannery workers—from calling it Dutch Harbor, or simply "Dutch." The folks who live in Unalaska take pride in their small city, but many others just view it as a place to get rich quick and get out. This is perhaps best symbolized by a T-shirt seen around town. On the front is a hand filled with hundred dollar bills, and below the picture it simply says, "Dutch Harbor."

Dutch Harbor today is an extremely busy place, consistently ranking in the top three American fishing ports. At any given time you're likely to see a dozen or more cargo ships waiting to load fish, *surimi,* or crab destined for Japan, Korea, the Lower 48, or elsewhere. Most impressive of all is the huge container crane at the American President Lines dock where truck-sized loads are dropped onto ships. Crab pots and nets line the roads, and seven different seafood processing plants—huge multi-unit complexes—are scattered around the harbors, processing pollock, king crab, opilio (snow) crab, salmon, halibut, cod, herring roe, and other seafood. All told, these plants churn through over 600 million pounds of seafood a year, valued at over $135 million. It's the nation's number-one port in both pounds of seafood caught and total dollar value. Most of the catch is processed during the hectic winter fishing season, Nov.-April. Despite this rowdy make-a-million-bucks present, Unalaska/Dutch Harbor is filled with history, and visitors will find a number of places worth exploring.

History

When the first Russians "discovered" Unalaska in 1759, it was already home to more than 1,000 Aleut people scattered in 24 settlements. Over the next century the Russians decimated the Aleut, enslaving many of them to harvest fur seals and sea otters. The first permanent Russian settlement of Unalaska began in 1772, and Captain Cook spent three weeks here six years later. Under the Russians, Unalaska quickly became the main trading center in the Aleutians. After America took over in 1867, the focus gradually shifted, and it became an important coaling and supply station for the Nome gold rush.

In the 1940s, the U.S. Navy appropriated Dutch Harbor. After the city was bombed by the Japanese in June 1942, all the Aleuts were shipped off to relocation camps in Southeast Alaska. Ten percent of them died in these refugee camps (generally abandoned canneries) due in part to unsanitary conditions and overcrowding. Once WW II ended, they returned to a vastly different place filled with military facilities. Many of their homes had been ransacked.

Boomtimes

Dutch Harbor's economy exploded in the 1960s and '70s with the rapid growth of the king crab fishery, but crashed almost as suddenly when crab stocks plummeted—partly due to overfishing—in 1982. A few years later a second boom came as the fleet began to focus on bottom fish (especially pollock), primarily for the production of *surimi.* Today the many seafood processing plants in Dutch Harbor service the rich fisheries of nearby Bristol Bay. But the ghost of past booms hangs over this get-it-all-now culture. There is increasing evidence that even the

UNALASKA AREA

© MOON PUBLICATIONS, INC.

seemingly inexhaustible Bering Sea cannot withstand the sort of harvest now taking place. Today's factory trawlers—some are over 350 feet long—are enormous killing machines capable of raking in up to 240 *tons* in a single tow. This sort of fishing can best be equated to clearcut logging; the only difference is that a clearcut area is obvious, but a decimated ocean still looks the same on the surface.

Commercial fishermen contend that they are simply catching what's legal, and that there is no proof that they are destroying the marine environment. But the numbers of Steller's sea lions (which depend upon pollock for food) have nosedived, and some species of bottom fish are also declining. And overfishing in the Bering Sea is compounded by illegal fishing by foreign fleets. Will anything be done about this mess before the fish stocks crash? Don't hold your breath; too many folks are living high on the hog right now, hoping it will last forever. Maybe it will. Maybe it won't.

The Americanization of fisheries production in recent years and the boom in bottom fishing has led to rapid growth in Unalaska/Dutch Harbor. The population now tops 4,000 people—double that of 15 years earlier—plus another 2,500 transient workers. Boom times have come to the Aleutians, and right now there are lots of blue-collar jobs paying relatively high wages. Dutch is also becoming a minor center for conventions and other activities in Alaska's far west.

Historic Sights
The most interesting attraction in Unalaska is the beautiful **Russian Orthodox Church of the Holy Ascension.** Built 1824-27, this is the oldest Russian church still standing in Alaska, and a National Historic Landmark. A $1.5-million restoration project completely rebuilt this marvelous cathedral in time for its centennial in 1996, though additional work is needed on the inside. Out front is a small graveyard, and not far away is the **Bishop's House,** built in 1882. It is closed and also in need of repair. Another historic site (built in 1890) is the **Jesse Lee Home** near the cemetery. It was built by Methodist missionaries.

Not far from the airport is **Sitka Spruce Park,** where you'll find four scraggly stolid spruce trees planted by Russian settlers in 1805. At their base lies a plethora of stunted, struggling,

younger spruce. These, plus a couple of other clusters of trees around town, make up the only "forest" in this otherwise treeless country. The park is a National Historic Landmark.

Exploring the Country
The countryside around Unalaska is pockmarked with all sorts of evidence from WW II, including underground bunkers, gun emplacements, buildings of all types, and flotsam and jetsam from the military. The best places to find these are on the northeast end of Amaknak Island near Ulakta Head, and in the Summer Bay area on Unalaska Island.

A popular hiking place is 1,634-foot tall **Mount Ballyhoo,** just northeast of the airport on Amaknak Island. The easiest way to the top is to drive or mountain bike up the steep and very rough dirt road (4WD recommended, unless you have a rental car that needs a workout) that ends at Ulakta Head. This area is packed with decaying military structures of all sorts, but the open country is very pretty in late summer, with flowers galore, plus Arctic ground squirrels and bald eagles. (Red foxes are the only other wild mammal found on these islands, though some of the fishermen could fall into the "wild mammal" category.) Climb up the ridge from the end of the road for more dramatic vistas out to sea and back to the mountain-rimmed harbors. The west side of Amaknak Island consists of a harrowing series of cliffs that plummet to the sea 1,500 feet below, so stay away from the edge. In the winter months Mt. Ballyhoo is a popular walk-up, ski-down summit.

For a good view of town, climb **Haystack Hill** on the south side of Iliuliuk River (filled with spawning pink salmon in late summer). More panoramic vistas (and military bunkers) are atop the 421-foot Bunker Hill. A road up this hill veers west of the bridge.

Get to **Summer Bay** by heading northeast out of town on Summer Bay Rd. past the dump (a good place to see eagles). Five miles out is a lagoon where you can swim on a sunny day or practice your long jumping form on the tall sand dunes. Nice place for a picnic. Continue out the progressively rougher road past bunkers, Quonset huts, and a gun emplacement that guarded Iliuliuk Bay. Keep your eyes open for the two horses—the only ones on Unalaska—that graze here.

Aleutian Adventures, tel. (907) 581-4489, sells and rents outdoor gear, including kayaks, bikes, snowboards, skis, and backpacking equipment. The Unalaska Department of Parks, Culture and Recreation also rents bikes.

Accommodations

When it comes to lodging, you'll quickly discover that nothing comes cheap in Unalaska. Camping is frowned upon, and the local Native corporation has been known to slap a stiff fine on those who get caught. Some folks certainly do camp for a few nights, but it's pretty hard to hide in this open country. Stop by the Ounalashka Corporation office, 400 Salmon Way, tel. (907) 581-1276, for permission to camp.

Most local lodging places offer free airport pickup; see the chart for a complete listing. Note that the least expensive places are shared-room bunkhouses at the major canneries. The elaborate **Grand Aleutian Hotel** (owned by Unisea Corporation) is the place to stay if you've got the bucks to go in style.

Finding longer-term housing is very difficult and very expensive ($1,300 a month for a one-bedroom apartment), and things are so bad here that some folks even make their homes in old Sealand containers. One reason for these

---

UNALASKA/DUTCH HARBOR ACCOMMODATIONS

Statewide Services Inc., OSI Bunkhouse; tel. (907) 581-1515; $49 pp in shared rooms; $79 pp in private rooms; $73 pp in shared rooms with three meals; $103 pp in private rooms with three meals

Alaska Ship Supply Guest House; tel. (907) 581-1640; $51 s, $81 d; bath down hall, weekly and monthly rates

Beach House B&B; tel. (907) 581-1717; $60 s, $75 d; four guest rooms, private baths, continental breakfast

Unisea Inn; tel. (907) 581-1325; $90 s, $100 d

Carl's Bayview Inn; tel. (800) 581-1230; $90 s or d in standard rooms; $125 s or d with kitchenettes; $150 s or d in one-bedroom apartment

The Grand Aleutian; tel. (907) 581-3844 or (800) 891-1194; $135 s, $150 d

---

sky-high prices is that 90% of the land belongs to Ounalashka Native Corporation. Most homeowners purchase 99-year property leases from the corporation. Fortunately, these high prices are reflected in a plethora of jobs paying better wages than in other parts of the nation.

For something very different, ask about **Chernofski Farm,** a huge sheep ranch on the west end of Unalaska Island. The owners, Milt and Cora Holmes, sometimes take visitors, but you'll have to pay well over $1,000 for the charter flight out and back. They do not have a phone but can be reached by radio through Reeve Aleutian Airways.

Located on Umnak Island near Nikolski, **Fort Glenn Lodge,** tel. (907) 522-4999, is the state's largest cattle, sheep, and horse ranch. The ranch contains buildings from a WW II air base, including a USO theater where Bob Hope once performed. Today, guests come to enjoy the open country, to watch birds and other animals, and to climb up Okmok caldera.

Food

The food scene in Unalaska/Dutch Harbor is not especially notable, except in terms of price. No fast food places yet, but given the rapid growth, it's probably only a matter of time till Big Macs are available. Best place for burgers? Try the restaurant at the airport. **Dutch Harbor Cafe and Pizzaria** in the Margaret Bay area serves a mixed bag of Italian, American, and Mexican specialties, including the best pizza in town. Try the cannelloni. Right next door are **Peking Restaurant,** tel. (907) 581-2303; and **Linh's Restaurant,** tel. (907) 581-1625, both of which serve barely tolerable Chinese, Korean, and Japanese food. The Peking also features a karaoke bar. **Ziggy's Homestyle Cooking,** tel. (907) 581-2800, serves good Mexican food. **Nicky's Place,** tel. (907) 581-1570, in downtown Unalaska sells books, music, and posters, along with the best espresso coffee in town. **Unisea Inn,** tel. (907) 581-1325, has a popular Sunday brunch, and fresh seafood specials nightly.

By far the fanciest local eating places—and the best spots for fresh fish—are inside the Grand Aleutian Hotel. Downstairs find **Margaret Bay Cafe** which serves reasonably priced breakfast and lunches, including an all-you-can-eat soup, salad, and dessert bar. Upstairs is **Chart**

Room, where white linen and fine china match the food quality and prices ($20 and up, though they also have buffets starting at $17). They have an impressive wine selection, and a nice wine bar here as well. Not at all what you might expect in such a blue-collar town.

Get groceries at either **Alaska Commercial Co.** (ACC) or **Eagle Quality Centers,** tel. (907) 581-4040. Both have in-store delis and bakeries. **Alaska Ship Supply** also sells food and other gear, but is mainly used by big commercial purchasers on fishing boats. They have a large warehouse packed with pulleys, lines, pots, buoys, and other fishing gear. Don't expect to pay Lower 48 food prices in Dutch; a gallon of milk will set you back $5!

Entertainment and Events

Given the nature of the population—especially the transient and often wealthy crab fishermen—it should come as no surprise that bars are the main attraction in Unalaska. (There are only half as many churches as places with liquor licenses.) In the 1970s, *Playboy* labeled Unalaska's **Elbowroom,** tel. (907) 581-1271, America's most notorious bar, the sort of place where drunken brawls were the norm. Things have calmed down considerably in recent years, but you'll be rubbing elbows with lots of other folks—including some tough cookies—at the Elbow. When the crews are in from the crab fleet, things quickly start to resemble the *Star Wars* bar scene, with characters who might just as well have crawled off a different planet. The Elbow has live rock music on weekends, as does **Unisea Sports Bar** (across from the ACC store). The Unisea is a bright, glitzy place, the opposite of the Elbow. Stop in for Monday night football games. **Cape Cheerful Lounge** in the new Grand Aleutian Hotel has a piano bar (with fresh sushi) for more romantic times.

For more summertime entertainment, you'll find very competitive softball games almost daily at the high school field. Another place to check out is the **Marco Roller Rink** run by the city. No movie theater in Unalaska, though the **Community Center** in Unalaska, tel. (907) 581-1297, often has G-rated flicks.

July Fourth is, not surprisingly, the biggest event in Unalaska, with a parade, softball tournament, and fireworks.

Information and Services

Get local information at the tiny **Henry Swanson's House Visitor Center,** tel. (907) 581-4242, on Broadway near Second St. in downtown Unalaska. It's open Thursday 1-7 p.m. and Saturday 1-4 p.m. only. When they're closed, try the city hall. Take a shower—and they throw in a free swim—at the **high school pool.** Get fast cash from **ATMs** inside the Eagle and ACC stores.

Transportation

Unalaska has not traditionally been a place for tourists, and most everyone comes here to make money, not to vacation. The high costs of transportation and accommodations will continue to keep most tourists away, though a few cruise ships are now starting to visit during the summer months. If you decide on a quick visit, try to schedule it around a period of good weather; check the *Anchorage Daily News* for the forecast. When the weather is clear, the countryside is stunning, but much more common are the rainy and windy days when the place doesn't look so great and you start to wonder why you spent so much cash to get here. Besides, you may find yourself stuck for days waiting for the weather to lift enough for planes to land. And it costs a bundle to stay here!

The ***Tustemena*** state ferry heads out once a month (April-Oct.) to Dutch Harbor, by way of Homer, Kodiak, Chignik (home to the most massive fish weir in America—it is put in with a pile driver), Sand Point, King Cove, and Cold Bay. The trip takes three and a half days one-way and can be somewhat rough, especially in September and October, ($242 one-way). The *Tustumena* has showers, cafeteria, bar, and gift shop. It's advisable to bring some food and drink, plus plenty of books, tapes, and other recreational items. Sleep in the solarium with the Therm-a-rest and Fiberfill crowd. Call (800) 642-0066 for ferry reservations. There is no ferry terminal in Unalaska, but the ship docks near the airport on Amaknak Island.

The other way to reach Unalaska is by air. **Reeve Aleutian Airways,** tel. (800) 243-4700, flies both jets and prop planes to the airport in Dutch. Landing or taking off is always an adventure since the runway is only 3,900 feet long—about 2,000 feet shorter than pilots (and passengers) would like. Nearly everyone who has flown into or out of Dutch has a hair-raising

Reeve Aleutian Airways, Inc.

story to tell. Because of this, many locals prefer to fly on Reeve's 1950s-era Super Electras rather than the 727s that come in fast and stop even faster. Besides, the old Electras fly lower and slower, and have wide seats and big windows!

Other companies flying into Dutch Harbor are **PenAir,** tel. (800) 448-4226; and **Alaska Airlines,** tel. (800) 426-0333. Rates for all these airlines are similar: approximately $860 roundtrip ($710 roundtrip with a 14-day advance purchase) to Dutch from Anchorage. Note that during the winter fishing season many flights are booked up far in advance. By the way, if the weather is good, try to get a seat on the right side of the plane when you fly out of Anchorage. The flight passes near the dramatic and volcanic summits of Mt. Iliamna and Mt. Redoubt. **Aleutian Air,** tel. (907) 581-1686, has charter flights.

Getting Around Dutch

The settlements of Dutch Harbor and Unalaska are spread over two islands, and the distances mean some sort of transport is needed. Mountain bikes are available at the **Community Center** (tel. 907-581-1297), and offer the most en-

joyable way to explore the many dirt roads leading into the hills. They are not, however, nearly as much fun in the rain. Some 21 different **taxi** companies cruise around town; it's very easy to get a ride to the airport or other places. Expect to pay $8-10 for most points. Car rentals are exorbitant, starting at $85 a day ($110 for the more practical 4WDs) from **Blue Checker Taxi,** tel. (907) 581-2186; **North Port Rentals,** tel. (907) 581-3880; and **Aleutian Truck Rental,** tel. (907) 581-1576. Unlimited miles, but there are only 38 miles of roads to drive anyway. For details on **charter fishing,** ask at the Grand Aleutian, tel. (907) 581-3844.

A.L.E.U.T. Tours, tel. (907) 581-6001, is really Patricia Lekanoff-Gregory, an Aleut woman from Unalaska who offers tours of the community from a Native perspective.

OTHER ALEUTIAN ISLANDS

Akutan (pop. 600), a small island 35 miles northeast of Dutch Harbor, is a much smaller fishing center. It has a general store, but not much else. Get here from Unalaska on PenAir, tel. (907) 243-2323 (in Anchorage). The Air Force maintains a low-level radar base on **Shemya** (pop. 660), but the Navy's anti-submarine warfare base on **Adak** has closed due to the reduced threat from Russia; security clearance is required to visit either island. If you still want to go, call the commanding officer at least a month in advance. For Shemya call (907) 552-4202, and for Adak call (907) 592-8051.

The Aleut villagers of **Attu** were deported to Japan in 1942 by the Japanese. On their return to Alaska after the war, the U.S. government refused to allow them to resettle on their island. Today the only inhabitants of Attu are the staff of the Coast Guard Loran station. Birders sometimes come here to look for Asian species that have strayed into the Aleutians. This is also the only place in America where the white-tailed eagle breeds.

Tiny Aleut villages exist at **Atka** (on Atka Island; pop. 70) and **Nikolski** (on Umnak Island; pop. 40). Despite its fragile geological situation, the remote volcanic island of Atka was used by the U.S. for underground nuclear testing until as late as 1971. In its first public action, the Vancouver-based environmental organization, Greenpeace, sent a protest vessel into the area, and the resulting controversy led to cancellation of the tests.

An excellent source for up-to-date info on the more remote Alaska Peninsula, Aleutian, and Pribilof settlements is the free **"Aleutian Accommodations"** brochure produced annually by Reeve Aleutian Airways, tel. (907) 243-4700 or (800) 544-2248. It covers such places as Port Moller, Sand Point, Nikolski, Port Heiden, King Cove, Chignik, Cold Bay, and other ports of call. Reeve offers air service to Dutch Harbor, Adak, King Salmon, Cold Bay, Port Heiden, and Sand Point.

PRIBILOF ISLANDS

The remote, teeming Pribilofs "sit like matzo balls amid the richest plankton soup north of the Galapagos." Lying in the middle of the Bering Sea 250 miles north of the Aleutians, 300 miles west of the mainland, and 1,000 miles from Anchorage, the two main islands—**St. Paul** (pop. 760; world's largest Aleut community) and **St. George** (pop.

190)—along with two minor ones, host what may be the largest concentration of mammals and seabirds anywhere on planet earth. Although both islands have abundant wildlife of all sorts, St. Paul is best known for its fur seal colonies; St. George for its seabird rookeries.

Volcanic in origin, two of the four islands in the Pribilof group are now inhabited. Tiny Walrus and Otter Islands also support thousands of seals and birds. St. Paul is the largest of the islands: 14 miles long and eight miles wide, with hills reaching 500 feet in elevation. St. George has a sheer wall rising from the sea to almost 1,000 feet, with millions of waterfowl breeding in its nooks and crannies. There are no trees on either island, but the rolling tundra becomes a dense rainbow of flowers in mid-July. The weather is similar to that of the Aleutians—cool, damp, foggy, and windy; summer temperatures average 47° F, with an occasional 60° F day in July.

Wildlife

Each summer some 800,000 northern fur seals—75% of the world's population—return to the Pribilofs (the majority to St. Paul) to breed and give birth. The "beachmasters" are first to arrive at the haul-out sites and rookeries (late May), with the females coming ashore in June to give birth. At 90-130 pounds, the females are far smaller than the largest males, which can reach 600 pounds. Harbor seals, sea otters, Steller's sea lions, and long-tusked walruses round out this brawling, bawling, and caterwauling marine mammalian gumbo. Nowhere else in North America, and arguably the world, is wildlife so easily seen in such numbers. If you're set on doing something really wild during your trip north, this would be it.

In addition to the sea mammals, over 210 species of birds have been identified on the Pribilofs, including millions of murres and thousands of puffins, cormorants, kittiwakes, and fulmars. The late birder and artist Rodger Tory Peterson called one of St. George's rookeries "probably the greatest single bird cliff anywhere in North America." Birders interested in adding to their life list may want to come early (mid-May to early June) for accidental Asian species that sometimes wander over from Siberia. Don't forget your bird book and binoculars!

History

Soon after Russian fur finder Gerassim Pribylov discovered the uninhabited islands in June 1786—and named them for himself—his fur company brought Aleut slaves to harvest the seals. Accounts vary, one claiming that the Russians slaughtered the seals here nearly to extinction; the other that in 1867 the population had regenerated to record numbers and that it was the Americans who trimmed their skins by the millions (these fur seal rookeries were a prime reason the U.S. government purchased Alaska from the Russians). In either case, by 1911 the seal population had dwindled to under 150,000 animals, less than 10% of what it had been. That same year, the U.S., Russia, England, and Japan signed a treaty banning ocean hunting and limiting the number allowed to be taken on land. But it wasn't until 1985 that commercial seal harvesting was finally halted, in large part due to pressure from environmental groups. The Aleut people were not given full control of their islands until 1983.

Today, the economy of St. Paul is booming due to the rapid development of seafood processing plants and floating processing ships. Part of this growth was spurred by the creation of a new $80 million harbor. This development has, unfortunately also brought increasing concerns of overfishing. There is strong evidence of declines in some fish populations, and sea lion and seal populations appear to also be on the skids.

St. Paul Practicalities

The small **St. Peter and Paul Church** is a focal point of life on St. Paul. This plain old Russian Orthodox church has a lavishly ornate interior. Stay at the rough-at-the-edges **King Eider Hotel,** tel. (907) 546-2477 or (907) 546-2312, for $80 pp. Camping is not allowed on the island, and there are no restaurants, but meals are available from a cafeteria in one of the local canneries. Your best bet is probably to bring food with you, though you won't be able to cook anything. There is also a small general store with limited and expensive supplies, plus a taxi service. Or, rent a car from **North Star Truck Rental,** tel. (907) 546-2645.

The vast majority of the 3,000 or so annual visitors to St. Paul arrive on one of the tours put on jointly by the local Native corporation (Tanadgusix) and **Reeve Aleutian Airways,** tel. (800) 544-2248. Choose from a range of trips out of Anchorage, starting at $735 for three days and two nights, with lodging, island transport, and experienced guide included. Three meals a day will cost approximately $38/day extra from the cafeteria. Be sure to schedule a buffer of several days since foggy weather sometimes prevents flights from landing for up to a week. The tours are offered Memorial Day to Labor Day.

Both **Reeve Aleutian Airways,** tel. (800) 544-2248; and **PenAir,** tel. (800) 448-4226, fly to St. Paul from Anchorage three times a week for around $770 roundtrip. The latter also connects St. Paul with St. George for $60 one-way, but getting on these may be tricky because of the weather and other difficulties; reserve ahead to be sure of space.

St. George Practicalities

St. George the Martyr Russian Orthodox Church is the most distinctive local structure, though the **St. George Tanaq Hotel,** tel. (907) 859-2255, is also a National Historic Landmark. The cost is $89 pp with a shared bath. Reserve ahead to be certain of a space, since there are only nine rooms. No restaurants on the island, but you can buy food locally and cook it at the hotel kitchen. Both **St. George Island Canteen** and **Alaska Ship Supply** have limited groceries at Bush prices; better to bring your own from Anchorage. The hotel also offers bus transportation from the airport. Camping is not allowed on St. George Island. **PenAir,** tel. (907) 243-2323 or (800) 448-4226, flies to St. George three times a week for around $770 roundtrip. They also offer flights from St. George to St. Paul for $60 one-way, but getting on these flights may be tricky because of the weather; reserve ahead to be sure of space.

For more on St. George, contact **Tanaq Corporation** in Anchorage, at (907) 272-9886. If you want to have someone else set everything up, **Joseph Van Os Photo Safaris,** tel. (206) 463-5383, offers pricey treks led by a professional photographer. For $2,495 all-inclusive you get three nights and four days on St. George, plus two nights in Anchorage.

Seeing it All

If you're going all the way out to one of the Pribilofs on your own, why not do a two-for-one deal? PenAir lets you fly to one of the islands, hop over to the other one, and then fly back to Anchorage for the same fare as a roundtrip to either island, plus $60 for the inter-island flight (total of $830). You'll have to set up all your own hotel and other arrangements, but you'll save a bundle over the package tours and see far more.

puffin

LOUISE FOOTE

BOB RACE

BERING SEA AND THE ARCTIC COAST

This part of Alaska is the state's true outback, far, far, from the reach of civilization. The scattered settlements—Dillingham, Bethel, Nome, Kotzebue, and Barrow—are really more like pinpricks on the map. The vast distances between the towns make them difficult and expensive to reach, but also exotic and fascinating to visit. Any trip into these areas means passing out hundred-dollar traveler's checks like candy, but you'll be rewarded with a unique and unforgettable experience.

Bristol Bay, on the southern end of the Bering Sea, is considered the world's most productive red salmon fishery. Dillingham—the main port town—is home to hundreds of salmon fishing boats, and dozens of sportfishing lodges, and is the gateway to remote Wood-Tikchik State Park, America's largest at 1.4 million acres. Also nearby are the Walrus Islands, with an extraordinary walrus haul-out on Round Island. Bethel and vicinity, in western Alaska, is a low-lying,

lake-filled delta through which the Kuskokwim and Yukon Rivers spread and finally empty into the Bering Sea. Yup'ik villages are scattered across the stark, treeless plain.

Farther north is Nome, a gold rush town where dredging continues today. Even farther northward, across the rounded mountains of the Seward Peninsula, is the large Eskimo town of Kotzebue. Several national parks surround Kotzebue, and more parks and refuges encompass the Brooks Range, offering exciting possibilities for hikers and river runners in search of adventure. At the top of the continent on the Arctic Ocean lies Barrow, famous as the summertime land of the midnight sun (and the land where the sun does not rise for two straight months in winter). Prudhoe Bay, the source of Alaska's oil wealth, is also here—an impressive indoors city in the frigid north. Remote Arctic National Wildlife Refuge holds down the far northeast corner, bordered by the Arctic Ocean and Yukon Territory.

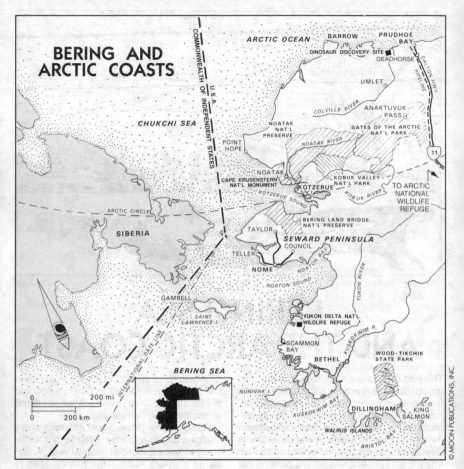

Visiting the Arctic

Traveling among the Eskimo, you might sense a certain tension. For the past 200 years, they have watched the marine mammals and caribou herds, once the foundation of their society, ruthlessly depleted by whites using advanced technology. Whenever a valuable resource has been discovered in their homeland—be it fur, gold, or oil—strangers have arrived to grab it for themselves. Also, the Eskimo subsistence lifestyle has been seriously undermined by alcohol, American education, and the consumer society. But, as is the case everywhere in the world, if you travel lightly, approach the people with sensitivity, and carry yourself with dignity, you'll learn a lot about traveling, the people, and yourself.

BERING SEA REGION

DILLINGHAM

The small city of Dillingham (pop. 2,100) is the regional center for Bristol Bay, Alaska's largest sockeye salmon fishery. A large portion of the world's salmon catch comes from this enormous bay on the southern end of the Bering Sea. During the peak of the season, set nets line Dillingham beaches while gillnetters catch fish just offshore, and the town's four canneries run full blast. You won't, however, see the big fishing boats found elsewhere in Alaska, since commercial boats are limited to a maximum of 32 feet in length throughout Bristol Bay.

History

Dillingham's origins came from the first Russian fur traders who established a fort (Alexandrovski Redoubt) on the other side of Nushagak Bay in 1822. After the Americans took over, canneries were established in the area to process the enormous runs of red (sockeye) salmon up the Nushagak and Wood Rivers. After an influenza epidemic decimated the Native villages around Nushagak Bay in the winter of 1918-19, many of the survivors moved to Dillingham. The result is a place composed of Yup'iks, Aleuts, Russians, and Americans. The local radio station, KDLG, still has Yup'ik language broadcasts. Today, the town is almost wholly dependent upon the rich salmon fisheries of Bristol Bay. With low prices (a measly 50 cents/pound for reds in 1996) and fierce competition, many fishermen are concerned for the future in what has been a highly lucrative fishery. Still, you're likely to see 500 boats crowded into Dillingham's harbor.

Sights and Sounds

Although there are many sportfishing lodges in the area, Dillingham is not much of a tourist town; most people come here to work. The small **Sam Fox Museum**, tel. (907) 842-5521, is on the corner of Seward and D Sts. in the same building as the library. The **visitor center**, tel. (907) 842-5115, is just a block away. The town

also has a number of gift shops that sell Native crafts such as Native-made baskets and dolls. Tours are available at the local cannery and cold storage facilities.

The main attractions for visitors—if they aren't fishermen—are Wood-Tikchik State Park and Walrus Island State Game Sanctuary (see below). **Togiak National Wildlife Refuge** begins just three miles west of Dillingham and covers 4.3 million acres. It is a vital staging area for migrating waterfowl, especially brant, emperor geese, common eiders, and Steller's eiders. Stop by the refuge office, tel. (907) 842-1063, in Dillingham before heading out. An enjoyable 25-mile dirt road leads out of Dillingham to the village of **Aleknagik** (pop. 190) on Lake Aleknagik. Wood-Tikchik Park begins at the upper end of this lake.

Accommodations and Food

Dillingham has several places to stay, including **Bristol Inn**, tel. (907) 842-2240 or (800) 764-9704; and **Dillingham Hotel**, tel. (907) 842-5316. Expect to pay around $110 s or $135 d at these places. **Wild Goose B&B**, tel. (907) 842-4052, has less expensive rooms for $50 s or $75 d, including a continental breakfast. They also rent skiffs and pickup trucks. Get showers at the boat harbor next to the A.C. Harbor store. For food, try **Fisherman's Cafe, Captain's Table,** or **Ricardo's.** There are two grocers: **N&N Market** and the larger **Alaska Commercial Company.**

Events

Dillingham's main event is the **Beaver Round-Up,** a five-day winter party that features a championship dogsled race, dances, and the locally heralded Miss Dillingham pageant. There's also a **Silver Salmon Derby** during the summer.

Transportation

The airport is a bit over two miles from Dillingham; get into town ($6) on **Yellow Cab,** tel. (907) 842-5833; or **Ernie's Cab,** tel. (907) 842-2606. Or call (907) 842-2266 for car rentals. **PenAir,** tel. (800) 448-4226; **Alaska Airlines,** tel. (800) 426-0333; **Reeve Aleutian Airways,** tel. (800) 544-2248; and **Yute Air,** tel. (907) 842-5333 or (888) 359-9883, all have daily flights between Anchorage and Dillingham. PenAir and Yute also have service to all the surrounding villages and towns (King Salmon, Clarks Point, Togiak, Aleknagik, etc.). Other local air taxi operators are **Wren Air,** tel. (907) 842-5630; **Manokotak Air,** tel. (907) 842-2486; and **Tucker Aviation,** tel. (907) 842-1023.

WALRUS ISLAND STATE GAME SANCTUARY

The Walrus Islands are a cluster of seven small rocky points of land in northern Bristol Bay. One of them—Round Island—is famous as a haul-out spot for upwards of 10,000 walrus during the summer (only the bulls come ashore here). The masses of walrus form what author Tom Kizzia called "a writhing mat of wrinkled, rust-colored leather" on the rocky beach where they come ashore to rest. There are also hundreds of thousands of nesting seabirds: black-legged kittiwakes, common murres, cormorants, and parakeet auklets, as well as tufted and horned puffins. Also on the island are inquisitive red foxes. Steller's sea lions come ashore on one beach.

Getting There
Contact the Alaska Department of Fish and Game in Dillingham, tel. (907) 842-1013, to request an information packet and permit application. You can apply as early as January, and it's a good idea to get your application in early to be sure of a place at the peak time (mid-June through July). To keep human impacts to a minimum, only 12 permits ($50 pp) are issued for each five-day period, so you won't have a lot of neighbors, other than the birds and bulls. (Two of the 12 permits are held open for those who apply within 10 days prior to a given time slot, so you may be able to get in at the last minute.) Access to Round Island is difficult and equally expensive. Because of rough seas, there is no air access.

To reach the sanctuary, first fly to Dillingham (around $400 roundtrip from Anchorage), then plunk down another $100 roundtrip for a half-hour flight from Dillingham to the village of Togiak. Don Winkelman of **Don's Round Island Charters,** tel. (907) 493-5127, ferries people

out to Round Island by boat from Togiak for approximately $300 roundtrip. It takes two hours to get to Round Island. Most visitors arrive in Togiak the night before, and stay in a Weatherport that Winkelman supplies.

You'll have to bring all your own camping gear, food, and supplies. The weather can be pretty wild—60-knot winds and pelting rain—so don't skimp on your tent and raingear. Be sure to take long tent stakes—and some extras—to hold everything down. Also bring enough food to last a week longer than you'd expected, since the weather can occasionally close in for long periods, making it impossible to leave. Trails lead from the camping area to outstanding cliffs where you can look down on the walrus or across to nesting puffins, murres, and other seabirds. The Alaska Dept. of Fish and Game has two research technicians on the island who will answer your questions (they aren't guides, however).

WOOD-TIKCHIK STATE PARK

This 1.6-million-acre state facility—the largest state park in the country—is 300 miles southwest of Anchorage, and a half-hour floatplane flight from Dillingham. The park preserves a vast system of rivers and lakes, including two long chains of interconnected waterways. There are eight different lakes at least 20 miles long, plus countless smaller ponds. These lakes offer some of the finest sportfishing to be found: trophy salmon, trout, Arctic char, northern pike. The east side of Wood-Tikchik is almost flat, wooded terrain, but to the west the rugged Wood River Mountains rise, some topping 5,000 feet. Canoeists or kayakers may want to float down such rivers as the Nuyakuk or Tikchik, where the unsurpassed scenery is untouched by development. See the *Alaska Wilderness Milepost* for details on running these rivers.

Practicalities
Wood-Tikchik is remote. Most access is by floatplane from Dillingham, but it's also possible to drive the 25 miles from Dillingham to the village of Aleknagik on Aleknagik Lake. From there, boat through a long series of connected lakes. There are no trails or other developed facilities within the park itself, but camping and hiking opportunities abound if you have the right gear and

a boat to get around. Many visitors to the park stay in one of the five fishing and hunting lodges. Wood River Lodge, for example, charges $4,000 pp per week. For more information and a list of local lodges, contact the park at Box 3022, Dillingham, AK 99576, tel. (907) 842-2375.

BETHEL

Flying to Bethel (pop. 5,000) from Anchorage hammers home a stunning appreciation of how vast this country is. The Alaska Range and Kuskokwim Mountains serve up a seemingly impenetrable set of summits for over 300 miles. Then, it ends abruptly in a range of hills that flattens into an enormous coastal plain. Far below, the land is pockmarked with thousands of ponds of all sizes, and the Kuskokwim River meanders its way toward the sea, past oxbows and brush-lined shores. The mixed Native and immigrant town of Bethel sprawls along the wide Kuskokwim River some 80 miles from its mouth.

Bethel is one of the largest settlements in the Alaskan Bush. It serves as a supply center, as well as a transportation and communication hub, for dozens of outlying villages. You're likely to meet many people fluent in both English and Yup'ik (the nightly TV news is in both languages) along with quite a few emigrants from Eastern Europe and Korea. The country here is essentially flat tundra with willows along the river banks and thin black spruce forests farther upriver. In the summer, the Kuskokwim provides boat access to villages all along the river; when winter comes, it becomes an ice road for villages hundreds of miles upriver. This is certainly one of the most unique roads in America. Each spring all commerce shuts down for a couple of weeks, when the river is too thin to drive on and the ice has not yet floated away in the big breakup.

Bethel is built on permafrost, so all buildings are constructed on stilts to prevent heat from thawing the ground and causing them to sink into a quagmire. Permafrost makes it very difficult to lay water lines, so water is trucked to holding tanks outside each home and business. For the visitor, this means you won't have a lot of water to waste on showers, and in some places the water is nearly undrinkable (this depends upon the source). This undrinkable water might partly explain the very high sales of soda pop at local grocery stores, and perhaps the abundance of vodka in a town where alcohol is not legally sold.

History and Sights

A trading post was established along the Kuskokwim River in the 1870s, and was followed a decade later by a Moravian Church mission. The town of Bethel, named for the scriptural directive "Arise, go to Bethel, and dwell there," grew up around this mission and trading post. The **Yup'ik Cultural Center,** in the same building as the University of Alaska's Kuskokwim campus, contains a fascinating collection of old Yup'ik clothing and tools along with photographic exhibits. There are seal-gut parkas, dolls, baskets, and beautiful carved ivory pieces. The old **Moravian Church,** built around 1885, is the most interesting and photogenic local structure. Other than this, the primary sights are the town itself and the wild country that reaches for an eternity in all directions from Bethel. The **hospital** is that strange yellow building you pass on the way into town from the airport. It looks like the old drawings of space stations once planned for Mars.

Hang around the Alaska Commercial Co. store for that most Bethel of all Bethel attractions, the legion of local taxi cabs—all waiting outside with their engines running while the Slavic, Albanian, and Korean drivers smoke cigarettes and talk. Imagine it as a scene from an old Western, except that the horses tied up out front have been replaced by taxis, and the cowboys speak with an eastern European or Asian accent.

Yukon Delta National Wildlife Refuge

The town of Bethel is encircled by this 20-million-acre refuge, largest in America. The refuge covers the widely spreading mouths of both the Yukon and Kuskokwim Rivers ("The Y-K Delta"), plus Nunivak Island. Nearly all this land is a potholed mélange of tundra marshes, lakes, and streams. Yukon Delta National Wildlife Refuge is a vital area for waterfowl. The numbers are staggering: more than two million ducks, 750,000 geese and swans, plus another 100 million shorebirds nest here each summer. Most outsiders come to the refuge to see the birds and other animals; most Yup'ik people come here to hunt and fish as they have for time immemorial.

Access to the refuge is by boat or floatplane. Hiking is difficult on this marshy terrain. There is a **visitor center** at the refuge headquarters in Bethel, tel. (907) 543-3151, with wildlife displays and photographs. They occasionally offer guided birdwatching tours in the summer.

Accommodations

The largest Bethel lodging place is the notorious **Kuskokwim Inn,** tel. (907) 543-2207. It has a reputation as a noisy place where folks come from outlying villages to party, and as a haven for bootleggers. The least expensive place is **Bethel Inn,** tel. (907) 543-3204, in simple trailers behind the Kusko. You're far better off staying in one of the three Bethel B&Bs. **Brown Slough B&B,** tel. (907) 543-4334, is a comfortable, large home along the slough, with four guest rooms and a full breakfast for $85-105 s or d. Recommended. **Bentley's Porter House B&B,** tel. (907) 543-3552, charges $78 s or $101 d for comfortable rooms and a nice view. Considerably larger, but also very nice, is **Pacifica Guest House,** tel. (907) 543-4305. Summer rates here are $90 s, $100 d in the rooms, and $115-125 s, $135-140 d in suites. Free airport transport, and unlimited water (they're on a well system; a luxury in Bethel). **Blueberry Motel,** tel. (907) 543-3392, has four guest rooms going for $75 s, $80 d.

Food

Get pizza, along with calzones and Greek specialties (such as gyros, shish kebab, and baklava) at **Dimitri's Restaurant,** tel. (907) 543-3434. **Datu's Place,** tel. (907) 543-2216, has both Chinese food and the standard staples of burgers and sandwiches. **Diane's Cafe,** tel. (907) 543-4305, at Pacifica Guest House, has the most expensive meals in town. It's the on-the-town place, but the food is not really special. **Shogun Japanese Seafood Restaurant,** tel. (907) 543-3720, is upstairs in the Alaska Commercial Co. building. **Kuskokwim Inn,** tel. (907) 543-2207, has a larger restaurant with a choice of standard American food. Be sure to try their shrimp. Several other places in town also offer the standard burgers and fries menu, starting at around $5 for a cheeseburger.

Two surprisingly large stores provide almost any supplies—from refried beans to refrigerators—that you might need: **Alaska Commer-**

cial Company (ACC) and **Swanson's.** You'll even find an espresso machine at the big ACC store! Prices are not nearly as bad as might be expected for most items, though they are higher than in Anchorage. Looking for something a bit different? Check out the frozen food section, where Kuskokwim River white fish and chunks of raindeer stew meat are available.

A note on alcohol. Bethel is a "damp" town where booze can not be sold, but can be brought in for "personal use." This creates a situation ripe for bootlegging. More than a few locals import booze—especially vodka—to sell for a high markup ($50 a fifth!) to others desperate for a drink. One man was recently caught with 108 bottles in his possession, but he managed to convince a jury that they were for the wedding of a long-lost daughter.

Events

Bethel's primary event is the **Kuskokwim-300 Sled Dog Race** held each January. It's a three-day mad dash up the frozen ice that attracts some of the fastest teams in the country. Call (907) 543-3300 for details. The **Camai Festival** in March is a three-day Native dance event with performers from all over Alaska and even as far away as Russia. This is a great time to buy Native crafts.

Local Crafts

Adjacent to the Moravian church, the **Tundra Art Gallery,** tel. (907) 543-3641, has works by local painters and cards. Next door is the **Moravian Book Store,** where you'll find books, postcards from all the surrounding villages, church pamphlets, locally made jewelry, and a dose of the religious radio station. The Bethel jail has a case displaying crude ivory carvings made

BOB RACE

by the inmates. Ask around and you might find someone to sew one of the beautiful and distinctive parkas ("parkys") worn by Native women or to knit a garment out of musk ox wool. Be ready to part with a large amount of cash for either of these one-of-a-kind items. Also in Bethel, visit talented dollmaker Joyce Tall. The finest Alaskan baskets come from the village of Hooper Bay, 100 miles northwest of Bethel.

Transportation
Bethel serves as the transportation hub for much of western Alaska, and has the third busiest flight service station in the state. **Reeve Aleutian Airways,** tel. (800) 544-2248; **Alaska Airlines,** tel. (800) 426-0333; **Era Aviation,** tel. (800) 866-8394; and **Yute Air,** tel. (907) 842-5333 or (888) 359-9883; have daily service between Anchorage and Bethel throughout the year. Much of the year, Alaska's jets are just a dozen or so seats jammed behind the containerized cargo section in a 727.

Several air taxi companies offer scheduled flights to Hooper Bay, Tooksook Bay, Scammon Bay, Tununak, Chevak, and other places whose names reveal much about their remoteness from the Lower-48 world of traffic jams and fast food restaurants. The companies include **ERA Aviation,** tel. (907) 543-3905 or (800) 866-8394; **Camai Air,** tel. (907) 543-4040; **YK Aviation,** tel. (907) 543-5550; and **Yute Air Alaska,** tel. (907) 543-3003. In addition, these companies offer charters to more remote places, as do **Yukon Aviation,** tel. (907) 543-3280; **Kusko Aviation,** tel. (907) 543-3279; **Larry's Flying Service,** tel. (907) 543-3304; Arctic Circle Air, tel. (907) 543-5906; and **Craig Air,** tel. (907) 543-2575. Yute Air also offers direct flights between Anchorage and Aniak.

Rent cars from **Practical Rent-A-Car,** tel. (907) 543-3610; or **National Car Rental,** tel. (907) 543-3555 or (800) 227-7368. Note that a clause in the rental contract prohibits driving on the ice road up the Kuskokwim. Oh yes, if you want a cab, just look around; one is bound to be within a couple hundred feet of any place in town.

Kuskokwim Wilderness Adventures, tel. (907) 543-3900, leads rafting trips down remote backcountry rivers.

THE ARCTIC COAST

NOME

The town of Nome (pop. 4,400, of whom nearly 2,500 are Native) sits on the south side of the Seward Peninsula on the edge of Norton Sound facing the Bering Sea, only 190 miles east of Siberia, and 2,300 miles north of Seattle. (Flying time is 90 minutes from Anchorage.) Nome was named when a cartographer marked its unnamed location on a map as "? Name," and a second mapmaker misread it as "C. [for Cape] Nome." One hundred fifty miles south of the Arctic Circle, Nome is on roughly the same latitude as Fairbanks, and shares similar hours of daylight, as well as warmer temperatures than its Arctic coast cousins, Kotzebue and Barrow—though the mercury rests around zero °F in January, and soars to a sizzling 50° F in the long days of July! Local motels advertise: "Visit picturesque Nome this summer. Three days—no nights." Like other Bush Alaska settlements,

Nome is far from pretty, with piles of junk strewn about the yards and more than a few drunks stumbling from the town's eight saloons.

History
Word reached Dawson in late spring 1899 of fabulous deposits of gold at Anvil Creek near Nome. By fall, 10,000 stampeders had arrived and set up tents on the beach, only to have them blown away by a fierce September storm that prompted a migration inland. There, more gold was found; in fact, placer deposits were carried by most streams that emptied into the Bering Sea. By 1900, 20,000 prospectors crowded the coast, a full third of the white population of Alaska at the time. A railroad had been built to Anvil Creek, which produced several dozen million-dollar claims. Judge James Wickersham brought law and order to Nome in 1902, after the first judge was convicted of corruption.

In 1925, a diphtheria epidemic required emergency delivery of serum from Nenana 650 miles

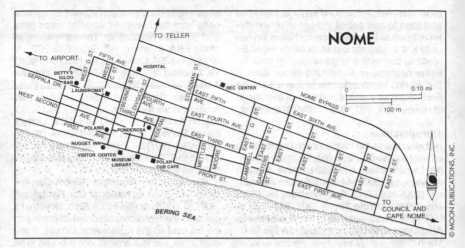

© MOON PUBLICATIONS, INC.

overland by dogsled, the forerunner of today's famous Iditarod Sled Dog Race from Anchorage to Nome. The race takes place every March and turns Nome into a late winter carnival. During WW II Nome was a major transfer point for lend-lease aircraft being sent to Russia. Almost 8,000 planes were turned over to Soviet airmen at Nome airfield.

No Place Like Nome

Oil and gas leases to Norton Sound (Nome is on the edge of the sound along the Bering Sea) were sold in 1983. Reindeer herding occupies a significant portion of the Nome economy, as do ivory carving and the arrival of 12,000 tourists every season. Nome is considered a good place to purchase ivory in the various gift shops. Of course, the Iditarod Race focuses international attention on Nome every March. Nome is still gold-dredge central—with over two dozen of the mechanical monsters nearby. Many visitors try their luck by panning along the beaches here; a few even find flakes of gold.

Sights

Start out at the **visitor center,** tel. (907) 443-5535, on Front St. across from city hall. Pick up the walking-tour brochure of Nome, mostly focusing on historical attractions, such as the nearby dredges. The center also dispenses informative local brochures and booklets. Spend some time with the scrapbooks and photo al-

bums. The center is open Mon.-Saturday. Step across the street to **city hall,** with its Victorian exterior and a massive wood burl (it is placed atop the arch to mark the Iditarod Race finish line). Check out the gift shops for Eskimo dolls, carved ivory and soapstone, grass baskets, and sealskin slippers.

The **Carrie McLain Museum,** in the basement of the library a few doors east on Front St., tel. (907) 443-2566, is open in summer Mon.-Fri. 1-7 p.m. and Saturday 1-6 p.m. It contains a fascinating collection of historical photos from the gold rush era, and exhibits on natural history, archaeology, and, of course, the gold rush. The **Kegoayah Kozga Library,** tel. (907) 443-5133, has an interesting rare books section.

There are quite a few old **gold dredges** within walking distance of Nome, but don't climb on them since they are unsafe. Gold is still being taken from the country around Nome, and two dredges operate 24 hours a day during the summer. Unfortunately, there are no tours or free samples of gold dust. The most impressive of these is the 14-story-tall dredge just offshore; it's the largest dredge in the world. With a little exploration, you're sure to find some of the more than 100 old dredges that remain in the surrounding country.

Also near Nome sits the rusting hulk of the **"Last Train to Nowhere."** The train consists of three locomotive engines from the Council City and Solomon River Railroad, begun in

1881. The engines originally served on the New York City Elevated before being shipped north in 1903, and are the only such engines still in existence. The site is a favorite of photographers.

Seeing the Country

The real treat in Nome is the opportunity to explore this expansive, far-as-the-eye-can-see landscape. Over 250 miles of roads fan out from town, allowing you to explore the vast Arctic countryside around Seward Peninsula. Wildlife—including musk ox, red foxes, wolves, moose, raindeer, and even a few grizzlies—can be seen. Good fishing for Dolly Varden, too. Birders come from all over the nation to spot unusual bird species. In midsummer the roads are lined with verdant tundra plants and a massive display of flowers. Some have likened it to driving through Denali National Park, but without anyone else there. The roads lead to the tiny settlements of Teller, Council, and Taylor, taking you past remnants from the gold rush—dredges, miner's cabins, and the ghost town of **Solomon.**

The most interesting route leads north along Nome River into the spectacular **Kigluaik Mountains.** The road parallels part of the historic **Wild Goose Pipeline,** built of metal hoops and redwood slats in 1920 to carry water to Nome gold mines. There's a free Bureau of Land Management campground at Salmon Lake, 40 miles out, and a hike-in cabin in the Mosquito Pass area. Contact the BLM office in Nome, tel. (907) 443-2177, for the access route.

Events

Nome's main attraction is the **Iditarod Trail Sled Dog Race.** Beginning in Anchorage on the first Saturday in March, the race covers 1,049 miles to the finish point in Nome. It generally takes 10-12 days for the first team to reach Nome. Reserve far ahead to be sure of a motel room for the hectic finish. Everyone comes out to cheer the winning mushers and also-rans. Other March events include the **Iditarod Basketball Tournament;** with over 50 different high school teams, this is said to be the largest in the nation. And, of course, there's the famous **Bering Sea Ice Golf Classic.** The golf classic is played on the frozen sea off Nome, a place with hazards not common to most courses. They use orange golf balls and green-dyed ice for the "greens." Another goofball event is the annual **Memorial**

Day Polar Bear Swim in the Bering Sea. If you aren't so foolhardy, there's always the indoor swimming pool at the high school.

Accommodations and Camping

Cheapest accommodation is at the **Polaris Hotel** downtown, tel. (907) 443-2268, $40 s, $80 d in the old section, shared bath. But things get loud at night with all the drunks; this is Nome's "party hotel." A far better bet is **Ponderosa Inn,** tel. (907) 443-5737, $85 s or $95 d, and the AAA-approved **Nugget Inn,** tel. (907) 443-2323, $85 s or $92 d. **Ocean View Manor B&B,** tel. (907) 443-2133, has three guest rooms with shared or private baths and a continental breakfast for $50-60 s, $55-65 d. Also try **Betty's Igloo B&B,** tel. (907) 443-2419. If you can't find a place to stay during the Iditarod, call the visitor center for help.

Anyone can **camp** on Nome's beaches or along the road system that fans out from town, but there are no official campsites. The abundant beach driftwood makes for great campfires. Showers are available at the recreation center.

Food and Entertainment

Eat at the popular **Polar Cub Cafe.** Nome also has a couple of pizzerias, a Chinese restaurant, a Mexican restaurant, and a handful of diners. Get groceries at **Alaska Commercial Company,** which now also houses a **Burger King** outlet! Nome is a hard-drinking town with eight different bars, including the **Board of Trade** on Front Street. This place opened as the Dexter Saloon in 1901 under the proprietorship of gunslinger Wyatt Earp. Residents from outlying villages come to Nome to drink, and do a very thorough job of it. It could be worse though—in the town's early days three-foot-thick urine glaciers were reported outside some saloons.

Transportation and Tours

Alaska Airlines, tel. (800) 426-0333, has daily flights into Nome from Anchorage and Fairbanks. **Cape Smythe Air,** tel. (907) 443-2414; **Bering Air,** tel. (907) 443-5464; **Olson Air Service,** tel. (907) 443-2229; **Baker Aviation,** tel. (907) 443-3081; **Ryan Air,** tel. (907) 443-5482; and **Anvil Aviation,** tel. (907) 443-2010 all have flightseeing and air taxi services out of Nome. **Alaska Sightseeing/Gray Line,** tel. (800) 666-7365, has hurried overnight trips to Nome and Kotzebue out of Anchorage. Prices start at $469 pp. The Nome airport is 1.5 miles away from town, but taxis are available: $5 to town, or $3 around town.

Rent pickups or 4WD vehicles from **Alaska Cab Garage,** tel. (907) 443-2939; **Bonanza,** tel. (907) 443-2221; **Budget,** tel. (907) 443-5598; and **Stampede Rent-a-Car,** tel. (907) 443-5252. Nome has just one parking meter, located right in front of the newspaper office.

For local tours, contact **Nome Custom Adventures,** tel. (907) 443-5134; or **Grantley Harbor Tours,** tel. (800) 478-3682. **Inua Expedition Co.,** tel. (907) 443-4994, offers sea kayak river trips down the Pilgrim River. **Gray Line,** tel. (800) 628-2449, has a trip that includes a day in Kotzebue, a night and day in Nome, and roundtrip transportation from Anchorage for $497 pp.

ST. LAWRENCE ISLAND

This hundred-mile-long island is about 200 miles west of Nome and just 40 miles from Siberia. On a clear day, residents can see across to the mountains of Russia. The village of **Gambell** (pop. 550) is the primary settlement, and is home to Siberian Eskimos who have lived here for centuries. Most people still speak Yup'ik and depend upon subsistence hunting of bowhead and gray whales (using harpoons), seal, walrus, fish, birds, and even polar bears. This is

BOB RACE

one place where walrus-hide (umiak) boats are still used. Because of its location, St. Lawrence Island is a good place to find unusual bird species. Limited lodging is available in Gambell and the island's other village of Savoonga, but anyone wanting to camp should contact the Native corporation for permission to go outside the city limits ($25 fee). Beautifully carved ivory and other crafts are available locally, but visitors should refuse to purchase any Eskimo artifacts. These priceless cultural relics are looted from ancient village sites around the island.

There is a well-stocked general store in town, thanks to daily flights from Nome. **Gray Line,** tel. (907) 277-5581 or (800) 628-2449, has a three-day, two-night "Gambell Adventure" tour Anchorage-Kotzebue-Nome-Gambell-Nome-Anchorage ($940 pp), including nights in Nome and Gambell. There are no cars on St. Lawrence Island; folks get around by foot or on four-wheelers.

KOTZEBUE

Kotzebue (pop. 3,000) on Kotzebue Sound, near the mouths of the Noatak, Kobuk, and Selawik Rivers, is 26 miles north of the Arctic Circle. The town covers a three-mile-long sandy spit occupied by Inupiat Eskimos for the last six centuries. The sun rises on June 3 and doesn't set for 36 days. Otto von Kotzebue, a Russian sailor, happened upon this Inupiat village in 1816, then called Kikiktagruk ("Almost An Island") at the edge of Baldwin Peninsula. The Natives today lead a traditional lifestyle (with all the amenities, including snowmobiles and VCRs) which includes herding reindeer. They make use of the entire animal for food; for mukluks, parkas, mittens, and socks from the hide; and for aphrodisiac powders from the ground-up antlers sold to Asians. Kotzebue is Alaska's largest Native settlement and serves as the primary commercial hub for northwest Alaska.

The big news around Kotzebue these days is the **Red Dog Mine,** largest zinc mine in the world, 100 miles north of town. Half a billion dollars have been invested in the giant operation—$175 million by the state, the rest by a consortium of international bankers. Red Dog is jointly owned by Cominco Canada and Northwest Alaska Native Association (NANA), which owns the land near the Noatak Preserve. The storage warehouse can hold eight million tons ($5 billion worth) of lead and zinc and is the largest building north of the Arctic Circle. A new borough was created to oversee and profit from this massive project.

Sights

Kotzebue boasts two museums. **NANA Museum of the Arctic,** on Second Ave., has an impressive multimedia show, crafts demonstrations, Native dancing, and the famous blanket toss. All this costs $20 pp, but entrance to the museum itself is free. The museum is open daily 8:30 a.m.-5:30 p.m. in the summer, or by appointment the rest of the year. **Ootukahkuktuvik** ("place having old things") is on First Ave., and you have to be able to pronounce the name to get in. Stop by city hall for access. Stroll around town to absorb the Native flavor. Of interest is the old **cemetery** with colorful spirit houses on some graves. See below for details on national parks in the Kotzebue area. Park Service area headquarters are in the same building as the NANA Museum. Inside are displays on the various parks.

Practicalities

Kotzebue's only lodging place is the **Nullagvik Hotel,** tel. (907) 442-3331. Reserve ahead, since tour groups often book it solid in midsummer. If those prices don't agree with you, you can pitch your tent out past the airport on the beach. The hotel's restaurant features fresh fish and raindeer stew, or try the other local eateries: **Dairy Queen, Hamburger Hut, Pizza House,** or **Arctic Dragon.** Dance at the **Ponderosa.** Kotzebue does not allow alcohol sales, so bring your own if you want to tip a few. Native arts and crafts—especially carved ivory pieces—are sold in the NANA Museum, the Nullagvik Hotel, and other gift shops.

Transportation

Alaska Airlines, tel. (800) 426-0333, has daily service to Kotzebue from Anchorage or Fairbanks. **Cape Smythe Air,** tel. (907) 442-3020; **Bering Air,** tel. (907) 443-5464; **Alaska Island Air,** tel. (907) 442-3205; **Arctic Air Guides,** tel. (907) 442-3030; **Northwestern Aviation,** tel. (907) 442-3525; and **Ram Aviation,** tel. (907) 442-3205, all offer flightseeing and air taxi service

to the area. **Tour Arctic,** tel. (907) 442-3301, provides ground tours around Kotzebue year-round. **Alaska Sightseeing Tours/Gray Line,** tel. (800) 628-2449, flies you Anchorage-Kotzebue, then on to Nome where you overnight, and back to Anchorage the next day for $497 pp. A too-quick day-trip to Kotzebue is $377 pp.

NORTHWEST ALASKA NATIONAL PARKS

Kotzebue is almost surrounded by four little-known national parks: Bering Land Bridge National Preserve, Cape Krusenstern National Monument, Kobuk Valley National Park, and Noatak National Preserve. Noatak and Kobuk abut Gates of the Arctic National Park, creating a massive 16-million-acre wilderness (this doesn't include the two-million-acre Selawik National Wildlife Refuge immediately south of Kobuk Valley). The **National Park Service Office** for the northwest area parks is in the NANA Museum building in Kotzebue. Contact them at Box 287, Kotzebue, AK 99752, tel. (907) 442-3890, for details on these rarely visited parks. They can provide a listing of local air taxi and guiding services for all three parks.

Bering Land Bridge

The 2.8-million acre Bering Land Bridge National Preserve is 90 miles north of Nome and 50 miles south of Kotzebue on the Seward Peninsula. Access is mainly by air taxi, though it is possible to drive from Nome to Teller and hike 20 miles to the preserve border. The Seward Peninsula is considered a remnant of the land bridge that connected Siberia with Alaska during the ice age. It was used as a migratory corridor by people as well as animals, and the preserve has many archaeological sites, some of which date back 10,000 years. Bering Land Bridge has no developed trails, though there is a public use cabin at Serpentine Hot Springs. Other attractions include interesting lava flows near Imuruk Lake, and volcanic craters.

Cape Krusenstern

The 660,000-acre Cape Krusenstern National Monument is 10 miles northwest of Kotzebue and accessible by foot, boat, or air charter. It contains significant archaeological sites on a

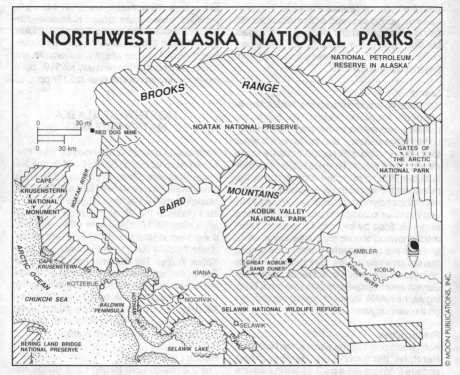

NORTHWEST ALASKA NATIONAL PARKS

NATIONAL PETROLEUM RESERVE IN ALASKA

BROOKS RANGE

NOATAK NATIONAL PRESERVE

RED DOG MINE

GATES OF THE ARCTIC NATIONAL PARK

CAPE KRUSENSTERN NATIONAL MONUMENT

BAIRD MOUNTAINS

KOBUK VALLEY NATIONAL PARK

AMBLER

KOBUK

CAPE KRUSENSTERN

GREAT KOBUK SAND DUNES

KOBUK RIVER

ARCTIC OCEAN

KOTZEBUE

KIANA

CHUKCHI SEA

BALDWIN PENINSULA

NOORVIK

SELAWIK NATIONAL WILDLIFE REFUGE

HOTHAM INLET

SELAWIK

BERING LAND BRIDGE NATIONAL PRESERVE

SELAWIK LAKE

© MOON PUBLICATIONS, INC.

series of 114 beach ridges that were formed over a period of 6,000 years. There are no developed facilities or trails within the national monument, but hikers enjoy the chance to look for a wide variety of waterfowl along with grizzlies, Dall sheep, and caribou.

Kobuk Valley

The 1.7-million acre Kobuk Valley National Park lies on the south side of the Baird Mountains 80 miles east of Kotzebue. Kobuk Valley is best known for the **Great Kobuk Sand Dunes** that cover 25 square miles near the Kobuk River. Some reach to 100 feet in height. Other areas of dunes dot the park, and the mountain passes are traversed by herds of caribou. Most visitors to the park arrive by floatplane from Kotzebue and float the Kobuk River in canoes or kayaks. Start with a flight from Bettles or Ambler into Walker Lake within Gates of the Arctic National Park. The 125-mile float trip to the village of

Kobuk generally takes six days. Contact the Park Service for more on running the river, or for a list of outfitters offering guided float trips. There are no developed facilities within Kobuk Valley National Park itself, though several Native villages dot the riverbanks.

Noatak National Preserve

The 6.6-million-acre Noatak National Preserve covers the enormous Noatak River drainage northeast of Kotzebue. Its northern edge is the crest of the DeLong Mountains, while to the south lie the Baird Mountains and Kobuk Valley National Park. Gates of the Arctic National Park lies immediately east of Noatak National Preserve. There are no developed trails or other facilities within the preserve. Most visitors float the river in kayaks or rafts, with the put-in point in the upper reaches. Fly in from Bettles and get picked up in the village of Noatak, approximately 350 miles away. Expect to take at least two weeks for this extraordinary and memorable trip. Contact the Park Service in Kotzebue for more information.

BARROW

Located 350 miles north of the Arctic Circle, at 71° latitude, and 800 miles northeast of Nome, the small city of Barrow (pop. 3,800) is filled with paradoxes. Barrow has a $72-million high school with room for 2,000 students, an indoor playground at the grade school (useful in the winter, when typical temperatures are -20° F outside), and a first-rate hospital, but all the streets are unpaved, and yards are cluttered with old snowmachines, barking sled dogs, four-wheelers, skin boats, polar bear hides, and racks filled with dead ducks, caribou, and seal meat. Barrow's population is predominantly Inupiat, and many people still speak their native tongue, but the taxi drivers are Filipinos, and many restaurants are owned by Koreans. One Native woman I met sews gorgeous traditional Eskimo parkas and has dead eider ducks on her front porch, but she also spends a month or two lying on the beach in Hawaii each year.

Most visitors to Barrow arrive as part of a package tour, some staying just a few hours, and others overnight. Few independent travelers visit the town since the cost of airfare alone is often higher than the tour price. Barrow receives 84 days of uninterrupted sunlight in summer, 67 days of darkness in winter. It sits on the edge of the Arctic Ocean, which remains virtually frozen 10 months of the year—an amazing sight in itself. Wintertime temperatures plummet far below zero, and the windchill can push them as low as - 80° F! Even in the summer, the weather is often chilly, wet, and windy. By mid-August it can be downright cold; be sure to bring warm clothes no matter when you visit. The dirt roads and wind also make for dusty conditions much of the summer. Few travelers get to see the events that are so important to Barrow— the whale hunts during the spring and the fall bowhead migrations. When a whale is brought in, the entire community comes out to see. Many help in the butchering process, and the whale's fatty meat is shared. Afterward, the carcasses are dragged far out Point Barrow to keep polar bears from wandering into town.

History
This stretch of coast was first mapped in 1826 by Captain Beech of the British Navy, who named it after Sir John Barrow, an English nobleman who encouraged and outfitted numerous Northwest Passage and polar expeditions. Whalers began arriving in the 1870s, and many of their ships became trapped in the ice; relief expeditions helped survey the North Slope. The first plane reached Barrow in 1926, and famous bush pilot Wiley Post and humorist Will Rogers crashed and died there in 1935. Today, Barrow is the seat of the vast 88,000-square-mile North Slope Borough, and has profited greatly (a $100 million annual budget) from the oil pipeline—as can be seen in the modern buildings, services, and very high wages.

Sights
The main attraction in Barrow is simply the place and its people. Located on the Arctic Ocean (technically the town is on the Chukchi Sea; the Beaufort Sea lies just east of Point Barrow), it has long been occupied by the Inupiat. The remains of old whale-bone and sod houses are visible on the shore at the west end of town, and are fascinating to explore—but do not disturb any artifacts. Walk the eroding shoreline to the east past skin-covered wooden boats and a pair of arched whale bones at Brower's Cafe. More bones, along with a "milepost" sign, can be found outside the historic **Utqiagvik Presbyterian Church,** established in 1898. The **North Slope Borough Office** has a big bowhead whale skull out front, and an impressive collection of artifacts—including parkas and carved walrus tusks—inside. They also sell carved ivory, garments, and other items.

Wander around Barrow and you're bound to find something of interest. There's always something dead hanging in somebody's yard, and the sophisticated above-ground piping system is distinctively Alaskan. (Barrow's gas comes from nearby fields and is very cheap, but water must be desalinated from brackish ponds, and costs a typical household $200 a month.) East of town is a mostly inactive Distant Early Warning (D.E.W.) site and Naval Arctic Research Lab (N.A.R.L.), now used primarily as a community college. A bowhead whale skull sits outside the college.

A monument to Wiley Post and Will Rogers stands next to the small information center near the airport. Another monument is at the actual

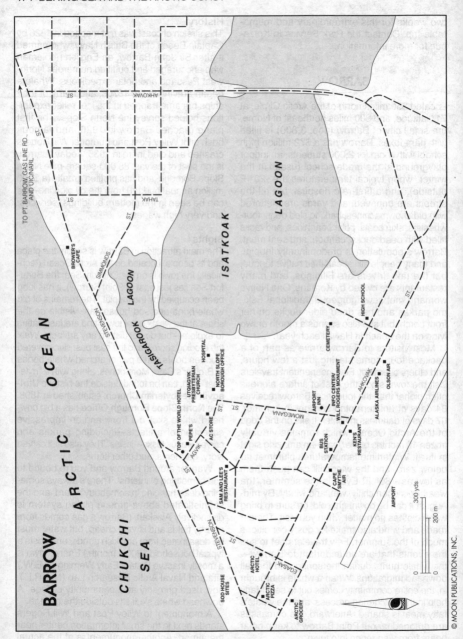

BARROW

ARCTIC OCEAN

CHUKCHI SEA

ISATKOAK LAGOON

TASIGAROOK LAGOON

TO PT. BARROW, GAS LINE RD.,
AND UIC/NARL

AHKOVAK ST

TAHAK ST

SIMMONDS ST

STEVENSON ST

BROWER'S CAFE

HIGH SCHOOL

CEMETERY

HOSPITAL

UTQIAGVIK
PRESBYTERIAN
CHURCH

NORTH SLOPE
BOROUGH OFFICE

TOP OF THE WORLD HOTEL

PEPE'S

AC STORE

AGVIK ST

AHKOVAK ST

MOMEGANA

AIRPORT
INN

INFO CENTER/
WILL ROGERS MONUMENT

ALASKA AIRLINES

OLSON AIR

BUS
STATION

KEN'S
RESTAURANT

CAPE
SMYTHE
AIR

AIRPORT

SAM AND LEE'S
RESTAURANT

STEVENSON ST

EGASAK ST

SOD HOUSE
SITES

ARCTIC
HOTEL

ARCTIC
PIZZA

ARCTIC
GROCERY

300 yds

200 m

0

0

© MOON PUBLICATIONS, INC.

crash site, 16 miles away and accessible only by foot or four-wheeler (or skis, dog team, or snow-machine in the winter). Gas Line Road extends 10 miles into the tundra from Barrow, providing good access for folks who want to wander or watch for birds.

Accommodations

Barrow has several places to stay. The largest and best-known is the **Top of the World Hotel,** tel. (907) 852-3900 or (800) 478-8520, where rooms run a budget-busting $159 s or $179 d. Lodging here, combined with a Barrow tour (see below), is $194 s or $239 d. The least expensive place is the **U.I.C./N.A.R.L. Hotel,** tel. (907) 852-7800, where dorm room space costs $60 s, $80 d. It's out of town, but offers free transport. **Airport Inn,** tel. (907) 852-2525, has clean and comfortable rooms with microwaves and fridges for $130 s or d. Other places to stay include **Siniktaq B&B, 2177 Itta St., tel. (907) 852-2177 and the** Arctic Hotel, tel. (907) 852-7786 (not recommended). These rooms are often completely filled by construction workers.

Food

For the most expensive Mexican food you could ever imagine, eat at **Pepe's North of the Border**—a taco-enchilada combination plate is $16, and worth it! Or just order a bean burrito for $4, and fill up on chips and salsa. In business since 1978, Pepe's is run by Fran Tate, who has filled this spacious place with the trappings of Mexico. It's made the front page of The Wall Street Journal and other newspapers, and even has a gift shop selling Pepe's shirts, hats, and jackets.

Arctic Pizza, tel. (907) 852-4222, bakes surprisingly good pizzas for reasonable prices; their medium (equal to a large elsewhere) costs $16, and they offer a big-screen TV to catch up on sports or CNN. **Ken's Restaurant,** upstairs in the old MarkAir building, tel. (907) 852-8888, has Chinese and American food, including $9 lunch specials. More Chinese food can be had at **Sam & Lee's Restaurant,** tel. (907) 852-5555. Both are open till 2 a.m., and are owned by members of Barrow's strong Korean community. Also try **Brower's Cafe** for all-you-can-eat lunch buffets Mon.-Thursday. Outside you'll see two arched whalebones and several skin boats.

For do-it-yourself meals, head to the **Alaska Commercial (AC) Store,** tel. (907) 852-6711, where you'll find everything from ice cream to sofas. (And yes, they do sell refrigerators, even at the top of the world.) They also have a deli with espresso coffee and an **ATM.** But hold onto your wallet, food prices are sky-high: butter $4.35/pound, milk $3.75/gallon, corn flakes $4.67/box, soda pop $4.79/6-pack, apples $2.49/pound, mushrooms $4.99/pound, and porterhouse steaks $6.39/pound. Many of these items arrive by air—which explains the high prices—but anything that won't spoil comes in aboard the barges that arrive during the brief ice-free period each August.

Information and Services

Visitor information is available summer weekdays at the **Convention and Visitors Association,** tel. (907) 852-8687, across from the old MarkAir terminal. Outside stands a monument to Wiley Post and Will Rogers, who died nearby in 1935. Get arts and crafts from **Mugsie's Arts 'N Crafts 'N Things,** 386 Ogrook St., tel. (907) 852-3106; or ask locally for artists who make Inupiaq clothing and jewelry. Barrow's excellent indoor **swimming pool** is at the high school, or you may want to check out the town's fine recreation center.

Transportation and Tours

Alaska Airlines, tel. (800) 426-0333, has daily flights to Barrow from Fairbanks. Alaska Airlines Vacations, tel. (800) 468-2248, offers excursions from Fairbanks that include a tour, plus an overnight in Barrow, for $492 pp. The same trip from Anchorage is $662 pp. If you're really in a hurry—and have tons of cash—take a 12-hour quick trip from Fairbanks to Barrow and back with a tour of the town for $383 pp ($553 from Anchorage). These tours are offered by **Tundra Tours/Top of the World Hotel,** tel. (907) 852-3900 or (800) 478-8520, and cost $58, if taken independently. Tours last 10:30 a.m.-5:30 p.m. (with a lunch break), and include a very informative cruise around town and out to the end of the road near Point Barrow; the point itself is several more miles. The tour ends with a rather hurried Eskimo blanket toss; get your photos fast since they generally do just a couple of tosses. Then you're treated to Inupiat dancing, drumming, and singing, followed by demonstrations of how traditional items are made. Afterwards, locals sell handmade arts and crafts. **Extreme Tours,** tel. (907) 852-2375, offers more personalized tours to the end of Point Barrow ($100), to the Will Rogers monument ($200), and to other places far off the beaten path. Dog mushing tours ($30 in summer using wheeled sleds, $40 in winter on the real thing) are offered by **Arctic Mushing Tours,** tel. (907) 852-6874.

Cape Smythe Air, tel. (907) 852-8333, is the biggest local carrier, providing scheduled service to Atqasuk ($67), Barter Island ($283), Deadhorse ($210), Kotzebue ($370), Nuiqsut ($155), Point Hope ($278), Point Lay ($144), and Wainwright ($72). **Olson Air Service,** tel. (907) 443-2229, has scheduled flights to Atqasuk ($65), Point Lay ($120), and Wainwright ($65). Both of these companies, along with **Alaska Island Air,** tel. (907) 852-2726, offer charter flights throughout the North Slope Borough.

One of the big surprises in Barrow is the excellent **public bus** service that transports folks throughout the area for just 50 cents. Buses are frequent and provide a cheap way to get around this surprisingly sprawling town. Rent used cars and pickups for $100 a day from **North Slope General Auto,** tel. (907) 852-7325.

PRUDHOE BAY/DEADHORSE

This is the place that makes Alaska run, home to the massive Prudhoe Bay Oilfield, and starting point for the Trans-Alaska Pipeline. Prudhoe Bay is home to some 3,500 oilfield and related workers. Lodging is available at **North Star Inn,** tel. (907) 659-3160, and there's a general store in Deadhorse. North Star also has a restaurant and health club. Keep your eyes open for the caribou that graze amid the small city of buildings, pump stations, and other equipment.

Getting There
Alaska Airlines, tel. (800) 426-0333, has daily flights to Prudhoe Bay/Deadhorse. **Northern Alaska Tour Company,** tel. (907) 474-8600, offers two-day van tours to Prudhoe Bay from Fairbanks that include overnight stops in Coldfoot and Prudhoe for $599 pp. Add $289 to this if you tack on a flight from Prudhoe to Barrow, where you'll stay overnight before flying back

to Fairbanks. They also offer a $159 day-trip to the Arctic Circle from Fairbanks, including a flight back. **Polar Tours,** tel. (907) 479-0751; **Tour Arctic,** tel. (907) 265-4100; and **Prudhoe Bay Adventures,** tel. (907) 474-4767, provide similar tours of the North Slope.

Princess Tours, tel. (907) 276-7711 or (800) 835-8907; and **Gray Line,** tel. (800) 544-2206, both offer three-day tours that run up the Dalton Highway, overnight at Coldfoot, then continue on to Prudhoe Bay where you spend another night before flying back to Fairbanks. Total cost is around $700 pp from Fairbanks, or $1,000 from Anchorage. See "Dalton Highway" under "Vicinity of Fairbanks" in the Interior chapter for information on heading up the 414-mile Dalton Highway from Fairbanks.

ARCTIC NATIONAL WILDLIFE REFUGE

It doesn't get any wilder or more remote than this. Arctic National Wildlife Refuge (ANWR) covers almost 20 million acres of country in the far northeastern part of Alaska, a landscape of flat and marshy coastal tundra, rolling hills, and tall, glaciated peaks topping 8,000 feet in elevation. Other than a few summertime travelers in search of the ultimate wilderness experience, this treeless country has almost no human presence. There has, however, been intense pressure from the oil companies and their allies (including a majority of Alaskan politicians from both parties) to "unlock" this wilderness. The oil wealth that lies beneath ANWR is undoubtedly great, but the loss of this last great wilderness would be greater. Fortunately, the government has been able to block development schemes; hopefully the land will remain protected. The battle has pitched Native people against each other—the Inupiat-owned Arctic Slope Regional Corporation is a big proponent of development (they stand to gain many millions of dollars in oil revenues), and the Gwich'in people are adamantly opposed, fearing that development would destroy the vital caribou herds upon which they depend.

The main reason people come to ANWR—other than to experience the stunning beauty of this place—is the wildlife. During the long and fierce winter, only the hardiest animals venture out of their dens, but in summer, the refuge

JURASSIC PARK ALASKA

Dinosaurs in Alaska? Unlikely as it may sound, dinosaurs did live here during the Triassic, Jurassic, and Cretaceous periods (66 million to 248 million years ago). The first discovery of dinosaur bones came in 1961 when a Shell Oil geologist happened upon strange bones along the Colville River. Thinking they were just mammoth bones from the last ice age, the company shelved them for two decades. When government scientists finally took a look, they were stunned to discover that these were instead the bones of dinosaurs. This discovery is now regarded as one of the most important dinosaur finds of the last 30 years, and one of the greatest Cretaceous vertebrate deposits anywhere on earth.

Over the last few years, scientists have flocked to the Colville site—right along the Arctic Ocean—to discover how the supposedly cold-blooded dinosaurs could survive such a harsh northern climate. Their findings have thrown several scientific theories into question, and some paleontologists now believe the dinosaurs were warm-blooded and could move fast enough to migrate long distances, much as the caribou do on today's north slope.

Temperate Times

The world the dinosaurs inhabited was vastly different from that of northern Alaska today. A warm inland sea ran from the tropics to the polar regions east of Alaska. The Arctic land was covered with dense, fern-filled redwood forests, and winter temperatures

rarely dropped below freezing. This moderate climate and abundant food source allowed the dinosaurs to survive for millions of years. The largest animals were the four-ton horned pachyrinosaurs and the three-ton duck-billed hadrosaurs, both of which were vegetarians. They were preyed upon by such meat-eaters as the tyrannosaurs. Why the dinosaurs disappeared is one of the ongoing mysteries in science, though the prevailing theory is that a giant comet slammed into the earth some 65 million years ago, causing the planet to cool so rapidly that the dinosaurs could not survive.

And what of the possibility of a "Jurassic Park" in Alaska? The dinosaur discoveries along the Colville River are unique in that some of the bones were never mineralized (turned into stone). Some of these are still the original bones, and it is even possible that some of the original DNA is present. Don't expect to see mutant dinosaurs roaming around Alaska anytime soon, but the bones could potentially provide information on what the dinosaurs ate and whether or not they were cold-blooded.

BOB RACE

erupts with life like there is no tomorrow. (The ubiquitous mosquitoes are the best example of this; bring headnets and insect repellents.) Best-known are the annual migrations of the 150,000-strong Porcupine caribou herd—they are the reason the reserve was established—but also here are millions of nesting ducks, geese, swans, loons, and other birds. Large mammals include musk ox, wolves, polar and grizzly bears, moose, and Dall sheep. Several major rivers drain ANWR on both sides of the Phillip Smith Mountains that split the refuge. The Sheenjek and Wind Rivers are favorites of experienced kayakers and rafters.

Visiting ANWR

Access to ANWR is by floatplane out of the surrounding settlements of Fort Yukon, Kaktovik, and Deadhorse. There are no developed facilities or trails within the refuge. Several companies offer expensive wilderness treks into ANWR; the refuge office has a listing. One of the best is Juneau's **Alaska Discovery,** tel. (907) 780-6226 or (800) 586-1911; they offer a 10-day ANWR trip out of Fairbanks for $2,900 pp. For more on this magnificent wild place, contact the Fish and Wildlife Service at: **Arctic National Wildlife Refuge,** 101 12th Ave. Fairbanks, AK 99701, tel. (907) 456-0250.

BOOKLIST

Note: An excellent place to order Alaskan books is through the **Alaska Natural History Association,** 605 W. Fourth Ave., Suite 85, Anchorage, AK 99501, tel. (907) 274-8440. Their catalog lists several hundred nature books, geographic volumes, maps, calendars, guides, and other titles.

DESCRIPTION AND TRAVEL

Alaska Geographic. Alaska Geographic Society, P.O. Box 4-EEE, Anchorage, AK 99509. A quarterly magazine with the emphasis on color photography.

Alaska Wilderness Milepost. Anchorage: Alaska Northwest Publishing. This extraordinarily detailed guide provides general information on all of Alaska's villages and cities, along with the many wild places. Great for background information and as a companion to this more specific guide. Updated annually.

Belous, Robert, et al. *The Sierra Club's Guide to the National Parks of the Pacific Northwest and Alaska.* New York: Stewart, Tabori, and Chang, 1985. Available from Sierra Club bookstores.

Bodeau, Jean. *Katmai National Park and Preserve.* Anchorage: Alaska Natural History Association, 1992. Describes the park's history, sights, access, hiking, bears, etc.

Buryn, Ed. *Vagabonding in the U.S.A.* Berkeley, CA: And/Or Press, 1980. A cornucopia of bizarre travel ideas, guaranteed to turn your wanderlust into a lifelong trip; a kaleidoscope of Americana.

Colby, Merle. *A Guide to Alaska.* New York: MacMillan, 1939. This Federal Writers' Project guide to Alaska half a century ago has never been surpassed. Look for it in a good library.

Exploring Alaska's Mount McKinley National Park. Anchorage: Alaska Travel Publications, 1976. This outstanding guidebook makes up for the lack of trails in the park by mapping and describing 25 recommended hikes off the road. Unfortunately, it is presently out of print.

Higgins, John. *The North Pacific Deckhand's and Alaska Cannery Worker's Handbook.* Available from Albacore Press, P.O. Box 355, Eastsound, WA 98245. Get this book for the evocative photographs, its description of the fishing industry, and practical instructions on how to become part of it all.

Lopez, Barry. *Of Wolves and Men.* New York: Scribner, 1978. Excellent discussion of the hunter/hunted dynamic.

Marshall, Robert. *Alaska Wilderness.* Berkeley: University of California Press, 1970. A thrilling account of the author's exploration of the Central Brooks Range.

Matsen, Brad. *Ray Troll's Shocking Fish Tales.* Anchorage: Alaska Northwest Books, 1991. Illustrated by Ray Troll—outrageous fish artist par excellence—the book offers a mix of scientific and philosophic ramblings about creatures of the sea. Great fun.

McGinniss, Joe. *Going to Extremes.* New York: New American Library, 1980. One man's journey to Alaska leads him to a series of characters as diverse as the state itself.

McPhee, John. *Coming into the Country.* New York: Bantam Books, 1979. Perhaps the best portrayal of Alaskan lifestyles ever written. Read it before your trip.

The Milepost. Alaska Northwest Publishing Co., P.O. Box 4-EEE, Anchorage, AK 99509, USA. For motorists, the best guidebook to Alaska and Western Canada. The highway maps and description make *The Milepost* a must if you're driving north. Although the information is accurate and comprehensive, specific listings of hotels, bars, and restaurants are limited to advertisers.

A Moneywise Guide to North America. Available from Presidio Press, 31 Pamaron Way, Novato, CA 94947. Although short on maps and necessarily selective in what it covers, this book is an indispensable companion on any trip across or around the United States or Canada. It contains a wealth of the most interesting and unusual information, as well as specific instructions on how to survive on a tight budget. Concise and delightful.

Moore, Terris. *Mt. McKinley: The Pioneer Climbs.* Seattle: The Mountaineers, 1981. An exciting history of the challenge to climb North America's highest mountain.

Muir, John. *Travels in Alaska.* New York: Houghton Mifflin Co., 1915. Muir's classic narration of his experiences on the Stikine River and at Glacier Bay during 1879, 1880, and 1890.

Murie, Adolph. *A Naturalist in Alaska.* New York: Devin-Adair, 1961. Excellent insight into the fauna of Alaska.

Murie, Adolph. *The Wolves of Mount McKinley.* Seattle: University of Washington Press, 1985. Originally published in 1944.

Nienhueser, Helen, and Nancy Simmerman. *55 Ways to the Wilderness in Southcentral Alaska.* Seattle: The Mountaineering Club of Alaska, 1985. Available from The Mountaineers, 300 Third Ave. W, Seattle, WA 98119. A compact trail guide, complete with maps, photos, and descriptions of the best the region has to offer.

O'Clair, Rita M., Robert H. Armstrong, and Richard Carstensen. *The Nature of Southeast Alaska.* Anchorage: Alaska Northwest Books, 1992. See the world through the naturalists' eyes in this beautifully illustrated guide to the lives of animals and plants in Southeast Alaska.

Piggot, Margaret. *Discover Southeast Alaska with Pack and Paddle.* Seattle: The Mountaineering Club of Alaska, 1974. Available from The Mountaineers, 300 Third Ave. W, Seattle, WA 98119. A superb guide to the trails and canoe routes of Southeast—full of photos, hiking maps, and useful tips. Highly recommended.

Walker, Spike. *Working on the Edge.* New York: St. Martin's Press, 1991. Harrowing tales from the edge of the abyss—working the king-crab boats of the Bering Sea in the boom years of the 1970s and early '80s when the financial stakes were almost as high as the risks to life. Read it before you even consider working on a crab boat!

Walker, Tom. *River of Bears.* Stillwater, Minnesota: Voyageur Press, 1993. The story of McNeil River and the bears that have made it a favorite of photographers. Photos by Larry Aumiller, the Fish and Game employee who guides hundreds of visitors here each summer.

Wayburn, Peggy. *Adventuring in Alaska.* Available from Sierra Club Books, 530 Bush St., San Francisco, CA 94108. A 1988 guide to the remote wilderness regions of Alaska and how to get there. This book is recommended for anyone planning a major canoe, kayak, or rubber-raft expedition of the state.

Williams, Howel, ed. *Landscapes of Alaska.* Berkeley: University of California Press, 1958. A superb geography text.

Wynne, Kate. *Guide to Marine Mammals of Alaska.* Fairbanks: University of Alaska, 1992. An outstanding, easy-to-use guide to the whales, seals, porpoises, sea lions, and other mammals of the seas around Alaska's shores. Perfect for anyone riding the ferry boats or heading out on a wildlife tour.

Zimmerman, Jenny. *A Naturalist's Guide to Chugach State Park, Alaska.* Anchorage: AT Publishing, 1993. Everything you ever wanted to know about Anchorage's wonderful next-door neighbor, from history to hikes to ski treks.

HISTORY

Berton, Pierre. *The Klondike Fever.* New York: Carroll & Graf, 1985. Originally published in 1958.

Berton, Pierre. *Klondike: The Last Great Gold Rush.* Toronto: McClelland and Stewart, 1972. Brings alive the unforgettable characters who came out of the last great gold rush.

Chevigny, Hector. *Lord of Alaska*. Portland: Binford & Mort, 1971. The biography of Alexander Baranof, manager of the Russian American Company from 1791 to 1817.

Cohen, Stan. *The Forgotten War*. Pictorial Histories Publishing Co., 713 South Third W, Missoula, MT 59801. A pictorial history of WW II in Alaska and northwestern Canada.

Greiner, James. *Wager with the Wind: The Don Sheldon Story*. New York: St. Martin's Press, 1982.

Heller, Herbert L. *Sourdough Sagas*. Cleveland: World Publishing Co., 1967. Colorful tales of mishap and adventure about Alaska's prospecting pioneers.

Morgan, Murray. *One Man's Gold Rush: A Klondike Album*. Seattle: University of Washington Press, 1967. A feast of gold-rush photography.

Okun, S.B. *The Russian-American Company*. Cambridge: Harvard University Press, 1951. This translation from the Russian gives a different view of Alaska in the period up to 1867.

Sherwood, Morgan B. *Exploration of Alaska, 1865-1900*. New Haven: Yale University Press, 1965. The story of the opening of the interior.

Speck, Gordon. *Northwest Explorations*. Portland: Binford & Mort, 1954. Fascinating tales of the early explorers.

POLITICS AND GOVERNMENT

Alaska magazine. Alaska Northwest Publishing Co., P.O. Box 4-EEE, Anchorage, AK 99509. A monthly magazine of life in the last frontier.

Hanrahan, John, and Peter Gruenstein. *Lost Frontier: The Marketing of Alaska*. New York: Norton & Co., 1977. A piercing analysis of what the transnationals have in store for Alaska.

Kresge, David T. *Issues in Alaska Development*. Seattle: University of Washington Press, 1977. A scholarly examination of the issues facing the state today.

Mixon, Mim. *What Happened to Fairbanks?* Boulder, CO: Westview Press, 1978. The social impact of the Trans-Alaska Oil Pipeline on Fairbanks, Alaska.

Watkins, Mel, ed. *Dene Nation: The Colony Within*. Toronto: University of Toronto Press, 1977. The struggle of the Athabascan Indians of Canada for a settlement similar to the one granted their brothers in Alaska.

ANTHROPOLOGY

Boas, Franz. *Race, Language, and Culture*. New York: MacMillan, 1940. Boas' s anthrolopological work on the Northwest Coast Indians was definitive.

Bruemmer, Fred. *Seasons of the Eskimo: A Vanishing Way of Life*. Greenwich, New York: Geographic Society, 1971. A photo essay on the Eskimos of Canada today.

Dekin, Albert A., Jr. *Arctic Archeology, A Bibliography and History*. New York: Garland Publishing, 1978.

Fejes, Claire. *Villagers*. New York: Random House, 1981. An account of contemporary Athabascan Indian life along the Yukon River.

Swanton, John R. *The Indian Tribes of North America*. Washington: Smithsonian Institution, 1952. Specifically identifies all native groups.

ART AND LITERATURE

Bancroft-Hunt, Norman. *People of the Totem: The Indians of the Pacific Northwest*. New York: Putnam's Sons, 1979. A beautifully illustrated history of the art of these people.

Bodett, Tom. *As Far As You Can Go Without a Passport*. Reading, MA: Addison & Wesley Publishing Co., 1986. A collection of wry, bring-a-smile-to-your-face tales from this Homer-based humorist and sometime Motel 6 promoter. His other books include *The End of the Road* and *Small Comforts*.

The Far North: 2000 Years of American Eskimo and Indian Art. Washington: National Gallery of Art, 1977. A catalog of an exhibition of Native art.

Kizzia, Tom. *The Wake of the Unseen Object.* New York: Henry Holt and Co., 1991. A beautifully written journey through the wild heart of today's Alaskan Bush. Filled with insights into the clashing cultures of Native and white America.

London, Jack. *The Call of the Wild.* This gripping tale of a sled dog's experience along the gold rush trail was Jack London's most successful rendering of the spirit of the North.

Masterpieces of Indian and Eskimo Art from Canada. Paris: Musee de l'Homme, 1969.

Service, Robert. *Collected Poems.* New York: Dodd, Mead & Co., 1959. No one has ever better captured the flavor of northern life than the poet Robert Service.

Stewart, Hilary. *Looking at Indian Art of the Northwest Coast.* Seattle; Universtiy of Washington Press, 1979. A concise analysis of the artforms of this powerful culture.

REFERENCE

The Alaska Almanac. Alaska Northwest Publishing Co., P.O. Box 4-EEE, Anchorage, AK 99509. A rich source of useful information about the state, all in one compact volume.

Alaska Atlas & Gazetteer. Freeport, ME: DeLorme Mapping, 1992. This $20 book of up-to-date topographic maps is a wise investment if you plan to explore the more remote parts of Alaska. Very easy to use.

Hulten, Eric. *Flora of Alaska and Neighboring Territories.* Stanford: Stanford University Press, 1968. A huge manual of the vascular plants—highly technical, but easy to consult.

Lada-Mocarski, Valerian. *Bibliography of Books on Alaska Published Before 1868.* New York: Yale University Press, 1969.

Murie, Olaus. *A Field Guide to Animal Tracks.* Boston: Houghton Mifflin, 1954. All North American mammals are included in this valuable publication.

Orth, Donald J. *Dictionary of Alaska Place Names.* Washington, D.C.: U.S. Government Printing Office, 1967.

Robbins, Chandler S., et al. *Birds of North America.* New York: Golden Press, 1966. A guide to field identification.

Tourville, Elsie A. *Alaska, A Bibliography, 1570-1970.* Boston: G.K. Hall & Co., 1974. Includes a simplified subject index.

Wickersham, James. *A Bibliography of Alaskan Literature, 1724-1924.* Fairbanks: Alaska Agricultural College, 1927.

INDEX

Page numbers in **boldface** indicate the primary reference; numbers in *italics* indicate information in captions, illustrations, special topics, charts, or maps.

Y
Yellow Hill: 134
Young, Samuel Hall: 212
Yukon-Charley Rivers National Preserve: 270
Yukon Conservation Society: 240
Yukon Crossing Visitor Station: 300
Yukon Delta National Wildlife
   Refuge: 465-466
Yukon Gardens: 239
Yukon Government Building: 238

Yukon Historical & Museums
   Association: 240
Yukon Quest: 278, *280*
Yukon Transportation Museum: 239-240
Yukon Visitor Reception Center: 239
Yup'ik Cultural Center (Bethel): 465

Z
zinc mining: 35

ABOUT THE AUTHORS

Don Pitcher

authoring this book, he wrote *Wyoming Handbook* and *Washington Handbook* (Moon Publications), along with *Berkeley Inside/Out* (Heyday Books). He has photographed books on Wyoming and Alaska for Compass American Guides, and his photographs have appeared in many books, calendars, magazines, posters, and other publications. Don bases his travels around Alaska and the world from his Anchorage home, where he lives with his wife, Karen Shemet.

Deke Castleman

Born in Atlanta, Georgia, Don Pitcher grew up all over the East Coast—from Florida to Maine. He moved west to attend college, and immediately fell in love with its wild places. Don holds a bachelor's degree in biology from Pacific Union College and a master's degree in fire ecology from the University of California, Berkeley. Once out of school, he traveled north to Alaska to work for the National Park Service, U.S. Forest Service, and Alaska Department of Fish and Game.

Trained as an ecologist, Don Pitcher's love of travel led him to work on various guidebooks as both a writer and photographer. In addition to co-

When Deke Castleman first visited Alaska in 1977, he became enchanted with McKinley (now Denali) National Park. For the next six summers, he was employed there as a shuttle and tour bus driver, waiter, luggage handler, and hotel locksmith. Thereafter, he worked as bell captain for four years at the Travelers Inn (now Westmark Fairbanks). Deke is also the author of *Nevada Handbook* and *Compass Las Vegas.* He lives in Las Vegas with his wife and two children.

NOTES

MOON TRAVEL HANDBOOKS
THE IDEAL TRAVELING COMPANIONS

Moon Travel Handbooks provide focused, comprehensive coverage of distinct destinations all over the world. Our goal is to give travelers all the background and practical information they'll need for an extraordinary travel experience.
Every Handbook begins with an in-depth essay about the land, the people, their history, art, politics, and social concerns—an entire bookcase of cultural insight and introductory information in one portable volume. We also provide accurate, up-to-date coverage of all the practicalities: language, currency, transportation, accommodations, food, and entertainment. And Moon's maps are legendary, covering not only cities and highways, but parks and trails that are often difficult to find in other sources.
Below are highlights of Moon's North America and Hawaii Travel Handbook series. Our complete list of Handbooks, covering North America and Hawaii, Mexico, Central America and the Caribbean, and Asia and the Pacific, is on the order form on the accompanying pages. To purchase Moon Travel Handbooks, please check your local bookstore or order by phone: (800) 345-5473 Monday-Friday 8 a.m.-5 p.m. PST.

MOON OVER NORTH AMERICA
THE NORTH AMERICA AND HAWAII TRAVEL HANDBOOK SERIES

> "Moon's greatest achievements may be the individual state books they offer. . . . Moon not only digs up little-discovered attractions, but also offers thumbnail sketches of the culture and state politics of regions that rarely make national headlines."
> —*The Millennium Whole Earth Catalog*

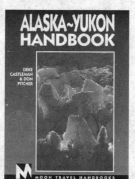

ALASKA-YUKON HANDBOOK
by Deke Castleman and Don Pitcher, 500 pages, **$17.95**
"Exceptionally rich in local culture, history, and reviews of natural attractions. . . . One of the most extensive pocket references. . . . An essential guide!" — *The Midwest Book Review*

ALBERTA AND THE NORTHWEST TERRITORIES
by Nadina Purdon and Andrew Hempstead, 466 pages, **$17.95**
"*Alberta and the Northwest Territories Handbook* provides strong coverage of the most rugged territories in Canada."
—*The Bookwatch*

ARIZONA TRAVELER'S HANDBOOK
by Bill Weir and Robert Blake, 486 pages, **$17.95**
"If you don't own this book already, buy it immediately"
—*Arizona Republic*

ATLANTIC CANADA HANDBOOK

by Nan Drosdick and Mark Morris, 436 pages, **$17.95**
New Brunswick, Nova Scotia, Prince Edward Island,
Newfoundland and Labrador.
"The new *Atlantic Canada* is the best I've seen on the region—
superior maps, travel tips, and cultural essays."
—Peter Aiken, *Providence Journal-Bulletin*

BIG ISLAND OF HAWAII HANDBOOK

by J.D. Bisignani, 349 pages, **$13.95**
"The best general guidebooks available." —*Hawaii Magazine*

BRITISH COLUMBIA HANDBOOK

by Jane King, 375 pages, **$15.95**
"Deftly balances the conventional and the unconventional, for both
city lovers and nature lovers."
—*Reference and Research Book News*

COLORADO HANDBOOK

by Stephen Metzger, 447 pages, **$18.95**
"Hotel rooms in the Aspen area, in the height of winter sports
season, for $20-$30? . . . who but a relentless researcher from
Moon could find it?" —The New York *Daily News*

GEORGIA HANDBOOK

by Kap Stann, 360 pages, **$17.95**
"[a] gold medal winner . . . Anyone who is interested in the South
should get this book." —*Eclectic Book Review*

HAWAII HANDBOOK

by J.D. Bisignani, 1004 pages, **$19.95**
Winner: Grand Excellence and Best Guidebook Awards, Hawaii
Visitors' Bureau
"No one since Michener has told us so much about our 50th
state." —*Playboy*

HONOLULU-WAIKIKI HANDBOOK

by J.D. Bisignani, 365 pages, **$14.95**
"The best general guidebooks available." —*Hawaii Magazine*

IDAHO HANDBOOK

by Don Root, 600 pages, **$18.95**
"It's doubtful that visitors to the Gem State will find a better, more
detailed explanation anywhere."
—*The Salt Lake Tribune*

KAUAI HANDBOOK
by J.D. Bisignani, 330 pages, **$15.95**
"This slender guide is tightly crammed. . . . The information
provided is staggering." —*Hawaii Magazine*

MAUI HANDBOOK
by J.D. Bisignani, 393 pages, **$14.95**
Winner: Best Guidebook Award, Hawaii Visitors' Bureau
"*Maui Handbook* should be in every couple's suitcase. It
intelligently discusses Maui's history and culture, and you can
trust the author's recommendations for best beaches, restaurants,
and excursions." —*Bride's Magazine*

MONTANA HANDBOOK
by W.C. McRae and Judy Jewell, 454 pages, **$17.95**
"Well-organized, engagingly written, tightly edited, and chock-full
of interesting facts about localities, backcountry destinations,
traveler accommodations, and cultural and natural history."
—*Sierra Magazine*

NEVADA HANDBOOK
by Deke Castleman, 473 pages, **$16.95**
"Veteran travel writer Deke Castleman says he covered more
than 10,000 miles in his research for this book and it shows."
—*Nevada Magazine*

NEW MEXICO HANDBOOK
by Stephen Metzger, 320 pages, **$15.95**
"The best current guide and travel book to all of New Mexico"
—New Mexico Book League

NEW YORK HANDBOOK
by Christiane Bird, 615 pages, **$19.95**
Contains voluminous coverage not only of New York City, but also
of myriad destinations along the Hudson River Valley, in the
Adirondack Mountains, around Leatherstocking Country, and
elsewhere throughout the state.

NORTHERN CALIFORNIA HANDBOOK
by Kim Weir, 779 pages, **$19.95**
"That rarest of travel books—both a practical guide to the region
and a map of its soul." —*San Francisco Chronicle*

OREGON HANDBOOK
by Stuart Warren
and Ted Long Ishikawa, 520 pages, **$16.95**
". . . the most definitive tourist guide to the state ever published."
—*The Oregonian*

TENNESSEE HANDBOOK
by Jeff Bradley, 500 pages, **$17.95**
Features nonpareil coverage of Nashville and Memphis, as well as the Appalachian Trail, Great Smoky Mountains National Park, Civil War battlefields, and a wide assortment of unusual amusements off the beaten path.

TEXAS HANDBOOK
by Joe Cummings, 598 pages, **$17.95**
"Reveals a Texas with a diversity of people and culture that is as breathtaking as that of the land itself."
—*Planet Newspaper,* Australia

"I've read a bunch of Texas guidebooks, and this is the best one."
—Joe Bob Briggs

UTAH HANDBOOK
by Bill Weir and W.C. McRae, 500 pages, **$17.95**
" . . . a one-volume, easy to digest, up-to-date, practical, factual guide to all things Utahan. . . . This is the best handbook of its kind I've yet encountered."
—*The Salt Lake Tribune*

WASHINGTON HANDBOOK
by Don Pitcher, 866 pages, **$19.95**
"Departs from the general guidebook format by offering information on how to cope with the rainy days and where to take the children. . . . This is a great book, informational, fun to read, and a good one to keep."
—*Travel Publishing News*

WISCONSIN HANDBOOK
by Thomas Huhti, 400 pages, **$16.95**
Lake Michigan, Lake Superior, and Wisconsin's 65 state parks and national forests offer unrivaled outdoor recreational opportunities, from hiking, biking, and water sports to the myriad pleasures of Door County, the "crown jewel of the Midwest."

WYOMING HANDBOOK
by Don Pitcher, 570 pages, **$17.95**
"Wanna know the real dirt on Calamity Jane, white Indians, and the tacky Cheyenne gunslingers? All here. And all fun."

—The New York *Daily News*

Hit The Road With Moon Travel Handbooks

ROAD TRIP USA
Cross-Country Adventures on America's Two-Lane Highways
by Jamie Jensen, 800 pages, **$22.50**
This Handbook covers the entire United States with 11
intersecting routes, allowing travelers to create their own
cross-country driving adventures

Packed with both practical information and entertaining
sidebars, *Road Trip USA* celebrates the spontaneity and culture of
the American highway without sacrificing the essential comforts of
bed and bread.

The World Wide Web edition of *Road Trip USA* features the
entire text plus links to local Internet sites. WWW explorers are
encouraged to participate in the exhibit by contributing their own
travel tips on small towns, roadside attractions, regional foods,
and interesting places to stay. Visit *Road Trip USA* online at:
http://www.moon.com/rdtrip.html

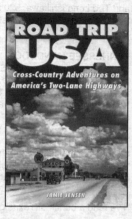

"Essential for travelers who are more interested in finding the real America than the fastest way
from points A to B. Highly recommended."   *—Library Journal*

"For budding myth collectors, I can't think of a better textbook than Moon Publications' cross-
country adventure guide."   *—Los Angeles Times*

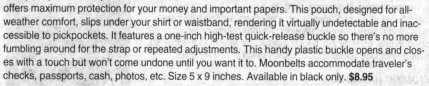

MOONBELT

A new concept in moneybelts. Made of
heavy-duty Cordura nylon, the Moonbelt
offers maximum protection for your money and important papers. This pouch, designed for all-
weather comfort, slips under your shirt or waistband, rendering it virtually undetectable and inaccessible to pickpockets. It features a one-inch high-test quick-release buckle so there's no more
fumbling around for the strap or repeated adjustments. This handy plastic buckle opens and closes with a touch but won't come undone until you want it to. Moonbelts accommodate traveler's
checks, passports, cash, photos, etc. Size 5 x 9 inches. Available in black only. **$8.95**

Travel Matters

Smart Reading for the Independent Traveler

Travel Matters is Moon Publications' free newsletter, loaded with specially commissioned travel articles and essays that get at the heart of the travel experience. Every issue includes:

Feature Stories covering a wide array of travel and cultural topics about destinations on and off the beaten path. Past feature stories in *Travel Matters* include Mexican professional wrestling, traveling to the Moon, and why Germans get six weeks vacation and Americans don't.

The Offbeat Path exploring unusual customs and practices from toothfiling ceremonies in Bali to the serving of deep fried bull testicles in a small Colorado bar.

Health Matters, by Dirk Schroeder, author of *Staying Healthy in Asia, Africa, and Latin America*, focusing on the most recent medical findings that affect travelers.

Reviews providing readers with assessments of the latest travel books, videos, multimedia, support materials, and Internet resources.

Travel Q&A, a reader question-and-answer column for travelers written by an international travel agent and world traveler.

To receive a free subscription to *Travel Matters,* call (800) 345-5473, e-mail us at travel@moon.com, or write to us at:

> Moon Publications
> P.O. Box 3040
> Chico, CA 95927-3040

Current and back issues of *Travel Matters* can also be found on our web site at
http://www.moon.com

Please note: Subscribers who live outside of the United States will be charged $7 per year for shipping and handling.

MOON TRAVEL HANDBOOKS

NORTH AMERICA AND HAWAII

Alaska-Yukon Handbook (0897) $17.95
Alberta and the Northwest Territories Handbook (0463) $17.95
Arizona Traveler's Handbook (0714). $17.95
Atlantic Canada Handbook (0072) $17.95
Big Island of Hawaii Handbook (0064). $13.95
British Columbia Handbook (0145). $15.95
Colorado Handbook (0447) $18.95
Georgia Handbook (0390) $17.95
Hawaii Handbook (0005) $19.95
Honolulu-Waikiki Handbook (0587) $14.95
Idaho Handbook (0889). $18.95
Kauai Handbook (0919) $15.95
Maui Handbook (0579) $14.95
Montana Handbook (0498). $17.95
Nevada Handbook (0641) $16.95
New Mexico Handbook (0862). $15.95
New York Handbook (0811) $19.95
Northern California Handbook (3840) $19.95
Oregon Handbook (0102) $16.95
Road Trip USA (0366). $22.50
Tennessee Handbook (0439) $17.95
Texas Handbook (0633) $17.95
Utah Handbook (0870) $17.95
Washington Handbook (0455). $19.95
Wisconsin Handbook (0927) $16.95
Wyoming Handbook (0854) $17.95

ASIA AND THE PACIFIC

Australia Handbook (0722) $21.95
Bali Handbook (0730). $19.95
Bangkok Handbook (0595) $13.95
Fiji Islands Handbook (0382) $13.95
Hong Kong Handbook (0560) $15.95
Indonesia Handbook (0625). $25.00
Japan Handbook (3700) $22.50
Micronesia Handbook (0773) $14.95

Nepal Handbook (0412) $18.95
New Zealand Handbook (0331) $19.95
Outback Australia Handbook (0471) $18.95
Pakistan Handbook (0692) $22.50
Philippines Handbook (0048) $17.95
Singapore Handbook (0781) $15.95
Southeast Asia Handbook (0021) $21.95
South Korea Handbook (0749) $19.95
South Pacific Handbook (0404) $22.95
Tahiti-Polynesia Handbook (0374) $13.95
Thailand Handbook (0420) $19.95
Tibet Handbook (3905) $30.00
Vietnam, Cambodia & Laos Handbook (0293) $18.95

MEXICO
Baja Handbook (0528) $15.95
Cabo Handbook (0285) $14.95
Cancún Handbook (0501) $13.95
Central Mexico Handbook (0234) $15.95
Mexico Handbook (0315) $21.95
Northern Mexico Handbook (0226) $16.95
Pacific Mexico Handbook (0323) $16.95
Puerto Vallarta Handbook (0250) $14.95
Yucatán Peninsula Handbook (0242) $15.95

CENTRAL AMERICA AND THE CARIBBEAN
Belize Handbook (0307) $15.95
Caribbean Handbook (0277) $16.95
Costa Rica Handbook (0358) $19.95
Jamaica Handbook (0706) $15.95

INTERNATIONAL
Egypt Handbook (3891) $18.95
Moon Handbook (0668) $10.00
Moscow-St. Petersburg Handbook (3913) $13.95
Staying Healthy in Asia, Africa, and Latin America (0269) $11.95
The Practical Nomad (0765) $17.95

PERIPLUS TRAVEL MAPS
All maps $7.95 each

Bali
Bandung/W. Java
Bangkok/C. Thailand
Batam/Bintan
Cambodia
Chiangmai/N. Thailand
Hong Kong
Indonesia
Jakarta
Java
Ko Samui/S. Thailand
Kuala Lumpur
Lombok
Penang
Phuket/S. Thailand
Sabah
Sarawak
SIngapore
Vietnam
Yogyakarta/C. Java

INTERNATIONAL TRAVEL MAPS
Price as indicated

Alaska	$6.95
Australia	$7.95
Barbados	$7.95
Belize	$7.95
British Columbia	$3.95
Central America	$8.95
Costa Rica	$7.95
Jamaica	$6.95
Mexico	$7.95
Mexico: Baja California	$7.95
Mexico City	$4.95
Mexico: South Coast	$7.95
San Juan Islands (WA)	$4.95
Vancouver Island	$3.95
Virgin Islands	$7.95
Yucatán Peninsula	$7.95
Yukon	$4.95

www.moon.com

MOON PUBLICATIONS

Welcome to Moon Travel Handbooks, publishers of comprehensive travel guides to North America, Mexico, Central America and the Caribbean, Asia, and the Pacific Islands. We're always on the lookout for new ideas, so please feel free to e-mail any comments and suggestions about these exhibits to travel@moon.com.

If you like Moon Travel Handbooks, you'll enjoy our travel information center on the World Wide Web (WWW), loaded with interactive exhibits designed especially for the Internet.

Our featured exhibit contains the complete text of *Road Trip USA*, a travel guide to the "blue highways" that crisscross America between the interstates, published in paperback in 1996. The WWW version contains a large, scrollable point-and-click imagemap with links to hundreds of original entries; a sophisticated network of links to other major U.S. Internet sites; and a running commentary from our online readers contributing their own travel tips on small towns, roadside attractions, regional foods, and interesting places to stay.

Other attractions on Moon's Web site include:

- Excerpted hypertext adaptations of Moon's bestselling *New Zealand Handbook, Costa Rica Handbook,* and *Big Island of Hawaii Handbook*

- The complete 75-page introduction to *Staying Healthy in Asia, Africa, and Latin America,* as well as the *Trans-Cultural Study Guide,* both coproduced with Volunteers in Asia

- The complete, annotated bibliographies from Moon's Handbooks to Japan, South Korea, Thailand, the Philippines, Indonesia, Australia, and New Zealand

- Current and back issues of Moon's free quarterly newsletter, *Travel Matters*

- Updates on the latest titles and editions to join the Moon Travel Handbook series

Come visit us at: **http://www.moon.com**

WHERE TO BUY MOON TRAVEL HANDBOOKS

BOOKSTORES AND LIBRARIES: Moon Travel Handbooks are sold worldwide. Please contact our sales manager for a list of wholesalers and distributors in your area.

TRAVELERS: We would like to have Moon Travel Handbooks available throughout the world. Please ask your bookstore to write or call us for ordering information. If your bookstore will not order our guides for you, please contact us for a free catalog.

> **Moon Publications, Inc.**
> **P.O. Box 3040**
> **Chico, CA 95927-3040 U.S.A.**
> **tel.: (800) 345-5473**
> **fax: (916) 345-6751**
> **e-mail: travel@moon.com**

IMPORTANT ORDERING INFORMATION

PRICES: All prices are subject to change. We always ship the most current edition. We will let you know if there is a price increase on the book you order.

SHIPPING AND HANDLING OPTIONS: Domestic UPS or USPS first class (allow 10 working days for delivery): $3.50 for the first item, 50 cents for each additional item.

EXCEPTIONS: *Tibet Handbook, Mexico Handbook,* and *Indonesia Handbook* shipping $4.50; $1.00 for each additional *Tibet Handbook, Mexico Handbook,* or *Indonesia Handbook.*

Moonbelt shipping is $1.50 for one, 50 cents for each additional belt.

Add $2.00 for same-day handling.

UPS 2nd Day Air or Printed Airmail requires a special quote.

International Surface Bookrate 8-12 weeks delivery: $3.00 for the first item, $1.00 for each additional item. Note: Moon Publications cannot guarantee international surface bookrate shipping. Moon recommends sending international orders via air mail, which requires a special quote.

FOREIGN ORDERS: Orders that originate outside the U.S.A. must be paid for with an international money order, a check in U.S. currency drawn on a major U.S. bank based in the U.S.A., or Visa or MasterCard.

TELEPHONE ORDERS: We accept Visa or MasterCard payments. Minimum order is US$15. Call in your order: (800) 345-5473, 8 a.m.-5 p.m. Pacific standard time.

ORDER FORM

Prices are subject to change without notice. Be sure to call (800) 345-5473
8 a.m.–5 p.m. PST for current prices and editions, or for the
name of the bookstore nearest you that carries Moon Travel Handbooks.
(See important ordering information on preceding page.)

Name: _____ Date: _____

Street: _____

City: _____ Daytime Phone: _____

State or Country: _____ Zip Code: _____

QUANTITY	TITLE	PRICE

Taxable Total_____

Sales Tax (7.25%) for California Residents_____

Shipping & Handling_____

TOTAL_____

Ship: ☐ UPS (no P.O. Boxes)   ☐ 1st class   ☐ International surface mail

Ship to: ☐ address above   ☐ other _____

_____

Make checks payable to: **MOON PUBLICATIONS, INC.**, P.O. Box 3040, Chico, CA 95927-3040 U.S.A.
We accept Visa and MasterCard. **To Order**: Call in your Visa or MasterCard number, or send a written order with your Visa or MasterCard number and expiration date clearly written.

Card Number: ☐ **Visa**   ☐ **MasterCard**

☐ ☐ ☐ ☐ ☐ ☐ ☐ ☐ ☐ ☐ ☐ ☐ ☐ ☐ ☐ ☐

Exact Name on Card: _____

Expiration date:_____

Signature: _____

THE METRIC SYSTEM

1 inch = 2.54 centimeters (cm)
1 foot = .304 meters (m)
1 mile = 1.6093 kilometers (km)
1 km = .6124 miles
1 fathom = 1.8288 m
1 chain = 20.1168 m
1 furlong = 201.168 m
1 acre = .4047 hectares
1 sq km = 100 hectares
1 sq mile = 2.59 square km
1 ounce = 28.35 grams
1 pound = .4536 kilograms
1 short ton = .90718 metric ton
1 short ton = 2000 pounds
1 long ton = 1.016 metric tons
1 long ton = 2240 pounds
1 metric ton = 1000 kilograms
1 quart = .94635 liters
1 US gallon = 3.7854 liters
1 Imperial gallon = 4.5459 liters
1 nautical mile = 1.852 km

To compute celsius temperatures, subtract 32 from Fahrenheit and divide by 1.8. To go the other way, multiply celsius by 1.8 and add 32.

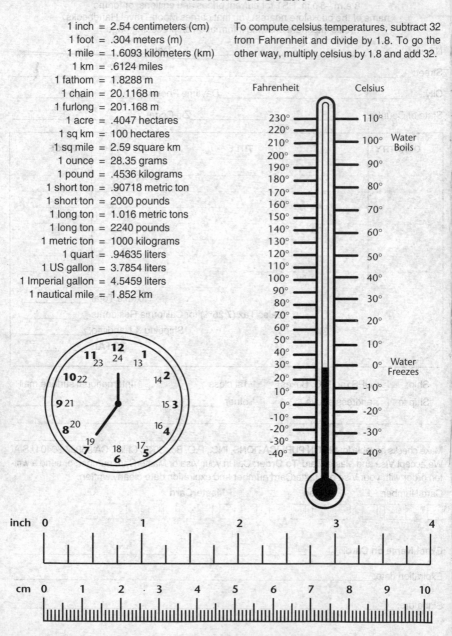